Using Statistics in Economics

R L Thomas

The **McGraw·Hill** Companies

London Boston Burr Ridge, IL Dubuque, IA Madison, WI New York San Francisco
St. Louis Bangkok Bogotá Caracas Kuala Lumpur Lisbon Madrid Mexico City
Milan Montreal New Delhi Santiago Seoul Singapore Sydney Taipei Toronto

Using Statistics in Economics
R L Thomas
ISBN 0-07-710743-8

Published by McGraw-Hill Education
Shoppenhangers Road
Maidenhead
Berkshire
SL6 2QL
Telephone: 44 (0) 1628 502 500
Fax: 44 (0) 1628 770 224
Website: www.mcgraw-hill.co.uk

British Library Cataloguing in Publication Data
A catalogue record for this book is available from the British Library

Library of Congress Cataloguing in Publication Data
The Library of Congress data for this book has been applied for from the Library of Congress

Acquisitions Editor: Kirsty Reade
Editorial Assistant: Laura Dent
Marketing Director: Petra Skytte
Production Editor: James Bishop

Text Design by Jonathan Coleclough
Cover design by Fielding Design
Typeset by Mathematical Composition Setters Ltd, Salisbury, Wiltshire
Printed and bound in Great Britain by Bell and Bain Ltd, Glasgow

ISBN 0-07-710743-8

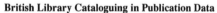

The McGraw-Hill Companies

Using Statistics in Economics

Brief table of contents

Detailed table of contents

Preface

This text is aimed specifically at *economics* students rather than, for example, business or accountancy students. Most published introductory statistics texts in the area contain material that is of little interest to economists and the exclusion of such material leaves room for topics of more relevance to economics. In particular, many current statistics texts give insufficient space to regression analysis, a vital technique of obvious interest to economics students. This book attempts to remedy such omission by shifting the balance of material firmly in favour of econometrics, as the table of contents indicates. This text should therefore serve as good preparation for specialized econometrics options served by, for example, my own text *Modern Econometrics*, Maddala's *Introduction to Econometrics* or Ramanathan's *Introductory Econometrics with Applications*.

This book is an intermediate text, stressing an easier but proper understanding of difficult topics. Although it is aimed at second-year students at British universities, it is obvious that, nowadays, the complexity of second-year statistics courses varies considerably across institutions. Firstly, course content must depend on the background of students and/or the syllabus that they have followed in their first year. Secondly, second-year statistics may be taught for one or two semesters. The text could be therefore be used by three types of student.

(i) Students studying statistics for two semesters with a strong quantitative background should omit the prerequisites section and spend most of their time on Part II (econometrics), with the intention of going on to tackle third-year econometrics options.

(ii) Students with a reasonable quantitative background and/or studying statistics for two semesters would be set a similar syllabus but omitting Chapter 7 and the sections marked with a double star (**) in Part II.

(iii) Students with a weaker quantitative background and/or studying statistics for just one semester should spend time on the prerequisites section, omit Chapter 7 and also omit all single-starred (*) and double-starred (**) material in Part II.

(Note that the star and double-star notation is not used in Part I. Also, double-starred sections are not necessarily more difficult than single-starred sections, but lack of time may mean that they have to be omitted.) Mixtures of options (i), (ii) and (iii) are, of course, also possible.

Long experience of teaching both statistics and econometrics has taught me that it is most unwise to introduce students to computer software too early in their studies. Thus, both in Part I and particularly in Part II of the text, students are required first to work through some fairly lengthy numerical examples, using nothing more than a hand calculator. Only then are they asked to repeat the examples using a computer. Hand-calculator work enables a student to get a feel for what is really going on in regression analysis. Without such preparatory work, I have found students have little idea of what a computer actually does for them. They can therefore become very competent at obtaining printouts from a computer yet lack any idea of how to interpret their results!

I have resisted the temptation of tying this text to any specific computer software. Some printouts from MICROFIT4 software are presented, but their general presentation of basic results is very similar to printouts obtained from virtually all popular econometric software.

I am grateful to all of the anonymous McGraw-Hill reviewers for comments on drafts of this text. Any remaining errors are, of course, my own.

Leighton Thomas, June 2004

Guided tour

Part openers

There are two Part Openers, which introduce the topics and themes covered throughout the two Parts of the text.

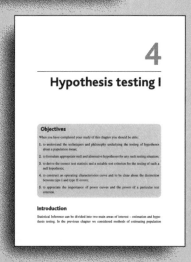

Objectives

Each chapter identifies the skills and abilities you will have gained after reading the chapter.

Figures and tables

Each chapter provides a number of figures and tables to help you to visualise the various economic models, and to illustrate and summarise important concepts.

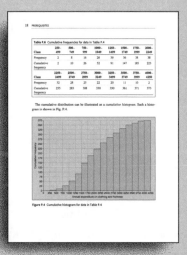

Worked examples with solutions

Each chapter includes a number of Worked Examples and their solutions. These help you practice the concepts discussed in the text.

End of chapter summary

This briefly reviews and reinforces the main topics you will have covered in each chapter to ensure you have acquired a solid understanding of the key topics.

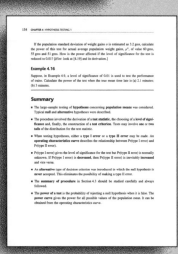

Technology to enhance learning and teaching

Online Learning Centre (OLC)

After completing each chapter, log on to the supporting Online Learning Centre website. Take advantage of the study tools offered to reinforce the material you have read in the text, and to develop your knowledge of marketing in a fun and effective way.

Resources for students include:

- Learning Objectives
- Self-test Questions
- Datasets
- Useful Weblinks

Also available for lecturers:

- PowerPoint Slides
- Lecture Outlines

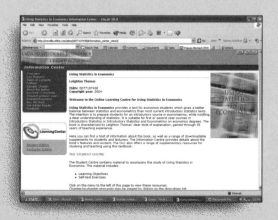

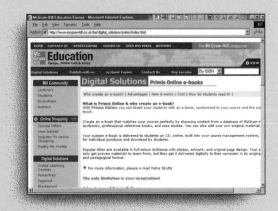

Prerequisites

P.1 The algebra of summations

Summations are often used in statistics. In this section we shall take as our variable of interest the annual expenditure, X, on clothing and footwear of married couples with two children of school age. The data set in Table P.1 refers to the expenditures (rounded to the nearest pound sterling), of 373 such families in a small UK town in the year 2001. We number the families from 1 to 373, beginning at the top left-hand corner of the table, then moving rightwards along the top row before moving to the second row, ending eventually with family 373 at the bottom right of the table. We let X_i denote the expenditure of the ith family, where i goes from 1 to 373. Thus, for example, $X_8 = 1745$ is the expenditure of the eighth family. Similarly, $X_{28} = 786$ represents expenditure by family 28, $X_{276} = 1873$ that by family 276, and so on.

Given all the X_i, their sum is indicated by the capital Greek letter Σ. Thus

$$\sum_{i=1}^{373} X_i = X_1 + X_2 + X_3 + X_4 + \cdots + X_{373}. \qquad [\text{P.1}]$$

Thus $\sum_{i=1}^{373} X_i$ is simply shorthand for adding up all the X_i from 1 to 373. Thus, using Table P.1, $\sum_{i=1}^{373} X_i = 788\ 224.$[1] Similarly,

$$\sum_{i=1}^{14} Y_i = Y_1 + Y_2 + Y_3 + \cdots + Y_{14} \quad \text{and} \quad \sum_{i=1}^{3} Z_i = Z_1 + Z_2 + Z_3.$$

The indices on the summation sign Σ are often omitted to remove clutter, particularly if the range of i is obvious. Thus, in this text, the following are identical:

$$\sum_{i=1}^{n} X_i = \sum_i X_i = \sum X_i. \qquad [\text{P.2}]$$

The sum does not always have to include all the X_i. For example, $\sum_{x=2}^{5} X_i = X_2 + X_3 + X_4 + X_5$. Also the 'sum over all i' is simply written as $\sum X_i$. For example, if we have $Y_1 = 3$, $Y_2 = 7$, $Y_3 = -2$, $Y_4 = 5$ and $Y_5 = -7$, then the sum over all i is $\sum Y_i = 3 + 7 - 2 + 5 - 7 = 6$.

Table P.1 Clothing expenditure of 373 families

1648	458	1256	3066	3069	2356	1862	1745	1056	852	2064
2657	1762	2813	1258	2712	1373	2613	3126	1006	3246	2274
1763	3411	1632	2709	1789	786	3888	1702	2056	3078	2318
711	3286	2913	1485	2489	1967	2776	3156	1311	2660	1212
2067	1673	2377	2178	2616	1715	2668	856	2729	1578	2510
1463	2178	1838	2206	1274	3333	2984	1496	3032	3111	1534
3682	1908	2178	1563	1745	2335	1187	3765	2408	1176	1788
1241	1998	1303	2555	1765	3488	1341	2813	912	2533	1089
3273	3687	2256	1620	1476	1838	3267	1202	2693	3167	2375
1567	1911	3756	948	2204	564	1732	2401	1506	2148	3086
2095	1829	1298	1808	2774	2281	3134	3765	1994	1007	2333
683	3509	2616	3367	1312	3842	2838	1134	2024	2482	2187
1592	2338	1591	3221	3712	3284	1722	1788	1086	3412	1523
3862	1631	2567	1476	688	1508	2912	3398	1413	913	2086
1754	1748	2806	1743	3201	2401	3567	1666	2111	2848	1572
2651	793	1583	2337	1616	2267	2392	2769	1406	2718	1154
2283	1386	2251	732	2916	2224	1441	1206	838	3298	3131
1784	1672	2106	1573	2888	1532	2187	2306	1154	1265	2156
3481	1811	1956	887	1234	274	3987	1362	1971	3210	915
1674	3408	2793	1502	4132	1723	2664	767	3087	2713	1591
2045	889	3371	1672	1603	2443	1313	2813	1583	3792	1902
2874	3067	694	1437	2993	3694	2313	1296	1934	2209	1243
1452	2197	3426	1562	1634	1354	1812	2834	1006	2278	3412
1674	1387	1808	2234	1276	2065	3524	2907	1498	2414	1034
2064	1573	1874	3145	1706	2176	1642	2043	741	1543	3276
1873	1505	2593	2008	1365	4208	2187	1486	1753	1965	1300
1205	3176	1538	2887	771	2153	1673	2271	2019	1356	3628
3063	2208	1267	1876	3376	3078	1734	2691	3801	1576	848
1482	1914	515	1498	1791	2167	1134	2757	3675	1010	3576
2052	2143	1772	1691	3654	2803	1585	2578	1832	2867	1598
1592	2096	998	2700	1386	3332	2613	1165	1208	2043	2381
1944	2688	1652	3002	2424	831	2937	2116	2478	1706	1591
2651	2507	2234	1204	2666	1098	2345	1472	1647	2731	2778
1012	3342	1261	3842	1352	2312	1808	2281	1935	1951	

As noted at the outset, summations are often used in statistics and several properties are well worth remembering. Firstly, if a is any constant, then

$$\sum_{i=1}^{n} aX_i = aX_1 + aX_2 + aX_3 + \cdots + aX_n$$
$$= a(X_1 + X_2 + X_3 + \cdots + X_n).$$

Thus

$$\sum_{i=1}^{n} aX_i = a \sum_{i=1}^{n} X_i. \tag{P.3}$$

For example, $\sum 6X_i = 6 \sum X_i$ and $\sum(-13X_i) = -13 \sum X_i$.

Sometimes you may encounter expressions like $\sum a$, where a is again some constant. But $\sum a$ simply means we must add up a series of constants a, one for each i, from 1 to n. Thus

$$\sum_{i=1}^{n} a = a + a + a + \cdots + a.$$

Hence,

$$\sum_{i=1}^{n} a = na. \tag{P.4}$$

For example, $\sum 6 = 6n$ and $\sum(-8) = -8n$.

Often we require quantities such as $\sum(X_i + Y_i)$. In fact, as we shall now show,

$$\sum_{i=1}^{n} (X_i + Y_i) = \sum_{i=1}^{n} X_i + \sum_{i=1}^{n} Y_i. \tag{P.5}$$

Using the definition of a summation, we have

$$\sum_{i=1}^{n} (X_i + Y_i) = (X_1 + Y_1) + (X_2 + Y_2) + (X_3 + Y_3) + \cdots + (X_n + Y_n)$$

$$= X_1 + X_2 + X_3 + \cdots + X_n$$
$$+ Y_1 + Y_2 + Y_3 + \cdots + Y_n$$

$$= \sum_{i=1}^{n} X_i + \sum_{i=1}^{n} Y_i.$$

Thus, the summation of the sum of two series is the sum of the summations!

Combining the results [P.3] and [P.5] leads to the more general result

$$\sum_{i=1}^{n} (aX_i + \beta Y_i) = a \sum_{i=1}^{n} X_i + \beta \sum_{i=1}^{n} Y_i. \tag{P.6}$$

Results [P.5] and [P.6] can, in fact, be extended to more than two variables, as the following worked example indicates.

> ### Worked Example
>
> Simplify the expressions
>
> **(a)** $\sum(8 + 3X_i + 7Y_i - 5Z_i)$,
>
> **(b)** $\sum(2X_i + 6X_i^2)$.
>
> ### Solution
>
> **(a)** $\sum(8 + 3X_i + 7Y_i - 5Z_i) = \sum 8 + \sum 3X_i + \sum 7Y_i + \sum(-5Z_i)$
> $$= 8n + 3 \sum X_i + 7 \sum Y_i - 5 \sum Z_i.$$
>
> **(b)** $\sum(2X_i + 6X_i^2) = \sum 2X_i + \sum 6X_i^2 = 2 \sum X_i + 6 \sum X_i^2.$
>
> [*Note*: it is not possible to simplify (b) further, since it is *not* generally the case that $\sum X_i^2 = (\sum X_i)^2$. For example, if $X_1 = 3$, $X_2 = 7$, $X_3 = 2$ and $X_4 = 0$, then $\sum X_i^2 = 3^2 + 7^2 + 2^2 + 0^2 = 62$, but $(\sum X_i)^2 = (3 + 7 + 2 + 0)^2 = 144$.]

P.2 Descriptive statistics

The subject of statistics can be divided into two areas of study – descriptive statistics and statistical inference. When all observations on the variable(s) of interest are available for analysis, all that is necessary is to describe the data. This is the process covered in this section. The more interesting part of statistics, statistical inference, occurs when not all observations on variable(s) are available. We then have to make do with 'samples' of data, from which we have to infer things about the complete data set, that is, the unavailable 'population'. Basic statistical inference is covered in Chapters 3–5.

In this section we shall again take the variable X, defined in the previous section, as our variable of interest. Its 373 values were shown in Table P.l.

There is a problem in digesting a data set such as that in Table P.1, and we immediately feel the need to *summarize* it. This feeling would obviously have been even greater had we been faced with, for example, data on 373 000 families! It would be impossible to obtain a 'feel' for such a data set. However, we shall illustrate the process of summarization using the more manageable data set of Table P.1.

Firstly, we shall define and then compute a series of *summary statistics* that will describe the data in a much more compact manner.

Measures of central tendency

The summary statistics computed in this subsection are all answers to the general question, 'what is a typical value for X in this data set?'.

One obvious answer to the above question would be take the arithmetic mean or 'average' of the values for X in Table P.1. The (arithmetic) *mean* of X is, therefore, defined as

$$\bar{X} = \frac{\sum x_i}{n}, \qquad \text{[P.7]}$$

where the summation sign $\sum$ simply implies that we are 'adding up' all the 373 X_i, that is, all the family expenditures in Table P.1. The total number of observations in a data set is given the symbol n. Thus $n = 373$ in this case. Performing this addition yielded $\sum X_i = 788\ 224$, so that, using [P.7], we obtain the mean value of X as

$$\bar{X} = \frac{788\ 224}{373} = 2113 \qquad \text{(to the nearest £).}$$

Thus we can say that a typical value for a family's expenditure on clothing and footwear is £2113.

A second answer to the question concerning typicality is to compute the so-called *median*, to which we shall give the symbol M. To obtain the median, it is first necessary to arrange the observations in ascending order, beginning with the smallest, which is $X_{204} = 274$, and finishing with the largest, $X_{281} = 4208$. That is, we obtain a sequence beginning and ending with the observations

274, 458, 515, 564, ..., 3888, 3987, 4132, 4208.

The above values are *tinted* in Table P.1.

The median of this data set is defined as the 'middle' number in this ascending list of observations. It is, in fact, the 187th smallest observation, because there are 186 expenditures below the median and 186 expenditures above it. The median for the data in Table P.1 is $M = 2019$. It is, in fact, given by X_{295}, which is *boxed* in Table P.1. The ascending sequence can therefore now be represented by

274, 458, 515, 564, ..., 2019, ..., 3888, 3987, 4132, 4208.

Clearly, if the total number of observations happens to be an even number, there is no 'middle number' and the median is then defined as the average of the two 'middle numbers'. For example, if we had 374 observations instead of 373, there would be 186 observations smaller than the two middle numbers and 186 observations larger.

The median, $M = 2019$, is therefore a second answer to the question about typicality posed earlier. Notice that the median has a different value from the mean and that this is almost always the case.[2] But which measure, mean or median, gives the better answer? While the mean is usually selected, the median is occasionally preferred if data sets contain one or a few *extreme* observations. An extreme observation is one whose value is either much larger or much smaller than the typical observations in the data set.

For example, suppose that the first observation in Table P.1 were 201 648 rather than 1648 (the head of this family happens to be a multimillionaire!). The sum of the observations would now be 988 224 rather than 788 224, so that the mean would now be $\bar{X} = 2649$ rather than 2113. The extreme observation 201 648 is clearly not typical of the data set and, consequently, there has been a large change in the value of $\bar{X}$. In fact, the value $\bar{X} = 2649$ is no longer a very good answer to our question about typicality.

In such a situation the median is a better measure of central tendency because it is far less affected by the presence of the occasional extreme observation. For example, if again we replace our first observation 1648 by 201 648, we need to move just one observation in our above ascending sequence (the 201 648 has to be moved to the far right in the list). The 187th smallest observation now becomes $X_{130} = 2024$ rather than 2019, which becomes the 186th smallest. Consequently, the median is now $M = X_{130} = 2024$, which is also boxed in Table P.1. The new ascending sequence is is

$$274, 458, 515, \ldots, 2019, 2024, \ldots, 3987, 4132, 4208, 201\ 648.$$

Thus, although the mean changes markedly, there is little change in the value of the median. Indeed, if the original observation had been larger than the median, rather than smaller, then the median would have been left unchanged. Thus, in situations where the data set contains the occasional extreme observation, we normally prefer the median rather than the mean as our measure of central tendency.

A third measure of central tendency is the so-called *mode*. The mode is simply defined as the *most frequent observation*. That is, it is the value of X that occurs most often in the data set. In fact there are just three families in the data set of Table P.1 that have the same income. This expenditure is £2616. Since there are *less* than three families with any other particular expenditure, the mode is therefore £2616 for this data set. In this case, since the number of expenditure *levels* is relatively large compared with n, the total number of *observations*, the mode has little meaning as a measure of central tendency. In fact, the mode is used much less as a measure of central tendency than the mean and median. It is included here for the sake of completeness and is not referred to again in this text.

Example P.1

Find the mean, median and mode of the following set of observations:

$$12, 3, 23, 8, 17, 24, 7, 11, 7, 23, 9, 9, 15, 7, 12, 4.$$

If the fourth observation of 8 is changed to 108, how does this affect the three measures of central tendency?

Other measures of central tendency

The mean, median and mode are probably the best-known measures of central tendency, but we now describe two further measures which we will encounter later. First, we consider the geometric mean of a data set.

Recall that, to obtain the (arithmetic) mean, we add up all the observations in a data set and divide by n, the total number of observations. The *geometric mean* is obtained by an analogous process but here we *multiply* all the observations together and then take the nth root of the resulting quantity. That is, we calculate

$$\tilde{X} = \sqrt[n]{\prod_i X_i} \qquad\qquad [P.8]$$

where $\prod$ is a symbol similar to Σ and indicates that the X_i are all to be multiplied together.

Worked Example

Find both the mean and the geometric mean of the observations

$$11, 4, 8, 3, 13, 8, 6.$$

Solution

Summing the observations yields $\sum_i X_i = 53$, while multiplying them together gives $\prod_i X_i = 658\,944$. The mean is therefore given by [P.7] as

$$\bar{X} = 53/7 = 7.57.$$

To compute the geometric mean, we use [P.8], which gives

$$\tilde{X} = \sqrt[7]{658\,944} = 658\,944^{1/7} = 6.78.$$

Thus the geometric mean is somewhat smaller than the mean. In fact, except for the unlikely situation where all the X_i are identical, the geometric mean will always be smaller than the (arithmetic) mean.

Example P.2

Find the arithmetic and geometric means of the observations

$$24, 103, 61, 8, 42.$$

Compare the two summary statistics.

Example P.3

Find the geometric mean of the observations in Example P.1. Compare it with the arithmetic mean.

We conclude this subsection by considering the so-called weighted mean. Suppose we were dealing with a variable X, identical to that used above, but were faced with a rather different data set of, say, just eight observations, in which each observation consisted of the (arithmetic) mean clothing expenditure of a group of households all of the same size and composition. Such a data set is shown in Table P.2. There are 309 households in total in this data set and, if we required the mean expenditure of the 309 households, one way of obtaining a rough estimate of its mean would be to take the average of the eight observations in the second row of Table P.2. This gives a value of 20 920/8 = £2615.

Table P.2 Clothing expenditure of groups of households							
No of households	8	32	74	69	56	44	21	5
Mean expenditure	1 034	1 502	1 871	2 033	2 634	3 322	4 071	4 453
Total expenditures	8 272	48 064	138 454	140 277	147 504	146 168	85 491	22 265

But we can do better than this. The £2616 value just obtained takes no account of the fact that, for example, there are as many as 74 households in the group with mean £1871, whereas there are only five households in the group having mean £4453. Similarly, there are 56 households in the group with mean £2634 but only eight in the group that has mean £1034. Clearly, we should give more *weight* to the larger groups of households than we do to smaller groups.

We can, in fact, find the exact value for the (arithmetic) mean of spending for the 309 households, by finding first the sum of the clothing expenditures in each of the groups. Clearly, the eight households in the first group must have a total expenditure of 8 × 1034 or £8272. This follows from the definition of a group mean. Further total expenditure values for each of the groups are given in the third row of Table P.2 by, in each case, multiplying the group size by the group mean. To find the sum of the expenditures of all 309 households, we simply have to add up all the values in the third row. This yields a value of £736 495. Overall mean clothing expenditure is therefore given by 736 495/309 or £2383.

Our exact value of £2383 for mean expenditure is fairly far away from our rough estimate £2615, obtained earlier. The difference is the result of our original failure to take account of the different sizes of the various groups.

If we refer to the size of the ith group as n_i and refer to the ith group mean as $\bar{X}_i$, then it can be seen that, to obtain the true mean value £2383, we had to first sum all the products $n_i\bar{X}_i$ and then divide this sum by n, the total number of households. That is, the overall (arithmetic) mean is given by

$$\bar{X} = \frac{\sum n_i\bar{X}_i}{n} = \sum\left(\frac{n_i}{n}\right)\cdot\bar{X}_i$$
$$= \sum w_i\bar{X}_i, \qquad\qquad\qquad\text{[P.9]}$$

where $w_i = n_i/n$ for all i. The w_i, are known as *weights* and measure the proportions of the households in the various groups. Notice that, since $\sum n_i/n = 1$, the sum of the weights must be unity.

To obtain the exact value of $\bar{X} = $ £2383, we gave greater weight to the larger groups in the data set and for this reason, [P.9] is referred to as a *weighted mean*.

In general, if we have n observations, X_i, on a variable, (whether X happens to be a group mean or any other variable), and we assign a weight, w_i, to the ith observation, such that $\sum w_i = 1$, then the weighted mean of the X_i is given by

$$\bar{X}' = \sum w_i X_i. \qquad\qquad\qquad\text{[P.10]}$$

Normally, we use a weighted mean rather than a simple (arithmetic) mean whenever we believe that different observations in a data set are of varying importance and should therefore be given different weights.

Example P.4

Consider the following 10 observations on a variable X

$$23 \quad 8 \quad 14 \quad 11 \quad 45 \quad 24 \quad 10 \quad 32 \quad 16 \quad 23.$$

(a) If the respective weights 0.11, 0.07, 0.06, 0.12, 0.03, 0.03, 0.03, 0.24, 0.13 and 0.18 are given to the observations, find the weighted mean of X.

(b) If instead the weights are made proportional to the size of each observation, what is the new weighted mean?

(c) If instead the weights are made inversely proportional to the size of each observation, what is the new weighted mean?

Measures of variation

Measures of variation are summary statistics that provide an answer to the question 'to what extent do the observations vary about their central value?'. That is, how large is the spread or *dispersion* of the observations? There are a number of such measures,[3] but we will concentrate on just three of them, the first of which, the so-called *variance*, has great importance in statistics.

In the above question concerning variability, we referred to the 'central value' of observations. In this subsection, we select the (arithmetic) mean as the central value. Consequently, an obvious way of measuring the variability of observations in a data set is to consider the 'distances' or *deviations* of given observations from their mean $\bar{X}$. The size of such deviations will be dependent on the variability in the data. Let us define x_i as the deviation of the *i*th observation, X_i, from the mean, $\bar{X}$. That is,

$$x_i = X_i - \bar{X}, \qquad \text{for all } i. \tag{P.11}$$

There will be n values of x_i for any data set, some of them positive and the rest negative, depending on whether the X_i are greater or less than $\bar{X}$. An obvious way of obtaining an overall measure of variability is therefore to work out, in some way, the 'average value' of the x_i deviations. The simplest way to do this might seem to be to calculate the mean value of the x_i; that is, to take $\sum x_i/n = \sum(X_i - \bar{X})/n$ as our measure of variability. Unfortunately, it turns out that $\sum x_i$ always equals zero. We can demonstrate this fact by using the results concerning summations we obtained in the previous section:

$$\sum(X_i - \bar{X}) = \sum X_i - \sum \bar{X} = \sum X_i - n\bar{X} \qquad \text{(since } \bar{X} \text{ does not depend on } i\text{)}$$
$$= \sum X_i - n(\sum X_i/n) = 0.$$

Thus $\sum(X_i - \bar{X})/n = \sum x_i/n$ must always be zero. Effectively, positive values of x_i cancel out with negative values of x_i. But a quantity which always comes out as zero is hardly much use as a measure of the variability in the data set!

There are basically two ways in which we can get round this problem. Firstly, a negative number can be always transformed into a positive number, by squaring it. Thus $x_i^2 = (X_i - \bar{X})^2$ will always be positive for any observation, regardless of whether $x_i = X_i - \bar{X}$ is positive or negative. Thus, we can obtain a more appropriate measure of variability by taking the average value of the x_i^2 rather than the x_i. This yields the *variance* of the observations in a data set as

$$v^2 = \frac{\sum x_i^2}{n} = \frac{\sum(X_i - \bar{X})^2}{n}. \tag{P.12}$$

Such statistics are automatically produced by many statistical packages, and a scheme for calculating v^2 is illustrated in Table P.3, which involves the data in Table P.1. Firstly, the mean $\bar{X}$ is subtracted from each of the X_i observations in turn, to yield the $x_i = X_i - \bar{X}$ column. Notice that the sum of the values in this column comes to zero, as expected. The values are then, however, all squared to give the $x_i^2 = (X_i - \bar{X})^2$ column. The sum of the values in the $(X_i - \bar{X})^2$ column yields $\sum x_i^2 = 252\,126\,000$ (to six significant figures) so that, using [P.12], the variance v^2 is given by $252\,126\,000/373$ or $675\,941$. If you have available software such as Excel, for example, you can check these calculations for yourself but, if not, you can regard the value of v^2 as given. We shall interpret this value shortly.

Table P.3 Scheme for calculating squared and absolute deviations

X_i	$X_i - \bar{X}$	$(X_i - \bar{X})^2$	X_i^2	$|X_i - X|$
1 648	−465	216 225	2 715 904	465
458	−1 655	2 739 025	209 764	1 655
1 256	−857	734 449	1 577 536	857
3 066	953	908 209	9 400 356	953
3 069	956	913 936	9 418 761	956
2 356	243	59 049	5 550 736	243
$\vdots$	$\vdots$	$\vdots$	$\vdots$	$\vdots$
788 224	0	252 126 078	1 917 801 880	322 272

An alternative way of computing the variance of a set of observations is to use

$$v^2 = \frac{\sum X_i^2}{n} - \left(\frac{\sum X_i}{n}\right)^2. \tag{P.13}$$

This will always give the same value as [P.12],[4] and is often computationally quicker (particularly if you are reduced to using a hand calculator!) Since $\sum X_i/n = \bar{X}$, to use [P.13] the only other quantity required is $\sum X_i^2$. Schematically, this can be obtained by summing the X_i^2 column in Table P.3. This yields a value of $1.917\,80 \times 10^9$ (to 6 sig. figs). Thus, using [P.13], we obtain

$$v^2 = \frac{1.917\,8 \times 10^9}{373} - 2113.2^2 = 675\,941,$$

which gives the same value as given above by [P.12].

Example P.5

Find the variance of the observations in Example P.1, using both expressions [P.12] and [P.13].

Most beginners in statistics have conceptual difficulties in interpreting values for a variance. For example, if told that $v^2 = 675\,941$, how should we interpret this number? If the variance had been, for example, $463\,941$ rather than $675\,941$, we could have said that $675\,941$ implied a greater spread or dispersion in the observations than a value of $463\,941$. But what is implied by an absolute value of $675\,941$, when we have nothing to compare it with? We can go some way to interpreting values for the variance by computing the so-called standard deviation.

The *standard deviation*, v, of a set of observations is defined simply as the positive square root of the variance. That is, using [P.12],

$$v = \sqrt{\frac{\sum x_i^2}{n}}.$$ [P.14]

Thus for the data set of Table P.1, the standard deviation is given by $v = \sqrt{675\,941} = 822$ (to 3 sig. figs).

It is possible to give a rough idea of how we should interpret this value. Recall that the variance and standard deviation are based on the deviations or 'distances' between the observations X_i and their mean X. Some observations are obviously very 'far away' from the mean of 2113 but others are much 'closer'. Roughly, we can interpret v as being the 'average' deviation or 'distance' of observations from their mean value. Thus, roughly, the observations in Table P.1 are on average 822 away from their mean of 2113.

Example P.6

Consider the following set of examination marks:

$$34, 51, 68, 43, 57, 81, 28, 64.$$

Find the mean and standard deviation of the marks.

Suppose the marks were changed by (a) adding 5 to each mark; (b) increasing all marks by one-fifth. What effect will these changes have on the mean and standard deviation of the marks?

This rough interpretation of the standard deviation leads naturally to the third main summary statistic for measuring the variability of a data set. Recall that the quantities $X_i - \bar{X}$ can be negative or positive. Their sum is always zero, so we had to square all the $X_i - \bar{X}$ values, before we took their average, to obtain the variance. An alternative way of transforming the $X_i - \bar{X}$, so that they all become positive, is to take their *absolute value*.[5] The absolute value of $X_i - \bar{X}$ is normally written as $|X_i - \bar{X}|$. Such values are shown in the far right-hand column of Table P.3, and their sum is given at the foot of that column as

$\Sigma\,|\,X_i-X\,|$ = 322 272. The *mean deviation* is defined, as its name suggests, by

$$\text{mdev} = \frac{\Sigma\,|\,X_i-X\,|}{n}. \tag{P.15}$$

Hence, for the data in Table P.1, mdev = 322 272/373 = 864.

From its definition, it can be seen that the mean deviation is *exactly* equal to the average of the deviations of the X_i observations from their mean, whereas the standard deviation, as noted above, is only *roughly* equal to this average distance. As a summary statistic, the mean deviation is therefore a more precise measure of the dispersion of a set of observations than is the standard deviation. However, in practice you will find that the standard deviation is more often used. The reason for this is that, as we shall see on many occasions in this text, statistical theory concerning the variance, and hence the standard deviation, is well developed, unlike that of the mean deviation. This is simply because it is mathematically easier to handle squared values than absolute values.

Example P.7

Find the mean deviation of the observations in Example P.1 and compare it with the standard deviation.

Example P.8

Find the mean deviation of the exam marks in Example P.6 and compare it with the standard deviation.

Frequency distributions

It is often the case that summary statistics for central tendency and variation summarize a data set to too great an extent. So sometimes we require a 'halfway house' between raw data, such as that in Table P.1, and the summary statistics that we computed above.

A so-called *frequency distribution* of the data set in Table P.1 is shown in Table P.4 and provides such a halfway house. Notice that all 373 observations from Table P.1 have now been allocated to various 'ranges' or *classes*. For example, 26 of the observations have been allocated to the class, denoted 1000–1249, 38 have been allocated to the class 1750–1999, and so on. The numbers in the first column in Table P.4 are referred to as *class limits*,[6] while those in the third column are the *class frequencies*, which of course sum to 373. The middle column contains the tallies that have been used to count the numbers of observations in the various classes. Notice that there are more observations (56) in the class 1500–1749 than in any other class and, for this reason, such a class is termed the *modal class*.

Table P.4 Frequency distribution for data in Table P.1

Class	Tally	Frequency
250–499	‖	2
500–749	JHT ‖‖	8
750–999	JHT JHT JHT ‖	16
1000–1249	JHT JHT JHT JHT JHT ‖	26
1250–1499	JHT JHT JHT JHT JHT JHT JHT ‖‖‖	39
1500–1749	JHT JHT JHT JHT JHT JHT JHT JHT JHT JHT JHT ‖	56
1750–1999	JHT JHT JHT JHT JHT JHT JHT ‖‖	38
2000–2249	JHT JHT JHT JHT JHT JHT JHT ‖‖	38
2250–2499	JHT JHT JHT JHT JHT JHT ‖	32
2500–2749	JHT JHT JHT JHT JHT ‖‖	28
2750–2999	JHT JHT JHT JHT JHT	25
3000–3249	JHT JHT JHT JHT ‖	22
3250–3499	JHT JHT JHT JHT	20
3500–3749	JHT JHT ‖	11
3750–3999	JHT JHT	10
4000–4249	‖	2

Figure P.1 shows a *histogram*, which is a pictorial representation of the frequency distribution. In Fig. P.1, it is important to realize that *areas*, not heights, have been made proportional to frequencies, when constructing the histogram. To illustrate the reason for this, suppose the frequency distribution of Table P.4 had been given unequal class sizes, as shown in Table P.5. In this table, we have combined the first two classes of Table P.4 into a single class of 250–749, and combined the last four classes in Table P.4 into two single classes of 3250–3749 and 3750–4249. These new classes are twice the size of the original classes.

Taking the new Table P.5, if we now allowed heights to represent frequencies, we would obtain the histogram shown in Fig. P.2a whereas, if we make areas proportional to frequencies, we obtain the histogram of Fig. P.2b. It should be very clear that Fig. P.2b gives a much better approximation to the true underlying histogram than was illustrated in Fig. P.1. Consequently, it is very important to make areas and not heights proportional to frequencies, when constructing histograms of frequency distributions with unequal class sizes.

Histograms can take almost any shape, but in Fig. P.3 we show three histogram 'outlines' that are fairly common. In Fig. P.3a we have a frequency distribution or histogram outline that is perfectly symmetrical. In Fig. P.3b we have a frequency distribution which is

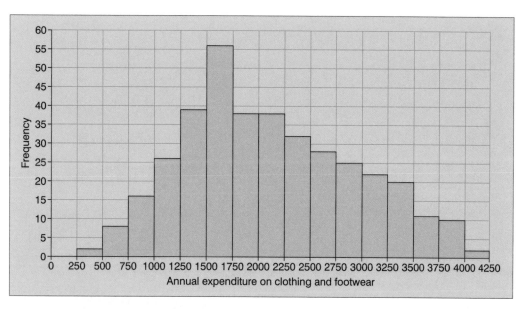

Figure P.1 Histogram of data in table P.1

non-symmetrical, with a longish 'right-hand tail'; such a distribution is said to be *skewed to the right*. On the other hand, in Fig. P.3c we have a histogram outline with a longish 'left-hand tail', that is, one that is *skewed to the left*.

The relationship between the three measures of central location, mean, median and mode, defined earlier in this section, depends on the skewness of the relevant frequency

Table P.5	
Class	**Frequency**
250–749	10
750–999	16
1000–1249	26
1250–1499	39
1500–1749	56
1750–1999	38
2000–2249	38
2250–2499	32
2500–2749	28
2750–2999	25
3000–3249	22
3250–3749	31
3750–4249	12

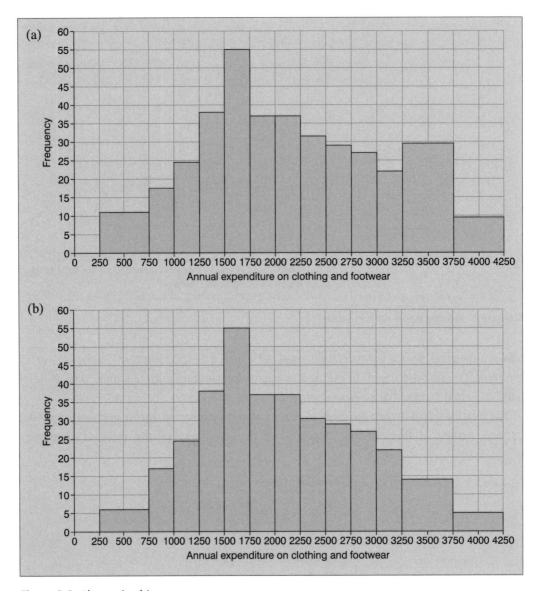

Figure P.2 Alternative histograms

distribution. A skew to the left implies the existence of some small extreme observations, and this will reduce the mean of the distribution but have little effect on the median. In fact, it turns out that for such a distribution

$$\text{mean} < \text{median} < \text{mode},$$

as illustrated in Fig. P.3c. In contrast, for a distribution that is skewed to the right,

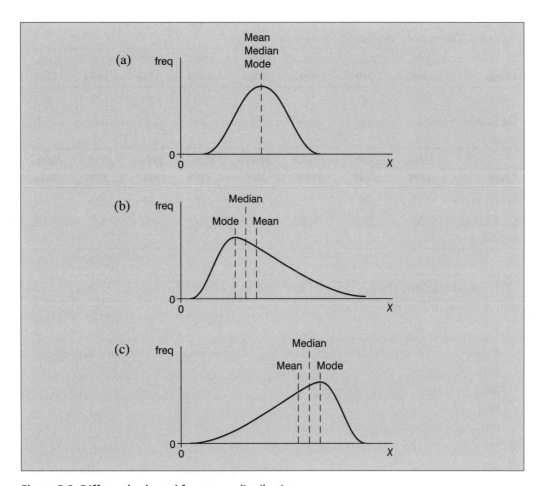

Figure P.3 Differently shaped frequency distributions

we always have

$$\text{mean} > \text{median} > \text{mode},$$

as illustrated in Fig. P.3b. Finally, for a completely symmetrical distribution all the measures of central tendency are equal, as indicated in Fig. P.3a.

Cumulative frequencies

It is often useful to display frequencies such as those in Table P.4 as a *cumulative frequency distribution*. In Table P.6, the frequencies from Table P.4 are shown in the second row, while the figures in the third row give the total number of observations below any given upper class limit in the first row. These make up the cumulative frequency distribution.

Table P.6 Cumulative frequencies for data in Table P.4

Class	250–499	500–749	750–999	1000–1049	1250–1499	1500–1749	1750–1999	2000–2249
Frequency	2	8	16	26	39	56	38	38
Cumulative frequency	2	10	26	52	91	147	185	223
Class	2250–2499	2500–2749	2750–2999	3000–3249	3250–3499	3500–3749	3750–3999	4000–4250
Frequency	32	28	25	22	20	11	10	2
Cumulative frequency	255	283	308	330	350	361	371	373

The cumulative distribution can be illustrated as a *cumulative histogram*. Such a histogram is shown in Fig. P.4.

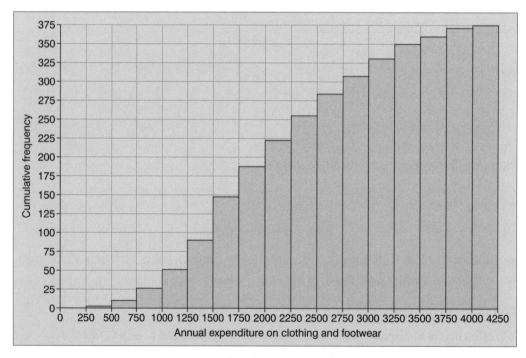

Figure P.4 Cumulative histogram for data in Table P.4

Example P.9

Consider the following observations:

40, 43, 46, 59, 64, 67, 68, 69, 75, 76, 78, 80, 82, 82, 86, 90, 92.

Classifying the observations into fives (40–44, 45–49, etc.) construct a frequency distribution for the data. Hence construct a cumulative frequency distribution.

Construct a cumulative histogram for the data.

Example P.10

Consider the following frequency distribution. Note that the class size varies in this distribution.

Class	25–29	30–39	40–49	50–59	60–69	70–89
Frequency	12	10	8	6	4	3

All observations have been rounded to the nearest whole number. Construct a histogram for the distribution.

P.3 Basic probability

It is sometimes useful to replace the frequencies in Table P.4 by what are termed *relative frequencies*. Relative frequencies are simply the *proportions* of the total number of observations that belong to the various classes in the distribution. For example, for Table P.4, we can obtain relative frequencies by dividing each of the original frequencies by $n = 373$. This yields the *relative frequency distribution* shown in Table P.7. Notice that the sum of the relative frequencies must, inevitably, equal unity.

Suppose now that the total number of observations had been not 373 but $n = 373\,000$ and that the number of observations occurring in the class 1750–1999 had been, for example, $f = 36\,844$. The proportion or relative frequency of observations lying in the class 1750–1999 would now be given (to 2 sig. figs) by

$$f/n = 36\,844/373\,000 = 0.099.$$

When n is as large as this, the relative frequency 0.099 is usually referred to as a *probability*. Thus we say that there is a probability of 0.099 that an observation will lie in the class 1750–1999. We summarize this by writing

$$\Pr(X \text{ in class } 1750\text{–}1999) = 0.099.$$

Table P.7 Relative frequency distribution for data in Table P.1

Class	250–499	500–749	750–999	1000–1049	1250–1499	1500–1749	1750–1999	2000–2249
Frequency	2	8	16	26	39	56	38	38
Relative frequency	0.005	0.021	0.043	0.070	0.105	0.150	0.102	0.102
Class	2250–2499	2500–2749	2750–2999	3000–3249	3250–3499	3500–3749	3750–3999	4000–4250
Frequency	32	28	25	22	20	11	10	2
Relative frequency	0.086	0.075	0.067	0.059	0.054	0.029	0.027	0.005

There is more than one way of defining a probability, but in this text we will use the above approach. More precisely, we will define a probability as a *limiting relative frequency*. If an *event E* has n opportunities of occurring but actually occurs just f times, then we define the *probability* of E occurring as the value that the relative frequency f/n approaches as n becomes very large. In mathematical language, that probability is called the *limit* of f/n as n tends to infinity. We write this as

$$\Pr(E) = \lim_{n \to \infty} (f/n). \qquad [\text{P.16}]$$

As an example, we apply the definition [P.16] to events in the following simple 'experiment'. Each *trial* of the experiment involves both rolling a six-sided die and tossing a coin. The possible *outcomes* are listed in Table P.8, where H denotes 'heads' and T 'tails'. Thus, for example, if a trial of the experiment results in a 5 rolled on the die and a head tossed with the coin, we say that the outcome H5 has occurred.

Table P.8 Outcomes for die-coin experiment

H1	H2	H3	H4	H5	H6
T1	T2	T3	T4	T5	T6

Consider what would happen if the number of trials, n, of the experiment is made larger and larger. Provided both the die and the coin are 'fair', each of the 12 outcomes in Table P.8 can be expected to occur one-twelfth of the time. That is, the relative frequency of H5 will gradually approach $\frac{1}{12}$ as n becomes larger and larger. The definition [P.16] thus yields

$$\Pr(\text{H5}) = \lim(f/n) = \tfrac{1}{12},$$

where f, this time, is the number of trials in which outcome H5 occurs. The probability of outcome H5 occurring is therefore $1/12$. In fact, it must be the case that

$$\text{Pr(H1)} = \text{Pr(H2)} = \text{Pr(H3)} = \text{Pr(H4)} = \text{Pr(H5)} = \text{Pr(H6)} = \text{Pr(T1)}$$
$$= \text{Pr(T2)} = \text{Pr(T3)} = \text{Pr(T4)} = \text{Pr(T5)} = \text{Pr(T6)} = 1/12.$$

That is, all the outcomes must be 'equally likely' and have the same probability, all occurring $1/12$ of the time, provided the number of trials, n, is extremely large.

Mutually and non-mutually exclusive events

In the above experiment, consider the outcomes H3 and T5. It is impossible to obtain both these outcomes on the same trial of the experiment. That is, the probability of obtaining both H3 and T5 on the same trial must be zero. Hence, we write

$$\text{Pr(H3 } and \text{ T5)} = 0.$$

H3 and T5 are examples of *mutually exclusive* events. Two such events are mutually exclusive if the occurrence of one precludes the possibility of the other occurring.

Next, consider two rather more complicated events, E_1 and E_2, each of which might occur on any trial of the experiment. Suppose E_1 is the event of obtaining a tail and die score of 5 or more, E_2 that of obtaining a tail and an even die score. There are in fact two outcomes, T5 and T6 (ringed in Table P.8), that result in the event E_1 occurring. Recalling that over very many trials of the experiment, each outcome occurs one-twelfth of the time, it follows that the event E_1 will occur $2 \times \frac{1}{12} = \frac{1}{6}$ of the time and hence has a probability of $\frac{1}{6}$.

There are three outcomes, T2, T4 and T6 (boxed in Table P.8) that result in the event E_2 occurring. Thus the event E_2 occurs $3 \times \frac{1}{12} = \frac{1}{4}$ of the time and will have a probability of $\frac{1}{4}$.

Now suppose we require the probability that *either E_1 or E_2 or both* occur. We can obtain such a probability by noting all the outcomes in Table P.8 that are either ringed or boxed or both ringed and boxed. There are four such outcomes and we know that, over very many trials, each of these outcomes will occur one-twelfth of the time. The required probability must therefore be $4/12$ and we therefore write

$$\text{Pr}(E_1 \text{ } or \text{ } E_2) = \tfrac{4}{12} = \tfrac{1}{3}. \qquad\qquad [\text{P.17}]$$

Note that the notation 'or' implies that, in [P.17], we are including the probability that *both* events have occurred. In fact, if the single outcome T6 is obtained then clearly both E_1 and E_2 will have occurred and this is the only outcome that has this property. We write this as

$$\text{Pr}(E_1 \text{ } and \text{ } E_2) = \tfrac{1}{12}.$$

Notice that, since $\text{Pr}(E_1 \text{ } and \text{ } E_2) \neq 0$ in this case, the events E_1 and E_2 cannot, by definition, be mutually inclusive. They are examples of *non-mutually exclusive events*.

The addition rule

In general, for any two events E_1 and E_2, the probability of either E_1 or E_2 or both occurring can be obtained by considering the so-called *Venn diagram* in Fig. P.5. The Venn diagram and its annotation are a symbolic representation of the probabilities associated with the two events E_1 and E_2. Notice, in particular, that the shaded area represents situations where *both* events have occurred.

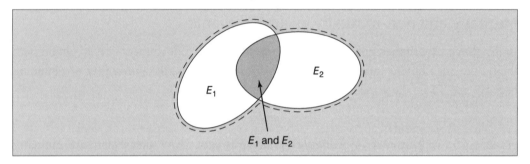

Figure P.5 Venn diagram for events E_1 and E_2

It should be clear that the total area inside the dotted boundary represents $\Pr(E_1 \text{ or } E_2)$, whereas the shaded area represents $\Pr(E_1 \text{ and } E_2)$. However, it is not the case that the sum of the E_1 and E_2 areas yields the $(E_1 \text{ or } E_2)$ area. That is, we cannot simply write

$$\Pr(E_1 \text{ or } E_2) = \Pr(E_1) + \Pr(E_2),$$

since this would imply including the shaded area twice. So, to find $\Pr(E_1 \text{ or } E_2)$, we need to subtract the shaded area, representing $\Pr(E_1 \text{ and } E_2)$:

$$\Pr(E_1 \text{ or } E_2) = \Pr(E_1) + \Pr(E_2) - \Pr(E_1 \text{ and } E_2). \qquad \text{[P.18]}$$

This is a completely general relationship between probabilities concerning any two events E_1 and E_2. We can check [P.18] for the given above events. We have

$$\Pr(E_1) = \tfrac{1}{6}, \qquad \Pr(E_2) = \tfrac{1}{4}, \qquad \Pr(E_1 \text{ and } E_2) = \tfrac{1}{12}.$$

Substituting in the right-hand side of [P.18] verifies that

$$\Pr(E_1 \text{ or } E_2) = \tfrac{1}{6} + \tfrac{1}{4} - \tfrac{1}{12} = \tfrac{4}{12} = \tfrac{1}{3},$$

as obtained above.

Example P.11

The probability that a patient visiting his dentist will have a tooth extracted is 0.06, the probability that he will have a cavity filled is 0.23 and the probability that he will have both a tooth extracted and a cavity filled is 0.02. Find the probability that a patient:

(a) will have a tooth extracted but no cavity filled;

(b) will have either a tooth extracted or a cavity filled;

(c) will have either a tooth extracted or a cavity filled but not both;

(d) will have neither a tooth extracted nor a cavity filled.

[*Hint*: draw the Venn diagram.]

Often of more use than [P.18] is a special case of this equation. Suppose the two events E_1 and E_2 are mutually exclusive. If this were the case, then we would have $\Pr(E_1 \text{ and } E_2) = 0$ by definition. In a such case, [P.18] becomes

$$\Pr(E_1 \text{ or } E_2) = \Pr(E_1) + \Pr(E_2). \qquad \text{[P.18a]}$$

Equation [P.18a] is referred to as the *addition rule* for probabilities. It implies that, *provided the two events are mutually exclusive*, the probability of either E_1 or E_2 occurring can be found by simply adding the probabilities corresponding to the two events. In terms of the Venn diagram in Fig. P.5, there is no shaded area and, to find the total area, the individual areas corresponding to the probabilities can simply be added, as in Fig. P.6.

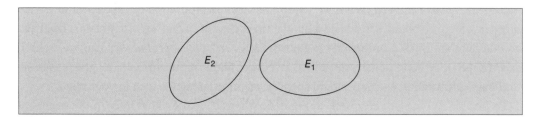

Figure P.6 Venn diagram for mutually exclusive events

It should be stressed that this is the only occasion when it is permitted to add probabilities! Addition of probabilities can be validly performed *only* when events are mutually exclusive *and* when we are seeking a probability of the kind $\Pr(E_1 \text{ or } E_2)$. Remember, however, that if two events are not mutually exclusive, then we have to resort to the general rule [P.18].

The addition rule can be extended to more than two events, provided they are all mutually exclusive. For example, to find the probability that one of the mutually exclusive events E_1, E_2, E_3 occurs, we can use

$$\Pr(E_1 \text{ or } E_2 \text{ or } E_3) = \Pr(E_1) + \Pr(E_2) + P(E_3).$$

Example P.12

If a single card is drawn from a normal pack of playing cards, the probability of any particular card being drawn is, obviously, 1/52. Find the probability that a single card drawn is:

(a) an ace;

(b) the ace or king of spades;

(c) a red card;

(d) a black king;

(e) an ace or king of the same suit.

Although you might not have realized it, for which answers were you using the addition rule [P.18a]?

Conditional probabilities

Referring back again to our coin/die experiment, consider the events E_1, tossing a head and rolling an odd number, and E_2, tossing a head and rolling a number that exceeds 2. Suppose we wish to obtain the probability of event E_1 occurring on a trial, *given that we already know that event E_2 has occurred*. What we require here is the proportion of times (out of all the times in which we obtain a head and a number in excess of 2) that we *also* obtain a head and an odd number. Such a probability is known as a *conditional probability* and we write it as $\Pr(E_1 | E_2)$. A conditional probability is conceptually more difficult to grasp than an 'ordinary' probability, and you should spend some time fixing the idea in your mind.

To find $\Pr(E_1 | E_2)$ we refer back to Fig. P.5, where E_1 and E_2 now refer to the events of this subsection. The occasions on which E_2 (head and number greater than 2) occur can be represented by all points lying within the area E_2 in Fig. P.5. But the occasions on which E_1 (head and odd number) *also* occur are given by the shaded area in Fig. P.5. Thus, out of all the occasions on which E_2 occurs, the proportion of times that E_1 also occurs can be represented by the shaded area *divided by* the total E_2 area. Thus we have

$$\Pr(E_1 | E_2) = \frac{\Pr(E_1 \text{ and } E_2)}{\Pr(E_2)}. \tag{P.19}$$

We can now make use of Table P.8 to obtain the required conditional probability. E_2 occurs whenever the outcome of the experiment is either H3, H4, H5 or H6. Hence $\Pr(E_2) = 4/12 = 1/3$. Both E_1 and E_2 occur only when the outcome is either H3 or H5. Thus $\Pr(E_1 \text{ and } E_2) = 2/12 = 1/6$. We therefore have, using [P.19], $\Pr(E_1 \mid E_2) = \frac{1}{6}/\frac{1}{3} = \frac{1}{2}$. Thus, one half of the times that we obtain a head and a number greater than 2, we also obtain a head and an odd number.

We can also obtain the conditional probability

$$\Pr(E_2 \mid E_1) = \frac{\Pr(E_2 \text{ and } E_1)}{\Pr(E_1)}. \qquad \text{[P.20]}$$

From Table P.8, it should be clear that $\Pr(E_1) = 3/12 = 1/4$. Since $\Pr(E_1 \text{ and } E_2) = \Pr(E_2 \text{ and } E_1) = 1/6$ we therefore obtain $\Pr(E_2 \mid E_1) = \frac{1}{6}/\frac{1}{4} = \frac{2}{3}$. Hence two-thirds of the occasions on which we obtain a head and an odd number we also obtain a head and a number greater than 2.

Equation [P.18] gave us a general method of finding $\Pr(E_1 \text{ or } E_2)$. We can find a general way of obtaining $\Pr(E_1 \text{ and } E_2)$ by using the definitions [P.19] and [P.20]. In fact, rearranging these equations gives two alternative expressions for $\Pr(E_1 \text{ and } E_2)$.

$$\Pr(E_1 \text{ and } E_2) = \Pr(E_1 \mid E_2)\Pr(E_2) = \Pr(E_2 \mid E_1)\Pr(E_1). \qquad \text{[P.21]}$$

Worked Example

Among third-year students, 60% are male and 12% are econometricians. The probability that such a student is both male and an econometrician is 0.07. Find the probabilities that:

(a) a student is both female and an econometrician;

(b) a female student is an econometrician;

(c) an econometric student is male.

Solution

The main problem with this type of question is in translating the words into precise probability statements. This is particularly difficult if English is not your first language! Let us define the following events: M, student is male; F, student is female; E, student is an econometrician; and N, student is a non-econometrician. Clearly

$$\Pr(M) = 0.6, \qquad \Pr(F) = 0.4 \qquad \Pr(E) = 0.12, \qquad \Pr(N) = 0.88.$$

We are also given

$$\Pr(M \text{ and } E) = 0.07.$$

(a) There two kinds of econometrician. Students can be either be male econometricians or they can be female econometricians. But being a male econometrician and being a female econometrician are mutually exclusive, so that we can use result [P.18a] and add probabilities. That is,

$$\Pr(E) = \Pr(M \text{ and } E) + \Pr(F \text{ and } E).$$

It follows that

$$\Pr(F \text{ and } E) = \Pr(E) - \Pr(M \text{ and } E) = 0.12 - 0.07 = 0.05.$$

(b) Here, we are asked what proportion of females are also econometricians. Recalling the meaning of a conditional probability, we therefore require $\Pr(E \mid F)$. To obtain this, we have to use the definition of a conditional probability given earlier. That is,

$$\Pr(E \mid F) = \frac{\Pr(E \text{ and } F)}{\Pr(F)} = \frac{\Pr(F \text{ and } E)}{\Pr(F)}$$

$$= \frac{0.05}{0.4} = 0.125.$$

(c) On this occasion we require the proportion of econometric students who are male, that is, $\Pr(M \mid E)$. Thus,

$$\Pr(M \mid E) = \frac{\Pr(M \text{ and } E)}{\Pr(E)} = \frac{0.07}{0.12} = 0.583.$$

In result [P.21], which of the two expressions for $\Pr(E_1 \text{ and } E_2)$ we use depends on what information is available, as the next example illustrates.

Example P.13

A company has a large stock of replacement parts for a machine. Twenty per cent of the parts are defective and the rest are good. Sixty per cent of the parts were bought from another company but the rest were made internally. Of those parts that were internally made, 90% are good. If a part is selected from stock:

(a) find the probability that it is both good and internally made;

(b) given that the part is good, find the probability that it is internally made.

Independent events

We begin this subsection with a definition. Two events are said to be *independent* if, and only if, the occurrence or non-occurrence of one of them has no influence on the probability of occurrence of the other. For example, suppose in a trial of our usual experiment we had the events E_1, tossing a head on the coin, and E_2, rolling a throw greater than 4 on the die. Clearly, what happens to the coin has no effect on what happens to the die and vice versa. Thus the events E_1 and E_2 are independent events.

Make sure you do not confuse independent events with mutually exclusive events (described earlier). For example, while the E_1 and E_2 in this subsection are independent, they are certainly not mutually exclusive, since there is no reason why E_1 and E_2 could not both occur on the same trial of the experiment.

Independent events have an important property. For two independent events, it must be the case that

$$\Pr(E_1|E_2) = \Pr(E_1) \quad \text{and} \quad \Pr(E_2|E_1) = \Pr(E_2). \tag{P.22}$$

That is, conditional probabilities reduce to 'ordinary' unconditional probabilities.

A moment's reflection should convince you that the results in [P.22] must be true. For example, $\Pr(E_1)$, the probability of tossing a head, is obviously one-half. But $\Pr(E_1|E_2)$, the probability of obtaining a head given that we have a roll in excess of 2, must also be one-half because what happens with the die has no effect on the coin. Whatever happens to the die, we will still obtain a head half of the time! Similarly, $\Pr(E_2) = 1/3$ regardless of what happens with the coin.

If we substitute from [P.22] into the general result [P.21], we see that, *for independent events*,

$$\Pr(E_1 \text{ and } E_2) = \Pr(E_1) \times \Pr(E_2). \tag{P.21a}$$

This is referred to as the *multiplication rule* for probabilities. In fact, this is the only occasion when it is permitted to multiply two probabilities together. Multiplication gives a valid result only if two events are independent *and* if we seek the probability that both events will occur.

In this case, since $\Pr(E_1) = 1/2$ and $\Pr(E_2) = 1/3$, it follows that $\Pr(E_1 \text{ and } E_2) = \frac{1}{2} \times \frac{1}{3} = \frac{1}{6}$. We can check this by referring back to Table P.8, where it can be seen that only the two outcomes, H5 and H6, imply that both events have occurred.

Of course, if two events are not independent, so that [P.21a] does not hold, then, to obtain $\Pr(E_1 \text{ and } E_2)$ we have to resort to the more general result [P.21].

Do not confuse the addition rule [P.18a] and the multiplication rule [P.21a]. The former is valid only for finding $\Pr(E_1 \text{ or } E_2)$ when E_1 and E_2 are mutually exclusive, whereas the latter can only be used to find $\Pr(E_1 \text{ and } E_2)$ when E_1 and E_2 are independent.

The multiplication rule extends to the case of more than two independent events. For example, if E_1, E_2 and E_3 are all independent events, then the probability that all three events will occur is given by

$$\Pr(E_1 \text{ and } E_2 \text{ and } E_3) = \Pr(E_1) \times \Pr(E_2) \times \Pr(E_3).$$

Worked Example

An unbiased six-sided die is rolled twice. Find the probability of obtaining:

(a) two 5s;

(b) an odd number on the first roll and a number greater than 1 on the second;

(a) a total score of 10.

Solution

(a) For each roll $Pr(5) = 1/6$. Since the 5s are independent events,

$$Pr(5 \text{ and } 5) = \tfrac{1}{6} \times \tfrac{1}{6} = \tfrac{1}{36}.$$

(b) $Pr(odd) = 1/2$, whereas $Pr(X > 1) = 5/6$. Again the events are independent, so that

$$Pr(odd \text{ and } X > 1) = \tfrac{1}{2} \times \tfrac{5}{6} = \tfrac{5}{12}.$$

(c) There are three ways in which we can end up with a total score of 10: (4 and 6), (6 and 4), (5 and 5). Now

$$Pr(4 \text{ and } 6) = \tfrac{1}{6} \times \tfrac{1}{6} = \tfrac{1}{36} \qquad \text{(independent events)}.$$

Similarly $Pr(6 \text{ and } 4) = Pr(5 \text{ and } 5) = 1/36$. The three ways of obtaining a total of 10 are all mutually exclusive. Hence,

$$Pr(\text{total of } 10) = 1/36 + 1/36 + 1/36 = 1/12.$$

Example P.14

Five independent firms can be either successful or unsuccessful during the forthcoming year, the probabilities of success being 0.7, 0.2, 0.4, 0.6 and 0.3, respectively. Find the probability that:

(a) all the firms are successful;

(b) all the firms are unsuccessful;

(c) at least one of the firms is successful.

Summary

- The algebra of **summation** provides a useful tool and shorthand for the study of statistics.

- The study of statistics can be divided into **statistical description** and **statistical inference**. In statistical description we frequently make use of various **summary statistics**.

- When summarizing a data set, the best-known measures of **central tendency** are the (arithmetic) **mean**, the **median** and the **mode**. However, the **geometric mean** and **weighted mean** are also used.

- The most important measures of **variation** are the **variance** and its positive square root, the **standard deviation**. Another measure is the **mean deviation**.

- **Frequency distributions** provide a useful 'halfway house' between raw data and summary statistics. **Histograms** provide a pictorial representation of frequency distributions.

- The **probability** of an event occurring can be defined as the limit of the **relative frequency** of the event occurring.

- The **addition rule** for probabilities can only be applied when two events are **mutually exclusive** and we require the probability that *either* one *or* the other of the events occurs.

- The **conditional probability** that an event occurs, given that we know that a second event has occurred, is given by the proportion of times that the first event also occurs.

- The **multiplication rule** for probabilities can only be applied when two events are **independent** and we require the probability that both events occur.

Notes

1. You do not need to check this value on a hand calculator! Any statistical software will have a facility for summing the observations in a data set.

2. As we shall see later, only if the dispersion of the observations is perfectly symmetric about its central point will the mean and median be identical. But if there is a substantial 'tail' of large observations, then the mean will exceed the median. Similarly, if there is a tail of small observations, then the median will exceed the mean.

3. For example, the simplest measure of variability is the *range*. The range is the difference between the smallest and largest observations in a data set. For other similar measures, see Bowers (1991, pp. 56–7).

4. Note that

$$\Sigma(X_i - \bar{X})^2 = \Sigma(X_i^2 - 2X_i\bar{X} + \bar{X}^2)$$
$$= \Sigma X_i^2 - 2\bar{X} \Sigma X_i + n\bar{X}^2$$
$$= \Sigma X_i^2 - 2n\bar{X}\frac{\Sigma X_i}{n} + n\bar{X}^2$$
$$= \Sigma X_i^2 - n\bar{X}^2.$$

Dividing this result throughout by n yields [P.13].

5. The absolute value of any number is obtained by ignoring any negative sign before the number. Thus the absolute value of -8 is simply 8. This is written as $|-8| = 8$. Similarly, $|-56| = 56$ and so on. If a number is positive, then its absolute value is just that number. Thus $|6| = 6$, $|324| = 324$, and so on.

6. The class limits should be distinguished from the *class boundaries* which are the 'true' class limits. Since the observations in Table P.1 have been rounded to the nearest pound, this implies that any expenditures lying between, for example, £1749.50 and £1999.49 will, after rounding, be included in the class £1750–£1999. The class boundaries are, therefore, £1749.50–£1999.49 in this case and differ from the quoted class limits.

Part I

Statistics

1

Discrete probability distributions

Objectives

After completing your study of this chapter you should be able:

1. to understand the concepts of a sample space and a discrete random variable;

2. to build up the probability distribution for a variable from knowledge of a sample space;

3. to understand the idea of a mathematical expectation and know how to compute the mean and variance of a probability distribution;

4. to construct pictorial representations of probability distributions and understand the concept of a probability density;

5. to calculate the expected monetary value of a decision and appreciate the limitations of this concept;

6. to recognize some well-known probability distributions and be able to make use of them.

Introduction

The concepts you will meet in this chapter are best grasped by using simple chance mechanisms such as dice and coins. Building on these ideas, we can then go on to analyse situations that are closer to the more real-world situations we meet in economics.

Much of modern statistics is built on the notion of probability distributions and the associated concept of mathematical expectation. It is assumed that the student has read the material on basic probability in the prerequisites chapter, but before we can discuss probability distributions and expectations, we first need to discuss the concepts of *sample spaces* and *stochastic variables*. We then consider the construction of *probability histograms*, which requires the discussion of the rather difficult concept of a *probability density*. Finally, we consider some well-known probability distributions, in particular the *binomial* distribution and the *Poisson* distribution.

1.1 Sample spaces and stochastic variables

Consider a simple so-called *experiment* where a coin is tossed three times. Each *trial* of the experiment results in an *outcome*. There are eight possible outcomes to the experiment.

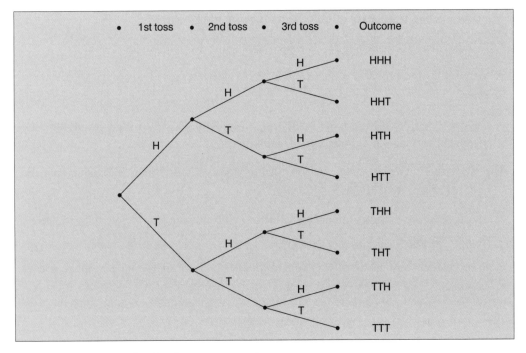

Figure 1.1 Outcomes for the three-toss experiment

The simplest way of finding all possible outcomes is to construct a tree diagram like that in Fig. 1.1. Note that there are $2^3 = 8$ outcomes in all, which are listed in Table 1.1.

Table 1.1 Sample space for three-toss experiment

HHH (3)	HHT (2)	HTH (2)	HTT (1)
THH (2)	THT (1)	TTH (1)	TTT (0)

In general, the *sample space* of an experiment simply consists of a listing of all the possible outcomes of that experiment. Thus the outcomes in Table 1.1 define the sample space for the present experiment.

Suppose we define a variable, X, which equals the number of heads obtained on one trial of the experiment. The value of X will vary according to the outcome of the experiment. The values obtained for each of the possible outcomes are shown in parentheses in Table 1.1.

The variable X is an example of what is called a *random* or *stochastic variable*. A stochastic variable is a variable the values of which are determined by some chance mechanism. In the current example the chance mechanism is simply the tossing of a coin.

Notice that the stochastic variable X can only take certain integer values. For example, in any given trial of the experiment it is impossible to obtain $X = 3.21$. A variable such as X is therefore referred to as a discrete variable.[1]

It is frequently possible to attach probabilities to individual outcomes in a sample space. For example, in our coin tossing experiment, if the coin is a fair one, then the probabilities of obtaining 'heads' (H) and 'tails' (T) are both 0.5 and individual 'tosses' can be regarded as independent events. It follows that the probability of obtaining the sequence HHT is simply $0.5 \times 0.5 \times 0.5 = 0.125$ or 1/8. Similarly, each and every outcome in this sample space has a probability of 1/8 of occurring.

The sample space in Table 1.1 can also be used to find the probability of more complicated 'events' occurring. For example, suppose we require the probability that, on one trial of our experiment, more heads than tails are obtained. Of the outcomes in the sample space, four (HHH, THH, HTH, and HHT) yield the required result. Each of these outcomes has a probability of $\frac{1}{8}$. But all outcomes are mutually exclusive, so that the probability of getting more heads than tails must be $4 \times \frac{1}{8} = \frac{4}{8}$ or 0.5.

Finally, note that, since all outcomes in a sample space are mutually exclusive, the sum of the probabilities for all the outcomes must always be unity. For example, in our experiment all eight outcomes have probability $\frac{1}{8}$ so that the sum of the probabilities in the distribution is $8 \times \frac{1}{8} = 1$.

Example 1.1

Suppose the coin is tossed four times. What is the sample space for this experiment? If Y is the number of heads obtained, find $\Pr(Y = 3)$.

Example 1.2

A six-sided die is rolled twice. Set up the sample space for this experiment. Hence find the probability:

(a) of getting a double 6;

(b) of getting a value on the second roll that is greater than the value on the first roll;

(c) that the sum of the two values obtained is an even number;

(d) of getting a 4 at least once in the two rolls.

1.2 **Probability distributions**

In this section we derive what is called the *probability distribution* for the stochastic variable X, defined above as the number of heads obtained in three tosses of a coin. The probability distribution for a variable involves, firstly, a *listing* of all the possible values that the variable can take. Thus, in this case, the variable X can take any of the values 0, 1, 2, and 3, as indicated in Table 1.2.

Table 1.2 Probability distribution for X			
X	0	1	2	3
$\Pr(X)$	0.125	0.375	0.375	0.125

Secondly, deriving a probability distribution involves the computation of the *probabilities* of obtaining each and all the possible values that X can take. For example, to compute $\Pr(X = 3)$, we simply note that only the outcome HHH gives us $X = 3$ and this has a probability of 1/8 of occurring. Thus $\Pr(X = 3) = \frac{1}{8}$.

Suppose, however, we wish to compute $\Pr(X = 2)$. Assuming the coin is a fair one, we know that each outcome has a probability of 1/8 of occurring. From Table 1.1, it can be seen that three of the eight outcomes lead to our getting the result $X = 2$. Since all outcomes are mutually exclusive, it follows from the addition rule [P.18a] that

$$\Pr(X = 2) = \Pr(HHT) + \Pr(HTH) + \Pr(THH)$$
$$= \tfrac{1}{8} + \tfrac{1}{8} + \tfrac{1}{8} = \tfrac{3}{8} = 0.375.$$

One way of interpreting this result is to say that, if we considered very many trials of the experiment, we would obtain each and every of the above three outcomes $\frac{1}{8}$ of the time. Hence, we would obtain the result, $X = 2$, a proportion $\frac{3}{8} = 0.375$ of the time.

Probabilities for all possible values of X are shown in Table 1.2. Notice that, in Table 1.2, we have introduced the notation that $p(X)$ represents the probability of obtaining X tosses. Thus $\Pr(X = 2) = p(2)$ and so on.

Since we cover all possible values of X, the probabilities in a probability distribution should always sum to unity. That is, $\sum p(X) = 1$. If the probabilities do not sum to unity then either an arithmetic error has been made or the range of values for X has not been correctly specified.

Example 1.3

Use the sample space obtained in Example 1.1 to obtain the probability distribution for Y, the number of heads in four tosses of a coin.

Worked Example

In the next three years' trading, depending on market conditions, a firm may make either an annual profit (P) or an annual loss (L). If the market is booming, then annual profit is £80 million, and there is a probability of 3/4 that this happens. But if the market slumps, there is an annual loss of £20 million with probability 1/4.

Assuming that probabilities remain unchanged throughout, and that T is the aggregate profit/loss over the three years, find the probability distribution for T.

Solution

The sample space in this case is shown in the first column of Table 1.3. For example, the outcome LPL implies losses in the first and third years but a profit in the second.

Table 1.3 Sample space and values for T

Outcome	T	Probability
PPP	$80 + 80 + 80 = 240$	$\frac{3}{4} \times \frac{3}{4} \times \frac{3}{4} = \frac{27}{64}$
LPP	$-40 + 80 + 80 = 140$	$\frac{1}{4} \times \frac{3}{4} \times \frac{3}{4} = \frac{9}{64}$
PLP	$80 - 20 + 80 = 140$	$\frac{3}{4} \times \frac{1}{4} \times \frac{3}{4} = \frac{9}{64}$
PPL	$80 + 80 - 20 = 140$	$\frac{3}{4} \times \frac{3}{4} \times \frac{1}{4} = \frac{9}{64}$
PLL	$80 - 20 - 20 = 40$	$\frac{3}{4} \times \frac{1}{4} \times \frac{1}{4} = \frac{3}{64}$
LPL	$-20 + 80 - 20 = 40$	$\frac{1}{4} \times \frac{3}{4} \times \frac{1}{4} = \frac{3}{64}$
LLP	$-20 - 20 + 80 = 40$	$\frac{1}{4} \times \frac{1}{4} \times \frac{3}{4} = \frac{3}{64}$
LLL	$-20 - 20 - 20 = -60$	$\frac{1}{4} \times \frac{1}{4} \times \frac{1}{4} = \frac{1}{64}$

Our random variable in this example is aggregate profit T. The various values of T are shown in the second column of Table 1.3. For example, the outcome LPL results in a total profit (in £m) of $T = -20 + 80 - 20 = 40$. Similarly the outcome PPL yields $T = 80 + 80 - 20 = 140$.

The tricky part of this problem is finding the probabilities of the eight outcomes. Unlike the above coin tossing example, the outcomes do not all have the same probabilities. But, since we know that the probabilities of profit and loss remain unchanged, we can compute the probability of PLL, for example, as $\frac{3}{4} \times \frac{1}{4} \times \frac{1}{4}$ or 3/64. Similarly, the probability of PPP is $\frac{3}{4} \times \frac{3}{4} \times \frac{3}{4} = 27/64$. All such probabilities are, in fact, evaluated in the third column of Table 1.3.

To obtain the probability distribution for T, we must first list all possible values of T. From Table 1.3, it can be seen that T can take the values 240, 140, 40 and −60 as listed below. To obtain the probabilities in the distribution it is clear, from Table 1.3, that $\Pr(T = 240) = 27/64$ and $\Pr(T = -60) = 1/64$. $\Pr(T = 140)$ can be found by adding the probabilities corresponding to the three (equally likely) mutually exclusive outcomes that yield $T = 140$. Thus $\Pr(T = 140) = 3 \times 9/64 = 27/64$. Similarly, $\Pr(T = 40) = 3 \times 3/64 = 9/64$. The full probability distribution is therefore as follows:

T	−60	40	140	240
$p(T)$	1/64	9/64	27/64	27/64

Notice that, as expected, the sum of the probabilities in the distribution is unity.

Cumulative distributions

Consider again the probability distribution in Table 1.2, for $X = $ the number of heads obtained in three tosses of a coin. Let

$$C(X) = \Pr(\text{obtaining } X \text{ } or \text{ } fewer \text{ heads in 3 tosses}).$$

Thus, for example, $C(2)$ is the probability of obtaining 0 or 1 or 2 heads out of 3. It follows from Table 1.2 that

$$C(0) = 0.125,$$
$$C(1) = 0.125 + 0.375 = 0.5,$$
$$C(2) = 0.125 + 0.375 + 0.375 = 0.875,$$
$$C(3) = 0.125 + 0.375 + 0.375 + 0.125 = 1.$$

These probabilities are known as *cumulative probabilities* and their distribution is referred to as the *cumulative distribution* for X. The distribution is summarized in Table 1.4. As we shall see, cumulative distributions can be a useful tool for tackling certain problems.

Table 1.4 Cumulative distribution for X

X	0	1	2	3
C(X)	0.125	0.500	0.875	1.000

Example 1.4

Use the probability distribution in Example 1.3 to obtain the cumulative distribution for Y.

Example 1.5

Four travelling salesmen are employed by a firm. The probability that a salesman makes a sale on his first visit of the day is 0.4. This is the same for each salesman. The 'experiment' in this case involves observing the four salesmen making their first visits of the day. What is the 'sample space' for this experiment? What is the probability that at most two salesmen make sales on their first visits of the day?

Worked Example

A four-sided die has the numbers 1, 2, 4, 8 on its sides. It is tossed twice. List the elements of the sample space for this experiment. If X is the sum of the numbers obtained on the two tosses, derive the probability distribution for X. Find the cumulative distribution for X.
 If Y is the product of the numbers obtained, derive the probability distribution for Y.

Solution

The sample space is shown below, together with the resultant X and Y numbers.

	X	Y		X	Y		X	Y		X	Y
(1, 1)	2	1	(2, 1)	3	2	(4, 1)	5	4	(8, 1)	9	8
(1, 2)	3	2	(2, 2)	4	4	(4, 2)	6	8	(8, 2)	10	16
(1, 4)	5	4	(2, 4)	6	8	(4, 4)	8	16	(8, 4)	12	32
(1, 8)	9	8	(2, 8)	10	16	(4, 8)	12	32	(8, 8)	16	64

The possible values of X are 2, 3, 4, 5, 6, 8, 9, 10, 12 and 16. Since all 16 outcomes of the experiment are equally likely, the probability distribution for X is therefore

X	2	3	4	5	6	8	9	10	12	16
$p(X)$	0.0625	0.125	0.0625	0.125	0.125	0.0625	0.125	0.125	0.125	0.0625

The cumulative distribution for X is hence

X	2	3	4	5	6	8	9	10	12	16
$C(X)$	0.0625	0.1875	0.25	0.375	0.5	0.5625	0.6875	0.8125	0.9375	1

The possible values of Y are 1, 2, 4, 8, 16, 32 and 64 and its probability distribution, which we write as $q(Y)$, is

Y	1	2	4	8	16	32	64
$q(Y)$	0.0625	0.125	0.1875	0.25	0.1875	0.125	0.0625

Example 1.6

A box contains eight electric bulbs taken from stock, two of which are faulty and the rest satisfactory. Three bulbs are drawn from the box, each bulb being replaced and 'mixed' with the other bulbs before the next is drawn. What is the sample space for this experiment? If X is the number of satisfactory balls drawn, find the probability distribution for X. [*Hint*: look at the worked example on page 37.]

Suppose that when a bulb is removed from the box it is *not* replaced. What will the probability distribution for X be now? [*Hint*: if S = satisfactory, then $\Pr(SSS) = \frac{6}{8} \times \frac{5}{7} \times \frac{4}{6}$ *not* $\left(\frac{6}{8}\right)^3$].

1.3 **Mathematical expectations**

Suppose our coin tossing experiment was performed very many times. It is fairly clear that 'on average', over very many such trials, we would obtain 1.5 heads out of the three tosses. However, deducing the 'average' result of an experiment is not always so easy. It is easy in this case because of the symmetric nature of the probability distribution in Table 1.2, with the highest probabilities being for $X = 1$ and $X = 2$.

With non-symmetric probability distributions, we need a more general approach. It is not normally enough to take the average or mean value of the X values in a probability distribution such as that in Table 1.2. Some values of X occur more often than others so, usually, it is necessary to take not the simple arithmetic mean but a *weighted mean*[2] of the X values. The weights we use in this case are the probabilities, $p(0)$, $p(1)$, $p(2)$ and $p(3)$, that is, the proportion of times each value of X occurs. Since these weights sum to unity, we therefore use [P.10] and compute a weighted mean as

$$\text{average value of } X = 0p(0) + 1p(1) + 2p(2) + 3p(3)$$
$$= \Sigma\, Xp(X),$$

where the summation is over all values of X. Computing this for the distribution in Table 1.2 yields

$$\Sigma\, Xp(X) = 0(0.125) + 1(0.375) + 2(0.375) + 3(0.125)$$
$$= 1.5$$

as expected. The advantage of using this method of finding the 'average' is, as we shall see, that it can be employed for non-symmetric probability distributions.

The quantity $\Sigma\, Xp(X)$ is known as the *mean* of the probability distribution for X and is normally given the symbol μ. It is also referred to as the *expected value* or *mathematical expectation* of X, written E(X). That is,

$$\mu = \text{E}(X) = \Sigma\, Xp(X). \tag{1.1}$$

The symbol E in [1.1] is known as the *expectations operator*.

For a reason that will be clear in a moment, suppose that on each trial of our experiment, we not only count the number of heads, X, obtained but also square this number and obtain a value for X^2. What would the average value of these X^2 values be over very many trials? That is, what is the expected value of X^2?

The possible values of X^2 are 0, 1, 4, and 9. We can find E(X^2) by taking a weighted mean of these X^2 values, again using the respective probabilities as weights. That is,

$$\text{E}(X^2) = \Sigma\, X^2 p(X). \tag{1.2}$$

Thus, for the probability distribution in Table 1.2, we have

$$\text{E}(X^2) = 0(0.125) + 1(0.375) + 4(0.375) + 9(0.125)$$
$$= 3.$$

Notice that E(X^2), the average value of X^2 over many trials of the experiment, equals 3 not 2.25, which is the square of E(X) = 1.5. In fact in general *it is not the case* that E(X^2) = [E(X)]^2. This result illustrates the fact that one has to be very careful when manipulating mathematical expectations. What may seem to follow from the normal rules of arithmetic does not necessary follow.

Notice also that, although the possible values of X^2 are 0, 1, 4 and 9, it is not possible to obtain $E(X^2)$ by taking the simple arithmetic mean of the X^2 values. That would yield a value of $14/4 = 3.5$. Because of the non-symmetrical nature of the X^2 values, we have to be careful to take a weighted mean of these values. The weights used are, as explained, the probabilities in Table 1.2.

The technique of using weighted means can be used for finding the expected value of any function of a stochastic variable, X. For our example, if we require $E(X^3)$, the average value of X^3 over many trials, then we use

$$E(X^3) = \sum X^3 p(X) = 0(0.125) + 1(0.375) + 8(0.375) + 27(0.125)$$
$$= 6.75$$

Notice that $E(X^3)$ is not the same as $[E(X)]^3$, which is $(1.5)^3 = 3.375$. Again we have to be cautious when handling the expectations operator. Similarly, for example,

$$E(X^4) = \sum X^4 p(X),$$
$$E(X + 3)^2 = \sum (X + 3)^2 p(X),$$
$$E(X + 1)^{-1} = \sum (X + 1)^{-1} X p(X),$$

where, in all cases, the summation is over all values of X.

In general the expected value of any function of X, $f(X)$, is given by

$$E(X) = \sum f(X)p(X). \qquad [1.3]$$

Example 1.7

Find the mean of the probability distribution in Example 1.3. Find also $E(Y^2)$, $E(Y^3)$ and $E(Y + 2)$. Verify that $E(Y^2) \neq [E(Y)]^2$ and $E(Y^3) \neq [E(Y)]^3$, but $E(Y + 2) = E(Y) + 2$.

The variance of a probability distribution

A very useful mathematical expectation is the *variance* of a probability distribution, sometimes written $V(X)$, given the symbol σ^2 and defined as the expected value of $(X - \mu)^2$, μ being, as usual, the mean of the distribution. Thus, using [1.3],

$$\sigma^2 = V(X) = E(X - \mu)^2 = \sum (X - \mu)^2 p(X). \qquad [1.4]$$

In our coin tossing example, X is the number of heads obtained and $\mu = 1.5$ is the expected number of heads per trial, so that σ^2 equals $E(X - 1.5)^2$. The variance, in this case, is thus based on the quantity $X - 1.5$ and is therefore a measure of the 'average' distance of X from its mean value of 1.5. In fact, it measures the extent to which all the values of X that we would obtain from many trials spread themselves about their central value of 1.5. Since the extent of this spread or dispersion depends on the probabilities in Table 1.2, σ^2 is therefore a measure of the spread or dispersion of probabilities in the distribution. The mean of a probability distribution will not of course always equal 1.5, but we can use [1.4] to measure the dispersion of probabilities in any distribution.[3]

One way of computing a variance is to use the expression given by [1.4]. The computations required are shown in the various rows of Table 1.5. By summing the bottom row in Table 1.5, it can be seen that the variance $\sigma^2 = 0.75$ for this probability distribution.

Table 1.5 Computation of variance

X	0	1	2	3
$p(X)$	0.125	0.375	0.375	0.125
$X - 1.5$	-1.5	-0.5	0.5	1.5
$(X - 1.5)^2$	2.25	0.25	0.25	2.25
$(X - 1.5)^2\, p(X)$	0.28125	0.09375	0.09375	0.28125
	$\Sigma(X - 1.5)^2 p(X) = 0.75$			

In fact, the variance is more easily computed using

$$\sigma^2 = E(X^2) - \mu^2. \qquad [1.5]$$

We have already found $E(X^2) = 3$ in the previous subsection so that, using [1.5], we have $\sigma^2 = 3 - 1.5^2 = 0.75$ as before. In fact the expressions [1.4] and [1.5] will always give identical values for a variance.[4]

While it is usually easy to give a clear meaning to the value of the mean of a probability distribution, interpreting the variance is not quite so straightforward. The variance is easy enough to compute and we know that a variance measures the dispersion of probabilities in a distribution, but it is not easy to attach any absolute meaning to a value such as $\sigma^2 = 0.75$. However, it is also useful to define the *standard deviation*, σ, of a probability distribution as the positive square root of the variance, and this quantity is easier to interpret.

In our coin tossing example, the standard deviation is clearly $\sigma = \sqrt{0.75} = 0.866$. The advantage of the standard deviation over the variance is that the standard deviation gives a very rough and ready idea of the dispersion of probabilities in a distribution. We can say that over many trials of our experiment, the values of X obtained will 'on average' be roughly about a distance of 0.866 units away from their mean of 1.5. Sometimes we will get values of $X = 0$ or $X = 3$, which are relatively far away from their mean of $E(X) = 1.5$, but other times we will get values of $X = 1$ or $X = 2$, which are relatively close to E(X). But on average we will get values of X which are roughly 0.866 units away from E(X).[5]

Example 1.8

Use the probability distribution for X obtained in the worked example on p. 39 to find its mean E(X) and variance σ^2. Interpret these values. Find also E($1/X$). Compare $1/$E(X) and E($1/X$).

Example 1.9

In the worked example on p. 37, find the expected value of T. Find also E(T^2) and hence V(T). Find and interpret the standard deviation of T.

Example 1.10

For the experiment in Example 1.6, find E(X) and V(X) (a) when bulbs are replaced and (b) when bulbs are not replaced. Find also E(X^4) in each case and compare it with $[E(X^2)]^2$.

Example 1.11

Thirty per cent of a business's long distance telephone calls are charged for 5 minutes, 60% of calls are charged for 10 minutes, while the remaining calls are zero-charged. If the business has to pay £5 per minute, what is the expected charge for a call?

Example 1.12

For Example 1.5, find the probability distribution for the number of sales made on the first visit. Find the expected value and variance of first-visit sales.

1.4 Pictorial representations and probability densities

It is often helpful to provide a pictorial representation of a probability distribution such as that in Table 1.2. In Fig. 1.2a this has been done by presenting a *probability histogram*.

In a probability histogram, values of the variable X are shown on the horizontal axes and it may seem, at first, that in Fig. 1.2a we are measuring simple probabilities on the vertical axis. However, what appears on the vertical axis are values of something rather more complicated than simple probabilities. The crucial point to grasp, at this stage, is that it is the *areas* rather than the *heights* of the blocks in a histogram that represent probabilities.[6]

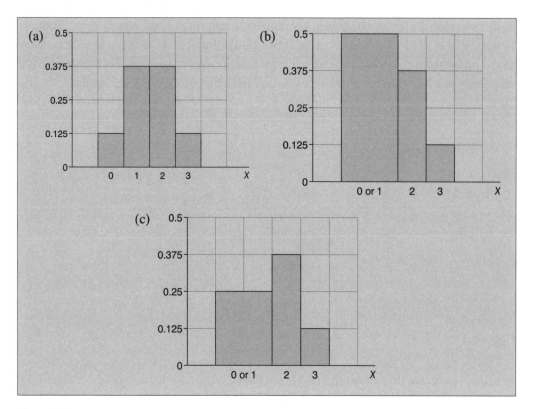

Figure 1.2

Suppose, for example, we were unaware of the individual values for $p(0)$ and $p(1)$ in Table 1.2 but that we did know that $\Pr(X = 0 \text{ or } 1) = 0.5$. If we attempted to represent this in a histogram, with heights rather than areas representing probabilities, we would obtain Fig. 1.2b. It should be clear that this gives a false impression of the true probability of getting $X = 0$ or $X = 1$. However, if we allow *areas* to represent probabilities we obtain Fig. 1.2c. Since the width of the combined $X = 0$ or 1 block is twice that of the $X = 0$ and $X = 1$ blocks in Fig. 1.2a, we give the combined block a height of half the 0.5 in Fig. 1.2b. In fact the *area* of the $X = 0$ or 1 block in Fig. 1.2c is exactly equal to the sum of the areas of the $X = 0$ and $X = 1$ blocks in Fig. 1.2a. Thus Fig. 1.2c gives a better representation of the unknown values than does 1.2b.

The question arises of what is actually being measured on the vertical axis of Fig. 1.2a. In fact we are measuring probability *per unit distance along the horizontal axis*. This is referred to as the *probability density* for X.

For example, consider Fig. 1.3, which illustrates a probability distribution for the take-home pay per week of a large population of four-person households. On the horizontal axis is measured pay in pounds sterling and on the vertical axis probability density per pound. Remember that it is areas rather than heights that represent probabilities in such diagrams. Hence the area of block A represents the probability of a household receiving a take-home pay, X, of between zero and £200. Since the probability density per pound is 0.0015 over the range zero to £200, the area of the block A is given by $0.0015 \times 200 = 0.3$, so that[7]

$$\Pr(0 < X < 200) = 0.30.$$

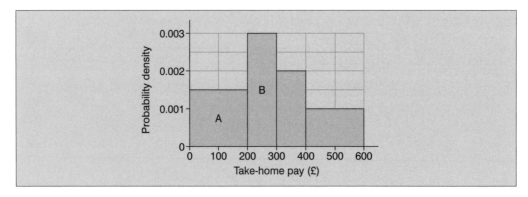

Figure 1.3

Similarly, to obtain the probability of a household getting take-home pay of between £200 and £300, we need to find the area B. Over this range, probability density is 0.003 per pound, so that the area B equals $0.003 \times 100 = 0.3$. That is,

$$\Pr(200 < X < 300) = 0.3.$$

Notice that the two probabilities that we have calculated are the same. This reflects the fact that the blocks A and B have the same areas, although they have different heights. Similarly, we can calculate the remaining probabilities in the distribution as

$$\Pr(300 < X < 400) = 0.002 \times 100 = 0.2,$$
$$\Pr(400 < X < 600) = 0.001 \times 200 = 0.2.$$

Note that the four probabilities in the distribution sum to unity as they should.

Example 1.13

Consider the following probability distribution.

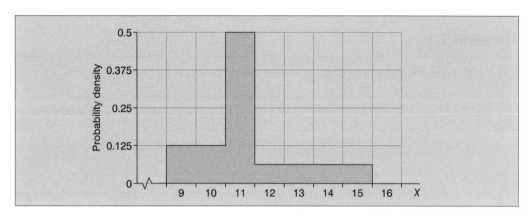

Find the probability that: (a) $X = 11$; (b) $X =$ either 9 or 10; (c) X lies between 12 and 15, inclusive.

Example 1.14

The probability histogram for the output of a firm, Y, measured in tonnes, is shown below. As usual, probability densities are shown on the vertical axis.

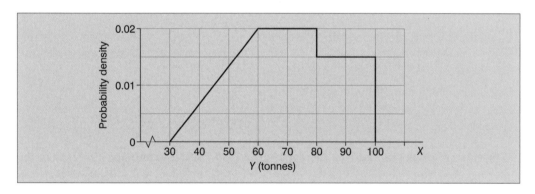

Find the probability that output (a) lies between 80 and 100 tonnes; (b) lies between 60 and 80 tonnes; (c) is less than 60 tonnes.

If weights are measured in units of 0.1 tonne instead of tonnes, how will this affect the probability densities on the vertical axis?

We introduced the expectations operator earlier in this chapter and saw, for example, that it was not the case that $E(X^2) = [E(X)]^2$. We shall make much use of mathematical expectations in this text and great care must be taken over how they are handled. We will therefore present a number of theorems concerning the use of both expected values and variances in this and the next chapters. The first such theorem is the following.

Theorem 1.1

If X is a random variable and a and b are constants such that $Z = a + bX$, then

$$E(Z) = a + bE(X)$$

and

$$V(Z) = b^2 V(X).$$

The proof of the above theorem can be found in the appendix to this chapter but we are more concerned here with its implications. We will illustrate this with a simple example.

Worked Example

Suppose that a firm's total costs are given by $C = 2 + 15Q$, where Q represents the firm's output. The expected value and variance of output, $E(Q)$ and $V(Q)$ respectively, are known to be 10 and 5 respectively. But what are the expected value and variance of total cost, C?

Solution

Using the first part of Theorem 1.1, we have

$$E(C) = E(2 + 15Q) = 2 + 15E(Q) = 2 + 15(10) = 152.$$

Using the second part of the theorem yields

$$V(C) = V(2 + 15Q) = 15^2 V(Q) = 225(5) = 1125.$$

Students are often confused by the appearance of b^2 in the expression for $V(Z)$ in the above theorem. But remember that the square root of the variance is the standard deviation (which we shall write as Stdev here), and this is also a measure of the spread or dispersion in values of a variable. That is, $\text{Stdev}(Z) = \sqrt{V(Z)}$. Thus, if we take the square root of $V(Z) = b^2 V(X)$, we obtain

$$\text{Stdev}(Z) = b\text{Stdev}(X).$$

Thus, if the values of a variable X are all multiplied by some constant b to give another variable Z, then the standard deviation is also multiplied by b. That is, the spread of the Z values is b times the spread of the original X values.

Example 1.15

(a) Suppose E(X) = 12 and V(X) = 5. If Z = 8 + 3X, find E(Z) and V(Z). If the standard deviation of X doubles, what will happen to the standard deviation of Z?

(b) Suppose Y = 6 − 5X. If E(X) = 4 and V(X) = 2, find E(Y) and V(Y).

Example 1.16

A builder has to bid for a contract for a house extension. He knows that his fixed costs are certain to be £800. His additional costs will depend on weather conditions. His experience tells him that, if the weather is hot and dry, his additional costs will be £12 000. However, if the weather is wet, his additional costs will be £20 000. Finally, if he is lucky and the weather is cool and dry, his additional costs will be only £10 000.

The builder checks the weather forecast and estimates that hot and dry weather, wet weather, and cool and dry weather have probabilities of 0.6, 0.1 and 0.3, respectively. Find the expected value and the standard deviation of the builder's total costs.

1.5 Expected monetary values

Probability theory can be very useful as a guide to decision-making, when we are faced with 'games of chance' involving money. Suppose, when Ms Punter purchases a raffle ticket, she knows that she may win a first prize of £500 or one of three second prizes of £200. The price of a raffle ticket is 20p and Punter (being very mercenary) wants to work out whether it is worth her while to purchase a ticket.

Punter knows that 10 000 tickets are to be sold in all and therefore deduces that the probability of winning the first prize is 1/10 000 = 0.0001, so that the probability of winning one of the second prizes must be 0.0003.

To solve Punter's problem it will help to derive the probability distribution for X, Punter's net winnings from the raffle. The distribution is shown below:

X	−£0.20	£199.80	£499.80
p(X)	0.9996	0.0003	0.0001

Recall that a probability distribution involves a listing of *all* possible values of X, Punter's *net* winnings. Thus, when Punter wins, X equals the prize minus the price of the ticket. However, when she fails to win a prize her net winnings are negative and simply equal minus the price of a ticket. The possible values of X are therefore those shown above.

Given the above probability distribution, we can now compute the expected value of X in the usual way. That is, we can find Punter's *expected winnings*, given by

$$E(X) = -0.20 \times 0.9996 + 0.003 \times 199.80 + 0.001 \times 499.80$$
$$= -£0.09.$$

Thus the expected winnings are −9 pence. That is, Punter expects to lose 9p from the purchase of the ticket.

A valid interpretation of the value of −9 pence is to say that, if Ms Punter bought a single ticket in each of many thousands of raffles, all with identical rules and structure, she would lose, 'on average', an amount equal to 9 pence per raffle. The value of −£0.09 is often referred to as the *expected monetary value* (EMV) of the ticket.

It is easy to slip from the negative EMV to the conclusion that Ms Punter should not buy the ticket because it involves her in an expected loss. But, of course, many people do purchase such raffle tickets. Some may do so for altruistic reasons to help in a 'good cause', while others may simply like a 'flutter'. However, there are more fundamental reasons why entirely rational individuals may be guided in their decision-making by factors other than EMV.

To explain this, we must realize that Ms Punter is unlikely to partake in many thousand raffles and is solely concerned with a *single* raffle like the one above. Should she buy a ticket in this one?

Firstly, imagine Punter has a relatively small income but has debts totalling £400. She faces a court appearance and possible imprisonment next week unless she pays her debts in full. In such a situation Punter will purchase the ticket (maybe several!). Even though there is only a slim chance of winning first prize, this may be the only way in which she can avoid jail. In fact Punter might well be prepared to pay £20 (if she has got it) rather than 20p for a ticket, if this is the only way in which she can avoid prison. But it is easy to calculate that the EMV of a ticket, when its price is £20, is −£19.89. Yet Punter will still purchase the ticket. Clearly, expected monetary value is not the only criterion that guides Punter's decisions.

Suppose, however, Ms Punter has no ready money at all. Since purchasing a ticket involves an expected monetary loss she would probably refuse a ticket. She would be even less likely to purchase a ticket if the price was £20. In fact even if the prizes were trebled in value, so that the EMV was *positive*, she might still refuse a ticket since she regards £20 as too high a price, because of the risk (0.9996) of losing the stake. Again, expected monetary value is not the sole criterion of decision-making.

Example 1.17

In Example 1.16, to ensure an expected profit of £2000, the contractor must make a bid that is in excess of his expected total costs. Use EMV analysis to decide how much the builder should bid for the contract. Under what circumstances might EMV be an inappropriate criterion to use?

Example 1.18

A publisher is considering printing and publishing a novel by an unknown author. If the book is badly reviewed, the publisher will make a loss of £10 000. The probability of bad reviews is 0.8. On the other hand, if the book is well reviewed then two outcomes are possible. There is a probability of 0.9 that the book sells well but a probability of 0.1 that the book does not sell well. These outcomes would result in a profit of £70 000 in the first case but a loss of £30 000 in the second. The structure of the problem is illustrated in Fig. 1.4. Should the novel be published?

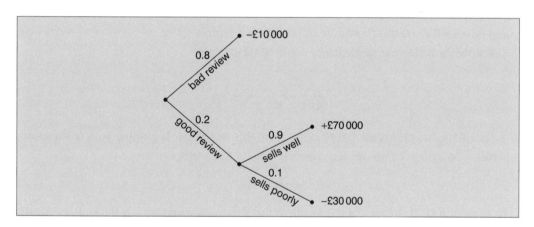

Figure 1.4 Structure of the publisher's problem

1.6 **The binomial distribution**

The binomial distribution describes situations which arise remarkably often in everyday life. Suppose that a trial of an experiment can result in just two outcomes, which we will refer to as *success* and *failure*. Suppose, furthermore, that trials of this experiment can be regarded as totally independent of one other. That is, the outcome of any trial is totally uninfluenced by any other previous or future trial. Under such conditions it is possible for the probabilities of success and failure to remain constant from trial to trial. When this is the case the trials are said to be *binomial*. Such trials are also often referred to as Bernoulli trials (after the statistician James Bernoulli).

An obvious example of Bernoulli trials concerns the tossing of a coin. If a toss results in a 'head' and we regard this as 'success', then the probability of a success clearly equals one-half and remains one-half no matter what the outcomes of previous tosses. The outcome is totally independent of the outcomes of previous trials.

A further example might refer to the possibility of whether a group of firms are still trading in 20 years' time. 'Success' occurs if the firm is still trading 20 years later, 'failure' implying that it has gone bankrupt. If the probability of survival is 0.6, for example, then provided that the firms are all independent, this can be regarded a sequence of binomial trials. Each trial involves checking whether a given firm has survived.

Consider n independent trials of such a binomial experiment and let X be the number of successes in the n trials. Thus X could take any of the values 0, 1, 2, 3, 4 ... , n.

Suppose the constant probability of 'success' is π. Obviously the probability of 'failure' is $1 - \pi$. It is the probability distribution for X, the number of successes in n independent trials, with $\Pr(\text{success}) = \pi = \text{constant}$, that is referred to as the *binomial distribution*. What we seek is a 'formula' for the probabilities in such a distribution that we can use, without going through the tedious procedure of setting up a sample space.

Consider the following sequence of n independent trials.

$$
\begin{array}{cc}
\overset{X}{\overleftrightarrow{\text{SSS ... S}}} & \overset{n-X}{\overleftrightarrow{\text{FFF ... F}}}
\end{array}
\tag{1.6}
$$

If S stands for 'success' and F for failure, then this sequence, beginning with X successes and followed by $n - X$ failures, has a probability P of occurring, where

$$
P = \pi^{X}(1 - \pi)^{n-X}
\tag{1.7}
$$

Note that, in [1.7], we have a π for each of the X successes and a $1 - \pi$ for each $n - X$ failures. Moreover, the πs and $(1 - \pi)$s in [1.7] have all been multiplied together, because the n trials are independent by assumption.[8]

Of course there are many other sequences apart from [1.7] that will yield X successes and $n - X$ failures. But the probability of each such sequence will always contain X probabilities π and a further $n - X$ probabilities $1 - \pi$, again all multiplied together. Thus each such sequence will have the same probability, given by [1.7], of occurring. It is possible to show that the total number of different sequences that yield X successes in n trials is given by

$$
{}^{n}C_{X} = \frac{n!}{(n - X)!X!}
\tag{1.8}
$$

Because all the different sequences that yield X successes are mutually exclusive, we can find the overall probability of obtaining X successes by multiplying [1.8] by [1.7] to give[9]

$$p(X) = \frac{n!}{(n-X!)X!} \pi^X (1-\pi)^{n-X}.$$ [1.9]

Equation [1.9] defines the *binomial distribution*. For given values of π, the probability of success, and n, the number trials, [1.9] can be used to the find the values of $p(X)$ for all $X = 1, 2, 3, \dots, n$.

Worked Example

Sixty per cent of a large workforce is in favour of strike action over a pay claim. Six members of the workforce are selected at random and interviewed. If X is the number in the sample who are in favour of strike action, find the probability distribution for X. Hence, find the mean and variance of the distribution.

Solution

The binomial distribution is applicable to this problem for two reasons. Firstly, we are dealing with a success/failure situation. We shall regard interviewing a person and finding them in favour of strike action as a 'success'. Secondly, because we are dealing with a large workforce, we can regard the probability of success as a constant. That is, Pr(success) is given by $\pi = 0.6$ and remains 0.6 for each interview. It is the six interviews that constitute the binomial trials in this case.

Notice that the assumption of a large workforce is crucial. For example, suppose the work force is 200 000, of whom 60% or 120 000 are in favour of strike action. When the first person in the sample is selected, the probability of their being a 'success' is clearly 0.6. If this person is a success, this leaves 199 999 in the work force, of whom 119 999 are in favour of strike action. Thus, when the second person is selected, the probability of success is 119 999/199 999 which equals 0.599 998, which is virtually identical to 0.6. Thus, because of the size of the workforce, we can regard the 0.6 as unchanged.

Notice, however, that if we had a small workforce of, for example, 20 persons of whom 12 were in favour of strike action, then the probability of success could not then be regarded as constant. When making the first random selection, the probability of success would again be 0.6. However, if the person selected were a 'success', this would leave 19 in the workforce, of whom 11 were in favour of strike action. The probability of 'success' for the second selection is therefore now 11/19 or 0.58, which cannot be approximated by 0.6. On the other hand, if the first person selected were a 'failure', this would leave 12 out of the remaining 19 in favour of strike action. Thus the probability of 'success' on the next trial would be 12/19 or 0.63, which also cannot be approximated by 0.6. In this situation, it should clear that the outcome on any one trial will be very much influenced by what has occurred on previous trials. Thus the trials cannot be independent and neither can be the probability of 'success' remain constant.[10] In such a situation we could not make use of the binomial distribution.

Recapping, for this example, we have $n = 6$ trials and, since we are dealing with a large population, we can treat π as constant and equal to 0.6. Thus, using the binomial distribution [1.9], we obtain

$$p(X) = \frac{6!}{(6-X)!X!}(0.6)^X(0.4)^{6-X}. \tag{1.10}$$

Substituting the values $X = 0, 1, \ldots, 6$ into [1.10] gives the binomial probability distribution in Table 1.6. For example, $p(4)$ is given by (to 3 sig. figs)

$$p(4) = \frac{6!}{2!4!}0.6^4\,0.4^2 = 15 \times 0.1296 \times 0.16 = 0.311.$$

Similarly,

$$p(3) = \frac{6!}{3!3!}0.6^3\,0.4^3 = 20 \times 0.216 \times 0.064 = 0.276$$

and so on.

Table 1.6 Binomial distribution with $n = 6$ and $\pi = 0.6$

X	0	1	2	3	4	5	6
$p(X)$	0.004	0.037	0.138	0.276	0.311	0.187	0.047

Notice that it is not really necessary to use [1.10] to obtain $p(0)$ and $p(6)$. Clearly the probability of getting six successes in n independent trials must be $p(6) = 0.6^6$ or 0.047. Similarly, $p(0) = 0.4^6$ or 0.004. If expression [1.10] is to be used to obtain $p(0)$ or $p(6)$ then it is necessary to remember that 0! has to be given the value of unity. For example

$$p(0) = \frac{6!}{6!0!}0.6^0\,0.4^6 = 1 \times 1 \times 0.0041 = 0.004.$$

Note that in Table 1.6 the probability distribution again consists of a listing of all possible values for X, together with the computing of probabilities for each such value for X.

The mean of the distribution is, using [1.1]

$$\mu = \Sigma\, Xp(X) = 0 \times 0.004 + 1 \times 0.037 + 2 \times 0.138$$
$$+ 3 \times 0.276 + 4 \times 0.311 + 5 \times 0.187$$
$$+ 6 \times 0.047 = 3.6.$$

This result is as expected since a proportion 0.6 of the six members of the workforce is known to be in favour of strike action. In fact the mean of the binomial distribution is always given by

$$\mu = \mathrm{E}(X) = n\pi. \qquad\qquad [1.11]$$

To obtain the variance of the distribution, it is simplest to first obtain

$$\mathrm{E}(X^2) = \Sigma\, X^2 p(X) = 0^2 \times 0.004 + 1^2 \times 0.037 + 2^2 \times 0.138$$
$$+ 3^2 \times 0.276 + 4^2 \times 0.311$$
$$+ 5^2 \times 0.187 + 6^2 \times 0.047 = 14.4.$$

Thus, using [1.5], we have

$$V(X) = \mathrm{E}(X^2) - \mu^2 = 14.4 - (3.6)^2 = 1.44.$$

In general, the variance of the binomial distribution is given by

$$V(X) = n\pi(1 - \pi). \qquad\qquad [1.12]$$

Thus in this case $V(X) = 6 \times 0.6 \times 0.4$ or 1.44, as already calculated.

Example 1.19

Use the binomial distribution to check the probability distribution of Table 1.2, for $X =$ the number of heads obtained in three tosses of a coin. Why is the binomial distribution a valid tool to use in this situation?

Example 1.20

Use Table 1.6 to obtain the cumulative distribution for X in the above worked example. Hence find $C(3)$. Sketch the cumulative distribution.

Example 1.21

It is believed that 70% of applications for a job in a travel agency are successful. Five such applicants are selected at random. What is the probability that (a) all five obtain a job; (b) three obtain a job but two do not; (c) at least one gets a job?

If it turns out that only one of the five applicants prove successful, what might you conclude?

Example 1.22

A burglar alarm in a supermarket makes use of three electronically activated 'eyes'. The alarm is triggered if one or more of the eyes is activated. Each eye has a probability of 0.7 of being activated when a burglar breaks in. Let X be the number of eyes activated by a break-in. Use the binomial model to find the probability distribution of X. What is the probability that the alarm is triggered if there is a break-in?

Example 1.23

A box contains six eggs, two of which are bad. Suppose three eggs are taken from the box (without replacement). Find the probability distribution for X, the number of bad eggs drawn. Find the expected value of X and interpret it. [*Hint*: you cannot use the binomial distribution. Why not?]

Example 1.24

An airline operates a small eight-seater passenger plane. It follows a procedure of accepting $R > 8$ bookings for each flight because 20% of expected passengers fail to show. The opportunity cost of having an empty seat on a flight is £205, whereas the value of goodwill forfeited if a passenger has booked but cannot obtain a seat is £420. If the airline is a cost minimizer, should it accept $R = 9$ or $R = 10$ bookings on each flight?

1.7 **Some other discrete probability distributions**

We shall introduce the *Poisson distribution* via a simple example. Suppose there are 100 000 dwellings in a city. The fire brigade estimates that there is a probability of 0.000 02 that a dwelling will suffer a fire on any given night. The brigade regards itself as 'over-stretched' if it has to deal with more than four fires a night. Suppose we wish to find, firstly, the probability of a fire-free night and, secondly, the proportion of nights the brigade is overstretched.

One way of tackling this problem would be to make use of the binomial distribution. Each dwelling can be regarded as a trial, so that $n = 100\,000$, while the constant probability of a fire (a success!) is $\pi = 0.000\,02$. We could then use [1.9] to find the probability distribution for X, the number of fires per night. However, since [1.9] involves dealing with quantities such as 100 000!, this can be somewhat messy, so we shall use an approximation.

It can be shown that, provided n is very large and π, the probability of success, is very small, the binomial distribution [1.9] can be approximated by

$$p(X) = \frac{(n\pi)^X \, e^{-n\pi}}{X!}, \qquad [1.13]$$

where $n\pi$ = the mean number of successes in the n trials. That is, in our example, $n\pi = 2$ is the mean number of fires per night.

Noting that $e^{-2} = 0.135\,34$ and remembering that $0! = 1$, we can use [1.13] to obtain $p(X)$ for $X = 0, 1, 2, 3, 4, \dots$: These probabilities are shown below

$$p(0) = \frac{2^0 \, e^{-2}}{0!} = 0.1353,$$

$$p(1) = \frac{2 \, e^{-2}}{1!} = 0.2707,$$

$$p(2) = \frac{2^2 \, e^{-2}}{2!} = 0.2707,$$

$$p(3) = \frac{2^3 \, e^{-2}}{3!} = 0.1804,$$

$$p(4) = \frac{2^4 \, e^{-2}}{4!} = 0.0902, \text{ etc.}$$

Clearly, we could use [1.13] to calculate $p(5), p(6)$, etc. But the above probabilities are the only ones we require to answer the questions posed. The probability of a fire-free night is 0.1353 and the probability that the brigade is not overstretched is

$$\Pr(X \leqslant 4) = p(0) + p(1) + p(2) + p(3) + p(4) = 0.9473.$$

Hence, we can say that

$$\Pr(\text{overstretched}) = 1 - 0.9473 = 0.0527$$

Thus the fire brigade will be overstretched on roughly 5% of nights.

Expression [1.13] has applications that may appear to be unconnected to the binomial distribution. For example, as we shall see, it can be applied to problems concerning infrequent events in both time and space. In such cases $n\pi$ is replaced by the parameter λ = mean number of successes per unit of time, length, area or space. [1.13] then becomes

$$p(X) = \frac{\lambda^X \, e^{-\lambda}}{X!} \qquad [1.14]$$

Expression [1.14] is the Poisson distribution. It is particularly useful in situations where, firstly, n is very large and π is very small and, secondly, when n and π are unknown but their product $\lambda = n\pi$ is known. An example should make the usefulness of [1.14] clear.

Worked Example

A bank branch receives on average three dud cheques per day. Calculate the probability that, on a given day, (a) the bank gets at least one dud cheque, and (b) the bank gets exactly three dud cheques.

Solution

In this case, we let π be the probability that the bank gets a dud cheque at any particular 'split-second' of the day. Clearly there are very many such 'split-seconds' in a working day so that, although it is unknown, π must be very small since the bank only gets three dud cheques a day on average. In this case, n is simply the number of 'split-seconds' in a working day. The number of such 'split-seconds' is clearly very large but unspecified. (How long is a 'split-second'?) Fortunately, although we do not know π or n, we do know the value of $\lambda = n\pi$, the mean number of dud cheques per day. In fact, λ was given above as 3. Provided π can be regarded as a constant, we can therefore make use of the expression [1.14].

A constant π implies that the probability of receiving a dud cheque remains unchanged over the working day. That is, it is the same at 11.20 in the morning as it is at 3.10 in the afternoon. Hence [1.14] becomes

$$p(X) = \frac{3^X e^{-3}}{X!} \qquad [1.15]$$

Since $e^{-3} = 0.050$, it follows that

$$p(3) = \frac{3^3 e^{-3}}{3!} = 0.224.$$

That is, there is a probability of 0.224 of the bank receiving exactly three dud cheques in any given day. The probability of the bank receiving at least one dud cheque is given by $1 - p(0)$, where $p(0)$ is the probability of receiving no such cheques. Using [1.15],

$$p(0) = \frac{3^0 e^{-3}}{0!} = 0.050,$$

so that

$$p(X \geqslant 1) = 1 - 0.050 = 0.950.$$

Thus there is a 0.950 probability that the bank receives at least one dud cheque in any working day.

Example 1.25

Two per cent of the TV sets produced by a firm are faulty in some way. Use the Poisson distribution to approximate the probability that in a production run of 5000 TV sets exactly 20 are faulty.

Example 1.26

A type of automobile tyre has a puncture on average once every 5000 miles. Find
(a) the probability that, on a 5000-mile run, four punctures occur.
(b) the probability that, on a 500-mile run, no punctures occur.

Example 1.27

Medical records indicate that births in a town occur at a mean rate of 8.3 per week. Births can occur at any time of day or night with constant probabilities. What is the probability that in a given week: (a) there are 22 births; (b) there is at least one birth?

Another well-known discrete probability distribution is the so-called *geometric distribution*. One simple experiment that gives rise to this distribution is that of our old friend the binomial trial. Recall that in binomial trials there can only be two outcomes, 'success' or 'failure', and that successive trials are independent of one another. Suppose X is the number of trials that are performed *before* the first *failure* is encountered. That is, if $X = 6$, for example, then the first failure arises after seven trials.

In general, to obtain a failure *after* X trials, we require X successful trials, followed by a failure. If π and $1 - \pi$ are probabilities of success and failure, then the probability of the X successful trials is π^X, since the trials are independent. The probability of the failure is simply $1 - \pi$, so that the probability of getting X trials before the failure is given by

$$p(X) = (1 - \pi)\pi^X. \tag{1.16}$$

Expression [1.16] is the geometric distribution.

As an example, consider a sequence of tosses of a coin, and suppose we wish to find the probability of obtaining the first head after six tosses of a coin. In this situation, $X = 6$ and $\pi = 0.5$. Hence

$$p(6) = 0.5 \times 0.5^6 = 0.007\ 812\ 5.$$

Example 1.28

Two villages play an annual cricket match, the winner being awarded the Battenbowl trophy for a year. Village A wins four times as often as village B and is the current holder of the trophy. Find the probability that village A finally loses the trophy in the last of six further matches.

Finally, in this section, we consider the *discrete uniform* or *rectangular* distribution. Suppose a random variable X can take any of n discrete values within the range A and B, inclusive, and probabilities are given by

$$p(X) = \frac{1}{n} = \text{constant}, \qquad \text{for all } A \leqslant X \leqslant B. \qquad [1.17]$$

Expression [1.17] defines the discrete uniform distribution.

For example, if X can take only the discrete values 6, 6.5, 7, 7.5, 8, 8.5 and 9, then $n = 7$ and [1.17] becomes

$$p(X) = \tfrac{1}{7} = \text{constant}, \qquad \text{for all } 6 \leqslant X \leqslant 9.$$

Summary

- The **sample space** of an experiment consists of a listing of all the possible outcomes of the experiment. A **stochastic** or **random** variable is a variable whose values are determined by some **chance mechanism**. A **discrete** variable can take only certain particular values.

- The **probability distribution** for a random variable, X, consists of a listing of all the possible values that X can take, matched with the probabilities associated with each such value of X. A **cumulative probability distribution** yields the probabilities that X is either equal to or less than each of the above possible values.

- The concept of a **mathematical expectation** (also known as an **expected value**) enables us to find the 'average value' of functions of X, when X is subject to a probability distribution. Important expected values are the **mean** and **variance** of a probability distribution.

- Probability distributions can be represented pictorially by **probability histograms**, in which **probability densities** are measured on the vertical axis.

- **Expected monetary values** can be used to deal with problems concerning monetary quantities, when variables are subject to probability distributions.

- **The binomial distribution** arises when an experiment has only two possible outcomes, 'success' and 'failure', and successive trials of the experiment are all **independent**. The binomial formula yields the probability of *x* **successes in** *n* **trials**.

- Other well-known discrete probability distributions are the **Poisson distribution**, the **geometric distribution** and the **discrete uniform distribution**.

Appendix 1A

Proof of Theorem 1.1

If X is a random variable and a and b are constants, such that $Z = a + bX$, then

$$E(Z) = E(a + bX)$$
$$= \Sigma(a + bX)p(X) \quad \text{(using definition of an expected value).}$$
$$= \Sigma \, ap(X) + \Sigma \, bXp(X)$$
$$= a \, \Sigma \, p(X) + b \, \Sigma \, Xp(X) \quad \text{(since } a \text{ and } b \text{ are constants).}$$
$$= a + bE(X).$$

Also

$$V(Z) = V(a + bX)$$
$$= E\{[a + bX - E(a + bX)]^2\} \quad \text{(using definition of variance).}$$

But

$$E(a + bX) = a + bE(X) = a + b\mu, \quad \text{where } \mu = E(X).$$

Hence

$$V(Z) = E[(a + bX - a - b\mu)^2]$$
$$= E[b(X - \mu)]^2 = E[b^2(X - \mu)^2]$$
$$= b^2 E(X - \mu)^2 = b^2 V[X].$$

Notes

1. Note that a discrete variable is not necessarily the same as an integer variable. For example, a variable taking only the values 0.5, 1, 1.5, 2.0, 2.5, ... is discrete but not integer.

2. See Section P.2 in the prerequisites section for a discussion of weighted means.

3. An alternative measure of the spread of probabilities in a distribution is based not on $(X - \mu)^2$ but on the absolute value of $X - \mu$, that is, $|X - \mu|$. This is analogous to using the mean deviation rather than the variance for measuring the dispersion of a set of

numerical observations. (See prerequisites section.)

4. Using the algebra of summations, and recalling that $\sum p(X) = 1$ and that $\sum Xp(X) = \mu =$ constant, we have

$$
\begin{aligned}
V(X) = \sum(X - \mu)^2 p(X) &= \sum(X^2 + \mu^2 - 2X\mu)p(X) \\
&= \sum X^2 p(X) + \sum \mu^2 p(X) - \sum 2X\mu p(X) \\
&= \sum X^2 p(X) + \mu^2 \sum p(X) - 2\mu \sum Xp(X) \\
&= E(X)^2 + \mu^2 - 2\mu^2 \\
&= E(X^2) - \mu^2.
\end{aligned}
$$

5. See note 3. Another measure of dispersion in a probability distribution is the so-called *mean deviation*, defined as $\sum |X - \mu| p(X)$, where $|X - \mu|$ is the absolute value of $X - \mu$. The mean deviation is *exactly* equal to the average distance of X from μ. However, for reasons of statistical theory the standard deviation is usually preferred to the mean deviation as a measure of dispersion.

6. This is directly analogous to the use of areas rather than heights in frequency histograms. (See the prerequisites section.)

7. Incomes *exactly* equal to £200 have been allocated to the 200–300 block. Similarly for incomes exactly equal to £300 and £400. However, as we shall see in Chapter 2, when a variable is continuous rather than discrete then the probability that, for example, $X = 200$, can be treated as zero. Thus there is no difference between $\Pr(0 < X < 200)$ and $\Pr(0 < X \leqslant 200)$.

8. See the prerequisites section for the multiplication rule that holds when events are independent.

9. See the prerequisites section for the addition rule that holds when events are mutually exclusive.

10. The probability distribution in this situation is known as the *hypergeometric* distribution. See Hoel (1962, p. 116).

2

Continuous variables

Objectives

After completing your study of this chapter you should be able:

1. to appreciate the difference between continuous and discrete variables and understand the concept of a probability density function;

2. to recognise the normal distribution;

3. to use standard normal tables to compute area (and hence probabilities) underneath any normal distribution curve;

4. to obtain normal curve approximations to binomial probabilities.

Introduction

In this chapter, we consider continuous variables and their probability distributions. In particular, we examine the well-known normal distribution and its uses.

In the first section of the chapter, we take, as our variable X, the weight of a male student in the United Kingdom. Notice that X is what is termed a *continuous* variable. In the previous chapter we dealt only with discrete variables, that is, variables that could only take certain values (e.g., 0.5, 1.0, 1.5, 2.0, …). However, the weight of a student, provided it can be measured sufficiently accurately, can take any value within a given range. For example, there is no reason why the weight of a male student could not be 65.857 323 kg.

Early in the chapter we discover that the distribution of student weights has a shape that occurs frequently in nature. This common shape or curve has a known equation, that of the normal distribution. Then, later in the chapter, we consider the various uses to which this normal distribution can be put.

2.1 Probability distributions for continuous variables

Let us assume that we carry out a complete survey of all the thousands of male students in the UK and obtain the weights of all such students. Suppose, initially, we measure these weights to the nearest kilogram. Given these data, we could compute the proportion or relative frequency of students with various weights. For example, the relative frequency of students with a weight of 63 kg (i.e., the proportion between 62.5 kg and 63.5 kg)[1] might be 0.044. We saw in Section P.3 that, when dealing with large data sets, it is possible to interpret relative frequencies as probabilities. Since we are dealing with many thousands of students, we can therefore interpret the value 0.044 as the probability of getting a student of weight 63 kg.

When interpreting a value such as 0.044 as a probability, we are in effect saying that, if we select a male student at random, then the probability that such a student has a weight of

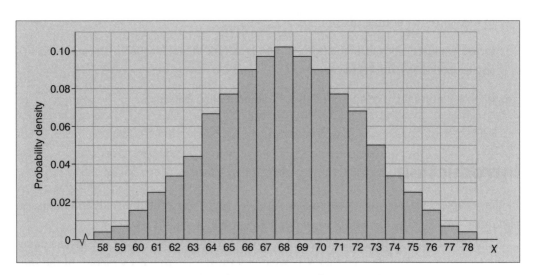

Figure 2.1 Probability histogram of heights measured to the nearest kg

63 kg is 0.044. In other words we are treating X as a random or stochastic variable, in which case we can treat any relative frequencies obtained from our survey as part of the probability distribution of X. The histogram for such a probability distribution might look something like that in Fig. 2.1.

Remember that in probability histograms it is areas, not heights, that represent probabilities and, as we saw in the previous chapter, it is probability densities that are measured on the vertical axis. For example, the width of the $X = 63$ kg block is 1 kg and $\Pr(X = 63) = 0.044$. It follows that the probability density at this value of X must be 0.044 per kilogram and that the *area* of the block must be $1 \times 0.044 = 0.044$ as required.

Next, suppose we measure the weights of students not to the nearest kilogram but to the nearest half kilogram. We can again compute relative frequencies and interpret them as probabilities. For example, the relative frequency of $X = 63$ kg (i.e., the proportion of students with weights between 62.75 and 63.25 kg) might be 0.021.[2] Given such extra accuracy, it is now this value that must be interpreted as the probability of a student, selected at random, having a weight of $X = 63$ kg. Such values can be used to form a probability histogram such as that in Fig. 2.2.

Notice that the probability of obtaining a weight of $X = 63$ kg is much smaller when we measure weights to the nearest half kilogram than when we measure them to the nearest kilogram. This is because there are fewer students with weights within the range 62.75 to 63.25 kg than there are students with weights within the range 62.5 to 63.5 kg.

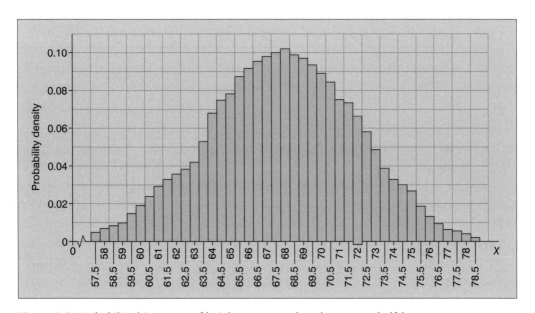

Figure 2.2 Probability histogram of heights measured to the nearest half-kg

Since we have used the same scale on the horizontal axis in Fig. 2.2 as we have in Fig. 2.1, the width of the blocks in Fig. 2.2 is 0.5 kg, only half the width of those in Fig. 2.1. In Fig. 2.2, the probability density at $X = 63$ kg is 0.042 per kilogram, so that the area of the $X = 63$ block is $0.5 \times 0.042 = 0.021$, which is the probability of obtaining $X = 63$ given above. Notice, again, that it is areas that represent probabilities. This is why the heights of the blocks in Fig. 2.2 are similar to those in Fig. 2.1.

Obviously, the accuracy of weight measurements can be increased further. For example, we could measure weights to the nearest quarter of a kilogram, then to the nearest eighth and so on. As we increase the accuracy of measurement, the resultant histograms will have narrower and narrower blocks and, although each successive histogram will have roughly the same shape, they will become less and less jagged in outline.

As the accuracy of weight measurement is increased even further, that is, to the nearest hundredth of a kilogram and even (if it were feasible) to the nearest millionth of a kilogram, the outline of the probability histogram will become smoother and smoother and will, almost certainly, approach the symmetrical bell-shaped curve illustrated in Fig. 2.3. The outline of the curve can be thought of as being the result of millions of blocks all of very tiny width.

We have continually stressed that it is areas, and not heights, that represent probabilities in histograms such as Figs 2.1 and 2.2. It follows that it is the areas under the curve in Fig. 2.3 that give probabilities. Therefore if we wish to find, for example, the probability that a male student has a weight between 64 and 73 kg, then we have to find the area beneath the curve between 64 and 73.

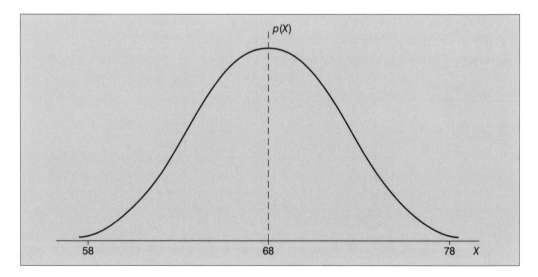

Figure 2.3 The limiting case

The areas beneath curves are normally found by integrating the equation of the curve between the required definite limits.[3] To do this it is necessary to know the equation of the curve. Fortunately, this equation was deduced by statisticians as early as the nineteenth century. It is given, by

$$p(X) = (2\pi\sigma^2)^{-0.5} \exp[-(X - \mu)^2/2\sigma^2], \qquad [2.1]$$

where $\mu = E(X)$ is the mean of the distribution and $\sigma^2 = V(X)$ is its variance.[4] Since π and e are known constants this means that, for given values of μ and σ^2, the expression in [2.1] is a function of X alone and, hence, has been written as $p(X)$. You do not need to reproduce or even remember equation [2.1] since, as we shall see, tables, enabling us to compute areas under normal curves, are readily available. All you need to appreciate is that, if we selected a range of values for X, computed the corresponding values of $p(X)$ using [2.1], and plotted points on some graph paper, we would in fact obtain a curve of the form showed in Fig. 2.3.

The probability distribution [2.1] is the most famous in statistics and is known as the *normal distribution*. Many variables in nature turn out to be normally distributed – for example, heights, foot sizes, the diameters of coconuts, and the weights of rabbits. But the real importance of the normal distribution, as we shall see, in the next chapter, is its usefulness in statistical theory.

Since it is probability density that is measured on the vertical axis in Fig. 2.3, probability distributions for continuous variables are usually referred to as *probability density functions*.[5] A normally distributed variable with mean μ and variance σ^2 is usually written in shorthand as $N(\mu, \sigma^2)$. For example, if

$$X \text{ is } N(12, 133), \qquad [2.2]$$

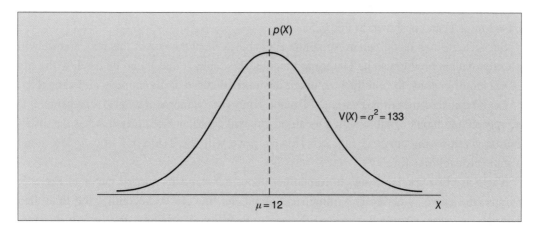

Figure 2.4 The normal distribution with mean 12 and variance 133

then this implies that X has a probability density function [2.1] with mean $\mu = 12$ and variance $\sigma^2 = 133$. It has the characteristic smooth symmetric bell-shaped distribution illustrated in Fig. 2.4.

There are, obviously, other probability distributions for continuous variables; that is, there are other probability density functions apart from the normal distribution. We will introduce two later in this chapter.[6]

2.2 Using the normal distribution

We have seen that many natural variables have a normal distribution and that, if we wish to compute probabilities concerning them, then we have to calculate areas below the normal curve between the relevant points. In principal, such areas can always be found by integrating the normal probability density function [2.1] between the required limits. Unfortunately, integrating [2.1] is not easy and, consequently, special tables have been constructed to assist with the calculation of areas below normal curves.

It should be clear that there are very many different normal distributions, since the μ and σ^2 in $N(\mu, \sigma^2)$ can take many different values. Obviously, it is not practical to construct tables for each and every normal distribution. However, tables are readily available giving values beneath a very special normal curve, that referring to the so-called *standard normal distribution*.

The standard normal distribution

This distribution is, simply, the normal distribution that has mean $\mu = 0$ and variance $\sigma^2 = 1$. That is, in the notation just introduced, it is the $N(0, 1)$ distribution. The probability density function for this variable, normally designated as Z, can be obtained by setting $\mu = 0$ and $\sigma^2 = 1$ in [2.1] and is shown in Fig. 2.5.[7]

Such a table is in fact given in Appendix A (Table A.1), at the end of this text, and we will shortly explain how to use it. The importance of this table is that it can be used, with only slight modifications, to find the area under any normal curve of given mean and variance.

Let Z be a standard normal variable. Do not worry for the moment what Z represents. It is simply a continuous variable with a mean of zero and a variance of unity that has the distribution given by the curve in Fig. 2.5. However, we will use Table A.1 to calculate some simple probabilities for Z.

There are two crucial things to remember about the standard normal curve of Fig. 2.5. Firstly, the curve is perfectly symmetrical about the line $Z = 0$. Secondly, the total area beneath the curve must equal unity. Like any probability distribution, the sum of its probabilities must be unity, and it is areas beneath the normal curve that represent probabilities.

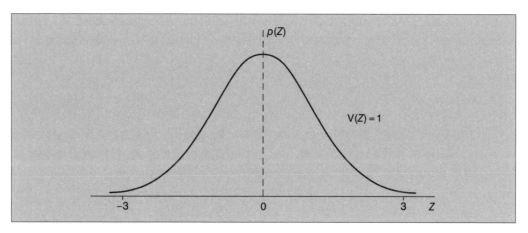

Figure 2.5 The standard normal distribution

Since the total area beneath the symmetrical curve is unity, it follows that the area under each so-called 'tail' must be 0.5.

The values in the main body of Table A.1 give various areas beneath the normal curve. The values in the far left-hand column and along the top row of the table indicate various values for the Z variable. Areas are given in the main body of the table and are those beneath the curve between the line $Z = 0$ and the indicated value of Z. Such an area, marked as A, is shown in the diagram above Table A.1.

Worked Example

Use Table A.1 to find the probabilities that:
(a) $Z > 0.86$;   (b) $Z > -1.36$;   (c) $-0.43 < Z < 1.74$;   (d) $1.45 < Z < 1.94$.

Solutions

(a) $\Pr(Z > 0.86)$
The value 0.86 is positive and hence lies to the right of the centre line $Z = 0$ in Fig. 2.6.[8] To find the required probability we must find the area beneath the curve and to the right of $Z = 0.86$. This has been shaded in Fig. 2.6. If we are to use the standard normal table we need to find, first, the area beneath the curve between $Z = 0$ and $Z = 0.86$. This is our area A in this case.

Using Table A.1 we obtain, in fact, area $A = 0.3051$. To find the probability that $Z > 0.86$, we make use of the fact that the total area beneath the right-hand tail of the curve is 0.5. It follows that

$$\Pr(Z > 0.86) = 0.5 - \text{Area } A = 0.5 - 0.3051 = 0.1949.$$

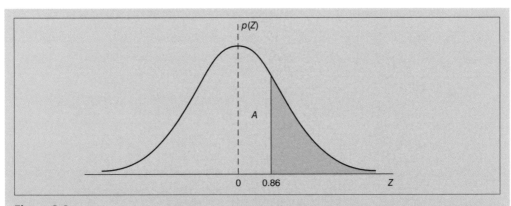

Figure 2.6

(b) $\Pr(Z > 1.36)$

The value -1.36 is negative and hence lies to the left of the centre line $Z = 0$ in Fig. 2.7. In this example, we require the total area under the normal curve to the right of $Z = -1.36$. This of course includes the whole area beneath the right-hand tail of the curve. The required area is shaded in Fig. 2.7. We now use the fact that the normal curve is symmetrical about $Z = 0$. It follows that the area beneath the curve between 0 and $+1.36$ must be identical to the area beneath the curve between 0 and -1.36. In Fig. 2.7 we have denoted the area between 0 and -1.36 by B.

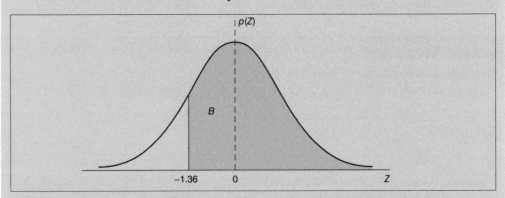

Figure 2.7

Using Table A.1, we find that area $B = 0.4131$. Since the total area beneath the right-hand tail is 0.5, we therefore have

$$\Pr(Z > -1.36) = \text{Area } B + 0.5 = 0.9131.$$

(c) $\Pr(-0.43 < Z < 1.74)$

We require the area beneath the normal curve between the points $Z = -0.43$ and $Z = 1.74$, that is, the sum of the shaded areas A and B, in Fig. 2.8. The area A can be read directly

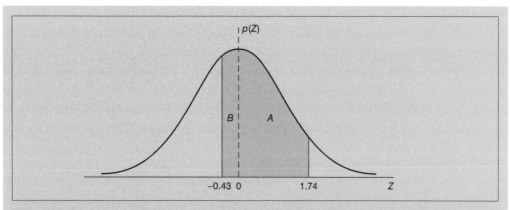

Figure 2.8

from Table A.1 and is 0.4591. To find the area B, we make use of the fact that the normal curve is symmetrical, so that the area between 0 and +0.43 must be the same as that between 0 and −0.43. Thus the area B is 0.1664. Hence

$$\Pr(-0.43 < Z < 1.74) = \text{Area } A + \text{Area } B$$
$$= 0.4591 + 0.1664 = 0.6255.$$

(d) $\Pr(1.45 < Z < 1.94)$

We require the shaded area in Fig. 2.9 lying beneath the normal curve between 1.45 and 1.94. To obtain it, we first use Table A.1 to find the area A which lies between 0 and 1.45. That is, area $A = 0.4265$. Secondly, we find the area C which lies beneath the curve and between 0 and 1.94. That is, area $C = 0.4738$. Subtracting the first area from the second gives the required probability. That is

$$\Pr(1.45 < Z < 1.94) = \text{Area } C - \text{Area } A$$
$$= 0.4738 - 0.4265 = 0.0473.$$

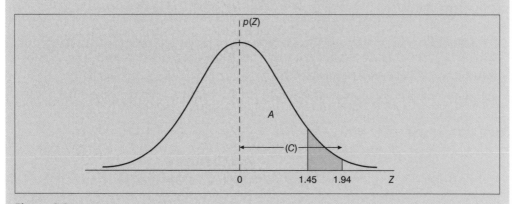

Figure 2.9

Notice that the area beneath the standard normal curve between $Z = 0$ and $Z = 3.09$, the final Z value in Table A.1, is 0.4990, which is very close to 0.5. In fact, since the total area beneath the right-hand tail of the curve is 0.5, the probability of getting $Z > 3.09$ is only $0.5 - 0.4990 = 0.0010$, which is very small. Similarly, because of the symmetry of the normal curve, the probability of getting $Z < -3.09$ is also only 0.0010. This implies, as illustrated in Fig. 2.10, that virtually all the area beneath the standard normal curve is contained between $Z = -3$ and $Z = +3$. That is, we can treat both $P(Z > 3)$ and $\Pr(Z < -3)$ as being virtually zero.

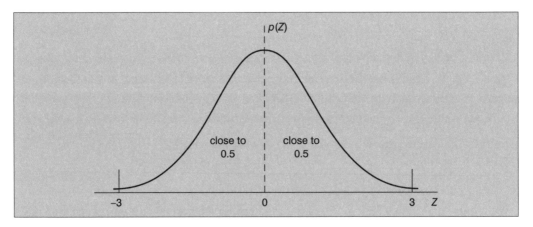

Figure 2.10 Areas under the normal curve between −3 and +3

Worked Example

Find the probability that $1.36 < Z < 6.13$.

Solution

The idea behind this example is the same as that of the last part of the previous worked example. We have to take the area A beneath the normal curve between $Z = 0$ and $Z = 1.36$ from the area C between $Z = 0$ and $Z = 6.13$.

As shown in Fig. 2.11, the point $Z = 6.13$ lies far out under the right-hand tail. Hence, the area C is, to four significant figures, 0.5000. Table A.1 gives the area A, in this case, as 0.4131. Hence

$$\Pr(1.36 < Z < 6.13) = \text{Area } C - \text{Area } A$$
$$= 0.5000 - 0.4131 = 0.0869.$$

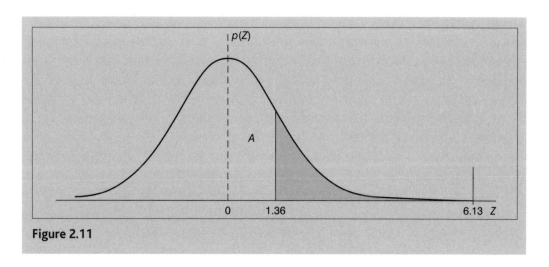

Figure 2.11

Since the variance and hence the standard deviation of the standard normal distribution equals unity, it is possible to calculate the probability of getting a value for Z which lies within k standard deviations of its zero mean. It is customary to let k take any of the values 1, 2 or 3. For example, since

$$\Pr(-3 < Z < 3) = 0.4987 + 0.4987 = 0.9974,$$

we can say that 99.74% of Z values lie within three standard deviations of their mean of zero. Similarly,

$$\Pr(-2 < Z < 2) = 0.4772 + 0.4772 = 0.9544$$

and

$$\Pr(-1 < Z < 1) = 0.3413 + 0.3413 = 0.6826.$$

It follows that 95.44% of Z values lie within two standard deviations of their zero mean and that 68.26% of Z values lie within one standard deviation of their mean. These ranges are illustrated in Fig. 2.12, and their relevance will be explained shortly.

Example 2.1

Using Table A.1, find the probability that a standard normal variable lies within the ranges:
(a) 0 to 2.00;   (b) −1.56 to 0;   (c) −2.00 to 1.56;   (d) > 2.00;   (e) > −1.56.

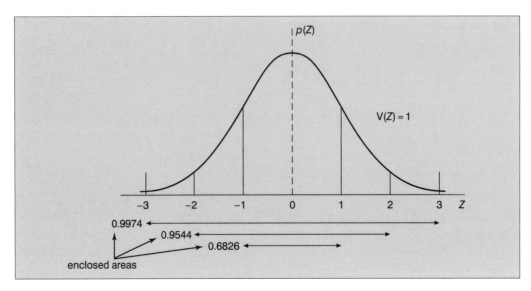

Figure 2.12 Areas within one, two and three standard deviations of the mean

Example 2.2

If Z is a standard normal variable, find the following probabilities:
(a) $\Pr(Z < -2.45)$;   (b) $\Pr(Z > 2.87)$;   (c) $\Pr(-1 < Z < 1.5)$;   (d) $\Pr(-1.87 < Z < 1.87)$;
(e) $\Pr(-4.2 < Z < -1.3)$;   (f) $\Pr(0.21 < Z < 0.84)$;   (g) $\Pr(-2.3 < Z < 4.6)$.

Example 2.3

Z is a standard normal variable. Find: (a) $\Pr(Z > 1.6)$;   (b) $\Pr(Z < 1.6)$;   (c) $\Pr(Z = 1.6)$.

Example 2.4

If Z is a standard normal variable, find the value of k such that:
(a) $\Pr(Z > k) = 0.23$;   (b) $\Pr(Z > k) = 0.77$;   (c) $\Pr(Z < -k) = 0.11$;
(d) $\Pr(-k < Z < k) = 0.95$;   (e) $\Pr(-k < Z < k) = 0.99$.
[*Hint*: in these examples, it is probabilities that are given and you need to find these values in the main body of Table A.1.]

Example 2.5

X has an $N(12, 25)$ distribution. Suppose $Y = X - 3$ and $W = Y/5$. Y and W are clearly both linear functions of the normally distributed X. It is well known that linear functions of normally distributed variables are themselves normally distributed. By using Theorem 1.1 in the previous chapter to find the mean and variance of Y and then the mean and variance of W, show that W has an $N(1.8, 1)$ distribution.

The standard normal distribution does not itself arise often in everyday life. In practice, normal distributions usually have a mean, μ, that is non-zero and a variance, σ^2, that is not equal to unity. But it is possible to use standard normal tables to answer probability questions about any normal distribution.

Consider the example with which we began this chapter, concerning the weights of male students. Suppose we find that the mean weight of such students is $\mu = 68.7$ kg and that the variance of student weights is $\sigma^2 = 49.3$, so that the standard deviation is $\sigma = 7.02$ kg. Since we are dealing with very many students, we are able to assume that the weight X of a male student is normally distributed. We can sum up this information by writing

$$X \text{ is } N(68.7, 49.3), \tag{2.3}$$

using the notation introduced earlier.

Now suppose we wish to find the proportion of students who have a weight in excess of 74 kg. This is the same as finding the probability that a given student has a weight X that exceeds 74 kg. That is, we require $\Pr(X > 74)$.

The first step in any problem of this kind is to discover what quantity can be regarded as a Z variable, that is, a standard normal variable, for which we have a table of areas.

It is possible to convert [2.3] to an $N(0, 1)$ distribution by taking two simple steps. Firstly, suppose we subtract from each student weight a value equal to the mean weight 68.7. That is, we create a new variable $Y = X - 68.7$. It should be clear that, since X has a mean of 68.7, Y must have a mean of zero. We are in fact using the first part of Theorem 1.1, in the previous chapter.[9] We can therefore write

$$Y = X - 68.7 \text{ is } N(0, 49.3). \tag{2.4}$$

Note that we write $N(0, 49.3)$ because, although the mean of our variable has become zero, as yet the variance is unchanged.

The second step of the procedure is to turn the variance into unity. It is possible do this by dividing the Y variable by its standard deviation, 7.02. That is, we form the variable $Z = Y/7.02$. By using the second part of Theorem 1.1, it is easy to show that Z must have a standard deviation of unity.[10] Thus, since the variance is the square of the standard deviation, it must also be unity. We can therefore write that

$$Z = \frac{X - 68.7}{7.02} \text{ is } N(0, 1).$$
[2.5]

Note that it is possible to take any normally distributed variable, such as [2.3], and convert it into a standard normal variable by first subtracting its mean and then dividing by its standard deviation.[11] That is, if X is $N(\mu, \sigma^2)$ then

$$Z = \frac{X - \mu}{\sigma} \text{ has an } N(0, 1) \text{ distribution.}$$
[2.6]

The question we set ourselves earlier was to find the probability that a male student would have a weight in excess of 74 kg. This was a question about the distribution [2.3], namely $\Pr(X > 74)$. The trick is to change the question about X into a question about the standard normal variable Z, for which we have Table A.1. In this case we must use [2.5], that is subtract 68.7 from X and then divide by 7.02 and write

$$\Pr(X > 74) = \Pr\left(\frac{X - 68.7}{7.02} > \frac{74 - 68.7}{7.02}\right)$$
$$= \Pr(Z > 0.755).$$
[2.7]

Notice that, when evaluating $\Pr(X > 74)$, we carry out, within the parentheses, the same operations on the 74 as we do on the X, that is we subtract 68.7 and divide by 7.02. We do this because this is the way we can convert an X into a Z.

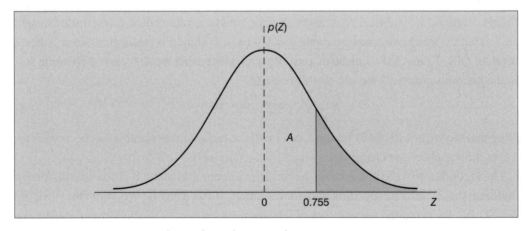

Figure 2.13 Area showing $\Pr(X > 74) = \Pr(Z > 0.755)$

We have now converted our original question about X into the question about Z given by [2.7]. Now we can use Table A.1 to answer the question [2.7] in the usual way. From Fig. 2.13, we have

$$\Pr(Z > 0.755) = 0.5 - \text{Area } A$$
$$= 0.5 - 0.2759 = 0.2241.$$

Thus about 22% of male students have weights in excess of 74 kg.

Worked Example

The times taken by a factory operative to assemble plastic cartons are normally distributed with mean 167.3 secs and standard deviation of 20.3 secs. Find:

(a) the probability that an operative will take less than 140 secs to assemble a particular carton.

(b) the proportion of cartons that take between 150 and 170 secs to assemble.

Solution

Suppose we let X be the time taken to assemble a carton. We therefore have

$$X \text{ is } N(167.3, 412.09). \qquad [2.8]$$

Note that it is the variance $\sigma^2 = (20.3)^2 = 412.09$ that, using the usual notation, appears in [2.8], although at the moment we are more interested in the standard deviation.

Following the usual procedure, we can convert our X variable into a standard normal Z variable by subtracting the mean value of X and dividing by its standard deviation. That is, we subtract the 167.3 and divide by the 20.3. Hence

$$Z = \frac{X - 167.3}{20.3} \text{ is } N(0, 1). \qquad [2.9]$$

The questions about X are to find (a) $\Pr(X < 140)$ and (b) $\Pr(150 < X < 170)$. We now need to convert these questions about X into questions about our standard normal variable Z, given by [2.9]. Firstly,

$$\Pr(X < 140) = \Pr\left(\frac{X - 167.3}{20.3} < \frac{140 - 167.3}{20.3}\right)$$
$$= \Pr(Z < -1.34)$$
$$= 0.5 - \text{Area } B = 0.5 - 0.4099 = 0.0901,$$

where B is the area under the curve between -1.34 and 0 in Fig. 2.14. Thus approximately 9% of cartons are assembled in less than 140 secs.

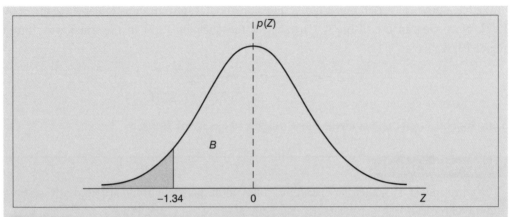

Figure 2.14

Secondly, since finding the required proportion implies finding the equivalent probability, we have

$$\Pr(150 < X < 170) = \Pr\left(\frac{150 - 167.3}{20.3} < \frac{X - 167.3}{20.3} < \frac{170 - 167.3}{20.3}\right)$$
$$= \Pr(-0.85 < Z < 0.13)$$
$$= \text{Area } B + \text{Area } A = 0.3023 + 0.0517 = 0.3540.$$

The required areas beneath the normal curve are shown in Fig. 2.15. Thus, roughly 35% of cartons are assembled in between 150 and 170 s.

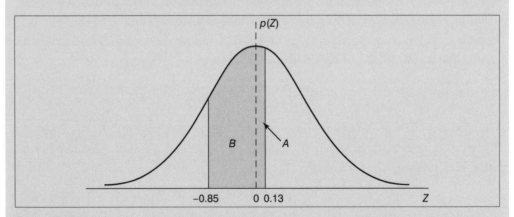

Figure 2.15

In tackling examples such as this, it is always a good idea to sketch a rough distribution. It is also more helpful to sketch the distribution for the standard normal Z rather than the distribution for the original X, since it is the former distribution for which we have a table of areas.

Example 2.6

The lengths of aluminium-coated sheets are normally distributed with a mean of 30.5 cm and a variance of 0.04 cm^2. Find: (a) the probability that a given sheet has a length in excess of 30.7 cm; (b) the proportion of such sheets that are less than 30.6 cm.

Example 2.7

A manufacturer of tin cans produces can lids with widths (in centimetres) that are known to have a $N(8, 1.44 \times 10^{-6})$ distribution. Cans with width greater than 8.0021 cm or less than 7.9979 cm are deemed to be defective. What proportion of the manufacturer's can lids will be defective?

Worked Example

Marks in a nationwide examination have a normal distribution with mean 53.4 and standard deviation of 8.8. It is decided to give an A grade to the best 20% of students. How high a mark must a student get to qualify for an A grade?

Solution

If we let X equal a student mark in the examination, then clearly X has a $N(53.4, 77.4)$ distribution, where the variance of marks is $8.8^2 = 77.4$. To convert X into a standard normal Z, we follow our usual procedure of subtracting the mean 53.4 and dividing by the standard deviation, 8.8. Thus

$$Z = \frac{X - 53.4}{8.8} \text{ has an } N(0, 1) \text{ distribution.}$$

Suppose m is the mark needed to get an A grade. That is, we have to find m such that

$$\Pr(X > m) = 0.2.$$

As usual, we now turn the question about X into a question about Z, by subtracting the mean and dividing by the standard deviation. Thus we have to find m such that

$$\Pr\left(\frac{X - 53.4}{8.8} > \frac{m - 53.4}{8.8}\right) = \Pr\left(Z > \frac{m - 53.4}{8.8}\right) = 0.2.$$

Letting $k = (m - 53.4)/8.8$, what we have to find is a value for k such that

$$\Pr(Z > k) = 0.2. \qquad [2.10]$$

To find k we have to use Table A.1 in reverse. Recall that the values in the main body of the table give areas beneath the normal curve, whereas Z values appear around the edges. Normally, we are given a Z value and have to read off an area. In this case we are given an area and have to find the relevant Z value.

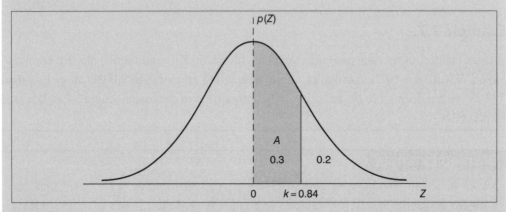

Figure 2.16

The required calculation is illustrated in Fig. 2.16. Note that the area A equals 0.3 (not 0.2!) so that the required Z value is 0.84, since,

$$\Pr(Z > 0.84) = 0.2.$$

Comparison with [2.10] indicates that $k = 0.84$, so that

$$0.84 = \frac{m - 53.4}{8.8}$$

Thus

$$m = 8.8 \times 0.84 + 53.4 = 60.8$$

In other words, a student has to get a mark of about 61 to qualify for an A grade.

Example 2.8

An electrical firm manufactures light-bulbs that have a length of life that is normally distributed with a mean of 800 hours and a standard deviation of 40 hours. Find the probability that a bulb burns out after between 778 and 834 hours.

If a bulb burns out before s hours, it is said to be substandard. If 10% of bulbs are substandard, find the value of s.

Example 2.9

A supermarket sells 1 litre bottles of milk. Demand per day for its milk has an $N(250, 625)$ distribution. The supermarket plans to have a stock of bottles of 300 at the start of each day. What proportion of its customers will have to do without? If the proportion of dissatisfied customers is to be reduced to 0.01, what starting stock will be needed each day?

If it costs the supermarket 1p per bottle to store milk and it is estimated that loss of good-will is 0.5p per every unsatisfied customer, does it make sense to reduce the proportion dissatisfied to 0.01?

Example 2.10

Annual incomes in a developing country are normally distributed with a mean of £118 with a variance of 144. Find the probability that a citizen of this country has an income: (a) less than £95; (b) greater than £95; (c) equal to £95.

Example 2.11

When fully fuelled, airplane A can fly for an average of 21 hours with a standard deviation of 3.5 hours, whereas airplane B can fly for an average of 22 hours with a standard deviation of 2.5 hours. In an emergency, one of the planes has to attempt to fly 26 hours to fetch help. Which airplane should be selected? You may assume that flight times for both aircraft are normally distributed.

We saw earlier that, if Z is a standard normal variable, then 99.74% of Z values will lie within three standard deviations of their mean of zero, 95.44% of Z values will lie within two standard deviations of their mean and 68.26% will lie within just one standard deviation. Since any normally distributed variable can be expressed as a linear function of the standard normal variable, these percentages carry over to all normal distributions.

For example, suppose X is $N(28, 16)$. Since X has a standard deviation $\sigma = 4$, we can say that

(i)   99.74% (that is virtually all) of X values must lie within $3\sigma = 12$ of their mean of 28, that is, between 16 and 40.

(ii) 95.44% (about 95%) of X values must lie within $2\sigma = 8$ of their mean of 28, that is, between 20 and 36.

(iii) 68.26% (about two-thirds) must lie within $\sigma = 4$ of their mean of 28, that is, between 24 and 32.

The distribution is illustrated in Fig. 2.17. These percentages enable us to gain a clear idea of the dispersion of values for any normally distributed variable.

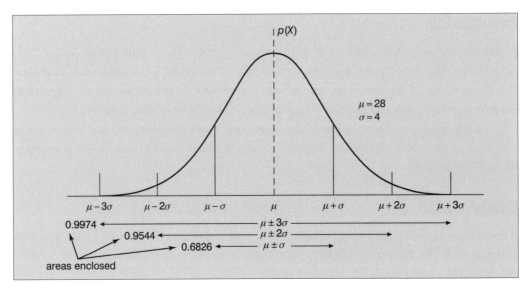

Figure 2.17 Areas within one, two and three standard deviations of $\mu = 28$

Example 2.12

Young couples' annual expenditures on durable goods have a mean of £2048 with a standard deviation of £408. Within which range of expenditures would you find approximately 95% of young couples? Within which range would you find approximately two-thirds of couples?

Example 2.13

The mean breaking strength (in kilograms) of plastic bin liners has a $N(5, 0.0004)$ distribution.

(a) Find: (i) the probability that a given bin liner has a breaking strength of less than 4.95 kg; (ii) the proportion of bin liners that have a breaking strength in excess of 5.03 kg.

(b) A bin liner is tested and found to break when filled with rubbish weighing only 4.9 kg.
(i) Would this make you doubt that the bin liners have the stated mean and variance?
(ii) If it were known that the breaking strengths were not normally distributed, would you still doubt the stated mean and variance of bin liners? [Use *Chebyshev's theorem*, which states that the probability of a variable differing from its mean by k or more standard deviations cannot exceed $1/k^2$.]

2.3 **Other continuous distributions**

Obviously, not all continuous variables are normally distributed. For example, the probability density function

$$p(X) = \lambda e^{-\lambda X} \qquad [2.11]$$

is known as the *negative exponential distribution* (or, more simply, as the *exponential distribution*) and is illustrated in Fig. 2.18. This distribution occurs frequently in the real world. The mean of the distribution can be shown to be $E(X) = 1/\lambda$ and the variance $V(X) = 1/\lambda^2$. For example, the interval X between successive arrivals at a queue is likely to have a negative exponential distribution.

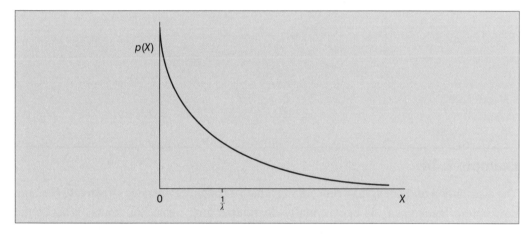

Figure 2.18 The negative exponential distribution

Worked Example

The time taken to serve customers is known to have a negative exponential distribution with a mean of 5 minutes. What proportion of customers spend more than 10 minutes being served?

Solution

As is always the case with probability density functions, areas under the curve represent probabilities. Unfortunately, we do not have a table of areas for the exponential distribution, so we have to compute the required area by finding the definite integral of [2.11], between the limits 10 and infinity. That is, we require the shaded area under the curve in

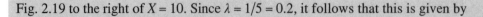

Fig. 2.19 to the right of $X = 10$. Since $\lambda = 1/5 = 0.2$, it follows that this is given by

$$\int_{10}^{\infty} 0.2\, e^{-0.2X}\, dx = {}_{10}^{\infty}[-e^{-0.2X}] = 0 - (-0.135) = 0.135.$$

Thus 13.5% of customers spend more than 10 minutes being served.

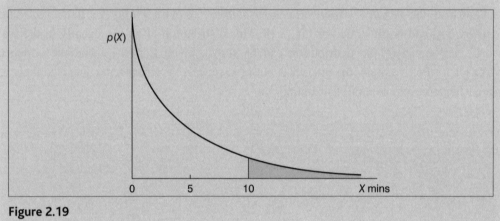

Figure 2.19

Example 2.14

The distribution of the length of time during which a computer operates effectively (i.e., the time before breakdown), is exponentially distributed with mean 360 hours. What is the probability that the computer will operate effectively for only 180 hours or less?

The discrete uniform distribution of the last chapter has a continuous counterpart, the so-called *continuous uniform distribution*. The density function for this distribution can be written as

$$p(X) = \begin{cases} 1/(b-a), & \text{for } a < X < b, \\ 0, & \text{otherwise.} \end{cases}$$

The density function is illustrated in Fig. 2.20. a and b are, respectively, the minimum and maximum possible values of X. The distribution has mean $E(X) = (a+b)/2$ and variance $V(X) = (b-a)^2/12$.

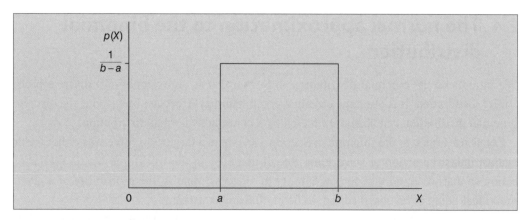

Figure 2.20 The continuous uniform distribution

Worked Example

Annual earnings of middle managers in a large company have a continuous uniform distribution with minimum earnings £53 257 and maximum £78 843. What proportion of middle managers earn more than £75 000?

Solution

The density function for this example is shown in Fig. 2.21. Since the horizontal range of the distribution is $b - a = 25\ 586$, and the total rectangular area is unity, the probability density on the vertical axis must be $1/25\ 586 = 0.000\ 039$. The proportion required is given by area A, which has a width of $78\ 843 - 75\ 000 = 3843$, and so equals $3843 \times 0.000\ 039 = 0.15$. Hence 15% of middle managers earn more than £75 000.

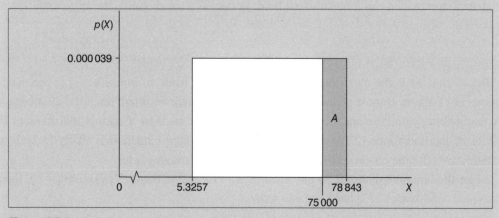

Figure 2.21

2.4 **The normal approximation to the binomial distribution**

We introduced the binomial distribution in Section 1.6 as an example of a discrete probability distribution. It is often the case that computational effort can be saved if the discrete binomial distribution can be approximated by a continuous normal distribution.

Let us refer back to the situation in Section 1.6, where a large workforce was either for or against industrial action of some kind. Recall that 60% of the workforce was in favour of action so that we could take the probability of 'success', that is, the probability of a given individual being in favour of action, to be $\pi = 0.6$ and constant.

Now suppose not 6 but 100 individuals are interviewed. If X is the number of the $n = 100$ interviewees who favour industrial action, then the binomial formula [1.9] gives

$$p(X) = \frac{100!}{(100 - X!)X!} 0.6^X 0.4^{100-X} \qquad [2.12]$$

as the probability of getting X interviewees in favour of industrial action. That is, X successes in the 100 trials.

Suppose, however, that we required the probability that X lies between 50 and 65 inclusive. One way of obtaining this would be to use [2.12] 16 times, that is, for every value of X from 50 to 65, and then add all the resultant probabilities. This would be rather tedious and it is possible to use an alternative and quicker method which will give a good approximation to the true answer. Notice, however, that we cannot use the Poisson distribution to approximate binomial probabilities in this case, because, as we saw in Section 1.7, this approximation is only valid for large n and small π. In this case $\pi = 0.6$ and is large.

It is possible to approximate the discrete binomial distribution by a continuous normal distribution provided certain conditions hold. In fact, as a rough guide, the approximation is a good one if

$$n\pi > 5 \quad \text{and} \quad n(1 - \pi) > 5. \qquad [2.13]$$

Recall that $n\pi$ is the mean number of successes in n trials so that $n(1 - \pi)$ is the mean number of failures. If these quantities both exceed 5, then the resultant binomial distribution is reasonably symmetric and can be approximated quite well by a normal distribution. If either of the conditions [2.13] does not hold, then the approximation is likely to be less satisfactory. But the conditions [2.13] are meant only as rough guides.

Since the binomial distribution has mean $E(X) = n\pi$ and variance $V(X) = n\pi(1 - \pi)$, then provided conditions [2.13] hold, we can write

X has an approximate $N(n\pi, n\pi[1 - \pi])$ distribution. [2.14]

Recall that we wish to find the probability that between 50 and 65, inclusive, of the 100 interviewees are in favour of industrial action. Since $n = 100$ and $\pi = 0.6$, we have $n\pi = 60$ and $n(1 - \pi) = 40$ so that the normal approximation is valid and we can say that X is approximately normally distributed with mean $n\pi = 60$ and variance $n\pi(1 - \pi) = 24$. That is, [2.14] becomes

$$X \text{ has an approximate } N(60, 24) \text{ distribution,} \qquad [2.15]$$

with a standard deviation of 4.90.

We can now proceed to use Table A.1 in the usual manner, apart from one slight modification which we will outline in a moment. As usual, we can convert our X variable into a standard normal Z variable by subtracting the mean and dividing by the standard deviation. That is

$$Z = \frac{X - 60}{4.9} \text{ has an approximate } N(0, 1) \text{ distribution.} \qquad [2.16]$$

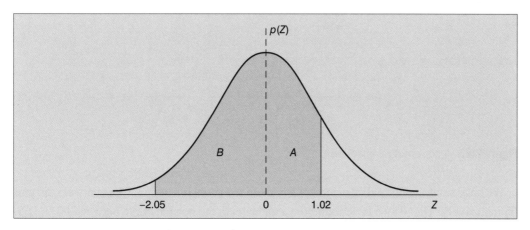

Figure 2.22 Area showing Pr(50 < X < 65)

The required probability can therefore be approximated by

$$
\begin{aligned}
\Pr(50 < X < 65) &= \Pr\left(\frac{50 - 60}{4.9} < \frac{X - 60}{4.9} < \frac{65 - 60}{4.9}\right) \\
&= \Pr(-2.04 < Z < 1.02) \\
&= \text{area } B + \text{area } A \text{ (see Fig. 2.22)} \\
&= 0.4793 + 0.3461 = 0.8254.
\end{aligned}
\qquad [2.17]
$$

This value 0.8254 is, in fact, quite a good approximation to the probability required, but it can be improved on.[12] Recall that X is a discrete variable, whereas the normal distribution normally refers to continuous variables. In Fig. 2.23, we have shown that part of the true binomial distribution that refers to the values of X for 48 to 52. Each block in the distribution refers to a particular value of X and the areas of the blocks, as usual, refer to probabilities. The smooth curve in Fig. 2.23 refers to the normal curve [2.15] that we are using to approximate the binomial distribution.

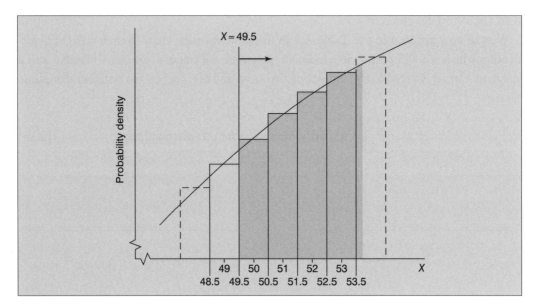

Figure 2.23 A continuity correction

We have used the normal curve to approximate the probability that X lies between 50 and 65 inclusively. That is, we have found the area beneath the normal curve between 50 and 65. But the blocks are 'centred' about their relevant X values. That is, the $X = 49$ block is centred on 49 and so on. Thus, for example, the $X = 49$ block stretches from 48.5 on the horizontal axis to 49.5 and so on. Hence, in the above calculation for the area beneath the curve between 50 and 65, we have included only half of the area of the $X = 50$ block. Since we are required to find the probability of X lying between 50 and 65 *inclusive*, a better approximation would be to take the area to the right of $X = 49.5$, thus including the whole of the $X = 50$ block. This argument is illustrated in Fig. 2.23, where the required area is shaded. Similarly, at the other limit of required X, we should include the area beneath the curve to the left of $X = 65.5$ since we want to include the whole of the $X = 65$ block. We can therefore improve our approximation by using

$$\Pr(49.5 < X < 65.5). \qquad [2.18]$$

Using [2.18] rather than [2.17] is usually referred to as applying a *continuity correction*, since the need for it arises because we are approximating a discrete distribution by a continuous distribution.

Since [2.16] still holds, we have, from [2.18],

$$\Pr(49.5 < X < 65.5) = \Pr\left(\frac{49.5 - 60}{4.9} < \frac{X - 60}{4.9} < \frac{65.5 - 60}{4.9}\right)$$
$$= \Pr(-2.14 < Z < 1.12)$$
$$= \text{area } B + \text{area } A$$
$$= 0.4838 + 0.3686 = 0.8524. \qquad [2.19]$$

This is a slightly larger value than we obtained earlier, and will be a better approximation to the true probability of X lying in the range 50 to 65.

Worked Example

A coin is tossed eight times. Let X be the number of heads obtained. Using, firstly, the binomial distribution formula [1.9] and, secondly, a normal approximation, find the probability of getting: (a) two or three heads; (b) eight heads.

Solution

In this binomial example, $n = 8$ and $\pi = 0.5$ is the probability of getting a head on a given toss. Firstly, using the binomial formula, we obtain

$$P(2) = \frac{8!}{6!2!} 0.5^2 0.5^6 = \frac{28}{256},$$

$$P(3) = \frac{8!}{5!3!} 0.5^3 0.5^5 = \frac{56}{256}.$$

Thus the exact probability of getting two or three heads is 84/256 which is 0.3281.

We can now rework this probability using the normal approximation. Although $n\pi$ and $n(1 - \pi)$ both equal 4, so that condition [2.13] does not strictly hold, we can check how good an approximation the normal distribution gives. Using [2.14], we have

$$X \text{ has an } N(4, 2) \text{ distribution} \qquad [2.20]$$

so that

$$Z = \frac{X - 4}{1.414} \text{ has an } N(0, 1) \text{ distribution.}$$

Using the continuity correction, we approximate the probability of getting two or three heads by

$$\Pr(1.5 < X < 3.5) = \Pr\left(\frac{1.5-4}{1.414} < \frac{X-4}{1.414} < \frac{3.5-4}{1.414}\right)$$
$$= \Pr(-1.77 < Z < -0.35)$$
$$= 0.4616 - 0.1368 = 0.3248.$$

This is clearly a very close approximation to the true probability 0.3281 obtained above.

The true probability of getting eight heads out of eight is clearly $0.5^8 = 0.003\,906$. If we were to approximate the probability of getting eight heads by the normal approximation we would use

$$\Pr(7.5 < X < 8.5) = \Pr\left(\frac{7.5-4}{1.414} < \frac{X-4}{1.414} < \frac{8.5-4}{1.414}\right)$$
$$= \Pr(2.48 < Z < 3.18)$$
$$= 0.5 - 0.4934 = 0.0066.$$

This time the relative error in the approximation is greater. This is because, firstly, the restrictions [2.13] do not quite hold and, secondly, we are trying to approximate a probability at one of the tails of the distribution where the approximation is less accurate. If you are unclear about the reasoning behind the calculations in this example, you should sketch both the binomial distribution and its normal approximation on the same diagram. This will make it easier to figure out the areas you require.

Example 2.15

In a major chain of supermarkets, it is estimated that 40% of shoppers buy a non-biological detergent. To check this a random sample of 200 shoppers is interviewed. If X is the number of shoppers in the sample who use non-biological detergents, find the probability that X is greater than 65 but less than 85. Find the probability that X is 70 or less. (Remember to apply continuity corrections.)

Suppose the above 40% figure was merely the supermarket's 'best guess'. If the sample reveals that fewer than 60 of the 200 shoppers use non-biological detergents, should the supermarket revise its estimate?

Example 2.16

A basketball player is successful with 60% of his shots from the floor. What is the probability that he makes less than one-half of his next 100 such shots?

Example 2.17

A firm manufactures components for an automobile company. Of these components 2% are defective. If a sample of 10 000 components is to be taken, use the normal approximation to the binomial distribution to calculate the probability that the number of defective components will lie between 204 and 206 inclusive. What is the probability that the number of defective components is 201 exactly?

Example 2.18

A multiple-choice quiz has 200 questions each with four possible answers, of which only one is correct. What is the probability that pure guesswork will yield from 25 to 30 correct answers for the 80 of the 200 questions about which a student has no knowledge?

Summary

- Unlike discrete variables, **continuous variables** are not restricted to taking particular values. Probability distributions for continuous variables are termed **probability density functions**.

- The best-known probability density function is the so-called **normal distribution** which arises frequently in the natural world. It is also of considerable importance in statistical theory.

- The **standard normal distribution** is the normal distribution that has a mean of zero and a variance of unity. Areas under the standard normal **curve** are **tabulated**.

- Any normally distributed variable can be transformed into a standard normal variable by **subtracting** its **mean** and then **dividing** the result by its **standard deviation**. This enables us to compute probabilities concerning any normally distributed variable, using the standard normal table.

- Other examples of continuous variables are the **negative exponential distribution** and the **continuous uniform distribution**.

- The binomial distribution can be **approximated** by a normal distribution, provided $n\pi$ and $n(1 - \pi)$ both exceed 5. This can facilitate the computation of probabilities concerning binomial variables. Such probabilities are approximated better if **continuity corrections** are made.

Notes

1. There may seem to be some ambiguity about whether a student of weight 62.5 kg would be measured as 62 kg or 63 kg. But remember that X is a continuous variable which, in principle (if not in practice), could be measured to the nearest millionth of a kilogram. With such precision measurements, the proportion of students with a weight of *exactly* 62.5 kg can be treated as virtually zero.

2. Using the same arguments as in note 1, the probability of obtaining a student with the exact weight 62.75 kg or 63.25 kg can be regarded as zero.

3. See, for example, Thomas (1999, p. 168).

4. In [2.1] the 'exp' stands for exponential and indicates that the exponential constant e is to be raised to $-(X - \mu)^2/2\sigma^2$.

5. Although the probability histograms for discrete variables, which we considered in the previous chapter, also have probability densities on the vertical axis, these distributions are normally referred to as *probability mass functions*. This is because, in these cases, the 'masses' of the various probability values are concentrated at given discrete values.

6. In general, if a continuous variable has probability density function $p(X)$, then its mean and variance are given by

$$E(X) = \mu = \int_{-\infty}^{+\infty} Xp(X)\,dx \quad \text{and} \quad V(X) = \int_{-\infty}^{+\infty} (X - \mu)^2 p(X)\,dx.$$

These expressions are analogous to the discrete variable formulae [1.1] and [1.4]. However the above expressions are more difficult to use and, consequently, we do not make use of them in this text.

7. In fact, its formula is $p(Z) = (2\pi)^{-0.5} \exp[-Z^2/2]$.

8. For the moment you need not be concerned exactly where you draw the line $Z = 0.86$, in Fig. 2.6, provided you draw it to the *right* of the $Z = 0$ line. The precise positions of positive and negative Z values will gradually become clear.

9. Using the first part of Theorem 1.1, we have

$$E(Y) = E(X - 68.7) = E(X) - 68.7 = 68.7 - 68.7 = 0.$$

10. Using the second part of Theorem 1.1, we have

$$V(Z) = V(Y/7.02) = (1/7.02)^2 V(Y) = (1/49.3)49.3 = 1.$$

Thus the standard deviation of Z must also be unity.

11. It might seem more convenient to use a notation $N(\mu, \sigma)$, where σ is the standard deviation. However, you will find that all statistics texts that you may consult will use the $N(\mu, \sigma^2)$ notation, so to avoid confusion we have adopted the traditional notation as well.

12. Use of the binomial formula [2.12] 16 times gives the actual probability as 0.8532.

3

Basic statistical inference

Objectives

When you have completed your study of this chapter, you should be able:

1. to appreciate the difference between population parameters and sample statistics;

2. to understand what is meant by statistical inference and appreciate the problem of sampling variability;

3. to understand thoroughly the concept of a sampling distribution and, particularly, the distribution of the sample mean;

4. to solve numerical problems regarding the sample mean by making use of the central limit theorem;

5. to compute point estimates of population parameters and construct confidence intervals for population means and proportions;

6. to recognize the different kinds of random sample and have some knowledge of their relative merits.

Introduction

In this chapter we take a first look at the relationship between 'samples' and 'populations'. In particular, we consider the problems that arise when we attempt to deduce or *infer* things about a population when the only information we possess refers to the sample rather than a population. That is, we consider problems of *statistical inference*.

A key concept in this chapter is that of a sampling distribution. Knowledge of the sampling distribution of the mean of a random sample enables us to make estimates of population parameters and, at least for large samples, construct what are termed 'confidence intervals' for such parameters.

3.1 **Populations and samples**

Most people are familiar with the everyday concept of a 'population'. For example, the population of Birmingham can be defined as all the individuals who live and work there. But, the statistical definition of a population is a little more complicated. Considering a random or stochastic variable, X, we can also define a population in terms of probabilities.

Suppose X has the simple discrete probability distribution, shown in Table 3.1. Suppose we have very many values for X (millions!), all determined by this distribution. One-tenth of all the X values will equal 4, one-fifth of the X values will equal 5, and so on. We can define the *population* for X as the set of all X values obtained by 'drawing' values from the distribution in Table 3.1. We talked above about 'very many' values of X, although strictly speaking a statistician would talk of an infinite number of X values drawn from this population.

Table 3.1 A simple discrete distribution

X	4	5	6	8
$p(X)$	0.1	0.2	0.3	0.4

It is very easy to link the everyday notion of a population to the statistical definition. Suppose X is the annual income of a given resident in a large city (perhaps measured to the nearest £10). Since there are thousands or millions of residents and each resident has an annual income, we have thousands or millions of values for X. Moreover if, for example, one-thousandth of the population have an income of £18 940 then we can write $\Pr(X = 18\ 940) = 0.001$. Clearly, other probabilities could be determined in this manner so that, in principle, we could derive the whole probability distribution for X.[1]

Populations can be characterized by certain constants in which we are often interested. These constants are referred to as *population parameters*. For example, the population of X, described in Table 3.1, has a mean X value given by $E(X)$ or

$$\mu = 4(0.1) + 5(0.2) + 6(0.3) + 8(0.4) = 6.4.$$

In this context, μ is a parameter and is referred to as the *population mean*.

Similarly, if X is the annual income of a city resident, then the population mean μ is simply the mean income of the population of residents. It is also equal to the mean of the implied probability distribution for X.

We shall encounter many population parameters in this text. Another such parameter is the *population variance*, σ^2. The population variance is simply the variance of all the X values in the population, that is, the variance of the probability distribution describing the population. For example, the variance of the probability distribution in Table 3.1 can be found using $\sigma^2 = E(X^2) - \mu^2$. Clearly,

$$E(X^2) = 4^2(0.1) + 5^2(0.2) + 6^2(0.3) + 8^2(0.4) = 43.$$

Thus

$$\sigma^2 = 43 - (6.4)^2 = 2.04.$$

As always, the variance measures the spread or dispersion of X values about their mean, which in this case was 6.4. Similarly, in our annual income example, σ^2 measures the dispersion of the annual incomes of city residents about their mean μ.

We stress that population parameters are *constants*. Unfortunately, it is often the case that population parameters are also *unknown*. For example, it might be infeasible to interview all the residents in the city and determine their annual incomes. It might be too costly or too time-consuming. But, obviously, we might still be interested in the values of certain population parameters; an obvious example would be mean annual income. In such situations statisticians have to resort to taking a *sample*.

In a sample, we have data on a finite number of members of the population. For example, the sample might consist of 100 or 1000 residents of the city. In practice, the size of the sample is likely to depend, firstly, on the precision with which we wish to estimate various population parameters and, secondly, on the difficulty and/or the cost of obtaining it.

Statistical inference

In the absence of knowledge about the population, a statistician has to infer things about the population from the sample information that is available.

As an example of a typical problem in statistical inference, consider the situation of the previous subsection, where we had a city of perhaps millions of residents. Suppose that, in the twentieth week of the year 2004, a survey is carried out of all residents in the city to ascertain, possibly among many other things, their annual incomes. Suppose that the mean annual income of such residents is found to be £17 670. Since we have data on all residents, we therefore know that the population mean $\mu = £17\,670$ and, if necessary, we could compute the population variance, σ^2.

Suppose now, three years later, in the twentieth week of 2007, we wish to check whether there has been any rise in income in the past three years. This time, however, we do not have time to carry out a complete survey of the whole population, or maybe it is too costly, so we therefore contact a sample of just 400 residents. The mean income of residents in the sample turns out to be £19 110.

The problem now is, on the basis of the known *sample mean* of £19 110, whether we can say that mean income for the population has risen from the value of £17 670 it took three years ago.[2] If our sample mean had been as high as £25 000 we would, almost certainly, infer that mean income for the population as a whole had risen. On the other hand, if our sample mean had been just £17 800 we might strongly suspect that population income had not risen – after all, the rise in income is fairly small, and we only have data on 400 residents rather than the whole population. But, in our sample, the mean is £19 110 which is definitely higher than the population mean of £17 670 three years ago, but is not that much higher. Since our sample is as small as 400 residents, how confident can we be that the sample mean of £19 110 is sufficiently large, compared with three years ago, for us to believe that income for the population as a whole has risen? Exactly how large must the sample mean be before we can conclude that population earnings have risen?

The above is typical of the many problems of statistical inference that we shall encounter in this text. We can summarize our first problem in statistical inference very briefly. We have to find some level of income £k such that

$$\text{if } \bar{X} \geq k \text{ then we will conclude that } \mu \text{ has risen,}$$
$$\text{but if } \bar{X} < k \text{ then we will conclude that } \mu \text{ is unchanged.}$$

Normally we give the symbol $\bar{X}$ to a sample mean such as that above. In statistical inference, population parameters are normally represented by Greek symbols such as μ for the population mean and σ^2 for the population variance, whereas *sample statistics* such as $\bar{X}$ are usually denoted by English letters. Any quantity computed from sample data only is referred to as a sample statistic. For example, the variance of all the values in a sample is a sample statistic and we give it the symbol v^2.

Sampling variability

The great difficulty that statisticians face when tackling problems of inference is the fact that different samples will almost certainly yield different outcomes. For example, in the resident income problem of this section, when we took a sample of residents we obtained a mean income of $\bar{X} = £19\ 110$. But if we took a second sample (involving different residents), again of size 400, it is highly unlikely that we would get an identical outcome. We might instead obtain a sample mean of, for example, £18 210. A third sample might yield $\bar{X} = £20\ 880$, and so on. The problem of different samples yielding different outcomes is referred to as that of *sampling variability*. It is important since, clearly, there is a great danger that the conclusion reached about a problem in inference will depend very much on what actual sample is obtained and how it is drawn.

It is clear that, to get sensible results from a sample, we need this sample to be 'representative' of the population in some sense. Fortunately, the problem of sampling variability can be tackled in a probabilistic manner, provided the samples taken are what is known as *random*. When this is the case, sampling variability follows known and systematic laws.

A sample is said to be random *if every combination of* n *members of the population has the same probability of becoming the sample that is actually drawn.*

Great care has to be taken over drawing a random sample and, obviously, no one set of members of the population can be allowed to have a greater chance of being drawn than any other member. In practice, to select a random sample, use has to be made of some chance device. We shall return to the problem of selecting such a sample at the end of this chapter but, for the moment, we simply assume that all samples taken are random in the sense defined above.

3.2 The sampling distribution of the mean

Recall that the problem of sampling variability refers to the fact that different samples, taken from the same population, normally yield different information. For example, our samples of city residents, discussed earlier, provided different values for mean sample income. Let us suppose that we take a whole series of such samples, all of fixed size 400. The samples will yield different values for the sample mean $\bar{X}$ of, say, £20 460, £18 740, £18 520, £19 230, etc.

If it were possible to take very many such samples, we would clearly obtain very many different values for $\bar{X}$. Suppose that we obtained a value for $\bar{X}$ between £18 000 and £19 000 one-tenth of the time. Since we took very many such samples, we could interpret this proportion, 0.1, as the probability of obtaining such a sample mean. That is,[3]

$$\Pr(18\ 000 < \bar{X} < 19\ 000) = 0.1.$$

Similarly, if we obtained a sample mean $\bar{X}$ between £21 000 and £22 000 one-fifth of the time, we could also interpret this as a probability and write

$$\Pr(21\ 000 < \bar{X} < 22\ 000) = 0.2.$$

In principle, there is no reason why we could not build up the whole probability distribution for $\bar{X}$ in this way. A probability histogram for such a distribution might look like that in Fig. 3.1.

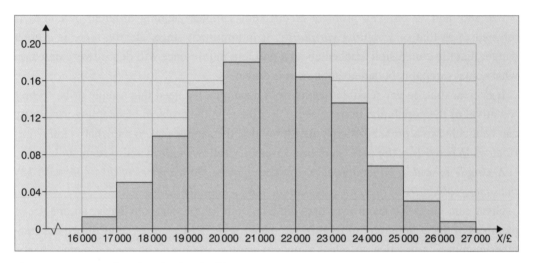

Figure 3.1 A sampling distribution for $\bar{X}$

Since we have measured resident income within £1000 bands in Fig. 3.1, the outline of the histogram is fairly jagged. However, it should be clear that if we had measured income to the nearest £100 or even to the nearest £1, the outline of the histogram would gradually become smoother.

The probability distribution we have just described is usually referred to as the *sampling distribution of the mean* of a random sample. It is simply the probability distribution for $\bar{X}$ we would obtain if we took 'very many' samples, all of the same size n, from the given population. The concept of a sampling distribution is one of the most important in statistics. We shall encounter it many times in this text, not only for a sample mean but for many other sample statistics. It is therefore worth your pausing for a moment and reflecting back on how the sampling distribution for $\bar{X}$, shown in Fig. 3.1, was built up out of all the $\bar{X}$s obtained from the 'very many' samples.

Obviously we cannot, in practice, build up a sampling distribution, such as that in Fig. 3.1, empirically. Normally, we can take just one sample (or possibly two or three) from a population. We do not have the time or resources to take 'very many' such samples.

Fortunately, there are known theoretical results available, concerning the sampling distribution of the mean, which we shall consider shortly. Despite the fact that, normally, we are only able to take a single sample, it is possible, on the basis of a single *random* sample, to use these theoretical results to *deduce* the sampling distribution for $\bar{X}$ that we *would* obtain if we had been able to take 'very many' random samples. Note that we are talking about *random* samples. Only if samples are random will the following results be valid.

Theorem 3.1

If random samples of size n are taken from an infinitely sized population with mean μ and variance σ^2 then the sample distribution of the sample mean $\bar{X}$ will have mean

$$E(\bar{X}) = \mu$$

and variance[4]

$$V(\bar{X}) = \sigma_{\bar{X}}^2 = \frac{\sigma^2}{n}.$$

A proof of Theorem 3.1 will be provided in Chapter 6, but an intuitive understanding of it is possible now. The theorem is illustrated in Fig. 3.2. It is important to realize that Theorem 3.1 involves *three* different means and *three* different variances. We will consider the three means first.

Firstly, we have μ, which is the mean of all the X values in the population. Secondly, we have $\bar{X}$, which is the mean of all the X values in the single sample that we have taken. Finally and most importantly, we have $E(\bar{X})$ which is really a kind of 'hypothetical mean', since it is the mean of all the $\bar{X}$ values we would get if we took very many different random samples all of the same size n.

The first statement that Theorem 3.1 makes is that the first and third of these means are always the same. That is, $E(\bar{X}) = \mu$. In other words, the 'average' of all sample means obtained from the many samples must equal the population mean.

There are also three variances involved in the above process. Firstly, we have σ^2, which is the variance of all the X values in the population. Secondly, although not mentioned in the theorem, we have v^2, which is the variance of the X values in the single sample taken. Notice that, again, we have used an English letter for a sample statistic as opposed to the Greek σ^2 used for the population variance. As we shall see later, v^2 is most useful because as a sample statistic it can always be computed and, with modification, then used to estimate[5] the unknown population variance σ^2.

The third variance involved is $\sigma_{\bar{X}}^2$, which is a 'hypothetical' quantity like $E(\bar{X})$. It is the variance $V(\bar{X})$ of all the $\bar{X}$s we would obtain if very many samples of size n were taken. The

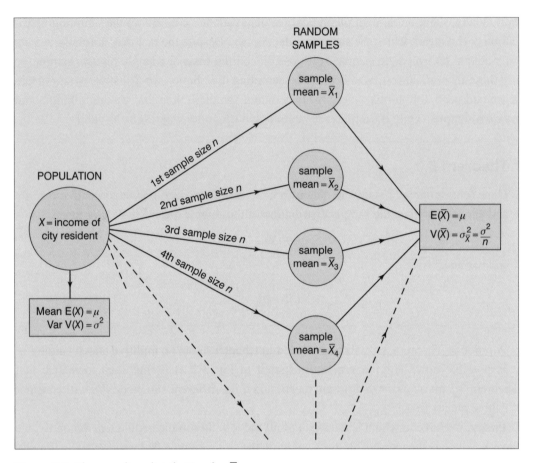

Figure 3.2 The sampling distribution for $\bar{X}$

second statement that Theorem 3.1 makes is that the two variances, σ^2 and $\sigma_{\bar{X}}^2$ are intimately linked, because $\sigma_{\bar{X}}^2 = \sigma^2/n$, where n is the sample size.

The first result in the theorem, $E(\bar{X}) = \mu$, is probably the most intuitively obvious. It is not surprising that the average value of all the $\bar{X}$s, $E(\bar{X})$, we would obtain if we took very many samples, should equal the average value of all the Xs, μ, in the population. However, the second result in Theorem 3.1 is less obvious and needs some explaining, because it has two implications.

Firstly, consider a situation where the sample size n is a fixed constant. We can then write the result $\sigma_{\bar{X}}^2 = \sigma^2/n$ as

$$\sigma_{\bar{X}}^2 = k\sigma^2, \qquad \text{where } k = 1/n = \text{constant.} \qquad [3.1]$$

This implies that $\sigma_{\bar{X}}^2$ is directly proportional to σ^2. For example, a doubling of σ^2 results in a doubling of $\sigma_{\bar{X}}^2$. Recall that variances measure the dispersion of the values of variables.

Hence, [3.1] simply means that the greater the dispersion of the X values in the population, the greater will be the dispersion of all the $\bar{X}$s obtained when very many samples are taken.

Now let us consider a situation where the population variance σ^2 is a fixed constant but the sample size is allowed to vary. For example, firstly we might take very many samples all size $n = 10$ and calculate $\sigma_{\bar{X}}^2$. Next we take very many samples size $n = 20$ and again observe $\sigma_{\bar{X}}^2$, then very many samples size $n = 30$ and so on. Since σ^2 is fixed we can, in this case, write the basic result $\sigma_{\bar{X}}^2 = \sigma^2/n$ as

$$\sigma_{\bar{X}}^2 = k/n, \qquad \text{where } k = \sigma^2 = \text{constant} \qquad\qquad [3.2]$$

It should be clear from [3.2] that $\sigma_{\bar{X}}^2$ varies inversely with n. That is, as the constant sample size is increased, the variance of all the $\bar{X}$s we would obtain, if we took very many samples, falls. A moment's reflection should reveal that this result is not surprising. Very many samples of size just $n = 2$ are likely to yield sample means $\bar{X}$ that show considerable variation. That is, $\sigma_{\bar{X}}^2$ is likely to be large. But, provided σ^2, the variance of the X values in the population, remains unchanged, very many samples of size, for example, $n = 20$, are likely to show $\bar{X}$s with much less variability. That is, $\sigma_{\bar{X}}^2$ is likely to be much smaller. This is because occasional 'rogue' or 'extreme' values of $\bar{X}$ will have much more effect on the sample mean $\bar{X}$ in samples of size $n = 2$ than they will have in samples of size $n = 20$.

Example 3.1

In city A, the expenditure per week, X, on alcohol by adult males has a mean of £31.24 and a standard deviation of £8.26. A random sample of 20 such males is taken. Let $E(\bar{X})$ and $V(\bar{X})$ be the mean and variance of the average expenditure of men in such samples. Find and then interpret $E(\bar{X})$ and $V(\bar{X})$. What would $V(\bar{X})$ be: (a) if the sample size was 40? (b) if the standard deviation of $\bar{X}$ were £4.13?

Example 3.2

A long series of random samples, all of size 12, is taken from a population of X values with mean μ and variance σ^2. For each sample, the sample mean $\bar{X}$ is calculated. The average value of all the $\bar{X}$s obtained turns out to be 20 with a standard deviation of 2. Guess the values of μ and σ^2.

Theorem 3.1 tells us a lot about the sampling distribution of the mean. But it tells us nothing about its shape. For example, is the distribution shaped like the normal distribution or does it have a uniform distribution, or an exponential distribution – or what? The following theorem, normally referred to as the *central limit theorem*, goes some way towards answering that question.

Theorem 3.2 (The central limit theorem)

If *sufficiently large* samples are randomly drawn from a population with mean μ and variance σ^2, then the sampling distribution of the mean will be approximately normally distributed with mean $E(\bar{X}) = \mu$ and variance $\sigma_{\bar{X}}^2 = \sigma^2/n$, *regardless of the shape of the distribution of the population.*

A proof of Theorem 3.2 is beyond the scope of this text, but theorems of this kind are of great importance in statistical inference. At first, it might appear that Theorem 3.2 says little more than Theorem 3.1, but that 'little more' turns out to be crucially useful. Theorem 3.2 implies that, provided the sample size is sufficiently large, then even if the population values of X are *non-normally distributed* (e.g., they could take any of the shapes illustrated in Fig. 3.3), the sampling distribution for $\bar{X}$ can still be approximated by a normal distribution. In fact, the larger the sample size, the better the approximation. It is because of this that the meaning of the phrase 'sufficiently large' is deliberately left vague in the theorem. There is no hard-and-fast distinction between what is a 'large' sample and what is a 'small'

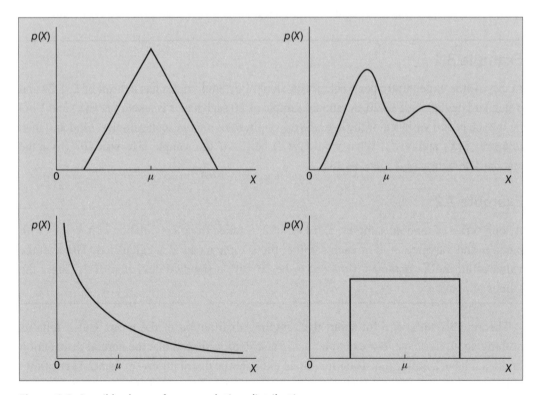

Figure 3.3 Possible shapes for a population distribution

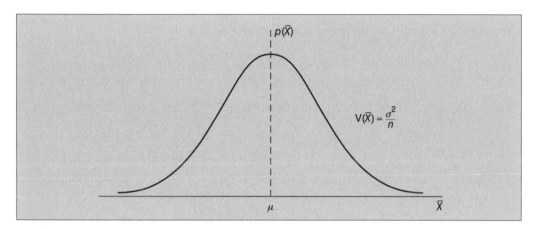

Figure 3.4 Sampling distribution for $\bar{X}$ when n is 'large'

sample. In practice, even for samples size 25, the sampling distribution for the mean has a shape roughly resembling the normal distribution.[6] For samples of size 50, the shape is very close to the normal, and with samples of size 100 or more the approximation is virtually exact, as in Fig. 3.4.

As we pointed out earlier, population parameters such as μ and σ^2 are frequently unknown. But, to enable you to grasp the ideas behind Theorems 3.1 and 3.2 thoroughly, in the following example μ and σ^2 are taken as given.

Worked Example

The residents of a large city have a mean income of £40 250 with a standard deviation of £12 500.

(a) If incomes in the city are normally distributed, find the probability that a given resident's income exceeds the poverty level, defined as half mean income.

(b) Assuming that city incomes have a roughly exponential distribution and that a random sample of 100 city residents is interviewed, find the probability that mean income in the sample will lie between £38 000 and £40 000.

Solution

Part (a) is in fact similar to the examples covered in Chapter 2. If we let X be the income of a resident, then since σ^2 equals $12\ 500^2 = 1.5625 \times 10^8$, we can write

$$X \text{ has an } N(40\ 250, 1.5625 \times 10^8) \text{ distribution.} \qquad [3.3]$$

The standard normal variable in this part of the question is therefore

$$Z = \frac{X - 40\,250}{12\,500}.$$

Turning the question about X into a question about Z, in the usual manner, yields

$$\Pr(X > 20\,125) = \Pr\left(\frac{X - 40\,250}{12\,500} > \frac{20\,125 - 40\,250}{12\,500}\right)$$
$$= \Pr(X > -1.61)$$
$$= 0.5 + \text{area } A \qquad (\text{see Fig. 3.5})$$
$$= 0.5 + 0.4463 = 0.9463.$$

Thus 94.63% of residents have incomes above the poverty level.

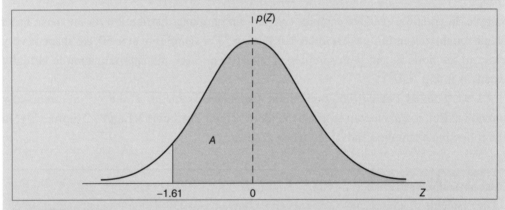

Figure 3.5

Part (b) of this question involves the use of the central limit theorem. Note that here you are required to answer a question not about X, the income of a single resident, but about $\bar{X}$, the mean of a random sample of residents. The fact that the income of residents has an exponential distribution does not matter, since the sample size n is sufficiently large for the central limit theorem to be invoked. That is, the sampling distribution for $\bar{X}$ has an approximate $N(\mu, \sigma^2/n)$ distribution.

Using the central limit theorem, we therefore have

$$E(\bar{X}) = \mu = 40\,250$$

and

$$\sigma_{\bar{X}}^2 = \frac{\sigma^2}{n} = \frac{1.5625 \times 10^8}{100} = 1.5625 \times 10^6,$$

so that we can write

$$\bar{X} \text{ has an } N(40\,250, 1.5625 \times 10^6) \text{ distribution.} \qquad [3.4]$$

The standard deviation of $\bar{X}$ is, therefore, £1250.

In this case we have to turn our question about $\bar{X}$ into a question about Z. We can do this by using [3.4]:

$$\Pr(38\,000 < \bar{X} < 40\,000) = \Pr\left(\frac{38\,000 - 40\,250}{1250} < \frac{\bar{X} - 40\,250}{1250} < \frac{40\,000 - 40\,250}{1250}\right)$$

$$= \Pr(-1.8 < Z < -0.2)$$

$$= \text{Area } B - \text{Area } A \qquad (\text{see Fig. 3.6})$$

$$= 0.4641 - 0.0793 = 0.3848.$$

Thus the probability of getting a sample mean income value of between £38 000 and £40 000 is 0.3848.

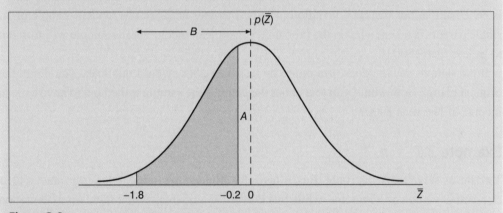

Figure 3.6

Notice that, in this question, we made use of two different standard normal Z variables. Expression [3.3] involved X, whereas [3.4] involved $\bar{X}$. To answer part (a) of the question we used [3.3], but to answer part (b) we used [3.4].

Example 3.3

A population has a mean of 75 and a variance of 25. A random sample of 80 is drawn from the population. Find the probability that the sample mean $\bar{X}$:
(a) lies between 74 and 76;   (b) exceeds 100;   (c) equals 75.

Example 3.4

The tensile strength of lengths of wire is normally distributed with a mean of 98 kg and variance 16 kg^2. A sample of size 64 lengths of wire is to be taken. Find the probability: (a) that a given length of wire has a tensile strength less than 90 kg; (b) that the mean strength of the sample of lengths exceeds 99 kg.

Example 3.5

A bridge can withstand a total weight of 1700 kg before collapsing. A group of children have a mean weight of 23.5 kg with a standard deviation of 3 kg. If a total of 70 children walk across the bridge at the same time, what is the probability that the bridge will collapse?

Example 3.6

It is claimed that the weekly incomes of single parents in a city have a mean of £600 and it is believed that the standard deviation of these incomes is £250. If a random sample of 50 single parents is taken, what is the probability that mean income in the sample will turn out to be less than £500?

   If the sample income does turn out to be less than £500, would this make you doubt the original claim? How would you feel about the claim if the sample turned out to have a mean income of less than £400?

Example 3.7

Two buses serve the same route. Bus A takes 80 minutes to complete the full route, with a standard deviation of 2 minutes, while bus B takes 75 minutes, with a standard of deviation of 10 minutes. A commuter expects to use the service 46 times in the next year. If he wishes to make the probability of a mean journey time of more than 82 minutes as small as possible, which bus should he take?

3.3 Estimating population parameters

The previous examples involved known values of the population parameters μ and σ^2 and required answers concerning the sample mean $\bar{X}$. The more usual situation occurs when population parameters such as μ are unknown but where we do have information about $\bar{X}$. That is, the situation is the reverse of Examples 3.3–3.7 and requires some statistical inference. That is, we have to infer things about the population from known information in the sample.

There are two ways in which we can estimate an unknown population mean μ and both involve, not surprisingly, the use of the known sample mean $\bar{X}$. Firstly, we may use a *point estimate*, which involves a single number. Secondly, we can employ a *confidence interval*, which requires the specifying of a range of values within which we are 'confident' the true mean μ lies. We shall look at both procedures in turn.

Point estimates

The obvious single-number estimate of a population mean μ is the sample mean $\bar{X}$. For example, if we want to estimate mean resident income in a city, and we find that the mean income of a random sample of 50 residents is $\bar{X} = £23\ 000$, then it makes sense to estimate the population mean by the single figure £23 000.

In fact, there is a big advantage in using the *estimator*[7] $\bar{X}$. From Theorems 3.1 and 3.2, we know that $E(\bar{X}) = \mu$. So we know that, if we took very many samples of size $n = 50$ from the population, we would obtain a sampling distribution similar to that shown in Fig. 3.4 with a value for $\bar{X}$ 'on average' equal to the true but unknown μ.

It is important to note that we are *not* saying that $\bar{X}$ equals μ and you *must not* write $\bar{X} = \mu$; that is simply not correct. It is $E(\bar{X})$ that equals μ, that is, it is the 'average value' of all the $\bar{X}$s obtained from the very many samples taken that equals μ. Since areas under the curve in Fig. 3.4 give probabilities, it should be clear that there are, in fact, quite large probabilities of obtaining values of $\bar{X}$ that are considerably less than μ as well as values that are considerably greater than μ. Indeed, it would be unusual to obtain an $\bar{X}$ that was exactly equal to μ.

Although it is only the 'average value' of $\bar{X}$ over many samples that equals μ, and although in practice we normally take but a single sample, it is still of some comfort to know that $E(\bar{X}) = \mu$. It means that there will be no *systematic* tendency towards error when we use $\bar{X}$ to estimate μ. That is, there will be no systematic tendency to either overestimate or underestimate μ. When there is no such systematic tendency towards error, we say that there is no *bias* in our estimating procedure. Because of this – that is, because $E(\bar{X}) = \mu$ – we say that $\bar{X}$ is an *unbiased point estimator* of μ.

Frequently, we shall find that we need to estimate the population variance σ^2 as well as its mean μ. An obvious point estimate of σ^2 is the sample variance, given by

$$V(X) = v^2 = \frac{\Sigma(X_i - \bar{X})^2}{n}, \qquad [3.5]$$

where we are simply using the normal expression for the variance of a set of n values, explained in the prerequisites chapter.

The difficulty with the sample variance, v^2, is that it is *not* an unbiased point estimator. That is, $E(v^2)$ is not equal to the true population variance σ^2. It turns out that, if very many samples were taken, each yielding a different sample variance v^2, the mean of all the v^2s so obtained would be less than the true σ^2. In fact, it can be shown that[8]

$$E(v^2) = \frac{n-1}{n}\sigma^2 < \sigma^2. \qquad [3.6]$$

Thus v^2 'on average' underestimates σ^2. The sampling distribution for v^2 is in fact illustrated in Fig. 3.7.

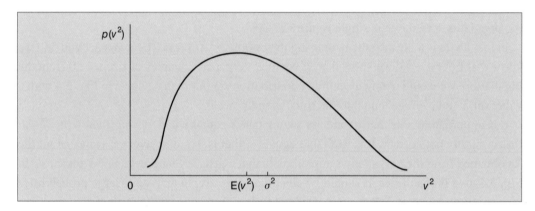

Figure 3.7 Sampling distribution for v^2

Notice that the distribution for v^2 centres itself about a point to the left of the population variance σ^2. Remembering that areas again always represent probabilities, it can be seen that there is a greater probability of obtaining a sample variance that is less than the true σ^2 than there is of getting one that is greater than σ^2. Thus, in this case, there is a *systematic tendency towards error* when we use v^2. The sample variance v^2 is therefore said to be a *biased point estimate* of the population variance σ^2.

To get round this problem of bias, the population variance is normally estimated by

$$s^2 = \frac{\Sigma(X - \bar{X})^2}{n-1}. \qquad [3.7]$$

The fact that $n-1$ appears in the denominator of [3.7], rather than n as in [3.5], means that s^2 always gives a slightly larger value than v^2. Using $n-1$ instead of n thus 'compensates' for the downward bias explained above. In fact,

$$s^2 = \frac{n}{n-1}v^2 \qquad [3.8]$$

so that, using Theorem 1.1,

$$E(s^2) = E\left(\frac{n}{n-1} v^2\right) = \frac{n}{n-1} \frac{n-1}{n} \sigma^2 = \sigma^2,$$

using [3.6]. Thus, since $E(s^2) = \sigma^2$, s^2 given by [3.7] is an unbiased point estimator of the population variance σ^2.

We will have a lot more to say about point estimators in later chapters.

Example 3.8

During May, a random sample of packages leaving a large wholesale store have weights in kilograms as follows:

$$250, 2000, 720, 1200, 310, 280, 1460, 180$$

Find unbiased estimates of the mean and variance of all packages leaving the store in May.

Example 3.9

X is the time taken by workers to complete an aptitude test and is normally distributed with a mean $\mu = 28$ minutes and standard deviation $\sigma = 4$ minutes. A random sample of 81 workers are tested and the mean test time, $\bar{X}$, of workers in the sample computed. Find k such that:
(a) $\Pr(\bar{X} > k) = 0.025$;   (b) $\Pr(\bar{X} > k) = 0.005$.

Confidence intervals

Very often point estimates alone are insufficient for our purpose and we need to specify the degree of confidence we have in our estimate. One method of doing this is to indicate a 'range' of possible values, within which we are '95% confident' that the true value of a parameter lies.

Suppose we require such a range for the population mean, μ. We begin our determination of this range by specifying two values $\bar{X} + E$ and $\bar{X} - E$ such that, before we take our sample, there is a 0.95 probability that the range eventually obtained will contain the unknown μ. That is, we require E such that

$$\Pr(\bar{X} - E < \mu < \bar{X} + E) = 0.95. \qquad [3.9]$$

E is simply an 'expression' which we have to derive. Notice that the centre of the range $\bar{X} - E$ to $\bar{X} + E$ is the sample mean $\bar{X}$. We can therefore write the range as $\bar{X} \pm E$. This makes sense since we know that $\bar{X}$ is an unbiased estimator of μ.

To find E we begin by making use of the central limit theorem. Provided the sample size n is large, $\bar{X}$ has an $N(\mu, \sigma^2/n)$ distribution. It follows that

$$\frac{\bar{X} - \mu}{\sigma/\sqrt{n}} \text{ has an } N(0, 1) \text{ distribution.} \qquad [3.10]$$

Notice that to obtain [3.10] we have subtracted the mean value of X (that is, μ) and then divided by its standard deviation (i.e., $\sqrt{\sigma^2/n} = \sigma/\sqrt{n}$) in the usual manner.

The next step is to compute what could be called a 95% confidence interval for the standard normal variable Z. That is, we find two numbers such that there is a 0.95 probability that Z lies between them. Table A.1 and Fig. 3.8a enable these two numbers to be found:

$$\Pr(-1.96 < Z < 1.96) = 0.95. \qquad [3.11]$$

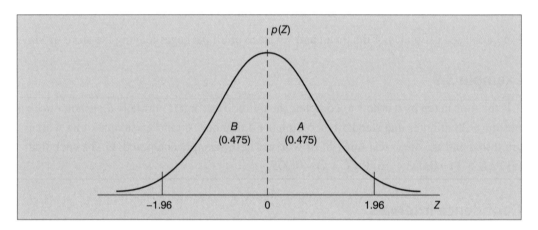

Figure 3.8a The area between +1.96 and −1.96 underneath the normal curve

The areas of both A and B in Fig. 3.8a equal 0.475, so that [3.11] follows. Notice that the interval −1.96 to +1.96 is not the only interval we could have found with an area beneath the normal curve that is 0.95. But it is the only such interval that has a centre of zero. The reason for selecting this particular interval is that ultimately we want to find an interval for μ of the kind $\bar{X} - E$ to $\bar{X} + E$, centred at $\bar{X}$.

We can now find the required confidence interval for μ by taking the expression for Z in [3.10] and substituting it into [3.11]:

$$\Pr\left(-1.96 < \frac{\bar{X} - \mu}{\sigma/\sqrt{n}} < +1.96\right) = 0.95. \qquad [3.12]$$

We now manipulate the quantities between the brackets in [3.12] until we have an interval for μ. Firstly, we multiply the bracketed terms through by $\sigma/\sqrt{n}$ to obtain

$$\Pr\left(-1.96\,\frac{\sigma}{\sqrt{n}} < \bar{X} - \mu < +1.96\,\frac{\sigma}{\sqrt{n}}\right) = 0.95. \qquad [3.13]$$

Next we subtract $\bar{X}$ from all terms between the brackets.

$$\Pr\left(-\bar{X} - 1.96\,\frac{\sigma}{\sqrt{n}} < -\mu < -\bar{X} + 1.96\,\frac{\sigma}{\sqrt{n}}\right) = 0.95 \qquad [3.14]$$

Finally, we multiply throughout by -1 to obtain

$$\Pr\left(\bar{X} + 1.96\,\frac{\sigma}{\sqrt{n}} > \mu > \bar{X} - 1.96\,\frac{\sigma}{\sqrt{n}}\right) = 0.95. \qquad [3.15]$$

Notice that when we multiply throughout by -1, the direction of the inequality sign changes.[9] That is, the $<$ sign becomes $>$.

We have now obtained an expression of the form [3.9], that is, a range which has a 0.95 probability of containing μ. Comparison of [3.15] with [3.9] indicates that the expression E that we require must be $1.96\sigma/\sqrt{n}$. The range we have obtained is usually referred to as a *95% large-sample confidence interval* for the population mean μ. We can write it as

$$\bar{X} \pm 1.96\,\frac{\sigma}{\sqrt{n}}.$$

A problem with this interval is that the expression $E = 1.96\sigma/\sqrt{n}$ depends on σ, the population standard deviation, which, like μ, is unknown. Hence, when computing a confidence interval, in practice it is necessary to replace σ by s, the *sample* standard deviation. s is computed using [3.7], which provides an unbiased estimator of σ. The 95% confidence interval for μ is therefore usually written as

$$\bar{X} \pm 1.96\,\frac{s}{\sqrt{n}}. \qquad [3.16]$$

If necessary, it is possible to increase the confidence of our estimate. For example, we might wish to be 99% confident that our range will contain μ. This simply means reading a different number from Table A.1. The areas A and B in Fig. 3.8a become 0.495 rather than 0.475 and the Z value becomes 2.58 rather than 1.96. This is illustrated in Fig. 3.8b. The 99% confidence interval for μ is thus

$$\bar{X} \pm 2.58\,\frac{s}{\sqrt{n}}. \qquad [3.17]$$

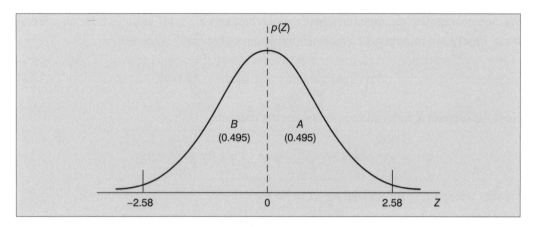

Figure 3.8b Area between +2.58 and −2.58 under the normal curve

It should be clear that confidence intervals for any percentage can be obtained in the above manner, simply by using Table A.1. However, as the degree of confidence required is increased, there is a price to pay, since it can be seen that the width of the interval also increases. That is, the *precision* of the estimate is less.

We will frequently have occasion to form confidence intervals for other parameters in this text. However, the process is usually similar to the above. The standard deviation of the relevant sampling distribution is known as the *standard error of the estimate*. For example, when estimating a population mean μ, the estimate is $\bar{X}$ and the standard error of the estimate is $\sigma/\sqrt{n}$. In general, providing the sampling distribution is symmetric, confidence intervals always take the form

$$\text{point estimate} \pm \text{critical value} \times \text{standard error of estimate.} \qquad [3.18]$$

The critical value in [3.18] is taken from the relevant table of distribution values. For example in the above example, the point estimate is $\bar{X}$ and the critical value comes from Table A.1.

Worked Example

A sample of 250 ten-year-old male children, from a developing country, were found to have a mean height of 138 cm with a standard deviation of 20.3 cm. Find a 95% confidence interval for the true mean height of such children. How large a sample would be necessary if we wished to estimate the true mean to within 2 cm with 95% confidence?

Solution

We have $n = 250$, $\bar{X} = 138$ and $s = 20.3$, so using [3.16] we obtain a 95% confidence interval as

$$138 \pm 1.96 \frac{20.30}{\sqrt{250}} = 138 \pm 2.52. \qquad [3.19]$$

Thus the range which we have found is from 135.48 to 140.52.

To obtain the required sample size for the second part of the question, note that there must be a 0.95 probability that the interval $\bar{X} \pm 2$ contains μ. If this is the case, then $\bar{X}$ must lie within 2 cm of the unknown μ, as required. Comparing $\bar{X} \pm 2$ with the confidence interval formula [3.16] we see that we must choose n so that

$$1.96 \frac{s}{\sqrt{n}} = 2. \qquad [3.20]$$

Since $s = 20.3$, we can use [3.20] to solve for n. That is

$$\sqrt{n} = \frac{20.3 \times 1.96}{2} = 19.89.$$

Thus we obtain a value of 395.77 for n. Notice that the larger we make n, the smaller we make $1.96s/\sqrt{n}$ and the narrower our confidence interval [3.16] becomes. We had to make n sufficiently large for the interval to be as narrow as $\bar{X} \pm 2$. Obviously the sample size n has to be a whole number. We cannot use $n = 395$, because this would yield an interval just a little wider than $\bar{X} \pm 2$. We therefore take $n = 396$, even though it gives an interval just a little narrower than that required.

The computation of confidence intervals involves straightforward arithmetic, requiring simple substitution into given formulae. But the interpretation of computed confidence intervals turns out to be much more slippery.

The key point in their interpretation is the fact that the unknown population mean μ is a fixed constant. It must therefore either lie inside any given range or it must lie outside that range. In the above worked example, we apparently found a range of 135.48 to 140.52 cm for the mean height μ of 10-year-old males. But if μ is a constant the probability of it lying in this range must be either unity or zero. If μ lies within the range 135.48 to 140.52 then the probability is unity. If it lies outside the range then the probability is zero. The probability certainly cannot be 0.95.

At this point you may feel somewhat baffled. What, then, was computed in the above worked example? The crucial point to remember is that different samples yield different values of $\bar{X}$ and different values of s and, consequently, different samples will yield, after substitution into [3.16], *different confidence intervals*. If very many samples were taken we would obtain very many different confidence intervals – one for each sample. The point is that, if we select the 95% confidence level, then 95% of the confidence intervals obtained will contain or 'bracket' the unknown μ, but the remaining 5% will not. Remember that μ is a fixed number, so that it is the confidence interval that varies, not the population mean μ.

In practice, of course, we do not take 'very many' samples. But before we take our single sample we can say, with 95% confidence, that there is a 0.95 probability that the interval we will eventually obtain will contain the fixed μ. Unfortunately, once we have taken the sample and obtained the interval we can no long say this! The fixed μ either lies within the interval we have computed or it does not. The interpretation of confidence intervals is therefore not quite as straightforward as you might think!

Example 3.10

In a diet trial 80 chickens were fed a high-carbohydrate diet for five days. The gains in weight of the chickens averaged 36 gms with a variance of 25 gms^2.

(a) Compute a 95% confidence interval for μ, the population mean weight gain.

(b) How large a sample has to be taken if the sample mean $\bar{X}$ is to differ from μ by less than 0.5 gms with 95% confidence?

Explain carefully what is meant by 95% confidence in the context of part (b).

Example 3.11

In 2002, the weekly food expenditure of couples with two children was £164 with a standard deviation of £28. To estimate the weekly food expenditure of such families in 2004, a sample is to be taken. How large should the sample be if the sample mean is to be within £2 of the true mean expenditure with 90% confidence?

Example 3.12

Consider a population with mean 200 and standard deviation 15. If it costs 50p to draw one member of a sample, how much does it cost to draw a sufficiently large sample to ensure that the probability of the sample mean lying within 1% of its true population value is 0.95?

Suppose the precision of the estimate of μ needed to be doubled. How much would it cost to draw a sufficiently large sample now? What if the precision needed was doubled a second time?

Estimating a population proportion

We return now to the large population of workers, last visited in Section 2.4, who were for or against industrial action of some kind. The population in this case is normally referred to as a *binomial* or *binary* population. This is because we can regard each worker in the population as having a value for a variable X which is permitted to take just one of two values, 0 and 1. We say that $X = 1$ when the worker is in favour of industrial action, whereas $X = 0$ when the worker is not in favour. Suppose

$$\Pr(X = 1) = \pi, \qquad \Pr(X = 0) = 1 - \pi. \qquad [3.21]$$

The parameter π is simply the probability of getting an X value equal to 1, that is, it is the probability of a given worker being in favour of industrial action. Since we are dealing with a large workforce, we can also interpret π as the *proportion* of workers in the population who favour industrial action. Obviously, $1 - \pi$ is the proportion of workers not in favour.

π, the *population proportion*, is another example of a population parameter. In fact, a population proportion is a special type of population mean. Equation [3.21] provides the probability distribution for X (remember X can take just two values). So, using the standard procedure for obtaining the mean of a probability distribution, μ, we have

$$\mu = \mathrm{E}(X) = 1\pi + 0(1 - \pi) = \pi. \qquad [3.22]$$

Thus, the population mean in this case is simply equal to the population proportion.

Although in Section 2.4 it was assumed that we knew that $\pi = 0.6$, generally a population proportion is unknown and has to be estimated. Fortunately, it is possible to make point estimates and construct confidence intervals for π from sample data.

Point estimates

The obvious point estimator of a population proportion π is the sample proportion. This is the proportion of workers in the sample who are in favour of industrial action. Following the usual procedure of using Greek letters for population parameters and English letters for sample statistics, we adopt p as the symbol for the sample proportion.

p is clearly a point estimator of π, but is it an unbiased point estimator? Suppose we have a sample of size n. Let us look closely at the n values in our sample. These values of X are all either equal to 1 or equal to 0: $X = 1$ if the particular member of the sample is in favour of industrial action, but $X = 0$ if they are against. If we sum all the X values in the sample, that is, sum the 1s and 0s, then this sum must equal

$$\Sigma X = \text{number of sample members who favour action.}$$

The proportion of sample members who favour industrial action is therefore

$$p = \frac{\Sigma X}{n}.$$ [3.23]

Notice from [3.23] that the sample proportion is in fact the mean of all the X values in the sample, that is, $\bar{X}$.

We have now seen that, just as the population proportion π is a special case of the population mean μ, the sample proportion p is a special case of the sample mean, $\bar{X}$. We can therefore make use of the first part of Theorem 3.1, which states that $E(\bar{X}) = \mu$. It follows that $E(p) = \pi$. That is, if 'very many' samples are taken, then the average value of all the ps obtained will equal the true population proportion π. p is therefore an unbiased estimator of π.

Confidence intervals

To obtain a confidence interval for π, akin to those of [3.16] and [3.17], we need to answer two questions. Firstly, what is the population variance σ^2, in this case? Secondly, does the sampling distribution for p have a normal distribution, so that we can use Table A.1?

We can obtain the population variance from the 'mini-probability distribution' [3.21] in the usual way, using $\sigma^2 = E(X^2) - \mu^2$. Since

$$E(X^2) = 1^2\pi + 0^2(1 - \pi) = \pi,$$

we have

$$\sigma^2 = \pi - \pi^2 = \pi(1 - \pi).$$ [3.24]

Thus the population variance also depends on the population proportion π.

We can now use the second part of Theorem 3.1 to obtain the variance of the sampling distribution for p. We simply rewrite $V(\bar{X}) = \sigma^2/n$ as

$$V(p) = \frac{\pi(1 - \pi)}{n}.$$ [3.25]

We saw in the previous chapter that, for a binomial population, the number of successes in n trials could be approximated by a normal distribution, provided both $n\pi$ and $n(1 - \pi)$ both exceeded 5. Since a sample proportion is no more than the number of successes, ΣX, divided by the sample size (or number of trials), it follows, for given n, that p is a constant multiple of ΣX. Hence, under the above conditions, p itself must have a normal distribution with mean π and variance given by [3.25]. That is,

$$p \text{ has an } N[\pi, \pi(1-\pi)/n] \text{ distribution.} \qquad [3.26]$$

We have thus derived the sampling distribution for p.

To obtain confidence intervals for π, firstly we simply slot values $\bar{X} = p$ and $\sigma = \sqrt{\pi(1-\pi)/n}$ into [3.16] or [3.17]. For example, a 95% confidence interval for π is

$$p \pm 1.96 \sqrt{\frac{\pi(1-\pi)}{n}}. \qquad [3.27]$$

The main problem with [3.27] is that the interval involves π which, of course, is unknown. In practice the unknown π has to be replaced by its unbiased estimate, the known sample proportion p. Expression [3.27] then becomes

$$p \pm 1.96 \sqrt{\frac{p(1-p)}{n}}. \qquad [3.28]$$

Intervals for other confidence levels can then be found using Table A.1 in the usual way.

Worked Example

A random sample of 100 workers in an economy reveals that 20% are unemployed. Obtain an unbiased point estimate of the true population unemployment level. Hence, find a 99% confidence interval for the true population unemployment level.

Solution

π is the true population proportion of workers who are unemployed. The sample proportion is 20%, so that $p = 0.20$ provides an unbiased point estimate of π. A 99% confidence level for π is therefore given by

$$p \pm 2.58 \sqrt{\frac{p(1-p)}{n}} = 0.2 \pm 2.58 \sqrt{\frac{0.2 \times 0.8}{100}}$$
$$= 0.2 \pm 0.10.$$

Example 3.13

Of the cows in a particular country, 21% have an infectious disease. If a random sample of 80 such cows is taken, what is the probability that more than 22 of these cows will be sick?

If it turned out that more than 28 cows in the sample were sick, what would you conclude?

Example 3.14

A random sample of 20 adults are numbered 1 to 20. Adults 4, 7, 16 and 18 fail a basic reading test and are termed 'illiterate'. Obtain an unbiased point estimate for the population proportion of adults who are illiterate. Find a 99% confidence interval for this population proportion.

Example 3.15

In a public opinion poll, 35% of a random sample of 1000 voters say they intend to vote for the government in a forthcoming election. Find a 95% confidence interval for the true proportion of the electorate who intend to support the government. How large a sample should the government take if it wishes to estimate its true level of support to within 1% with 95% confidence?

Example 3.16

A firm is surveying its former employees to determine the proportion π that left the firm because of conflict with their immediate supervisor. The firm wishes to estimate the true π to within 0.1 with 95% confidence. How large a sample of former employees should be taken: (a) if a small pilot sample suggests that 30% of employees left for this reason? (b) if no information about π is available?

In each case, determine the required sample size if the precision in the estimate of π is to be doubled.

3.4 **Random sampling**

We defined a random sample in Section 3.2 and throughout Section 3.3 we assumed that any samples taken were random. However, the taking of a random sample is not always an easy matter. For example, suppose we wished to select a random sample of 400 residents from the city of Sections 3.1 and 3.2. The first step to take would be to obtain a list of all residents. This could be constructed from, for example, the electoral register. The next step would be to assign a different number to each resident on the list, starting with 1, 2, 3, … and continuing until all residents have been assigned. The final step would be to use some chance mechanism to select 400 residents from the numbered list. For example, an appropriate chance mechanism might be a ten-sided die, with the numbers 0, 1, 2, …, 9 on its sides.

It should be clear that drawing a random sample can be a lengthy and costly process. Nowadays chance devices, such as dice, have been superseded by computer-generated sequences of random numbers but constructing full lists of the members of a population can still be time-consuming. Fortunately, economists are often able to make use of so-called secondary data sources. Many governments publish time series for various economic variables; for example, fairly reliable quarterly and annual GDP series are available for all developed countries. The extent to which these series can be regarded as random samples is discussed in Chapter 7. There are also cross-sectional secondary data sources available; for example, in the UK, the Family Expenditure Survey (FES) is a government survey published each year, describing households' individual income and expenditures in that particular year.

Other sampling methods

Clearly, the primary or raw data out of which secondary data series are constructed have to be collected. Because of the problems in obtaining random samples of a reasonable size, various techniques are often adopted in order to acquire less costly samples that are still representative of the population. For example, most public opinion polls use *quota samples*. Interviewers are expected to select their quota of individuals according to certain criteria determined by the characteristics of the population under study. For example, an interviewer may be required to find so many white-collar middle-class females, so many unemployed males, and so on. Obviously, interviewers need very thorough training if they are to be able to obtain reliable quotas. But provided quotas are well selected, this can ensure that the known characteristics of the population are replicated in the sample. Such samples are probably more representative than random samples but, unfortunately, since they do not have a probabilistic base, the statistical findings from such samples are less reliable. Since samples are no longer random, the central limit theorem cannot now be relied on and, consequently, there can be no guarantee that estimates of population parameters are unbiased. Moreover, it is not possible to use the usual confidence interval formulae.

Stratified samples do have a part-probabilistic basis. Firstly, the population is divided into *strata*. For example, the population might be divided into individuals with income in excess of £50 000, those with income between £40 000 and £50 000, those between £30 000 and £40 000, and so on. Random samples are then taken from each of the strata, the size of each such subsample depending on the relative numbers of individuals in each stratum. Such a stratified sample has the advantage over a simple random sample in that it rules out the possibility that the sample might not be representative of the population as far as incomes are concerned. Stratification is most beneficial when there are large between-strata differences in the variable of interest. For example, if low-income individuals tend to spend larger proportions of their income on food than do high-income individuals, then an overestimate of the average propensity to consume food will be obtained from a purely random sample in which low-income individuals are overrepresented. A sample stratified by income would avoid this possibility.

Cluster samples also have a probabilistic basis. Samples are drawn in two (sometimes more) stages. For example, in the first stage a random selection of towns (or maybe counties) is selected. Then, in the second stage, random samples of individuals can be drawn from each such town. Cluster samples are necessarily less efficient than true random samples, but can be very much cheaper to draw. Collecting a true random sample of, for example, 1000 people from the UK population would be very expensive, since the individuals are certain to be highly spread out geographically. Cluster sampling can reduce this expense dramatically. Two-stage or often multi-stage sampling is frequently used in practice; for example, the FES mentioned above uses a multi-stage process, involving both clustering and stratification.

Many would argue that better estimates of single-number population parameters can be obtained from stratified or cluster samples. But it remains the case that only when samples are totally random can we rely completely on properties such as those implied by Theorems 3.1 and 3.2, concerning sampling distributions. While estimators of population parameters are likely to remain unbiased, the usual confidence interval formulae can no longer be employed.

Summary

- **Populations** are to be distinguished from **samples**. Populations are characterized by certain population **parameters** which are fixed constants. These constants are often unknown.

- **Statistical inference** involves inferring things about populations and their parameters, using just sample information. The basic problem of inference is that of **sample variability**. However, provided samples are **random**, this problem can be dealt with.

- The **sampling distribution of the mean**, $\bar{X}$, arises if many samples of fixed size are taken from a population. The **central limit theorem** states that, provided the samples are 'large', then the mean, $\bar{X}$, will have a normal distribution.

- A population parameter can be estimated in two ways. Firstly, we could obtain a **point estimator**, that is, a single-number estimate. Preferably, we like point estimators to be **unbiased**, that is, the expected value of the estimator should equal the parameter being estimated.

- Secondly, **confidence intervals** specify a range of values within which we are, for example, 95% confident that an unknown parameter lies. Confidence intervals are easy to compute but much more slippery to interpret.

- Point estimators and confidence intervals can be computed both for population **means** and for population **proportions**.

- Totally random samples can be expensive to collect. This expense can be reduced by using **cluster** and/or **stratified samples**.

Notes

1. A population does not necessarily have to involve people. For example, let X be the weight of a parcel leaving a mail room. The population and the probability distribution for X could then refer to the large number of parcels leaving the mail room during a ten-week period.

2. We abstract from any price changes in this example.

3. Since we are assuming that income is a continuous variable, the probability of obtaining an X exactly equal to 18 000, for example, can be treated as zero.

4. For a finite population of size N, while $E(\overline{X})$ remains equal to μ, the variance of $\overline{X}$ is in fact

$$\sigma_{\overline{X}}^2 = \frac{\sigma^2}{n}\left(\frac{N-n}{N-1}\right).$$

But, as N becomes very large, $V(\overline{X})$ tends to σ^2/n.

5. As we shall see later, the modification is necessary because, if we use v^2 as an estimate of σ^2, v^2 will systematically underestimate the true σ^2.

6. For small samples, the distribution of $\overline{X}$ is naturally influenced by the shape of the population distribution. For a fairly extreme shape, such as the exponential distribution, the sample size has to be a little larger before the central limit theorem makes its influence felt. On the other hand, if the population itself is normally distributed, the sampling distribution for $\overline{X}$ will be normally distributed even for very small samples.

7. Formulae such as $\overline{X} = \sum X_i/n$, into which we substitute sample values to estimate population parameters, are referred to as *estimators*. However, once the substitution has been performed and a specific value obtained, that value is referred to as an *estimate*.

8. See, for example, Hoel (1962, p. 229).

9. It is always the case that, if an inequality is multiplied throughout by -1, then the direction of the inequality is reversed. For example, $6 > 4$ multiplied by -1 gives $-6 < -4$. Similarly, $-2 < 7$ but $2 > -7$, and $3 > -5$ but $-3 < 5$, and so on.

4

Hypothesis testing I

Objectives

When you have completed your study of this chapter you should be able:

1. to understand the techniques and philosophy underlying the testing of hypotheses about a population mean;

2. to formulate appropriate null and alternative hypotheses for any such testing situation;

3. to derive the correct test statistic and a suitable test criterion for the testing of such a null hypothesis;

4. to construct an operating characteristics curve and to be clear about the distinction between type I and type II errors;

5. to appreciate the importance of power curves and the power of a particular test criterion.

Introduction

Statistical Inference can be divided into two main areas of interest – estimation and hypothesis testing. In the previous chapter we considered methods of estimating population parameters, using either a point estimator or a confidence interval. Often, however, we may be more concerned about whether some parameter takes (or differs from) a given value. We then enter the area of hypothesis testing. For example, a store might wish to know whether the proportion of shoppers who regularly visit it exceeds 30%. That is, it wants to know whether π, the population proportion, exceeds 0.3 or not. A statistician would tackle such a situation by formulating *hypotheses*. One such hypothesis might be, for example, $\pi = 0.3$ and another $\pi > 0.3$. The next few chapters will be concerned with the statistical testing of such hypotheses. In this chapter, however, we will consider only situations regarding a population mean.

4.1 **Testing hypotheses about a population mean**

Recall our first problem of statistical inference, discussed towards the end of Section 3.1, concerning the income of residents of a large city. It was assumed that, in the 20th week of 2004, mean annual income was £17 670. However, in the 20th week of 2007, only a sample could be taken and, on the basis of this sample, a decision had to be made as to whether mean income had risen during the past three years.

We reduced the problem to that of finding a value k such that, if the sample mean $\bar{X} \geqslant k$, we would conclude that population incomes had risen since 2004, while if $\bar{X} < k$ we would conclude that they had not. Given the central limit theorem (Theorem 3.2), we are now in a position to find such k values.

Firstly, we construct two hypotheses, both concerning the new 2007 value of μ. The *null hypothesis* is that mean annual income in the population has remained unchanged since 2004. The null hypothesis is normally designated as H_0. In this case, therefore, we have

$$\text{null hypothesis } H_0: \mu = 17\ 670. \qquad [4.1]$$

Our second hypothesis covers *all reasonable possibilities other than the null hypothesis* and we refer to it as the *alternative hypothesis*, designated H_A. All possibilities other than $\mu = 17\ 670$ obviously imply $\mu \neq 17\ 670$ but, to simplify matters for now, we shall rule out the possibility $\mu < 17\ 670$, so that the alternative hypothesis becomes $\mu > 17\ 670$. We can justify this by arguing that, since we live in prosperous times, it is highly unlikely that annual incomes will have fallen since three years ago. Thus we have

$$\text{alternative hypothesis } H_A: \mu > 17\ 670. \qquad [4.2]$$

Clearly, we have to choose between H_0 and H_A. Let us suppose we must do this on the basis of information from a sample size $n = 400$. It should also be clear that if the sample mean income $\bar{X}$ turns out to be 'much larger' than 17 670, the 2004 population value of mean income, then we will be inclined to *reject* H_0 and *accept* H_A. The question that now has to be answered is how much larger than £17 670 $\bar{X}$ has to be before we can reject H_0.

As noted above, it is the central limit theorem that now enables us to tackle this problem. Since our sample is a large one, we can say that the sample mean $\bar{X}$ has a $N(\mu, \sigma^2/n)$ distribution. It follows that

$$Z = \frac{\bar{X} - \mu}{\sigma/\sqrt{n}} \text{ has a } N(0, 1) \text{ distribution.} \qquad [4.3]$$

As usual we denote a standard normal variable by the symbol Z.

If we assume, for the sake of argument, that H_0 is true and that annual incomes have remained unchanged, then we can substitute $\mu = 17\,670$ into [4.3] and obtain

$$TS = \frac{\bar{X} - 17\,670}{\sigma/\sqrt{n}} \text{ has a } N(0, 1) \text{ distribution.} \qquad [4.4]$$

The formula $(\bar{X} - 17\,670)/(\sigma/\sqrt{n})$ in [4.4] is an example of what is known as a *test statistic* (*TS*). We shall encounter many such test statistics in this text. The important thing about *TS* here is that it has an $N(0, 1)$ distribution *only when the null hypothesis H_0 is true*. That is, under H_0, *TS* has a standard normal distribution. If H_0 were false and $\mu > 17\,670$ so that H_A was true, then we could not make the substitution $\mu = 17\,670$ in [4.3] and move on to [4.4].

We call the quantity in [4.4] a test statistic for the simple reason that it enables us to test whether H_0 is true or not. Since, from [4.4], *TS* has an $N(0, 1)$ distribution, with much of the area beneath the normal curve (and hence most of the probability) centred around zero, under H_0, we expect *TS*, when it is computed, to turn out to have a value close to zero. Consequently, if the value of *TS* turns out to be 'sufficiently different' from zero, we reject H_0 and accept that incomes have risen since the previous year.

Notice that *TS* is based on $\bar{X} - 17\,670$, the difference between $\bar{X}$ and 17 670. That is, we are comparing the sample mean with the 17 670 in H_0. The greater this difference, the greater the difference between *TS* and zero. However, we earlier ruled out the possibility that $\mu < 17\,670$, so that in this situation we reject H_0 only if $\bar{X}$ is 'sufficiently *greater*' than 17 670. This implies that we reject H_0 if the test statistic *TS*, depending as it does on $\bar{X} - 17\,670$, is sufficiently *greater* than zero.

The problem, of course, is deciding on what we mean by 'sufficiently greater'. If H_0 is true, we know that *TS* has a standard normal distribution, as depicted in Fig. 4.1. As we saw above, when H_0 is true, there is a large probability of getting a value for *TS* which is close to zero. Consequently, there is only a very small probability of getting a value for *TS* which is much greater than zero.

Suppose, once our sample of 400 residents has been taken, we compute *TS* [4.4] and obtain a value which is rather greater than zero. Suppose, in fact, we get a value $TS > 1.64$.

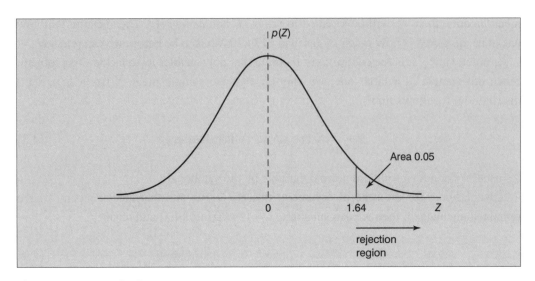

Figure 4.1 A test criterion

The number 1.64 has been carefully chosen, because the area beneath the standard normal curve, to the right of 1.64, in Fig. 4.1 is just 0.05. 1.64 is obviously a positive number, but is it 'sufficiently greater' than zero for us to be confident enough to reject H_0 and maintain that annual incomes have risen? In fact, if $TS > 1.64$, then, logically, we can make just one of two possible statements.

Firstly, we could insist that H_0 was true, despite the fact that $TS > 1.64$. But, if we insist on this, then we have to admit that a rather unusual event has occurred. If H_0 is true, then the test statistic has an $N(0, 1)$ distribution as in Fig. 4.1. It follows that the probability of getting a value $TS > 1.64$ is then as small as 0.05. That is, if H_0 is true, there is only a 1 in 20 chance of our sample yielding $TS > 1.64$. In the everyday world, many people would regard such a 1 in 20 chance just 'turning up' as somewhat unusual.

The alternative is to reject H_0 as false, whenever we get $TS > 1.64$. In this case we would accept H_A and conclude that annual incomes have risen. Note that, if it is H_A that is true, then the normal curve in Fig. 4.1 no longer represents the distribution of TS, since we can no longer make the transition from [4.3] to [4.4]. TS may well be distributed about 1.25 or 1.5, for example, rather than zero. That being the case, there would no longer be anything unusual in getting a value of $TS > 1.64$.

Suppose we do in fact reject H_0. In that case, we must still keep in the back of our minds the small probability (of up to 0.05) that H_0 was true all along. In other words, when we claim, as a result of $TS > 1.64$, that incomes have risen, we must admit a probability of up to 0.05 that we are in error when we make the claim.[1]

When we obtain $TS > 1.64$, we normally state that we 'reject H_0 at the 0.05 *level of significance*'. This statement is normally referred as a *test criterion* and can be paraphrased as 'we reject H_0 but we admit that there is a 5% chance that we are wrong to do so'. The values of Z that lie to the right of 1.64 are often referred to as a *rejection region*, as illustrated in Fig. 4.1.

The level of significance is simply the probability of error, when rejecting the null hypothesis. It is normally given the symbol α. That is,

level of significance $\alpha = \Pr(\text{reject } H_0 \,|\, H_0 \text{ is true})$.

A word of warning is in order at this point. Careful reading of the previous paragraphs should make clear that the level of significance, α, measures the probability of error only under certain circumstances. It gives the probability of error *only when the null hypothesis is true*. If H_0 were *false*, and if we *accepted* H_0, we would indeed be making an error but it would be a different kind of error and the probability of that error occurring would not be measured by the level of significance, α. The probability of making this second type of error, that of accepting a null hypothesis when it is false, is usually given the symbol β. We shall be having a lot more to say about α and β in the next section.

There is, of course, nothing unique about the number 1.64, used in the above problem. Suppose, instead, our sample resulted in a value for $TS > 2.33$. The area under the normal curve in Fig. 4.2, to the right of 2.33, is now as small as 0.01. In this situation, we can again say one of two things. Either we can accept H_0 but admit that a very unusual event has occurred, that event having a probability as low as 0.01, or we can reject H_0. But, if we do

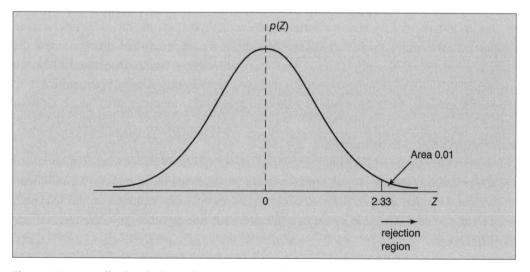

Figure 4.2 A smaller level of significance

reject H_0, we must remember that there is a very small probability (of up to 0.01) that we are in error. If $TS > 2.33$, a statistician would say that 'we reject H_0 at the 0.01 level of significance'. The rejection region for this case is shown in Fig. 4.2.

Notice that the smaller we make the level of significance at which we reject H_0, the more definite that rejection becomes. A rejection at the 0.01 level is a stronger rejection of H_0 than a rejection at the 0.05 level, because in the former case the chance of error is smaller. Of course, it would be possible to choose an even smaller level of significance if required. But there are two difficulties with this. Firstly, you can never reduce the probability of error to zero. Recall that the tails of the standard normal curve only approach the Z-axis as Z tends to plus or minus infinity. That is, however large we make the Z value, there is always some non-zero area under the curve to the right of it. Secondly, if you make the level of significance too small, you will find, as explained in the next section, that H_0 is virtually never rejected!

In tackling the above problem, we formulated a test criterion of the kind 'reject H_0 if $TS > 1.64$'. Writing the test criterion in full, using [4.4], gives

$$\text{reject } H_0 \quad \text{if } \frac{\bar{X} - 17\,670}{\sigma/\sqrt{n}} > 1.64. \qquad [4.5]$$

Rearranging [4.5] then yields

$$\text{reject } H_0 \quad \text{if } \bar{X} > 17\,670 + 1.64\sigma/\sqrt{n}. \qquad [4.6]$$

This implies that we reject H_0 (at the 0.05 level of significance) when our sample results in a mean $\bar{X}$ which exceeds some level k, where

$$k = 17\,670 + 1.64\sigma/\sqrt{n}. \qquad [4.7]$$

If σ, the population standard deviation, were known then, for given n, we could compute k. This is, in fact, exactly how we formulated our first problem in statistical inference in Section 3.1. We said we would reject the hypothesis that incomes had risen provided the sample mean exceeded some given k that was 'sufficiently larger' than the 2004 mean income of £17 670. We now know what is meant by 'sufficiently larger'. We require $\bar{X} > k$, where k is given by [4.7]. However, we need to qualify this by saying that, since we have selected a level of significance of 0.05, if we do reject H_0 when $\bar{X} > k$ then there is a 0.05 probability that we will be in error.

It is time we actually worked out the value of a test statistic. We have a random sample of $n = 400$ residents and suppose the sample gives a mean annual income of $\bar{X} = £17\,890$ with a standard deviation of $s = £2048$. If we use s as an unbiased estimate of the unknown population standard deviation σ, we can substitute the above values into the test statistic [4.4] and obtain

$$TS = \frac{17\,890 - 17\,670}{2048/\sqrt{400}} = 2.15.$$

The test statistic is clearly greater than 1.64 but not greater than 2.33. Thus we can reject H_0 (the hypothesis of unchanged income) at the 0.05 but not at the 0.01 level of significance.

How do we interpret this? Firstly, we can say that if we allow ourselves a 0.05 probability of error, we can safely reject H_0 and maintain that incomes have risen. Secondly, however, when we allow ourselves only a 0.01 probability of error, we find that, according to our test criterion, we are unable to reject H_0 and claim a rise in incomes. In fact, if we did reject H_0, then the probability of error would exceed the 0.01 that we originally permitted ourselves.

Worked Example

A driving school claims that the mean age of its pupils is 22. A sample of 60 pupils proves to have a mean of 20.7 years with a variance $s^2 = 2.2$ years^2. Test at the 0.05 level of significance whether the true mean age of pupils is in fact less than 22.

Solution

The first step, in this example, is to formulate null and alternative hypotheses. Firstly, we adopt a null hypothesis that the claim is true:

$$H_0: \mu = 22. \qquad [4.8]$$

(As will become increasingly clear, it makes life much less complicated if we can manage to formulate a null hypothesis which contains the equality sign '=', rather than an inequality sign '<' or '>' or even '≠'. In this example we therefore set up the null hypothesis that the school's claim is true.)

We are asked to test whether mean pupil age is less than 22, so we set up an alternative hypothesis that the claim is untrue:

$$H_A: \mu < 22. \qquad [4.9]$$

(Notice that hypotheses always involve the unknown population *mean. The population in this case refers to all pupils that ever have been or ever will be taught at the driving school. The value 20.7 in the question refers to the* sample *mean $\bar{X}$ which is obviously known. Resist the temptation to write things like '$H_0: \bar{X} = 20.7$' which is simply silly and leads nowhere. You know the value of $\bar{X}$, so why on earth should you want to test a hypothesis about it?)*

To perform the required hypothesis test, we need to construct a test statistic. We can do this by using [4.3]. Under H_0, $\mu = 22$ so that [4.3] becomes

$$TS = \frac{\bar{X} - 22}{\sigma/\sqrt{n}} \text{ has a } N(0, 1) \text{ distribution.} \qquad [4.10]$$

(Since TS has a standard normal distribution, as illustrated in Fig. 4.3, we expect its value to turn out to be close to zero if H_0 is true. However, if TS proves to be very different from zero, we shall start thinking that H_0 may be false. Expression [4.10] is therefore an appropriate test statistic.)

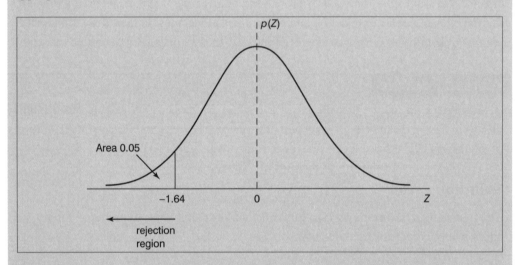

Figure 4.3

We now select a significance level, that is, we specify a permitted probability of error for the situation 'reject H_0'. Since the consequences of error are not particularly serious in this case, we shall select the 0.05 rather than the 0.01 level of significance. Figure 4.3 indicates that our test criterion should be

$$\text{reject } H_0 \text{ if } TS < -1.64. \qquad [4.11]$$

(Since the alternative hypothesis is H_A: $\mu = 22$, in this situation we should reject the null hypothesis $\mu = 22$ if the sample mean $\bar{X}$ is sufficiently smaller than 22, that is, if $\bar{X} - 22$ is sufficiently less than zero. Thus we require that the test statistic, given by [4.10], be sufficiently negative. We made use of Table A.1 to determine how negative it should be.)

We are now in a position to work out the test statistic [4.10] and reach some conclusion about the validity of H_0. Substituting for $\bar{X}$ in [4.10] and replacing σ by its unbiased estimate, s, we obtain

$$TS = \frac{20.7 - 22}{\sqrt{2.2/60}} = -6.79.$$

Hence we reject H_0 at the 0.05 level of significance. That is, we reject the driving school's claim, remembering, however, that we allowed ourselves a 0.05 probability of error.

Two-tail tests

Recall that, in our example concerning the annual incomes of city residents, we ruled out the possibility that incomes might have fallen since the year 2004. We justified this by arguing that we were living in prosperous times. Suppose, however, perhaps because of an economic recession, that this possibility could no longer be ignored. In such a situation, we could retain our null hypothesis $H_0: \mu = 17\ 670$, that incomes had remained unchanged, but would have to modify our alternative hypothesis. Because the alternative hypothesis needs to cover all other reasonable possibilities, apart from H_0, we now require $H_A: \mu \neq 17\ 670$. That is, H_A implies that incomes have *changed* since 2004.

We also need to modify our criterion for rejecting H_0. It now makes sense to reject H_0, not only if the sample mean $\bar{X}$ is sufficiently *greater* than £17 670, but also if $\bar{X}$ is sufficiently *smaller* than £17 670, to allow for the possibility that, in 2007, $\mu <$ £17 670. In terms of the test statistic [4.4], which remember is based on the difference between $\bar{X}$ and £17 670, this implies that we should reject H_0, either if *TS* is sufficiently positive, or if it is sufficiently negative.

To find out what is meant by 'sufficiently positive or negative' we refer, as usual, to Table A.1. If we were to adopt a 0.05 level of significance, Fig. 4.4 indicates that we should reject H_0 either if $TS > 1.96$ or if $TS < -1.96$. In Fig. 4.4 note that the 0.05 probability of error is now split equally into two 0.025 areas, one beneath each tail of the standard normal curve. For obvious reasons, such a test is normally referred to as a *two-tail test*. Tests such as that described by Figs 4.1–4.3 are normally referred to as *one-tail tests*.

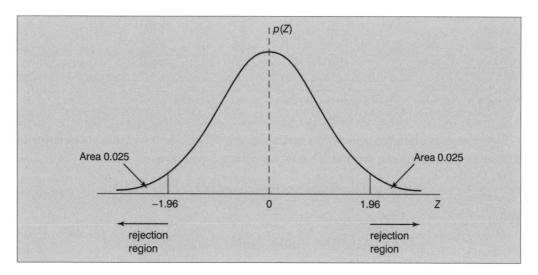

Figure 4.4 A two-tail test criterion

The argument behind the two-tail test is identical to that behind the one-tail test. Suppose a sample were taken and a value for the test statistic [4.4] was found to be either greater than 1.96 or less than −1.96. If it is maintained that H_0 is true, in which case the distribution for the test statistic would be that described in Fig. 4.4, then it would have to be accepted that something rather unusual had happened. Under H_0 there is a probability of only $0.025 + 0.025 = 0.05$ of getting a value of the test statistic either greater than 1.96 or less than −1.96. Since such events are so unusual, we therefore normally reject H_0, although we admit that there is a probability of up to 0.05 that we may have made an error.

As with one-tail tests, the level of significance does not have to be 0.05. A more stringent requirement would be to reject H_0 only at the 0.01 level of significance. As Fig. 4.5 indicates, rejection at this level of significance requires either that $TS > 2.58$ or that $TS < −2.58$. Now it is the $0.005 + 0.005 = 0.01$ probability that is split equally between the two tails of the standard normal curve.

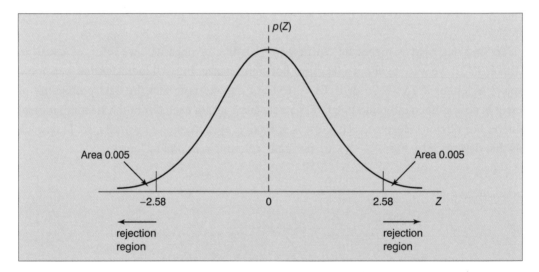

Figure 4.5 A smaller level of significance when the test is two-tail

Note that it is often convenient to express the test criteria for two-tail tests in terms of absolute values of the test statistic. That is, we write the criteria as

reject H_0 at the 0.05 level of significance if $|TS| > 1.96$

and

reject H_0 at the 0.01 level of significance if $|TS| > 2.58$,

where $|TS|$ is the absolute value of the test statistic.

Suppose, next, that a sample of 400 city residents is taken and yields an average annual income of only $\bar{X} = £17\,550$ with standard deviation £1985. This value is clearly less than the 2004 value of £17 670. Replacing σ by s, in the usual manner, the test statistic [4.4] now yields a value

$$TS = \frac{17\,550 - 17\,670}{1985/\sqrt{400}} = -1.21.$$

Since the value of the test statistic is $-1.23 > -1.96$ (i.e., $|TS| < 1.96$), we are unable, in this case, to reject the null hypothesis that annual incomes have remained unchanged.

Notice the careful wording of the last sentence. We stated not that we accepted H_0 but that we were *unable to reject H_0*. Whether we should actually accept H_0 is the subject of the next section.

One-tail versus two-tail tests

When testing hypotheses concerning a population mean, it is the two-tail test that is the 'default option'. This is because the alternative hypothesis, covering all possibilities other than H_0: $\mu = $ constant, is logically H_A: $\mu \neq$ constant. One-tail tests with H_A: $\mu >$ constant (upper tail) or with H_A: $\mu <$ constant (lower tail) really only occur in either of the two following situations.

(a) When the situation specifically requires a one-tail test. For example, in the above worked example, the question actually asked was that we should test whether the average age of drivers was less than 22 years. We therefore used H_A: $\mu < 22$ and adopted a one-tail test (lower tail in this case).

(b) When it is possible to rule out on *a priori* grounds either $\mu >$ constant or $\mu <$ constant. For example, in our first example concerning city residents, it was possible to rule out $\mu < 17\,670$ on the grounds that we were living in prosperous times. Consequently, we used H_A: $\mu > 17\,670$, which implied a one-tail test (upper tail in this case). One-tail tests are actually fairly frequent in economics where it is often possible to restrict, on *a priori* grounds, the form of H_A.

It is in case (b) that beginners often come unstuck. Suppose we have H_0: $\mu = q$, where q is some appropriate constant. To test this hypothesis we take a sample and obtain a value for $\bar{X}$, the sample mean. At this point, we will know whether $\bar{X} < q$ or $\bar{X} > q$ and it becomes tempting to use an alternative hypothesis H_A: $\mu > q$, if it turns out that $\bar{X} > q$, and to use H_A: $\mu < q$ if we obtain $\bar{X} < q$. That is, even if we begin with H_A: $\mu = q$, we still end up using a one-tail test.

This is incorrect for two linked reasons. Firstly, the alternative hypothesis always involves the *population* mean μ, whereas the sample gives us $\bar{X}$, the *sample* mean. Just because $\bar{X} < q$ does not necessarily mean that $\mu < q$. Similarly, $\bar{X} > q$ does not necessarily imply that $\mu > q$.

Secondly, and more importantly, you should not allow your sample evidence to influence your choice of hypotheses. In the real world, good statistical practice is to decide on the hypotheses to be tested, and the level of significance for your test, *before you take your sample*. Thus, at this stage you will not know what $\bar{X}$ is! The statistician resists the temptation to go back and change hypotheses once he has seen the sample evidence. Otherwise, this would be the first step on the slippery path to a world in which statistics can be used to prove anything!

Two crucial ideas

It is important to grasp two important ideas when tackling hypothesis testing situations. Firstly, in all tests in this text, we proceed by comparing what we expect to find when the null hypothesis is true with what we actually obtain. If the difference between the two is large enough, we conclude that H_0 cannot be true. For example, in this chapter, we expect our test statistic to be near zero when the null hypothesis is true. If it is not near zero, then we are likely to reject that null hypothesis.

Secondly, in all tests we require an appropriate test statistic. Such a test statistic is always found by taking some *basic result* and seeing what happens to that result when the null hypothesis is true. For example, when testing a hypothesis about a population mean, the appropriate basic result is the fact that $(\bar{X} - \mu)/(\sigma/\sqrt{n})$ is a standard normal Z variable. But the basic result is not yet the test statistic. The test statistic is only found when we substitute the H_0 value for μ into the basic result. Thus, if we have $H_0: \mu = q$ then the test statistic is $(\bar{X} - q)/(\sigma/\sqrt{n})$, and *not* $(\bar{X} - \mu)/(\sigma/\sqrt{n})$.

This second point often appears quite trivial to many students but, in fact, it is fundamental to the whole idea of hypothesis testing. The quantity $(\bar{X} - \mu)/(\sigma/\sqrt{n})$ *always* has a standard normal distribution (in large samples) and is expected to take a value near zero, *whether H_0 is true or not*. Thus, it can hardly be used to test whether H_0 is true or not! But $(\bar{X} - q/(\sigma/\sqrt{n})$ is a standard normal variable *only when H_0 is true*, and this is why it can be used as a test statistic.

In the following examples you are expected to do more than just get the arithmetic correct. Make sure you are absolutely clear about which numbers refer to the population and which refer to the sample.

Example 4.1

A consumer watchdog receives numerous complaints from customers that boxes of a company's detergent contain less than the 3200 gms advertised. To check the complaints, the watchdog purchases 50 boxes and finds that their mean weight is 3197.3 gms with a variance of 173.2 gms^2. Test whether the company is selling detergent boxes below the advertised weight.

Example 4.2

A bank is aware that in the past the time taken for its clients to clear overdrafts was 23 days. To test whether, nowadays, clients are still clearing their overdrafts at the previous rate, the bank takes a sample of 40 new overdrafts which prove to take a mean of 26 days to clear, with a standard deviation of 7 days. What should the firm conclude? Be careful in your selection of alternative hypothesis.

Example 4.3

The breaking strength of steel cables produced by a firm has a mean of 850 kg with a standard deviation of 50 kg. It is claimed that a new manufacturing process leads to an increased breaking strength. A sample of 60 cables produced by the new method proves to have a mean breaking strength of 875 kg. Can this claim be supported at the 0.01 level of significance? Justify the alternative hypothesis adopted.

4.2 Two types of error

In the examples in the previous section, we adopted a test criterion of the kind 'reject H_0 if $|TS| > Z'$' where Z' depended on the level of significance and was taken from the standard normal table. Rejection of H_0 implied acceptance of H_A. But what if our test criterion is such that we are unable to reject H_0? Do we then simply *accept* H_0 and reject H_A?

Suppose we extend our test criterion to

$$\text{reject } H_0 \text{ if } |TS| > Z' \text{ but accept } H_0 \text{ if } |TS| < Z'. \qquad [4.12]$$

Under [4.12], rejection of H_0 implies acceptance of H_A while acceptance of H_0 means rejection of H_A. With such a criterion, there are *two* different kinds of error that can be made. Firstly, we make an error whenever we reject H_0 but in fact H_0 is true. This is the kind of error we have concentrated on so far, and it is referred to as a *type I error*. It is the probability of a type I error that is termed the level of significance, α.

The other kind of error that can be made, when using the criterion [4.12], is that of accepting H_0 when it is in fact false. This is referred to as a *type II error*. Note that the probability of a type II error (referred to as β) is not given by the level of significance. Unfortunately, as we shall see, this second probability is normally unknown.

The two types of error are illustrated in Table 4.1. Note that the two situations marked with a 'tick' involve either accepting H_0 when it is true or rejecting H_0 when it is false. In these situations no errors are made.

Table 4.1 Types of error

	H_0 is true	H_0 is false
Reject H_0	Type I error	✓
Accept H_0	✓	Type II error

Ideally we would like to be able to find a value of Z' in [4.12] such that the probabilities of making type I or type II errors were as small as possible. Obviously, no one likes making mistakes, particularly since mistakes might prove costly. Unfortunately, as we shall now see, it turns out that it is normally impossible to make α and β very small simultaneously. We will find that the smaller we make α the larger β inevitably becomes. Similarly as β becomes smaller, the larger becomes α.

To explain these difficulties, we revert to our annual incomes example where we make the null and alternative hypotheses

$$H_0: \mu = 17\,670, \qquad H_A: \mu \neq 17\,670 \tag{4.13}$$

The test statistic is, as usual,

$$TS = \frac{\bar{X} - 17\,670}{\sigma/\sqrt{n}}. \tag{4.14}$$

Adopting a 0.05 level of significance, the test criterion [4.12] therefore becomes (using the two-tail test),

$$\text{reject } H_0 \text{ if } |TS| > 1.96 \text{ but accept } H_0 \text{ if } |TS| < 1.96. \tag{4.15}$$

The rejection and acceptance zones were shown in Fig. 4.4.

Given this framework, we now consider the probability of committing type I and type II errors. For the sake of clarity, we assume for the moment that the population standard deviation σ is known.

Type I errors

This type of error is fairly easily dealt with. Recall that, under H_0, the test statistic in [4.14] has a $N(0, 1)$ distribution, that is, it is a standard normal Z variable. Hence,

$$\begin{aligned}
\Pr(\text{type I error}) &= \Pr[\text{reject } H_0 \,|\, H_0 \text{ is true}] \\
&= \Pr[\,|TS| \,>\, 1.96 \,|\, TS \text{ is } N(0, 1)] \\
&= \Pr(\,|Z| \,>\, 1.96) \\
&= 0.05 = \text{level of significance.} \qquad\qquad [4.16]
\end{aligned}$$

This confirms that the probability of a type I error is simply the level of significance. In fact, we have merely gone round in a circle because, once the level of significance has been selected as 0.05, the number 1.96 taken from the standard normal table is bound to appear in the test criterion [4.15].

Type II errors

This type of error is more difficult to handle. They only occur when H_0 is false. The problem is that, when H_0 is false, we do not know the value of μ. If it is H_A that is true, then from [4.13], all we can say is that $\mu \neq 17\,670$. Suppose we let the 'new' unknown value of μ be μ^*, that is, $\mu = \mu^* \neq 17\,670$.

  In these circumstances (when H_0 is false) we can no longer regard the test statistic [4.14] as having a $N(0, 1)$ distribution. However, by the central limit theorem, it is still the case that $\bar{X}$ has a $N(\mu, \sigma^2/n)$ distribution, regardless of the true value of μ. When H_0 is false and $\mu = \mu^*$, $\bar{X}$ will therefore have a $N(\mu^*, \sigma^2/n)$ distribution. It follows that

$$\frac{\bar{X} - \mu^*}{\sigma/\sqrt{n}} \text{ has a } N(0, 1) \text{ distribution.} \qquad\qquad [4.17]$$

  Compare the two cases [4.14] and [4.17]. In the first case H_0 is *true*, so that $\mu = 17\,670$ and [4.14] holds. That is, TS has a $N(0, 1)$ distribution. But, in the second case, H_0 is *false*, so that $\mu = \mu^*$ (where $\mu^* \neq 17\,670$) and [4.17] holds. In this second case, it is *not TS* that has the $N(0, 1)$ distribution.

  We can now set about trying to compute the probability of making a type II error. Recall that

$$\Pr(\text{type II error}) = \Pr(\text{accept } H_0 \,|\, H_0 \text{ is false})$$

Since we have adopted the test criterion [4.15], it follows that

Pr(type II error)

$$= \Pr(-1.96 < TS < 1.96 \,|\, \mu = \mu^*)$$

$$= \Pr\left(-1.96 < \frac{\bar{X} - 17\,670}{\sigma/\sqrt{n}} < 1.96 \,\bigg|\, \frac{\bar{X} - \mu^*}{\sigma/\sqrt{n}} \text{ is } N(0, 1)\right). \qquad [4.18]$$

In [4.18] we have substituted equation [4.14] for TS, and used the fact that, when $\mu = \mu^*$, [4.17] holds. Equation [4.18] requires us to answer a question about $TS = (\bar{X} - 17\,670)/(\sigma/\sqrt{n})$ when, unfortunately, it is not TS but $(\bar{X} - \mu^*)/(\sigma/\sqrt{n})$ that is the standard normal variable. We therefore need to manipulate [4.18] in order to obtain $(\bar{X} - \mu^*)/(\sigma/\sqrt{n})$ between the equality signs.

Firstly, we add $17\,670/(\sigma/\sqrt{n})$ to all terms to the left of the 'conditional sign' in [4.18]. This gives

Pr(type II error)

$$= \Pr\left(-1.96 + \frac{17\,670}{\sigma/\sqrt{n}} < \frac{\bar{X}}{\sigma/\sqrt{n}} < 1.96 + \frac{17\,670}{\sigma/\sqrt{n}} \,\bigg|\, \frac{\bar{X} - \mu^*}{\sigma/\sqrt{n}} \text{ is } N(0, 1)\right).$$

Next, we subtract the unknown quantity $\mu^*/(\sigma/\sqrt{n})$ from all terms to the left of the conditional sign. This yields

Pr(type II error)

$$= \Pr\left(-1.96 + \frac{17\,670 - \mu^*}{\sigma/\sqrt{n}} < \frac{\bar{X} - \mu^*}{\sigma/\sqrt{n}} < 1.96 + \frac{17\,670 - \mu^*}{\sigma/\sqrt{n}} \,\bigg|\, \frac{\bar{X} - \mu^*}{\sigma/\sqrt{n}} \text{ is } N(0, 1)\right).$$

We have now turned the question about TS in [4.18] into a question about the quantity $(\bar{X} - \mu^*)/(\sigma/\sqrt{n})$ which is a standard normal Z variable. Thus we can write

Pr(type II error)

$$= \Pr\left(-1.96 + \frac{17\,670 - \mu^*}{\sigma/\sqrt{n}} < Z < 1.96 + \frac{17\,670 - \mu^*}{\sigma/\sqrt{n}}\right). \qquad [4.19]$$

Suppose that the sample size is $n = 400$ and that the population standard deviation happens to be $\sigma = £1700$. Thus, $\sigma/\sqrt{n} = 85$ in [4.19], which then becomes

Pr(type II error)

$$= \left(-1.96 + \frac{17\,670 - \mu^*}{85} < Z < 1.96 + \frac{17\,670 - \mu^*}{85}\right). \qquad [4.20]$$

Recall that μ^* is the unknown value that μ takes when it is H_A that is true rather than H_0. The great problem with [4.20] is that we cannot use it to work out the probability of a type II error because we do not know μ^*. This a serious problem because no one wishes to make decisions that have an unknown (possibly high) probability of being wrong.

One approach to this problem is to consider some possible values that the unknown μ^* might take. Suppose, for example, that $\mu = \mu^* = £18\ 500$. H_0 is therefore false. If we were to accept H_0 in these circumstances, then substituting for μ^* in [4.20] gives

$$\text{Pr(type II error)} = \text{Pr}(-11.72 < Z < -7.80) = 0$$

The two Z values of -7.80 and -11.72 are so far away under the left-hand tail of the normal curve that the probability of a type II error is virtually zero. This is reassuring as far as it goes because we now know that if $\mu^* = £18\ 500$ then there is a probability of virtually zero of our accepting H_0 in these circumstances. But the problem is that we do not *know* that $\mu^* = £18\ 500$. What if, instead, μ^* were £17 750?

If $\mu^* = £17\ 750$, H_0 would still be false, but now, again substituting into [4.20], we obtain

$$\text{Pr(type II error)} = \text{Pr}(-2.90 < Z < 1.02)$$
$$= 0.4981 + 0.3461 = 0.8442.$$

In this case there is now a massive probability of 0.8442 that we would accept H_0 even though it was false. Obviously if we knew that μ^* were £17 750 we would take care not to make this error. But, as we have stressed, unfortunately μ^* is unknown.

The problem is not, however, quite as bad as it might seem. When H_0 is false, and average population income differs from £17 670, it may matter little when μ^* lies close to £17 670 but it may matter a great more when μ^* lies far away. Luckily, when μ^* lies far away from £17 670, the probability of accepting H_0 and making a type II error is close to zero as we saw above. It is only when μ^* is close to £17 760 that Pr(type II error) becomes worryingly large. Thus our test criterion is able to 'pick up' large differences in μ^* from the H_0 value, but is unlikely to 'pick up' smaller differences.

Operating characteristics curves

Table 4.2 shows values of Pr(accept H_0), calculated using [4.20], for various values of μ^* from £17 000 to £18 500. Notice, however, that the second row of values has been labelled Pr(accept H_0) rather than Pr(type II error), as in equation [4.20]. For all values μ^* other than £17 670, which has been circled, H_0 is false so that Pr(accept H_0) does indeed give Pr(type II error). But, for one value of μ^*, £17 670 (circled), H_0 is true, so that Pr(accept H_0) no longer gives the probability of error. It is therefore more appropriate to label the second row Pr(accept H_0) rather than Pr(type II error).

Table 4.2 Pr(accept H_0) for various values of μ^*

μ^*	17 000	17 250	17 450	17 550	(17 670)	17 750	17 850	17 950	18 500
Pr(accept H_0)	0	0.001	0.265	0.708	0.950	0.844	0.437	0.091	0

The values in Table 4.2 have been plotted in Fig. 4.6 with values of μ^* on the horizontal axis and probabilities ranging from zero to unity on the vertical axis. The resultant curve is the *operating characteristics* (OC) *curve* for the test criterion [4.15]. The OC curve gives the best overall picture of the advantages and disadvantages of this particular test criterion. Firstly, for values of μ^* other than $\mu^* = 17\,670$, it provides

$$\text{Pr(accept } H_0 | \mu^* \neq 17\,670)$$
$$= \text{Pr(accept } H_0 | H_0 \text{ is false)} = \text{Pr(type II error)}.$$

However, for the single central value $\mu^* = 17\,670$, the curve in Fig. 4.6 gives

$$\text{Pr(accept } H_0 | \mu^* = 17\,670)$$
$$= \text{Pr(accept } H_0 | H_0 \text{ is true)}$$
$$= 1 - \text{Pr(reject } H_0 | H_0 \text{ is true)} = 1 - \text{Pr(type I error)}.$$

This last follows from the fact that, when H_0 is true and $\mu^* = 17\,670$, the probabilities of rejecting and of accepting H_0 must sum to unity.

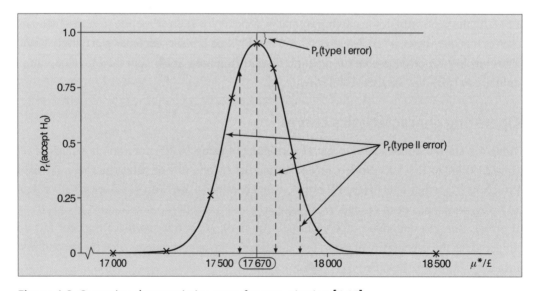

Figure 4.6 Operating characteristics curve for test criterion [4.15]

Summarizing, for all values of μ^* on the horizontal axis, apart from the central value of 17 670, the vertical height of the OC curve gives Pr(type II error). But for the single central value $\mu^* = 17\,670$, the vertical height of the OC curve gives $1 - $ Pr(type I error). That is, Pr(type I error) is given by the small distance labelled as such in Fig. 4.6.

Consideration of the OC curve confirms the point made earlier, that Pr(type II error) depends on μ^*, which is generally unknown. Different μ^*s imply different probabilities of type II error. Since μ^* is unknown, we do not know which type II error probability applies. A number of possible values for Pr(type II error) are marked in Fig. 4.6.

In contrast, for our particular test criterion, Pr(type I error) is fixed and known. This is the consequence of having a null hypothesis that specifies a definite value for the population mean.

It is important to realize that different test criteria result in different OC curves. Suppose we replaced [4.15] by the criterion

$$\text{reject } H_0 \text{ if } |TS| > 1.64 \text{ but accept } H_0 \text{ if } |TS| < 1.64. \qquad [4.21]$$

(You should be able to confirm that the level of significance for this criterion is $\alpha = 0.10$.) If the OC curve for this test criterion were drawn, it would be found to lie beneath the OC curve for [4.15] at all points. In fact, in Fig. 4.6, it would pass through the central line $\mu^* = 17\,670$ at the point where Pr(accept H_0) = 0.90, so that Pr(type I error) = 0.10 as expected. Hence, although Pr(type I error) is larger for the test criterion [4.21], the lower OC curve [4.21] implies *smaller* probabilities of type II errors.

It should now be clear that, as the level of significance is varied, so the OC curve will drift upwards and downwards, and this reveals a basic conflict. As the OC curve drifts downwards, values of Pr(type II error) will *decline* but Pr(type I error) must *increase*. Conversely, if the OC curve is pushed upwards, Pr(type I error) will *fall* but only at the expense of *higher* values of Pr(type II error). Normally, with a given sample size, it is impossible to design a test criterion which yields small probabilities for *both* types of error.[3]

In concluding this section, we can say that test criteria of the kind we have been describing give rise to two major difficulties.

(a) Since μ^* is unknown, this means that the probability of a type II error remains unknown.[4]

(b) The smaller we make Pr(type I error), that is, the lower the level of significance, the higher become the probabilities of type II errors. Conversely, the lower we make the probabilities of type II errors, the larger becomes Pr(type I error).

Example 4.4

In the above example, the following decision criterion is adopted:

$$\text{reject } H_0 \text{ if } |TS| > 2.58, \text{ but accept } H_0 \text{ if } |TS| < 2.58.$$

Find the level of significance implied by this criterion and roughly sketch its OC curve on Fig. 4.6, using the equivalent version of equation [4.20].

Worked Example

The null hypothesis $H_0: \mu = 150$ is to be tested against an alternative $H_A: \mu > 150$. The test statistic $TS = (\bar{X} - 150)/(\sigma/\sqrt{n})$ is employed and a test criterion,

$$\text{reject } H_0 \text{ if } TS > 1.8 \text{ but accept } H_0 \text{ if } TS < 1.8,$$

is adopted. If the test statistic has a standard normal distribution when H_0 true, calculate Pr(type I error). If $n = 80$ and $\sigma = 11$, calculate Pr(type II error) when (a) $\mu^* = 160$, (b) $\mu^* = 155$ and (c) $\mu^* = 150.5$.

Solution

We are told that, under H_0, TS has an $N(0, 1)$ distribution. Hence

$$\begin{aligned}
\text{Pr(type I error)} &= \text{Pr[reject } H_0 | H_0 \text{ is true]} \\
&= \text{Pr}[TS > 1.8 \,|\, TS \text{ is } N(0, 1)] \\
&= \text{Pr}[Z > 1.8] = 0.0359,
\end{aligned}$$

using Table A.1.

Under H_A, $\mu = \mu^* > 150$, and $(\bar{X} - \mu^*)/(\sigma/\sqrt{n})$ has an $N(0, 1)$ distribution. Hence

$$\begin{aligned}
\text{Pr(type II error)} &= \text{Pr[accept } H_0 | H_0 \text{ is false]} \\
&= \text{Pr}\left(TS < 1.8 \,\middle|\, \frac{\bar{X} - \mu^*}{\sigma/\sqrt{n}} \text{ is } N(0, 1) \right) \\
&= \text{Pr}\left(\frac{\bar{X} - 150}{\sigma/\sqrt{n}} < 1.8 \,\middle|\, \frac{\bar{X} - \mu^*}{\sigma/\sqrt{n}} \text{ is } N(0, 1) \right) \\
&= \text{Pr}\left(\frac{\bar{X} - 150}{\sigma/\sqrt{n}} - \frac{\mu^*}{\sigma/\sqrt{n}} < 1.8 - \frac{\mu^*}{\sigma/\sqrt{n}} \,\middle|\, \frac{\bar{X} - \mu^*}{\sigma/\sqrt{n}} \text{ is } N(0, 1) \right) \\
&= \text{Pr}\left(\frac{\bar{X} - \mu^*}{\sigma/\sqrt{n}} < 1.8 + \frac{150 - \mu^*}{\sigma/\sqrt{n}} \,\middle|\, \frac{\bar{X} - \mu^*}{\sigma/\sqrt{n}} \text{ is } N(0, 1) \right) \\
&= \text{Pr}\left(Z < 1.8 + \frac{150 - \mu^*}{\sigma/\sqrt{n}} \right).
\end{aligned}$$

When $n = 80$ and $\sigma = 11$, $\sigma/\sqrt{n} = 1.23$, so that we have

$$\Pr(\text{type II error}) = \beta = \Pr\left(Z < 1.8 + \frac{150 - \mu^*}{1.23}\right).$$

Thus, using Table A.1,

when $\mu^* = 160$, $\quad \beta = \Pr[Z < -6.33] = 0$,

when $\mu^* = 155$, $\quad \beta = \Pr[Z < -2.27] = 0.0116$,

when $\mu^* = 150.5$, $\quad \beta = \Pr[Z < 1.39] = 0.5 + 0.4177 = 0.9917$.

Again we find that, when μ^* is close to the H_0 value of 150, the probability of a type II error becomes very large. That is, this criterion 'picks up' a false H_0 only when μ^* differs greatly from 150.

Example 4.5

A landlord owns many thousands of two-bedroom flats. He maintains that the average weekly rent he charges his tenants is £80. In contrast, a group of tenants claim that the landlord charges more than the £80 average and a resulting sample of 50 tenants are found to pay on average £82, with a standard deviation of £9.2. Using a 0.05 level of significance, what do you conclude?

If the true (but unknown) average rent was $\mu = 82$, what is the probability of a type II error?

Example 4.6

Null and alternative hypotheses are $H_0: \mu = 50$ and $H_A: \mu = 48$ (there are only two possible values for μ).

It is believed that the population variance is 25 and a sample of size 80 is taken. A decision criterion is adopted of the form

reject H_0 if $\overline{X} < 49$ but accept H_0 if $\overline{X} \geq 49$,

where $\overline{X}$ is the sample mean. Calculate the probabilities of type I and type II errors for this criterion. Do you think this criterion is a sensible one?

Example 4.7

In a national examination, a random group of 100 children take the exam early, to see if the exam paper is of the correct degree of difficulty (defined as a mark of 50% for an average child). The children obtain an average mark of 48% with a variance of 95. Using 0.05 and 0.01 levels significance, test whether the exam paper is of the correct degree of difficulty. How would you explain your result to a non-statistician?

4.3 **An alternative approach**

Because of the difficulties of handling type II errors, pointed out above, many statisticians use a test criterion slightly different from that of previous sections. Like them, we shall adopt a criterion of the kind

$$\text{reject } H_0 \text{ if } |TS| > Z' \text{ but reserve judgement if } |TS| < Z'. \qquad [4.22]$$

Notice the crucial but subtle difference between the test criteria [4.22] and [4.12]. In [4.22], we reserve judgement on the hypotheses when $|TS| < Z'$, rather than accept H_0. In fact, if we use a test criterion of the kind [4.22], then we will never accept the null hypothesis H_0. We either reject H_0 or reserve judgement. The vital point is that, since we never accept H_0, *we can never make a type II error* (recall that a type II error can only occur when we accept H_0).

Having eliminated the possibility of a type II error, we can now concentrate on type I errors and choose a value for Z' in [4.22] that makes Pr(type I error) as small as we like. This involves selecting an appropriate level of significance. We usually adopt 0.05 and/or 0.01 levels of significance but, in practice, if the cost of making such an error were very serious (as it could be in certain medical decisions, for example) the level of significance might be set very low indeed.

English and Scottish systems of jury trials

A defendant must be either innocent (null hypothesis H_0) of the crime of which he is accused, or guilty (alternative hypothesis H_A). In England and Wales a jury has a choice between finding the defendant guilty (that is, rejecting H_0) or not guilty (that is, *accepting H_0*). A not guilty verdict presumes innocence. The English system is therefore akin to decision criterion [4.12] since H_0 must either be accepted or rejected.

In the Scottish system, however, a jury can give a third verdict. Instead of finding a defendant guilty or not guilty, the jury can find the case *not proven*. The three possibilities are in fact reject H_0 (guilty), accept H_0 (not guilty) or *reserve judgement* on H_0 (not proven), this last possibility being that which appears in test criterion [4.22]. In giving a 'not proven' verdict, a jury presumably feels that the defendant may well be innocent but does not bring in a 'not guilty' verdict because the probability of a type II error (finding the defendant innocent when he is in fact guilty) is thought to be non-negligible.

Large-sample tests for μ: summary of procedure

Although this summary deals with a population mean, μ, we will find that similar systematic procedures need to be followed for testing hypotheses about any population parameter. The type of procedure we adopt in this text involves six steps, which should be rigorously followed.

I. *State null and alternative hypotheses.* The null hypothesis should normally contain an equality.

$$H_0: \mu = q,$$

where q is some appropriate constant. The alternative hypothesis should cover *all* other reasonable possibilities. The 'default' alternative hypothesis is therefore

$$H_A: \mu \neq q.$$

However, on *a priori* grounds, and/or because of a direct instruction, we may wish to rule out $\mu > q$ or $\mu < q$ and perform a one-tail test. The alternative hypothesis will then be either

$$H_A: \mu < q \quad \text{or} \quad H_A: \mu > q.$$

II. *Construct an appropriate test statistic.* This can always be obtained from the basic result [4.3] and using the fact that, under H_0, $\mu = q$. Thus

$$TS = \frac{\overline{X} - q}{\sigma/\sqrt{n}} \text{ has an } N(0, 1) \text{ distribution.}$$

III. *Decide on the level of significance.* This is the permitted level of Pr(type I error) and will depend on the seriousness of making such an error.

IV. *Formulate a test criterion* of the kind

reject H_0 if $|TS| > Z'$ but reserve judgement if $|TS| < Z'$.

The value of Z', taken from the standard normal Table A.1, will depend on the level of significance and whether a one- or two-tail test is performed.

V. *Take the sample and examine the sample information,* calculating the sample mean $\overline{X}$ and the sample standard deviation s, using the latter as an estimate of σ. At this stage, resist the temptation to change any of the steps I–IV above!

VI. *Compute the value of TS* derived in step II and apply the test criterion formulated in step IV.

It cannot be stressed too much how important it is to approach hypothesis testing in a systematic and sequential manner, following the steps outlined above. We shall encounter more complicated hypothesis testing situations later in this text, and it is therefore important to get used to using a systematic approach early in your studies.

Worked Example

Small firms in a county were known to have spent on average £6500 on capital equipment during 1995. Five years later, to determine whether there has been any change in capital spending patterns, 100 firms were surveyed by the County Council. It was found that (after allowing for inflation) the 100 firms spent an average of £6200 on investment, with a standard deviation of £2000. What should the Council conclude?

Solution

We shall follow the steps in the procedural outline. We formulate

$$H_0: \mu = 6500 \text{ (no change in capital spending)},$$
$$H_A: \mu \neq 6500 \text{ (change in capital spending)}$$

Under H_0, $(\bar{X} - 6500)/(\sigma/\sqrt{n})$ has a $N(0, 1)$ distribution and hence may be used as a test statistic.

Level of significance = 0.05.
The decision criterion is

reject H_0 if $|TS| > 1.96$ but reserve judgement if $|TS| < 1.96$.

(We use a two-tail test, because of the form of the alternative hypothesis. The situation is as in Fig. 4.4.)

For the given sample we have $\bar{X} = £6200$, and $s = 2000$ can be used as an unbiased estimate of σ. Hence

$$TS = \frac{6200 - 6500}{2000/\sqrt{100}} = -1.5.$$

Since $|1.5| < 1.96$, we are unable to reject H_0 but have to reserve judgement at the 0.05 level of significance. There is insufficient evidence to say that mean capital spending is any different from what was found five years ago.

Notice that, in the above worked example, we did not allow the finding that $\bar{X} < 6500$ to change our procedures and retained the alternative hypothesis $H_A: \mu \neq 6500$ and a two-tail test.

We permitted ourselves a 0.05 probability of error when rejecting H_0 but found that we could not in fact reject H_0 because, if we had done so, the probability of error would have been greater than the allowed 0.05. Another way of expressing this would be to say that we would only have rejected H_0 if we had been 95% confident we were correct. Since we were less than 95% confident, we did not reject H_0. We did not actually accept H_0 because, if we had, we would not have known the probability of error. Pr(type II error) might have been large.

Example 4.8

A student tackles the following example in an examination:

The government in a developed country believes that the mean level of savings of its senior citizens is at least $80 000. A social science foundation investigates and finds that, in a random sample of 200 senior citizens, mean savings are only $76 000 with a standard deviation of $30 500. Using a 0.01 level of significance, test whether the government's belief is correct.

The student's answer was as follows:

$$H_0: \bar{X} > 80\ 000 \qquad H_A: \bar{X} < 80\ 000$$

Under H_0, the test statistic $(\bar{X} - \mu)/(s/\sqrt{n})$ has an $N(0, 1)$ distribution.
Level of significance = 0.01.
Reject H_0 if $TS > 2.58$.
Since $\bar{X} = 76\ 000$, $s = 30\ 500$ and $n = 200$,

$$TS = \frac{76\ 000 - 80\ 000}{30\ 500/\sqrt{200}} = -1.85.$$

Accept H_0 at the 0.01 level of significance. The government's belief is correct, but there is a 0.01 probability that I am wrong to claim this.

List the mistakes made in this student's answer and provide a better answer.

Trying not to make the sort of mistakes by the student in Example 4.8, tackle the following examples.

Example 4.9

A train company claims that an inter-city service is on average only 2 minutes late in arriving at its destination. A random sample of 40 trains on this route turn out to be 3 minutes late on average with a standard deviation of 3.5 minutes. Test the company's claim. Interpret your answer.

Example 4.10

A random sample of 81 adults proves to be, on average, 71 kg overweight, with a standard deviation of $s = 2.51$ kg. Does such evidence contradict a claim that the population as a whole is on average 6 kg overweight?

Composite null hypotheses

In Example 4.8, the question asked appears to require

$$H_0: \mu > 80\,000 \text{ (government's belief is correct)},$$

$$H_A: \mu < 80\,000 \text{ (government's belief is incorrect)}.$$

As formulated, the null hypothesis is a *composite* hypothesis as is, normally, the alternative hypothesis. A composite hypothesis specifies some possible range of values for μ, whereas a simple hypothesis specifies just one particular value for μ.

In the examples presented in this chapter, we have always used a simple hypothesis as H_0. For example, we suggest you use $H_0: \mu = 80\,000$ in Example 4.8. There was a good reason for this. If the null hypothesis is $H_0: \mu = q$, then it is a simple matter to derive a test statistic for testing H_0 against H_A. Since, using the central limit theorem, we know that $(\bar{X} - \mu)/(\sigma/\sqrt{n})$ has a $N(0, 1)$ distribution, it follows that, under $H_0: \mu = q$, $(\bar{X} - q)/(\sigma/\sqrt{n})$ must also have a $N(0, 1)$ distribution. For the reasons outlined earlier, $(\bar{X} - q)/(\sigma/\sqrt{n})$ may then be used as a test statistic.

Things become more difficult with a composite null hypothesis. With $H_0: \mu > q$, for example, since we no longer have a particular value for μ to substitute into $(\bar{X} - \mu)/(\sigma/\sqrt{n})$ under H_0, strictly speaking, we can no longer derive a test statistic. This is why we have always adopted a simple hypothesis for H_0.

Frequently, as in Example 4.8, a composite H_0 may seem more appropriate, but it is always the case that if we are able to reject a hypothesis $H_0: \mu = q$ in favour of $H_A: \mu < q$ at a given level of significance, then we must certainly be able to reject $H_A: \mu > q$. Furthermore, if we are unable to reject $H_0: \mu = q$ and have to reserve judgement, then it reasonable to reserve judgement on $H_A: \mu > q$. Thus we can accommodate such test situations and recommend, again, that you always formulate null hypotheses that contain the 'equals' sign.

Example 4.11

A farmer's 20-acre wheat field has always yielded 24 bushels or more per acre, with a variance of 10 bushels^2. This year, however, the field yields just 19 bushels per acre. The farmer believes that the reduction in yield is the result of global warming. Is the fall in yield consistent with the farmer's belief, or is the reduction more likely to be the result of chance?

Example 4.12

A manufacturer of automobile tyres claims that its tyres will last for more than 25 000 miles under normal driving conditions. However, a sample of 150 such tyres turns out to last an average of only 23 856 miles with a standard deviation of 5500 miles. Is there evidence here that the manufacturer's claim is excessive?

Example 4.13

A firm claims that the average bonus paid to its employees exceeds £500. A random sample of 200 employees is found to have an average bonus of £511 with a standard deviation of £95. Using a 0.05 level of significance, test whether the firm's claim is valid. How would you explain such a result to a non-statistician?

Example 4.14

Regulations require that bottles of lager should contain an average volume of 0.75 litres but customers complain that the manufacturer is underfilling bottles. A random sample of 100 bottles is examined and found to have a mean content of 0.735 litres with a variance of 0.01 litres^2. Test at the 0.05 and 0.01 levels of significance whether the customers' complaint is justified. Assess the probabilities of any errors you might make in your conclusions.

4.4 **The power of a test**

When we adopt a test criterion of the kind [4.22] then, obviously, we hope that we will reject H_0 in favour of H_A whenever H_0 is false. Unfortunately, the likelihood of our doing so may not always be as high as we would wish.

Returning to our resident income example, suppose that $\mu^* = 17\ 750$ in Fig, 4.6, so that H_0: $\mu = 17\ 670$ is false. Recall that, for an OC curve, the vertical distance from the μ^*-axis to the curve measures Pr(accept H_0). Since we have adopted a criterion of the kind [4.22], in which we never accept H_0, the probabilities of type II error marked in Fig. 4.6 are not relevant. But the distances downwards to the OC curve from the 'probability equals one' line, which measure Pr(reject H_0) for various values for μ^*, remain highly relevant.

Such distances are measured using Fig. 4.6 and Table 4.2. For example, when $\mu^* = 17\ 750$ the probability of rejecting H_0 is $1 - 0.844 = 0.156$. For the central value of μ^*, 17 670, the downward distance is, of course, Pr(reject H_0 | H_0 is true) which is Pr(type I error) $= 0.05$, the level of significance. But, for any other value of μ^*, the downward distance gives the probability of rejecting H_0 when it is false – that is, it is the probability of not making an error! For any such given value for μ^*, this probability is referred to as the *power* of the test. That is,

$$\text{power of test} = \text{Pr}(\text{reject } H_0 | H_0 \text{ is false}).\qquad [4.23]$$

Power is therefore the probability of *making the correct decision when H_0 is false*. Since the power of a test is a probability, it must lie between 0 and 1. When the power is unity, the rejection of a false null hypothesis is certain. But when the power is zero, a false H_0 is never rejected.

In Fig. 4.7 we have turned the OC curve 'upside down' and plotted the power of our test against various values of μ^*. The result is known as a *power curve* or *power function*.

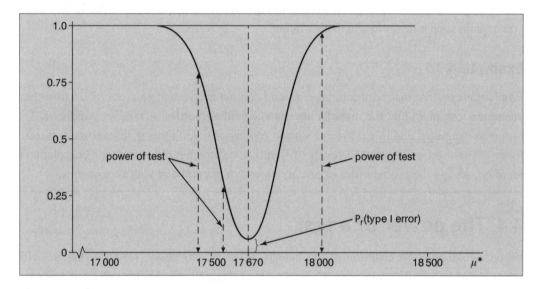

Figure 4.7 The power curve

Obviously we would like the probabilities in [4.23] to be large, ideally very close to unity. That is, we like tests that have a high power. Unfortunately, this is not always possible. We can see from Fig. 4.7 that, while for values μ^* that are far away from the H_0 value of 17 670 the power of the test is large, for values of μ^* close to 17 670 the power is very low. That is, in this latter case, our test criterion is unlikely to 'pick up' the false H_0.

When $\mu^* = 17\,670$, H_0 is in fact true and the power curve then gives us Pr(type I error). For other values of μ^*, however, the power curve gives us the probability of detecting the false H_0.

The shape of the power curve in Fig. 4.7 indicates that, if the probability of a type I error is to be kept small (e.g., 0.01 or 0.05), then the power of the test is bound to be small for values close to the H_0 value. If the size of the sample is given, then increased power inevitably means a rise in Pr(type I error). Our problem of Section 4.2 of balancing type I and type II errors has returned, albeit in a different guise; the alternative approach of never accepting H_0 does not solve all problems after all. If we make α, the probability of a type I error, very small, then the power of the test will be low for μ^* near 16 670, the H_0 value. That is, we are very likely to end up reserving judgement in such situations.

It is true that the problem can be reduced somewhat by increasing the sample size n. Referring back to equations [4.19] and [4.20], it can be seen that a rise in n will reduce Pr(accept H_0), and hence increase Pr(reject H_0), for all values for μ^* apart from 17 670. Thus the power of the test is increased, as illustrated in Fig. 4.8, but the problems of low power at values of μ^* close to 17 670 remain. We have to comfort ourselves that lower power arises only when H_0 is only 'slightly incorrect'.

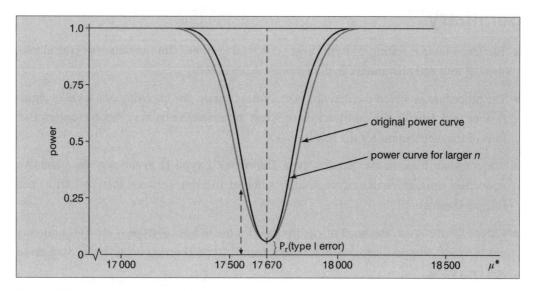

Figure 4.8 Increasing the sample size

Example 4.15

A goat breeder is experimenting with a new feed. It is claimed that the new feed will increase the average weight of goats by more than 50 gms per week. To test this, a random sample of $n = 64$ goats is given the feed. If a 0.05 level significance is used in the test, show that the power of this test is given by

$$P = \Pr\left(Z > 1.64 + \frac{50 - \mu^*}{\sigma/\sqrt{n}}\right),$$

where μ^* is the true population mean weight.

If the population standard deviation of weight gains σ is estimated as 3.2 gms, calculate the power of this test for actual average population weight gains, μ^*, of value 60 gms, 55 gms and 51 gms. How is the power affected if the level of significance for the test is reduced to 0.01? [*Hint*: look at [4.19] and its derivation.]

Example 4.16

Suppose, in Example 4.9, a level of significance of 0.01 is used to test the performance of trains. Calculate the power of the test when the true mean time late is (a) 2.1 minutes; (b) 3 minutes.

Summary

- The large-sample testing of **hypotheses** concerning **population means** was considered. Typical **null** and **alternative** hypotheses were described.

- The procedure involved the derivation of a **test statistic**, the choosing of a **level of significance** and, finally, the construction of a **test criterion**. Tests may involve **one** or **two tails** of the distribution for the test statistic.

- When testing hypotheses, either a **type I error** or a **type II error** may be made. An **operating characteristics curve** describes the relationship between Pr(type I error) and Pr(type II error).

- Pr(type I error) gives the level of significance for the test but Pr(type II error) is normally unknown. If Pr(type I error) is **decreased**, then Pr(type II error) is inevitably **increased** and vice versa.

- An **alternative** type of decision criterion was introduced in which the null hypothesis is **never** accepted. This eliminates the possibility of making a type II error.

- The **summary of procedure** in Section 4.3 should be studied carefully and always followed.

- The **power of a test** is the probability of rejecting a null hypothesis when it is false. The **power curve** gives the power for all possible values of the population mean. It can be obtained from the operating characteristics curve.

Notes

1. There is a probability of 'up to' 0.05 because, if the test statistic takes a value of 1.8, for example, then the probability of error will be less than 0.05. The larger the test statistic, the lower the probability of error. We deal with this point in greater depth at the end of the next chapter.

2. When you are given a value of the sample variance in any question, you may assume that it has been computed as s^2 as in [3.6] rather than as v^2 as in [3.4]. That is, the given sample variance is always an unbiased estimate of the population variation σ^2.

3. As we shall see later, increasing the sample size does improve matters somewhat.

4. However, more simple cases can arise where, for example, μ can take just two values, say q_1 and q_2. Then, if we postulate $H_0\colon \mu = q_1$, all other possibilities are given by $H_A\colon \mu = q_2$. See, for example, Example 4.6.

5

Hypothesis testing II

Objectives

Having completed your study of this chapter, you should be able:

1. to recognize the Student's t distribution and be aware of the conditions under which it arises;

2. to use the Student's t distribution for small-sample inference regarding a population mean;

3. to use the χ^2 distribution to test hypotheses concerning a population variance;

4. to test hypotheses about a population proportion, using the methods of the last chapter;

5. to test hypotheses using p-values, rather than using levels of significance.

Introduction

In the previous chapter we spent considerable time introducing the idea of hypothesis testing. We used the example of the population mean μ and we assumed that our sample was random with a size that was 'large', so that we could make use of the central limit theorem. In this chapter we examine, firstly, the problems that arise when we wish to test hypotheses about population means in situations where samples are 'small'. Secondly, we consider the testing of hypotheses concerning population parameters other than μ, namely population variances and population proportions. Finally, we introduce the idea of probability values or p-values, which can be used as an alternative to levels of significance in the testing of hypotheses.

5.1 **Small samples and the Student's t distribution**

In the previous chapter, we made use of the central limit theorem to construct a procedure for testing hypotheses about a population mean. That is, we made use of the fact that, *provided the sample size n was 'large'*,

$$Z = \frac{\bar{X} - \mu}{\sigma/\sqrt{n}} \text{ has a } N(0, 1) \text{ distribution.} \qquad [5.1]$$

The problem is that, frequently in economics, samples are not large and we have to deal with samples as small as 30 or even 15. When this is the case, the question of whether the population variance σ^2 is known or not becomes important. We have been quite cavalier so far about replacing σ^2 by the sample variance s^2 in [5.1], when computing test statistics. For large samples this is quite permissible, since not only is s^2 an unbiased estimator of σ^2, but also its 'precision' as an estimator improves as the sample size increases. But in small samples problems arise if σ^2 has to be replaced by its unbiased estimator, s^2.

Firstly, if the population variance σ^2 is known then, *provided the values in the population are normally distributed*, $(\bar{X} - \mu)/(\sigma/\sqrt{n})$ will always have a standard normal distribution *regardless of sample size.*[1] That is, [5.1] is still true, even for small samples. Secondly, however, if σ is unknown (which is the usual situation) and we have to replace it by its unbiased estimate s, the sample standard deviation, then [5.1] *is no longer true for small samples*. That is, $(\bar{X} - \mu)/(s/\sqrt{n})$ is no longer a standard normal Z variable. In fact, *provided the population is normally distributed*, then

$$\frac{\bar{X} - \mu}{s/\sqrt{n}} \qquad \text{has a Student's } t \text{ distribution with } n - 1 \text{ degrees freedom.} \qquad [5.2]$$

Result [5.2] obviously needs some explaining – some may think it needs translating into English! Firstly, recall the notion of a sampling distribution. Just as 'very many' samples of fixed size n (taken from a population with mean μ and variance σ^2) will yield a sampling distribution of values for $\bar{X}$, the sample mean, so they will also yield a sampling distribution of values for s^2, the sample variance. Thus, for every sample we will obtain a different value for $(\bar{X} - \mu)/(s/\sqrt{n})$. It is this distribution of values over many samples that is called the

Student's t distribution.[2] The term 'degrees of freedom' is defined in the Appendix to this chapter and the t distribution is also defined properly there. As can be seen there, a t variable is built up out of a series of standard normal variables. For the moment, however, it is probably best to revert to paraphrase and, in your mind, replace the words 'Student's t distribution with $n - 1$ degrees of freedom' with the words 'the Student's t distribution obtained from samples size n'. That is if, for example, we have a t distribution with 22 degrees of freedom (often written as 22 d.f.), then it follows that it must have been obtained by taking samples of size $n = 23$. The main point to grasp is that we obtain different t distributions for each value of n. Actually, it is the precise shape of the t distribution that depends on the sample size n, and this complicates the situation, as we shall now see.

The Student's t distribution

Like the standard normal distribution, the Student's t distribution is symmetrical and centred about zero. However, it is more peaked, with 'fatter' tails that the normal distribution, the two distributions being illustrated in Fig. 5.1.

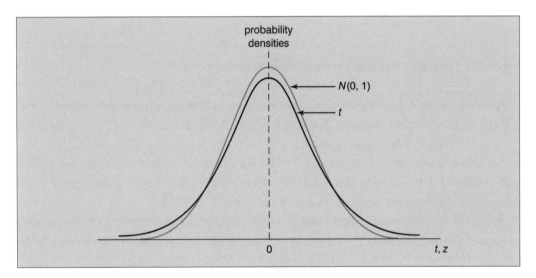

Figure 5.1 The standard normal and Student's t distributions

As noted above, the shape of the t distribution depends on the degrees of freedom, that is, on the size n of the samples taken. In fact, as n becomes larger, the shape of the t distribution gradually approaches the shape of the standard normal distribution, and for $n > 50$ the two curves are virtually indistinguishable.

Note that it is *not* simply that the t distribution arises when samples are small and the Z distribution when samples are larger. For small samples we require the *population* to be normally distributed before we are able to use the t distribution. Also, the dividing line between 'small' and 'large' samples is a blurred one. With a normally distributed population, the shape of the t distribution approximates the standard normal distribution gradually, as n increases. As illustrated in Fig. 5.2, for samples of size $n = 5$ the approximation to the standard normal is very rough, for $n = 20$ the approximation is much better and, for $n = 100$, it is virtually exact. Remember also that, as n becomes large, the central limit theorem comes into play, so the assumption of a normally distributed population is no longer required.

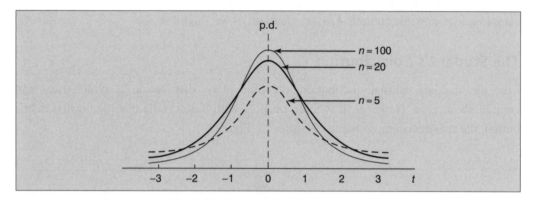

Figure 5.2 Student's t distributions for different values of n

Areas under the t distribution curve, as usual, measure probabilities, and critical values for the distribution are given in Table A.2 of the Appendix at the end of the text. For example, a critical value $t_{0.025}$ represents a point on the horizontal axis such that the area under curve to the right of the point is 0.025. As can be seen from the table, the critical values depend on the degrees of freedom which are shown down the left-hand column of the table. Thus, for example, with $v = 15$ d.f., we obtain $t_{0.025} = 2.131$.

We stress again that the t distribution is only employed in cases where (a) the population is normally distributed and (b) we have to replace the population standard deviation σ by its sample estimator s. If the population is non-normally distributed and its shape is unknown, then there is little that can be done when the sample size is small. For larger samples it is, of course, possible to make use of the central limit theorem, in the manner of the previous chapter.

Worked Example

The mean annual income of residents in a large city is claimed to exceed £18 000. To test this claim, a random sample of 10 residents were interviewed and found to have the following incomes:

19 200	20 300	18 100	19 700	16 800
19 600	15 400	19 900	20 800	18 200

Use these data to test the claim.

Solution

We formulate the hypotheses

$$H_0: \mu = 18\ 000,$$
$$H_A: \mu > 18\ 000 \qquad \text{(claim is valid)}.$$

Under H_0,

$$TS = \frac{\bar{X} - 18\ 000}{s/\sqrt{n}} \qquad \text{has a Student's } t \text{ distribution with } n - 1 \text{ d.f.}$$

(Notice that the test statistic is derived in the usual manner, by taking a general result, this time [5.2], and seeing what happens to it under H_0).

For this test we will take 0.05 as our level of significance. Note also that d.f. $= n - 1 = 9$. The decision criterion is, therefore:

reject H_0 if $TS > t_{0.05} = 1.833$, but reserve judgement otherwise.

(See Fig. 5.3 and Table A.2. A one-tail test is used because of the form of H_A.)

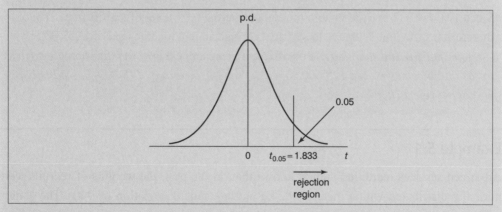

Figure 5.3

To compute TS, we need first to calculate $\bar{X}$ and s^2. Using the sample data, we have $\bar{X} = \sum X_i/n = 188\,000/10 = 18\,800$. The sample variance is calculated as shown in Table 5.1.

(Notice that $n-1$ has been used as denominator for s^2 since we require an unbiased estimator of the population variance.)

Table 5.1

X_i	$X_i - \bar{X}$	$(X_i - \bar{X})^2$
19 200	400	160 000
20 300	1500	2 250 000
18 100	−700	490 000
19 700	900	810 000
16 800	−2000	4 000 000
19 600	800	640 000
15 400	−3400	11 560 000
19 900	1100	1 210 000
20 800	2000	4 000 000
18 200	−600	360 000
188 000		25 480 000

$$s = \sqrt{\frac{\sum (X_i - \bar{X})^2}{n-1}} = \sqrt{\frac{25\,480\,000}{9}} = 1682.6$$

We therefore obtain $s = \sqrt{2\,831\,111} = 1682.6$, so that

$$TS = \frac{\bar{X} - 18\,000}{s/\sqrt{n}} = \frac{18\,800 - 18\,000}{1682.6/3.16} = 1.50.$$

Since $1.50 < 1.833$, we are unable to reject H_0 at the 0.05 level of significance. There is therefore insufficient evidence to say that average annual incomes exceed £18 000.

(Note that we said that there is insufficient *evidence. Clearly we have* some *evidence to say that incomes exceed £18 000, since the sample mean was £18 800, but statistically we cannot reject H_0.)*

Example 5.1

An armed services recruiting station knows that, in the past, the weights of recruits were normally distributed with a mean of 82 kg and a standard deviation of 9 kg. The station wishes to test whether this year's recruits have weights that are on average different from 82 kg. A random sample of 12 recruits turns out to have a mean weight of 87 kg. How would you proceed?

Example 5.2

A car manufacturer claims that one of its models averages 40 miles per gallon under normal driving conditions. Exhaustive tests on eight examples of the model give the following fuel consumption figures:

38.6, 37.9, 37.8, 39.3, 39.9, 38.8, 40.6, 39.1.

Test whether the manufacturer's claim is valid. What assumptions have you made in reaching your answer?

Example 5.3

In the past, a firm's output has been normally distributed with a mean of 2050 items per month and a standard deviation of 150 items. It is hoped that new working practices will increase monthly output but it is known that the standard deviation of output will not change. Twelve months of working with the new practices results in an average output of 2124 items. Using a 0.05 level of significance, test whether the new working practices have been successful.

Worked Example

A supervisor notices that one of his workers is arriving late. While it is permitted for a worker to arrive up to 5 minutes late, the supervisor notes that over a 10-day period this worker clocks up the following late arrivals (in minutes):

7.3, 3.8, 7.1, 6.4, 4.9, 6.6, 9.1, 5.7, 5.5, 6.3.

Assuming that the time late is normally distributed, compute a 95% confidence interval for the mean time late of this worker.

Solution

We can use the confidence interval expressions [3.15] and [3.17], replacing the Z value of 1.96 by the critical t value, $t_{0.025}$. Thus the required 95% confidence interval is

$$\bar{X} \pm t_{0.025} s/\sqrt{n}$$

Since the sample size is 10 we have 9 d.f., giving $t_{0.025} = 2.262$. The given sample data yield a sample mean $\bar{X} = 6.27$ with $\Sigma(X - \bar{X})^2$ equal to 18.78. Thus the sample variance is $s^2 = 2.087$. The interval is therefore

$$6.27 \pm 2.262(1.445/3.162) \quad \text{or} \quad 6.27 \pm 1.03.$$

Example 5.4

Use the data in Example 5.2 to obtain a 98% confidence interval for mean fuel consumption. How large does the sample have to be if you wish to estimate mean fuel consumption to within 0.1 miles per gallon with 98% confidence?

5.2 **Testing hypotheses about population variances**

Suppose that components produced in a factory have an effective life of X hours with a mean of μ and variance σ^2. The mean life is believed to be $\mu = 200$, and this is regarded as satisfactory. However, there is a concern about the variance of X, with some components having very long lives, counterbalanced by other components which have unacceptably short lives. It is felt that a satisfactory value for the variance of lives is $\sigma^2 = 400$, giving a standard deviation of 20

A random sample of 25 components unfortunately proves to have lifetimes with variance $s^2 = 605$. How do we test whether the true population variance of lifetimes, σ^2, is greater than the 400 that is regarded as satisfactory? We shall use the following result. Provided the population of X values is normally distributed, then

$$\frac{(n-1)s^2}{\sigma^2} \text{ has a } \chi^2 \text{ distribution with } n-1 \text{ degrees of freedom.} \qquad [5.3]$$

To interpret [5.3], recall again that if 'very many' samples of fixed size n are taken from a population with mean μ and variance σ^2, then they will yield sample distributions of values not only for $\bar{X}$, but also for s^2, the sample variance. Sampling variability ensures this. So, provided the population variance σ^2 is known, different samples will also yield different values for the statistic $\chi^2 = (n-1)s^2/\sigma^2$. That is, we obtain a sampling distribution of values for χ^2. We consider the sampling distribution for χ^2 rather than the sampling distribution of s^2, because χ^2 (pronounced chi-squared) is a very well-known variable in statistics.

The general definition of a χ^2 variable is given in the Appendix to this chapter; suffice to say that, like the Student's t distribution, it is built up out of a series of standard normal Z variables. A typical distribution for χ^2 is shown in Fig. 5.4.

Because the χ^2 variable depends on σ^2 and s^2, its values are always positive (this is why it is referred to as χ^2 rather than χ), so that the distribution lies to the right of the vertical probability density axis. Since there is no upper limit to the value of χ^2, the distribution is non-symmetrical and has a long right-hand tail as illustrated. Because the χ^2 distribution is a probability density function, areas beneath the curve measure probabilities, with the total area, as usual, equalling unity.

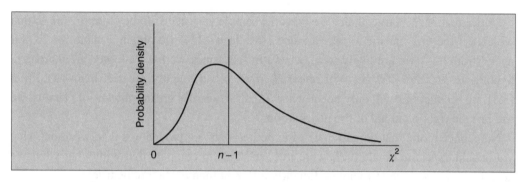

Figure 5.4 A χ^2 distribution

Notice that in [5.3] we have referred to the χ^2 distribution with $n-1$ degrees of freedom. As noted in the previous section, the meaning of degrees of freedom is explained in the Appendix to this chapter. At this stage it is probably best if you regard the phrase as just a bit of statistical jargon and simply take the words 'the χ^2 distribution with $n-1$ d.f.' and paraphrase them in your mind as 'the χ^2 distribution obtained when the sample size is n'. Thus, in this situation, a χ^2 distribution with 24 d.f., for example, is obtained when samples of size 25 are taken. The main point to appreciate is that we obtain a different χ^2 distribution for each value of n. The situation is therefore akin to that found when using the Student's t distribution.

It is easy to obtain the mean of the distribution [5.3]. Since we know that s^2 is an unbiased estimator of σ^2, it follows that $E(s^2) = \sigma^2$ and $E(s^2/\sigma^2) = 1$. Hence,

$$E(\chi^2) = (n-1)E(s^2/\sigma^2) = n-1. \qquad [5.4]$$

Thus the mean of the distribution is $n-1$. This is illustrated in Fig. 5.4. It follows that, the larger the sample size, the further to the right lies the peak of the χ^2 distribution.[3]

We are now in a position to tackle the problem posed at the beginning of this section. We formulate the hypotheses

$$H_0: \sigma^2 = 400 \qquad \text{(components variance is satisfactory),}$$
$$H_A: \sigma^2 > 400 \qquad \text{(components variance not satisfactory).}$$

We have employed a '>' sign in the alternative hypothesis because, as indicated earlier, the variance of lives is only regarded as unsatisfactory if it exceeds 400.

As usual, to obtain a test statistic we refer back to some basic result and see what happens when the relevant H_0 is true. In this case the basic result is [5.3] which, when H_0 is true, becomes

$$TS = \frac{(n-1)s^2}{400} \text{ has a } \chi^2 \text{ distribution with } n-1 \text{ d.f.} \qquad [5.5]$$

We can therefore use [5.5] as a test statistic.

Notice that, if H_0 is true, then we expect the sample variance s^2 to be close to 400, so that we expect the test statistic to take a value close to $n - 1$. If we obtain a value for TS 'far away' from $n - 1$ we are likely to reject H_0. In fact, since we have adopted an alternative hypothesis, $H_A: \sigma^2 > 400$, we will reject H_0 if s^2 is 'sufficiently greater' than 400. From [5.5], we see that this will only occur when TS is sufficiently greater than $n - 1$. That is, we use just the right-hand tail of the distribution.

Note, once more, that the rationale of hypothesis testing procedures is to work out what you would expect to obtain if H_0 were true, and then to compare that with what you have actually obtained. If the two are sufficiently different then H_0 cannot be true.

To decide what we mean by 'sufficiently' greater in this context, we refer to Fig. 5.5 and Table A.3 in the Appendix at the end of this text. Suppose we adopt a 0.05 level of significance. This means we require a value on the horizontal axis such that the area beneath the χ^2 curve to the right of that value is 0.05. This value is designated $\chi^2_{0.05}$. Such *critical values* are given in the main body of Table A.3 in the appendix. Notice that the value obtained for $\chi^2_{0.05}$ depends on n, the sample size. The left-hand column in the table in fact gives values for $v = n - 1$, the degrees of freedom.

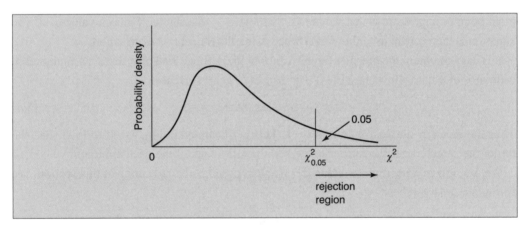

Figure 5.5 A χ^2 test

For our example $n = 25$, so under H_0 our test statistic has a χ^2 distribution with $n - 1 = 24$ d.f. Thus if the text statistic is sufficiently greater than 24 we will reject H_0. Table A.3 gives $\chi^2_{0.05} = 36.415$, so we therefore adopt the decision criterion

reject H_0 if $TS > 36.415$, but reserve judgement if $TS < 36.415$.   [5.6]

All that remains now is to compute the test statistic [5.5]. We have, since $s^2 = 605$,

$$TS = \frac{(n-1)s^2}{400} = \frac{24 \times 605}{400} = 36.3$$

Applying the test criterion [5.6], we are unable to reject H_0 at the 0.05 level of significance. We have to reserve judgement on whether or not the variance of component life times is satisfactory. The value of TS is certainly greater than the $n - 1 = 24$ we expect under H_0, but not quite large enough to reject H_0. So we do not quite have sufficient evidence to conclude that $\sigma^2 > 400$.

Worked Example

The time it takes to serve a customer in a shoe shop is believed to be normally distributed. Management is quite happy with the mean service of 18 minutes, but is concerned that the standard deviation of service times seems to be as large as 6 minutes. After a request for more consistent service patterns by staff, a random sample of 16 service times provides a standard deviation of 4.1 minutes. Test whether management's request has had any effect.

Solution

We formulate the hypotheses

$$H_0: \sigma^2 = 36 \qquad \text{(request has had no effect)},$$
$$H_A: \sigma^2 < 36 \qquad \text{(request has had some effect)}.$$

(Note the alternative hypothesis. Management's request is proven effective only if σ^2 is now smaller than before.) Under H_0,

$$TS = \frac{(n-1)s^2}{36} \text{ has a } \chi^2 \text{ distribution with } n-1 \text{ d.f.}$$

At a level of significance of 0.05, the required decision criterion (with $n - 1 = 15$ d.f.) is

reject H_0 if $TS < 7.261$, but reserve judgement if $TS > 7.261$.

(We use a one-tail test because of the form of the alternative hypothesis. The idea behind the test is that we reject H_0 if s_2 is sufficiently less than σ^2, i.e., if TS is sufficiently less than $n - 1 = 15$. We therefore use the lower tail of the distribution. The value $\chi^2_{0.95} = 7.261$ has to be taken from Table A.3 (see Fig. 5.6).)[4]

The sample information gives us $s^2 = (4.1)^2 = 16.81$ from a sample size $n = 16$. The test statistic is therefore

$$TS = \frac{(n-1)s^2}{36} = \frac{15 \times 16.81}{36} = 7.00$$

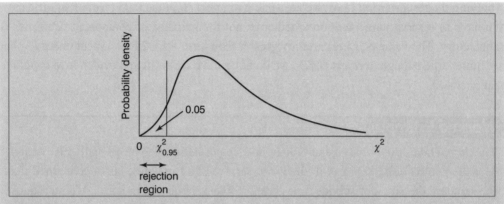

Figure 5.6

Since $TS < 7.261$, we reject H_0 at the 0.05 level of significance. The evidence suggests that σ^2 is indeed now less than 36, so management's request appears to have been effective.

Example 5.5

It is important that the time taken over one of the operations in a production line should be no more than 10 seconds on average and that the standard deviation of such times should not exceed 0.01 secs. If these standards are not met then the line is deemed to be faulty. A random check of 100 times has a mean of 10.002 secs with a standard deviation of 0.013 secs. Using a 0.05 level of significance, determine whether the production line is faulty.

Example 5.6

It is specified that the variance in the shear stress of a particular spot weld must be 150 kg or less. A random sample of 12 spot welds proves to have a variance of $s^2 = 205$ kg^2. Does this sample suggest that the specification is not being met?

5.3 Testing hypotheses about a population proportion

In this section we return to our population of trade unionists, last visited in Section 3.3. Recall that each trade unionist could be either in favour of industrial action or against it. We defined a variable X such that, if $X = 1$, the trade unionist was in favour of action but if $X = 0$, then s(he) was against.

The *population* parameter π was the proportion of trade unionists who were in favour of industrial action, whereas we used the symbol p for the proportion of trade unionists in a given random *sample*, size n, who favoured action. We saw that provided $n\pi$ and $n(1-\pi)$ both exceeded 5, then we could say that

$$p \text{ has a } N\left(\pi, \frac{\pi(1-\pi)}{n}\right) \text{ distribution.} \qquad [5.7]$$

That is, p has a sampling distribution that is normal with mean π and variance $\pi(1-\pi)/n$. We can now use this basic result to test hypotheses regarding any population proportion π.

Suppose that, with the possibility of industrial action looming, an employers' association claims that no more than 40% of workers are in favour of the action. The trade union concerned says that this claim is ludicrous and arranges for 1000 of its members to be interviewed. Of these, 638 prove to be in favour of industrial action. How can we use this information to test the employers' claim?

Our first step, as always, is to formulate hypotheses. We formulate

$$H_0: \pi = 0.4, \qquad H_A: \pi > 0.4.$$

H_0 implies that the employers' claim is a valid one. Note that we have adopted the usual procedure of making H_0 a simple hypothesis, containing the equality sign. We use a one-sided composite hypothesis for H_A, since only if H_A were to be found true could the union say that the employers' claim was invalid.

To obtain a test statistic, firstly we obtain from [5.7]

$$\frac{p-\pi}{\sqrt{\pi(1-\pi)/n}} \text{ has a } N(0, 1) \text{ distribution} \qquad [5.8]$$

Substituting the H_0 value $\pi = 0.4$ into [5.8], we can then say that, under H_0,

$$TS = \frac{p-0.4}{\sqrt{0.24/n}} \text{ has a } N(0, 1) \text{ distribution.} \qquad [5.9]$$

Thus, we can use [5.9] as a test statistic, rejecting H_0 when TS is sufficiently greater than zero, that is, when the sample proportion p is sufficiently greater than 0.4.

Notice that, as usual, we obtain a test statistic by substituting an H_0 value into a basic result, this time the result [5.8]. We stress that it is [5.9] and not [5.8] that is the test statistic.

Adopting a 0.05 level of significance and using the standard normal Table A.1, our test criterion is

$$\text{reject } H_0 \text{ if } TS > 1.64. \qquad [5.10]$$

We have used a one-tail test because of the form of the alternative hypothesis, reserving judgement for values of $TS < 1.64$.

Notice that the test statistic is based on the difference between the sample proportion and 0.4, the hypothesized value of p. Under H_0, what we expect is a value for the test statistic relatively close to zero. We compare this with the value we actually get.

Our sample consists of $n = 1000$ trade unionists, of whom 638 proved to be in favour of industrial action. The sample proportion p is therefore 0.638, so we compute the test statistic [5.9] as

$$TS = \frac{0.638 - 0.4}{\sqrt{0.24/1000}} = 15.36.$$

It is clear that we can reject H_0. The employers' claim appears to be invalid.

The following examples also involve proportions. Make sure you follow the strict procedural plan outlined in the previous chapter. As usual, it is not enough just to get the arithmetic correct.

Example 5.7

A governing political party claims that one of its opponents will obtain less than 30% of the vote in a forthcoming by-election. An opinion survey of 800 voters indicates 208 of them will vote for the opposition party. Assess the governing party's claim, using non-statistical language as far as you can.

Example 5.8

In an experiment to test ESP, one individual rolls a normal six-sided die 600 times and on each occasion thinks hard about the number obtained and writes it down. A second individual, visually screened from the first, tries to read the thoughts of the first and writes down what he believes is the outcome of each roll of the die. A comparison of outcomes indicates that the second individual 'guesses' correctly on 112 occasions. Is this evidence of ESP? Suppose the correct number of 'guesses' had been 72, what would have you concluded?

Example 5.9

A washing powder manufacturer claims that over 40% of home-makers use its product. The claim is regarded as excessive, and to test it, at the 0.05 level of significance, a consumer watchdog organization interviews a sample of 300 home-makers, of whom 124 admit to using the product. What should the watchdog organization conclude? (Be careful in formulating your hypotheses!)

5.4 **The use of *p*-values**

In statistics, we frequently apply decision criteria of the kind 'reject H_0 at the 0.05 level of significance when $TS > k$', where k is some critical value. Occasionally, however, we obtain a value for the test statistic that exceeds k by some margin. For example, in our test about a population proportion in Section 5.3, we obtained a test statistic of 15.36 compared with a critical value of only 1.64. In such cases, it is clear that we could have rejected H_0 at a level of significance considerably less than 0.05 (i.e., with a probability of error less than 0.05). This is why, when rejecting H_0 at the 0.05 level of significance, you will find statisticians saying that there is a probability of error of *up to* 0.05. In fact we have used the phrase 'up to' on a number of occasions already in this text.

Similarly, in the first worked example of Section 5.1, we obtained $TS = 1.50$ whereas the critical *t*-value was 1.833. We were, therefore, unable to reject H_0 at the 0.05 level of significance. Consequently we said there was *insufficient* evidence to say that annual incomes exceeded £18 000. However, if we had chosen a somewhat higher level of significance and consequently a smaller critical value, we could have ended up rejecting H_0 and concluding that incomes exceeded £18 000. For example, at a 0.10 level of significance we would have rejected H_0. (Check this using Table A.2.) This is why we pointed out that there was some evidence (but not sufficient) in favour of H_A.

We have stressed that it is not a particularly good statistical procedure to change your level of significance and test criterion *after* you have computed a test statistic. After all, you can usually find *some* level of significance that will give you the result that you want! But knowledge of the level of significance at which you *could* have rejected H_0 is often interesting. For this reason, statisticians often compute what are known as probability values or *p-values* when conducting hypothesis tests.

A *p*-value may be defined as the level of significance at which, for a given value of a test statistic, we can reject a null hypothesis. In fact, as the value of the test statistic falls, the required *p*-value increases.

We can always reformulate test criteria in terms of *p*-values. For example, a test criterion 'reject H_0 at the α level of significance if $TS > k$' can always be reformulated as:

$$\text{reject } H_0 \text{ if } p\text{-value} < \alpha. \qquad [5.11]$$

The level of significance is usually set at 0.01 or 0.05, but how do we find the *p*-value?

p-values for a *t*-test, for example, can be found by *interpolating* values from Table A.2. For example, we saw, in the first worked example of Section 5.1, that the test statistic had a value of 1.50. With the 9 degrees of freedom in this example, Table A.2 gives critical values of $t_{0.05} = 1.833$ and $t_{0.10} = 1.383$. Our test statistic lies between these two critical values. We can therefore say immediately that the *p*-value lies between 0.10 and 0.05. For any given degrees of freedom, the values in Table A.2 show an inverse relationship between the probability α and the critical value t_α. For 9 d.f., this relationship is shown in Fig. 5.7.

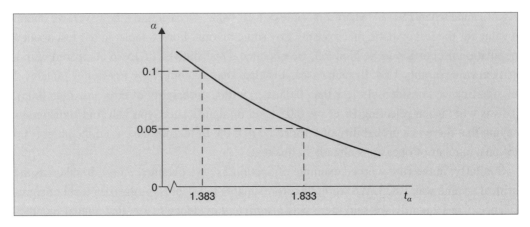

Figure 5.7 Interpolating a p-value

Since the value of the test statistic of 1.50 lies closer to $t_{0.10}$ than it does to $t_{0.05}$, the p-value must lie closer to 0.10 than it does to 0.05. The absolute value of the slope of the relationship in Fig. 5.7 is roughly

$$\frac{0.05 - 0.1}{t_{0.05} - t_{0.10}} = \frac{0.05 - 0.10}{1.833 - 1.383} = -0.111$$

Hence, by interpolation, we can estimate the p-value as

$$p = 0.10 - 0.111(1.50 - 1.383) = 0.087$$

Thus, in the worked example, we *could* have rejected H_0 had we adopted a 0.087 level of significance! However, because we in fact decided on a 0.05 level of significance, (i.e., a 0.05 probability of type I error), we did not reject H_0 because the p-value 0.087 exceeded 0.05.

Working out p-values in this rather cumbersome way takes a little while but it is always easy to find the range within which the p-value lies. Moreover, as we shall see in later chapters, many 'canned' statistical computer packages provide p-values as part of their standard output.[5]

Example 5.10

In Example 5.2, we rejected H_0 at the 0.05 level of significance. Calculate the p-value. Is $p < 0.05$? How you do interpret this result?

Example 5.11

In Example 5.3, calculate the p-value corresponding to the value found for the test statistic. Interpret this p-value.

5.5 **Some mixed revision examples**

Example 5.12

The owner of a shopping centre claims that 50% of householders within a radius of 3 miles have at least one member who shops at the centre. In a random sample of 300 shoppers from this region, 131 shop at the centre.

(a) Find a 95% confidence interval for the true proportion who shop at the centre.

(b) Test at the 0.05 level of significance whether the owner's claim is invalid.

Example 5.13

π is the proportion of the UK population in favour of the UK adopting the euro. To test the hypothesis H_0: $\pi = 0.5$, a random sample of 100 people is taken and the following decision criterion is employed:

$$\text{reject } H_0 \text{ if } p < 0.4 \text{ but accept } H_0 \text{ if } p > 0.4$$

where p is the sample proportion.

(a) Find the probability of a type I error;

(b) Find the probability of a type II error (i) when $\pi = 0.45$; (ii) when $\pi = 0.35$.

   What happens to these probabilities when the sample size is increased to 10 000?

Example 5.14

A headmaster at a high school is concerned that sixth-formers, taking part-time jobs, may be working for more than 6 hours per week. He questions nine randomly selected sixth-formers and finds they work the following hours:

$$7.5, \quad 5.8, \quad 10.3, \quad 6.3, \quad 5.6, \quad 6.7, \quad 1.8, \quad 6.4, \quad 8.1.$$

Is the headmaster's concern justified?

Example 5.15

The operating temperature of a device is supposed to have a mean of 190 °C with a variance not exceeding 3 °C^2. Twenty random checks on the device yield temperatures with a mean of 189 °C with a variance of 6 °C^2. Is the device in proper working order? Use a 0.01 level of significance.

Example 5.16

A mail order company delivers packets that have a mean weight of 0.4 kg with a standard deviation of 0.05 kg. It calculates its total cost per packet as being made up of a fixed cost of 5p plus a variable cost of 80p per kilogram. However, it decides to charge a flat rate per package, regardless of weight. The flat rate is set at 40p per packet, yielding a profit of 3p per packet.

Two years later, the company has expanded and now believes that its fixed costs are 6p per packet but that variable costs have remained unchanged. The company therefore retains its fixed charge of 40p. Despite this, the company finds that it is no longer making a profit. It suspects that the reason for this is that the mean weight of packets has risen. If the firm surveys 800 packets, how large must the mean weight of these packages be before the firm can safely conclude that this is the reason for its profit failure? [*Hint*: set up the null hypothesis that the company is correct in its suspicions.]

Example 5.17

A firm wishes to test the effectiveness of a new TV commercial. The commercial is regarded as effective if 25% of viewers can recall seeing it. Telephone interviews with 200 viewers show that only 42 can recall the commercial. Was the commercial effective? What is the *p*-value associated with the value of the appropriate test statistic?

Summary

- When samples are **small**, hypothesis tests about a population mean can be conducted using the **Student's *t* distribution**, with the appropriate number of degrees of freedom, provided the population is normally distributed.

- It is also possible to test hypotheses regarding a **population variance**. This involves the use of the χ^2 **distribution**, with an appropriate number of **degrees of freedom**.

- Hypothesis tests regarding a **population proportion** can be conducted in a manner similar to large sample tests about a population mean.

- Statisticians often use **p-values**, rather than levels of significance, when deciding whether to reject a null hypothesis.

- The appendices to this chapter explain the meaning of **degrees of freedom** and give the definitions of the χ^2 **distribution** and the **Student's *t* distribution**.

Appendix 5A

5A.1 **Degrees of freedom**

The phrase 'degrees of freedom' has cropped up frequently in this chapter, and students ought to have at least some feel for its meaning. Suppose we have a sum of squares

$$\sum_i (Y_i - \bar{Y})^2, \qquad [5A.1]$$

obtained from a random sample of n values, $Y_1, Y_2, Y_3, \ldots, Y_n$, with sample mean $\bar{Y}$. We therefore have n so-called 'deviations', $Y_1 - \bar{Y}, Y_2 - \bar{Y}, Y_3 - \bar{Y}, \ldots, Y_n - \bar{Y}$. Degrees of freedom are a property of a sum of squares such as [5A.1].

As a simple example of the idea, suppose we have just four $Y_i - \bar{Y}$ deviations, so that $n = 4$. Suppose that the values of three of the deviations were known and that, in fact, $Y_1 - \bar{Y} = -3$, $Y_3 - \bar{Y} = +5$ and $Y_4 - \bar{Y} = -4$. The sum of these three deviations is obviously -2. Since it is always the case that $\sum_i (Y_i - \bar{Y}) = 0$ (see the prerequisites chapter if this is not clear), the remaining deviation $Y_2 - \bar{Y}$ has to equal $+2$. In such a case the deviations and hence the sum of squares $\sum_i (Y_i - \bar{Y})^2$ are said to have just 3 degrees of freedom.

In general, a sum of n squared deviations, $\sum_{i=1}^{n} (Y_i - \bar{Y})^2$, will have $n - 1$ degrees of freedom. Whenever you come across the term 'degrees of freedom' in statistics, you can be certain that there is a sum of squares of the above kind lurking somewhere behind the scenes. The sum of squares may not always be obvious but it will be there nevertheless.

Suppose, however, the population mean μ were known and we formed the sum of squares

$$\sum_i (Y_i - \mu)^2. \qquad [5A.2]$$

Then, since there is no reason why $\sum_i (Y_i - \mu) = 0$, knowledge of $n - 1$ of the deviations $Y_i - \mu$ will not now enable us to deduce the nth. The sum of squares [5A.2] therefore has not $n - 1$, but n degrees of freedom.

Note that, in replacing a population parameter μ in [5A.2] by a sample statistic $\bar{Y}$ to obtain [5A.1], we 'lose' one degree of freedom and we place one restriction on the deviations. The restriction is that the sum of the deviations must sum to zero. Such results are quite general. Every time a population parameter is replaced by a sample statistic in a sum of squares, a restriction is inevitably placed on the deviations so that a degree of freedom is lost. In fact, we can best define the degrees of freedom associated with a sum of squares as *the sample size minus the number of parameters that have to be estimated by sample statistics when computing the sum of squares.*

Grasping the concept of degrees of freedom is hard for a beginner, because at this stage in the study of statistics there are very few examples that can be helpfully introduced. However, two more examples will occur later in the text.

5A.2 Two important statistical distributions

The χ^2 distribution

In Chapter 2 you were introduced to the standard normal distribution. Since a standard normal Z variable is a continuous variable, its distribution is an example of a probability density function. The standard normal variable is an important building brick in statistics, in that a number of well-known and important variables and their density functions are built up out of standard normal variables. In Section 5.2, we made use of the χ^2 distribution. In fact, a χ^2 variable is defined as the sum of the squares of n *independent* standard normal Z variables. That is,

$$\chi^2 = Z_1^2 + Z_2^2 + Z_3^2 + \cdots + Z_n^2. \qquad [5A.3]$$

The χ^2 variable defined in [5A.3] has the 'full' n degrees of freedom. This is because the Z variables all have independent $N(0, 1)$ distributions, the underlying sum of squares being of the kind [5A.2] with $\mu = 0$.

It is easy to derive the mean of a χ^2 distribution. Since $\mu = 0$,

$$V(Z_i) = E(Z_i^2) - \mu^2 = E(Z_i^2) \qquad \text{for all } i.$$

Because $V(Z_i) = 1$ for all i (remember that all the Z variables are $N(0, 1)$), it follows that $E(Z_i^2) = 1$ for all i, so that

$$E(\chi^2) = E(Z_1^2 + Z_2^2 + Z_3^2 + \cdots + Z_n^2) = n.$$

Thus, the mean of a χ^2 distribution equals its degrees of freedom.[6] Some examples of χ^2 distributions are illustrated in Fig. 5A.1. As noted in Section 5.2, the larger the degrees of freedom, the further from the vertical axis lies the peak of the distribution.

In Section 5.2 we used the fact that $(n-1)s^2/\sigma^2$ has a χ^2 distribution to test hypotheses about population variances. We are now in a position to demonstrate this result.

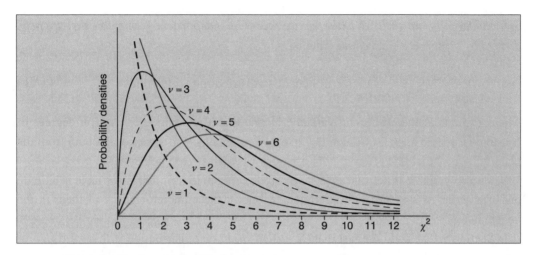

Figure 5A.1 Some χ^2 distributions (ν = number of degrees of freedom)

Consider n sample values, $X_1, X_2, X_3, \ldots, X_n$, drawn from an $N(\mu, \sigma^2)$ population. It follows that

$$\text{each } \frac{X_i - \mu}{\sigma} \text{ has a } N(0, 1) \text{ distribution.} \qquad [5A.4]$$

Given that the sample variance is

$$s^2 = \frac{\Sigma(X_i - \overline{X})^2}{n - 1},$$

we can write

$$\frac{(n - 1)s^2}{\sigma^2} = \frac{\Sigma(X_i - \overline{X})^2}{\sigma^2}. \qquad [5A.5]$$

Using [5A.4], $\Sigma((X - \mu)/\sigma)^2$ has a χ^2 distribution with n degrees of freedom, since it is the sum of the squares of n standard normal variables. However, if we replace the parameter μ by its sample estimator $\overline{X}$, we lose a degree of freedom. Hence, using [5A.5], $(n - 1)s^2/\sigma^2$ must have a χ^2 distribution with just $n - 1$ degrees of freedom. This is the result used in Section 5.2.

The Student's *t* distribution

In Section 5.1, we made use of the *t* distribution to conduct hypothesis tests about population means using small samples. A Student's *t* variable can, in fact, be defined as *the ratio* *of a standard normal variable to the square root of an independent χ^2 variable that has been divided by its degrees of freedom.* That is,

$$t = \frac{Z_0}{\sqrt{\chi_n^2/n}} \text{ has a Student's } t \text{ distribution with } n \text{ d.f.} \qquad [5A.6]$$

where Z_0 is the standard normal variable. Notice that a χ^2 distribution with n degrees of freedom is written as χ_n^2. A Student's t distribution obtains its degrees of freedom from the underlying χ^2 variable. Different t distributions were illustrated in Fig. 5.2.

Since a χ^2 variable is defined as [5A.3], it follows from [5A.6] that a t variable is built up out of a series of standard normal variables, one in the numerator and n of them in the denominator.

In Section 5.1 we used the fact that $(\bar{X} - \mu)/(s/\sqrt{n})$ has a t distribution with $n - 1$ d.f., provided samples are taken from a normally distributed population. We can now demonstrate this. Regardless of sample size, for a normal population,

$$\frac{\bar{X} - \mu}{\sigma/\sqrt{n}} \text{ has an } N(0, 1) \text{ distribution} \qquad [5A.7]$$

We saw above that

$$\frac{(n-1)s^2}{\sigma^2} \text{ has a } \chi^2 \text{ distribution with } n - 1 \text{ d.f.} \qquad [5A.8]$$

Using the definition of a t distribution given above, we can therefore say that

$$\frac{\dfrac{\bar{X} - \mu}{\sigma/\sqrt{n}}}{\sqrt{\dfrac{(n-1)s^2/\sigma^2}{n-1}}} = \frac{\bar{X} - \mu}{\sqrt{(\sigma^2/n)(s^2/\sigma^2)}} = \frac{\bar{X} - \mu}{s/\sqrt{n}} \qquad [5A.9]$$

must have a Student's t distribution with $n - 1$ degrees of freedom. The degrees of freedom of the t distribution are obtained from the $n - 1$ d.f. of the χ^2 distribution in the denominator obtained from [5A.8]. Equation [5A.9] is the result used in Section 5.1.

Notes

1. Note that $\bar{X} = \sum X_i/n$ is a linear function of the sample observations, that is, of the X_i. Thus, if the population of values of X_i is normally distributed, then $\bar{X}$ itself must have a normal distribution. It follows that $(\bar{X} - \mu)/(\sigma/\sqrt{n})$ must have a standard normal distribution.

2. The t distribution was discovered by W.S. Gosset in the early twentieth century. His work was published under the pen name 'Student' and the distribution is named after him.

3. The variance of the χ^2 distribution is $2(n-1)$.

4. Notice χ^2_a gives the point on the horizontal axis such that the total area under the curve to the right of χ^2_a equals a. a can be either a small area such as 0.05 or a large area such as 0.95.

5. In fact the true p-value in the above example is 0.084, close to the value of 0.087 obtained by interpolation.

6. Thus, in Section 5.2, the χ^2 distribution had $n-1$ degrees of freedom and, hence, a mean of $n-1$.

6

More about probability and inference

Objectives

After completing your study of this chapter you should be able:

1. to distinguish between joint and marginal probability distributions and construct such distributions from the sample space of an experiment;

2. to compute the expected values of functions of more than one variable;

3. to define, compute and interpret population covariances and correlations;

4. to appreciate the difference between non-correlation and independence, and understand the conditions necessary for each;

5. to recognize the difference between sample and population correlations;

6. to test hypotheses about the difference between two population means, for both 'large' and 'small' samples;

7. to use the F distribution to test hypotheses about the difference between two population variances;

8. to test hypotheses about the difference between two population proportions using standard normal tables.

Introduction

Often in statistics we need to compare parameter values relating to two or more different populations. For example, consider two cities, A and B. Suppose we needed to know whether mean annual income in city A was any different from that in city B. Clearly we could, if necessary, take samples from each city. But before we can draw any inferences from such samples, we need to introduce some more probability theory. This additional probability theory is the purpose of the early sections of this chapter. For clarity, we again resort, first, to simple experiments involving chance. Then we move on to more practical situations. Finally, in the last section of the chapter, we consider the testing of hypotheses concerning the difference between two parameters relating to two different populations.

6.1 Joint and marginal probability distributions

Consider an experiment in which a four-sided die[1] is rolled twice. The sample space for this experiment is shown in Table 6.1, and consists of 16 outcomes. If the die is a fair one, then the probability of each outcome will be 1/16. We consider two random variables, X and Y. Suppose

> X is the product of the numbers obtained on the two rolls, and Y is the absolute value of the difference between the numbers obtained on the two rolls.

In Table 6.1, values for X and Y have been entered against each sample outcome. For example if the outcome (3, 4) is obtained then $X = 12$ and $Y = 1$. Similarly, the outcome (4, 1) gives $X = 4$ and $Y = 3$, and so on.

Table 6.1 Sample space for two rolls of a four-sided die

	X	Y		X	Y		X	Y		X	Y
(1, 1)	1	0	(2, 1)	2	1	(3, 1)	3	2	(4, 1)	4	3
(1, 2)	2	1	(2, 2)	4	0	(3, 2)	6	1	(4, 2)	8	2
(1, 3)	3	2	(2, 3)	6	1	(3, 3)	9	0	(4, 3)	12	1
(1, 4)	4	3	(2, 4)	8	2	(3, 4)	12	1	(4, 4)	16	0

Now consider Table 6.2. Values along the top row of the table relate to X and values down the far left column relate to Y. More importantly, the values entered in the main body of this table are known as *joint probabilities*. For example, the value on the top left-hand side of the main array gives the joint probability of getting both $X = 1$ and $Y = 0$ on any given trial of the experiment. Since only one outcome, that of (1, 1), will give this combination for X and Y, this joint probability is 1/16. Similarly, the value in the $X = 6$ column and the $Y = 1$ row gives the joint probability of obtaining both $X = 6$ and $Y = 1$ on a given trial. Referring back to the sample space, it can be seen that two outcomes, (2, 3) and (3, 2), result in $X = 6$ and $Y = 1$. Since each outcome has the same probability 1/16 of occurring, it follows that the joint probability of obtaining these values for X and Y is 2/16.

Table 6.2 Joint and marginal probability distributions

X \ Y	1	2	3	4	6	8	9	12	16	g(Y)
0	1/16	0	0	1/16	0	0	1/16	0	1/16	4/16
1	0	2/16	0	0	2/16	0	0	2/16	0	6/16
2	0	0	2/16	0	0	2/16	0	0	0	4/16
3	0	0	0	2/16	0	0	0	0	0	2/16
f(X)	1/16	2/16	2/16	3/16	2/16	2/16	1/16	2/16	1/16	

Notice that a number of the joint probabilities are zero, because it is impossible for some of the X and Y combinations to occur. For example, if we have a product of $X = 3$, which implies an outcome of either (1, 3) or (3, 1), then the difference Y obviously cannot be 0 or 1.

The array of joint probabilities in Table 6.2 makes up what is referred to as the *joint probability distribution for X and Y*. Any joint probability distribution for two variables consists, therefore, of

(a) a listing of all the possible combinations of values that the two variables can take and

(b) the joint probabilities associated with each such combination.

For convenience, joint probability distributions are usually presented in a two-dimensional array as in Table 6.2.

We denote a joint probability distribution as $p(X, Y)$, for all X and all Y. That is, we use the shorthand

$$\text{Pr(both } X = 3 \text{ and } Y = 2) = p(3, 2),$$
$$\text{Pr(both } X = 6 \text{ and } Y = 1) = p(6, 1), \text{ etc.}$$

Notice that the sum of all the probabilities in the joint distribution is equal to unity. This will always be the case, provided we include all the possible combinations of X and Y.

Another way of looking at joint probabilities is to consider 'very many' trials of the experiment, each trial providing a value for X and a value for Y. Since, from Table 6.2, $p(8, 2) = 2/16 = 1/8$, we can say that, over very many trials, the outcome (8, 2) will occur one-eighth of the time.

For the moment, let us concentrate solely on the variable Y, the difference between the two numbers obtained on the two rolls of the die. That is, for now, we ignore the value of X. The probability of Y taking a particular value, regardless of X, is known as a *marginal probability*.

We can compute marginal probabilities for Y directly from the sample space in Table 6.1. For example, the marginal probability that $Y = 2$ is simply 4/16 since, ignoring the values for X, there are four outcomes of the experiment that yield $Y = 2$. Similarly, the marginal probability that $Y = 1$ is 6/16, since there are six outcomes yielding $Y = 1$. These marginal probabilities are entered in the far right-hand column of Table 6.2 and constitute what is known as the *marginal probability distribution for Y*. We denote this marginal distribution as $g(Y)$. That is, our shorthand is such that, for example, we write

$$Pr(Y = 2) = g(2) = 4/16,$$
$$Pr(Y = 1) = g(1) = 6/16.$$

It is also possible to obtain marginal probabilities for X, the product of the two numbers. For example, this time ignoring the values of Y, the marginal probability of obtaining $X = 4$ can be found by referring back to the sample space in Table 6.1. In fact $Pr(X = 4) = 3/16$ because there are three outcomes that will result in $X = 4$.

The marginal probabilities for X are entered in the bottom row of Table 6.2, marked $f(X)$. That is, $f(X)$ represents the marginal probability distribution for X. Again our notation is such that $Pr(X = 4) = f(4) = 3/16$ and so on.

The sum of the probabilities in each marginal distribution equals unity, as do those in the joint distribution. But can you see any other relationships between the probabilities in Table 6.2?

There is a clear relationship *between* the marginal and joint distributions. In fact each *row* of joint probabilities sums to the marginal probability in the right-hand *column*. Similarly, each *column* of joint probabilities sums to the marginal probability in the bottom *row*.

A moment's reflection should reveal why these relationships between marginal and joint probabilities must hold. Any value for X and Y can be obtained in a number of ways. For example, $Y = 2$ can be obtained either if the event ($X = 3$, $Y = 2$) occurs or if the event ($X = 8$, $Y = 2$) occurs. These two events are mutually exclusive and there are no other combinations of X and Y that will yield $Y = 2$. Hence, to find the marginal probability $g(2)$ we need to add up the joint probabilities $p(3, 2)$ and $p(8, 2)$. But that is exactly what we do when we sum the joint probabilities in the $Y = 2$ row to obtain $g(2)$.

Because of the relationships between joint and marginal distributions that we have uncovered, we do not normally have to refer back to the sample space when computing marginal probability distributions.

> Provided we know the joint distribution for X and Y, we can find the marginal distributions just by summing rows and columns of joint probabilities.

Means and variances can be calculated for marginal distributions in the same way as they were calculated for 'ordinary' probability distributions in Chapter 1.3. For example, the marginal distributions for X and Y in Table 6.2 have means

$$E(X) = \sum Xf(X) = 6.25,$$
$$E(Y) = \sum Yg(Y) = 1.25.$$

Also, since $E(X^2) = \sum X^2 f(X) = 56.25$ and $E(Y^2) = \sum Y^2 g(Y) = 2.5$, we have

$$V(X) = E(X^2) - [E(X)]^2 = 56.25 - 6.25^2 = 17.19,$$
$$V(Y) = E(Y^2) - [E(Y)]^2 = 2.5 - 1.25^2 = 0.94.$$

Worked Example

One four-sided die has the numbers 1, 3, 5 and 7 on its sides, while a second such die has the numbers 2, 4, 6 and 8. Both dice are rolled. Suppose X is the higher of the two numbers obtained and Y the lower. Find the joint probability distribution for X and Y. Hence find the expected values and the variances of X and Y.

Solution

The sample space for this solution is shown below, as are the values of X and Y for each possible outcome of the experiment.

	X	Y		X	Y		X	Y		X	Y
(1, 2)	2	1	(3, 2)	3	2	(5, 2)	5	2	(7, 2)	7	2
(1, 4)	4	1	(3, 4)	4	3	(5, 4)	5	4	(7, 4)	7	4
(1, 6)	6	1	(3, 6)	6	3	(5, 6)	6	5	(7, 6)	7	6
(1, 8)	8	1	(3, 8)	8	3	(5, 8)	8	5	(7, 8)	8	7

Since all outcomes are equally likely, each outcome has a probability of 1/16. The joint and marginal probability distributions are shown in Table 6.3.

Using Table 6.3, the means of the marginal distributions are given by

$$E(X) = 2(\tfrac{1}{16}) + 3(\tfrac{1}{16}) + 4(\tfrac{1}{8}) + 5(\tfrac{1}{8}) + 6(\tfrac{3}{16}) + 7(\tfrac{3}{16}) + 8(\tfrac{1}{4}) = 5.875$$
$$E(Y) = 1(\tfrac{1}{4}) + 2(\tfrac{3}{16}) + 3(\tfrac{3}{16}) + 4(\tfrac{1}{8}) + 5(\tfrac{1}{8}) + 6(\tfrac{1}{16}) + 7(\tfrac{1}{16}) = 3.125$$

Table 6.3

X \ Y	2	3	4	5	6	7	8	$g(Y)$
1	1/16	0	1/16	0	1/16	0	1/16	4/16
2	0	1/16	0	1/16	0	1/16	0	3/16
3	0	0	1/16	0	1/16	0	1/16	3/16
4	0	0	0	1/16	0	1/16	0	2/16
5	0	0	0	0	1/16	0	1/16	2/16
6	0	0	0	0	0	1/16	0	1/16
7	0	0	0	0	0	0	1/16	1/16
$f(X)$	1/16	1/16	2/16	2/16	3/16	3/16	4/16	

To obtain the variances, we first compute

$$E(X^2) = 4(\tfrac{1}{16}) + 9(\tfrac{1}{16}) + 16(\tfrac{1}{8}) + 25(\tfrac{1}{8}) + 36(\tfrac{3}{16}) + 49(\tfrac{3}{16}) + 64(\tfrac{1}{4}) = 37.875,$$
$$E(Y^2) = 1(\tfrac{1}{4}) + 4(\tfrac{3}{16}) + 9(\tfrac{3}{16}) + 16(\tfrac{1}{8}) + 25(\tfrac{1}{8}) + 36(\tfrac{1}{16}) + 49(\tfrac{1}{16}) = 13.125.$$

Hence,

$$V(X) = 56.625 - (5.875)^2 = 3.36,$$
$$V(Y) = 13.125 - (3.125)^2 = 3.36.$$

Example 6.1

A coin is tossed four times. Suppose X is the number of tails on the *first* three tosses and Y is the number of heads on the *last* three tosses. Set up the sample space for this experiment and hence find the joint probability distribution for X and Y. Next, find the marginal distributions for X and for Y, without referring back to the sample space. Find the variances of the two marginal distributions.

Example 6.2

Two firms produce identical output. Firm I can produce output X of between 200 and 600 units, while firm II can produce output Y of only between 100 and 300 units. Joint probabilities for all possible combinations of output are shown in Table 6.4. Obtain the marginal distributions for X and Y. Hence, find the mean outputs $E(X)$ and $E(Y)$ of the two firms. Find the distribution for total output $Z = X + Y$ and verify that $E(Z) = E(X) + E(Y)$.

Table 6.4

X Y	200	300	400	500	600
100	0.01	0.05	0.10	0.07	0.02
200	0.04	0.12	0.20	0.14	0.05
300	0.01	0.04	0.08	0.06	0.01

Example 6.3

A large company can sell its output either in the home market or overseas. Home output can take any of the values $X = 10, 20, 30, 40, 50$, whereas overseas output Y must be either 20 or 40. The joint probability distribution for X and Y is given in Table 6.5. Find $E(X)$, $V(X)$, $E(Y)$ and $V(Y)$.

Table 6.5

X Y	10	20	30	40	50
20	0.07	0.10	0.12	0.20	0.08
30	0.05	0.07	0.10	0.15	0.06

6.2 More about expected values

We saw in Chapter 1.3 that, if X has a probability distribution $p(X)$, then the expected value of any function of X can be found by taking a weighted mean of the function values, with probabilities used as weights. For example, $E(X) = \Sigma\, Xp(X)$ and $E(X - 4)^4 = \Sigma(X - 4)^4 p(X)$.

Often in statistics we need to find the expected value or mathematical expectation of a function which contains *more than one variable*. For example, in the die rolling of the last section we might want to find, for a reason that will be clear later, $E(XY)$ or $E(X + Y)$ or $E(X^2 Y^2)$.

Suppose we require the expected value of XY, which is a function of just two variables. Let us, first, consider what we actually mean by $E(XY)$. In any trial of the experiment in the previous section, we obtain values for both X (the product of the two numbers) and Y (their difference). Suppose we compute their product XY for each such trial. $E(XY)$ is simply the 'average value' of all the XYs we would obtain if we performed 'very many' trials of the experiment.

The way of obtaining E(XY) is analogous to the way used to obtain E(X). Just as E(X) = Σ $Xp(X)$, to find E(XY) we have to compute the *double summation*

$$E(XY) = \Sigma(XY)p(X, Y) \qquad [6.1]$$

where $p(X, Y)$ is now the joint probability distribution for X and Y. The double summation in [6.1] simply means that, for every possible combination of X and Y, we multiply XY by the joint probability of obtaining that combination (i.e., $p(X, Y)$) and then sum. That is, we are merely taking a *weighted* average of the XYs with the joint probabilities used as weights.

In Table 6.6 we have simply reproduced Table 6.2 but omitted the marginal probabilities and placed each joint probability in a 'box'. The simplest way of computing E(XY) is to write above each $p(X, Y)$ the relevant value of XY. These are entered as the numbers in Table 6.6 in the top right-hand corner of each box. For example, for the box corresponding to $X = 8$ and $Y = 2$ we enter $XY = 16$. Each box will now contain an XY in the top right-hand corner and a $p(X, Y)$ in the middle. For each box in the table we now multiply the former number by the latter and sum these products. This yields the required double summation and, hence, E(XY). That is,

$$E(XY) = 4/16 + 12/16 + 24/16 + 12/16 + 32/16 + 24/16$$
$$= 6.75 \qquad [6.2]$$

(Notice that many of the $XYp(X, Y)$ terms are zero and have been omitted.)

Table 6.6 The evaluation of E(XY)

X \\ Y	1		2		3		4		6		8		9		12		16	
0	1/16	0	0	0	0	0	1/16	0	0	0	0	0	1/16	0	0	0	1/16	0
1	0	1	2/16	2	0	3	0	4	2/16	6	0	8	0	9	2/16	12	0	16
2	0	2	0	4	2/16	6	0	8	0	12	2/16	16	0	18	0	24	0	32
3	0	3	0	6	0	9	2/16	12	0	18	0	24	0	27	0	36	0	48

Thus the average value of XY over many trials is 6.75. Note, however, that although, from the last section, E(X) = 6.25 and E(Y) = 1.25, it is not the case that $6.25 \times 1.25 = 6.75$. Thus, it is *not* generally the case that E(XY) = E(X)E(Y). As we noted in Chapter 1, care is needed when handling expected values. To the uninitiated it is sometimes the case that what seems to be obvious is not obvious at all! We will discover, later in this chapter, the conditions under which E(XY) actually will equal E(X)E(Y).

It is possible to obtain the expected value of any function of X and Y, $h(X, Y)$, by computing the relevant double summation. That is,

$$E[h(X, Y)] = \sum h(X, Y)p(X, Y).$$

Worked Example

For the die-rolling example, find:

(a) $E(XY^2)$;

(b) $E(X + Y)$.

Verify that $E(XY^2) \neq E(X)E(Y^2)$ but that $E(X + Y) = E(X) + E(Y)$

Solution

(a) To obtain $E(XY^2)$ we need to find the double summation $\sum XY^2 p(X, Y)$. Hence, we compute XY^2 for all possible combinations of X and Y. These are shown in the top right-hand corner of each box in Table 6.7. For example, when $X = 2$ and $Y = 3$, we have $XY^2 = 18$ and this value is shown in the ($X = 2$, $Y = 3$) box. The joint probabilities, in the middle of each box, are of course unchanged. The double summation is obtained, in the usual manner, by multiplying the numbers in the top right-hand corner by the numbers in the middle (this time using Table 6.7) and then summing. This gives

$$E(XY^2) = 4/16 + 24/16 + 72/16 + 12/16 + 64/16 + 24/16 = 12.5$$

In the previous section we obtained $E(X) = 6.25$ and $E(Y^2) = 2.5$ so that $E(X) \times E(Y^2) = 6.25 \times 2.5 = 15.625$, which is clearly different from 12.5. Thus $E(XY^2) \neq E(X) \times E(Y^2)$ in this case.

Table 6.7

Y \ X	1	2	3	4	6	8	9	12	16
0	1/16 $^{0}_{1}$	0 $^{0}_{2}$	0 $^{0}_{3}$	1/16 $^{0}_{4}$	0 $^{0}_{6}$	0 $^{0}_{8}$	1/16 $^{0}_{9}$	0 $^{0}_{12}$	1/16 $^{0}_{16}$
1	0 $^{1}_{2}$	2/16 $^{2}_{3}$	0 $^{3}_{4}$	0 $^{4}_{5}$	2/16 $^{6}_{7}$	0 $^{8}_{9}$	0 $^{9}_{10}$	2/16 $^{12}_{13}$	0 $^{16}_{17}$
2	0 $^{4}_{3}$	0 $^{8}_{4}$	2/16 $^{12}_{5}$	0 $^{16}_{6}$	0 $^{24}_{8}$	2/16 $^{32}_{10}$	0 $^{36}_{11}$	0 $^{48}_{14}$	0 $^{64}_{18}$
3	0 $^{9}_{4}$	0 $^{18}_{5}$	0 $^{27}_{6}$	2/16 $^{36}_{7}$	0 $^{54}_{9}$	0 $^{72}_{11}$	0 $^{81}_{12}$	0 $^{108}_{15}$	0 $^{144}_{19}$

(b) We can obtain $E(X + Y) = \Sigma(X + Y)p(X, Y)$ in the usual way. This time the relevant $X + Y$ values are shown in the bottom right-hand corner of each box in Table 6.7. The double summation is this time given by

$$E(X + Y) = 1/16 + 6/16 + 10/16 + 4/16 + 14/16 + 14/16 + 20/16$$
$$+ 9/16 + 26/16 + 16/16$$
$$= 7.5.$$

We already know that $E(X) = 6.25$ and $E(Y) = 1.25$, so the sum of $E(X)$ and $E(Y)$ is 7.5, which is equal to $E(X + Y)$. This is obviously one of those occasions when manipulating expected values actually produces an unsurprising result!

The above worked example demonstrates the general rule that, while the addition of expected values never causes any problems, the multiplication of expected values usually leads to complications. We now present a further theorem concerning expected values. Although you do not need to remember the proof in this theorem (it is presented in the Appendix to this chapter), you should become aware of what it states. An ability to manipulate expected values is important in statistics and particularly econometrics.

Theorem 6.1

If X and Y are two random variables and a and b are any two constants, then

$$E(aX + bY) = aE(X) + bE(Y).$$

Worked Example

If $E(X) = 10$ and $E(Y) = 20$, find the expected value of $Z = 3X + 2Y$.

Solution

Using Theorem 6.1, we have

$$E(Z) = E(3X + 2Y) = 3E(X) + 2E(Y) = 30 + 40 = 70.$$

Example 6.4

For the joint probability distribution in Example 6.1, find $E(X)$ and $E(Y)$ and verify, *using the joint probability distribution*, that $E(X + 2Y) = E(X) + 2E(Y)$.

Show that $E(XY) \neq E(X)E(Y)$. Find $E(X^2)$ and $E(Y^2)$ and show that $E(X^2Y^2) \neq E(X^2)E(Y^2)$.

Example 6.5

For the joint probability distribution in Example 6.3, find $E(XY)$. Given $E(X)$ and $E(Y)$, check whether $E(XY) = E(X)E(Y)$. Show that $E(2X - Y) = 2E(X) - E(Y)$ and check whether $E(X/Y) = E(X)/E(Y)$.

Example 6.6

In Example 6.2, total profits for firm I and firm II for every combination of X and Y are given in Table 6.8. Find the expected profits of each firm.

Table 6.8											
	Profits of firm I						Profits of firm II				
X \\ Y	200	300	400	500	600	X \\ Y	200	300	400	500	600
100	24	32	36	37	32	100	8	7	5	4	2
200	19	28	34	35	29	200	15	12	9	7	4
300	16	25	31	33	24	300	20	15	12	10	6

Example 6.7

In Example 6.3, suppose that the firm's total profit is given by $Z = 10X + 12Y$. Find the mean total profit.

6.3 Covariances and correlations

We define the *covariance* between two random variables as

$$\text{Cov}(X, Y) = E[X - E(X)][Y - E(Y)]. \tag{6.3}$$

As we shall see, the covariance measures the strength of any *linear association* between X and Y that is present. For example, in our two-dice experiment in the previous sections, we had $E(X) = 6.25$ and $E(Y) = 1.25$. The covariance [6.3] therefore becomes $E[X - 6.25][Y - 1.25]$ and measures the average value of the quantity $[X - 6.25][Y - 1.25]$ over 'very many' trials of the experiment.

  To see why a covariance measures the strength of the association between X and Y, recall that each trial of the experiment yields a value for X and a value for Y. 'Very many' trials will therefore give us 'very many' pairs of values of X and Y. Suppose there is a positive (linear) association between X and Y (i.e., X rises as Y rises). This implies that positive values of $X - 6.25$ (i.e., 'above average' values of X) will *tend* to coincide with positive values of $Y - 1.25$ (i.e., 'above average values' of Y). Similarly, negative values of $X - 6.25$ (i.e., 'below average' values of X) will *tend* to coincide with negative values of Y (i.e., 'below average' values of Y). Consequently, the product $(X - 6.25)(Y - 1.25)$ will *tend* to consist of either two positive quantities multiplied together or two negative quantities, and hence will *tend* to be positive. Since, the covariance measures the 'average' value of the product over 'very many' trials, it follows that the covariance will be a *positive* quantity. Moreover, the stronger the positive linear association between X and Y, the stronger will be the tendency for the product $[X - 6.25][Y - 1.25]$ to be positive, and the larger will be the covariance.

If instead there is a negative or inverse linear association between X and Y, there will be a *tendency* for positive values of $X - 6.25$ to coincide with negative values of $Y - 1.25$. Conversely, negative values of $X - 6.25$ will *tend* to coincide with positive values for $Y - 1.25$. In such a situation, the product $[X - 6.25][Y - 1.25]$ will normally consist of one positive quantity and one negative quantity multiplied together and, hence, will *tend* to be negative. Its 'average value', the covariance, will therefore be a negative quantity. Moreover, the stronger is the negative linear association between X and Y the more negative is the covariance [6.3].

One way of computing a covariance is to use definition [6.3] to obtain

$$\text{Cov}(X, Y) = \Sigma[X - E(X)][Y - E(Y)]p(X, Y). \qquad [6.4]$$

Since $E(X) = 6.25$ and $E(Y) = 1.25$, and the joint probabilities for this experiment are given in Table 6.2, we could compute all the $(X - 6.25)(Y - 1.25)$s in the usual way and then obtain the double summation in [6.4]. However, it is usually less tedious to obtain a covariance by using the following relationship:[2]

$$\text{Cov}(X, Y) = E(XY) - E(X)E(Y). \qquad [6.5]$$

Expressions [6.4] and [6.5] will always result in the same value. In fact, we have already calculated $E(X)$, $E(Y)$ and $E(XY) = 6.75$ for our die-rolling example. Expression [6.5] thus gives

$$\text{Cov}(X, Y) = 6.75 - (6.25)(1.25) = -1.0625.$$

Notice that the covariance is negative. Thus it appears that the larger is X, the product of the numbers on the dice, the smaller is Y, their difference.

Example 6.8

Verify that expression [6.4] for the covariance also gives the value -1.0625.

Example 6.9

Find the covariance between X and Y for the experiment in Examples 6.1 and 6.4. Explain the value obtained.

Example 6.10

For Example 6.2, find the covariance between the profits of firm I and firm II.

Example 6.11

For Example 6.3, find the covariance between output for the home market and output for overseas.

Having defined and interpreted the concept of a covariance, we can now consider the following theorem on variances. Once again you do not have to understand the proof of this theorem (it can be found in the appendix to this chapter), but you should understand clearly what it states.

Theorem 6.2

If X and Y are two random variables and a and b are constants, then

$$V(aX + bY) = a^2 V(X) + b^2 V(Y) + 2ab \, \text{Cov}(X, Y).$$

There are several useful special cases of Theorem 6.2. In particular, if $\text{Cov}(X, Y) = 0$, so that there is no linear association between X and Y, then Theorem 6.2 reduces to

$$V(aX + bY) = a^2 V(X) + b^2 V(Y). \qquad [6.6]$$

Thus, if two variables have no linear association, then the variance of, for example, $2X + 4Y$ depends *only* on the variances of X and Y.

Example 6.12

Use Theorem 6.2 to find $V(2X - Y)$ for the experiment in Examples 6.1, 6.4 and 6.9.

Worked Example

Suppose X and Y are two random variables with known variances $V(X)$ and $V(Y)$ and covariance $\text{Cov}(X, Y)$. Obtain expressions for $V(X + Y)$ and $V(X - Y)$.

If there is no linear association between X and Y, how does this affect $V(X + Y)$ and $V(X - Y)$?

Solution

Setting $a = 1$ and $b = 1$ in Theorem 6.2 gives

$$V(X + Y) = 1^2 V(X) + 1^2 V(Y) + (2 \times 1 \times 1)Cov(X, Y)$$
$$= V(X) + V(Y) + 2\,Cov(X, Y). \qquad [6.7]$$

Setting $a = 1$ and $b = -1$ in Theorem 6.2 then yields, remembering that $(-1)^2 = +1$,

$$V(X - Y) = 1^2 V(X) + (-1)^2 V(Y) + (2 \times 1 \times (-1))Cov(X, Y)$$
$$= V(X) + V(Y) - 2\,Cov(X, Y). \qquad [6.8]$$

If there is no linear association between X and Y, then $Cov(X, Y) = 0$, so that [6.7] and [6.8] become

$$V(X + Y) = V(X) + V(Y), \qquad [6.9]$$
$$V(X - Y) = V(X) + V(Y). \qquad [6.10]$$

Note that *it is not the case that* $V(X - Y) = V(X) - V(Y)$!

Correlations

We obtained a value of -1.0625 for the covariance in our die-rolling example. Although this negative value tells us that there is a negative linear association between X and Y, it tells us nothing about the strength of this association. Does a value of -1.0625 imply a strong association or a weak association? How do we judge the strength of an association anyway? Working out the correlation between two variables goes some way to answering these questions.

The *correlation coefficient* (or simply the *correlation*), ρ, between X and Y is defined as

$$\rho = \frac{Cov(X, Y)}{\sqrt{V(X)}\sqrt{V(Y)}} = \frac{E[X - E(X)][Y - E(Y)]}{\sqrt{E[X - E(X)]^2}\sqrt{E[(Y - E(Y)]^2}}. \qquad [6.11]$$

The usefulness of the correlation coefficient lies in the fact that, unlike the covariance, it can only take values within a definite finite range. While a covariance can take any value between $-\infty$ and $+\infty$, the correlation is restricted to values within the range -1 and $+1$. In fact, as we shall see in a moment, when there is an *exact* positive linear association between X and Y, the correlation takes the value $\rho = +1$. Similarly, when there is an *exact* negative linear association between X and Y, the correlation is $\rho = -1$. Furthermore, when there is no linear association between X and Y at all, then $\rho = 0$.

The correlation coefficient, ρ, gives us a standard by which we can judge the strength of any linear association between two variables. Clearly, if ρ were to take a value close to zero, we would judge the association to be a very weak one. However, values close to $+1$ or -1 would imply strong positive and negative linear associations, respectively.

To understand why, for example when $\rho = 1$, there is an exact positive association between two variables X and Y, suppose that the exact association $Y = 3 + 6X$ holds. That is, when X takes the value 2, for example, Y *always* takes the value 15. Similarly, whenever $X = -4$, Y *always* takes the value -21, and so on.

Since $Y = 3 + 6X$, it follows[3] that $E(Y) = 3 + 6E(X)$. Substituting for Y and $E(Y)$ in the numerator of [6.11], we therefore have

$$E[X - E(X)][3 + 6X - 3 - 6E(X)] = 6E[X - E(X)]^2. \qquad [6.12]$$

Similarly, substituting into the denominator of [6.11] yields

$$\sqrt{E[X - E(X)]^2}\sqrt{E[3 + 6X - 3 - 6E(X)]^2}$$
$$= \sqrt{E[X - E(X)]^2}\sqrt{E6^2[X - E(X)]^2}$$
$$= \sqrt{36\{E[X - E(X)]^2\}^2}$$
$$= +6E[X - E(X)]^2, \qquad [6.13]$$

where we always take the *positive* value of the square root. Comparing [6.12] and [6.13], we see that, in this case, the correlation [6.11] does indeed come out to $+1$.

Example 6.13

If a relationship between X and Y of the kind $Y = 12 - 3X$ holds exactly, show that the correlation $\rho = -1$.

We can now calculate the correlation between X and Y for the die-rolling example. We have already computed the covariance as -1.0625, whereas we found $V(X) = 17.19$ and $V(Y) = 0.94$ in Section 6.1. Hence, substituting into the first expression in [6.11], we obtain the correlation as

$$\rho = \frac{-1.0625}{\sqrt{17.19}\sqrt{0.94}} = -0.26.$$

The correlation is negative, as expected, but the value of ρ is rather closer to 0 than to -1. So we can say that there is a fairly weak negative linear association between X and Y in this case. This is not unexpected because, intuitively, we would not expect a close relationship between X, the product of the two numbers on the two dice, and Y, their difference.

Example 6.14

For the experiment of Examples 6.1, 6.4 and 6.9, you have found V(X), V(Y) and Cov(X, Y). Find the correlation between X and Y and comment on the value you have found.

Example 6.15

A coin is tossed three times. Let X be the number of heads obtained, and Y the number of tails. Find the joint probability distribution for X and Y. What is unusual about this joint distribution? Find the covariance between X and Y. Hence, show that the correlation coefficient for these variables is -1 and explain why this is the case.

Example 6.16

(a) For Examples 6.2 and 6.10, find the correlation between firm I's profit and firm II's profit.
(b) For Example 6.3, find the correlation between home output and overseas output.
   Comment on the correlations found in (a) and (b)

Independence

In the previous subsection we concentrated on assessing the strength of any linear association between two variables. From the definitions [6.5] and [6.11], it can be seen that

whenever the condition

$$E(XY) = E(X)E(Y)$$

is satisfied, the correlation between X and Y will be zero.   [6.14]

Unfortunately, condition [6.14] refers only to linear relationships and, in economics, relationships are rarely linear. Consequently, we frequently need to discover whether any nonlinear relationships between variables are present.

In the prerequisites chapter, we saw that independence between two *events A* and *B* implied that Pr(A and B) equals Pr(A) × Pr(B). That is, the joint probability of two independent events occurring is given by the product of the marginal probabilities of the individual events.

Two random *variables*, X and Y, are said to be *independent* if joint probabilities are the product of the relevant marginal probabilities *for all possible combinations of* X *and* Y. That is,

X and Y are independent if and only if $p(X, Y) = f(X)g(Y)$ for all X and Y.   [6.15]

In Table 6.9, we have an example of two *independent* variables. Notice that relationship [6.15] holds for all combinations of X and Y. For example, $p(5, 4) = f(5)g(4)$ and $p(10, 1) = f(10)g(1)$. We stress that [6.15] must hold for *all* combinations of X and Y if the variables are to be independent. If just one combination of X and Y were to fail to obey condition [6.15], then the variables could no longer be called independent.

Table 6.9 Two independent variables

Y X	1	2	3	4	5	f(X)
5	0.06	0.04	0.04	0.04	0.02	0.2
10	0.09	0.06	0.06	0.06	0.03	0.3
15	0.15	0.10	0.10	0.10	0.05	0.5
g(Y)	0.3	0.2	0.2	0.2	0.1	

While non-correlation ($\rho = 0$) implies the absence of any *linear* association between X and Y, independence is a stronger condition. It implies the absence of *any* association between X and Y, linear or nonlinear. Thus independence implies non-correlation, but non-correlation does not necessarily imply independence. Thus condition [6.14] implies $Cov(X, Y) = 0$, and hence non-correlation, but it does not necessarily imply independence. For independence we also require condition [6.15]. Thus, if two variables are non-correlated, they are not linearly associated but they could still be non-independent if there were some nonlinear, possibility tenuous, association present.

Example 6.17

Compute E(X), E(Y) and E(XY) for the following joint probability distribution

X Y	1	2	3
0	1/8	0	0
1	0	1/4	1/8
2	0	1/4	1/8
3	1/8	0	0

Are X and Y uncorrelated? Are X and Y independent?

Example 6.18

Two firms A and B have outputs X and Y that are independently distributed with the following marginal distributions.

X	10	20	40	80
$f(X)$	0.1	0.4	0.3	0.2
Y	30	40	50	
$g(Y)$	0.2	0.5	0.3	

Write down the joint distribution for X and Y. Show that $E(XY) = E(X)E(Y)$ for this joint distribution. Are the two outputs correlated?

Example 6.19

Compute $E(X)$, $E(Y)$ and $E(XY)$ for the following joint distribution:

Y \ X	0	1	2	3
1	0.125	0	0	0.125
2	0	0.25	0.25	0
3	0	0.125	0.125	0

Do your results mean that X and Y are independent?

Although the discussion in this chapter has been restricted to discrete variables, the concepts of independence and non-correlation apply equally well to continuous variables. However, it can be shown that the *distinction between the two concepts disappears when continuous variables are normally distributed.* In fact, it turns out that if two normally distributed variables X and Y are uncorrelated then they must be independent.

There is one further useful property of normally distributed variables, given by the following theorem, which we present without proof.

Theorem 6.3

Any linear function of a series of independently and normally distributed variables is itself normally distributed.

The above property is a very useful one. For example, if X, Y and Z are all independent normally distributed variables, then it follows that $W = 2X + 4Y - 3Z$ will also be normally distributed.

Example 6.20

Suppose X and Y are two independently distributed variables. If X is $N(5, 4)$ and Y is $N(4, 9)$ find the distribution for $Z = 2X - 3Y$. Hence find the probability that Z exceeds 2.5.

Sample correlations

The term 'correlation' will be familiar to even beginners in the study of statistics. However, they may be confused to encounter it in the world of probability. This is because correlations are usually computed only for *samples*.

Consider our die-rolling example of previous sections, where we worked with two random variables X, the product of the two numbers obtained, and Y, the difference between them. Let us consider 10 trials for this experiment. Each trial will yield a pair of values, a value for X and a value for Y. The 10 trials can be regarded as a sample, size $n = 10$, taken from an infinitely large population of such trials, each trial resulting in X and Y values. This *population* is described by the joint probability distribution for X and Y, first given in Table 6.2.

A typical *sample* of the above kind is given by the second and third columns in Table 6.10. For the population, we worked out in previous sections (using the joint distribution for X and Y) values for the means and variances of X and Y and for the covariance and

Table 6.10 A sample of size $n = 10$

Trial	X	Y	$X - \bar{X}$	$Y - \bar{Y}$	$(X - \bar{X})^2$	$(Y - \bar{Y})^2$	$(X - \bar{X})(Y - \bar{Y})$
(1, 3)	3	2	−2.8	0.7	7.84	0.49	−1.96
(2, 1)	2	1	−3.8	−0.3	14.44	0.09	1.14
(4, 3)	12	1	6.2	−0.3	38.44	0.09	−1.86
(3, 1)	3	2	−2.8	0.7	7.84	0.49	−1.96
(2, 2)	4	0	−1.8	−1.3	3.24	1.69	2.34
(1, 4)	4	3	−1.8	1.7	3.24	2.89	−3.06
(2, 3)	6	1	0.2	−0.3	0.04	0.09	−0.06
(4, 3)	12	1	6.2	−0.3	38.44	0.09	−1.86
(2, 2)	4	0	−1.8	−1.3	3.24	1.69	2.34
(4, 2)	8	2	2.2	0.7	4.84	0.49	1.54
Total	58	13			121.60	8.10	−3.40

correlation between these variables. It is also possible to compute analogous quantities, termed *sample statistics*, from the sample in Table 6.10. Firstly, corresponding to the *population* means E(X) and E(Y), we have *sample* means

$$\bar{X} = \Sigma X/n = 58/10 = 5.8, \qquad \bar{Y} = \Sigma Y/n = 16/10 = 1.3, \qquad [6.16]$$

where n is the sample size (10 in this case).

Next, notice that the *population* variances E$[X - E(X)]^2$ and E$[Y - E(Y)]^2$ can both be expressed in words as 'the average value of the variable minus its mean, all squared'. *Sample* variances are defined in the same manner, except that, instead of working out averages over an infinite number of trials, we compute averages over the n trials that form our sample. Thus the *sample* variances of X and Y are defined as

$$v_X^2 = \frac{\Sigma(X - \bar{X})^2}{n} \quad \text{and} \quad v_Y^2 = \frac{\Sigma(Y - \bar{Y})^2}{n}. \qquad [6.17]$$

Notice that, just as the population variances measure the dispersion of X values and Y values, respectively, in the population, so the sample variances measure the dispersion of X and Y values in the sample.[4]

For the sample in Table 6.10, values of $(X - \bar{X})^2$ and $(Y - \bar{Y})^2$ are given in the sixth and seventh columns with the relevant sums at the foot. Dividing by $n = 10$ gives the sample variances as, using [6.17],

$$v_X^2 = 121.60/10 = 12.16 \quad \text{and} \quad v_Y^2 = 8.10/10 = 0.81. \qquad [6.18]$$

The *population* covariance was defined by [6.3]. In words, the definition can be expressed as 'the average value of $[X - E(X)][Y - E(Y)]$' over an infinite number of trials of the experiment. The *sample* covariance is defined in exactly the same way, except that this time we take the average over just the n trials in our sample and use the sample means, $\bar{X}$ and $\bar{Y}$, instead of E(X) and E(Y). It is therefore given by

$$v_{XY} = \frac{\Sigma(X - \bar{X})(Y - \bar{Y})}{n}, \qquad [6.19]$$

where the summation is over all pairs of X and Y.

For the sample in Table 6.10, values for $(X - \bar{X})(Y - \bar{Y})$ are given in the eighth column of the table, again with their sum at the foot. Using [6.19] we therefore obtain

$$v_{XY} = -3.40/10 = -0.34. \qquad [6.20]$$

Like the population covariance, v_{XY} measures the strength of any linear association between X and Y, but this time over the sample values.

Finally, we can compute a *sample* correlation coefficient, R. To obtain R, the population covariance and variances in [6.11] have to be replaced by the sample covariance and variances defined above. That is, using [6.17] and [6.19],

$$R = \frac{\Sigma(X - \bar{X})(Y - \bar{Y})}{\sqrt{\Sigma(X - \bar{X})^2}\sqrt{\Sigma(Y - \bar{Y})^2}} = \frac{v_{XY}}{\sqrt{v_X^2}\sqrt{v_Y^2}}. \qquad [6.21]$$

For the sample values [6.18] and [6.20], given above, the sample correlation is therefore given by

$$R = \frac{-0.34}{\sqrt{12.16}\sqrt{0.81}} = -1.08.$$

Like the population correlation, R must lie between 1 and -1. A value of $R = -0.108$ indicates a weak negative linear relationship between X and Y.

Our values for sample measures, such as R, differ from the corresponding population measures obtained earlier. For, example, the population correlation was found to be $\rho = -0.260$. But there is nothing unusual about such differences, because our sample measures are obtained from a sample of just 10 pairs of X and Y values. If we carried out a further 10 trials of the die-rolling experiment, we would, almost certainly, obtain differing values for sample means, variances, covariance and correlation. In fact, if we took 'very many' samples, generated in the above manner, we would obtain *sampling distributions* for each of the sample statistics defined earlier. For example, knowledge of the sampling distribution for R would enable us to obtain confidence intervals for the population correlation, ρ, defined earlier. We will return to correlations later in this book when we discuss regression analysis.

6.4 Tests concerning two populations

In Chapters 4 and 5 we considered the testing of hypotheses about the parameters of a single population. In this section we apply these ideas to situations where we compare the means and variances of two different populations.

Tests about two means

Consider two cities, one, city A, perhaps in a more undeveloped part of a country and the other, city B, in a more industrial part. Suppose that a Social and Economic Institute suspects that mean annual income in city B is greater than that in city A, and wishes to test whether this is actually the case.

As always, we begin by formulating hypotheses. If μ_1 and μ_2 are the population mean incomes in cities A and B, respectively, we can formulate a null hypothesis

$$H_0: \mu_1 = \mu_2 \quad \text{(no difference between mean incomes).}$$

Notice that we have inserted the equality sign in H_0 because, as we shall see shortly, this will enable us to derive a suitable test statistic for tackling the problem we face.

Because we are specifically asked to test whether incomes in city B are greater than in city A, we make the alternative hypothesis

$$H_A: \mu_1 < \mu_2 \quad \text{(mean incomes are greater in city B).}$$

Let us pause at this point and consider the structure of the problem we face. This is illustrated in Fig. 6.1. We let X_1 be the annual income of a resident from city A, and X_2 the annual income of a resident in city B. We therefore have a population of 'very many' values for X_1 from city A, with a mean μ_1 and a variance we designate as σ_1^2. Similarly, we have a second population of 'very many' values for X_2 from city B, with mean μ_2 and variance designated as σ_2^2. Notice that the absolute sizes of the populations in the two cities are unimportant, provided both cities are 'large'.

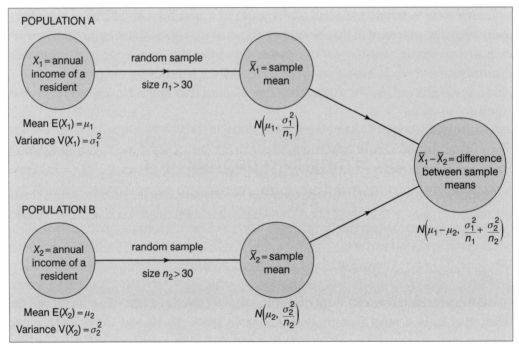

Figure 6.1 The sampling distribution for $\overline{X}_1 - \overline{X}_2$

We can now apply the central limit theorem (Theorem 3.2) to both populations in turn. Suppose we take a sample size n_1 from the first population, city A, and compute its mean income $\bar{X}_1$, as indicated in Fig. 6.1. If we imagine taking a whole series of such samples, all size n_1, from city A, we will obtain a sampling distribution of values for $\bar{X}_1$. Provided the sample size n_1 is large, (e.g., $n_1 > 30$), then the sampling distribution for $\bar{X}_1$ will have the normal distribution. Thus, combining Theorems 3.1 and 3.2, we can write

$$\bar{X}_1 \text{ has a } N(\mu_1, \sigma_1^2/n_1) \text{ distribution,} \tag{6.22}$$

as shown in Fig. 6.1.

An identical approach can be applied to the second population. If we take many samples of size n_2 from city B, computing $\bar{X}_2$ in each case, we will obtain a sample distribution for $\bar{X}_2$, where

$$\bar{X}_2 \text{ has a } N(\mu_2, \sigma_2^2/n_2) \text{ distribution.} \tag{6.23}$$

This is again shown in Fig. 6.1.

Since we are interested in the difference between the two unknown *population* means, $\mu_1 - \mu_2$, it makes sense to base any test statistic we develop on the quantity $\bar{X}_1 - \bar{X}_2$, the difference between the two *sample* means, which we can calculate. If we imagine that, whenever we take a sample of size n_1 from the first population, we also take a sample of size n_2 from the second population, we will obtain, each time, a pair of values for $\bar{X}_1$ and $\bar{X}_2$. Thus, as illustrated in Fig. 6.1, from each pair of samples, we could compute a value for $\bar{X}_1 - \bar{X}_2$. If 'very many' pairs of such samples were taken, each yielding a value for $\bar{X}_1 - \bar{X}_2$, we would obtain a sampling distribution for $\bar{X}_1 - \bar{X}_2$, from which we could derive a suitable test statistic.

We therefore need to find the sampling distribution for $\bar{X}_1 - \bar{X}_2$. Since $\bar{X}_1$ and $\bar{X}_2$ are both normally distributed, it follows from Theorem 6.3 that $\bar{X}_1 - \bar{X}_2$ must also be normally distributed. We can derive the mean and variance of $\bar{X}_1 - \bar{X}_2$ using [6.22] and [6.23]. Since $E(\bar{X}_1) = \mu_1$ and $E(\bar{X}_2) = \mu_2$, it follows that

$$E(\bar{X}_1 - \bar{X}_2) = E(\bar{X}_1) - E(\bar{X}_2) = \mu_1 - \mu_2. \tag{6.24}$$

Again using [6.22] and [6.23], we have $V(\bar{X}_1) = \sigma_1^2/n_1$ and $V(\bar{X}_2) = \sigma_2^2/n_2$. If we assume that the two samples are generated by completely independent processes (which is likely if we are dealing with two cities, some way apart), we can treat $\bar{X}_1$ and $\bar{X}_2$ as two independent variables so that $\text{Cov}(\bar{X}_1, \bar{X}_2) = 0$. We can now use [6.10] to obtain

$$\text{Var}(\bar{X}_1 - \bar{X}_2) = V(\bar{X}_1) + V(\bar{X}_2) = \frac{\sigma_1^2}{n_1} + \frac{\sigma_2^2}{n_2}. \tag{6.25}$$

Since we know that $\bar{X}_1 - \bar{X}_2$ is normally distributed, it follows from [6.24] and [6.25] that

$$\bar{X}_1 - \bar{X}_2 \text{ has a } N\left(\mu_1 - \mu_2, \frac{\sigma_1^2}{n_1} + \frac{\sigma_2^2}{n_2}\right) \text{ distribution.} \qquad [6.26]$$

This is the required sampling distribution, shown in Fig. 6.1. This is our 'basic result' which we can now use to derive an appropriate test statistic.

Firstly, from [6.26] we have that

$$\frac{\bar{X}_1 - \bar{X}_2 - (\mu_1 - \mu_2)}{\sqrt{\dfrac{\sigma_1^2}{n_1} + \dfrac{\sigma_2^2}{n_2}}} \text{ has a } N(0, 1) \text{ distribution} \qquad [6.27]$$

To derive the test statistic, we adopt our usual procedure of considering the consequences of the basic result, when H_0 is true. Under H_0, $\mu_1 = \mu_2$, so that [6.27] becomes

$$TS = \frac{\bar{X}_1 - \bar{X}_2}{\sqrt{\sigma_1^2/n_1 + \sigma_2^2/n_2}} \text{ has a } N(0, 1) \text{ distribution.} \qquad [6.28]$$

We can use [6.28] as a test statistic because, if H_0 is true, we expect TS, as an $N(0, 1)$ variable, to take a value close to zero. Values far away from zero will lead us to reject H_0.

Notice that the test statistic is based on $\bar{X}_1 - \bar{X}_2$, the difference between the sample means. It makes obvious sense to reject the hypothesis that the population means are the same if the sample means are very different.

As usual, we resort to standard normal tables to decide what is meant by 'very different'. In this case we are asked to test whether μ_1 is *less* than μ_2. We will therefore reject H_0 if $\bar{X}_1$ is sufficiently *smaller* than $\bar{X}_2$. This implies that $\bar{X}_1 - \bar{X}_2$ must be sufficiently negative, so that we need to use a one-tail test.

Adopting a 0.05 level of significance, our test criterion is therefore (see Fig. 6.2)

$$\text{reject } H_0 \text{ if } TS < -1.64, \text{ but reserve judgement if } TS > -1.64. \qquad [6.29]$$

Now, suppose we take samples of size 200 from both cities and that these samples yield the following information:

$$\text{city A: } n_1 = 200, \bar{X}_1 = 14\,860, s_1 = 1655;$$
$$\text{city B: } n_2 = 200, \bar{X}_2 = 17\,230, s_2 = 2108.$$

Since sample standard deviations are unbiased estimators of the corresponding population standard deviations,[5] we can use s_1 and s_2, instead of σ_1 and σ_2, and then substitute into [6.28] to obtain a value for the test statistic. This yields

$$TS = \frac{14\,860 - 17\,230}{\sqrt{\dfrac{1655^2}{200} + \dfrac{2108^2}{200}}} = -12.52.$$

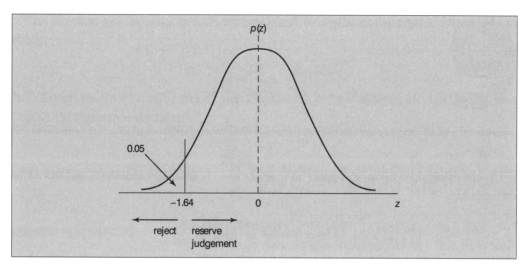

Figure 6.2 Test criterion for two-cities problem

Applying the test criterion [6.29] we therefore reject H_0 at the 0.05 level of significance, since -12.52 is quite clearly less than -1.64. Since H_0 is the hypothesis that incomes are the same in both cities, we appear to have strong evidence that average income in city B is greater than that in city A.

Example 6.21

A study of 200 patients in a hospital catchment area reveals that the average waiting time (in weeks) before a patient gets to see a heart specialist is 7.53 with standard deviation 2.5. In a second separate study of 100 patients near a second hospital, average waiting time is 6.73 weeks with a standard deviation of 1.2. Test whether there is any difference between waiting times in the two hospitals.

[*Note*. As in all examples of this type, do not be happy just because you have the 'arithmetic' correct! Set out your answer properly in the manner of the testing procedure of Chapter 4.]

Small samples

When sample sizes are large, we can resort to the central limit theorem to test for a difference in two population means. For small samples, the test is a little more complicated. Just as when testing hypotheses about a single mean, it turns out that we have to switch to the Student's t distribution.

The structure of the testing procedure is identical to that depicted in Fig. 6.1. However when n_1 and n_2 are 'small', some additional conditions are required before a valid test can be performed. Provided both populations

(a) have values that are normally distributed about their respective means, and

(b) have the same variance σ^2 (i.e., $\sigma_1^2 = \sigma_2^2 = \sigma^2$), then [6.27] becomes

$$\frac{\bar{X}_1 - \bar{X}_2 - (\mu_1 - \mu_2)}{\sigma\sqrt{1/n_1 + 1/n_2}}, \quad\quad [6.30]$$

which can be shown still to have a standard normal distribution, even when samples are small.

Unfortunately, the common population variance σ^2 is normally unknown and has to be estimated by

$$s^2 = \frac{(n_1 - 1)s_1^2 + (n_2 - 1)s_2^2}{n_1 + n_2 - 2}, \quad\quad [6.31]$$

where s_1^2 and s_2^2 are the respective sample variances.

We shall have more to say about [6.31] in a moment, but the main point is that, if σ is estimated in this way and then replaced by s in [6.30], it can be shown that [6.30] has a Student's t distribution with $n_1 + n_2 - 2$ degrees of freedom. This is the basic result we require if we are to construct a valid test statistic.

s^2 in [6.31] is a weighted average of the two sample variances,[6] s_1^2 and s_2^2. Since the two sample variances are both unbiased estimators of the common population variance, σ^2, it follows that s^2 must also be unbiased. It might seem more sensible to weight the two sample variances by the sample sizes n_1 and n_2 and estimate σ^2 by

$$v^2 = \frac{n_1 s_1^2 + n_2 s_2^2}{n_1 + n_2}. \quad\quad [6.32]$$

This is identical to [6.31], except that n_1 and n_2 have replaced $n_1 - 1$ and $n_2 - 1$ respectively, but, for reasons of statistical theory, [6.31] is necessary if we are to obtain a Student's t distribution.

Summarizing, substituting s for σ in [6.30] yields

$$\frac{\bar{X}_1 - \bar{X}_2 - (\mu_1 - \mu_2)}{s\sqrt{1/n_1 + 1/n_2}} \text{ has a Student's } t \text{ distribution with } n_1 + n_2 - 2 \text{ d.f.} \quad [6.33]$$

An explanation of the term 'degrees of freedom' was provided in the Appendix to Chapter 5. However, students who found that section difficult may simply paraphrase the above as 'the Student's t distribution obtained when the sample sizes are n_1 and n_2'.

We are finally in a position to obtain the test statistic needed to test for a difference between means in the small-sample case. The null hypothesis is $H_0: \mu_1 = \mu_2$, as in the previous subsection, so that, substituting into the basic result [6.33], gives us the required test statistic. Under H_0,

$$TS = \frac{\bar{X}_1 - \bar{X}_2}{s\sqrt{\dfrac{1}{n_1} + \dfrac{1}{n_2}}} \text{ has a Student's } t \text{ distribution with } n_1 + n_2 - 2 \text{ d.f.} \qquad [6.34]$$

Worked Example

Two groups of children are taught arithmetic by two methods, one traditional and the other progressive. It is required to test whether there is any difference between the mean percentage marks of the two groups when both are given the same examination. The following results were obtained:

	Traditional group	Progressive group
Mean mark	78	72
Standard deviation	12	14
Size of group	8	11

How would you proceed?

Solution

The population parameters, μ_1 and μ_2, here refer to the average marks that would be obtained if a 'very large group' of children were taught by the traditional method and if a different 'very large' group of children were taught by the progressive method.

We formulate null and alternative hypotheses

$$H_0: \mu_1 = \mu_2 \quad \text{(no difference in methods),}$$
$$H_A: \mu_1 \neq \mu_2.$$

(As usual, the 'equals' sign appears in H_0 and we place a 'not equals' sign in H_A, since we are asked to test for a difference between means.)

Under H_0,

$$TS = \frac{\bar{X}_1 - \bar{X}_2}{s\sqrt{1/n_1 + 1/n_2}} \text{ has a Student's } t \text{ distribution with } n_1 + n_2 - 2 \text{ degrees of freedom.}$$

For a 0.05 level of significance, we construct the decision criterion

$$\text{reject if } |TS| > t_{0.025} = 2.11, \text{ but reserve judgement if } |TS| < 2.11.$$

(since $n_1 = 8$ and $n_2 = 11$, d.f. = 17).

For the samples, we have $\bar{X}_1 = 78$, $\bar{X}_2 = 72$, and [6.31] gives

$$s^2 = \frac{7 \times 144 + 10 \times 196}{17} = 174.6.$$

Thus

$$TS = \frac{78 - 72}{\sqrt{174.6}\sqrt{\dfrac{1}{8} + \dfrac{1}{11}}} = 0.98.$$

Applying the above decision criterion, since $0.98 < 2.11$ we cannot reject H_0 at the 0.05 level of significance. We have to reserve judgement and conclude that we have insufficient evidence to say that the two teaching methods differ.

Example 6.22

A Japanese car manufacturer is considering two locations for a new production line in the UK. A Development Council claims that skilled engineering mean wages are lower in location A than in location B. The car manufacturer interviews five engineers from location A and seven from location B with the following results:

Location A (weekly wages/£)   600, 680, 570, 590, 560;
Location B (weekly wages/£)   605, 725, 618, 630, 705, 660, 635.

(a) Obtain unbiased estimates of the means and variances of engineering wages in the two locations.
(b) Using a 0.05 level of significance, test whether mean wages are lower in location A.

Tests about two variances

When testing for a difference between two population means we saw that, with small samples, it is necessary that the populations should have the same variance if a valid test is to be performed. It is therefore sensible actually to *test* whether the variances, σ_1^2 and σ_2^2, are the same before proceeding to the testing of the difference between the means. Using the same notation as in the previous subsection, suppose we formulate the hypotheses

$$H_0: \sigma_1^2 = \sigma_2^2, \qquad H_A: \sigma_1^2 \neq \sigma_2^2.$$

A suitable statistic for testing H_0 against H_A is, in fact, the ratio of the two sample variances, s_1^2/s_2^2. Clearly, if s_1^2 is sufficiently different from s_2^2, then we will want to reject H_0.

Under H_0, the population variances are the same, so that

$$\frac{s_1^2}{s_2^2} = \frac{s_1^2/\sigma_1^2}{s_2^2/\sigma_2^2} = \frac{s_1^2(n_1-1)/\sigma_1^2(n_1-1)}{s_2^2(n_2-1)/\sigma_2^2(n_2-1)}. \qquad [6.35]$$

Careful study of [6.35] reveals that, under H_0, s_1^2/s_2^2 can be expressed as the ratio of two χ^2 distributions, each of which has been divided by its respective number of degrees of freedom. In the numerator of [6.35], we have

$$\chi^2_{n_1-1} = \frac{s_1^2(n_1-1)/\sigma_1^2}{n_1-1}$$

and in the denominator we have

$$\chi^2_{n_2-1} = \frac{s_2^2(n_2-1)/\sigma_2^2}{n_2-1}.$$

The ratio of two independent χ^2 distributions defines what is known as the F *distribution* with (n_1-1, n_2-1) d.f. Notice that the degrees of freedom of an F distribution are obtained from the underlying χ^2 distributions. For this reason the n_1-1 is referred to as the *degrees of freedom in the numerator* while the n_2-1 is referred to as the *degrees of freedom in the denominator*. Thus, under H_0, our test statistic is given by

$$TS = \frac{s_1^2}{s_2^2} \text{ has an } F \text{ distribution with } (n_1-1, n_2-1) \text{ d.f.} \qquad [6.36]$$

A typical F distribution is shown in Fig. 6.3. In the present case, since $\sigma_1^2/\sigma_2^2 = 1$ under H_0, this F distribution in centred about unity. As we noted above, we will reject H_0 if s_1^2 and s_2^2 are sufficiently different, that is if TS is either sufficiently greater than unity or sufficiently

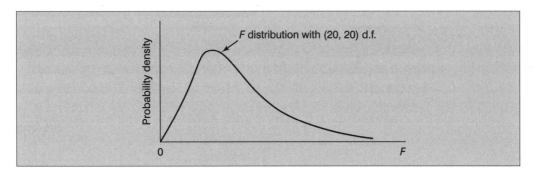

Figure 6.3 The F-distribution with (20, 20) degrees of freedom

smaller than unity. Thus we undertake a two-tail test using Table A.4 in the Appendix, which provides critical F values.

Worked Example

Two independent populations are both normally distributed and it is believed that they have the same variance. Samples, which yield the following information, are available from each population:

$$n_1 = 26 \text{ with } s_1^2 = 8.38, \qquad n_2 = 28 \text{ with } s_2^2 = 13.16.$$

Test the hypothesis that the population variances are indeed equal.

Solution

$$H_0: \sigma_1^2 = \sigma_2^2, \qquad H_A: \sigma_1^2 \neq \sigma_2^2$$

Under H_0, s_1^2/s_2^2 has an F distribution with $(n_1 - 1, n_2 - 1)$ d.f.
Level of significance = 0.05.

To derive a decision criterion, we make use of Table A.4 which gives values for F_α, where α is the probability area to the right of F_α underneath the F-curve. Thus, as illustrated in Fig. 6.4, we require $F_{0.025}$ and $F_{0.975}$, since we have a two-tail test.

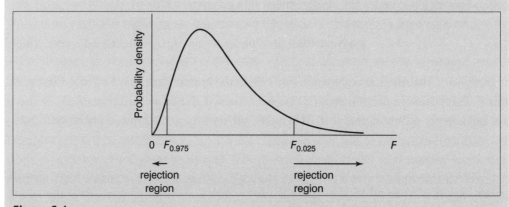

Figure 6.4

The degrees of freedom in this case are $(25, 27)$. Degrees of freedom in the numerator are listed along the top of Table A.4, while degrees of freedom in the denominator are listed down the right-hand side. We can therefore read off, directly, the value $F_{0.025} = 2.18$. Unfortunately, values for $F_{0.975}$ are not given in the table, so we have to make use of a known property of the F distribution.

Although the F curve is not symmetrical, it can be shown that $F_{1-\alpha} = 1/F_{\alpha}$ for any α. That is, the area to the right of F_{α} always equals the area to the left of the value $1/F_{\alpha}$. We have $\alpha = 0.025$, and hence $F_{0.025} = 2.18$. Thus, since $1 - \alpha = 0.975$, we find that

$$F_{0.975} = 1/F_{0.025} = 1/2.18 = 0.46.$$

Thus our decision criterion becomes

reject H_0 either if $TS > 2.18$ or if $TS < 0.46$.

For our data, $TS = s_1^2/s_2^2 = 8.38/13.16 = 0.64$. Thus since $TS > 0.46$, we cannot reject the hypothesis that the population variances are equal.

Example 6.23

Use the data in the worked example of the previous subsection to test for a difference in the variances of the two populations of children.

Tests about two proportions

In Sections 3.3 and 5.3, we considered the sampling distribution for a sample proportion, p. We saw, for a given population proportion π, that provided the sample size n was such that $n\pi$ and $n(1 - \pi)$ both exceeded 5, then p was normally distributed. In fact

$$p \text{ has a } N\left(\pi, \frac{\pi[1 - \pi]}{n}\right) \text{ distribution.} \qquad [6.37]$$

We can use this result to construct a test statistic for testing hypotheses concerning the difference between two population proportions.

As an example, assume we have sample information on the proportion of families with a single parent, for two counties, I and II, and assume further that we wish to test whether the proportion of single-parent families is greater in county I.

Suppose that, in a sample of size $n_1 = 346$ families from county I, 22.3% have a single parent, whereas in county II, in a sample of size $n_2 = 237$ families, the percentage is only 15.1%. That is,

$$n_1 = 346, \quad p_1 = 0.223, \qquad n_2 = 237, \quad p_2 = 0.151, \qquad [6.38]$$

where p_1 and p_2 are the sample proportions.

We let π_1 and π_2 be the *population* proportions for counties I and II, respectively, and formulate null and alternative hypotheses as

$$H_0: \pi_1 = \pi_2, \qquad H_A: \pi_1 > \pi_2.$$

We use [6.37] to find the sampling distributions for p_1 and p_2, the *sample* proportions. This situation is illustrated in Fig. 6.5.

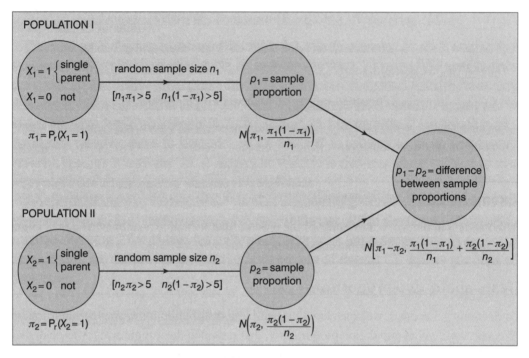

Figure 6.5 The sampling distribution for $p_1 - p_2$

As in the previous subsections, we now visualize the taking of a series of pairs of samples, one from each county. For each such pair of samples we calculate p_1, p_2 and then $p_1 - p_2$, as illustrated in Fig. 6.5. If very many pairs of such samples were taken, then we would obtain a sampling distribution for the quantity $p_1 - p_2$. As usual, however, we do not need to take very many samples. In this case, we can derive the sampling distribution for $p_1 - p_2$ in a similar manner to that used to derive the distribution for $\bar{X}_1 - \bar{X}_2$, earlier in this section. Making use of Theorem 6.2 leads, as demonstrated in Fig. 6.5, to a basic result:

$$\frac{p_1 - p_2 - (\pi_1 - \pi_2)}{\sqrt{\dfrac{\pi_1(1-\pi_1)}{n_1} + \dfrac{\pi_2(1-\pi_2)}{n_2}}} \text{ has a } N(0,1) \text{ distribution.} \qquad [6.39]$$

We can now use the basic result [6.39] to derive an appropriate test statistic. Under $H_0: \pi_1 = \pi_2 = \pi$, where π is the common population proportion, it follows from [6.39] that

$$TS = \frac{p_1 - p_2}{\sqrt{\pi(1-\pi)\left(\dfrac{1}{n_1} + \dfrac{1}{n_2}\right)}} \text{ has a } N(0,1) \text{ distribution.} \qquad [6.40]$$

This is the required test statistic. Notice that it is based on the difference between the *sample* proportions $p_1 - p_2$. If this difference is sufficiently large we shall reject the null hypothesis that the *population* proportions are equal. Since we wish to test whether the proportion of single-parent families in county I is greater than that in county II, we use a one-tail test.

If we adopt a 0.05 level of significance, our decision criterion becomes: reject H_0 if $TS > 1.64$. To compute the test statistic, we need to estimate the common proportion π. Since, under H_0, π_1 and π_2 are identical, the two samples can be pooled and π estimated by p, where p is the overall proportion of single-parent families in the pooled sample. That is, since the *total* number of single-parent families in the *pooled* samples is $n_1 p_1 + n_2 p_2$, we estimate π by

$$p = \frac{n_1 p_1 + n_2 p_2}{n_1 + n_2}. \qquad [6.41]$$

Substituting the data in [6.38] into [6.41] gives

$$p = \frac{346 \times 0.223 + 237 \times 0.151}{346 + 237} = 0.194.$$

Finally, substituting in the test statistic [6.40] yields

$$TS = \frac{0.223 - 0.151}{\sqrt{0.194(1 - 0.194)\left(\dfrac{1}{346} + \dfrac{1}{237}\right)}} = 2.16.$$

Since $2.13 > 1.64$, our decision criterion indicates that we should reject the null hypothesis that $\pi_1 = \pi_2$, at the 0.05 level of significance. Thus we have sufficient evidence to say that the proportion of families that have one parent is greater in county I than in county II.

Example 6.24

A polling organization is asked to determine whether more people oppose increased fuel duties in rural areas than do those in urban areas. Of a sample of 684 rural residents, 488 oppose increased duties and, in a sample of 731 urban residents, 465 feel the same. Test whether there is any difference between rural and urban residents in this regard.

6.5 **Some mixed revision examples**

When dealing with hypothesis testing situations, often the first difficulty is to identify the structure of the problem faced. For example, are we dealing with one or two population parameters? Furthermore, are we dealing with population mean(s) or population proportion(s)?

Only when you have answered these questions is it possible to formulate the correct null hypothesis and conduct the appropriate test. Trying the following examples should help you in this regard.

Example 6.25

Two working designs are being considered for adoption in a factory. A time and motion study showed that eight workers using design A had the following assembly times, in seconds:

300, 320, 290, 310, 280, 305, 295, 300.

A further eight workers, using design B, had the following assembly times, also in seconds:

285, 295, 310, 290, 275, 285, 290, 290.

Prior to the time and motion studies, management believed that design B would result in shorter average assembly times, and now maintains that the studies fully support this belief. Test whether management is correct, stating carefully any assumptions you have made.

Example 6.26

On a proposal of national importance, 38 out of 100 Labour voters are in favour of the proposal but 137 out of 200 Conservative voters are opposed. Using a 0.05 level significance, test whether there is any difference in attitudes between Labour and Conservative voters.

Example 6.27

A sample of 140 brand A light-bulbs show a mean lifetime of 1400 hours, with a standard deviation of 120 hours. A sample of 180 brand B light-bulbs show a mean life time of 1350 hours, with a standard deviation of 105 hours.
(a) Test the hypothesis that the mean lifetime of brand A light bulbs exceeds that of brand B light bulbs.
(b) Find a 95% confidence interval for the difference between the true mean lifetimes of brand A and brand B.
[*Hint*: look at equation [3.17] in Chapter 3.3.]

Example 6.28

In an investigation of unfair trade practice, a random sample of 40 bars of chocolate with a stated weight of 200 grams is examined and found to have a mean of 196.3 g, with a standard deviation of 10.8 g. All previous such investigations had indicated that the bars were of the correct mean weight of 200 g. Test whether the current investigation constitutes evidence of unfair practice. Use a 0.01 level of significance and carefully interpret your answer.

Example 6.29

A random sample of 12 workers from industry A is found to have mean weekly earnings of £484 with a standard deviation of £14. A random sample of 9 workers from industry B, carrying out similar work, is found to have mean weekly earnings of £494, with standard deviation £18. Assume both populations are normally distributed.
(a) Test for a difference in population variances.
(b) Test the hypothesis that mean weekly earnings in industry B exceed mean worker earnings in industry A by £4.
(c) Find a 90% confidence interval for the true difference in mean earnings.

Example 6.30

As the managing director of a small family concern, you have decided to buy a particular new machine only if it has a higher mean output than the old machine you already own. Random samples from each of the two machines result in the following outputs.

Old machine: 28, 39, 26, 35, 42.
New machine: 29, 31, 39, 35, 42, 46.

Test the hypothesis that the outputs of the two machines have a common variance. Use an estimate of this common variance to decide whether or not to buy the new variance. Are any other assumptions necessary?

Summary

- The **joint probability distribution** for X and Y consists of a listing of all the possible combinations of X and Y accompanied by the probabilities associated with all such combinations.

- The probability of X taking a given value, regardless of the value of Y, is known as a **marginal probability**. The distribution of such probabilities is referred to as **the marginal probability distribution** for X.

- For any function of X and Y, $h(X, Y)$, the **expected value of $h(X, Y)$** can be obtained by the summation $\sum h(X, Y)p(X, Y)$, the summation being over all values of X and Y. For example, $E(XY) = \sum XYp(X, Y)$.

■ The **covariance** between two random variables, X and Y, measures the strength of any **linear** association between them. However, a better measure of such strength is the **correlation** between the two variables, since this must always lie between 0 and 1. Both the covariance and the correlation will be zero whenever $E(XY) = E(X)E(Y)$.

■ **Independence** between two random variables is a stronger condition than non-correlation, since it requires not only that $E(XY) = E(X)E(Y)$ but also that joint probabilities should always equal the product of the relevant marginal probabilities.

■ If X and Y are two random variables and a and b are constants, then **Theorem 6.1** enables us to evaluate $\mathbf{E}(aX + bY)$ and **Theorem 6.2** enables us to evaluate $\mathbf{V}(aX + bY)$. Remember the special cases of Theorem 6.2, particularly $V(X - Y) = V(X) + V(Y)$.

■ The concepts of joint probability distributions and the expected values of functions of two variables enable us to develop procedures for testing hypotheses about the **difference between two population means**, the **difference between two population variances** and the **difference between two proportions**.

Appendix 6A

6A.1 **Proof of Theorem 6.1**

If X and Y are two random variables and a and b are any two constants, then

$$
\begin{aligned}
E(aX + bY) &= \sum \sum (aX + bY)p(X, Y) \\
&= \sum \sum aXp(X, Y) + \sum \sum bYp(X, Y) \\
&= a \sum X \sum p(X, Y) + b \sum Y \sum p(X, Y) \\
&= a \sum Xf(X) + b \sum Yg(Y) \\
&= aE(X) + bE(Y). \tag{6A.1}
\end{aligned}
$$

(In [6A.1] we have used the fact that marginal probabilities are always the sums of relevant joint probabilities.)

Special case

If $Y = 1 =$ constant, then $E(Y) = 1$, so that Theorem 6.1 becomes

$$
E(aX + b) = aE(X) + b. \tag{6A.2}
$$

6A.2 **Proof of Theorem 6.2**

If X and Y are two random variables and a and b are two constants, then

$$\begin{aligned}
V(aX + bX) &= E[aX + bY - E(aX + bY)]^2 \\
&= E[aX - aE(X) + bY - bE(Y)]^2 \\
&= E\{a^2[X - E(X)]^2 + b^2[Y - E(Y)]^2 \\
&\quad + 2ab[X - E(X)][Y - E(Y)]\} \\
&= a^2 E[X - E(X)]^2 + b^2 E[Y - E(Y)]^2 \\
&\quad + 2ab E[X - E(X)][Y - E(Y)] \\
&= a^2 V(X) + b^2 V(Y) + 2ab \, \text{Cov}(X, Y). \quad\quad [6A.3]
\end{aligned}$$

(In the proof of Theorem 6.2, we have repeatedly made use of Theorem 6.1 and its special case.)

Notes

1. Unlike the die in the worked example of Section 1.1, this die has the numbers 1, 2, 3, 4 inscribed on its faces.

2. Using definition [6.3], $E[X - E(X)][Y - E(Y)] = E[XY - XE(Y) - YE(X) + E(X)E(Y)]$. Remembering that $E(X)$ and $E(Y)$ are constants and applying the expectations operator to each term on the right-hand side of the above gives

$$\begin{aligned}
\text{Cov}(X, Y) &= E(XY) - E[XE(Y)] - E[YE(X)] + E[E(X)E(Y)] \\
&= E(XY) - E(Y)E(X) - E(X)E(Y) + E(X)E(Y) \\
&= E(XY) - E(X)E(Y),
\end{aligned}$$

where we have made use of result [6A.2] in Appendix 6A.

3. Using [6A.2] in Appendix 6A.

4. Notice that the sample variances [6.17] have the sample size n in their denominators. If we had wished to use them to estimate the population variances, we would have had to replace the ns by $(n - 1)$s.

5. This is always assuming that the sample variances have been calculated with $n - 1$ in the denominator.

6. Weighted means are described in the prerequisites section. In this case, the weights attached to s_1^2 and s_2^2 are $(n_1 - 1)/(n_1 + n_2 - 2)$ and $(n_2 - 1)/(n_1 + n_2 - 2)$, respectively. As required, these weights sum to unity.

7

Chi-squared tests and nonparametric statistics

Objectives

After completion of your study of this chapter you should be able:

1. to appreciate the usefulness of nonparametric statistics in cases where the usual small-sample tests are not valid;

2. to construct contingency tables and use the χ^2 distribution to test hypotheses concerning independence and homogeneity;

3. to use the χ^2 distribution to test the 'goodness of fit' of sample data with appropriate theoretical distributions;

4. to use various nonparametric statistics to test hypotheses about population means when samples are small and the usual assumptions about populations are invalid;

5. to test for randomness in sequential event data;

6. to appreciate the strengths and weaknesses of nonparametric tests.

Introduction

In previous chapters we have considered a series of situations in which we carried out hypothesis tests regarding various population parameters. However, in many small-sample tests, it is necessary that relevant population distributions should be of known form if standard test statistics are to be appropriate. For example, the small-sample t-test for a single population mean requires that the population be normally distributed. In this chapter we deal, mainly, with statistical inference for cases in which hypotheses do not involve any population parameter(s) and/or situations where we have no knowledge of the underlying population distribution(s). The methods described are usually called nonparametric methods.[1]

The advantage of using nonparametric tests is that they depend on a minimum number of underlying assumptions and, hence, can be regarded as valid in a wide range of situations. Such methods are also often appropriate for circumstances where we have to deal with frequency or count data – that is, instead of using variables such as the income of a household, we have to use variables such as the number of households in a given income range.

7.1 A nonparametric χ^2 test for independence

A very useful application of the χ^2 distribution occurs in connection with what are called *contingency tables*. Such tables involve the two-way classification of a data set. An example is given in Table 7.1, where a random sample of 800 individuals are classified both by income range and how many years they spent in full-time education.

Table 7.1 A two-way classification

Education (years)	Income range (£'000)		
	5–10	**10–20**	**20–80**
8–10	56	46	35
11–13	134	145	126
14–18	81	85	92

Clearly the information in Table 7.1 is an example of count data. For example, we have 253 individuals out of 800 with an income in the range £20 000 to £80 000.[2]

Suppose we wish to test whether an individual's income Y is influenced by duration of full-time education E, using the information in Table 7.1. Casual observation of the data suggests that income may well be higher for better-educated individuals. For example, a slightly larger proportion of the better educated, and a slightly smaller proportion of the poorly educated, have high incomes. But this finding could be purely the result of chance, and we need to test more rigorously whether or not Y and E are indeed linked. We shall therefore adopt a nonparametric test to deal with this set of count data.

We formulate the null hypothesis

H_0: Y is independent of E.

The alternative hypothesis in this case is simply that the two classifications are not independent. The test we now devise is a nonparametric test, since H_0 involves no population parameters.

The idea behind the following test is, first, that we compute the number of individuals we would expect to find, *if H_0 were to be true*, in each of the nine *cells* in the contingency Table 7.1. We then compare the *observed* frequencies in the cells (that is, those in Table 7.1) with the *expected* frequencies we have just computed. If the expected frequencies are 'sufficiently different' from the observed frequencies, then we reject H_0 and conclude that Y is not independent of E.

As an example, the cell in the top left-hand corner of Table 7.1 has an observed frequency of 56 individuals with income £5000–£10 000 and 8–10 years in full-time education. To find the expected frequency in this cell, we proceed as follows.

Provided H_0 is true, it must be the case that

$$\Pr(Y = 5000\text{--}10\,000 \,|\, E = 8\text{--}10)$$
$$= \Pr(Y = 5000\text{--}10\,000 \,|\, E = 11\text{--}13)$$
$$= \Pr(Y = 5000\text{--}10\,000 \,|\, E = 14\text{--}18).$$

These three probabilities must all be the same, since Y is independent of E. We can estimate this common probability by 271/800, the proportion of all individuals in the sample that have an income of £5000–£10 000. That is, we lump together all individuals who have an income in this range, regardless of their education, and estimate $\Pr(Y = 5000\text{--}10\,000)$ by 271/800.

Next, whether H_0 is true or not, we can estimate $\Pr(E = 8\text{--}10)$ by the proportion, 137/800, of all individuals in the sample who have 8–10 years of full-time education. Given the null hypothesis of independence, we now use the rule [P.22] to find the probability of getting an individual who has *both* an income of £5000–£10 000 *and* 8–10 years in full-time education

$$\Pr(Y = 5000\text{–}10\ 000 \text{ and } E = 8\text{–}10)$$
$$\Pr(Y = 5000\text{–}10\ 000 \mid E = 8\text{–}10) \times \Pr(E = 8 - 10)$$
$$= \frac{271}{800} \times \frac{137}{800}.$$

Finally, we can interpret this joint probability as an estimate of the *proportion* of individuals in the sample who have both an income Y of £5000–£10 000 and years in full time education E of 8–10. Since the total sample size is 800, to find the expected *number* of individuals in this cell, we therefore need to multiply the 800 by the joint probability or proportion found above. That is, we expect the number of individuals in this cell to be

$$800 \times \frac{271}{800} \times \frac{137}{800} = \frac{271 \times 137}{800} = 46.4. \tag{7.1}$$

Thus, although the observed number in the top left-hand cell, that is the cell $(Y = 5000\text{–}10\ 000, E = 8\text{–}10)$, is 56, if the null hypothesis were true we would expect to find, on average, 46.4 individuals in such a cell. The *expected frequency* 46.4 has been inserted (in parentheses) after the *observed frequency* 56 in the top left-hand cell in the redrawn contingency Table 7.2.

Table 7.2 Inserting the expected frequencies

		Income range (£'000)			
		5–10	**10–20**	**20–80**	
	8–10	56 (46.4)	46 (47.3)	35 (43.3)	137
Education (years)	**10–13**	134 (137.2)	145 (139.7)	126 (128.1)	405
	14–18	81 (87.4)	85 (89.0)	92 (81.6)	258
		271	276	253	800

Obviously, a fairly long chain of argument was needed to find the above expected frequency of 46.4. Fortunately, it is possible to find such expected frequencies by using a fairly rapid short-cut method. Notice that the expected frequency [7.1] is simply given by

$$\frac{271 \times 137}{800} = \frac{(\text{column total } 271)(\text{row total } 137)}{\text{sample size } 800},$$

where the column and row totals refer to the row and column in which the cell

$(Y = 5000\text{--}10\,000, E = 8\text{--}10)$ is to be found. In fact, it is always possible to find the expected frequencies in a contingency table by this method. That is,

$$\text{expected frequency} = \frac{\text{column total} \times \text{row total}}{\text{sample size}}. \qquad [7.2]$$

For example, the observed frequency of individuals in the cell $(Y = 10\,000\text{--}20\,000, E = 14\text{--}18)$ is 85 but the expected frequency for this cell is $(276 \times 258)/800 = 89.0$, where 276 and 258 are the relevant column and row totals.

All the expected frequencies have been inserted in parentheses after the observed frequencies in Table 7.2. Notice that summing the rows and columns of the expected frequencies yields the same row and column totals that were obtained by summing the observed frequencies. Thus, this is a useful method of checking arithmetic when computing the expected frequencies.

It is clear that there are some obvious differences between the observed and expected frequencies. Recall that we intend to reject the null hypothesis of independence if the difference between the observed frequencies and what we expect, under H_0, is sufficiently great. What we now require is some *overall* measure of the differences between the two arrays of frequencies and some way of judging what we mean by 'sufficiently great'.

Firstly, we derive an appropriate overall measure. Letting o_i and e_i represent the observed and expected frequencies for the ith cell, an obvious overall measure of the differences might seem to be $\Sigma(o_i - e_i)$, where the summation is over all cells. Unfortunately, since both the observed and the expected frequencies sum to their respective row and column totals, $\Sigma(o_i - e_i)$ is always identically equal to zero, with some of the $o_i - e_i$ terms negative and the others positive. Thus $\Sigma(o_i - e_i)$ is not a useful measure. A better measure of the overall difference between the o_i and e_i is $\Sigma(o_i - e_i)^2$, all the terms now becoming positive. One further adjustment to the measure has to be made; each of the differences $o_i - e_i$ is 'deflated' by the relevant expected frequency e_i. That is, we compute

$$\sum \frac{(o_i - e_i)^2}{e_i}. \qquad [7.3]$$

Deflation by e_i ensures that we consider *relative* differences between the o_i and e_i rather than *absolute* differences.[3]

It is possible to show that, under the null hypothesis of independence between the two classifications, the quantity [7.3] can be approximated by a χ^2 distribution. Hence, we can use [7.3] as a test statistic. Since we reject H_0 if the differences between observed and expected frequencies are sufficiently *large*, we employ an upper-tail χ^2 test, as illustrated in Fig. 7.1.

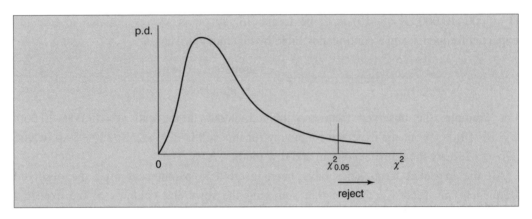

Figure 7.1 χ^2 test for independence

The degrees of freedom associated with this χ^2 distribution depend on the number of columns c and rows r in the table, (excluding both the total column and row). In fact, it can be shown that the relevant degrees of freedom are given by $(c - 1)(r - 1)$.[4] Summarizing, we can say that,

> under H_0 the above statistic has an approximate χ^2 distribution with $(c - 1)(r - 1)$ degrees of freedom and hence may be used as a test statistic.

This is the χ^2 *test for independence*.[5]

For the current example we have $c = 3$ and $r = 3$ so that the degrees of freedom for this χ^2 distribution are $2 \times 2 = 4$. Consequently, if we wish to test H_0 at the 0.05 level of significance, then, using Table A.3 in the Appendix, our decision criterion becomes:

> reject H_0 if $TS > \chi^2_{0.05} = 9.488$.

Finally, we compute the test statistic. The $(o_i - e_i)^2/e_i$ terms for the cells are given in Table 7.3, all given to one decimal place. The sum of all the nine terms gives a value for the test statistic [7.3] of 5.9 so that, since $TS < 9.488$, we are unable to reject the null hypothesis of independence. There is, therefore, insufficient evidence to say that income and years in full-time education are linked.

Table 7.3 Calculating the test statistic

		Income range (£'000)		
		5–10	**10–20**	**20–80**
	8–10	2.0	0.0	1.6
Education (years)	**11–13**	0.1	0.2	0.0
	14–18	0.5	0.2	1.3

Example 7.1

In a survey to determine whether attitudes to the euro are affected by party political allegiance, a random sample of 600 voters is taken with the following results.

	Conservative	Labour	Lib Dem
In favour	56	72	38
Against	143	95	52
Unsure	38	75	31

What would you conclude?

Example 7.2

A sample survey, designed to determine whether there is a link between annual income levels and shopping habits, provided the following information.

		Store used			
		A	B	C	D
	10–20	238	25	113	116
Income £'000	20–40	186	148	155	126
	40–60	71	249	108	96

Test whether there is any link between income level and shopping habits. [*Hint:* you do not need to compute all the $(o_i - e_i)^2/e_i$ terms.]

7.2 Some further chi-squared tests

The χ^2 test for homogeneity

The χ^2 test of this subsection is closely related to the χ^2 test for independence. Consider a situation in which a contingency table such as Table 7.1 is constructed, not by taking a single random sample of n individuals from the whole population, but by first identifying three separate subpopulations, those individuals with 8–10 years of full-time education, those with 11–13 years and those with 14–18 years. Suppose we wished to test whether incomes were distributed identically for all three subpopulations, regardless of years of full-time education. That is, we want to test whether the whole population is *homogeneous* with respect to income distribution. Suppose, further, that random samples of sizes n_1, n_2 and n_3 individuals were taken from the respective subpopulations. If all individuals selected were allocated to one or other of the three income ranges £5000–£10 000, £10 000–£20 000, £20 000–£80 000, a contingency table similar to Table 7.1 could be constructed.

Let π_{ij} be the proportion of the ith subpopulation that is in income range j. If the three populations are identical with regard to income distribution, this must imply that the proportions of each subpopulation ($i = 1, 2, 3$) that are in a given income range j must be the same. Hence, for income range £5000–£10 000, that is, if $j = 1$, we have

$$\pi_{11} = \pi_{21} = \pi_{31}. \tag{7.4}$$

Similarly, for the income ranges £10 000–£20 000 and £20 000–£80 000, that is for $j = 2$ and $j = 3$, we have

$$\pi_{12} = \pi_{22} = \pi_{32} \tag{7.5}$$

and

$$\pi_{13} = \pi_{23} = \pi_{33}. \tag{7.6}$$

Recapping, if a null hypothesis that the subpopulations are homogeneous with respect to income distribution is to be valid, then we require [7.4], [7.5] and [7.6] all to be true.

As with the test for independence, to test for homogeneity we deduce what numbers we would expect to find in the cells of a contingency table, such as Table 7.1, if this hypothesis were to be true. We then compare these expected values with the actual values in the table and, if the differences are sufficiently large, the hypothesis of homogeneity is rejected.

It turns out that the expected frequencies in this test can be found in exactly the same way as in the test for independence in the previous section. That is, we can use [7.2].[6] Moreover, we can still use [7.3] as our overall measure of the difference between observed and expected frequencies and it can be shown that, under the null hypothesis of homogeneity, [7.3] is again distributed as a χ^2 distribution with the same number of degrees of freedom, $(c - 1)(r - 1)$. It can, therefore, also be used as the test statistic for homogeneity.

If it were the case that the three samples from the three subpopulations were of sizes $n_1 = 137$, $n_2 = 405$ and $n_3 = 258$ respectively, it should be clear that we could obtain an identical contingency table to Table 7.2. It follows that, if we wish to test for homogeneity using the data in this table, then we would obtain a test statistic of 5.9 as we did for the test for independence. Since we must again use an upper-tail test, the decision criterion will be identical to that in the last subsection and, again, we will fail to reject the null hypothesis since $5.9 < \chi^2_{0.05} = 9.488$. The difference is that now we will be testing the hypothesis of homogeneity rather than that of independence.

The arithmetic involved in the χ^2 tests for independence and homogeneity is clearly identical but there are subtle differences in the two procedures. Firstly, the homogeneity test has a null hypothesis given by equations [7.4], [7.5] and [7.6] which involve nine population *parameters*, the various population proportions. Thus the homogeneity test is not, strictly, a nonparametric test. Secondly, the sampling procedure in the two tests is rather different. In the independence test a single sample size $n = 800$ was taken from the whole population. But in the homogeneity test, three separate samples of sizes n_1, n_2 and n_3 are taken from each of the three subpopulations defined above. In our example it just happened that $n_1 = 137$, $n_2 = 405$ and $n_3 = 258$, so that $n_1 + n_2 + n_3 = 800$ and we could obtain the same contingency Table 7.1.[7]

Example 7.3

Random samples of size 250 are taken from the employees of four firms. The numbers of workers asked to work part-time or full-time last month were as follows.

	Firm A	Firm B	Firm C	Firm D
Working part-time	65	71	68	59
Working full-time	185	179	182	191

Test whether the incidence of part-time working varies between the firms.

Worked Example

During an epidemic, a new drug is used to test whether it gives protection from disease. A group of 500 individuals are treated with the drug, while a further group of 500 are observed but not treated with the drug. Of the 1000 individuals, 280 in all catch the disease. Of the 500 who are treated with the drug, only 125 get the disease.

(a) Construct the appropriate contingency table and use the χ^2 distribution to test whether there is any difference between the proportions of the treated and untreated groups who catch the disease.

(b) How would you test the hypothesis that the proportion of the treated group who catch the disease is less than the proportion of the untreated group who catch it?

Solution

(a) The required contingency table can be partly filled used the information in the question.

	Diseased	Not diseased	
Treated individuals	125		500
Untreated individuals			500
	280		

Since all rows and columns in the table must sum to their respective totals, the completed contingency table must, therefore, be

	Diseased	Not diseased	
Treated individuals	125	375	500
Untreated individuals	155	345	500
	280	720	1000

The null hypothesis required in (a) is that of homogeneity over the two populations of treated and untreated individuals. That is, the proportion of treated individuals, π_1, who get the disease must equal the proportion of untreated individuals, π_2, who do. Thus

$$H_0: \pi_1 = \pi_2.$$

In the χ^2 test for homogeneity, the alternative hypothesis is that of non-homogeneity, which implies that the two populations are different with regard to the proportion of individuals who get the disease:

$$H_A: \pi_1 \neq \pi_2.$$

We can now obtain expected frequencies e_i in the usual way, using [7.2]. This yields the following table:

	Diseased	Not diseased	
Treated individuals	125 (140)	375 (360)	500
Untreated individuals	155 (140)	345 (360)	500
	280	720	1000

Our level of significance is 0.01. Since we have $(c - 1)(r - 1) = 1$ degree of freedom, we reject H_0 if the test statistic [7.3] exceeds $\chi^2_{0.01} = 6.635$, as shown in Fig. 7.2.

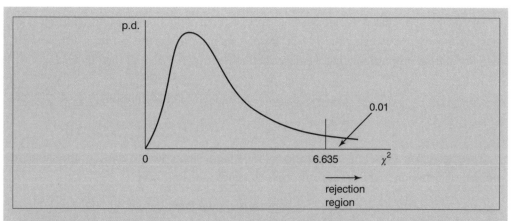

Figure 7.2

For the given contingency table,

$$TS = \frac{(125-140)^2}{140} + \frac{(375-360)^2}{360} + \frac{(155-140)^2}{140} + \frac{(345-360)^2}{360}$$
$$= 4.464$$

Thus, since $4.464 < 6.635$, we are unable to reject H_0 at the 0.01 level of significance. That is, there is insufficient evidence to suggest that there is a difference between the two groups.

(Students are frequently confused by this test. The alternative hypothesis is $\pi_1 \neq \pi_2$ (i.e., it contains the 'not equal' sign), yet Fig. 7.2 indicates that we have performed a one-tail test! But recall that the test statistic [7.3] involves only squared terms and hence must always be positive. The idea of the test is that we reject H_0 if the difference between the observed and expected frequencies is sufficiently large, that is, if [7.3] is sufficiently positive. Hence, we use the upper tail of the χ^2 distribution, which lies to the right of the vertical axis.)

(b) A problem with the above χ^2 test is that it tests only for a *difference* between the treated and untreated groups of individuals. It is, therefore, conceivable that a situation could arise where the treated group actually has a larger proportion of individuals contracting the disease, leading to a rejection of H_0. If we wish to test whether the treatment succeeds in reducing the *proportion* of individuals who get the disease, then we need to test the hypotheses

$$H_0: \pi_1 = \pi_2, \qquad H_A: \pi_1 < \pi_2.$$

The problem is that it is not possible to test for a reduction in the proportion contracting the disease by using the χ^2 test. Instead we have to use the test for a difference in two population proportions that we described in Section 6.4. Recall that, under H_0,

$$TS = \frac{p_1 - p_2}{\sqrt{\pi(1-\pi)\left(\dfrac{1}{n_1} + \dfrac{1}{n_2}\right)}} \text{ has an } N(0,1) \text{ distribution.} \qquad [6.38]$$

If we again use a level of significance of 0.01 then, using the lower tail of the standard normal distribution, our decision criterion becomes (see Fig. 7.3)

reject H_0 if $TS < -2.33$, but reserve judgement if $TS > -2.33$.

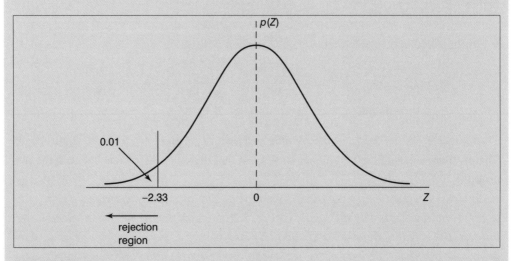

Figure 7.3

The sample sizes are $n_1 = 500$ and $n_2 = 500$. The sample proportions are $p_1 = 125/500 = 0.25$ for the treated group and $p_2 = 155/500 = 0.31$ for the untreated group. The common proportion, π, is estimated by $(125 + 155)/1000 = 0.28$. Substituting in [6.38] then gives

$$TS = \frac{0.25 - 0.31}{\sqrt{0.28 \times 0.72\left(\dfrac{1}{500} + \dfrac{1}{500}\right)}} = -2.113.$$

Since $-2.113 > -2.33$, we are unable to reject H_0 at the 0.01 level of significance. There is insufficient evidence to say that the treatment reduces the proportion of individuals who contract the disease.

(*Not surprisingly, the tests in (a) and (b) are closely linked. Recall, from the previous chapter, that the sum of the squares of n independent Z variables has a χ^2 distribution with n degrees of freedom. Thus, the square of a single Z variable must have a χ^2 distribution with just one degree of freedom. Consequently, the square of the test statistic in (b) above should equal the value of the test statistic in (a). If you check back, you will see that this is indeed the case, because $(-2.113)^2 = 4.464$, allowing for slight rounding error. In fact if, in part (b), we had adopted $H_A: \pi_1 \neq \pi_2$ as in part (a) and, hence, used a two-tail text, our decision criterion would have been 'reject H_0 if $|TS| > 2.58$'. Now, not only are the two test statistics linked by $\chi^2 = Z^2$, but it is also the case that the critical values obey the relationship $\chi^2_{0.01} = Z^2_{0.005}$, since $6.635 = 2.58^2$, again allowing for slight rounding error. Hence, since the alternative hypotheses are the same in each case, the two tests will always give the same result. Which is as it should be!*)*

Example 7.4

A study is set up to analyse the newspaper reading habits of different social classes. Separate random samples of 'working-class' households, 'middle-class' households and 'upper-class' households are taken and their newspaper purchases analysed with the following results.

	Purchases	Tabloid	Broadsheet	Both
	Working	148	32	20
Class	**Middle**	105	73	22
	Upper	5	61	14

(a) Test whether reading habits differ between the social classes.

(b) Test whether the proportion of middle-class households who purchase a broadsheet exceeds the proportion of working-class households who purchase such a newspaper.

The χ^2 test for goodness of fit

Often there are other situations in statistical work where we wish to test the compatibility between sets of observed and expected frequencies, using the χ^2 statistic of the previous subsections. For example, suppose a six-sided die is rolled $n = 900$ times and we obtain the observed frequency distribution of Table 7.4. Suppose, further, on the basis of these results, we wished to test whether the die is fair or not.

Table 7.4 A goodness of fit test

Number obtained	1	2	3	4	5	6
Observed freq o_i	128	145	132	172	159	164
Expected freq e_i	150	150	150	150	150	150
$(o_i - e_i)^2/e_i$	3.23	0.17	2.16	3.23	0.54	1.31

The null hypothesis of fairness implies

$$H_0: \pi_1 = \pi_2 = \pi_3 = \pi_4 = \pi_5 = \pi_6 = \tfrac{1}{6}.$$

where π_i is the probability of rolling the number i.

Under H_0, it is easy to compute the expected frequencies for all numbers after 900 rolls of the die. We expect each number to occur $900/6 = 150$ times. These frequencies are also shown in Table 7.4.

It can be shown that, under H_0,

> as n becomes very large, the quantity [7.3] approaches a χ^2 distribution with $k-1$ degrees of freedom, where k is the number of possible outcomes to the relevant experiment.

Since $n = 900$, we can use this result with $k = 6$ in this case. Thus, under H_0, $TS = \Sigma(o_i - e_i)^2/e_i$ has an approximate χ^2 distribution with $k - 1 = 5$ d.f. and can hence be used as a test statistic.[8]

We reject the null hypothesis of a fair die if the difference between the frequencies observed and those expected, under H_0, is sufficiently large. Thus, using a 0.05 level of significance, the decision criterion in this case is to reject H_0 if $TS > \chi^2_{0.05} = 11.07$.

Using the data in Table 7.4, the terms in the test statistic are given in the third row. Their sum gives $TS = 10.64$, which is less than 11.07, so we cannot reject H_0 at the 0.05 level of significance. Consequently, the die cannot be said to be unfair.

The above test is known as the χ^2 *goodness-of-fit test*. Since it involves the six population π parameters it is again, strictly speaking, not a nonparametric test.

In the previous example, the expected frequencies were known because the cell probabilities were assumed known (all $\tfrac{1}{6}$). It is often the case, however, that the cell probabilities depend on one or more population parameters. Fortunately, the χ^2 distribution can still be used in such situations, provided that one further degree of freedom is deducted for *each* parameter that has to be estimated from sample data.

Worked Example

The number of new cases per day, X, in a flu epidemic has the frequency distribution shown in the first two columns of Table 7.5. Assuming that new cases follow a Poisson distribution, estimate the mean number of cases a day. Test whether the Poisson distribution provides a good 'fit' to the above data.

Table 7.5

No. of new cases	Obs. freq o_i	Exp prob $p(X_i)$	exp freq e_i	$\dfrac{(o_i - e_i)^2}{e_i}$
0	17	0.0517	22.4	1.30
1	54	0.1532	66.3	2.28
2	103	0.2269	98.2	0.23
3	108	0.2241	97.0	1.25
4	86	0.1660	71.9	2.77
5	43	0.0984	42.6	0.00
6	17	0.0486	21.0	0.76
7	2	0.0206	8.9	5.35
8	3	0.0076	3.3	0.03
9	0	0.0025	1.1	1.10
10	0	0.0007	0.3	0.30
⋮	⋮	⋮	⋮	⋮

Solution

The mean of the Poisson distribution can be estimated by $\lambda = \sum X_i(o_i/n)$, where $n = 433$ is the total number of days. Thus, we obtain a mean of $\hat{\lambda} = 2.963$ cases per day. We can now estimate the probabilities in the Poisson distribution using the usual formula, given in Chapter 1.7, $p(X) = \lambda^X e^{-\lambda}/X! = 2.963^X e^{-2.963}/X!$. This yields the third column in Table 7.5. The expected frequencies e_i can then be obtained by multiplying the expected probabilities by 433 to get the fourth column in Table 7.5.

The statistic [7.3] has a χ^2 distribution under the null hypothesis of a Poisson distribution. There are nine frequencies that have to be estimated in Table 7.5, but we lose one degree of freedom since the frequencies must sum to 433, and one further degree of freedom because we had to replace one population parameter λ by its sample estimate $\hat{\lambda} = 2.963$. Thus we have just seven degrees of freedom, so we reject the Poisson distribution, at the 0.05 level of significance, if the test statistic exceeds $\chi^2_{0.05} = 14.067$. The terms in [7.3] are given in the final column in Table 7.5 and their sum eventually gives a value for the test statistic of 15.4. Hence, at the 0.05 level of significance, we reject the hypothesis that new cases follow a Poisson distribution.

Example 7.5

The number of girls X in families with six children is found to have the following distribution.

No. of girls	0	1	2	3	4	5	6
Frequency	4	21	48	64	44	17	2

(a) Assuming that Pr(child is a girl) = 0.5, check whether the distribution is the result of a binomial process.
(b) Use the frequencies to estimate Pr(child is a girl) and then recheck whether the distribution is the result of a binomial process.

Example 7.6

An invoice clerk makes X errors per week with a frequency distribution observed to be as follows:

X	0	1	2	3	4	5	6
Frequency	6	13	12	11	8	2	0

Estimate the mean number of errors per week and check whether the frequencies can be approximated by a Poisson process. Use a 0.05 level of significance.

7.3 The sign test

The small-sample tests concerning population means, which we studied in previous chapters, were based on the assumption that we were sampling from normally distributed populations. Indeed, when testing for the difference between two means, we needed the additional assumption that the two populations should have the same variance. One way to overcome the problem of such requirements is to take large samples and then rely on the central limit theorem. But it is often the case that the only samples that are available happen to be small and, in such cases, we have to rely on nonparametric statistics.

One of the simplest nonparametric tests is the *sign test*, which can be used for testing hypotheses concerning a single population mean. Suppose that we wish to test whether the mean income μ of single mothers, under 25 years of age, is greater than £200 per week, but have available a sample of 'only' 18 such mothers.

If it is possible to assume that we are dealing with a symmetric population distribution then, provided H_0: $\mu = 200$ is valid, the probability of obtaining an income less than £200 must equal the probability of finding an income greater than £200. Obviously, both probabilities must equal 0.5. The test proceeds by replacing each sample observation by a plus sign when an income is above £200 and by a minus sign when an income is less than £200. For example, if our sample is as follows, then the plus and minus signs will be as illustrated:

197	206	212	189	206	212	190	199	225
–	+	+	–	+	+	–	–	+
204	213	187	206	221	205	203	200	195
+	+	–	+	+	+	+		–

Notice that, since the seventeenth observation is exactly equal to £200, this observation has no sign and has to be removed from the sample, leaving just $n = 17$ observations. Under H_0: $\mu = 200$, the number of plus signs must have a binomial distribution with parameter $\pi = 0.5$. On the other hand, if $\mu > 200$, then we expect $\pi > 0.5$, that is, the proportion of observations with plus signs should exceed 0.5.[9]

Our sample yields 11 plus signs out of 17, that is, a sample proportion of $p = 11/17$. Hence, since np is 11 and $n(1 - p)$ is 6, we can use the normal approximation to the binomial distribution.

If X is the number of pluses obtained, then under H_0: $\mu = 200$ (implying $\pi = 0.5$), the mean and variance of X must be $n\pi = 8.5$ and $n\pi(1 - \pi) = 4.25$, respectively. The standard deviation of X is therefore 2.06. Hence, under H_0,

$$Z = \frac{X - 8.5}{2.06} \text{ has a N}(0, 1) \text{ distribution.} \qquad [7.7]$$

Thus, we can use [7.7] as a test statistic, rejecting H_0 at the 0.05 level of significance if the test statistic exceeds 1.64. We use a one-tail test since we wish to test whether incomes exceed £200. Since our sample has $X = 11$ pluses, the test statistic [7.8] takes the value $(11 - 8.5)/2.06 = 1.21$. Thus, since $1.21 < 1.64$, we cannot reject H_0 at the 0.05 level of significance. That is, we have insufficient evidence to suggest that mean incomes exceed £200.

Example 7.7

Fifteen visitors to a theme park spend the following amounts (in pounds).

22, 15, 12, 35, 8, 12, 28, 31, 13, 12, 24, 10, 33, 22, 30.

Use the sign test to test the hypothesis that, on average, visitors spend less than £25 on a visit.

Retest this hypothesis using the small-sample t-test and comment.

7.4 The median test

This test may be applied when testing for a difference between two means (or medians), under circumstances in which the two populations are not normally distributed and/or do not have a common variance. In such a situation, if the samples are small, then the usual t-test cannot be applied.

Suppose we wish to ascertain whether 18-year-old leavers from a well-known public school, Harroweton, have an initial earned income different from similar leavers from a local high school, Bogstan. Two random samples are taken. From Harroweton $n_1 = 9$ school leavers have monthly initial incomes (in pounds) of

1610, 1770, 1440, 1920, 1680, 2150, 1770, 2010, 1830.

From Bogstan, $n_2 = 7$ leavers have monthly initial incomes (again in pounds) of

1480, 1370, 1580, 1670, 1360, 2010, 1550.

To perform the so-called *median test*, the two samples from the schools are, first, combined into one single sample. Then, we divide all leavers into those for whom initial income is above the median income of the combined sample and those for whom initial income is below. If we list the combined sample in order of ascending order, we obtain

£1360, £1370, £1440, £1480, £1550, £1580, £1610, £1670, £1680,
£1770, £1770, £1830, £1920, £2010, £2010, £2150.

The two 'middle numbers' in the combined sample are, therefore, £1670 and £1680, so that the median is £1675. If X is the number of incomes in the *first* sample that fall below the median of the combined sample, then, provided $n_1 + n_2$ is an even number, we can construct the 'contingency table' shown in Table 7.6a, where $k = (n_1 + n_2)/2$ is the number of observations both below and above the median. [10]

Table 7.6a is a 2×2 table, in which both the column and row totals are fixed, being determined by the two sample sizes. For our two-school example we obtain Table 7.6b.

Table 7.6 The median test contingency table

(a)

	Population 1	Population 2	
Below median	X	$k - X$	k
Above median	$n_1 - X$	$n_2 - k + X$	k
	n_1	n_2	

(b)

	Harroweton	Bogstan	
Below median	2 (4.5)	6 (3.5)	8
Above median	7 (4.5)	1 (3.5)	8
	9	7	16

Under the null hypothesis that the two schools have the same mean initial incomes, we can obtain expected frequencies for the four cells in Table 7.6b in the normal manner, utilizing [7.2]. The expected frequencies are shown in parentheses in Table 7.6b in the usual way.

Under the null hypothesis, the χ^2 statistic [7.3] has just $(2 - 1)(2 - 1) = 1$ degree of freedom, so we reject the null hypothesis if $TS > \chi^2_{0.05} = 3.841$.

Substituting in [7.3] yields a value for the test statistic of

$$TS = \frac{(2 - 4.5)^2}{4.5} + \frac{(6 - 3.5)^2}{3.5} + \frac{(7 - 4.5)^2}{4.5} + \frac{(1 - 3.5)^2}{3.5} = 6.35.$$

Thus we can reject, at the 0.05 level of significance, the hypothesis that leavers from the two schools have equal initial incomes.

Example 7.8

The average yields of two varieties of wheat are to be compared. Samples from the two varieties gave the following results:

Variety 1: 93 89 91 87 90 94 89 78 92 84 88 101 98.
Variety 2: 102 97 94 101 92 97 104 88 95.

Use the median test to determine whether there is sufficient evidence to suggest that variety 1 gives different yields from variety 2.

Use the small sample t-test to re-examine whether variety 1 results in different yields. Comment on your results.

Example 7.9

Ten students, who have studied economics at A level, obtain the following marks in a first-year university examination:

$$64, 34, 56, 34, 46, 61, 57, 48, 61, 51.$$

Nine students without A level obtain the marks

$$39, 44, 60, 54, 38, 54, 55, 36, 47.$$

Use the median test to determine whether average marks differ between the two groups of students.

7.5 The Mann–Whitney rank-sum test

In this section we describe a further nonparametric statistic that can be used to test whether two populations have the same mean and/or the same variance.

Suppose 11 automobile salesmen receive the following bonus payments (in pounds):

$$2140, 2500, 2280, 3520, 2710, 2610, 2840, 2330, 2380, 3140, 2650.$$

Similarly, nine vacuum cleaner salesmen receive bonuses of:

$$2130, 2530, 2630, 2880, 2270, 2230, 2400, 2510, 2160.$$

The mean bonus of auto salesmen, £2645, exceeds the mean bonus of cleaner salesmen, £2416, but we wish to know whether this difference is statistically significant. Unfortunately, study of the data suggests that the variances of the two populations may well be unequal, so we cannot use the normal t-test, but will apply the *Mann–Whitney* test.

Firstly, we jointly rank, in ascending order, the 20 bonuses of the combined sample. This yields:

2130	2140	2160	2230	2270	2280	2330	2380	2400	2500	2510
V	A	V	V	V	A	A	A	V	A	V

2530	2610	2630	2650	2710	2840	2880	3140	3520
V	A	V	A	A	A	V	A	A

where the letters beneath each bonus denote whether a salesman sells automobiles (A) or vacuum cleaners (V). The auto salesmen have ranks 2, 6, 7, 8, 10, 13, 15, 16, 17, 19, 20, in the pooled sample, whereas the cleaner salesmen have ranks 1, 3, 4, 5, 9, 11, 12, 14, 18.

Under the null hypothesis H_0, that the population means are the same, we would expect the average ranks of the two samples to be roughly the same. However, if the two population means were different, then we would expect one sample to have more of the low ranks and the other sample to have more of the high ranks. In the Mann–Whitney test, we use *rank sums* rather than average ranks, and base our decision on the statistic

$$U = n_1 n_2 + \frac{n_1(n_2 + 1)}{2} - R, \tag{7.8}$$

where n_1 and n_2 are the two sample sizes and R is the sum of the ranks in one of the samples. (It is immaterial which sample is used to work out R.)

Under the null hypothesis of equal population means, it can be shown that, provided both n_1 and n_2 are greater than 8, then the statistic [7.8] is normally distributed with mean

$$E(U) = \frac{n_1 n_2}{2}$$

and

$$\text{variance } V(U) = \frac{n_1 n_2 (n_1 + n_2 + 1)}{12}.$$

It follows that, under H_0,

$$TS = \frac{U - E(U)}{\sqrt{V(U)}} \text{ has an } N(0, 1) \text{ distribution.} \tag{7.9}$$

Thus, at the 0.05 level of significance, we will reject H_0 if $|TS| > 1.96$.

Using the above data, selecting the first sample to give a rank sum of $R = 133$, and with $n_1 = 11$ and $n_2 = 9$, we have

$$U = 21, \qquad E(U) = 49.5, \qquad V(U) = 173.25.$$

The test statistic therefore equals $(21 - 49.5)/13.2 = -2.16$. Thus, since $|TS| > 1.96$, we reject H_0 at the 0.05 level of significance. It appears that mean bonuses differ between the two types of salesmen.

Words of caution

The nonparametric tests discussed in this chapter are usually quick and easy to employ. Moreover, because they are not dependent on any underlying assumptions, they are often valid under a wide range of situations. They are particularly useful for samples taken from non-normally distributed populations. But it must be remembered that, under certain conditions, they are likely to be inefficient. That is, there may be alternative tests that possess greater power.[11] For example, when testing for a difference between two population means, if the populations are both normally distributed and have a common variance, then the small-sample t-test will be more powerful than either the median test or the Mann–Whitney test. This is because the Mann–Whitney test would fail to make use of the above information concerning the populations. However, if such assumptions are incorrect then the t-test is simply invalid and nonparametric methods have to be used. To make the correct choice of test requires a careful assessment of the assumptions underlying any statistical model.

Example 7.10

For the data of Example 7.9, use the Mann–Whitney U statistic to test whether there is any difference in average marks for the two groups of students.

Example 7.11

To test whether the average weekly wages (in pounds) of workers differ between two firms, two random samples of wages are taken.

> Firm A: 420, 450, 380, 460, 340, 430, 500, 470, 450.
> Firm B: 390, 370, 410, 380, 470, 380, 430.

Using the Mann–Whitney test, what would you conclude? Would your conclusion differ if you used the small-sample t-test for the difference between two means?

7.6 **Tests based on runs**

Consider a sequence of data observations in which each observation can be classified as being one of two possible types. For example, suppose morning arrivals at a post office are classified as either male (m) or female (f), and we observe the sequence of arrivals:

> m m m f m m f f f f m m f f f m m m m f m f m m m.

This sequence consists of a series of *runs*. For example, the sequence begins with a run of three males, followed by a run of just one female, followed by a run of two males, and so on. There are 11 runs altogether in the above sequence.

The *runs test* of this section may be used to test the null hypothesis that a sequential sample, drawn from a population, is a random sample. For example, suppose that we obtained the sequence

> m m m m m m m m m m m m m f f f f f f f f f f f.

Obviously, this sequence does not appear to be random. There appears to be some sociological reason why males arrive at the post office early in the morning! While non-randomness in a sequence is not always so obvious, it should be clear that we would view with some suspicion a sequence that had either too few or too many runs in it. Too few runs would clearly suggest non-randomness, while too many runs would suggest that the sequence might have been tampered with, to give the appearance of randomness.

To test H_0, the null hypothesis of randomness, we simply count the number of runs, u, in a sequence. If n_1, the number of outcomes of type m, and n_2, the number of outcomes of type f in a sequence, both exceed 10 then, under H_0, u can be shown to be approximately normally distributed with mean

$$E(u) = \frac{2n_1 n_2}{n_1 + n_2} + 1$$

and variance

$$V(u) = \frac{2n_1 n_2 (2n_1 n_2 - n_1 - n_2)}{(n_1 + n_2)^2 (n_1 + n_2 - 1)}.$$

It follows that, under H_0, the statistic

$$TS = \frac{u - E(u)}{\sqrt{V(u)}} \text{ has an } N(0, 1) \text{ distribution.} \qquad [7.10]$$

Thus, we will reject H_0, at the 0.05 level of significance, if the absolute value of the test statistic [7.10] exceeds 1.96.

Let us suppose that morning arrivals at the post office result in the following sequence:

m m f f f m f m m m f m f f m f m f f f f f m m f m
f f f m m m f m f f f m f m m f f m f m m f f f m f.

The number of m outcomes is $n_1 = 23$ and the number of f outcomes is $n_2 = 29$. Thus, using the above expressions, we have $E(u) = 26.7$ and $V(u) = 12.4$. The total number of runs in the above sequence is $u = 30$, so the value of the test statistic [7.10] is

$$TS = \frac{30 - 26.7}{\sqrt{12.4}} = 0.94.$$

It follows that we cannot reject the null hypothesis of randomness. There are more runs (30) than we would expect (26.7) but the difference is not significant at the 0.05 level.

Example 7.12

Parts coming off a production process can be good (g) or defective (d). Some proportion of parts is inevitably defective but, if it is found that once one defective is produced another is likely to follow immediately, then the process is regarded as faulty. The following sequence is observed:

$$g\ g\ g\ g\ g\ d\ d\ d\ g\ g\ g\ g\ g\ g\ g\ d\ g\ g\ g\ g\ g\ g\ g\ d\ d\ g\ g$$
$$g\ g\ g\ g\ d\ g\ g\ g\ g\ g\ g\ g\ g\ d\ d\ g\ g\ g\ g\ g\ g\ d\ g\ g\ g\ g\ g$$
$$g\ g\ d\ d\ d\ g\ g\ g\ g\ g\ g\ g\ g\ g\ g\ d\ g\ g\ g\ g\ d\ g\ g\ g\ g\ g\ g.$$

Use the runs test to determine whether the process is faulty.

Using the median to create a sequence of runs

It is also possible to use the runs test to check for randomness even when faced with a sequential sample that is not classified by type of observation. For example, suppose samples are taken from a production line, every morning and afternoon, to check the mean diameter of a specific item. It is suspected that diameters tend to be greater in the morning shift than in the afternoon. The following sequence of 32 mean diameters (in centimetres) is observed, beginning with a morning value and reading across each consecutive row in turn:

$$0.412 \quad 0.410 \quad 0.413 \quad 0.409 \quad 0.408 \quad 0.407 \quad 0.412 \quad 0.411$$
$$0.414 \quad 0.409 \quad 0.411 \quad 0.412 \quad 0.410 \quad 0.415 \quad 0.412 \quad 0.408$$
$$0.413 \quad 0.411 \quad 0.414 \quad 0.406 \quad 0.411 \quad 0.408 \quad 0.413 \quad 0.406$$
$$0.411 \quad 0.408 \quad 0.413 \quad 0.415 \quad 0.412 \quad 0.404 \quad 0.414 \quad 0.416.$$

The median observation is easily calculated as 0.411. We now classify the observations as either 'above median' (a) or 'below median' (b) which yields the following sequence of a's and b's:

$$a \quad b \quad a \quad b \quad b \quad b \quad a \quad - \quad a \quad b \quad - \quad a \quad b \quad a \quad a \quad b$$
$$a \quad - \quad a \quad b \quad - \quad b \quad a \quad b \quad - \quad b \quad a \quad a \quad a \quad b \quad a \quad a.$$

The dashes '−' denote an observation that is exactly equal to the median of 0.411. We can use the runs test to test for randomness, provided we define a run as a sequence of identical letters that is preceded and followed by a different letter or a dash. There are, in fact, as many as $u = 21$ such runs in this sequence.

We can now use the test statistic [7.10] to check for randomness in the sequence. With $n_1 = 15$ and $n_2 = 12$, we have

$$E(u) = 14.33, \qquad V(u) = 6.32.$$

The test statistic [7.10] therefore takes the value

$$TS = \frac{21 - 14.33}{\sqrt{6.32}} = 2.65.$$

Thus, since 2.65 > 1.96, we have to reject the null hypothesis of randomness at the 0.05 level of significance. Diameters appear to differ between the morning and afternoon shifts.

Example 7.13

The following data give the number of defective bricks for samples of 100 bricks each from day to day:

$$
\begin{array}{cccccccccc}
8 & 6 & 11 & 7 & 5 & 9 & 5 & 8 & 3 & 6 \\
6 & 4 & 6 & 7 & 4 & 3 & 10 & 5 & 8 & 4 \\
6 & 2 & 7 & 3 & 7 & 12 & 2 & 9 & 3 & 1
\end{array}
$$

(read down consecutive columns to obtain consecutive counts). Test for homogeneity of quality from day to day, using the total number of runs above and below the median.

Summary

- **Nonparametric** methods are used in statistical inference for cases in which hypotheses do not involve population parameters and/or situations where we have no knowledge of the underlying shape of population distributions. They are frequently used when handling **count data**.

- **Contingency tables** are used for testing for the **independence** of two classifications and for testing for **homogeneity** across two or more populations. In both cases the test statistic used has an approximate χ^2 distribution. The same χ^2 statistic can be used for testing the **goodness of fit** of empirical distributions when compared with theoretical distributions.

- The **sign test** is a non-parametric test for testing a hypothesis about a single population mean, when the sample size is small. The **median test** and the **Mann–Whitney test** are used for testing hypotheses about the difference between two means, when sample sizes are small. These tests are only used when the population distributions are believed to be non-normal.

- The **runs test** is used to test whether sequenced data is random or not.

Notes

1. Tests in which no knowledge of the underlying distribution is assumed should be termed 'distribution-free' tests. However, nowadays the general term 'nonparametric' is also used to describe distribution-free tests.

2. Incomes of £20 000 are allocated to the range 20–80 rather than the range 10–20. Similarly £10 000 is allocated to 10–20.

3. For example, the cells ($Y = 20$–80, $E = 8$–10) and ($Y = 10$–20, $E = 11$–13) have $o_i - e_i$ terms of 8.3 and 5.3, respectively, which are fairly similar. However, the sizes of $(o_i - e_i)^2$ terms relative to the values of e_i, that is $(o_i - e_i)^2/e_i$, are 1.6 and 0.2 respectively (see Table 7.3). This is a much larger difference.

4. The degrees of freedom in this case depend on the restrictions that have to be placed on the expected frequencies. Once $(c - 1)(r - 1)$ of the expected frequencies are determined, the remainder can be determined from the fact that the sums of all row and column frequencies must equal the respective row and column totals. Thus there are $(c - 1)(r - 1)$ degrees in freedom in total.

5. As stated, under H_0 the test statistic [7.3] has an approximate χ^2 distribution. It has been found that the approximation is usually satisfactory if each $e_i > 4$. This limitation is similar to that placed on the use of the normal approximation to the binomial in which np and $n(1 - p)$ are required to exceed 5.

6. The arguments required to compute the expected frequencies in the homogeneity test are subtlely different from those of the independence test, but this need not concern us here.

7. See also note 6.

8. One degree freedom is lost because of the restriction that the expected frequencies must sum to their known total. As with the previous χ^2 tests in this chapter, the approximation will be satisfactory provided all $e_i > 4$.

9. If the population distribution is non-symmetric then the method can still be used to test a hypothesis about the population median.

10. If $n_1 + n_2$ is even, the median value can be omitted, leaving an odd number of observations.

11. As explained in Chapter 5, the power of a test is the probability of rejecting H_0 when H_0 is false.

Part II

Econometrics

What is econometrics?

Introduction

Johnston (1984, p. 5) very succinctly defined the basic aim of econometrics as 'to put *empirical* flesh and blood on theoretic structures'. A more lengthy definition is that of Samuelson *et al.* (1954, pp. 141–6), who described econometrics as 'the application of mathematical statistics to economic data to lend empirical support to the models constructed by mathematical economists and to obtain numerical estimates'.

Chapters 3–7 provided material that partly satisfies the first part of Samuelson's definition; we have considered the application of statistical methods to certain types of economic data. But clearly we have some way to go if we are to cover the full definition.

8.1 The purpose of econometrics

Mathematical economists deduce or predict certain relationships between two or more economic data series. Obvious examples are the consumption function, demand curves and employment functions. Econometrics is concerned with:

(i)   quantifying such relationships and finding values for the parameters contained in them;
(ii) testing any theories implied by such relationships;
(iii) using such relationships as a basis for quantitative predictions or forecasts.

Mathematical economists express economic theories in mathematical form, but they do so in ways that are almost always qualitative rather than quantitative, that is, normally without involving numbers. Econometrics takes such theoretical/mathematical equations and, by confronting them with economic data, seeks to give them numerical form. An example should make the above clearer.

Consumer theory suggests that aggregate consumer expenditure in an economy depends on some 'scale' variable, such as income or wealth, and on the cost of borrowing to finance expenditure. For example, suppose

$$C = C(Y, I), \tag{8.1}$$

where C is consumer expenditure, Y is the scale variable and I is an appropriate interest rate. Theory specifies a relationship between real values of C and Y which is independent of prices. It also suggests that a rise in Y leads to a rise in C, whereas a rise in I normally results in a fall in C.

Unfortunately, theory leaves many other things unclear. Firstly, there is the problem of defining the variables C, Y and I. Do we use total consumption or consumption per head of population? Should consumer expenditure include spending on durable goods or do we limit it to spending on non-durables? In fact, it is the services obtained from durable goods that should theoretically be included in consumption, but normally we have no reliable data on such services. What scale variable, Y, should we include in [8.1]? Is Y to be defined as measured income or as some form of permanent income?. Should financial wealth be included as a separate variable in [8.1], or should we employ permanent income as an all-encompassing measure of total consumer wealth? Which of the many possible rates of interest should we include in [8.1]?

Secondly, economic theory almost never tells us anything about the precise functional form of an economic relationship. For the consumption function, it is often convenient to specify the simple linear function

$$C = \alpha + \beta Y + \gamma I, \qquad \beta > 0, \gamma < 0. \tag{8.2}$$

But there is no reason why a linear function should necessarily be valid. [8.1] could be specified in the equally convenient constant-elasticity form of

$$C = AY^\beta I^\gamma, \qquad \beta > 0, \gamma < 0, \qquad\qquad [8.3]$$

but there is no reason why any nonlinearity in [8.1] should be captured by this particular function rather than by any other.

Thirdly, theory provides no quantitative information about how Y and I affect C. What are the true values of β and γ in [8.2] or [8.3]? Such quantified values of β and γ are of the greatest importance for the formulation of government policy.

Fourthly, economic theory normally refers to the so-called *long run*. It tells us only about various possible equilibrium points. But economic systems are very rarely in equilibrium and, unfortunately, theory often provides little information about how an economic system behaves when it is not in equilibrium. That is, theory says little about the adjustment processes that may or may not take a system to its equilibrium. But economic data usually describe the adjustment process rather than a series of equilibrium points.

Econometrics, with varying success, seeks the answers to these questions that mathematical economics is unable to provide. It uses estimation techniques, similar to those introduced in Part I of this book, to attempt the placing of numerical values on parameters such as β and γ above. It also makes use of the hypothesis-testing procedures of the last few chapters to attempt the testing of some of the predictions of economic theory.

As an example of this process, consider again the statement made above that the relationship between real consumption and real income is independent of prices. For example, let us generalize [8.2], to allow for such price effects:

$$C = \alpha + \beta Y + \gamma I + \delta P, \qquad\qquad [8.4]$$

where P is the general price level. If $\delta = 0$ in [8.4], then it is a prediction of economic theory that the price level should have no influence on consumer expenditure.[1] The procedures (to be described in following chapters) that have to be employed to estimate β and γ can also be used to estimate the value of δ. We can then make use of the estimate δ to derive a test statistic which we can use to test the null hypothesis H_0: $\delta = 0$. If we find that H_0 has to be rejected at a specified level of significance, then this implies that the prediction of theory has been contradicted.

8.2 Social versus physical sciences

The ability to carry out planned experiments is one of the key differences between the social sciences, such as economics, and the physical sciences. Let us take two simple examples – one from physics and then one from economics.

Suppose we are interested in the effect on the volume V of a gas, of changes in its temperature T and changes in the pressure P under which it is maintained. For example, we might wish to test the hypothesis that a given proportionate increase in the temperature of the gas, with pressure held constant, leads to an equally proportionate increase in its volume. That is, resorting to the terminology of economics, we ask the question whether the elasticity of volume with respect to temperature is unity or not. Suppose we assume that a relationship of the form

$$V = AT^{\beta}P^{\gamma} \qquad [8.5]$$

exists, where A, β and γ are constants.[2] The parameters β and γ measure the elasticity of volume with respect to temperature and pressure respectively. The hypothesis we wish to test is therefore H_0: $\beta = 1$.

Equation [8.5] is an example of what is called a *maintained hypothesis*. In any hypothesis-testing situation, we have, typically, to make a number of assumptions not all of which we wish to test. Any assumptions that we are prepared to accept without test make up the maintained hypothesis. While we can never be certain that the relevant maintained hypothesis is valid (e.g., a simpler linear formulation might be preferable to [8.5]) some such assumptions are always necessary if hypothesis testing is to proceed at all. Of course, if the maintained hypothesis is invalid then the results of any investigation are necessarily unreliable. The form of [8.5] is, in fact, particularly convenient since, in this case, the implied elasticities are constants.

To estimate β a physicist might set up a laboratory experiment under which pressure is kept constant and the temperature of the gas is allowed to vary at will. Under such conditions, [8.5] becomes

$$V = A^*T^{\beta}, \qquad [8.6]$$

where $A^* = AP^{\gamma} = $ constant. The relationship [8.6], between temperature and volume alone, can then be observed by the experimenter, and perhaps sketched on a two-dimensional diagram.[3] Some conclusion can then be reached about the value of β.

To test a hypothesis about the value of γ, the elasticity of volume with respect to pressure, a second controlled experiment would have to be performed, in which the temperature of the gas was now held constant. In this experiment, [8.5] would become

$$V = A^{**}P^{\gamma}, \qquad [8.7]$$

where $A^{**} = AT^{\beta} = $ constant. By varying P and observing the resultant changes in V, information about the parameter γ could then be obtained.

Now let us take a second simple example, this time from the world of economics. Recall the consumption function of the previous section and suppose we accept the maintained hypothesis that the form of the function is that of [8.3] above. That is,

$$C = AY^\beta I^\gamma. \tag{8.8}$$

In this situation, β is the income elasticity of consumption, and testing H_0: $\beta = 1$ implies that we are testing the so-called *proportionality postulate* that, for given I, consumption C is exactly proportional to income Y.

Unfortunately, it is highly unlikely that we could ever set up a controlled experiment in which interest rates were held constant for a sufficiently long period for us to observe the relationship between C and Y with any precision. In economics it is virtually impossible to set up experiments in which all variables but two are held constant. Economists usually have to make do with data sets in which all variables are changing and the approach therefore has to be very different.

Fortunately, a statistical technique, normally referred to as *multiple regression analysis*, is available to economists in their attempt to overcome the handicap of not being able to perform controlled experiments. The technique enables us to estimate parameters such as β and γ not one by one but simultaneously, without the need to hold any variables constant. Multiple regression is covered in the later chapters of this text.

Most econometrics involves multiple regression in some form or other. It is the econometrician's substitute for the controlled experiment of the physical sciences. In many ways it is not a perfect substitute but it is usually the best we have. For example, the conditions under which various forms of multiple regression can be applied have to be studied very carefully. Much of this part of the text is given to analysing these conditions.

8.3 Deterministic and stochastic relationships

Economic relationships such as [8.2] or [8.3] are never exact. That is, they are not *deterministic* in the sense that given values of Y and I will *always* provide the same value of C. Human beings are by nature unpredictable in their behaviour and, for this reason, random or stochastic *disturbances* are usually added to such relationships. Therefore, we rewrite equations such as [8.2] as[4]

$$C = \alpha + \beta Y + \gamma I + \varepsilon, \tag{8.9}$$

where ε is a disturbance that can be either positive or negative. The disturbance can also be regarded as reflecting the effect (presumably small) of all other factors, apart from Y and I, on C.

The fact that a disturbance has to be included in [8.9] means that we cannot expect parameters such as α, β and γ in [8.9] to be measured exactly. Even if we were able to set up laboratory experiments to control the values of Y and I, the presence of the uncontrollable disturbance would mean that values of C will still vary, even if the values of Y and I remain the same. As can be seen from study of [8.9], C depends not only on Y and I but also on the stochastic disturbance ε. Thus C itself becomes stochastic because of the stochastic nature of the disturbance. There must therefore be uncertainty about the values of the parameters α, β and γ. The relationship is stochastic rather than deterministic. Similarly, when applying the multiple regression technique of later chapters, to different samples of C, Y and I data, we will find our estimates of α, β and γ varying from sample to sample.

It should now be clear that, in econometrics, estimates of parameters will have sampling distributions akin to the distributions for the sample mean $\bar{X}$ and the sample proportion π that we considered in earlier chapters. Consequently, estimating or testing hypotheses about parameters, such as the above α, β and γ, becomes as much an exercise in statistical inference as the situations we faced in Part I.

Notes

1. Do not fall into the trap of expecting a rise in P to lead to a fall in C. This is not the traditional 'demand equation'. A rise in P, with real income unchanged, should have no effect on C.

2. Those familiar with the laws of Boyle and Charles, concerning gases, will realize that the true relationship between V and T and P is $V = $ (constant) TP^{-1}, so that experiment-ation should yield $\beta = 1$ and $\gamma = -1$.

3. Taking natural logarithms of [8.6] gives

    $$\ln(V) = \ln(A^*) + \beta \ln(T).$$

    Thus plotting $\ln(V)$ against $\ln(T)$ should yield a straight-line graph. Measuring the slope of such a line will then give an estimate of β.

4. The simplest way to add a disturbance ε to [8.3] is to write $C = AY^{\beta}I^{\gamma}\varepsilon$. Taking natural logarithms then gives

    $$\ln(C) = \ln(A) + \beta \ln(Y) + \gamma \ln(I) + \varepsilon^*,$$

    where $\varepsilon^* = \ln(\varepsilon)$ is a disturbance playing the same role as ε in equation [8.9].

9

Two-variable correlation and regression

Objectives

When you have completed your study of this chapter, you should be able:

1. to understand that sample correlations between two variables may be high for spurious reasons, and that even non-spurious correlations may tell us nothing about causation;

2. to appreciate the difference between population and sample regression lines and the difference between disturbances and residuals;

3. to understand the ordinary least-squares (OLS) method of estimating the parameters of a two-variable regression equation and to compute OLS estimates;

4. to compute and interpret a coefficient of determination and understand its relationship to the correlation coefficient;

5. to use simple regression software to compute two-variable regression equations.

Introduction

In Chapter 6 we introduced the idea of the correlation between two variables, X and Y. In particular, we considered the *sample* correlation coefficient which could be regarded as an estimate of the underlying *population* correlation coefficient. When X and Y refer to variables such as the number of heads in four tosses of a coin or the number of spots on two rolls of a die, it is possible to compute the relevant population correlation. However, in economics matters are rarely that simple. While we are frequently interested in the strength of any association between two economic variables, we almost always have to assess this association from sample information. This involves, inevitably, computing sample rather than population correlations.

In this chapter, therefore, we begin with a second and more detailed look at sample correlations. Then we move on to consider regression analysis, in which an a priori assumption is made about the direction of causation between the two variables and an attempt made to quantify the assumed relationship between them.

9.1 **Sample correlations again**

For our first economic example concerning sample correlations, consider the information in Table 9.1. This contains data on the money stock, M, and the gross domestic product, G, (both measured per head of population and in thousands of current US dollars), of 30 countries for the year 1985. A *scatter diagram* of the data in Table 9.1 is presented in Fig. 9.1.

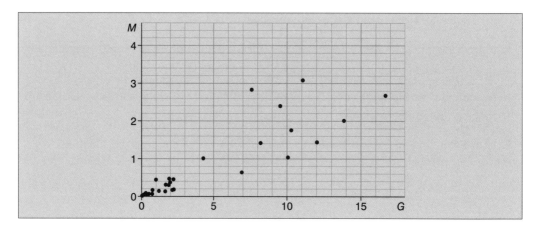

Figure 9.1 Scatter diagram for data in Table 9.1

Table 9.1 Data on 30 countries for 1985

Observation	M	G	Country
1	0.16470	2.1520	Argentina
2	1.0338	10.0014	Australia
3	0.12624	1.6730	Brazil
4	0.036328	0.17638	Burma
5	2.0096	13.7998	Canada
6	0.13388	1.2193	Columbia
7	0.43287	1.0077	Egypt
8	2.3912	9.4661	France
9	1.7531	10.2113	Germany
10	0.052155	0.46857	Ghana
11	0.45515	1.9366	Hungary
12	0.044403	0.28180	India
13	0.055788	0.52070	Indonesia
14	2.8369	7.4967	Italy
15	3.0892	10.9748	Japan
16	0.038689	0.28803	Kenya
17	0.36352	1.9942	Malaysia
18	0.17169	2.2609	Mexico
19	0.62824	6.8687	New Zealand
20	0.15670	0.77267	Nigeria
21	0.080302	0.31190	Pakistan
22	0.035168	0.60220	Philippines
23	0.44167	2.2118	Romania
24	0.30064	1.6932	South Africa
25	1.0065	4.2548	Spain
26	1.4314	11.9883	Sweden
27	0.064666	0.74743	Thailand
28	1.4137	8.1162	UK
29	2.6786	16.5921	US
30	0.29163	1.9151	Yugoslavia

Students of economics should be familiar with the famous equation of exchange, which was the basis of the quantity theory of money. We shall write it as

$$MV = PG, \qquad [9.1]$$

where P is the general price level and V is the income (or GDP) velocity of circulation. Rearranging [9.1] gives

$$M = kG, \qquad [9.2]$$

where $k = P/V$. If k could be regarded as a constant, then the money stock would be exactly and directly proportional to gross domestic product. In Chapter 6.3 we saw that, in these circumstances, the population correlation between two variables would be +1. The relation-ship $M = kG$ is a straight line passing through the origin with gradient k, as depicted in Fig. 9.2. In fact, if the population correlation between M and G actually were +1, this would imply that any scatter of (G, M) points would all lie exactly on such a line.[1]

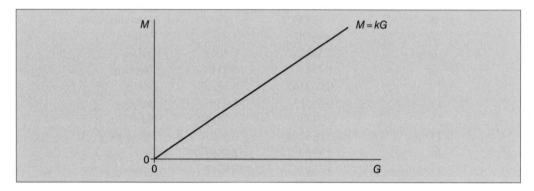

Figure 9.2 An exact and directly proportional relationship between M and G

Of course, it is highly unlikely that the ratio $k = P/V$ will be the same for all 30 countries, so M cannot be exactly proportional to G and, as can be observed from Fig. 9.1, the points in this scatter do not lie on any underlying straight line. However, we can still use the sample correlation coefficient to assess, for our 30 countries, the strength of the association between M and G.

We now use the data in Table 9.1 to compute the correlation coefficient [6.21]. Following a procedure identical to that in Chapter 6.3, we can obtain, letting Y represent M and X represent G,

$$\Sigma(X - \bar{X})(Y - \bar{Y}) = 116.60,$$
$$\Sigma(X - \bar{X})^2 = 666.86,$$
$$\Sigma(Y - \bar{Y})^2 = 26.403.$$

These values can be taken as given. Using [6.21], we then obtain a value $R = 0.8787$, or 0.879 to 3 sig. figs, for the sample correlation.

As noted in Chapter 6, in general the range of possible values for R lies between −1 and +1. This is illustrated in Figs 9.3a, 9.3b and 9.3c. Figure 9.3a depicts an exact *positive* linear association between the sample values of two variables, X and Y, with all points in a scatter lying exactly on an *upwardly* sloping straight line. In this case $R = +1$. In Fig. 9.3c the scatter of points for the sample all lie on a *downwardly* sloping line, implying an exact *negative* linear association. In this case $R = -1$. In Fig. 9.3b the points in the scatter are evenly spread and there appears to be no discernable association between the sample values of X and Y. This is the case where the correlation coefficient $R = 0$.

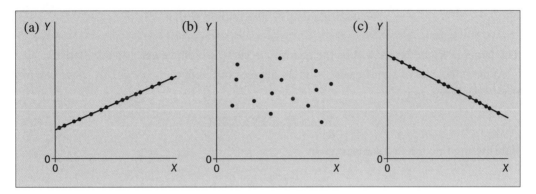

Figure 9.3a, b and c Scatters with $R = +1$, $R = 0$ and $R = -1$

Our value $R = 0.879$ is obviously much closer to +1 rather than 0, and suggests a strong underlying positive association between M and G. This reflects the fact that the points in the scatter in Fig. 9.1 all lie fairly close to some underlying upwardly sloping straight line.

Comparing a value for R with zero, +1 or −1 is obviously a very rough and ready method of assessing the strength of an association. Later we shall give a more precise interpretation of R. For the moment, however, recall from Chapter 6.3 that R is a sample statistic. If we took another sample of 30 countries or sampled the same 30 countries in 1992 instead of 1985, we would almost certainly obtain a different value for R. That is, R has a sampling distribution.[2] Thus, even if the population correlation coefficient $\rho = 0$, it is quite conceivable that a single sample value of R might turn out to be non-zero, purely by chance. In such a situation we need to decide whether R differs sufficiently from zero for us to be confident that the true population ρ is non-zero. We have faced this kind of situation often in earlier chapters. It is a typical problem in statistical inference, and we will begin, as usual, by formulating null and alternative hypotheses

$$H_0: \rho = 0, \qquad H_A: \rho > 0.$$

The null hypothesis states that there is *no* underlying population correlation between the money stock and GDP. Since we expect, on a priori grounds, that any correlation that may exist between M and G will be positive, we make the alternative hypothesis specify that ρ is positive.

Clearly, we shall reject H_0 if the sample correlation R is sufficiently greater than zero. Any test statistic must therefore be based on R and it can be shown that, under H_0,

$$\frac{R\sqrt{n-2}}{\sqrt{1-R^2}} \text{ has a Student's } t \text{ distribution with } n-2 \text{ d.f.} \qquad [9.3]$$

The larger is R, the larger will be the quantity in [9.3], which we use as a test statistic.

At the 0.05 level of significance, with 28 degrees of freedom, $t_{0.05} = 1.701$, so we can use the decision criterion

$$\text{reject } H_0 \text{ if } TS > 1.701. \qquad [9.4]$$

Substituting into the test statistic gives

$$TS = \frac{0.879\sqrt{28}}{\sqrt{1-0.879^2}} = 9.8.$$

Thus we reject H_0 at the 0.05 level of significant. There appears to be a clear positive association between M and G.

Notice that we have always been careful to say that there appears to be an 'association' between two variables X and Y. We have never suggested that X is caused by Y or vice versa. That is, a significant correlation R does not necessarily imply anything about causality. Firstly, a significant correlation between X and Y may be entirely *spurious*. That is, it may have occurred purely by chance and thus be meaningless. For example, many so-called time-series variables which move consistently upwards or downwards over time tend to be highly correlated even when there is no causal link between them.

To illustrate this problem consider Figs 9.4a and 9.4b in which time is measured on the horizontal axis. On the vertical axes we have, in Fig. 9.4a, the price of beer in the UK and, in Fig. 9.4b, the consumption of petrol in Japan. It should be clear that Figs 9.4a and 9.4b imply a high correlation between the two variables. When UK beer prices are low (in the 1950s), Japanese petrol consumption is low, whereas when UK beer prices are much higher (in the 1990s), Japanese petrol consumption is also much higher. In fact the sample correlation between these variables is as high as 0.93. Yet there is, at most, a very tenuous link between the two variables. The vast part of the correlation is misleading or spurious. No one would suggest that the rise in UK beer prices is caused by the rise in Japanese petrol consumption or vice versa. The problem of common trends, either upwards or downwards, in such time-series variables is, in fact, one that has bedevilled the statistical analysis of economic data for decades.

Even when we believe that at least part of a sample correlation may be non-spurious, it is still often difficult to say much about causality. If X and Y are correlated, is this because X influences Y or because Y influences X? We found a high correlation between the money stock and GDP in our numerical example above, and while most economists would agree

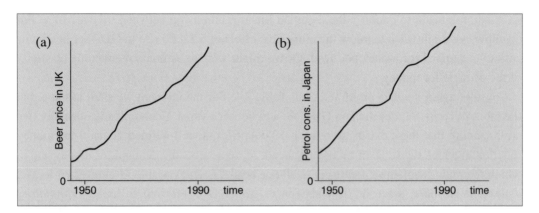

Figure 9.4a and b Time paths of UK beer price and Japanese petrol consumption

that much of the correlation we have found is real and not spurious, many would argue about the direction of causation in this case. In fact, it may well be that there is a two-way causation present, with M and G jointly influencing each other.

Another possibility is that two variables X and Y are highly correlated not because they are directly linked but because some other variable Z influences both X and Y. Taking our money stock and GDP example again, the population of the 30 countries in Table 9.1 varies from 3.25 million for New Zealand to 750.9 million for India. Clearly, the larger a country is, the bigger will be both its total money stock *and* its total GDP. The correlation between total money stock and total GDP must be at least partly the result of population factors. This is why we defined M and G as money stock and GDP *per head*. In fact the correlation between *total* money M and *total* G turns out to be 0.971. By failing to allow for population variations the correlation has been artificially boosted from 0.879 to 0.971.

We shall have more to say about correlations, spurious and non-spurious, in later chapters, but for the moment we just note that assessing a correlation coefficient is far more difficult than might first appear.

Example 9.1

In a sample of 250 heads of household it is found that the correlation between hours spent reading and disposable income is 0.28. Comment on this finding.

9.2 Two-variable regression analysis

Regression analysis differs from correlation analysis in two ways. Firstly, an *a priori* assumption is made about the direction of causation between the two variables. Secondly, an attempt is made to *quantify* the assumed linear relationship between the variables. For example, we might wish to know the numerical effect of a $1000 rise in GDP per head on a country's demand for money per head. Or we might wish to estimate the income elasticity of the demand for money.

Consider again the data on M and G in Table 9.1. For the moment we shall assume that the money supply, M, depends on GDP, G, and not vice versa. Economically speaking, we are assuming that there exists, across the 30 countries, a well-defined demand-for-money function in which the stock of money per head, M, represents the demand for money and in which the main 'explaining factor' is GDP per head, G. The variable M is referred to as a *dependent variable*, since it 'depends' on G, while G is referred to as an *explanatory variable* because it 'explains' M. A dependent variable is also sometimes referred to as a *regressand* and an explanatory variable as a *regressor*.

In regression analysis the dependent variable is normally given the symbol Y, while the explanatory variable is given the symbol X. So, for the rest of this chapter, we shall switch notation and write Y for demand for money and X for gross domestic product. In each case the variables are defined, as previously, in thousands of current US dollars per head of population.

The population regression line

In this subsection we develop a formal model to describe the relation between money stock and GDP. We assume that Y and X are linked by the *linear* relationship

$$E(Y) = \alpha + \beta X, \tag{9.5}$$

where $E(Y)$ is the *expected* demand for money of a country with a given GDP, X; α and β are *unknown population parameters*. $E(Y)$ could be described as the 'average' demand for money of 'many' countries, all with the same GDP, X. We refer to [9.5] as the *population regression equation*. Since [9.5] is a linear relationship its graph must be a straight line, which is shown in Fig. 9.5 as a broken line. The parameters α, β represent the intercept and gradient, respectively, of the line. Of course, it is possible that $\alpha = 0$, so that, as suggested earlier, the demand for money may be directly proportional to GDP.

The actual demand for money, Y, of a country is not always the same as the expected demand, $E(Y)$. The difference between the two is referred to as a deviation, error or *disturbance* to which we give the symbol ε. That is,

$$Y = E(Y) + \varepsilon. \tag{9.6}$$

The implication of [9.6] is that a country's demand for money may be 'disturbed' away from its normal or expected level $E(Y)$ by any number of random factors which we consider below.

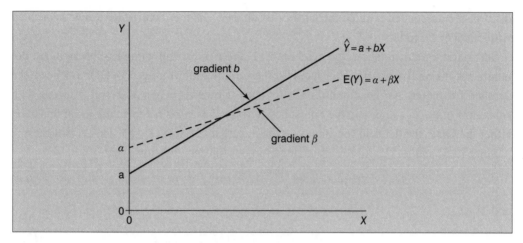

Figure 9.5 Population and sample regression equations

Substituting [9.5] into [9.6] gives

$$Y = \alpha + \beta X + \varepsilon. \tag{9.7}$$

The disturbance term ε in [9.7] is included to allow for two kinds of factor. First, it represents the influence on the demand for money of all variables other than GDP. We are implicitly assuming here that these influences are quantitatively small. Otherwise we would need to allow for other variables on the right-hand side of [9.7].[3]

Secondly, even if GDP were the only variable influencing the demand for money and even if GDP had been identical in all 30 countries in our sample, we would still expect some variation in the demand for money across countries. Almost certainly, we would still find some *random* variation in Y resulting from the basic unpredictability of economic agents. The disturbance ε is regarded as also representing all such random factors. We encountered such disturbances in the last chapter.

Disturbances can be either positive or negative. If $\varepsilon > 0$ in [9.6], then actual Y exceeds E(Y), whereas if $\varepsilon < 0$, then actual Y is less than its expected value E(Y).

In the above, we have been using the symbol Y as a shorthand for the words 'demand for money per head' and X as shorthand for 'GDP per head'. Also ε is simply our shorthand for the word 'disturbance'. However, we now extend our notation. As usual, we use n for the sample size (e.g., $n = 30$ in the current example). We can now number the countries in our sample from 1 to n. We write Y_i for the demand for money per head in country i, and X_i for the GDP per head of country i. For example Y_8 refers to country 8, France, and hence has the demand-for-money value 2.3912, taken from Table 9.1. Similarly X_{20} refers to country 20, Nigeria, and has the GDP value 0.772 67, again taken from Table 9.1. Finally, ε_i is the disturbance associated with country *i*. For example ε_{12} is the disturbance value associated with country 12, India.

Summarizing our notation, the symbols *X*, *Y* and ε occurring without subscripts are not numbers but simply a *general* shorthand for the variables they represent – GDP per head, the demand for money per head and the disturbance. However, when *X*, *Y* and ε appear with subscripts (e.g., X_{20}, Y_8 or ε_{12}) they must be interpreted as *numbers* referring to, in this case, either the GDP, the demand for money or the disturbance values for particular countries.

Since [9.5] and [9.7] hold for all countries in our sample, it follows that

$$E(Y_i) = \alpha + \beta X_i, \qquad \text{for } i = 1, 2, 3, ..., n, \tag{9.8}$$

and

$$Y_i = \alpha + \beta X_i + \varepsilon_i, \qquad \text{for } i = 1, 2, 3, ..., n. \tag{9.9}$$

The sample regression line

It is important to realize that the population regression equation [9.5] is unknown and remains unknown throughout any regression analysis. The investigator has to estimate it using sample data, for example, the data in Table 9.1 on the demand for money and GDP. One way of doing this is to fit a straight line to the scatter of points in Fig. 9.1. Such a line is fitted in Fig. 9.6. Notice that it is customary to place the dependent variable *Y* on the vertical axis in regression analysis. There are a number of ways of fitting lines to scatters such as that in Fig. 9.1, and we will discuss one shortly. For the moment, we assume such a line has been obtained by some unspecified method[4] and we write it as

$$\hat{Y} = a + bX. \tag{9.10}$$

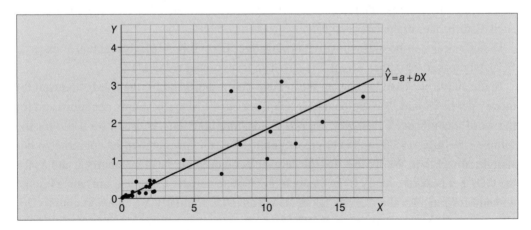

Figure 9.6 A sample regression line fitted to the scatter of Fig. 9.1

We refer to [9.10] as the *sample regression equation* and represent it by the unbroken line in Fig. 9.5. The intercept and slope of this line are given by a and b respectively, and can be regarded as estimates of the parameters α and β in the population regression equation. Thus, as usual, we use Greek letters for population parameters and English letters for the corresponding estimators. Recall that the broken line in Fig. 9.5 represents the population regression equation.[5]

$\hat{Y}$ in [9.10] is known as the *predicted value* of Y, because, once a sample regression equation has been obtained, (i.e., once we have estimates of α and β), we can compute predicted demand-for-money values for any country in the sample by substituting the relevant GDP values into the sample regression equation [9.10]. For example, country 15 (Japan) has GDP per head of $X_{15} = 10.9748$. Hence its predicted demand for money per head is equal to $\hat{Y}_{15} = a + 10.9748b$. Similarly, country 23 (Romania) has $X_{23} = 2.2118$, so that its predicted demand for money equals $\hat{Y}_{23} = a + 2.2118b$.

It should be clear that, given estimated values a and b, predicted values $\hat{Y}$ can be obtained for each and every country in our sample. That is, we have

$$\hat{Y}_i = a + bX_i, \qquad \text{for } i = 1, 2, 3, ..., n. \tag{9.11}$$

However, the predicted values, $\hat{Y}_i$, will rarely coincide exactly with the actual Y_i in Table 9.1. If they did then all the points in the scatter of Fig. 9.1 would lie exactly on the sample regression line, and this virtually never happens. The difference between an actual demand-for-money value, Y_i, and a predicted demand-for-money value, $\hat{Y}_i$, is referred to as a *residual*. Residuals are given the symbol e_i. That is,

$$Y_i = \hat{Y}_i + e_i, \qquad \text{for } i = 1, 2, 3, ..., n. \tag{9.12}$$

Thus there is a residual for every country (i.e., every observation) in the sample. A negative residual simply implies that predicted $\hat{Y}_i$ exceeds actual Y_i, whereas a positive residual implies $\hat{Y}_i$ is less than Y_i.

Worked Example

Suppose a sample regression equation $\hat{Y} = 5 + 20X$ is obtained from the following data:

Obs	1	2	3	4	5
X	5	12	7	-3	17
Y	84	279	129	-51	372

Calculate the predicted value of Y and the residual for every observation.

Solution

For observation 1, the sample regression equation gives a predicted value of

$$\hat{Y}_1 = 5 + 20X_1 = 5 + 20 \times 5 = 105.$$

Using [9.12], the residual for this observation is therefore

$$e_1 = Y_1 - \hat{Y}_1 = 84 - 105 = -21.$$

For observation 2, $\hat{Y}_2 = 5 + 20 \times 12 = 245$ and $e_2 = 279 - 245 = 34$. The residuals for observations 1 and 2 are illustrated in Fig. 9.7. Notice that the negative residual implies a point below the sample regression line, whereas the positive residual implies a point above.

Check that the remaining predicted values are $\hat{Y}_3 = 145$, $\hat{Y}_4 = -55$, and $\hat{Y}_5 = 345$, with residuals $e_3 = -16$, $e_4 = 4$ and $e_5 = 27$.

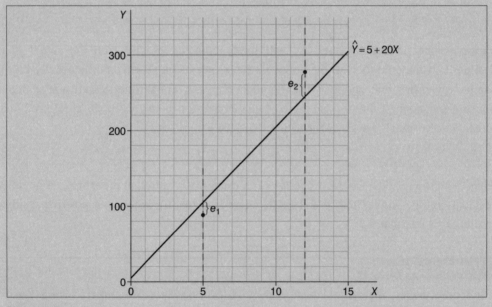

Figure 9.7

It is important to appreciate the difference between residuals and the disturbances introduced earlier. A failure to understand the distinction at the outset of studying regression analysis frequently leads to misunderstandings. Figure 9.8 should clarify the situation.

In Fig. 9.8 the broken line, as always, represents the population regression equation which is and always remains *unknown* to any investigator. The cross indicates the actual

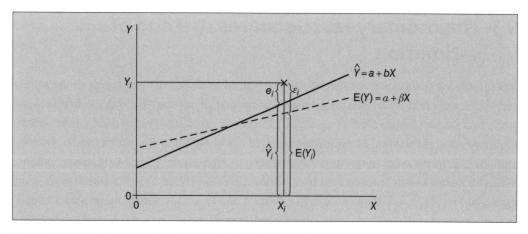

Figure 9.8 Disturbance and residual for the *i*th observation

values of Y, the demand for money, and X, GDP, for the *i*th country in the sample. It is therefore just one of the 30 points in the scatter of Fig. 9.1. From [9.8] and [9.9] we have

$$Y_i = \text{E}(Y_i) + \varepsilon_i, \qquad i = 1, 2, 3, ..., n \qquad [9.13]$$

Examination of [9.13] should make clear that the disturbance associated with the *i*th country is in fact the *vertical* distance between the cross and the *population* regression line in Fig. 9.8. That is $\varepsilon_i = Y_i - \text{E}(Y_i)$. Although the investigator is aware of the position of the cross in Fig. 9.8 (since it is he who has taken the sample), he does not know the position of the population regression line. That is, while he knows Y_i, he does not know $\text{E}(Y_i)$. The disturbance therefore is and remains *unknown*.

For each country in our sample there is a point in the scatter and therefore a disturbance, measured by the vertical distance between the point and the population regression line. Some points obviously may lie below the population line but, as we noted earlier, this simply means that the relevant disturbance $\varepsilon_i < 0$. We stress that all the ε_i, positive or negative, are and remain *unknown*.

As noted above, the unbroken line in Fig. 9.8 represents the sample regression line [9.10] that was fitted to the scatter. In fact, it should be clear from Fig. 9.8 and equation [9.12] that a residual e_i is the vertical distance between a point in the scatter and the *sample* regression line. Points below the sample line represent countries with negative residuals, whereas points above the line imply positive e_i.

Since the points in a scatter are known, as is the position of the sample regression line, residuals are *known* quantities. That is, they can be calculated. This is in contrast to the disturbances which are unknown because the population regression line is unknown. Frequently, however, as we shall see later, we shall find ourselves forced to use the known residuals as estimates of the unknown disturbances.

9.3 The ordinary least-squares method of estimation

In Fig. 9.8, the residuals are given by the vertical differences between points in the scatter and the sample regression line. It should be clear that, if we vary the sample line in some way, then we will obtain a different set of residuals. Consequently, the residuals we obtain will depend on the method of estimation adopted. Easily the best-known method of fitting a straight line to a scatter diagram is the *ordinary least-squares* (OLS) estimation method. When choosing a sample regression line we have, effectively, to choose values for its intercept a and its slope b. It makes sense to choose a and b so as to make the residuals 'small' in some sense. Small residuals imply that the differences between actual Ys and predicted $\hat{Y}$s are small. The OLS method chooses a and b so as to minimize the sum of the squares of the residuals.[6] That is, the method minimizes $\sum e_i^2$.

Using [9.12] and then [9.11], we can write this sum of squares as

$$S = \sum e_i^2 = \sum(Y_i - \hat{Y}_i)^2 = \sum(Y_i - a - bX_i)^2, \qquad [9.14]$$

where the summations are over all i, that is, over all countries in the sample. Since the X_i and Y_i are just numbers, [9.14] expresses the sum of squares S in such a way that it depends on a and b alone. So, to maximize [9.14], we need to partially differentiate S with respect to a and b alone and set these derivatives obtained to zero. This yields

$$\frac{\partial S}{\partial a} = -2\sum(Y_i - a - bX_i) = 0, \qquad [9.15]$$

$$\frac{\partial S}{\partial b} = -2\sum X_i(Y_i - a - bX_i) = 0. \qquad [9.16]$$

Since the X_i and Y_i are simply numbers we treat them as constants when performing the differentiation. We can rearrange [9.15] and [9.16] as

$$-2\sum Y_i = -2\sum a - 2\sum bX_i, \qquad [9.17]$$
$$-2\sum X_iY_i = -2\sum aX_i - 2\sum bX_i^2, \qquad [9.18]$$

referring, if necessary, to the material on the algebra of summations in the prerequisites section.

Dividing both [9.17] and [9.18] throughout by -2 and noting that $\sum a = na$, since all summations are from $i = 1$ to $i = n$, gives

$$\sum Y_i = na + b\sum X_i, \qquad [9.19]$$
$$\sum X_iY_i = a\sum X_i + b\sum X_i^2. \qquad [9.20]$$

Equations [9.19] and [9.20] are the so called *normal equations* of two-variable OLS regression analysis.[7] Since quantities such as $\sum Y_i$ and $\sum X_i^2$ are constants that can be computed from the sample data, they consist of two equations in just two unknowns a and b. Provided $n > 1$, the normal equations can therefore be solved to find expressions for a and b.[8]

To improve the flow of the analysis, the solution of the normal equations [9.19] and [9.20] has been relegated to Appendix 9A at the end of the chapter. While tedious, the solution procedure is not particularly difficult, and you should work through it at your leisure. Here, we just present the solution which, in its most compact and useful form, is as follows:

$$b = \frac{\sum x_i y_i}{\sum x_i^2},$$ [9.21]

where $x_i = X_i - \bar{X}$ and $y_i = Y_i - \bar{Y}$; and

$$a = \bar{Y} - b\bar{X}.$$ [9.22]

Equations [9.21] and [9.22] are the *OLS estimators* of the parameters β and α in the population regression equation. Note that, in [9.21], $x_i = X_i - \bar{X}$ is what is called the *deviation* of X_i from its mean $\bar{X}$, while $y_i = Y_i - \bar{Y}$ is the deviation of Y_i from its mean $\bar{Y}$.

We shall obtain values for a and b in a moment, but notice first that the term in parentheses in [9.15] and [9.16] is in fact the ith residual $e_i = Y_i - \hat{Y}_i = Y_i - a - bX_i$. We can therefore rewrite [9.15] and [9.16] as

$$\sum e_i = 0 \text{ and } \sum X_i e_i = 0.$$ [9.23]

The residuals in OLS regression must therefore always possess the properties [9.23]. It turns out that these properties are often very useful, and we shall make use of them later. But it must be remembered that it is only OLS residuals that satisfy [9.23]. That is, the equations [9.23] can only be obtained when we use the OLS method of estimation.

We can now use the data in Table 9.1 to compute values for a and b for our demand-for-money example. Basic calculations are shown in Table 9.2, where the sums of the columns give us the numerical quantities $\sum X_i$, $\sum Y_i$, $\sum Y_i^2$, $\sum X_i^2$ and $\sum X_i Y_i$.

We can now calculate the sample mean values for the demand for money per head and GDP per head as

$$\bar{Y} = \frac{23.718}{30} = 0.7906 \quad \text{and} \quad \bar{X} = \frac{132.004}{30} = 4.4001.$$ [9.24]

Table 9.2 Basic computations based to Table 9.1

OBS.	X	Y	X^2	Y^2	XY
1	2.1520	0.16470	4.6310	0.027126	0.35443
2	10.0014	1.0338	100.0284	1.0687	10.3392
3	1.6730	0.12624	2.7989	0.015936	0.21120
4	0.17638	0.036328	0.031108	0.0013197	0.0064074
5	13.7998	2.0096	190.4351	4.0385	27.7321
6	1.2193	0.13388	1.4868	0.017925	0.16325
7	1.0077	0.43287	1.0154	0.18738	0.43620
8	9.4661	2.3912	89.6078	5.7180	22.6358
9	10.2113	1.7531	104.2712	3.0733	17.9012
10	0.46857	0.052155	0.21955	0.0027202	0.024438
11	1.9366	0.45515	3.7503	0.20716	0.88143
12	0.28180	0.044403	0.079410	0.0019716	0.012513
13	0.52070	0.055788	0.27113	0.0031123	0.029049
14	7.4967	2.8369	56.2007	8.0479	21.2673
15	10.9748	3.0892	120.4463	9.5431	33.9032
16	0.28803	0.038689	0.082959	0.0014968	0.011143
17	1.9942	0.36352	3.9768	0.13215	0.72493
18	2.2609	0.17169	5.1116	0.029477	0.38817
19	6.8687	0.62824	47.1795	0.39469	4.3152
20	0.77267	0.15670	0.59702	0.024555	0.12108
21	0.31190	0.080302	0.097283	0.0064484	0.025046
22	0.60220	0.035168	0.36264	0.0012368	0.021178
23	2.2118	0.44167	4.8919	0.19507	0.97686
24	1.6932	0.30064	2.8668	0.090383	0.50903
25	4.2548	1.0065	18.1030	1.0130	4.2824
26	11.9883	1.4314	143.7194	2.0490	17.1603
27	0.74743	0.064666	0.55865	0.0041817	0.048333
28	8.1162	1.4137	65.8726	1.9984	11.4735
29	16.5921	2.6786	275.2992	7.1751	44.4445
30	1.9151	0.29163	3.6675	0.085050	0.55850
Σ	132.004	23.718	1247.66	45.154	220.956

Next, using the sums of the columns in Table 9.2, we calculate what we shall call the three basic building blocks of two-variable regression analysis:

$$\sum x_i^2 = \sum X_i^2 - \frac{(\sum X_i)^2}{n} \qquad [9.25]$$

$$= 1247.66 - \frac{132.00^2}{30} = 666.86;$$

$$\Sigma\, x_i y_i = \Sigma\, X_i Y_i - \frac{\Sigma\, X_i \Sigma\, Y_i}{n} \qquad\qquad [9.26]$$

$$= 220.96 - \frac{132.00 \times 23.718}{30} = 116.60;$$

$$\Sigma\, y_i^2 = \Sigma\, Y_i - \frac{(\Sigma\, Y_i)^2}{n} \qquad\qquad [9.27]$$

$$= 45.154 - \frac{23.718^2}{30} = 26.403.$$

The quantities [9.25] and [9.27] are sums of squares and must therefore always be positive. However, [9.26] can be either positive or negative. In fact, if $\Sigma\, x_i y_i$ turns out to be negative, then this is an early sign that the sample regression line must be downward sloping.

From now on, it is crucial to distinguish between X_i and x_i and between Y_i and y_i when making calculations. Recall that X_i and Y_i refer to the actual sample values of X and Y, whereas x_i and y_i refer to the *deviations* of actual values from their respective sample means. That is, $x_i = X_i - \bar{X}$ and $y_i = Y_i - \bar{Y}$.

The basic building blocks $\Sigma\, x_i^2$, $\Sigma\, x_i y_i$ and $\Sigma\, y_i^2$ crop up continually in two-variable regression. In fact, we can make use of two of them immediately. Using [9.21], the OLS estimate of β is

$$b = \frac{116.60}{666.86} = 0.174\,85. \qquad\qquad [9.28]$$

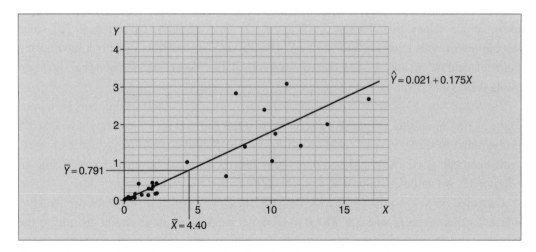

Figure 9.9 The OLS sample regression line fitted to the scatter of Fig. 9.1

Once b has been found, we can use [9.22] and [9.24] to find the OLS estimate of a. In fact

$$a = \bar{Y} - b\bar{X} = 0.790\,6 - 0.174\,85 \times 4.4001 = 0.021\,24. \qquad [9.29]$$

Our OLS sample regression equation is therefore

$$\hat{Y} = 0.021 + 0.175X, \qquad [9.30]$$

where we have expressed a and b to three decimal places.

This sample regression equation has been plotted against the original scatter diagram in Fig. 9.9. Notice that, as desired, the sample line passes fairly closely to each of the points.[9] For example, using [9.30], country 15 (Japan) has $\hat{Y} = 1.942$, compared with $Y = 3.089$. Recall that the vertical distances between points in the scatter and the fitted sample regression line are the sample residuals, defined by [9.12].

Example 9.2

Use the data in Table 9.1 and the OLS sample line [9.30] to obtain the predicted demand-for-money values for:

(a) Canada;

(b) Indonesia;

(c) Spain.

Find also the residuals associated with each of these countries.

An OLS sample regression line always passes through the point where X and Y take their mean sample values, that is where $X = \bar{X}$ and $Y = \bar{Y}$. This should be clear from [9.22], since we can rewrite this equation as $\bar{Y} = a + b\bar{X}$. For obvious reasons this point is known as the point of sample means. In the current example it has co-ordinates (to three sig. figs) (4.40, 0.791) and is shown in Fig. 9.9.

Notice that our sample regression line has an intercept $a > 0$, albeit a small one. However, at the beginning of this chapter we suggested that the demand for money might be exactly proportional to GDP. That is, the demand-for-money function could be written as $Y = bX$, with intercept $a = 0$. Although $a > 0$, it does indeed seem to be close to zero and, in Chapter 12, we will explain how to test whether the true a is zero or not.

The value $b = 0.175$ tells us that the demand for money per head will increase by $175 whenever there is an increase of $1000 in GDP per head. But a more useful quantity is the income (or GDP) elasticity of the demand for money. We will therefore use the above results to estimate this income elasticity.

The required elasticity is given by the usual formula

$$\eta = \frac{dY}{dX}\frac{X}{Y} \qquad [9.31]$$

However, we have estimated a linear demand-for-money function, and the income elasticity will therefore vary along our sample regression line, because the values of X and Y in [9.31] will vary along that line. dY/dX in [9.31] can be estimated by b, the slope of the sample regression line, and it is customary to work out the elasticity at values for X and Y that are equal to the sample means. Recall that the points $X = \bar{X}$ and $Y = \bar{Y}$ lie on the sample regression line, so we are actually calculating the elasticity roughly 'halfway' along it.

Since $b = 0.174\,85$ from [9.28] and the sample means are, from [9.24], $\bar{X} = 4.4001$ and $\bar{Y} = 079061$, we have

$$\eta = 0.174\,85 \, \frac{4.4001}{0.790\,6} = 0.973.$$

Thus we obtain an income elasticity relatively close to unity. That is, a 1% rise in GDP per head leads approximately to a 0.97% rise in demand for money per head.

Notice that the classical equation of exchange [9.1] implies not only an intercept of zero, but also an income elasticity of unity, when it is written in the form [9.2]. We have obtained an elasticity close to unity and, in Chapter 12, we will explain how it is possible to test the hypothesis of a unitary income elasticity. Firstly, however, in Chapter 10 we will consider alternative methods of estimating elasticities.

We have seen how it is possible to obtain predicted values, $\hat{Y}$, for all the countries in our sample. But we can also obtain predicted demand-for-money values for countries outside our sample. Suppose some imaginary country, Westeuro, has a GDP of $8500 per head and we wish to predict the demand for money per head in this country. We can set $X = 8.5$ in the sample regression equation [9.30]. This yields

$$\hat{Y} = 0.021 + 0.175(8.5) = 1.51.$$

Thus we predict that, at this level of GDP per head, Westeuro will have a demand for money of $1510 per head.

For obvious reasons such a prediction is known as an out-of-sample prediction. We shall have more to say about out-of-sample predictions in Chapter 12, when we show how it is possible to put confidence intervals on such predictions. This will give us some idea of the reliability or precision of our estimates and predictions.

Example 9.3

Easteuro has a GDP of $2230 per head. Predict the level of the demand for money in this country.

The following examples should enable you to obtain a good grasp of the numerical procedures that have to be followed in obtaining OLS estimators. In Examples 9.5 and 9.6 certain quantities are given so that you can concentrate on procedure rather than basic arithmetic.

Example 9.4

The data in the following table relate to 15 developed countries; Y is per-capita income (in thousands of dollars) and X is the percentage of the labour force engaged in agriculture.

Y	13	11	12	10	9	12	11	8	12	11	12	10	10	13	12
X	4	7	3	9	12	5	8	11	7	6	6	8	10	4	7

(a) Verify that $\sum X_i^2 = 859$, $\sum Y_i^2 = 1866$ and $\sum X_i Y_i = 1137$.

(b) Find $\sum x_i^2$, $\sum x_i y_i$ and $\sum y_i^2$.

(c) Estimate the OLS sample regression line $\hat{Y} = a + bX$.

(d) Plot a scatter diagram for the data and draw in the sample line estimated in (c).

(e) Estimate the elasticity of per-capita income with respect to agricultural employment at the point of sample means.

Example 9.5

The following data refer to the weekly consumption expenditure C (£) and disposable income Y (£) of 10 families.

C	150	70	155	65	110	115	95	90	140	120
Y	260	80	240	100	160	180	140	120	220	200

$\sum C_i^2 = 132\ 100$ $\sum Y_i^2 = 322\ 000$ $\sum C_i Y_i = 205\ 500$
[You do *not* need to check any of these calculations.]

(a) Calculate $\sum c_i^2$, $\sum y_i^2$ and $\sum c_i y_i$.

(b) Use the OLS method to estimate the marginal propensity to consume for these families.

(c) Predict the weekly expenditure of a family with a weekly income of £350.

[*Strong hint*: always rename your variables Y for the dependent variable and X for the explanatory variable. This saves needless confusion and minimizes the possibility of numerical errors. Thus, in this example, start by letting $Y = X$ and then $C = Y$.]

Example 9.6

Let U be the percentage unemployment rate and Q the quit rate in quits per 1000 employees. The following data refer to 180 consecutive quarters in a developed western economy:
$\bar{U} = 6.61$, $\bar{Q} = 14.84$, $\sum q_i^2 = 3237.7$, $\sum u_i^2 = 1745.2$, $\sum u_i q_i = -2084.3$.
[Lower-case letters denote deviations of variables from their means. For example, $u_i = U_i - \bar{U}$.]

(a) Use the OLS method to estimate a relationship of the kind $Q = a + bU + \varepsilon$, where ε is a disturbance.

(b) Interpret your estimate of β.

We mentioned earlier that ordinary least squares is, almost certainly, the best-known method of estimating a population regression equation. However, a word of caution is appropriate at this point. While OLS is well known, this does not mean that it is necessarily the best method of estimation. In fact, in many situations, it turns out that other methods prove to be superior. However, before we consider the relative merits of various estimating methods, we need to develop some criteria for judging various estimators. We shall do just that in Chapter 11, where we will also examine alternative estimating approaches. Then, in Chapter 12, we shall consider the specific conditions under which OLS estimation might be considered superior to other approaches.

9.4 Measuring goodness of fit

In the previous section (see Fig. 9.9) we fitted the sample regression line [9.30] to our scatter of points. We found that our line passed 'fairly closely' to each point in the scatter. However, we need to be rather more precise than this; that is, we require some numerical measure of *goodness of fit*. An obvious measure is the so-called *coefficient of determination* which is, in fact, equal to the square of the sample correlation coefficient, introduced in Chapter 6 as equation [6.21]. Since the correlation coefficient lies between 1 and −1, it follows that the coefficient of determination must lie between 0 and 1. We in fact computed the sample correlation for our demand-for-money example in Section 9.1, obtaining a value of $R = 0.8787$. In this case, the coefficient of determination must therefore be $R^2 = 0.772$.

In regression analysis it is possible to give a very precise interpretation of the value 0.772 obtained for R^2. To do this, we first pose the question: *What proportion of the variation in the demand for money for our 30 countries can be attributed to variations in their GDPs?* Clearly, if we are able to explain a high proportion of demand for money variations then this must imply a well-fitting sample regression line.

Consider Fig. 9.10, on which is plotted a single point from the data in Table 9.1. The point refers in fact to France, country 8, which has $Y_8 = 2.3912$, with predicted $\hat{Y}_8 = 1.6776$. The horizontal line refers to the mean level of the demand for money per head, $\bar{Y} = 0.7906$. What follows applies equally well to all points in the scatter.

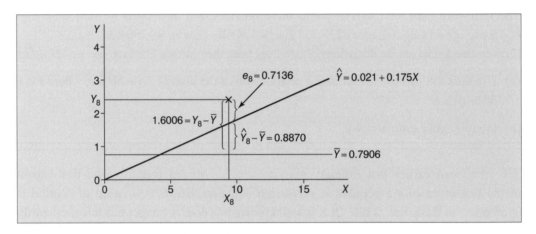

Figure 9.10 Total, explained and residual variations

We measure variations in demand-for-money values relative to their mean value $\bar{Y} = 0.7906$. For France, the *total variation* in the demand for money per head Y, from its mean, is therefore given by $Y_8 - \bar{Y} = 1.6006$, as shown in Fig. 9.10. However, we can also say that, for France, *the variation in Y that can be attributed to the influence of X* (i.e., that can be attributed to the regression line) is given by $\hat{Y}_8 - \bar{Y} = 0.8870$. The remaining variation in the demand for money, that is, the variation that cannot be attributed to X, is seen to be given by the residual associated with France, $e_8 = 0.7136$. For obvious reasons, this is referred to as the *residual variation*.

It should be clear from Fig. 9.10 and equation [9.12] that, for France,

$$\text{total variation} = \text{variation due to } X + \text{residual variation}$$
$$Y_8 - \bar{Y} \quad = \quad \hat{Y}_8 - \bar{Y} \quad + \quad e_8$$

or

$$1.6006 \quad = \quad 0.8870 \quad + \quad 0.7136.$$

In fact, for each point in a scatter (i.e., each country) it is possible to divide the total variation in Y into a variation due to X and a residual variation, just as we did for France. Thus, we have

$$Y_i - \bar{Y} \quad = \quad \hat{Y}_i - \bar{Y} + e_i, \qquad i = 1, 2, 3, ..., n. \qquad [9.32]$$

Note that it is possible for any of the three variations, $Y_i - \bar{Y}$, $\hat{Y}_i - \bar{Y}$ and e_i, to be negative. The total variation will be negative whenever Y_i lies below its mean. The residual variation will be negative, as usual, whenever a point lies below the regression line. Finally, the variation due to X will be negative whenever predicted $\hat{Y}_i$ lies below $\bar{Y}$. Variations can be negative because we are measuring variations from the sample mean $\bar{Y}$. Values above $\bar{Y}$ are regarded as positive and values below $\bar{Y}$ as negative.

The question we set ourselves at the outset referred to all countries in our sample, not to any particular country. We therefore require an overall equivalent of the division [9.32]. A measure, taken over *all* points in a scatter, of the total variation in Y about its mean $\bar{Y}$, is given by the sum of the squares of the individual total variations, $\Sigma(Y_i - \bar{Y})^2$. This is usually referred to as the *total sum of squares* (SST). Since it is a sum of squares, this measure will always be positive. Notice that if we divide the total sum of squares by n, we would obtain the sample variance, so SST is an obvious measure of variation to adopt.

A similar measure of the variation in Y that can be attributed to X, again taken over *all* points in the scatter, is given by $\Sigma(\hat{Y}_i - \bar{Y})^2$. That is, we take the sum of the squares of the individual variations due to X. This quantity is referred to as the *explained sum of squares* (SSE). Again, this quantity will always be positive.

Finally, the obvious measure of the overall residual variation is the positive quantity Σe_i^2, which is the *residual sum of squares* (SSR).

Next consider the following result. In a moment, we shall show that, over all points in the scatter, it is the case that

total sum of squares   =   explained sum of squares   +   residual sum of squares,

that is,

$$\Sigma(Y_i - \bar{Y})^2 = \Sigma(\hat{Y}_i - \bar{Y})^2 + \Sigma e_i^2 \qquad [9.33]$$

or

$$\text{SST} = \text{SSE} + \text{SSR}.$$

It may seem obvious that the above equation should hold. Simple common sense suggests that the total variation should be the sum of the variation that can be attributed to X and the variation that cannot be attributed to X (i.e., the residual variation). However, there are a number of ways in which we could have defined the above variations and there can be no guarantee that such a common-sense division will be valid for the definitions we have chosen.

We investigate the relationship [9.33] between the three sums of squares by squaring both sides of [9.32] and then summing over all sample observations. This gives

$$\Sigma(Y_i - \bar{Y})^2 = \Sigma(\hat{Y}_i - \bar{Y} + e_i)^2$$

or

$$\Sigma(Y_i - \bar{Y})^2 = \Sigma(\hat{Y}_i - \bar{Y})^2 + \Sigma e_i^2 + 2 \Sigma e_i(\hat{Y}_i - \bar{Y}). \qquad [9.34]$$

A comparison of [9.33] and [9.34] indicates that the result [9.33] will not normally be valid.[10] In fact the suggested division of the total sum of squares into explained and residual (unexplained) components will only be valid if, in [9.34],

$$\Sigma e_i(\hat{Y}_i - \bar{Y}) = 0. \qquad [9.35]$$

Under what conditions will the quantity $\Sigma e_i(\hat{Y}_i - \bar{Y})$ be zero as required? Using [9.10] gives

$$\begin{aligned}
\Sigma e_i(\hat{Y}_i - \bar{Y}) &= \Sigma e_i(a + bX_i - \bar{Y}) \\
&= a \Sigma e_i + b \Sigma X_i e_i - \bar{Y} \Sigma e_i. \qquad [9.36]
\end{aligned}$$

Recall the properties of the OLS residuals given by [9.23], that is, $\Sigma e_i = 0$ and $\Sigma X_i e_i = 0$. Given these properties, it can be seen from [9.36] that we do have $\Sigma e_i(\hat{Y}_i - \bar{Y}) = 0$, so that in this case the division [9.33] is valid. But note that [9.35] and hence [9.33] are valid *only if the method of estimation is OLS* because only then do equations [9.23] hold. If any other method of estimation is used, then [9.35] will not be true and the apparently obvious split of the total variation in Y into explained and unexplained components will not be valid. In such cases, if we want the common-sense division to be valid, then we have to define the three variations differently.

We can now answer the question set at the beginning of this section. We shall define the coefficient of determination R^2, mentioned earlier, as the proportion of the total sample variation in Y that can be attributed to the sample variation in X. That is, using the above terminology,

$$R^2 = \frac{\text{variation attributed to } X}{\text{total variation in } Y} = \frac{\text{SSE}}{\text{SST}}. \qquad [9.37]$$

To compute R^2 using [9.37] we require SST and SSE. We know that SST $= \Sigma y_i^2$, and we can find SSE as follows:

$$\text{SSE} = \Sigma(\hat{Y}_i - \bar{Y})^2 = \Sigma(a + bX_i - \bar{Y})^2,$$

where we have used the OLS sample regression line $\hat{Y}_i = a + bX_i$. Using [9.22], we can now substitute for a to obtain

$$SSE = \sum(\overline{Y} - b\overline{X} + bX_i - \overline{Y})^2$$
$$= \sum(bX_i - b\overline{X})^2 = \sum b^2(X_i - \overline{X})^2 = b^2 \sum x_i^2.$$ [9.38]

Substituting SSE and SST into [9.37] then gives

$$R^2 = \frac{b^2 \sum x_i^2}{\sum y_i^2}.$$ [9.39]

Equation [9.39] is the most convenient expression for the coefficient of determination R^2, since it involves only b and two of the basic building blocks, $\sum x_i^2$ and $\sum y_i^2$. Notice, though, that we have used OLS formulae to obtain it. It should therefore be stressed that we can interpret the R^2 in [9.39] as the proportion of the variation in Y that can be attributed to the variation in X, only if the method of estimation is standard OLS.

Since SST = SSE + SSR, an alternate expression for R^2 can be obtained if [9.37] is written as

$$R^2 = \frac{SST - SSR}{SST} = 1 - \frac{SSR}{SST};$$

that is,

$$R^2 = 1 - \frac{\sum e_i^2}{\sum y_i^2}.$$ [9.40]

Equation [9.40] is a less convenient expression than [9.39] since it requires the computation of $\sum e_i^2$. Recall also that the division SST = SSE + SSR, used to obtain [9.40], is only valid if the estimation method is OLS. Thus, like [9.39], [9.40] can only be given its usual interpretation when OLS is being used.

For our demand-for-money example, we already have $b = 0.174\,85$, $\sum x_i^2 = 666.86$ and $\sum y_i^2 = 26.403$. Thus, we can use [9.39] to obtain $R^2 = 0.772$. So we can say that close to 77% of the variation in the demand for money may be attributed to the variation in GDP. The 0.772 is, as pointed out earlier, the square of the correlation coefficient, $R = 0.8787$.

The relationship between the two coefficients can be demonstrated fairly easily. If we square expression [6.11] for R, we obtain

$$\frac{(\sum x_i y_i)^2}{\sum x_i^2 \sum y_i^2} = \frac{(\sum x_i y_i)^2 / \sum x_i^2}{\sum y_i^2}$$
$$= \frac{(\sum x_i y_i / \sum x_i^2)^2 \sum x_i^2}{\sum y_i^2} = \frac{b^2 \sum x_i^2}{\sum y_i^2},$$

which is expression [9.39] for R^2.

Since R^2 is a proportion, its value must lie between 0 and 1. Unlike R, it can never be negative. However, if we refer back to Figs 9.3, we can assign values for R^2 to each figure. In Fig. 9.3a, all the points in the scatter lie exactly on a positively sloping sample line, so that $R = +1$ and $R^2 = 1$. The value $R^2 = 1$ implies that 100% of the variation in Y can be attributed to variations in X. This reflects the fact that all points lie on a single line. In Fig. 9.3c, $R = -1$ and again we have $R^2 = 1$. Thus again all points lie on a straight line (this time negatively sloping) and again we can explain 100% of the variation. Finally, in Fig. 9.3b, the points are evenly spread, there is no correlation ($R = 0$) and we are unable to explain any of the variation in Y ($R^2 = 0$).[11]

The coefficients of determination and correlation are clearly closely linked statistically. However, statisticians tend to use the correlation coefficient simply as a measure of the strength of the association between two variables. Nothing about causation is implied, and it is recognized that much of the correlation present may be totally spurious. Furthermore, nothing is inferred about the direction of any causation that may be believed to be present.

In contrast, when a statistician uses the coefficient of determination, the underlying model is always the regression model in which it is *assumed* that Y is linearly dependent on X. That is, some assumption about causation is made at the outset. Then R^2 is interpreted as the proportion of the sample variation in Y that can be attributed to X. However, notice that we used the phrase 'can be attributed to X' not 'can be explained by X'. We stressed above the possibility of some spurious correlation between X and Y which is not the result of a direct causal link. At least part of R^2 may therefore be spurious, and it is wiser to refer to the proportion of variations in Y that can be *attributed* to X.

Example 9.7

Calculate the coefficient of determination, using [9.39], and the correlation coefficient, using [6.21], for the data in Example 9.4. Verify that the coefficient of determination is the square of the correlation coefficient.

Example 9.8

Calculate the coefficient of determination, R^2, for the data in Example 9.6. Interpret its value.

Computer Exercise 9.1

As a general principle we believe that, as far as possible, it is highly desirable that students should tackle numerical regression problems using hand calculators, before they make any use of regression software. Only then will they have a clear idea of what the computer is doing for them. Otherwise, as regression statistics become more numerous, it becomes increasingly difficult to understand them, let alone interpret them. This will be particularly the case when we come to tackle multiple regression in later chapters.

In the spirit of this approach we have therefore, firstly, obtained the values a, b and R^2 as in the main text for the data in Table 9.1. They were presented in [9.29], [9.28] and using [9.39]. For convenience sake we reproduce them here:

$$a = 0.021\ 22, \qquad b = 0.174\ 85, \qquad R^2 = 0.772. \tag{9.41}$$

You should make use of any regression software that is available to you to verify that the values obtained earlier were correct!

Having entered your regression program, access the file DATASET 1 from the learning centre and view the data held in it. You will find 33 observations on four variables. In this exercise, we will use just the first two variables M, which is demand for money per head, and G, which is GDP per head and the first 30 numbered observations. That is, we will use the data in Fig. 9.1. You should check these data.

Since we intend to compute a sample regression line with an intercept, you may have to create this intercept. This can be done using a facility in your regression program. You will probably have to provide the constant with a name, for example, *inter*.

Before estimating a two-variable regression equation it is always worthwhile taking a look at the two-dimensional scatter of observations. Your program will almost certainly have a facility enabling you to do this. The scatter obtained should look identical to that in Fig. 9.1.

You are now in a position to estimate a simple two-variable regression equation. You can do this by employing the *single equation estimation* section of your program. It will be necessary to specify whether you wish to use all the observations in the sample. It may be possible to use, for example, just the first 20 or the last 20. We shall use just the first 30 observations in the data set.

Next, you will have to enter the name of the dependent variable (regressand), followed by the names of explanatory variables (regressors), including the intercept. That is, you will have to type something like

$$M \quad inter \quad G$$

At this point you will probably be given a choice of estimation methods. Since OLS is the only method you are familiar with, at this stage, select ordinary least squares! You may also be asked to specify the number of observations to be used in a 'predictive failure test'. Ignore this by asking for none. Eventually you should find your OLS regression result on the screen.

In Fig. 9.11 you will see the top part of the regression result. This is, in fact, what you will find in the results window for the regression program Microfit 4. But all regression programmes will present the result in a similar manner. Very little of it will make much sense as yet, but three crucial quantities, a, b and R^2, have been highlighted and labelled in Fig. 9.11 and you will also find a value for the residual sum of squares quoted. Check that, allowing for possible rounding error, these values are the same as those in [9.41].

```
                    Ordinary Least Squares Estimation
*****************************************************************************
 Dependent variable is M
 30 observations used for estimation from   1 to 30
*****************************************************************************
 Regressor              Coefficient        Standard Error       T-Ratio[Prob]
 INTER                    .021258 ←―a              .11576         .18364[.856]
 G                        .174582 ←―b             .017950        9.7408[.856]
*****************************************************************************
 R-Squared          R²→  .77214   R-Bar-Squared                       .76400
 S.E of Regression        .46353   F-stat.    F( 1,   28)     94.8827[.000]
 Mean of Dependent Variable .79061 S.D. of Dependent Variable          .95416
 Residual Sum of Squares  6.0160   Equation Log-likelihood         -18.4665
 Akaike Info. Criterion -20.4665   Schwarz Bayesian Criterion      -21.8677
 DW-statistic            1.2825
*****************************************************************************


                          Diagnostic Tests
*****************************************************************************
    Test Statistics        LM Version              F Version
*****************************************************************************
 *                     *                   *                           *
 *A:Serial Correlation *CHSQ( 1)=  4.1520[.042] *F( 1,  27)=  4.3370[.047]*
 *                     *                   *                           *
 *B:Functional Form    *CHSQ( 1)=  2.1167[.146] *F( 1,  27)=  2.0497[.164]*
 *                     *                   *                           *
 *C:Normality          *CHSQ( 2)= 27.6684[.000] *    Not applicable      *
 *                     *                   *                           *
 *D:Heteroscedasticity *CHSQ( 1)=  2.5583[.110] *F( 1,  28)=  2.6103[.117]*
*****************************************************************************
    A:Lagrange multiplier test of residual serial correlation
    B:Ramsey's RESET test using the square of the fitted values
    C:Based on a test of skewness and kurtosis of residuals
    D:Based on the regression of squared residuals on squared fitted values
```

Figure 9.11

Work out how to save and then obtain a printout of your regression result. Obtain such a printout.

Computer Exercise 9.2

In this exercise you are asked to replicate the answers to Examples 9.4 and 9.5 This will involve you inputting data from the keyboard yourself.

Having entered your program, open a new data file. Your first task is then to enter the data on Y (per-capita income) and X (percentage of labour in agriculture) from Example 9.4. Firstly, you may have to choose the appropriate data frequency, but since your data is cross-sectional select an undated option. You will, almost certainly, have to enter the number of the observations (15) and the number of variables (2). You will now find that your two variables have been given standard names (maybe $X1$ and $X2$, for example). Change their names to Y and X (in that order!) and describe them as 'per capita income' and 'percent in agri'.

Next create an intercept as you did in Computer Exercise 9.1. It is most important, at this stage, to *check*, *edit* and *save* your data, before you rush on and start computing regression equations. If an error has been made when inputting your data and has not been corrected, then any regression results obtained are worthless. An apparently simple error, such as a misplaced decimal point in just one number, will totally invalidate your results. A lot of time and energy can be saved by getting your data right first time!

Check the Y and X data, making any necessary corrections. Notice that it is also possible to check the variable *inter* created earlier to provide your equation with an intercept. You should find that *inter* takes the same value of unity in each observation. In fact a in, for example [9.30], can be regarded as the coefficient on a variable (*inter*) that always takes the value unity. [12] When you have finished your data checking, close the data file, give it a name and save it, obeying the instructions given by your program. It is a good idea to save your data immediately in case you should forget to do so later.

You are now in a position to estimate the linear regression equation $Y = \alpha + \beta X + \varepsilon$. Following the same procedures as in Computer Exercise 9.1, you can now check the values for a, b and R^2 obtained in Example 9.4.

Now tackle Example 9.5 in the same way, entering the two data series for this example, giving them the names C and Y. As for Example 9.4, replicate the values for a, b and R^2.

Summary

- In economics we usually have to deal with **sample correlations** rather than population correlations. It is possible to *t*-test whether a sample correlation is significantly different from zero, but we must be aware of the possibility of **spurious correlations**.

- In **two-variable regression analysis** an assumption is made about the direction of causation between the two variables. An unknown **population regression equation**, assumed to be linear, links the variables X and Y.

- **Disturbances** represent the effects of (a) **random unpredictability** and (b) **variables other than X** on the **dependent Y variable**.

- Sample data are used to estimate the population regression equation by fitting a **sample regression equation** to a two-dimensional **scatter**.

- The values of **disturbances** are **unknown** but represent the distances between points in a scatter and the **population regression line**. However, **residuals** are **known** and measure the distances between points in the scatter and the known **sample regression line**.

- The best-known method of estimating a sample regression equation is that of **ordinary least squares (OLS)**. The **OLS estimators** are given by [9.21] and [9.22] and are obtained by minimizing the **residual sum of the squares**.

- In OLS regression, the **total variation** in Y can be divided into an **explained variation** and a **residual variation**. But the usual expressions for such variations are **only valid for OLS regression**.

- **Goodness of fit** is measured by the **coefficient of determination**, which is defined as the proportion of the total variation in Y that can be attributed to variations in the explanatory X variable. The **square** of the **correlation coefficient** equals the **coefficient of determination**.

Appendix 9A

Solving the normal equations

The normal equations [9.19] and [9.20] are reproduced here as

$$\sum Y_i = na + b \sum X_i, \qquad \text{[9A.1]}$$

$$\sum X_i Y_i = a \sum X_i + b \sum X_i^2. \qquad \text{[9A.2]}$$

The solution proceeds as follows. First, we divide [9A.1] throughout by n, the sample size, to obtain

$$\frac{\sum Y_i}{n} = a + \frac{b \sum X_i}{n}. \qquad \text{[9A.3]}$$

Rearranging [9A.3] yields

$$a = \bar{Y} - b\bar{X}, \qquad \text{[9A.4]}$$

where $\bar{Y} = \sum Y_i/n$ and $\bar{X} = \sum X_i/n$ are the sample mean values of Y and X.

Substituting for a in [9A.2] then gives

$$\sum X_i Y_i = \bar{Y} \sum X_i - b\bar{X} \sum X_i + b \sum X_i^2,$$

and hence,

$$\sum X_i Y_i = \frac{\sum X_i \sum Y_i}{n} + b\left[\sum X_i^2 - \frac{(\sum X_i)^2}{n}\right].$$

Thus we can now obtain b as

$$b = \frac{\sum X_i Y_i - (1/n)\sum X_i \sum Y_i}{\sum X_i^2 - (1/n)(\sum X_i)^2}. \qquad [9A.5]$$

Once b is known, a can be found using [9A.4].

Next, note that

$$\begin{aligned}
\sum(X_i - \bar{X})^2 &= \sum(X_i^2 - 2\bar{X}X_i + \bar{X}^2) \\
&= \sum X_i^2 - 2\bar{X} \sum X_i + n\bar{X}^2 \\
&= \sum X_i^2 - \frac{2(\sum X_i)(\sum X_i)}{n} + \frac{(\sum X_i)(\sum X_i)}{n} \\
&= \sum X_i^2 - \frac{(\sum X_i)^2}{n},
\end{aligned}$$

and similarly,

$$\sum(X_i - \bar{X})(Y_i - \bar{Y}) = \sum X_i Y_i - \frac{\sum X_i \sum Y_i}{n}.$$

It is therefore possible to write b in a more compact form as

$$b = \frac{\sum x_i y_i}{\sum x_i^2}, \qquad [9A.6]$$

where $x_i = X_i - \bar{X}$ and $y_i = Y_i - \bar{Y}$. We refer to x_i as the *deviation* of X_i from its mean $\bar{X}$. Similarly, y_i is the deviation of Y_i from its mean $\bar{Y}$.

Equations [9A.4] and [9A.6] are the expressions for the OLS estimators given in the main text. Although it is possible to obtain an expression for a in terms of the X_i and Y_i which does not involve b, it is computationally easier to first obtain b using [9A.6] and then use the estimator b to substitute in [9A.4] and obtain a.

Notes

1. Since the population of (G, M) points must all lie on the single straight line $M = kG$, any sample of such points much also lie on that line.

2. A deeper notion of the sampling distribution arises if we consider a whole series of different realizations or possible 'courses of history', where in each such realization the 30 countries have different values for M and G. There are an infinite number of possible realizations but we experience just one, which provides our sample data.

3. For example, one other obvious such variable might be the rate of interest.

4. The method could be as simple as taking a ruler and drawing a line through the points 'by sight'. It may not involve any complicated 'formulae'.

5. We have arbitrarily drawn the sample regression line with a greater gradient than the unknown population regression line. But the sample line is just as likely to have a smaller gradient.

6. The OLS method may seem a trifle arbitrary, but minimizing the sum of the absolute values of the residuals, $\sum |e_i|$, raises awkward mathematical difficulties. To try to minimize $\sum e_i$ is silly, as a moment's thought makes clear.

7. The word 'normal' is used here in the sense of 'perpendicular' and has no connection here with the 'normal' distribution.

8. If we have only one observation in our sample ($n = 1$), then [9.19] and [9.20] become

$$Y_1 = a + bX_1,$$
$$X_1Y_1 = aX_1 + bX_1^2$$

so that [9.20] is simply [9.19] multiplied by X_1. Thus, there is really only one equation from which we have to find solutions for two variables a and b. For $n = 1$, therefore, the equations do not yield a single unique solution. This is not too surprising since, with $n = 1$, we are trying to fit a regression line to a single point.

   If $n = 2$, then the normal equations will yield OLS estimators a and b but with a residual sum of squares of zero. There are now just two points in the scatter so the sample regression line will pass exactly through the two points with both residuals equal to zero.

9. Figure 9.9 differs from Fig. 9.6 in that in the later figure the OLS line has been fitted against the scatter, while in the earlier one a line has been fitted 'freehand'.

10. Simple algebra indicates that $(p + q)^2 = p^2 + q^2 + 2pq$. So it will not normally be the case that $(p + q)^2 = p^2 + q^2$ unless either p or q is zero.

11. Provided $\sum x_i^2$ is non-zero, [9.39] indicates that R and hence R^2 can only be zero if $b = 0$.

12. For example, [9.10] can be written as $\hat{Y} = aD + bX$, where D is a variable that always takes the value unity.

10

Introduction to nonlinear regression

Objectives

When you have completed your study of this chapter you should be able:

1. to recognize how and when variables need to be nonlinearly transformed before OLS estimation is performed;

2. to understand how various nonlinear curves can be fitted to a scatter of points;

3. to use simple econometric software to fit appropriate nonlinear functions to a given data set;

4. to recognize the limitations of R^2 when comparing the goodness of fit of linear and various nonlinear functions;

5. to use the Zarembka procedure for comparing the goodness of fit of linear and double-log functions;

6. to fit nonlinear time trends to data series;

7. to appreciate the problems that arise when an equation is 'nonlinear in its parameters'.

Introduction

In the two-variable regression model of the previous chapter, we assumed that the relationship between our two variables was always linear. We assumed a population regression equation of the form $E(Y) = \alpha + \beta X$ rather than, for example, $E(Y) = \alpha + \beta X^2$. That is, the sample regression equation we fitted to a scatter of points was always a straight line. But economic relationships are not normally linear. For example, the demand curve and the consumption function of the standard first-year economics textbook are almost always non-linear to a lesser or greater extent. In this chapter we therefore consider various nonlinear functions that can be fitted to two-dimensional scatters of points. We also consider the problem of deciding which functional form provides the best fit to a given data set.

10.1 A transformation technique

There is one very simple way of fitting a curve to a scatter of points, and this is to apply the so-called *transformation technique*. Consider the equation

$$Y^* = \alpha + \beta X^*, \tag{10.1}$$

where $X^* = X^*(X)$ and $Y^* = Y^*(Y)$ are simple functions or transformations of two variables X and Y, respectively. The transformations we choose will depend on the precise scatter that we are faced with. For example, in the next section, we shall let $X^* = \ln(X)$ and $Y^* = \ln(Y)$.

Since [10.1] is a linear equation when expressed in terms of the transformed variables X^* and Y^*, (but not in terms of X and Y), we can apply the regression techniques of Chapter 9 to population regression equations which we assume have the form $E(Y^*) = \alpha + \beta X^*$.[1] The expressions for the OLS estimators [9.21] and [9.22] and for the coefficient of determination [9.39] can then still be used but with X^* and Y^* replacing X and Y, however they are defined. That is,

$$b = \frac{\sum x_i^* y_i^*}{\sum x_i^{*2}}, \qquad a = \bar{Y}^* - b\bar{X}^*, \qquad R^2 = \frac{b^2 \sum x_i^{*2}}{\sum y_i^{*2}} \tag{10.2}$$

where x_i^* and y_i^* are the deviations of X_i^* and Y_i^* from their respective means $\bar{X}^* = \sum X_i^*/n$ and $\bar{Y}^* = \sum Y_i^*/n$. This procedure should become clearer as we look at a series of examples.

Consider the data in Table 10.1, which relates to the demand for carrots Y (in kilograms) in a supermarket and the price of carrots X (in pence) over 30 weeks. Suppose we wish to estimate the price elasticity of carrot demand and predict the demand for carrots when the price is 90p per kg. This is therefore an out-of-sample prediction in the sense described in the previous chapter.

Table 10.1 The price of, and the demand for, carrots

Obs	1	2	3	4	5	6	7	8	9	10
Y (kg)	99	83	68	80	69	55	66	58	59	44
X (pence)	25	25	27	28	30	32	35	38	41	43
Obs	**11**	**12**	**13**	**14**	**15**	**16**	**17**	**18**	**19**	**20**
Y (kg)	55	38	42	43	36	44	35	35	38	52
X (pence)	54	52	60	64	70	70	71	66	61	58
Obs	**21**	**22**	**23**	**24**	**25**	**26**	**27**	**28**	**29**	**30**
Y (kg)	40	41	37	45	36	56	45	48	44	56
X (pence)	56	52	48	51	46	45	40	39	39	41

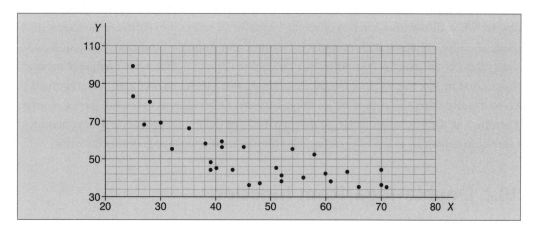

Figure 10.1 Scatter for data in Table 10.1

A scatter diagram of this data is shown in Fig. 10.1. It should be clear that it would be unwise to fit a straight line to this scatter of points. Some kind of curve is likely to fit the scatter better, since the relationship between X and Y appears to be nonlinear. In fact the fitting of a linear sample regression equation to the scatter, using the methods of the last chapter, yields

$$\hat{Y} = 92.9 - 0.881X, \qquad [10.3]$$

with a coefficient of determination $R^2 = 0.61$.

The out-of-sample prediction, obtained when $X = 90$, is $\hat{Y} = 92.9 - 0.881(90) = 13.6$ kg. Study of the scatter in Fig. 10.1, suggests that the demand for carrots is likely to be considerably higher than 13.6 kg, even though the price is as high as 90p. Clearly we need to allow for the nonlinearity in the data.

Since [10.3] is a linear relationship between demand and price, demand elasticity varies along this sample regression line and is given by

$$\eta = -\frac{dY}{dX}\frac{X}{Y}.$$

We can estimate dY/dX by b from [10.3] and we use the procedure, introduced in Chapter 9, of calculating the elasticity at the point of sample means, $\bar{X} = 46.9$, $\bar{Y} = 51.6$. The estimated elasticity is thus $-(-0.881)(46.9/51.6) = 0.801$. This value implies that a 1% rise in price results in a fall of about 0.80% in demand.

Unfortunately, since a linear regression line did not fit our scatter particularly well, the elasticity estimate obtained is unlikely to be too reliable. Better estimates should be obtainable by allowing for nonlinearity.

There are many relationships that give rise to curves of varying nonlinearity, and in this chapter we shall consider a series of them. Virtually all regression software packages allow users to adopt various transformation techniques and estimate nonlinear regression equations. But before using a computer, we believe it is crucial that such nonlinear methods should first be thoroughly understood. As always, when using a computer, it is important to know exactly what the computer is doing for you! Otherwise, much confusion can arise. Therefore, in the next sections we go through, in some detail, the process of fitting nonlinear regression equations to a scatter, using the transformation technique outlined earlier.

10.2 Double-logarithm functions

Consider the nonlinear function

$$Y = AX^\beta, \qquad A > 0, \qquad\qquad [10.4]$$

where A and β are constants. The possible shapes of the function [10.4] are shown in Figs. 10.2, for various values of the parameter β. It seems that the function in Fig. 10.2c, with $\beta < 0$, might fit the scatter in Fig. 10.1 reasonably well.

How can we estimate the parameters A and β from the scatter in Fig. 10.1? More specifically, is it possible to use the OLS estimation method of the last chapter to fit the function [10.4] to the scatter? Luckily, the function [10.4] has one particularly useful property; if we take logarithms of any base, [10.4] can be transformed into a convenient linear form. Taking natural logs of [10.4] results in

$$\ln(Y) = \alpha + \beta \ln(X), \qquad\qquad [10.5]$$

where $\alpha = \ln(A)$ is also a constant. Equation [10.5] expresses $\ln(Y)$ as a linear function of

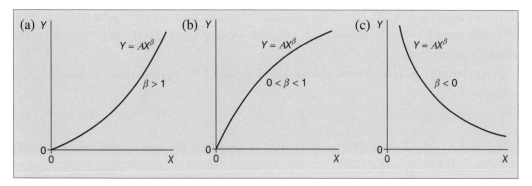

Figure 10.2 Double-logarithmic curves

$\ln(X)$, so we can rewrite it as

$$Y^* = \alpha + \beta X^*, \tag{10.6}$$

where $Y^* = \ln(Y)$ and $X^* = \ln(X)$. Equation [10.6] is identical to [10.1], so this is our first example of the transformation technique introduced in Section 10.1.

We can now apply the linear regression model of the previous chapter to the transformed variables X^* and Y^* because, from [10.6], these variables are *linearly* related. We proceed by defining a linear population regression relationship, analogous to [9.5], but in terms of the transformed variables:

$$E(Y^*) = \alpha + \beta X^*. \tag{10.7}$$

This is our population regression equation. Next we introduce a disturbance ε^* to account for any difference between the actual and expected values of Y^*. That is,

$$Y^* = \alpha + \beta X^* + \varepsilon^*. \tag{10.8}$$

Because [10.7] is a linear function[2] we can now use the OLS method of estimation to estimate it by a sample regression equation analogous to those estimated in Chapter 9. This will have the form

$$\hat{Y}^* = a + bX^* \tag{10.9}$$

where $\hat{Y}^*$ is the predicted value of Y^*, and a and b are the OLS estimators of α and β.

Notice that we can also write [10.9] in the form

$$\hat{Y} = AX^b, \tag{10.10}$$

where $\ln(A) = a$, since, taking natural logs of [10.10] leads back to [10.9]. Equation [10.10] is the estimated sample version of [10.4].

To obtain a and b in [10.9], we can simply use the general OLS estimators of [10.2] with $X^* = \ln(X)$ and $Y^* = \ln(Y)$. However, it is worth looking more closely at how a and b are obtained in this case.

In fact we choose a and b so as to minimize the sum of the squares of the residuals $\sum e_i^{*2}$, where now

$$e_i^* = Y_i^* - \hat{Y}_i^*, \qquad i = 1, 2, 3, \ldots, n, \qquad [10.11]$$

rather than $e_i = Y_i - \hat{Y}_i$ as in Chapter 9. In [10.11], the Y_i^* are the transformed values of Y and the $\hat{Y}_i^*$ found from [10.9].

Minimization of $\sum e_i^{*2}$ leads to normal equations identical to [9.19] and [9.20] except that X_i^* and Y_i^* replace X_i and Y_i. Their solution leads to OLS estimates a and b of the usual form of [9.21] and [9.22] except that they involve values of the transformed rather than the original variables. That is, as in [10.2],

$$b = \frac{\sum x_i^* y_i^*}{\sum x_i^*}, \qquad a = \bar{Y}^* - b\bar{X}^*, \qquad [10.12]$$

where, of course $x_i^* = X_i^* - \bar{X}_i^*$ and $y_i^* = Y_i^* - \bar{Y}_i^*$, so that x_i^* is the deviation of $\ln(X_i)$ from its mean and y_i^* is the deviation of $\ln(Y_i)$ from its mean.[3]

The basic calculations that are required for computation of [10.12] are given in Table 10.2. The summed columns can be used to compute the three basic building blocks. For example,

$$\sum x_i^{*2} = \sum X_i^{*2} - \frac{(\sum X_i^*)^2}{n} = 436.524 - \frac{114.059^2}{30} = 2.875$$

Similarly, $\sum y_i^{*2} = 2.239$ and $\sum x_i^* y_i^* = -2.140$.

We can now use [10.12] to obtain $b = -2.140/2.875 = -0.744$. From Table 10.2 we can obtain $\bar{X}^* = 3.802$ and $\bar{Y}^* = 3.903$. $\bar{X}^*$ and $\bar{Y}^*$ are the sample mean values of $\ln(X)$ and $\ln(Y)$ respectively, but note that the mean value of $\ln(X)$, for example, is not the same as the log of the mean value of X. In fact $\bar{X} = 46.9$, so $\ln(\bar{X}) = 3.848$ not 3.802.

Given X^* and Y^*, we can use [10.12] to obtain $a = 6.73$. Our sample regression equation [10.9] is therefore

$$\hat{Y}^* = 6.73 - 0.744X^*. \qquad [10.13]$$

Equation [10.13] is the sample equivalent of the population regression equation [10.7] and is expressed in terms of the transformed variables $X^* = \ln(X)$ and $Y^* = \ln(Y)$. It is of greater interest to express [10.13] in terms of the original variables Y, the demand for carrots, and X, the price of carrots:

$$\widehat{\ln(Y)} = 6.73 - 0.744 \ln(X). \qquad [10.14]$$

Table 10.2 Basic calculations for transformed data

OBS.	$X^* = \ln Y$	$Y^* = \ln Y$	X^{*2}	Y^{*2}	X^*Y^*
1	3.2189	4.5951	10.3612	21.1151	14.7911
2	3.2189	4.4188	10.3612	19.5262	14.2237
3	3.2958	4.2195	10.8625	17.8042	13.9068
4	3.3322	4.3820	11.1036	19.2022	14.6018
5	3.4012	4.2341	11.5681	17.9277	14.4010
6	3.4657	4.0073	12.0113	16.0587	13.8884
7	3.5553	4.1897	12.6405	17.5532	14.8957
8	3.6376	4.0604	13.2320	16.4872	14.7702
9	3.7136	4.0775	13.7906	16.6263	15.1422
10	3.7612	3.7842	14.1466	14.3201	14.2331
11	3.9890	4.0073	15.9120	16.0587	15.9852
12	3.9512	3.6376	15.6123	13.2320	14.3730
13	4.0943	3.7377	16.7637	13.9702	15.3033
14	4.1589	3.7612	17.2963	14.1466	15.6424
15	4.2485	3.5835	18.0497	12.8416	15.2246
16	4.2485	3.7842	18.0497	14.3201	16.0771
17	4.2627	3.5553	18.1704	12.6405	15.1553
18	4.1897	3.5553	17.5532	12.6405	14.8957
19	4.1109	3.6376	16.8993	13.2320	14.9537
20	4.0604	3.9512	16.4872	15.6123	16.0438
21	4.0254	3.6889	16.2035	13.6078	14.8490
22	3.9512	3.7136	15.6123	13.7906	14.6732
23	3.8712	3.6109	14.9862	13.0387	13.9786
24	3.9318	3.8067	15.4593	14.4907	14.9671
25	3.8286	3.5835	14.6585	12.8416	13.7200
26	3.8067	4.0254	14.4907	16.2035	15.3232
27	3.6889	3.8067	13.6078	14.4907	14.0423
28	3.6636	3.8712	13.4217	14.9862	14.1824
29	3.6636	3.7842	13.4217	14.3201	13.8636
30	3.7136	4.0254	13.7906	16.2035	14.9484
Σ	114.059	117.096	436.524	459.289	443.056

Remembering that $a = \ln(A)$ in [10.10], it follows that we can estimate A by $A = e^a = e^{6.73} = 837.1$. We can now write [10.13] in a form similar to our original [10.4] so that we can relate it to the scatter in Fig. 10.1:

$$\hat{Y} = 837.1X^{-0.744}. \qquad [10.15]$$

(Note that taking natural logs of [10.15] leads back to [10.14], so [10.15] must be valid.)

The function [10.15] is obviously a curve rather than a straight line when sketched on the (X, Y) plane. It is therefore trickier to fit it to a scatter such as that in Fig. 10.1. However, in Table 10.3, you will find a series of X values, together with the corresponding $\hat{Y}$ values, obtained using [10.15].

Table 10.3 Points on the log-linear curve					
X	22	34	46	58	70
$\hat{Y}$	84.1	60.9	48.6	40.9	35.6

In Fig. 10.3, the five points from Table 10.3 have been plotted as crosses against the background of the original scatter. The curve corresponding to [10.15] has been sketched from the five crosses. It is clear that the curve fits the scatter rather better than any straight line could.

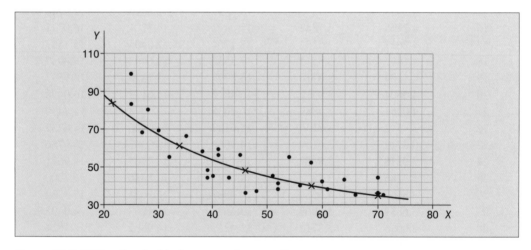

Figure 10.3 Fitting the double-log regression equation

Summarizing the above procedure, we have used the techniques of two-variable *linear* regression to fit a nonlinear relationship to the scatter in Fig. 10.1. The fact that we are still using linear regression can be seen by considering the scatter of points in Fig. 10.4. In Fig. 10.4, we have plotted values of the transformed variables rather than the original variables, using X^*- and Y^*-axes. That is, instead of plotting (on the (X, Y) plane) the X and Y values from Table 10.1, we have plotted (on the (X^*, Y^*) plane) the 30 pairs of X^* and Y^* values, obtained from the second and third columns of Table 10.2. Notice that a straight line now looks like fitting the redefined scatter as well as any curve.

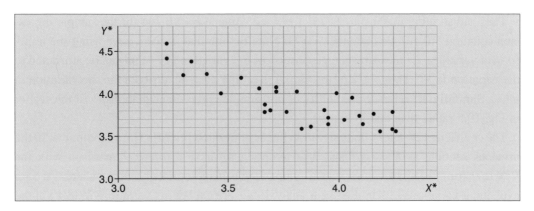

Figure 10.4 Scatter of X^* and Y^* values

Since we are now dealing with the (X^*, Y^*) plane, the relevant sample relationship is [10.13], which is linear in the transformed variables X^* and Y^*. In Fig. 10.5, we have therefore sketched the linear sample regression equation [10.13] onto the scatter, which it fits fairly well. The simple rule is that when we use X- and Y-axes, we express the scatter and the nonlinear sample regression equation in terms of the original variables but, when we use X^*- and Y^*-axes, we work with the transformed variables and a linear sample regression equation. Each approach is equally valid.

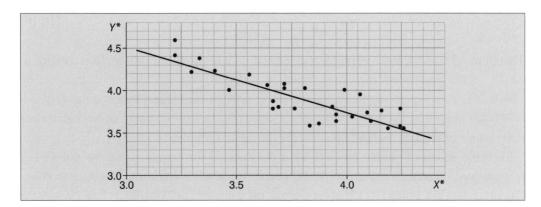

Figure 10.5 Fit of linear equation to transformed data

A coefficient of determination for the sample regression equation [10.13] can be computed using the general form for R^2 in [10.2]:

$$R^2 = \frac{b^2 \sum x_i^{*2}}{\sum y_i^{*2}},$$

where, in this case of course, $X^* = \ln(X)$ and $Y^* = \ln(Y)$.

Thus, substituting in $\sum x_i^{*2} = 2.875$, $\sum y_i^{*2} = 2.239$ and $b = -0.744$ for the sample regression equation [10.13] we obtain $R^2 = 0.71$. Note though that, since we are using the transformed variables, R^2 measures the proportion of the variation in Y^* that can be attributed to the variation in X^*. Thus, 71% of the variation in $\ln(Y)$ can be attributed to the variation in $\ln(X)$. Similarly, R^2 refers to the ability of our sample regression equations to fit the scatter in Fig. 10.5 rather than that in Fig. 10.3.

The coefficient of determination for the linear regression line [10.3] was computed, in the previous section, as $R^2 = 0.61$ and it is tempting to make a direct comparison with the $R^2 = 0.71$ for [10.13]. However, such a comparison is inappropriate because, whereas we are explaining variations in Y in the linear analysis, we are explaining variations in $\ln(Y)$ in the double-log regression. We would not be comparing like with like. We consider this problem further later in the chapter.

As we recalled in the previous section, elasticities vary along the straight line of a linear function. Nonlinear functions normally also have varying elasticities but the one exception is the double-logarithm function [10.4]. Differentiating [10.4] gives

$$\frac{\mathrm{d}Y}{\mathrm{d}X} = \beta AX^{\beta-1}.$$

Thus the elasticity of demand for carrots X with respect to their price Y is

$$\eta = -\frac{\mathrm{d}Y}{\mathrm{d}X}\frac{X}{Y} = -\frac{\beta AX^{\beta-1} X}{AX^{\beta}} = -\beta. \tag{10.16}$$

Therefore $-\beta$ in [10.4] is the required price elasticity; it is also the negative of the coefficient on X^* in the population regression equation [10.8]. Using [10.13], we estimate it by $-b = 0.744$. Thus we can say that a 1% rise in the price of carrots results approximately in a 0.74% fall in the demand for this vegetable. Notice that we have obtained an estimated elasticity rather lower than the 0.80 obtained for the linear formulation [10.3].

To make an out-of-sample prediction for the demand for carrots, using the double-log formulation, when their price rises to 90 pence, we need to substitute $X = 90$ into either [10.14] or [10.15]. Using [10.15] gives a predicted value of $\hat{Y} = 837.1/90^{-0.744}$ or 29.4 kg for a price of $X = 90$. Notice that, as we suggested in Section 10.1, this is a much higher value than the 13.6 kg that we obtained using the linear sample regression equation [10.3].

10.3 **Semi-logarithmic and exponential functions**

Semi-logarithmic functions

In the previous section we fitted a double-log function to the scatter in Fig. 10.1. While this function fitted the scatter rather better than a straight line, it is possible that an alternative function might do the job even better. For example, the *semi-logarithmic function* has the form

$$Y = \alpha + \beta \ln(X), \tag{10.17}$$

and is graphed in Figs 10.6a and 10.6b for positive and negative values of the parameter β. Notice that, unlike the double-log function, the semi-log cuts the X-axis. Moreover, there are no values of β that can approximate a curve like the double-log function for $\beta > 1$ in Fig. 10.2a. But our data does not suggest a curve of this form.

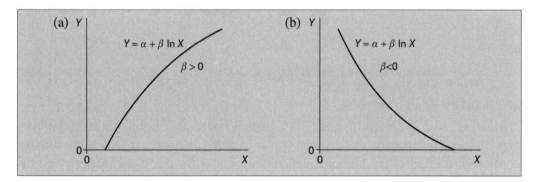

Figure 10.6 Semi-log curves

To fit nonlinear curves such as [10.17], we again have to transform the data. In this case, however, we need to transform the X variable only. We simply let $X^* = \ln(X)$ and $Y^* = Y$, that is, Y is left unchanged. Equation [10.17] then becomes

$$Y^* = \alpha + \beta X^*.$$

Y^* and X^* are therefore again related in the manner of [10.1], so that this is another example of the transformation technique at work. The population regression equation is again

$$E(Y^*) = \alpha + \beta X^*, \tag{10.18}$$

and the sample regression equation

$$\hat{Y}^* = a + bX^* \tag{10.19}$$

but remember that this time $Y^* = Y$ and $X^* = \ln(X)$.

The OLS estimators and R^2 are again given by [10.2], but since $Y^* = Y$ we can write them as

$$b = \frac{\sum x_i^* y_i}{\sum x_i^*}, \qquad a = \bar{Y} - \beta \bar{X}^*, \qquad R^2 = \frac{b^2 \sum x_i^{*2}}{\sum y_i^2} \qquad [10.20]$$

Notice that a and b are obtained this time by minimizing the sum of the squares of residuals of the type

$$e_i^* = Y_i - \hat{Y}_i \;\; = \;\; Y_i - a - b X_i^* \;\; = \;\; Y_i - a - b \ln(X_i).$$

For this formulation the data in table 10.1 yield the basic building blocks

$$\sum x_i^{*2} = 2.875, \qquad \sum y_i^2 = 7283.4, \qquad \sum x_i^* y_i = -120.99.$$

Using [10.20] then gives $b = -42.1$ and $a = 211.6$, so the sample regression equation [10.19] becomes

$$\hat{Y}^* = 211.6 - 42.1 X^* \qquad [10.21]$$

or

$$\hat{Y} = 211.6 - 42.1 \ln(X) \qquad [10.22]$$

in terms of the original variables.

Equation [10.22] is graphed against the original scatter in Fig. 10.7. A comparison of Figs 10.7 and 10.3 suggests that the semi-log function fits the scatter slightly worse than the double-log function of the previous section. One reason for this is the property that the

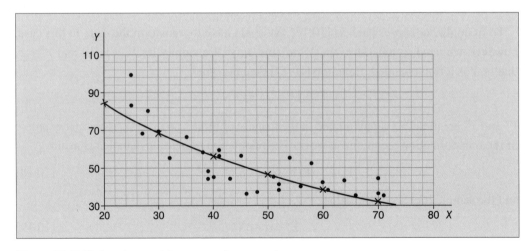

Figure 10.7 Fitting the semi-log regression equation

semi-log curve is forced eventually to intersect the X-axis. In fact, from [10.22], when $Y = 0$, $\ln(X) = 5.03$ so that $X = 153$. This gives the point of intersection (not shown) with the X-axis.

Again we can demonstrate the linear nature of our regression analysis by considering the scatter in Fig. 10.8, where the axes are X^* and $Y^* = Y$. In the (X^*, Y) plane the scatter looks rather more linear, and the linear sample regression line [10.21] fits this scatter relatively well.

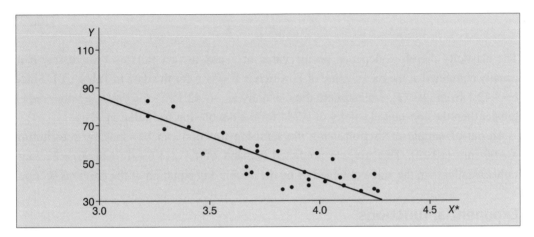

Figure 10.8 Fitting the semi-log regression equation to transformed data

We can compute a coefficient of determination for the semi-log equation by using [10.20]. In fact, this yields $R^2 = 0.70$. It is tempting but incorrect to conclude that this R^2 value and the $R^2 = 0.71$ obtained previously for the double-log function imply similar goodness of fit. But recall our warning, in the previous section, against making such direct comparisons of R^2s. The R^2s obtained refer to the sample regression equations [10.14] and [10.22]. But [10.14] has $\ln(Y)$ as dependent variable, whereas [10.22] has Y. Thus, in the previous section, we found that 71% of the variation in $\ln(Y)$ could be attributed to the variation in $\ln(X)$. But using the semi-log function, we find that 70% of the variation in Y (not $\ln(Y)$) can be attributed to the variation in $\ln(X)$. Consequently, if we compare the R^2s, we are again not comparing like with like. We shall return to this problem in a moment.

We can, however, compare the linear $R^2 = 0.61$, obtained from [10.3], with the semi-log $R^2 = 0.70$, because these equations have the same dependent variable. In each case we are explaining variations in Y. These relative R^2s confirm that nonlinear functions are able to fit the scatter better than any straight line.

Unlike the double-log function, the semi-log does not imply a constant elasticity. Differentiating [10.17] gives

$$\frac{dY}{dX} = \frac{\beta}{X}.$$

Hence the price elasticity of demand is

$$\eta = -\frac{dY}{dX}\frac{X}{Y} = -\frac{\beta}{Y}. \qquad [10.23]$$

The elasticity therefore depends on the value of Y and in fact falls as Y increases. It is usually computed at the mean value of Y, which is $\bar{Y} = 51.6$ for the data in Table 10.1. Since $b = -42.1$ from [10.22], we estimate the elasticity as $-(-42.1)/51.6 = 0.816$, a value rather greater than the constant elasticity of 0.744 for the double-log formulation.

An out-of-sample prediction using the semi-log function can be made by substituting $X = 90$ into [10.22]. This gives a predicted demand of $\hat{Y} = 211.6 - 42.1\ln(90) = 22.2$ kg, rather smaller than the value obtained using the double-log equation of the previous section.

Exponential functions

These functions have the form

$$Y = Ae^{\beta X}, \qquad A > 0. \qquad [10.24]$$

They are graphed in Figs 10.9a and 10.9b, for positive and negative values of β. Notice that these functions cut the Y-axis. So, confronted with a nonlinear scatter suggesting a Y-axis intercept, it would be worth searching for a linear version of [10.24].

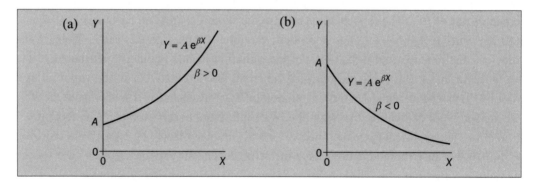

Figure 10.9 Exponential curves

The function [10.24] can, in fact, be linearized by again taking natural logarithms to obtain

$$\ln(Y) = \alpha + \beta X, \qquad \alpha = \ln(A). \tag{10.25}$$

In this case, we let $Y^* = \ln(Y)$ and $X^* = X$. That is, we leave X unchanged. Again we have a population regression equation[4]

$$E(Y^*) = \alpha + \beta X^*$$

and a sample regression equation

$$\hat{Y}^* = a + bX^*$$

which is equivalent to

$$\hat{Y}^* = A\,e^{bX}, \qquad \ln(A) = a. \tag{10.26}$$

[10.26] is comparable with [10.24].

To obtain the OLS estimates and R^2 we can again use [10.2]. Since $X^* = X$, in this case we have

$$b = \frac{\sum x_i y_i^*}{\sum x_i^2}, \qquad a = \bar{Y}^* - b\bar{X}, \qquad R^2 = \frac{b^2 \sum x_i^2}{\sum y_i^{*2}}. \tag{10.27}$$

The data in Table 10.1 can be combined with [10.27] to obtain the sample regression equation

$$\hat{Y}^* = 4.65 - 0.0158X \tag{10.28}$$

or

$$\widehat{\ln(Y)} = 4.65 - 0.0158X$$

which is plotted in Fig. 10.10 against the scatter in Fig. 10.1. Using [10.27], the coefficient of determination for the regression [10.28] is given by $R^2 = 0.64$.

As usual, we must be cautious in interpreting the value for R^2. The value of 0.64 implies that 64% of the variation in $\ln(Y)$ can be attributed to variations in X. We cannot make direct comparisons with the linear and semi-log equations because both these have Y rather than $\ln(X)$ as dependent variable. However, we can compare this exponential formulation with the double-log equation [10.13] which had $R^2 = 0.71$. The double-log fit appears superior, mainly because the exponential equation is constrained to intersect the Y-axis.

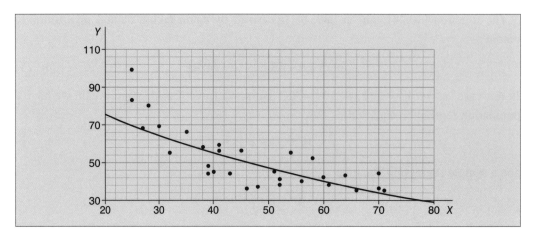

Figure 10.10 Fitting the exponential regression equation

Price elasticities are not constant along an exponential curve. Differentiating [10.24] yields

$$\frac{dY}{dX} = A\beta\,e^{\beta X} = \beta Y.$$

Thus the elasticity, in this case, is given by

$$\eta = -\frac{dY}{dX}\frac{X}{Y} = -\beta X \qquad [10.29]$$

The elasticity depends upon the value of X, and we calculate it at its mean value $\bar{X} = 46.9$. [10.29] gives a price elasticity of $-(-0.0158)46.9 = 0.74$, similar to the estimate obtained for the double-log formulation.

When price $X = 90$, the out-of-sample prediction is, using [10.28], $\widehat{\ln(Y)} = 4.65 - 0.0158 \times 90 = 3.228$, so that $\hat{Y} = 25.2$ kg, a value quite close to that obtained using the semi-log equation.

10.4 Other nonlinear functions

The *reciprocal function* has the form

$$Y = \alpha + \beta\left(\frac{1}{X}\right), \qquad [10.30]$$

and is graphed in Figs 10.11 for positive and negative values for β. When $\beta > 0$, as X increases Y gradually falls towards the constant α but can never fall below it. That is, the curve has an *asymptote* at $Y = \alpha$. But when $\beta < 0$, as X increases, Y gradually increases towards α but can never exceed it. Thus there is again an asymptote at $Y = \alpha$. Clearly [10.30], with $\beta > 0$, is a candidate for fitting to our original scatter in Fig. 10.1.

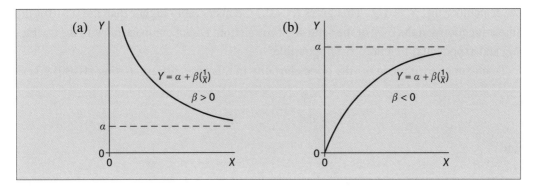

Figure 10.11 Reciprocal curves

To apply the transformation technique we let $X^* = 1/X$ and keep Y unchanged – that is, $Y^* = Y$. The OLS estimators and R^2 then take their usual form [10.2].

Again, using the data in Table 10.1, OLS estimation this time gives $b = 1801$ and $a = 9.33$ and hence a sample regression equation

$$\hat{Y} = 9.33 + 1801\left(\frac{1}{X}\right)$$ [10.31]

This equation is graphed in Fig. 10.12 against the original scatter of Fig. 10.1.

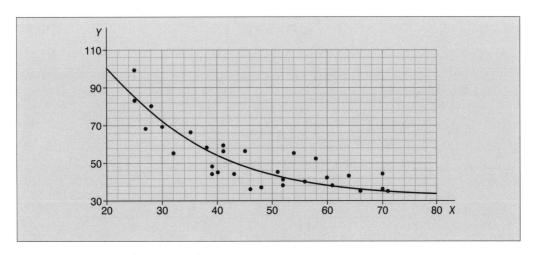

Figure 10.12 Fitting the reciprocal regression equation

Casual observation suggests that the reciprocal curve fits the scatter better than any previously tried. The positive asymptote $a = 9.33$ ensures that the predicted value of Y cannot fall below 9.33, which suits the data well.

We can also use [10.2] to obtain a coefficient of determination for this function, provided we remember that $X^* = 1/X$. This gives $R^2 = 0.77$, considerably higher than the 0.61 for the linear function and the 0.70 of the semi-log formulation. Direct comparison with the double-log and exponential functions is not possible.

To obtain an expression for the price elasticity in this case, differentiating [10.30] gives

$$\frac{dY}{dX} = -\beta X^{-2} = \frac{-\beta}{X^2}$$

and

$$\eta = -\frac{dY}{dX}\frac{X}{Y} = \frac{\beta}{XY}. \qquad [10.32]$$

Evaluating the elasticity at the point of sample means $\bar{X} = 46.9$, $\bar{Y} = 51.6$, gives a price elasticity of 0.74, rather lower than some of the previous estimates.

Finally, we can also use [10.31] to make an out-of-sample prediction. When $X = 90$, $\hat{Y} = 9.33 + 1801/90 = 29.3$ kg. A demand prediction of 29.3 kg is one of the highest found up to this point.

The *logarithmic-reciprocal function* has the rather complicated form

$$Y = e^{\alpha + \beta(1/X)}. \qquad [10.33]$$

Taking natural logs of each side gives

$$\ln(Y) = \alpha + \beta\left(\frac{1}{X}\right). \qquad [10.34]$$

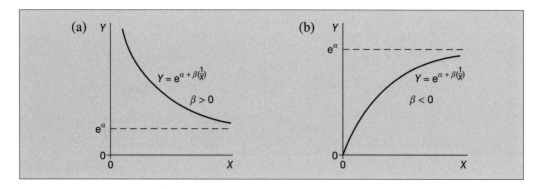

Figure 10.13 Log-reciprocal curves

Thus $\ln(Y)$ is a linear function of $1/X$. The function has asymptotes at $X = 0$ and at $Y = e^{\alpha}$. Its form is shown in Figs 10.13 for positive and negative β. For the scatter in Fig. 10.1, we would expect $\beta > 0$.

For linear regression we clearly need to use the transformed variables $Y^* = \ln(Y)$ and $X^* = 1/X$. The sample regression equation is, in fact,

$$\widehat{\ln(Y)} = 3.17 + 31.3\left(\frac{1}{X}\right), \tag{10.35}$$

with coefficient of determination $R^2 = 0.76$. It is fitted to the scatter of Fig. 10.1 in Fig. 10.14. Casual observation indicates that the log-reciprocal function fits the scatter better than all previous formulations apart from maybe the reciprocal function. The R^2 for [10.35] can be compared directly only with those for the double-log and exponential equations, [10.14] and [10.28], estimated earlier. However, it is clearly greater than the values of 0.71 and 0.64 obtained for these regressions.

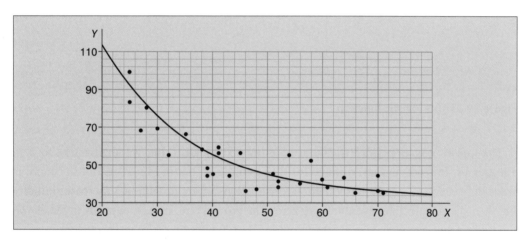

Figure 10.14 Fitting the log-reciprocal regression equation

The demand elasticity can be found by differentiating [10.33] and is given by

$$\eta = \frac{b}{X}.$$

At the mean value of X, $\bar{X} = 46.9$, it takes a value of 0.67, lower than any of the previous estimates. An out-of-sample prediction for demand when $X = 90$ can be found from [10.35] and gives $\widehat{\ln(Y)} = 3.52$. Thus the predicted demand for carrots is 33.8 kg, easily the highest value obtained for the models we have estimated.

The *logistic function* has a curve similar to the log-reciprocal function of Fig. 10.13b, with an upper Y-asymptote at $Y = k$, but it also has a lower asymptote at $Y = 0$. The function has the form

$$Y = \frac{k}{1 + \beta\, e^{-\alpha X}},$$ [10.36]

where α, β and k are all positive parameters. It is is graphed in Fig. 10.15.

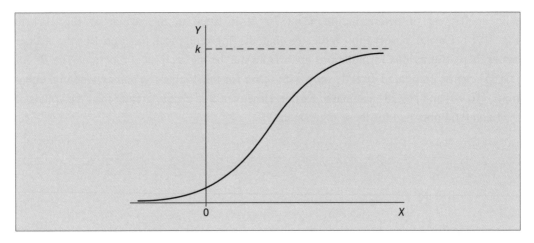

Figure 10.15 The logistic function

The logistic function [10.36] cannot be estimated by OLS, but we shall return to it in Chapter 14. It is not, in fact, suitable for fitting to the scatter in Fig. 10.1. But the curve is frequently used as a good approximation for situations where growth in X increases initially but then starts to decline, eventually to zero. The growth rate, in fact, depends inversely on the current distance from some 'saturation' level of Y determined by the parameter k.

There are many other functions that can be fitted to nonlinear-looking scatters. Some are given in Example 10.1 below. As noted earlier, any function of the form

$$E(Y^*) = \alpha + \beta X^*$$ [10.37]

where X^* and Y^* are suitable transformations of X and Y, can be estimated by OLS. In each such case the OLS estimators and the coefficient of determination are given by [10.2].

Example 10.1

Draw rough sketches of the following functions both for $\beta > 0$ and $\beta < 0$. In each case, it may be assumed that $\alpha > 0$.

(a) $Y = \alpha + \beta X^2$ (b) $Y = \alpha + \beta/X^2$ (c) $Y = \alpha + \beta X^{0.5}$ (d) $1/Y = \alpha + \beta(1/X)$

For each function derive an expression for the elasticity of Y with respect to X.

Example 10.2

Suggest suitable nonlinear functions that could be fitted to the scatters in Fig. 10.16.

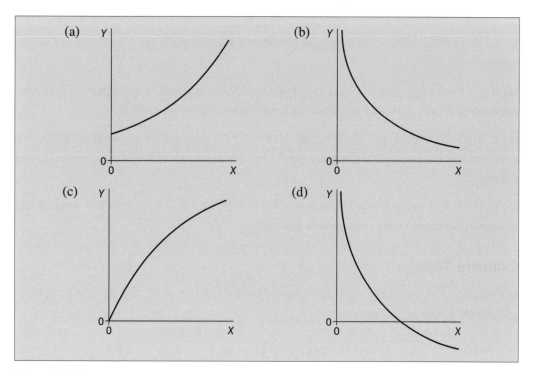

Figure 10.16

Example 10.3

Take the cross-sectional country data in Table 9.1 and fit a double-log function to its scatter. Estimate the income elasticity of the demand for money. Compare its value with that found in Chapter 9.

Example 10.4

Annual data for the UK economy, over the years 1953–9, on the percentage change in wages, W, and the percentage of the workforce unemployed, U, are given below:

W	4.4	5.4	7.1	6.2	4.2	3.1	2.6
U	1.5	1.3	1.1	1.2	1.4	2.1	2.2

In the following, lower-case letters denote deviations of variables from their respective means.

(a) If $\Sigma w^2 = 15.81$, $\Sigma u^2 = 1.137$ and $\Sigma uw = -3.934$, estimate a population regression equation $E(W) = \alpha + \beta U$ and calculate the coefficient of determination R^2.

(b) If $V = 1/U$ with $\Sigma v^2 = 0.1771$ and $\Sigma vw = 1.628$, estimate a population regression equation $E(W) = \alpha + \beta(1/U)$. Compare the R^2 for this equation with that obtained in (a) and comment.

(c) In 1964, $U = 1.6$ and $W = 4.4$, and in 1967 $U = 2.4$ and $W = 5.1$. Does this suggest any change in the relationship estimated in part (b)?

Example 10.5

Six months' data on a firm's average revenue per unit of output, P, and its sales/output, S, yielded the following information:

P	20.3	12.6	7.5	16.5	6.1	9.9
S	100	250	750	150	1000	400

$$\Sigma p^2 = 148.8, \qquad \Sigma s^2 = 647\,100, \qquad \Sigma ps = -8858.$$

Plot the data as a scatter diagram with P on the vertical axis. If $A = \ln(P)$ and $B = \ln(S)$, then

$$\Sigma A = 14.46, \qquad \Sigma B = 34.66, \qquad \Sigma a^2 = 1.063, \qquad \Sigma b^2 = 4.061, \qquad \Sigma ab = -2.076.$$

where, as usual, lower-case letters denote deviations from means.

(a) Estimate regression equations of the type
  (i) $P = \alpha + \beta S + \varepsilon$,   (ii) $P = KS^\beta \varepsilon$.

(b) Calculate the coefficient of determination for each of the regressions computed in (a) and comment.

(c) Plot both sample regression equations on the scatter diagram and comment.

(d) Obtain two estimates of the elasticity of sales with respect to price.

10.5 Comparing goodness of fit

We have stressed on a number of occasions that R^2s are not directly comparable when two sample regressions have different dependent variables. When it is obvious, from the scatter and the fitted functions, which is to be preferred, there is little problem. In such a situation the R^2 is likely to be much greater for the preferred equation. However, when the R^2s are fairly similar, we cannot rely on their relative sizes.

Box and Cox (1964) were the first to provide a method of judging the closeness of fit of alternative functions. Their general test is complicated, but Zarembka (1968) provides a version of the test that allows us to choose between linear and double-log formulations.

The problem with comparing linear and double-log equations is that the $\ln(Y)$ and predicted $\widehat{\ln(Y)}$ values are always much smaller than the corresponding Y and predicted $\hat{Y}$ values. Consequently, the residual sum of squares (SSR) for the double-log equation is bound to be much smaller than for the linear equation. Hence the SSR, and thus R^2, is not a valid way of comparing differences of fit.

Zarembka uses a transformation which enables the SSRs to be properly compared. The first step in his procedure is to obtain the *geometric mean* of the sample Y values:[5]

$$\tilde{Y} = (Y_1 Y_2 Y_3 \ldots Y_n)^{1/n} = \exp\left[\frac{1}{n} \sum \ln(Y_i)\right]. \qquad [10.38]$$

Next, we transform the original Y variable by dividing by the geometric mean $\tilde{Y}$. That is, we form

$$Y^* = \frac{Y}{\tilde{Y}}. \qquad [10.39]$$

Finally, we use OLS to estimate both linear and double-log equations, but with Y^* replacing the original Y in each case. That is, we compute the sample regression equations

$$\hat{Y}^* = a + bX \qquad [10.40]$$

and

$$\widehat{\ln(Y^*)} = a + b \ln(X). \qquad [10.41]$$

The residual sums of squares for [10.40] and [10.41] can be shown to be directly comparable, the equation with the smallest SSR providing the better fit.

We can use the Zarembka procedure to compare linear and double-log equations using the data in Table 10.1. First, we require the geometric mean of Y, the demand for carrots. This is best found using [10.38] and taking natural logs:

$$\ln(\tilde{Y}) = \frac{1}{n} \Sigma \ln(Y_i) = 3.903.$$

Hence, we have

$$\tilde{Y} = e^{3.903} = 49.55.$$

Y^* can now be constructed using [10.39], so that [10.40] and [10.41] can be estimated. This yields

$$\hat{Y}^* = 1.87 - 0.0178X \qquad\qquad (\text{SSR} = 1.165), \qquad\qquad [10.42]$$

$$\widehat{\ln(Y^*)} = 2.83 - 0.744 \ln(X) \qquad\qquad (\text{SSR} = 0.647). \qquad\qquad [10.43]$$

The coefficients in equations [10.42] and [10.43] are of no importance. It is the residual sums of squares that matter and it is clear that the SSR for the double-log formulation is considerably smaller than for the linear equation. Thus, as expected from the scatter in Fig. 10.1, the nonlinear double-log equation appears to provide the better fit.

It is possible, moreover, to test to see whether there is a statistically *significant* difference between the two SSRs. Under the null hypothesis of no difference in fit, it can be shown that *the quantity $(n/2)\ln(Z)$ is distributed as a χ^2 variable with one degree of freedom, Z being* the ratio of the larger SSR to the smaller. With 1 d.f., $\chi^2_{0.05} = 3.81$. In our case $(n/2)\ln(Z)$ equals $15(1.165/0.647) = 27.0$, so the null hypothesis can be strongly rejected. This confirms the superiority of the double-log formulation over the linear.

In Table 10.4 we present results for the six models we estimated in previous sections of this chapter. Of the three equations with Y as the dependent variable, the reciprocal model has the best fit, with $R^2 = 0.77$. Of the three equations with $\ln(Y)$ as dependent variable, the log-reciprocal proves best, with $R^2 = 0.76$.

Table 10.4 Comparison of fitted functions

Formulation	Y^*	R^2	η	$\hat{Y}$
Linear	Y	0.61	0.80	13.6
Semi-log	Y	0.70	0.82	22.2
Reciprocal	Y	0.77	0.74	29.3
Double-log	$\ln(Y)$	0.71	0.74	29.4
Exponential	$\ln(Y)$	0.64	0.74	25.2
Log-reciprocal	$\ln(Y)$	0.76	0.67	33.8

While we have demonstrated quite clearly that there are nonlinear models that are superior to a simple linear regression, unfortunately we have not tested whether, for example, the reciprocal or log-reciprocal function is preferable. The Box–Cox test mentioned earlier could be applied here, but unfortunately this is beyond our scope. Examination of Figs 10.12 and 10.14 suggests there is little to choose between the fits of the reciprocal and log-reciprocal models. All we can say, therefore, looking at Table 10.4, is that the elasticity of demand for carrots is around 0.70–0.72 and that, at a price of 90p per kilo, demand can be predicted to be about 30–34 kg.

Example 10.6

The data in Table 9.1 have been used, firstly, to compute a two-variable linear regression in Chapter 9 and, secondly, to compute a double-log regression in Example 10.3. Use the Zarembka procedure to compare the linear and double-log fits.

Example 10.7

Use the Zarembka procedure to compare the fits of the two equations estimated in Example 10.5(a).

Computer Exercise 10.1

By this time you should have a thorough knowledge of the transformation technique that we used earlier. Armed with this understanding, you should now return to your regression program. In fact it is far easier to compute simple nonlinear regressions using the facilities of a typical regression package than by means of a hand calculator. In fact, it is probably too easy! Without 'hand practice' of the kind given earlier in this chapter, students can very easily become totally confused about how to interpret any results they obtain.

In this exercise you will use your program to replicate all the equations you estimated earlier in this chapter. Firstly, therefore, you need to input the data in Table 10.1, labelling your dependent variable, the demand for carrots, as Q and the regressor, their price, as P. Remember to construct an intercept as you did in Computer Exercise 9.1. Check and if necessary edit the data, in the manner of Computer Exercise 9.2. Save the data in a data file with a suitable name. View the scatter of Q against P. It should be identical to that in Fig. 10.1.

Next move to the 'single equation' section of your program and estimate a linear regression of the form [10.3], using the full sample period. Check the computer result with the result at the beginning of the chapter and save it in a result file with a suitable name.

You should now construct the transformed variables used in sections 10.2–10.4. All regression packages will have a facility for doing this. For example, you can create the natural logarithms $\ln(Q)$ and $\ln(P)$ by keying in something like

$$lnQ = log(Q) \quad \text{and} \quad lnP = log(P)$$

Similarly, to construct the reciprocals of Q and P key in

$$RecQ = 1/Q \quad \text{and} \quad RecP = 1/P$$

It is now possible to replicate all the equations [10.14], [10.22], [10.28], [10.31] and [10.35]. For example, to replicate [10.14], key in the variables in the usual order, not forgetting the intercept. That is, type

lnQ inter lnP

Again, using the full sample period, estimate the double-log equation by OLS and save it in the result file opened earlier. Pick out the values of a, b and R^2 on the screen and compare these values with those in [10.14].

One by one, use OLS to replicate equations [10.22], [10.28], [10.31] and [10.35] and save them to the results file. Check the values of a, b and R^2 in each case. Print out your result file.

Before exiting your program, make sure you have saved all your variables, including those transformed, to the data file you opened earlier. This will overwrite your original file and gives you a single file containing both original and transformed data.

*10.6 **Fitting time trends**

Consider Table 10.5, which consists of seasonally adjusted quarterly data for UK disposable income over the period 1974–84. The data are in constant 1985 prices, measured in millions of pounds sterling. Suppose we want to estimate the average quarterly rate of growth in this variable and also predict the disposable income level in the fourth quarter of 1985, four quarters beyond our sample period. That is, we want to predict what can be called the *trend level* of income.

To perform the above task, we adopt the exponential function [10.24], using time, T, as our explanatory variable rather than the usual X-type variable:

$$Y = A\,e^{\beta T}, \tag{10.44}$$

where Y is income and T takes the values $1, 2, 3, 4, 5, \dots$. That is, T takes the value 1 in the first quarter of 1974, 2 in the second quarter, 3 in the third, and so on. Otherwise, we treat T just as any other explanatory variable.

Table 10.5 Data on UK disposable income

Observation	Y	Observation	Y	Observation	Y
1974Q1	48 856.0	1977Q4	51 164.0	1981Q3	55 520.0
1974Q2	48 921.0	1978Q1	50 232.0	1981Q4	55 962.0
1974Q3	50 727.0	1978Q2	52 379.0	1982Q1	55 325.0
1974Q4	50 929.0	1978Q3	53 388.0	1982Q2	55 568.0
1975Q1	51 138.0	1978Q4	54 314.0	1982Q3	55 419.0
1975Q2	51 695.0	1979Q1	53 412.0	1982Q4	56 232.0
1975Q3	50 061.0	1979Q2	55 033.0	1983Q1	55 950.0
1975Q4	49 525.0	1979Q3	55 014.0	1983Q2	57 203.0
1976Q1	49 371.0	1979Q4	58 841.0	1983Q3	57 563.0
1976Q2	49 445.0	1980Q1	55 814.0	1983Q4	58 234.0
1976Q3	51 344.0	1980Q2	56 151.0	1984Q1	57 961.0
1976Q4	49 539.0	1980Q3	56 968.0	1984Q2	58 954.0
1977Q1	47 278.0	1980Q4	56 949.0	1984Q3	58 975.0
1977Q2	47 895.0	1981Q1	56 736.0	1984Q4	61 041.0
1977Q3	48 996.0	1981Q2	55 902.0		

Notice that, when $T = 0$, [10.44] gives the value $Y = A$. Thus A can be regarded as a 'starting value' for income, being its value just before our sample period. A scatter diagram of the data with time on the horizontal axis is shown in Fig. 10.17. It demonstrates long-term growth in disposable income but with quite large fluctuations about the long-run trend. Despite these fluctuations, in a moment we shall fit an exponential curve with $\beta > 1$ (see Fig. 10.9a) to the scatter. You will learn how to deal with observations that lie far away from the long-term trend in a later chapter.

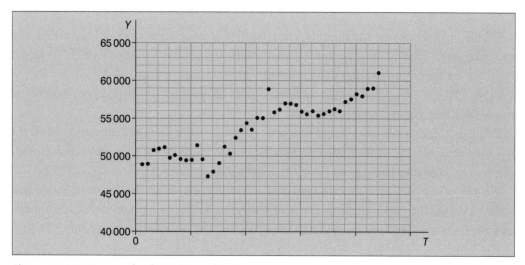

Figure 10.17 Time path of UK disposable income

How do we estimate the required rate of growth Y? Differentiating [10.49] with respect to time gives

$$\frac{dY}{dT} = \beta A \, e^{\beta T}$$

so that

$$\frac{dY}{dT} \frac{1}{Y} = \beta. \qquad [10.45]$$

Thus β is the *proportionate* rate of growth.

To estimate [10.44], we proceed as for any exponential function, taking natural logarithms to obtain

$$\ln(Y) = \alpha + \beta T \qquad [10.46]$$

or

$$Y^* = \alpha + \beta X^* \qquad [10.47]$$

where $Y^* = \ln(Y)$ and $X^* = T$. As usual, $\alpha = \ln(A)$.

We can now estimate a population regression equation of the usual form

$$E(Y^*) = \alpha + \beta X^* \qquad [10.48]$$

and use the general results [10.2]. Using the data in Table 10.5 together with a regression program, we obtain a sample regression equation

$$\widehat{\ln(Y)} = 10.78 + 0.004\,766T. \qquad [10.49]$$

Estimating a regression equation such as [10.49] is often referred to as *fitting a time trend* to a data series, T being the time trend. Equation [10.49] implies $\hat{Y} = 48\,050 \, e^{0.004\,776T}$ which is plotted on the original scatter in Fig. 10.18.

From [10.49] we estimate the quarterly rate of growth of disposable income as $b = 0.004\,776$ or about 0.48% per quarter.

To predict disposable income in the fourth quarter of 1985 (i.e., the quarter $T = 48$), we have to substitute $T = 48$ into [10.49]. This gives $\widehat{\ln(Y)} = 11.01$, so that we predict (trend) disposable income in 1985 Q4 as $\hat{Y} = e^{11.01} = £60\,476$ m.

We can, of course, also predict the trend income level for all the quarters within our sample period. The values obtained are sometimes interpreted as *permanent income* values. In economics we often split income into its *permanent* and *transitory* components.[6] That is,

$$Y = Y^p + Y^t, \qquad [10.50]$$

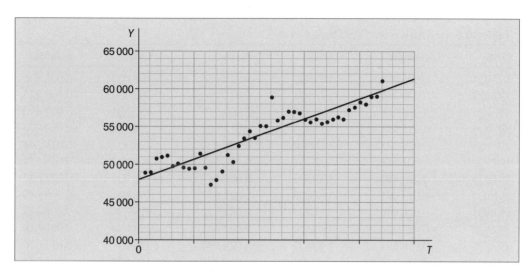

Figure 10.18 Fitting a log-linear trend

where Y^p and Y^t are the permanent and transitory components, respectively. However, it is just as plausible, and more convenient in this case, to define the relationship as

$$Y = Y^p Y^t, \qquad [10.51]$$

so that

$$\ln(Y) = \ln(Y^p) + \ln(Y^t). \qquad [10.52]$$

From [10.51] and [10.52], when $Y = Y^p$, $Y^t = 1$ and $\ln(Y^t) = 0$. Similarly, when $Y > Y^p$, so that income is above its permanent or trend level, we have $\ln(Y^t) > 0$, and when $Y < Y^p$ (income below its permanent level), $\ln(Y^t) < 0$. Thus, in this formulation, it is really $\ln(Y^t)$ that is the measure of transitory income.

For [10.51] and [10.52], $\ln(Y)$ can be found from the series in Table 10.5. $\ln(Y^p)$ we represent by the predicted $\ln(Y)$ values, $\widehat{\ln(Y)}$, obtained from [10.49]. $\ln(Y^t)$ is so far unknown, but we know that the residuals from a transformed OLS regression are, as always, given by $e^* = Y^* - \hat{Y}^*$. In this case,

$$e^* = \ln(Y) - \widehat{\ln(Y)} = \ln(Y) - \ln(Y^p). \qquad [10.53]$$

Comparison of [10.52] with [10.53] indicates that it is the residuals from the regression [10.49] that we can use as measures of transitory income values. The values are given in Table 10.6.

In Fig. 10.18, the vertical distances of points from the fitted curve also give an indication of transitory income values. But it is the logarithms of these vertical differences that are

Table 10.6 Residuals from fitted time trend

OBS.	residual	OBS.	residual	OBS.	residual
1974Q1	0.008 687	1977Q4	−0.016 650	1981Q3	−0.006 438
1974Q2	0.005 250	1978Q1	−0.039 300	1981Q4	−0.003 275
1974Q3	0.036 736	1978Q2	−0.002 713	1982Q1	−0.019 490
1974Q4	0.035 944	1978Q3	0.011 601	1982Q2	−0.019 874
1975Q1	0.035 273	1978Q4	0.024 030	1982Q3	−0.018 344
1975Q2	0.001 882	1979Q1	0.002 517	1982Q4	−0.017 528
1975Q3	0.004 454	1979Q2	0.027 549	1983Q1	−0.027 322
1975Q4	−0.011 077	1979Q3	0.022 537	1983Q2	−0.009 940
1976Q1	−0.018 958	1979Q4	0.085 022	1983Q3	−0.008 433
1976Q2	−0.022 226	1980Q1	0.027 441	1983Q4	−0.001 610
1976Q3	0.010 694	1980Q2	0.028 694	1984Q1	−0.011 076
1976Q4	−0.029 860	1980Q3	0.038 373	1984Q2	0.001 144
1977Q1	−0.081 342	1980Q4	0.033 273	1984Q3	−0.003 265
1977Q2	−0.073 142	1981Q1	0.024 760	1984Q4	0.026 400
1977Q3	−0.055 181	1981Q2	0.005 184		

equivalent to the transitory income measures obtained from [10.53]. Notice that the sign on the transitory income measure is dependent on the economic cycle. The values are negative (indicating that actual income is below its permanent value) during the recessions of 1976–8 and 1981–4. On the other hand, the values are positive during the boom conditions of 1974–5 and 1979–81, when actual income exceeds its permanent value. An exceptionally large positive value for transitory income occurs in the fourth quarter of 1979, and the relevant point is easily distinguished in the scatter of Fig. 10.18.

Of course, economic variables do not always grow exponentially in the manner shown above. But an exponential decline can be fitted by a curve of the kind [10.44], for which β is negative. Such a curve is illustrated in Fig. 10.9b.

Accelerating growth can be modelled using

$$Y = A \exp(\beta T^2)$$

or

$$\ln(Y) = \alpha + \beta T^2, \qquad \alpha = \ln(A). \qquad [10.54]$$

In [10.54] values of the variable T^2 would simply be 1, 4, 9, 16, … , and are entered into the computer just like any other variable.

More complicated time paths can also be modelled. For example, if the Y series is believed to have an asymptote at $Y = Y_a$ = constant, then the log-reciprocal function [10.33] and the logistic function [10.36] could be estimated, using time T as the X variable. Recall, however, that the logistic function cannot be estimated by OLS.

The *time-series models* of this section differ from the regression models of Chapter 9 and the earlier sections of this chapter in that they involve only one variable (apart from time T). In contrast, the *classical regression models* we estimated in Chapter 9 involved two genuine variables, Y and X. In classical regression an attempt is made to explain why the Y variable behaves as it does, and to determine the extent to which variations in Y can be attributed to variations in X. However, in time-series models no attempt is made to explain *why* the dependent variable moves in any particular way. Consequently, out-of-sample predictions made by a time-series model require the assumption that the future behaviour of a variable depends entirely on the way it has behaved in the past.

*10.7 **Some problems with OLS**

When estimating the double-log formulation [10.5], we assumed a population regression equation of the type [10.7] which implied that

$$\ln(Y) = \alpha + \beta \ln(X) + \varepsilon^* \qquad [10.56]$$

where ε^* is a disturbance. The problem now is that [10.56] in turn implies

$$Y = AX^\beta \varepsilon \qquad [10.57]$$

where $\varepsilon^* = \ln(\varepsilon)$ and, as usual, $\alpha = \ln(A)$.

In [10.57] we have what is known as a *multiplicative* disturbance. But what if the disturbance is *additive*? That is, what if

$$Y = AX^\beta + \varepsilon? \qquad [10.58]$$

There is no reason to believe that [10.58] is any less valid than [10.57]. While, as we have seen, it is possible to estimate [10.57] by the application of OLS, unfortunately [10.58] is much harder to estimate. In fact, [10.58] cannot be estimated by OLS.

In [10.57] and [10.58] there are three variables, Y, X and the disturbance ε. While it is possible to take logarithms of [10.57] and express $\ln(Y)$ as a linear function of $\ln(X)$ and $\ln(\varepsilon)$, it is not possible to do so with [10.58]. It is because the transformation technique does not work for [10.58] that the OLS method of estimation is inapplicable.

Population relationships such as [10.56] are said to be linear in the parameters. That is, they can be expressed as

$$Y^* = \text{parameter1} + (\text{parameter2})X^* + \varepsilon^*, \tag{10.59}$$

where Y^*, X^* and ε^* are suitable transformations of X, Y and ε. Only if a relationship is linear in the parameters, in this sense, is it possible to apply the transformation technique of this chapter and then apply OLS. For example, [10.57] is linear in the parameters because it can be transformed to [10.56] by taking logs. But [10.58] is not linear in the parameters and so cannot be estimated by OLS.

Unfortunately many functions are not linear in the parameters. For example, suppose

$$Y = \alpha + \frac{\gamma}{X - \beta}, \qquad \alpha > 0, \beta > 0, \gamma > 0. \tag{10.60}$$

This equation is illustrated in Fig. 10.19 and has asymptotes at $X = \beta$ and $Y = \alpha$. Unfortunately, [10.60] is not linear in the parameters because there are no transformations of X and Y that will yield an equation of the kind [10.59]. So OLS cannot be used to estimate the parameters of this equation.

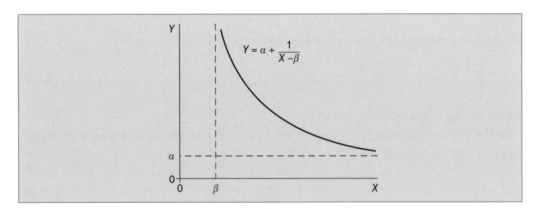

Figure 10.19 Non-linearity in parameters α and β

While the estimation of equations such as [10.60] is difficult, we can give some idea of how we might proceed. Suppose we choose a 'likely' value of β, for example $\beta = 8$. We could then construct a transformed variable $X^* = 1/(X - 8)$. We can now apply our transformation technique to this version of [10.60], regressing Y on X^*, and obtain a residual sum of squares, which we refer to as SSR_8.

Of course, we do not know whether $\beta = 8$ is the best value to choose. We have no idea whether 8 is a 'good' estimate of β or not. But we could go through the same procedure for $\beta = 6, 7, 9, 10$, etc., constructing a different X^* for each possible value of β. That is, we estimate [10.60] for each different X^*. This would give us a series of sample regression equations with residual sums of squares SSR_6, SSR_7, SSR_9, SSR_{10}, etc. The procedure normally adopted is then to select the best-fitting equation, that is, the one with the smallest residual sum of squares. The best value of β obtained is taken as the estimate of β, while the estimates of α and γ are taken from the best-fitting version of [10.60].

Computer Exercise 10.2

In this exercise we return to the data file DATASET1 containing data on the money stock, M, and GDP, G, concerning 30 countries, that we used in Computer Exercise 9.1. We estimated a linear demand-for-money regression, and obtained result [9.41] with SSR = 6.016.

In this exercise you will estimate a nonlinear equation similar to [10.60], but with γ expected to be negative since M increases as G increases.

$$M = \alpha + \frac{\gamma}{G + \beta}. \qquad \gamma < 0 \qquad\qquad [10.61]$$

Since [10.61] is non-linear in the parameters α, β and γ, we will adopt the estimation procedure suggested for [10.60]. That is, we select a series of possible values for β, construct a sequence of variables $R(\beta) = 1/(G + \beta)$ and then regress M on each R variable in turn. For example, if you make the arbitrary selection $\beta = 10$, then you must construct values for the variable $R(10) = 1/(G + 10)$. Regressing M on $R(10)$ should then yield the result

$$\hat{M} = 3.957 - 41.77R(10), \qquad SSR_{10} = 5.8137.$$

The idea of this estimating procedure is to find the value β that minimizes the SSR. We therefore need to choose a 'grid' of β values. Since we have no idea concerning the true value of β, you will need to start with large differences in β values. If you start by trying β values of 0, 10, 20, 30, ... , you should obtain the following SSRs:

β	0	10	20	30	40	50
SSR_β	19.05	5.814	5.628	5.646	5.585	5.720

The smallest SSR in this grid is that for $\beta = 20$. But we can be more precise than that.

Try a narrower grid with values of β equal to, for example, 18, 19, 20, ... You should obtain the following results:

β	18	19	20	21	22	23	24
SSR$_\beta$	5.6350	5.6309	5.6284	5.6273	5.6272	5.6279	5.6293

It should now be clear that the SSR is minimized for a value of β of around 22. In fact, for this value of β, the estimated version of [10.61] is

$$\hat{M} = 6.17 - \frac{132.2}{G + 22}, \qquad R^2 = 0.787 \qquad\qquad [10.62]$$

Thus we estimate α, β and γ in [10.61] by $\alpha^* = 6.17$, $\beta^* = 22$ and $\gamma^* = -132.2$. Of course, we could have used an even narrower grid of values for β and obtained an even more accurate estimate of β.

Notice that the nonlinear [10.62] has an R^2 of 0.787, compared with 0.772 for the linear regression quoted in [9.41]. Since both these equations have M as dependent variable, we can therefore say that the nonlinear fit is superior.

Summary

- Nonlinear curves can be fitted to a two-dimensional scatter of points by using a **transformation technique**.

- The transformation technique can be used to fit curves such as the **double-log**, **semi-log**, **exponential**, **reciprocal** and other functions.

- The **goodness of fit** of a curve can be judged by the **coefficient of determination**. But comparison of fits is **difficult** when different curves have **different dependent variables**.

- The **Zarembka procedure** can be applied to compare the goodness of fit of linear equations with those that have a double-log form.

- The **exponential function** can used to fit **time trends** to data on a single time series. This enables an estimate of the **growth rate** for such a variable to be obtained.

- **OLS estimation** is only feasible when a relationship is **linear in its parameters**. This usually implies that disturbances are **multiplicative** rather than **additive**.

Notes

1. A population regression equation of this kind implies that a full version of [10.1] is, in fact, $Y^* = \alpha + \beta X^* + \varepsilon^*$, where $E(\varepsilon^*) = 0$. As we shall see, ε^* itself may be a transformation of an underlying true disturbance, ε.

2. In the double-logarithm model it is usually conveniently assumed that $\varepsilon^* = \ln(\varepsilon)$ with the full version of [10.4] taking the form $Y = AX^\beta \varepsilon$. However, more awkward possibilities exist, as discussed in Section 10.7.

3. The mean of $X^* = \ln(X)$ is

$$\frac{1}{n}[\ln(X_1) + \ln(X_2) + \ln(X_3) + \cdots + \ln(X_n)] = \frac{1}{n}[\ln(X_1 X_2 X_3 \ldots X_n] = \ln(X_1 X_2 X_3 \ldots X)^{1/n}.$$

Thus the mean of $\ln(X_i)$ is, in fact, the log of the geometric mean of the X_i.

4. The implied full version of [10.24] is $Y = Ae^{\beta X}\varepsilon$ where ε is a disturbance. See Section 10.7 for an alternative possibility.

5. See the prerequisites chapter for a discussion of geometric means.

6. See, for example, Friedman (1957).

11

What makes a good estimator?

Objectives

After completing your study of this chapter you should be able:

1. to appreciate that population parameters usually have to be estimated and that all estimators have sampling distributions;

2. to understand the distinction between the small-sample and the large-sample (i.e., asymptotic) properties of estimators;

3. to recall the definition and meaning of (a) best linear unbiasedness, (b) efficiency and (c) the mean square error of an estimator;

4. to understand the concepts of an asymptotic distribution and a probability distribution;

5. to recall the definition and meaning of asymptotic unbiasedness, consistency and asymptotic efficiency;

6. to tackle simple algebraic problems regarding the properties and relative merits of different estimators;

7. to realize that there are three main methods of estimating a parameter.

Introduction

As we pointed out in Chapter 9, ordinary least squares is by no means the only way of estimating the parameters of a regression equation. In many circumstances other methods are preferred, and later in this text we will consider some of them. The reason why they are preferred is that they provide 'better' estimators than those provided by OLS. But before we can explain why this should be the case we need to define precisely what we mean by 'better'. Thus we shall spend much of this chapter defining the properties that we would like estimators to have. These properties can be divided into so-called 'small-sample' properties and so-called 'large-sample' or 'asymptotic' properties. Then at the end of the chapter we shall look briefly at some of the various methods of estimating parameters that are used by statisticians.

11.1 Background to estimation

To provide a background to discussing the properties of estimators, consider a population of values for a random variable X.[1] Effectively, we have a probability distribution for X, which may or may not be known. We shall assume that this population (or probability distribution) is characterized by a parameter θ, which is normally unknown. For example, θ might be the population mean μ or it might be the population variance σ^2. Alternatively, θ might be the slope, β, of a population regression line.[2] However, to keep the analysis general, we do not adopt a precise definition for θ.

Since θ is unknown, we have to estimate it using sample information. Suppose we have a random sample of n observations on the variable X, taken from our population. We represent the sample observations as

$$X_1, X_2, X_3, X_4, \dots, X_n, \qquad [11.1]$$

where X_1, is the ith sample observation. We will refer to our estimator of θ as Q. The estimator will be some function or formula involving some or all of the observations in [11.1]. That is,

$$Q = Q(X_1, X_2, X_3, \dots, X_n). \qquad [11.2]$$

For example, if θ were the population mean μ, then one obvious estimator would be the sample mean, $\bar{X}$, which clearly depends on all the X_i, since

$$\bar{X} = \frac{1}{n}(X_1 + X_2 + X_3 + \dots + X_n).$$

The important fact to recall is that *all* estimators will possess *sampling distributions*. In Chapter 3 we saw that, if very many samples were taken from a population, each sample would yield a different value for $\bar{X}$, the sample mean – that is, there exists a sampling distribution for $\bar{X}$. In general, when trying to estimate some parameter θ, if very many samples are drawn, there will exist a sampling distribution for its estimator Q. This distribution will have its own mean $E(Q)$ and its own variance $E[Q - E(Q)]^2$.

Although the situation is a little more complicated when we are dealing with two parameters, such as α and β in a two-variable population regression equation, the same concepts are valid. If we take very many samples and compute sample regression equations for each sample then each such sample will provide estimators a and b of the parameters α and β. Repeated sampling thus yields marginal sampling distributions for both a and b and a joint sampling distribution for these estimators.

The desired properties of estimators can be divided into two categories: small-sample properties and large-sample or asymptotic properties. Properties, the attributes of which are present regardless of the size of samples taken, are referred to as *small-sample* properties. That is, the desired attribute is present for both large samples and *even* for small samples. However, properties with desired attributes that only appear as the sample size becomes very large are referred to as *large-sample* or *asymptotic* properties.

11.2 Small-sample properties of estimators

The best-known desired small-sample property of an estimator is unbiasedness. We have, in fact, already introduced this idea in earlier chapters:

> An estimator Q is said to be an *unbiased estimator*
> of θ if and only if $E(Q) = \theta$.　　　　　　　　　　　[11.3]

[11.3] implies that an estimator can only be unbiased if its sampling distribution is such that its mean is equal to the parameter being estimated. This situation is illustrated in Fig. 11.1. In colloquial terms it means that, if we were to take very many samples, then the average of all the Qs obtained from these samples would equal θ, the true parameter value. Of course, when we take a single sample, this does not mean that Q will equal θ, except by an unlikely chance, but it does mean that there is no *systematic* tendency to error. That is, there is no tendency for Q regularly to overestimate θ and no tendency for Q regularly to underestimate θ.

We have already encountered unbiased estimators in Chapters 3–5. For example, we saw that $E(\bar{X}) = \mu$ so that $\bar{X}$ is an unbiased estimator of μ. Similarly, the sample proportion p is an unbiased estimator of the population proportion π since $E(p) = \pi$. Notice that no reference to the sample size is made in the definition [11.3]. The sample size could be large or small. Thus unbiasedness is a small-sample property.

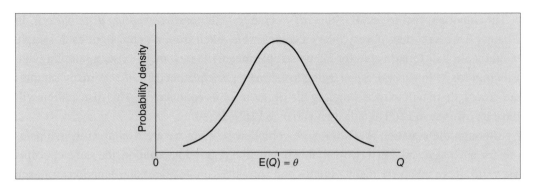

Figure 11.1 An unbiased estimator

If an estimator does not satisfy [11.3], that is if $E(Q) \neq \theta$, then that estimator is said to be *biased* and there is now a systematic tendency to error. In such a case, the difference between $E(Q)$ and θ is referred to as the *bias* in the estimator. That is,

$$\text{bias}(Q) = E(Q) - \theta. \qquad [11.4]$$

If Q tends to overestimate θ, so that $E(Q) > \theta$, then the estimator is said to have an *upward bias*. However, if Q tends to underestimate θ, with $E(Q) < \theta$, then the bias is *downward*.

As an example of a biased estimator, suppose we wish to estimate the population variance σ^2. The sample variance v^2, given by [3.4], we found to be a biased estimator of σ^2 since

$$E(v^2) = \left(\frac{n-1}{n}\right)\sigma^2 < \sigma^2.$$

That is, v^2 tends to underestimate σ^2 and so has a downward bias. The problem with v^2 is illustrated in Fig. 11.2. However, the estimator s^2, given by [3.6], is unbiased since

$$s^2 = \left(\frac{n}{n-1}\right)v^2$$

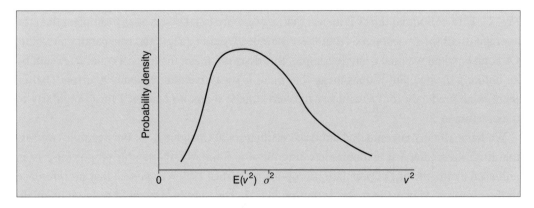

Figure 11.2 The downward bias of v^2

so that

$$E(s^2) = E\left(\frac{n}{n-1}v^2\right) = \left(\frac{n}{n-1}\cdot\frac{n-1}{n}\right)\sigma^2 = \sigma^2.$$

It is for this reason that we prefer s^2 to v^2 when estimating a population variance.

*Worked Example

A variable X is normally distributed with mean μ and variance σ^2. Three estimators of μ are proposed:

$$\hat{m} = \bar{X} - 10; \qquad \tilde{m} = \bar{X} + \frac{5}{n}; \qquad m^* = \left(\frac{n-1}{n-2}\right)\bar{X},$$

where $\bar{X}$ is the sample mean and n the sample size.

(a) Explain why all three estimators will have sampling distributions that are normal in shape.

(b) Recalling that $E(\bar{X}) = \mu$, use Theorem 1.1 to show that all the proposed estimators are biased and hence determine the bias in each case. If $n = 10$ and $\mu = 8$, which estimator has the smallest absolute bias?

(c) Recalling that $V(\bar{X}) = \sigma^2/n$, use Theorem 1.1 to find the variance of the sampling distribution for each estimator. Hence determine which estimator has the largest variance.

Solution

(a) We know, from the central limit theorem (Theorem 3.2), that $\bar{X}$ has a normal distribution. But $\hat{m}$, $\tilde{m}$ and m^* are all linear functions of $\bar{X}$. Since all linear functions of normally distributed variables are themselves normal distributions, it follows that the sampling distributions of $\hat{m}$, $\tilde{m}$ and m^* must all be of the normal form.

(b)
$$\begin{aligned}
E(\hat{m}) &= E(\bar{X} - 10) = E(\bar{X}) - 10 &&\text{(using Theorem 1.1)}\\
&= \mu - 10 \neq \mu &&\text{(since } E(\bar{X}) = \mu\text{).}
\end{aligned}$$

$$\begin{aligned}
E(\tilde{m}) &= E\left(\bar{X} + \frac{5}{n}\right) = E(\bar{X}) + \frac{5}{n} &&\text{(using Theorem 1.1)}\\
&= \mu + \frac{5}{n} \neq \mu &&\text{(since } E(\bar{X}) = \mu\text{).}
\end{aligned}$$

$$\begin{aligned}
E(m^*) &= E\left[\left(\frac{n-1}{n-2}\right)\bar{X}\right] = \left(\frac{n-1}{n-2}\right)E(\bar{X}) &&\text{(using Theorem 1.1)}\\
&= \left(\frac{n-1}{n-2}\right)\mu \neq \mu &&\text{(since } E(\bar{X}) = \mu\text{).}
\end{aligned}$$

Thus all the estimators are biased:

$$\text{bias}(\hat{m}) = E(\hat{m}) - \mu = \mu - 10 - \mu = -10$$

$$\text{bias}(\tilde{m}) = E(\tilde{m}) - \mu = \mu + \frac{5}{n} - \mu = \frac{5}{n}$$

$$\text{bias}(m^*) = E(m^*) - \mu = \left(\frac{n-1}{n-2}\right)\mu - \mu = \left(\frac{1}{n-2}\right)\mu.$$

When $n = 10$ and $\mu = 8$, the absolute value of the biases are $+10$, $+0.5$ and $+1$ respectively. Thus $\tilde{m}$ has the smallest bias.

(c) $\qquad\qquad V(\hat{m}) = V(\overline{X})$ (using Theorem 1.1)

$$= \frac{\sigma^2}{n}.$$

$$V(\tilde{m}) = V(\overline{X}) \qquad \text{(using Theorem 1.1)}$$

$$= \frac{\sigma^2}{n}.$$

$$V(m^*) = \left(\frac{n-1}{n-2}\right)^2 V(\overline{X}) \qquad \text{(using Theorem 1.1)}$$

$$= \left(\frac{n-1}{n-2}\right)^2 \frac{\sigma^2}{n} \qquad \text{(since } V(\overline{X}) = \sigma^2/n\text{).}$$

Thus since $(n-1)/(n-2) > 1$, it follows that m^* has the largest variance.

---

*Example 11.1

Let $X_1, X_2, X_3, \ldots, X_8$ be a random sample of size $n = 8$, taken from a normally distributed population with mean μ and variance σ^2. Suppose μ is estimated by

$$m^* = \frac{X_1 + X_8}{2}.$$

Show that m^* is a normally distributed and unbiased estimator of μ but has a variance greater than $V(\overline{X}) = \sigma^2/n$, where $\overline{X}$ is the sample mean.

Unfortunately, unbiasedness alone is not a particularly reassuring property. The fact that 'on average over many samples' $E(Q) = \theta$ is not particularly helpful when in practice we normally take but a single sample. Recall that, in Figs 11.1 and 11.2, it is areas under sampling distributions that represent probabilities. Even for unbiased estimators there is a non-zero probability of getting a value for our estimator Q that is 'far away' from the true parameter value θ. That is, some of the values for Q lie in the tails of the sampling distribution. If the variance of Q happens to be large, so that the distribution has a wide 'spread' of values, then the probability of getting a value of Q 'far away' from θ may be worryingly large. Since we only take one sample, it follows that we may be 'unlucky' in the precise sample that we take and (without realizing it) obtain a particular value for Q which lies far away from the unknown θ.

It should be clear from the above that we prefer an unbiased estimator to have a small rather than a large variance. In Fig. 11.3, Q_1 and Q_2 are alternative unbiased estimators of θ but Q_1 has the larger dispersion. That is, $V(Q_1) > V(Q_2)$. From Fig. 11.3 it can be seen that, for the single sample we take, the probability of obtaining a value in excess of a given value θ^* is greater for the estimator Q_1 than for the estimator Q_2. In such a situation we would prefer the estimator Q_2. This discussion leads us to our second desired small-sample property, which is that of *efficiency*.

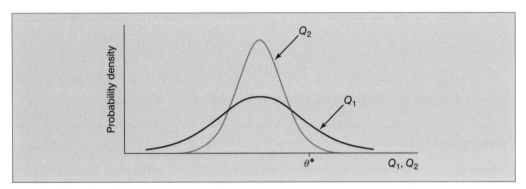

Figure 11.3 Unbiased estimators with $V(Q_1) > V(Q_2)$

An estimator Q is said to be an *efficient estimator* of θ if and only if

(i)   it is unbiased, that is, $E(Q) = \theta$;   [11.5]

(ii) no other unbiased estimator of θ has a smaller variance.

Notice that to be efficient an estimator must first be unbiased. Secondly if, out of all possible unbiased estimators, we select the one with the smallest variance we are, in effect, minimizing the probability of obtaining a value for Q that is 'far away' from θ. Note that there is no reference to the sample size in definition [11.5]. Thus, like unbiasedness, efficiency is a small-sample property. Because of its minimum-variance property, an efficient estimator is sometimes referred to as a *best unbiased estimator*.

Although it is often possible to prove that an estimator is unbiased, proving efficiency usually turns out to be more difficult. To establish efficiency involves comparing the variances of all unbiased estimators, and there may well be very many of them. The term 'efficient' is therefore also used in a relative manner. When two estimators of a parameter θ are unbiased but estimator Q_1 happens to have a smaller variance than estimator Q_2, then Q_1 is said to be *more efficient* than Q_2. For example, suppose we wish to estimate a population mean μ. One possible unbiased estimator of μ is the sample mean $\overline{X}$, since $E(\overline{X}) = \mu$. But the sample median $\overline{m}$ is also an unbiased estimator of μ, since $E(\overline{m}) = \mu$. However, as illustrated in Fig. 11.4, the sample mean turns out to be a more efficient estimator than $\overline{m}$ since $V(\overline{X}) < V(\overline{m})$. In fact the sample mean $\overline{X}$ can be shown to be *the* efficient estimator of μ, since there is in fact no unbiased estimator of μ that has a smaller variance.

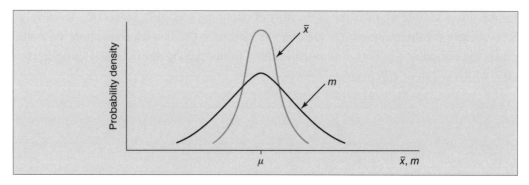

Figure 11.4 Sampling distributions for sample mean $\bar{x}$ and sample median $\overline{m}$

*Example 11.2

Suppose $[X_1, X_2, X_3]$ is a random sample taken from an $N(\mu, \sigma^2)$ population. Instead of using the sample mean $\overline{X}$ as an estimator of μ, a 'weighted' estimator of the kind

$$X^* = 0.6X_1 + 0.3X_2 + 0.1X_3$$

is proposed. Show that X^* is unbiased and will be normally distributed if many samples are taken. Show that $V(X^*)$ is less efficient as an estimator than $\overline{X}$, the sample mean.

If $\sigma^2 = 12$, find the probability that X^* lies at least two units away from the true μ.

As we noted above, it can be very difficult to find the unbiased estimator that has the smallest variance. However, the search often becomes much easier if we restrict ourselves to considering just linear estimators.

A *linear estimator* is simply an estimator that is a linear function of the sample observations. That is, [11.2] becomes

$$Q = a_1X_1 + a_2X_2 + a_3X_3 + \cdots + a_nX_n, \qquad [11.6]$$

where the a_i can be any constants.

One example of a linear estimator is the sample mean, since it can be written as

$$\bar{X} = \frac{1}{n} \sum X_i = \frac{1}{n} X_1 + \frac{1}{n} X_2 + \frac{1}{n} X_3 + \cdots + \frac{1}{n} X_n, \qquad [11.7]$$

where n, being the fixed sample size, is a constant. Thus, in this case, each $a_i = 1/n$ in [11.6].

---

*Example 11.3

Check whether the estimators $\hat{m}$, $\tilde{m}$ and m^* in the above worked example are linear estimators. Is X^* in Example 11.2 a linear estimator?

Of course, the general linear estimator [11.6] does not necessarily provide us with a 'good' estimate of the true θ. It is just that linear functions are usually easier to handle mathematically that nonlinear functions. As an example of a 'poor' linear estimator, consider $3\bar{X}$ as an estimator of a population mean μ. $3\bar{X}$ has $a_i = 3/n$, $i = 1, \ldots, n$, in [11.6] and is a linear estimator like $\bar{X}$. But $3\bar{X}$ is not a very sensible estimator of the population mean μ! Getting round this difficulty leads us to our third small-sample property, that of *best linear unbiasedness*.

> An estimator Q is said to be a *best linear unbiased estimator* (BLUE) of θ if and only if:
> (i) it is a linear estimator, that is, $Q = \sum_i a_i X_i$, where the a_i are constants;
> (ii) it is unbiased, that is $E(Q) = \theta$;   [11.8]
> (iii) no other linear unbiased estimator has a smaller variance.

Thus, to find the BLUE we have to search for that linear and unbiased estimator which has the smallest variance.

Notice that the BLUE of a parameter θ is not generally as 'good' as the efficient estimator of θ, since it is only the best of all linear unbiased estimators. There may be superior nonlinear unbiased estimators, although these can be difficult to derive. Only when the efficient estimator happens to be linear will the BLUE and the efficient estimator be identical. For example, we have already seen that the sample mean $\bar{X}$ is both a linear and an unbiased estimator of the population mean μ. It turns out that $\bar{X}$ is in fact the efficient estimator of μ. Since it also happens to be linear it must, therefore, be the BLUE of μ.

The mean square error of an estimator

As we saw above, we are generally concerned with two aspects of an estimator – whether or not it is biased and the size of its variance. However, so far we have given priority to unbiasedness and sought minimum variance only when unbiasedness is given. This was the idea behind both efficiency and BLUness. But it is sometimes sensible to balance the property of unbiasedness against that of efficiency. This is the case when there are no unbiased estimators with small variances.

Suppose a parameter θ has two estimators Q_1 and Q_2 with sampling distributions shown in Fig. 11.5. Q_2 happens to be the efficient estimator and therefore must be unbiased but, unfortunately, has a large variance. In contrast, Q_1 is biased upwards, just slightly, but has a much smaller variance. Which of the two estimators should we select? While Q_2 is unbiased, whereas Q_1 systematically overestimates θ, we must remember that areas under these sampling distributions measure probabilities. For the single sample we take, we are therefore much more likely to obtain an estimate 'far away' from θ if we use the estimator Q_2 than if we use Q_1. It may be more sensible to accept the small bias in Q_1 rather than the large variance of Q_2.

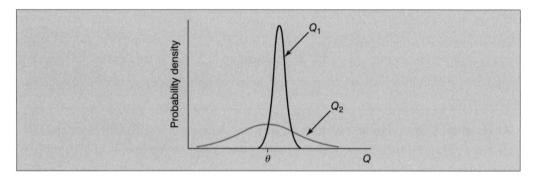

Figure 11.5 Unbiasness versus efficiency

To formalize this choice, it is helpful to define the *mean square error* (MSE) of an estimator. For any parameter θ, the *error* of an estimator is given by $Q - \theta$, so that

$$\text{MSE}(Q) = \text{E}[Q - \theta]^2. \tag{11.9}$$

Whereas the variance, $\text{E}[Q - \text{E}(Q)]^2$, of an estimator Q measures the dispersion of Q about its own mean $\text{E}(Q)$, the mean square error measures the dispersion of Q about the true parameter value θ. Only for unbiased estimators with $\text{E}(Q) = \theta$ will the variance and the MSE be the same. But, for biased estimators, the relationship between variance and MSE can be shown to be[3]

$$\text{MSE}(Q) = \text{V}(Q) + [\text{bias}(Q)]^2, \tag{11.10}$$

where the bias is given by [11.4].

One approach to estimation is simply to choose the estimator that has the smallest MSE. This has the attraction (as can be seen from [11.9]) that such an estimator minimizes the average squared distance between the estimator and the true parameter value. In addition, it provides a way of balancing the need for a small bias with the need for a small variance. From [11.10], when we minimize the MSE we are giving equal importance to the variance and the square of the bias. A more general procedure would be to calculate a weighted mean of $V(Q)$ and the squared bias. That is, minimize M where

$$M(Q) = \phi V(Q) + (1 - \phi)[\text{bias}(Q)]^2. \qquad [11.11]$$

Here the weights ϕ and $(1 - \phi)$ lie between 0 and 1. The greater we make ϕ, the greater the importance we wish to attach to the variance property and the less the importance given to bias.

We conclude this section by noting that, when estimating a parameter, it always makes good sense to make use of all the sample information that is available. In general, *the more information used, the more efficient it is possible for an estimator to be.*

For example, suppose two unbiased estimators are considered for the estimation of μ, the population mean. The first is $\bar{X}$, the sample mean, and the other has the formula $X^* = (X_L + X_S)/2$, where X_L is the largest observation in the sample and X_S the smallest. Both estimators are unbiased but, clearly, $\bar{X}$ makes use of more information than X^* and, hence, not surprisingly, it turns out to be more efficient. In fact, since $\bar{X}$ makes use of *all* the sample observations, $\bar{X}$ is, as noted above, *the* efficient estimator.

An estimator that utilizes all the sample information available is referred to as a *sufficient* estimator. A sufficient estimator may not be a particularly satisfactory estimator – for example, it may not use all the sample observations in a sensible way. But the point about sufficiency is that it is necessary for efficiency. An estimator *cannot* be efficient unless it is sufficient.

---

*Example 11.4

Find the mean square errors of the three estimators proposed in the above worked example. If $n = 10$, $\mu = 100$ and $\sigma^2 = 20$, which estimator has the smallest MSE?

---

*11.3 Asymptotic distributions and probability limits

Before we consider the large-sample properties of estimators, we need to become familiar with two important concepts. We shall introduce them via a well-known (non-numerical) example.

Asymptotic distributions

Suppose we wish to estimate the mean, μ, of a non-normally distributed population of values for X. We stress that this population is of unknown shape but is not normally distributed. For example, its probability distribution could take any of the shapes shown in Fig. 11.6. We estimate μ by $\bar{X}$, the mean of a random sample size n. We now consider the sampling distribution for $\bar{X}$.

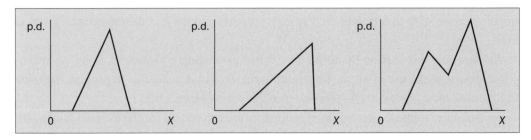

Figure 11.6 Possible population distributions

Firstly, suppose that our samples are all 'small' (e.g., of size $n = 8$). We know from Theorem 3.1 that, even for such small samples, the sampling distribution for $\bar{X}$ will have mean $\mathrm{E}(\bar{X}) = \mu$ and variance $s_{\bar{X}}^2 = \sigma^2/n$, where σ^2 is the population variance. However, for such samples, there is little we can say about the *shape* of the sampling distribution for $\bar{X}$. The shape of the sampling distribution will almost certainly reflect the shape of the population distribution, but this, of course, is unknown.

Suppose, however, we allow the size of samples taken gradually to increase. For example, suppose we now take many samples size $n = 20$ and examine the sampling distribution for $\bar{X}$. Then, suppose we take many samples size $n = 30$ and examine the sampling distribution. And then $n = 40$, $n = 50$ and so on, in each case examining the relevant sampling distribution. We know, from the central limit Theorem 3.2, that as n grows larger and larger, the sampling distribution for $\bar{X}$ gradually takes on the shape of a normal distribution with the above mean and variance. That is,

$$\text{as } n \rightarrow \infty, \qquad \bar{X} \rightarrow N(\mu, \sigma^2/n). \qquad [11.12]$$

This $N(\mu, \sigma^2/n)$ distribution is known as the *asymptotic distribution* for $\bar{X}$. Recall, from our discussion of the central limit theorem, that the shape of this asymptotic distribution is always the same, regardless of the shape of the underlying population distribution, whether that be, for example, any of the shapes illustrated in Fig. 11.6.

Estimators other than $\bar{X}$ can also have asymptotic distributions of this kind. In general, the asymptotic distribution of such an estimator Q is the distribution which the sampling distribution for Q approaches as the sample size n becomes larger and larger. Again, the shape of the asymptotic distribution is independent of the shape of the underlying population. Very often such asymptotic distributions have the normal shape, as in the case of $\bar{X}$. But this is not always the case.

In some cases, the sampling distribution for an estimator will have an unchanged shape regardless of sample size. For example, the sampling distribution for a sample mean $\bar{X}$ drawn from a normally distributed population will have an $N(\mu, \sigma^2/n)$ shape, even for small samples. Since, as n becomes larger and larger, there is no change in the sampling distribution, the asymptotic distribution in this case is simply the small-sample distribution $N(\mu, \sigma^2/n)$.

Probability limits

We now return to our original example concerning the non-normally distributed population and the sampling distribution of the mean $\bar{X}$. By the central limit theorem, we have the result [11.12]. But this is not, in this case, the final form taken by the sampling distribution. Clearly, as $n \rightarrow \infty$,

$$V(\bar{X}) = \sigma^2/n \rightarrow 0 \qquad [11.13]$$

[11.13] implies that, as the sample size n becomes infinitely large, the variance of the sampling distribution gets closer and closer to zero. That is, the sampling distribution for $\bar{X}$ actually collapses to a single value that is equal to μ, the population mean. (When $\bar{X}$ is distributed with mean μ and a zero variance, $\bar{X}$ can only take one possible value – that of μ.) This is illustrated in Fig. 11.7.

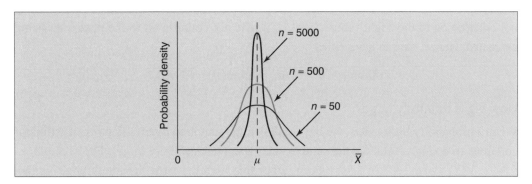

Figure 11.7 Collapse of the sampling distribution for $\bar{X}$ as $n \rightarrow \infty$

Note that, when considering Fig. 11.7, each curve represents a separate scenario. For example, the curve denoted $n = 50$ refers to a situation where 'very many' samples, all of size 50, are taken and a sampling distribution formed. Similarly, the $n = 500$ curve refers to the situation where 'very many' samples of size $n = 500$ are taken. The curve is not meant to refer to a situation where there is a single sample, size $n = 50$, which is increased in size to $n = 500$, $n = 5000$, and so on.

The particular shape of the curves in Fig. 11.7 arises from the fact that, firstly, areas under the curves represent probabilities and, secondly, as with all sampling distributions, the sum of the area under each curve must equal unity. Consequently, the 'narrower' the distribution, the 'higher' must be its maximum value.

As sample sizes increase in Fig 11.7, probability becomes more and more concentrated at the centre of the distribution until, ultimately, all probability is concentrated at the single point where $\bar{X} = \mu$. The sampling distribution then consists of a single vertical line of infinite height starting at the point $\bar{X} = \mu$. Thus, for 'infinitely large' samples, the probability of obtaining a value of $\bar{X}$ equal to μ is unity. In other words, if we were to take many 'infinitely large' samples we would find that the value of $\bar{X}$, the sample mean, obtained would be the same each time and would equal μ, the population mean.

When the sampling distribution for an estimate collapses to a single value, in the manner of Fig. 11.7, the estimator is said to *converge in probability* to that value. Thus $\bar{X}$ converges in probability to μ. The single value to which the estimator converges is then referred to as its *probability limit* (often written as 'plim'). Thus $\bar{X}$ has a probability limit of μ, and we write

$$\text{plim}(\bar{X}) = \mu. \tag{11.14}$$

It should be noted that sampling distributions do not always collapse to a point as in Fig. 11.7. That is, they do not converge in probability to a probability limit. Moreover, as we shall see in the next section, even when the probability limit of an estimator exists, it may not collapse on to the 'right' value. That is, it may not collapse on to the parameter being estimated. Hence, we can have either

$$\text{plim}(Q) = \theta \qquad \text{or} \qquad \text{plim}(Q) = \theta^* \neq \theta.$$

How big is infinitely large?

When a probability limit exists, we have said that the sampling distribution for an estimator collapses to a single value as the sample size 'becomes infinitely large'. For example, as $n \to \infty$, $V(\bar{X}) = \sigma^2/n \to 0$. We have been rather free with the term 'infinitely large' in this section. Clearly, in practical terms, we cannot take samples of infinite size. But can we regard the above concepts as useful when we have sample sizes that are merely 'very large'? For example, what if $n = 100\,000$, or $n = 10\,000$, or $n = 1000$?

It turns out that the sampling distributions of some estimators reach their asymptotic shape and finally approach their probability limits relatively quickly as the size of samples increases. For other estimators, the process takes much longer and, of course, as we have pointed out, some sampling distributions do not collapse to probability limits at all.

As we shall see in the next section, we prefer those estimators that approach their probability limits more quickly as the sample size increases. Frequently in econometrics we have to make do with sample sizes that are relatively small, so there are big benefits to be had if we can find estimators of this type.

Some properties of probability limits

Recall from Chapter 6 that, if X and Y have probability distributions, then $E(X + Y) = E(X) + E(Y)$. However, it was not generally the case, for example, that $E(XY) = E(X)E(Y)$ or that $E(X/Y) = E(X)/E(Y)$. That is, great care had to taken when manipulating the expectations operator.

Luckily, it can be shown that we can be much more flexible when dealing with probability limits. This is because, when dealing with expectations, we are faced with whole distributions of values for variables, whereas with probability limits we are dealing only with the single values to which the distributions have collapsed. Thus, if Q_1 and Q_2 are estimators (of two parameters θ_1 and θ_2) then, not only is it true that

$$\text{plim}(Q_1 + Q_2) = \text{plim}(Q_1) + \text{plim}(Q_2) \qquad [11.15]$$

but it is also possible to write

$$\text{plim}(Q_1 Q_2) = \text{plim}(Q_1)\text{plim}(Q_2) \qquad [11.16]$$

and

$$\text{plim}\left(\frac{Q_1}{Q_2}\right) = \frac{\text{plim}(Q_1)}{\text{plim}(Q_2)}. \qquad [11.17]$$

We shall not prove the results [11.15] to [11.17] and will take them as given, although the more intelligent student may find them intuitively obvious. The usefulness of the above properties will be apparent in the succeeding chapters.

*11.4 Large-sample or asymptotic properties

We shall see later that, in many situations, econometricians are unable to find *any* estimators with the small-sample properties described in Chapter 11.2. For example, it is very rare for the OLS estimators a and b, in two-variable regression, to be best linear unbiased or even simply unbiased. In such a situation, we have to make do with estimators that have, hopefully at least, desirable large-sample properties.

When an estimator has one of the following properties, it means that the estimator possesses the attributes of the property when the sample is 'very large' but does not possess these attributes for small samples. Strictly speaking, the attributes of the property hold only when the sample is 'infinitely large', but can be regarded as holding approximately when the sample size is 'very large'. As in the previous section, the interpretation of 'very large' is flexible, but the main point is that, when the sample size is 'small', the attributes of the property are not apparent at all. The first such property is *asymptotic unbiasedness*:

> an estimator Q is said to be an *asymptotically unbiased estimator* of θ if and only if $E(Q) \rightarrow \theta$ as $n \rightarrow \infty$.   [11.18]

Thus asymptotic unbiasedness implies that an estimator becomes unbiased as the size of the samples taken becomes 'very large'. Notice that such an estimator may well be biased for small samples. It is just that the bias gradually disappears as the size of the samples taken becomes larger. This process is illustrated in Fig. 11.8. For samples of size $n = 5$, the sampling distribution for Q has $E(Q) < \theta$ but, as n increases to 50, 500, 5000, 50 000, etc., the sampling distribution gradually shifts to the right, so that as $n \rightarrow \infty$, the bias disappears.

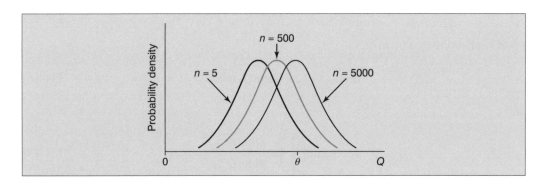

Figure 11.8 A biased but asymptotically unbiased estimator

We have already encountered an asymptotically unbiased estimator. We saw earlier in this chapter that the sample variance v^2 given by [3.4] is a biased estimator of the population variance σ^2 because

$$E(v^2) = \left(\frac{n-1}{n}\right)\sigma^2 < \sigma^2.$$

However, as $n \to \infty$, $(n-1)/n \to 1$ so that $E(v^2) \to \sigma^2$. That is, the bias disappears as the sample size increases; in other words, the distribution for v^2 gradually shifts to the right, eventually centring itself about σ^2. Thus v^2 is an asymptotically unbiased estimator of σ^2.

Notice that an unbiased estimator is necessarily asymptotically unbiased. This is because unbiasedness is a small-sample property. That is, the relevant attributes of the property hold regardless of the sample size and hence remain unchanged as the sample size becomes infinitely large. That is, $E(Q) = \theta$, for any n, and remains unchanged as $n \to \infty$.

An important and desirable large-sample property is that of *consistency*:

> an estimator Q is a *consistent estimator* of θ if and only if $\text{plim}(Q) = \theta$.   [11.19]

To understand [11.19], recall the definition of a probability limit given earlier. For an estimator to be consistent, it is necessary that the sampling distribution of that estimator should collapse on to the parameter being estimated as the size of the samples tends to infinity. That is, an estimator is consistent if it converges in probability to the parameter being estimated.

An estimator will be consistent if both the bias (if it exists) of the estimator and its variance tend to zero as the sample size becomes infinitely large. That is,

> sufficient conditions for consistency are that
> $$\text{bias}(Q) \to 0 \text{ and } V(Q) \to 0, \text{ as } n \to \infty.$$ [11.20]

It follows from [11.10] that an estimator will be consistent if the mean square error of the estimator tends to zero as the sample size n becomes infinitely large.

Sampling distributions for such consistent estimators are illustrated in Figs 11.9a and 11.9b. In Fig. 11.9b, the estimator happens to be unbiased in small samples (i.e., its bias does not exist). However, as n increases, the variance of the estimator becomes smaller and

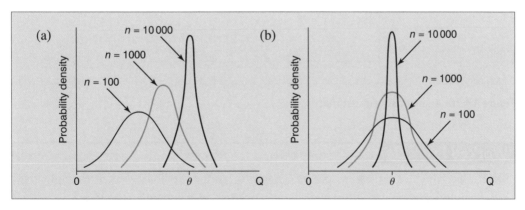

Figure 11.9a A biased but consistent estimator
Figure 11.9b An unbiased and consistent estimator

smaller so that the sampling distribution collapses on to the single value θ. Hence $\text{plim}(Q) = \theta$. In fact we have already encountered such a case. The sample mean $\bar{X}$ is unbiased in small samples and its variance σ^2/n tends to zero as $n \rightarrow \infty$. Thus $\bar{X}$ is a consistent estimator of the population mean μ, because $\text{plim}(\bar{X}) = \mu$.

In Fig. 11.9a, the estimator Q is biased for small samples but, as the sample size increases, both the bias and the variance of Q decline eventually to zero. That is, the sampling distribution for Q 'shifts over' towards θ and its dispersion becomes smaller and smaller. Again, the sampling distribution eventually collapses on to the single value θ.

As we saw in the previous section, the sampling distributions of estimators do not always collapse to the value that we would like. If the distribution of an estimator is such that $\text{plim}(Q) \neq \theta$, that is, if the distribution does not collapse on to the parameter being estimated, then the estimator is said to be *inconsistent*. Such an estimator is illustrated in Fig. 11.10. Here the estimator is biased, and this bias persists *however large the size of the samples taken*. But, although the bias remains as $n \rightarrow \infty$, the dispersion of the sample distribution still gets smaller and smaller. Recall again that areas under these curves represent probabilities. This means that, although there is at least some chance of getting a value of Q close to θ in smaller samples, the probability of this occurring becomes zero for large samples! Unfortunately, in many situations in economics, estimators turn out to be inconsistent. For example, except under fairly fortunate conditions, the OLS estimators a and b of Chapter 9 are *both biased and inconsistent*.

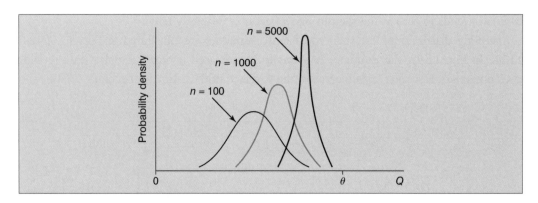

Figure 11.10 An inconsistent estimator

Worked Example

Determine which of the estimators, $\hat{m}$, $\bar{m}$ and m^*, in the previous worked example are:
(a) asymptotically unbiased; (b) consistent estimators of the population mean μ.

Solution

(a) To determine whether an estimator is asymptotically unbiased, we must consider what happens to its bias as $n \to \infty$. From the answer to the previous worked example, we see that as $n \to \infty$:

$$\text{bias}(\hat{m}) = -10, \qquad \text{and remains unchanged and non-zero;}$$

$$\text{bias}(\tilde{m}) = \frac{5}{n} \to 0;$$

$$\text{bias}(m^*) = \left(\frac{1}{n-2}\right)\mu \to 0.$$

Thus $\tilde{m}$ and m^* but not $\hat{m}$ are asymptotically unbiased.

(b) A sufficient condition for consistency is that both the bias and the variance of an estimator should tend to zero as $n \to \infty$. Since $\text{bias}(\hat{m})$ does not tend to zero, $\hat{m}$ cannot be consistent. From the previous worked example, we have, as $n \to \infty$,

$$V(\tilde{m}) = \sigma^2/n \to 0,$$

$$V(m^*) = \frac{(n-1)^2}{(n-2)^2} \frac{\sigma^2}{n} \to 0.$$

Thus $\tilde{m}$ and m^* are consistent estimators.

Consistency implies that the sampling distribution of an estimator collapses to the true parameter as n becomes very large. When the sampling distribution approaches such a collapse this means that, if many samples are taken, $\Pr(Q = \theta)$ approaches unity, so that each sample yields a value of Q very close or almost identical to the true parameter value θ. This is the real advantage of consistency. Although we take just one sample, *provided that sample is sufficiently large*, we are certain to get a value of Q very close, if not equal to, θ. Of course in econometrics, frequently we have to deal with samples that are not particularly large. However, if the sampling distribution of a consistent estimator reaches the 'point of collapse' on to the true parameter value relatively quickly as the sample size increases, then it is possible to reap the benefit of consistency even though n is 'fairly large' but not 'enormously large'.

Consider Fig. 11.11. In Fig. 11.11b, the estimator Q_2 is consistent but, for samples size $n = 1000$, its sampling distribution has still not reached the 'point of collapse'. However, in Fig. 11.11a, the estimator Q_1 is again consistent and, moreover, for samples of size only $n = 50$, its sampling distribution is just as close to the 'point of collapse'. That is, Q_1 has a sampling distribution approaching collapse more quickly than that of Q_2. Alternatively, we can say Q_1 is converging in probability to its probability limit more rapidly than Q_2. Thus Q_1 is said to be more *asymptotically efficient* than Q_2. Clearly, an econometrician faced with a sample of size maybe 100 or 200 will prefer the estimator Q_1.

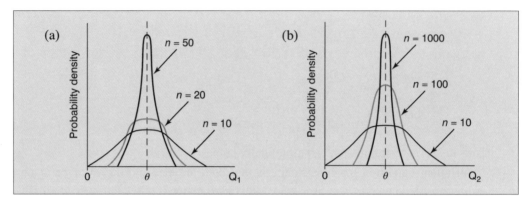

Figure 11.11 Q_1 is more efficient, asymptotically, than Q_2

Faced with a series of consistent estimators of a parameter, *the* asymptotically efficient estimator is simply the one that converges in probability *most* quickly. Thus, with such an estimator, it is easier to reap the 'benefit' of consistency. We can now give a concise definition of the large-sample property of asymptotic efficiency:

> Q is said to be an *asymptotically efficient* estimator of θ if and only if:
> (i) it is consistent, that is, plim(Q) = θ;
> (ii) no other consistent estimator of θ approaches its probability limit
> faster as $n \longrightarrow \infty$.   [11.21]

With time-series data, it is rare for a sample size to exceed $n = 100$. But modern cross-sectional data often involve sample sizes of many thousands. Although such samples are not 'infinitely large', obviously, they are often sufficiently large to make the use of an asymptotically efficient estimator well worth the effort.

Example 11.5

A random variable X has mean μ and variance σ^2. Two independent samples of observations on X, of sizes n and m, have means $\bar{X}_n$ and $\bar{X}_m$ respectively. Two possible estimators of μ are considered. The first is $\bar{X}_n$, the mean of the first sample, while the second is given by

$$\tilde{X} = \frac{n\bar{X}_n}{n + m} + \frac{m\bar{X}_m}{n + m}.$$

$\bar{X}_n$ obviously has mean μ and variance σ^2/n. Find the mean and variance of $\tilde{X}$. Which estimator is the more efficient?

Show that $\tilde{X}$ is a consistent estimator of μ. Is $\tilde{X}$ asymptotically more efficient than $\bar{X}_n$?

Example 11.6

A random variable has an $N(\mu, \sigma^2)$ distribution. Three samples from this population are available, with sizes n_1, n_2 and n_3. It is proposed to estimate μ by

$$\tilde{X} = \tfrac{1}{3}\bar{X}_1 + \tfrac{1}{3}\bar{X}_2 + \tfrac{1}{3}\bar{X}_3,$$

where $\bar{X}_1$, $\bar{X}_2$ and $\bar{X}_3$ are the respective sample means. A statistician, however, suggests that a better procedure would be to pool the samples and use $\bar{X}$, the mean of the $n = n_1 + n_2 + n_3$ observations in the pooled sample.

(a) What will be the shapes of the asymptotic distributions for $\bar{X}_1, \bar{X}_2, \bar{X}_3, \tilde{X}$ and $\bar{X}$?

(b) Show that $\tilde{X}$ is a consistent estimator of μ.

(c) Is $\tilde{X}$ a more asymptotically efficient estimator than $\bar{X}$?

Example 11.7

In Example 11.6, three estimators are used to estimate the population mean:
(i) $\tilde{X} = \tfrac{1}{3}\bar{X}_1 + \tfrac{1}{3}\bar{X}_2 + \tfrac{1}{3}\bar{X}_3$
(ii) $\hat{X} = (n_1\bar{X}_1 + n_2\bar{X}_2 + n_3\bar{X}_3 + 1)/n$
(iii) $X^* = 0.5\bar{X}_1 + 0.3\bar{X}_2 + 0.2\bar{X}_3$

(a) Which of the estimators are unbiased? If $n_1 = 30$, $n_2 = 20$ and $n_3 = 10$, which of the estimators is most efficient?
(b) Which of the estimators are consistent? Which of the estimators is asymptotically the most efficient?

*11.5 Methods of estimation

We have spent some time describing the properties that we would like our estimators to possess, so in this section we look, fairly briefly, how such estimators may be obtained.

The method of moments

This is the simplest method of estimating a parameter. Consider a population of values for a random variable X, with mean $E(X) = \mu$.

Statisticians refer to the quantity $E(X - \mu)$ as the *first moment of X about the mean μ*. Similarly, $E(X - \mu)^2$ is termed the *second moment about the mean* and $E(X - \mu)^3$ the *third moment about the mean*, and so on. Notice that the first moment about the mean is always equal to zero by definition, while the second moment about the mean is simply the population variance σ^2.

In addition, $E(X)$ is sometimes described by statisticians as the *first moment* of X about zero. Similarly, $E(X^2)$ is referred to as the *second moment about zero* and $E(X^3)$ the *third moment about zero*, and so on.

The point about moments is, firstly, that it is always possible to estimate the *population moments* defined above by the equivalent *sample moments* and, secondly, that such sample moments turn out, under very general conditions, to be consistent estimators of the corresponding population moments.

The first, second and third sample moments about the sample mean $\bar{X}$ are defined as $\Sigma(X_i - \bar{X})/n$, $\Sigma(X_i - \bar{X})^2/n$, $\Sigma(X_i - \bar{X})^3/n$, and so on. The sample moments about zero are defined as $\Sigma X_i/n$, $\Sigma X_i^2/n$, $\Sigma X_i^3/n$, and so on.

Notice that the first sample moment about zero is simply the sample mean. Also, for example, the first sample moment about the mean is identically zero and the second sample moment about the mean equals the sample variance as defined by equation [3.4].

The method of moments works by estimating any given population moment by the corresponding sample moment. For example, the population mean can be estimated by the sample mean, the population variance by the sample variance, and so on. As noted above, the method provides a very simple way of obtaining a consistent estimate of any population parameter. Unfortunately, however, such estimators are often biased in small samples. For example, while the sample mean is an unbiased estimator of the population mean, the sample variance (as defined by [3.4]) is a biased estimator of the population variance.

The least-squares method

Many students will be familiar with the use of least-squares estimation in regression analysis but it is, in fact, a very general method of estimating population parameters.

As a simple example, suppose we wish to estimate the mean, μ, of a population of X values. We simply select our estimator of μ so as to minimize the sum of squares,

$$S = \sum_i (X_i - \mu)^2. \qquad [11.22]$$

Clearly, we want our estimate of μ to be 'close' to the sample values, the X_i; that is, we want the 'distances' $X_i - \mu$ to be small. One way of achieving this is to minimize S in [11.22].

To minimize S, we differentiate with respect to μ and set the resulting derivative to zero:

$$\frac{dS}{d\mu} = -2 \sum (X_i - \mu) = 0, \qquad [11.23]$$

[11.23] implies

$$\sum X_i - n\mu = 0 \quad \rightarrow \quad \mu = \frac{\sum X_i}{n} = \bar{X}. \qquad [11.24]$$

Thus the least-squares estimator[4] of a population mean μ is the sample mean $\bar{X}$.

The problem with the least-squares estimation process is that it does not guarantee *any* of the desirable properties of estimators which we described in earlier sections of this chapter. For example, the least-squares estimators in two-variable regression are not necessarily unbiased in small samples or consistent in large samples. The properties of such estimators have to be investigated independently of the estimation process itself.

Maximum likelihood estimation

Maximum likelihood (ML) estimation has become increasingly popular with econometricians in recent decades, partly because it provides, under very general conditions, consistent and asymptotically efficient estimators. Unfortunately, its meaning and techniques are harder to grasp than the other approaches to estimation introduced above. This is particularly the case when ML estimation is used in regression analysis. Consequently, we adopt a mainly intuitive approach in this subsection and limit discussion to a few simple examples.

We begin by considering a normally distributed population of values for a random variable X, which has mean μ and variance σ^2. For simplicity, we assume for the moment that the variance is known to be $\sigma^2 = 16$, but wish to estimate the population mean μ. A sample size $n = 10$ is drawn from the population and yields the X values

$$(5, -3, 8, 12, -1, 6, -2, 4, 4, 7). \qquad [11.25]$$

Suppose we suspected that the unknown mean μ were 50. Given the known variance, inspection of the sample values [11.25] would make us realize that it was highly unlikely that this particular sample had come from a population with $\mu = 50$. Similarly, if we suspected that μ were 25, we would again realize that it was unlikely for this sample to have come from such a population. However, we might think that a value for μ of 25 is a better bet than one of 50. Suppose, however, μ were 8. In such a situation, we might think that there was a quite large probability that the above sample came from a population with a mean $\mu = 8$, since in this case all the values in [11.25] are relatively close to the suggested μ value.

It should be clear that a sensible approach would be to try to find the value of μ which is 'most likely' to have generated the above sample values. And it is this that ML estimation does. The *maximum likelihood estimator* (MLE) of μ is simply that value of μ that maximizes the probability of generating the sample values actually obtained. It is that value of μ that would generate the given sample [11.25] most often, if very many samples were taken.

Of course, the population variance σ^2 is also normally unknown and, usually, we face the problem of estimating two unknown parameters μ and σ^2. However, the principle of ML estimation remains unchanged. The given sample values could have come from a population with any pair of values for μ and σ^2, but clearly some pairs of values are more likely to have generated the sample than others. The MLEs of μ and σ^2 consist of that pair of values for μ and σ^2 that have the greatest probability (i.e., are 'most likely') to generate the given sample values.

A numerical example should make the ideas of ML estimation clearer. Suppose we have a population of values for X which is *binary* in character. That is, X can take only the values 0 and 1. We refer to the value $X = 1$ as 'success' and the value $X = 0$ as 'failure'. We encountered a number of such populations in Chapter 3.3. The probability of obtaining $X = 1$ is given by the population proportion π, while the probability of failure is $\Pr(X = 0) = 1 - \pi$.

Suppose a random sample of size $n = 5$ is drawn from this population. We represent this sample by the values

$$(Y_1, Y_2, Y_3, Y_4, Y_5).$$

Firstly, consider a situation where the five Y values are unknown, except that, of course, some are zero and the rest unity. If π were *known* it would be a relatively simple process to calculate the separate probabilities of all possible sets of Y values. There would in fact be $2^5 = 32$ such sets. For example, if the sample consisted of $Y_1 = 1$, $Y_2 = 0$, $Y_3 = 1$, $Y_4 = 1$, $Y_5 = 0$, then, since the Y_i are independent drawings from the given population, the probability of obtaining this sample would be

$$(\pi)(1 - \pi)(\pi)(\pi)(1 - \pi). \qquad [11.26]$$

Hence, if we knew that $\pi = 0.3$, for example, we would use [11.26] to compute the probability of drawing this particular sample as $0.3^3 0.7^2 = 0.013\ 23$.

Similarly, if the drawn sample turned out to be $Y_1 = 1$, $Y_2 = 0$, $Y_3 = 1$, $Y_4 = 1$, $Y_5 = 1$, then the probability of it being drawn would be

$$(\pi)(1 - \pi)(\pi)(\pi)(\pi). \qquad [11.27]$$

Again, if we knew that $\pi = 0.3$ then, using [11.27], we would compute the probability of obtaining this sample as $0.7 \times 0.3^4 = 0.005\ 67$.

It should now be clear that it is possible to compute the probability of *any* possible sample outcome, provided we know the value of π. Next, however, let us look at this process in reverse.

Suppose, as is usually the case, that the proportion of successes in the population π is *unknown*, but we have to estimate π from a *single* sample of size $n = 5$ for which the Y values are *known*. In such a situation, we could use the above procedure to compute, for all possible values of π, the probability of obtaining the known sample Y values. The MLE of π is then that value of π that has the highest probability of obtaining the given known sample values. That is, the MLE is that value of π that is 'most likely' to have generated the known sample. We denote the estimator as p^*.

For example, suppose we actually draw the random sample

$$Y_1 = 1, Y_2 = 1, Y_3 = 0, Y_4 = 1, Y_5 = 1, \qquad [11.28]$$

the probability of obtaining such a sample is $\pi^4(1 - \pi)$. We can therefore calculate, for all possible values of π between 0 and 1, the probability of obtaining the known sample [11.28]. Such probabilities, or sample likelihoods, are tabulated in Table 11.1 and sketched against π in Fig. 11.12. It is apparent from both table and graph that π takes its maximum value

Table 11.1 Sample likelihoods

π	0	0.1	0.2	0.3	0.4	0.5	0.6	0.7	0.8	0.9	1
L	0	0.000	0.001	0.006	0.015	0.031	0.052	0.072	0.082	0.066	0

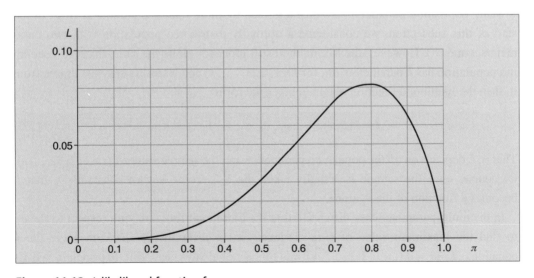

Figure 11.12 A likelihood function for π

when $\pi = 0.8$.[5] That is, the ML estimate of π is $p^* = 0.8$ and the probability of obtaining the given sample is $0.8^4 0.2 = 0.081\ 92$. The value $0.081\ 92$ is known as the *maximized likelihood*.

In practice, MLEs are not normally calculated in the above arithmetic manner. An MLE is usually obtained by first deriving a likelihood function.[6] This is simply a mathematical expression for the probability of obtaining a given sample. For example, in the current case, the probability or likelihood, L, of drawing a particular sample will depend on:

(a) the value of π, the population proportion;

(b) the sample values $(Y_1, Y_2, Y_3, Y_4, Y_5)$.

Thus, in this case the likelihood function has the form

$$L = L(\pi, Y_1, Y_2, Y_3, Y_4, Y_5). \qquad [11.29]$$

In practice, the precise algebraic form of a likelihood function [11.29] has to be found.[7] Next a random sample is taken and the actual Y values obtained. In the above example there would be only five sample values, all either zero or unity, depending on the distribution of successes and failures in the sample. Once these values are known, L in [11.29] becomes a function of the population proportion π only. The MLE of π can then be found by differentiating L with respect to π, setting the derivative $dL/d\pi$ to zero and solving the equation for π that results.[8] It turns out that the second-order derivative $d^2 L/d\pi^2$ is negative, so that the value of π found satisfies the conditions for a local maximum.[9] Thus the MLE of π, p^*, is simply that value of π that maximizes the likelihood function [11.29].

Many population parameters are characterized by more than one parameter (e.g., at the start of this subsection, we considered a normally distributed population with two parameters μ and σ^2). However, the ML method still proceeds along the same lines. In general, if a population has k parameters (θ_i, for $i = 1, 2, 3, \ldots, k$) and a sample size n is drawn from it, then the likelihood function obtained takes the form

$$L = L(\theta_1, \theta_2, \theta_3, \ldots, \theta_k, Y_1, Y_2, Y_3, \ldots, Y_n). \qquad [11.30]$$

That is, L depends on *all* the population parameters and the sample values $Y_i (i = 1, 2, 3, \ldots, n)$. Of course, once the sample is actually taken the Y_i become known constants so that L becomes a function of the θ_i alone.

In the multi-parameter case differentiating the likelihood function with respect to the θ_i, to find the maximum value of L is obviously more difficult. We have to solve the k equations $\partial L/\partial \theta_i = 0$ ($i = 1, 2, 3, \ldots, k$), and this is not always easy. But, in principle, MLEs of the θ_i can always be found.

As noted at the outset, ML estimation yields consistent and asymptotically efficient estimators under a very wide set of assumptions and thus provides a very powerful and useful technique, applicable in most situations. However, although MLEs are occasionally unbiased, this is not normally the case. That is, MLEs possess desired large-sample properties, but not necessarily desired small-sample properties.

One further point should be noted. The formulae for MLEs depend entirely on the form of the distribution assumed for the parent population. For example, in our population proportion case, we knew that the population was binary in form. It is this knowledge that makes it possible to derive a likelihood function such as [11.29]. If the relevant population is normally distributed, then again it is fairly easy to derive a likelihood function. Unfortunately, if the form of the parent population is unknown then it is not possible to derive the required likelihood function. In such cases MLEs cannot be obtained.

Worked Example

The number of customers arriving at a shopping till per minute, X, is believed to have a Poisson distribution

$$p(X) = \frac{\lambda^X e^{-\lambda}}{X!},$$

where λ is the mean number of arrivals per minute. In one interval of 1 minute it is observed that three customers arrive. Sketch the likelihood function for values of λ between 1 and 5. Hence find the MLE of λ.

How would you proceed if you had three observations on the number of arrivals per minute, for example, $X = 4$, $X = 7$ and $X = 5$?

Solution

We have a sample of just one value of X. Given $X = 3$, the likelihood function is therefore

$$L = p(3) = \frac{\lambda^3 e^{-\lambda}}{3!}.$$

L can now be computed for various possible values for λ, which are shown in Table 11.2. L appears to take its maximum value at around $\lambda = 3$. To make the estimate more precise, we calculate L for the values $\lambda = 2.9$ and $\lambda = 3.1$. This yields the value 0.2236 in each case, slightly less than the value for $\lambda = 3$. The MLE of λ therefore appears to be 3.[10] The likelihood function is sketched in Fig. 11.13.

Table 11.2

λ	1	2	3	4	5	6
L	0.0613	0.1804	0.2240	0.1954	0.1404	0.0892

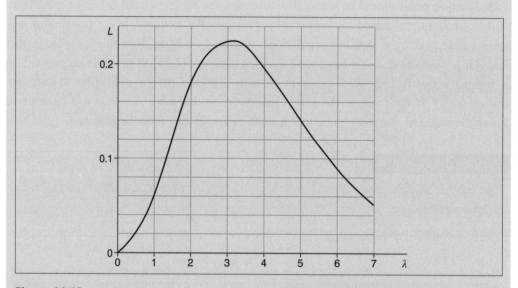

Figure 11.13

Given the three values 4, 7 and 5 for X, the number of arrivals per minute, the individual probabilities for these values are

$$p(4) = \frac{\lambda^4 e^{-\lambda}}{4!}, \qquad p(7) = \frac{\lambda^7 e^{-\lambda}}{7!}, \qquad p(5) = \frac{\lambda^5 e^{-\lambda}}{5!}.$$

Assuming that the three observations are all independent, the joint probability of obtaining 4, 7 and 5 is obtained by multiplying the probabilities together, to give a likelihood function

$$L = p(4)p(7)p(5) = \left[\frac{\lambda^4 e^{-\lambda}}{4!}\right]\left[\frac{\lambda^7 e^{-\lambda}}{7!}\right]\left[\frac{\lambda^5 e^{-\lambda}}{5!}\right].$$

$$= \frac{\lambda^{16} e^{-3\lambda}}{4!7!5!}.$$

This likelihood function could therefore be sketched for values of λ in the usual manner.

Example 11.8

A machine produces components which are either 'satisfactory' or 'defective'. The proportion π of components that are deemed defective is unknown. A sample of three components from the machine's output is examined and the first such component is found to be defective, while the others are satisfactory. Sketch the likelihood function for π and hence find its MLE.

Example 11.9

A variable X has a discrete uniform distribution with

$$\Pr(X = a) = \Pr(X = a + 1) = \Pr(X = a + 2) = 1/3.$$

A random sample of size $n = 5$ is drawn from this population and proves to have the values $(4, 4, 6, 5, 4)$. Find the MLE of a.

Example 11.10

The number of customers in a queue at a shop till, X, is known to have a geometric distribution

$$p(X) = \lambda^X(1 - \lambda), \qquad 0 < \lambda < 1$$

where $E(X) = \lambda/(1 - \lambda)$. At one single moment the number in the queue was observed to be $X = 2$. Sketch the likelihood function for λ and hence find its MLE.

Summary

- Estimators can have **small-sample properties** and **large-sample properties**. Small-sample properties have attributes that are present **regardless of the size of the samples** taken. Large-sample properties have attributes that only become apparent as the size of samples becomes '**very large**'.

- **Unbiasedness, efficiency and best linear unbiasedness** are small-sample properties. Minimizing the **mean square error** of an estimator is a way of balancing the need for a small bias with the need for a small variance.

- The **asymptotic distribution** of an estimator is that distribution to which its sampling distribution tends as the sample size n becomes very large. Some sampling distributions collapse to a single point as $n \to \infty$. This point is known as the **probability limit** of the estimator.

- **Asymptototic unbiasedness, consistency and asymptotic efficiency** are large-sample properties. In economics, it is often the case that estimators have no desirable properties even when the sample is very large. For example, an estimator can be **inconsistent**. That is, its sampling distribution may collapse to a probability limit that is not equal to the parameter being estimated.

- Three methods of estimation are: the **method of moments**, the **least-squares method** and **maximum likelihood estimation**. The last of these is a complicated method but yields estimators that are consistent and asymptotically efficient under a wide range of conditions.

Notes

1. We assume for the moment that the population is *univariate*, that is, it concerns just a single variable. However, populations may be *multivariate*. For example, a population could be *bivariate* and consist of values for two random variables, X and Y. The population would then be described by the joint probability for X and Y.

2. Normally the slope β of a regression line is estimated jointly with its intercept α. The two parameters would be estimated from a bivariate population of X and Y values. In practice, however, as we shall see in Chapter 12, the X values are often treated as a set of constant values, so that sampling can be regarded as from a univariate population of Y values. The same sample is used to estimate both α and β.

3. Equation [11.10] can be derived as follows:

$$\begin{aligned} \text{MSE}(Q) &= E[Q - \theta]^2 = E[(Q - EQ) + (EQ - \theta)]^2 \\ &= E(Q - EQ)^2 + 2E(Q - EQ)(EQ - \theta) + (EQ - \theta)^2 \\ &= V(Q) + 2E(Q - EQ)(EQ - \theta) + [\text{bias}(Q)]^2 \\ &= V(Q) + [\text{bias}(Q)]^2, \end{aligned}$$

since $E(Q - EQ) = E(Q) - E(Q) = 0$.

4. Since $dS/d\mu$ can be written as $-2 \sum X_i + 2n\mu$, where the X_i are known constants, the second-order derivative $d^2 S/d\mu^2 = 2n > 0$. Thus the second-order condition for minimum S is satisfied.

5. Of course $p^* = 0.8$ is not a particularly surprising result, given that the sample contained four 'successes' out of five!

6. The likelihood function for the above example was in fact sketched in Fig. 11.12.

7. In this case the likelihood function has the form $L = \pi^4(1 - \pi)$, the probability of obtaining the given sample [11.28].

8. The MLE is therefore found by setting the derivative $dL/d\pi$ to zero:

$$\frac{dL}{d\pi} = 4\pi^3(1 - \pi) - \pi^4 \rightarrow 4(1 - \pi) = \pi$$

Hence $5\pi = 4$, so that the MLE of π is 0.8.

9. The second-order derivative $d^2L/d\pi^2 = 4\pi^2(3 - 5\pi)$, which is negative when $\pi = 0.8$.

10. This is not a particularly surprising result, since our single observation resulted in $X = 3$.

12

The classical regression model with two variables

Objectives

When you have completed your study of this chapter, you should be able:

1. to list and understand the assumptions of the classical two-variable regression model;

2. to appreciate that the properties of the OLS estimators depend crucially on the validity of the above underlying assumptions;

3. to recall which OLS properties depend on which assumptions;

4. to test hypotheses about and find confidence intervals for the regression parameters α and β;

5. to apply the above simple inferential procedures in nonlinear regression;

6. to make out-of-sample predictions using the regression model and compute confidence intervals for such predictions;

7. to make further use of simple regression software to obtain quantities such as the estimated standard errors of a and b.

Introduction

In Chapter 9 we used the least-squares method to obtain estimators of the intercept α and slope β of a population regression line, such as that depicted in Fig. 9.5. This gave us the so-called *ordinary least-squares* (OLS) estimators of α and β as

$$b = \frac{\sum x_i y_i}{\sum x_i^2}, \qquad a = \bar{Y} - b\bar{X}. \qquad [12.1]$$

Recall that x_i and y_i are the deviations of X_i and Y_i from their respective sample means $\bar{X}$ and $\bar{Y}$.

We stressed in Chapter 9 that, like all sample statistics, a and b have *sampling distributions*. That is, any OLS estimates obtained are always specific to the particular sample that has been taken and, consequently, different samples will, almost certainly, yield different values for a and b. Unfortunately, as we saw in Chapter 11, the least-squares method of estimation does not necessarily provide us with estimators or sampling distributions possessing any of the desired properties that we listed there. In fact, in two-variable regression, it turns out that, if the OLS estimators are to be unbiased or even consistent estimators of α and β, then a whole series of quite rigorous conditions have to be valid.

The purposes of this chapter are, firstly, to describe these conditions. This involves defining the so-called *classical two-variable regression model*. Secondly, this model enables us to begin the application of the techniques of statistical inference to regression analysis. In particular, we shall introduce a procedure by which we can perform inference regarding regression parameters such as α and β.

12.1 Assumptions of the classical two-variable regression model

The classical regression model was originally constructed for use in the physical sciences. Not surprisingly, then, many of its assumptions are somewhat implausible when applied to social science data. However, the classical model remains a highly useful tool for introducing the inferential aspects of regression analysis. Also, a thorough knowledge of the classical model helps in identifying the conditions under which OLS regression remains appropriate.

In the classical model, it is assumed that there exists a population regression equation of the kind [9.5]. That is, the dependent variable Y is a linear function of the explanatory variable X and the disturbance ε. Equation [9.7] is assumed to be valid for all observations in a sample size n. We therefore have

$$Y_i = \alpha + \beta X_i + \varepsilon_i, \qquad i = 1, 2, 3, ..., n. \qquad [12.2]$$

Equation [12.2] is identical to [9.9]. The remainder of the classical model comprises a series of basic assumptions concerning, firstly, the explanatory variable X and, secondly, the disturbance ε. The passages that follow are some of the most important in this book. Some of the classical assumptions are conceptually difficult but a clear understanding of them is crucial to the proper application of regression analysis.

Assumptions concerning the explanatory variable

In the two-variable classical regression model, the explanatory variable X is assumed:

(IA) to be non-stochastic;

(IB) to have values that are fixed in repeated samples;

(IC) to be such that as $n \rightarrow \infty$ its variance $V(X) \rightarrow V^*$, where V^* is some fixed constant.

We will spend some time explaining the nature and purpose of these assumptions. In Chapter 1, we defined a random or *stochastic* variable as one whose values are determined by some chance mechanism. A *non-stochastic* variable must therefore simply be a variable which has values that are *not* determined by chance. In this context, this implies that the X values are determined by an experimenter or *investigator*. Recall that the classical model was originally developed for the physical sciences, where laboratory experiments are possible. It is therefore possible to envisage the investigator as choosing the X values in an experiment and then observing the Y values that result. Assumption IA implies that the X values (for example those in Table 9.1), have been chosen in this manner. Clearly, in most social sciences, it is not possible to carry out laboratory experiments, and in economics, for example, it is normally the case that both the X and the Y values in a random sample are stochastic. But the fiction of a non-stochastic X is a useful one and we shall retain it for now.

Notice that, although the values of the X variable are fixed, this is not true of the Y variable. From [12.2], Y depends not only on X but also on the unknown disturbance. Hence, unlike X, Y is a stochastic variable deriving its stochastic nature from the disturbance. Each Y value is determined, firstly, by the corresponding X value (chosen by the investigator) and, secondly, by the disturbance value over which the investigator has no control.

Assumption IB also implies the existence of an external investigator. It refers to a hypothetical situation where the investigator takes 'very many' samples, in which he retains exactly the same X values as in his first sample or experiment. For example, the experimenter could be thought to be checking his previous results or, alternatively, other scientists might be seeking to replicate the results of the first investigator. Notice, however, that although the X values remain unchanged in each sample or experiment, this is not the case for the Y values. As noted above, it is clear that the Y values depend not only on the chosen

X values but also on the values of the disturbance. Thus, while the X values remain fixed in repeated samples, the Y values will vary from sample to sample because the investigator has no control over the disturbances.

Because the Y values will vary, this means that the OLS estimators [12.1], which depend on both the X values and the Y values, must also vary from sample to sample. Thus a and b will have *sampling distributions*, although these distributions must be viewed in the context of repeated sampling with fixed X values.[1]

The significance of assumption IC will not become clear until later in the text. The assumption ensures that, as the sample size n increases, the variance of the X values, $V(X)$, does not increase without limit. Obviously as n increases the sum of squares $S = \sum_i (X_i - \bar{X})^2$ will, almost certainly, increase since we will have more X values to sum over.[2] However, $V(X) = S/n$ need not increase without limit, provided the investigator is careful about the X values that are chosen. It is when it is no longer plausible to maintain the fiction of such an investigator that assumption IC is likely to break down.

A breakdown in assumption IC is likely with time-series data, when we are dealing with variables that exhibit consistent trends (upwards or downwards) over time. In such time-series samples, as the sample size n increases, the range of X values in a typical sample must also increase. Consequently, the variance of X no longer tends to a finite value but can increase without limit. In such a case, assumption IC will not hold.

The importance of the assumption is that it conveniently rules out, for now, X variables which demonstrate strong trend behaviour. As we shall find later, making inferences about regression variables, for which assumption IC is not valid, is fraught with danger. For example, we saw in Chapter 9 that much of the correlation between trending variables can be largely spurious.

At this point we need to consider what we actually mean by 'repeated samples' when we are dealing with 'aggregate' economic data. For example, taking the data in Table 9.1, the idea of different samples occurring for the set of 30 countries in a given year may cause difficulty. Clearly, France only has one X_8 for 1984 – that of £9466. This is an aggregate value, and cannot be recomputed from another sample of French individuals. There is thus a problem of interpretation. While we could certainly envisage different X_8s for different years, it would be very likely that many economic factors, which we have excluded from our model, would vary across such years. It is therefore better to try and envisage a whole series of different alternative 'courses of history' or 'realizations' for France in 1984. Many such realizations were possible but only one actually occured, yielding the given value X_8. Any of the other realizations *could* have occurred but in fact *did not*. Generalizing, we can now visualize an infinite number of alternative realizations for the whole set of 30 countries. Each realization would result in a different sample of X values. It is in this framework that we seek to apply the classical assumptions. Of course, it now becomes even more difficult to accept the idea of an investigator holding fixed all the *X* values in every such realization. So, clearly, we will have to relax this assumption in later chapters.

Assumptions concerning the disturbances

In the two-variable classical regression model, the disturbances are assumed to have the following properties:

(IIA) $E(\varepsilon_i) = 0$, for all i;

(IIB) $V(\varepsilon_i) = E(\varepsilon_i - E[\varepsilon_i])^2 = E(\varepsilon_i^2) = \sigma^2 = $ constant for all i;

(IIC) $Cov(\varepsilon_i, \varepsilon_j) = E(\varepsilon_i - E[\varepsilon_i])(\varepsilon_j - E[\varepsilon_j]) = E(\varepsilon_i \varepsilon_j) = 0$ for all $i \neq j$;

(IID) each ε_i is normally distributed.

Study of Fig. 12.1, on which the population regression line [9.5] has been drawn, will assist understanding of the assumptions concerning the disturbances. Figure 12.1 also shows X_8, the value of the explanatory variable *X* pertaining to the eight-observation in the sample. For example, if we take the data set of Table 9.1, then X_8 is the GDP of the eighth country (France).

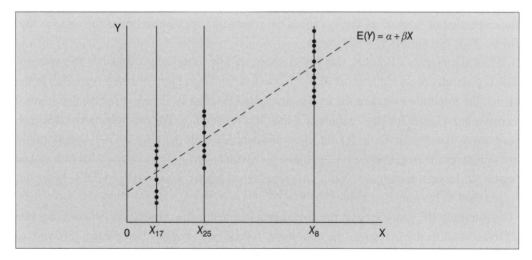

Figure 12.1 Repeated sampling under classical assumptions

Given assumptions IA and IB, X_8 has a fixed value, which would remain unchanged were it possible to take further samples. But the Y_8 value would *vary* if further samples were taken because of variations in ε_8, the disturbance pertaining to the eighth sample value or country. This fact is illustrated by points marked on the vertical line passing through X_8. Each of these points represents the eighth observation in a different sample, with a fixed X_8 but varying values for Y_8.

Recall that disturbances measure the vertical distances between points in Fig. 12.1 from the population regression line. Thus points on the line X_8 indicate the different values of the disturbance ε_8 in different samples. Points below the population regression line simply indicate negative ε_8 values.

Assumption IIA simply specifies that the mean value of the disturbances ε_8, taken over very many samples all with the same X_8, is equal to zero. That is, $E(\varepsilon_8) = 0$. Similarly, the mean value of the disturbances ε_{25}, ε_{17}, and so on, associated with the fixed X_{25}, X_{17}, and so on, are also assumed to be zero. That is, $E(\varepsilon_{25}) = 0$, $E(\varepsilon_{17}) = 0$, and so on. That is, in general $E(\varepsilon_i) = 0$ for all i, as stated by assumption IIA. (In fact, we have quietly made use of assumption IIA already, to move between [9.9] and the population equation [9.8] in Chapter 9.)

Assumption IIA implies that the varying Y_8s, Y_{25}s, Y_{17}s, and so on, obtained when repeated samples are taken, are 'equally spaced' above and below the population regression line, as illustrated in Fig. 12.1.

Assumption IIB states that, for example, the variance of the ε_8s, obtained over very many samples, is the same as the variance of the ε_{25}s, which is, in turn, equal to the variance of the ε_{17}s. That is, in general, $V(\varepsilon_i) = \sigma^2$, where σ^2 is a constant population parameter. The constant variance measures the equal dispersion of each set of disturbance values about their common zero mean. It follows, as illustrated in Fig. 12.1, that assumption IIB implies that the dispersion or 'spread' of the Y_8s about the population regression line is the same as that for the Y_{25}s, that for the Y_{17}s and so on.

When assumption IIB holds, the disturbances are said to be *homoscedastic*. The assumption is generally regarded as most likely to break down when there is a large variation in the size of the n sample values of the explanatory variable. The tendency is for the disturbance variance to be larger for large values of X than it is for small X. For example, in our demand-for-money example in Table 9.1, the largest countries with the largest GDP values might not only have the largest M values, but also the greatest *variation* in demand for money and hence the largest disturbance variation. Smaller countries with smaller GDPs, however, would tend to have smaller values for $V(\varepsilon_i)$.

Assumption IIC specifies that the covariance and hence the correlation between any two different disturbances is zero, (the condition 'for all $i \neq j$' implies that we are referring to *different* disturbances). Relating to *each* sample there will be disturbances for every observation, that is, values for ε_1, ε_2, ε_3, ..., ε_n. Assumption IIC implies that, over many samples, there must be no tendency, for example, for there to be 'large' positive ε_7s whenever there are 'large' positive ε_{10}s. Otherwise $Cov(\varepsilon_7, \varepsilon_{10})$ would be non-zero and positive. Negative correlations are also similarly ruled out. For example, there must no tendency for large positive ε_3s to occur whenever there are large negative ε_{12}s.

When assumption IIC holds, the disturbances are said to be *non-autocorrelated*. The assumption of non-autocorrelated disturbances is usually held to be violated most often for monthly or quarterly time-series data. Disturbances tend to 'spill over' from one time period to the next. For example, a positive disturbance in one month may well spill over into the next month. A simple case might involve a spell of hot weather leading to above average sales of ice-cream in two successive months. Autocorrelated disturbances are less likely to occur with annual time series, simply because spill-over effects across two years tend to be less important than spill-overs between two quarters or two months.

Assumption IID specifies that, for example, the ε_8s that would be obtained if very many samples were taken are normally distributed about their zero mean. Similarly for the ε_{25}s, the ε_{17}s, and so on. This assumption is illustrated in Fig. 12.2. It implies that, since areas under the normal curves in this figure represent probabilities, there is a larger probability of obtaining points close to the population regression line than there is of obtaining points far away from it. A more precise interpretation of assumption IID is provided by considering equation [12.2]. Since $E(\varepsilon_i) = 0$, for all i, and the X_i are assumed to be constants, it follows that, by taking expectations of [12.2], we have

$$E(Y_i) = \alpha + \beta X_i = \text{constant}.$$

Thus [12.2] can be written as

$$Y_i = E(Y_i) + \varepsilon_i.$$

Hence, since $E(Y_i)$ is a constant, if the ε_i are normally distributed, the Y_i must also be normally distributed.[3] In fact, each Y_i is normally distributed about its mean $E(Y_i)$.

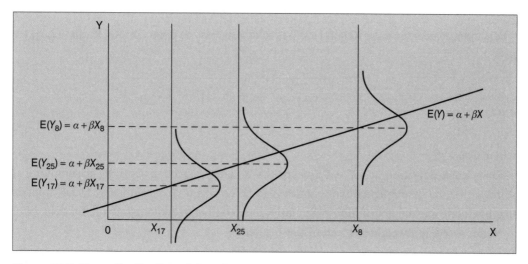

Figure 12.2 Normally distributed disturbances

Consequently, assumption IID implies there is a larger probability of getting a Y value close to its mean $E(Y_i)$ than there is of getting a value far from $E(Y_i)$.

12.2 **Properties of the OLS estimators**

In this section we shall be concerned with outlining *which* assumptions in the classical model are necessary and/or sufficient for the OLS estimators to possess the properties, such as best linear unbiasedness or consistency, that we described in Chapter 11. In addition, this will enable us to test hypotheses about, and to construct confidence intervals for, regression parameters such as α and β.

A thorough knowledge of the links between assumptions and properties is invaluable in applied regression work. Some of the results in this section will be given without proof, because they require a level of mathematics that is rather higher than that assumed in this book. We shall concentration on the OLS estimate of β rather than that of α, because β is usually of greater interest than α.

Linearity

If assumptions IA and IB hold, it is fairly easy to show that the OLS estimators are linear estimators. If the X values can be regarded as fixed constants in repeated samples then, in any given sample, it is *the Y values that are the sample observations*. Thus if b, for example, is to be a linear estimator, then it has to be a *linear function of the Y values*. That is, we require

$$b = \sum w_i Y_i, \quad\quad\quad [12.3]$$

where the w_is are constants. Result [12.3] is relatively easy to demonstrate. From [12.1], we have

$$b = \frac{\sum x_i y_i}{\sum x_i^2} = \frac{\sum x_i (Y_i - \overline{Y})}{\sum x_i^2} = \frac{\sum x_i Y_i}{\sum x_i^2} \quad (\text{since } \overline{Y} \sum x_i = 0)$$

$$= \sum w_i Y_i, \quad\quad\quad [12.4]$$

where $w_i = x_i / \sum x_i^2$.

Since each deviation $x_i = X_i - \overline{X}$, where the X_i and $\overline{X}$ are constants by assumption, it follows that the x_i and hence the w_i must also be constants. Consequently, [12.4] implies that b is a linear estimator of the Y_i. Similarly, it is possible to demonstrate the linearity of a.

Notice that b is a weighted mean of the Y values:

$$b = w_1 Y_1 + w_2 Y_2 + w_3 Y_3 + \cdots + w_n Y_n. \quad\quad\quad [12.5]$$

It is easy to show that the sum of the weights, w_i, has to be zero. If we let $A = \sum x_i^2$ where A is a constant, *independent of i*, then $w_i = x_i/A$, so that

$$\sum w_i = \sum x_i/A = \frac{1}{A} \sum x_i.$$

Thus, since $\sum x_i = 0$,

$$\sum w_i = 0. \qquad\qquad [12.6]$$

Unbiasedness and consistency

If we combine assumptions IA and IB with assumption IIA, the first of the assumptions concerning the disturbances, it is possible, without too much difficulty, to show that the OLS estimators a and b are unbiased estimators of the true α and β. That is, given the assumptions about X, if $E(\varepsilon_i) = 0$, then

$$E(b) = \beta \quad \text{and} \quad E(a) = \alpha. \qquad\qquad [12.7]$$

Proof the unbiasedness of b.

Taking expectations over [12.5] gives

$$E(b) = w_1 E(Y_1) + w_2 E(Y_2) + \cdots + w_n E(Y_n). \qquad\qquad [12.8]$$

But, using $E(\varepsilon_i) = 0$, we have $E(Y_i) = a + \beta X_i$ for all i. Hence, substituting in [12.8],

$$E(b) = w_1(\alpha + \beta X_1) + w_2(\alpha + \beta X_2) + \cdots + w_n(\alpha + \beta X_n)$$
$$= \alpha \sum w_i + \beta \sum w_i X_i. \qquad\qquad [12.9]$$

But, from [12.6], we know that $\sum w_i = 0$. Moreover, in [12.9],

$$\sum w_i X_i = \sum w_i(x_i + \bar{X}) = \sum w_i x_i \quad (\text{since } \sum w_i \bar{X} = \bar{X} \sum w_i = 0)$$
$$= \sum x_i^2/\sum x_i^2 = 1 \quad (\text{recall that } w_i = x_i/\sum x_i^2).$$

Hence, using these results in [12.9] we have $E(b) = \beta$, that is, b is an unbiased estimate of β.

Notice that, apart from $E(\varepsilon_i) = 0$, we did not require any of the other classical assumptions concerning the disturbances for the OLS estimators to be proved unbiased. That is, we did not need the assumptions of homoscedastic, non-autocorrelated and normally distributed disturbances. It also turns out that we do not require these assumptions to prove the large-sample property of consistency either. Provided *all* the classical assumptions about the explanatory variable X are valid and $E(\varepsilon_i) = 0$, then it can be shown that a and b are consistent estimators of α and β, respectively. That is, in the sense described in Chapter 11,

$$\text{plim}(a) = \alpha \quad \text{and} \quad \text{plim}(b) = \beta. \qquad\qquad [12.10]$$

This result implies that as the size of samples n becomes larger and larger, the sampling distributions for a and b collapse on to their probability limits, which happen to be the population parameters α and β, respectively. The proof of the consistency of the OLS estimators is beyond our scope,[4] but it is worth noting that one of the assumptions normally used to prove consistency is assumption IC, regarding the X variable. In time-series data, if X possesses a strong trend, then assumption IC is almost certain to be invalid and, in such circumstances, the standard proof of consistency breaks down. As we shall see in later chapters, this can sometimes have serious consequences.

Best linear unbiasedness

We stressed in the last chapter that unbiasedness was not a particularly reassuring property. Given that we usually take just a single sample, we normally like the variance of any unbiased estimator we use to have as small a variance as possible. But if the OLS estimators a and b are to be not merely unbiased, but best linear unbiased estimators of the regression parameters α and β, then there is an extra price to pay. For a and b to be BLUES, in the sense defined in Chapter 11, it turns out that not only assumptions IA, IB and IIA have to be valid but also IIB and IIC. That is, the disturbances must not only have zero mean but also be homoscedastic and non-autocorrelated.

The proof of the BLUness property is rather complicated, but it implies that, of all linear unbiased estimators, the OLS estimators are those that have the smallest variances. These minimum variances, normally written as σ_a^2 and σ_b^2, can be shown to be

$$V(a) = \sigma_a^2 = \frac{\sigma^2 \sum X_i^2}{n \sum x_i^2} \quad \text{and} \quad V(b) = \sigma_b^2 = \frac{\sigma^2}{\sum x_i^2}. \qquad [12.11]$$

It is worth pausing briefly to consider exactly what the expressions in [12.11] represent. We know that, if we were to take many samples, we would obtain sampling distributions for both a and b. Given the stated assumptions, the variances [12.11] are measures of the dispersion of these sampling distributions. As we shall see shortly, knowledge of these variances is vitally important if we are to make inferences about the unknown population parameters α and β (i.e., find confidence intervals for them, or test hypotheses about them). The square roots of the variances in [12.8] are known as *standard errors* and are written as σ_a and σ_b.

Efficiency

For an OLS estimator to be efficient and not merely the BLUE, that estimator has to have the minimum variance of *all* unbiased estimators, not just of *all linear* unbiased estimators. The extra assumption needed for efficiency is, in fact, assumption IID, which states that each disturbance has to be normally distributed. Thus given assumptions IA and IB regarding the X variable and assumptions IIA, IIB, IIC and IID concerning the disturbances, the OLS estimators a and b are efficient estimators of α and β.

Since efficiency is a small-sample property, the OLS estimators will also be efficient in large samples. This suggests that they must be asymptotically efficient. That is, out of all consistent estimators of α and β, the OLS estimators a and b should collapse most rapidly on to their probability limits. But, for an estimator to be asymptotically efficient, it must firstly be consistent. As we saw earlier, for the OLS estimators to be consistent we need the large-sample assumption IC. Therefore, for *asymptotic* efficiency, we have to add assumption IC to the assumptions required for small-sample efficiency.

Normality

Assumption IID, concerning normally distributed disturbances, has the important consequence that the OLS estimators a and b also then become normally distributed. Consider equation [12.2].

$$Y_i = \alpha + \beta X_i + \varepsilon_i \quad \text{for } i = 1, 2, 3, ..., n$$

Since the X values are non-stochastic fixed constants in repeated sampling, it follows that all the $\alpha + \beta X_i$ must be constants. Thus, each Y_i is the sum of a constant and a normally distributed disturbance ε_i. It follows that each Y_i has a normal distribution. (Adding a constant to normally distributed variable just shifts the distribution along the horizontal axis but does not change its shape. See Fig. 12.2.)

The links between the assumptions of the classical model and the properties of the OLS estimators are outlined in Box 12.1. It follows that we can summarize the small-sample

---

Box 12.1 Properties of the OLS estimators

1. **Small-sample properties**
Assumptions **IA, IB** ensure **linearity**.
Assumptions **IA, IB, IIA** ensure **unbiasedness**.
Assumptions **IA, IB, IIA, IIB, IIC** ensure **BLUness**.
Assumptions **IA, IB IIA, IIB, IIC, IID** ensure **efficiency**.
Assumptions **IA, IB, IID** ensure **normality**.

2. **Large-sample properties**
Assumptions **IA, IB, IC, IIA** ensure **consistency**.
Assumptions **1A, IB, IC, IIA, IIB, IIC, IID** ensure **asymptotic efficiency**.

properties by saying that, under classical assumptions,

$$a \text{ has a } N(\alpha, \sigma_a^2) \text{ distribution} \qquad [12.12]$$

and

$$b \text{ has a } N(\beta, \sigma_b^2) \text{ distribution,} \qquad [12.13]$$

where σ_a^2 and σ_b^2 are given in [12.11].

*Maximum likelihood estimation

ML estimation was discussed in Section 11.5. Provided the probability density function of each disturbance is known, it is possible to derive MLEs for the regression parameters α and β. In fact, it turns out, under classical assumptions, that the MLEs $\tilde{a}$ and $\tilde{b}$ are identical to the OLS estimators a and b. That is, of all possible estimators of α and β, $\tilde{a} = a$ and $\tilde{b} = b$ are the most likely to have generated a particular given sample, where a and b are given by [9.22] and [9.21].[5]

One advantage of maximum likelihood estimation is that they yield not only estimators of α and β but also of the other parameter in the classical regression model, σ^2, the common disturbance variance. The MLE of σ^2 is in fact

$$\tilde{s}^2 = \sum_i e_i^2 / n, \qquad [12.14]$$

where the e_i are the least-squares residuals. Notice that, since $\sum_i e_i = 0$, from [9.23], the mean of the residuals, $\bar{e}$, must be zero, so $\tilde{s}^2 = \sum_i (e_i - \bar{e})^2 n$ is, in fact, the variance of the residuals, which is a plausible estimator of σ^2, the variance of the disturbances.

Like all MLEs, $\tilde{s}^2$ is consistent but, unfortunately, it is *biased* in small samples[6] since

$$E(\tilde{s}^2) = \left(\frac{n-2}{n}\right)\sigma^2. \qquad [12.15]$$

Thus in small samples $\tilde{s}^2$ tends to underestimate the true σ^2. However, this is easily rectified since

$$s^2 = \frac{\sum e_i^2}{n-2} \qquad [12.16]$$

provides an unbiased estimator. From [12.14] and [12.16], $s^2 = [n/(n-2)]\tilde{s}^2$. Thus

$$E(s^2) = E\left(\frac{n}{n-2}\right)\tilde{s}^2 = \frac{n}{n-2} E(\tilde{s}^2) = \sigma^2,$$

using [12.15].

The easiest way to find the residual sum of squares, needed to compute [12.16], is to use

$$\sum e_i^2 = \sum y_i^2 - b \sum x_i y_i. \tag{12.17}$$

This equation can easily be derived, using the split of the total sum of squares into explained and residual sums of squares. Recall [9.33], which can be written as

$$\sum e_i^2 = \sum y_i^2 - \text{SSE}.$$

But, using [9.38], $\text{SSE} = b^2 \sum x_i^2 = b \sum x_i y_i$. Thus [12.17] follows.

12.3 Inference in the two-variable classical model

Provided the classical assumptions regarding the explanatory variable and the disturbances are valid, then [12.12] and [12.13] must be valid. It follows that

$$\frac{a - \alpha}{\sigma_a} \text{ and } \frac{b - \beta}{\sigma_b} \text{ have } N(0, 1) \text{ distributions.} \tag{12.18}$$

Unfortunately, the disturbance variance σ^2 is generally unknown, so we cannot use [12.18] as a basis for testing hypotheses or constructing confidence intervals. However, we know that $s^2 = \sum e_i^2 / (n - 2)$ is an unbiased estimator of σ^2, so we can estimate the variances in [12.11] by replacing σ^2 by s^2 to obtain

$$s_a^2 = \frac{s^2 \sum X_i^2}{n \sum x_i^2} \text{ and } s_b^2 = \frac{s^2}{\sum x_i^2}. \tag{12.19}$$

However, when we replace σ_a^2 and σ_b^2 by s_a^2 and s_b^2 in [12.18] we have to switch to the Student's t distribution.[7] That is, [12.18] becomes

$$\frac{a - \alpha}{s_a} \text{ and } \frac{b - \beta}{s_b} \text{ have Student's } t \text{ distributions with } n - 2 \text{ d.f.} \tag{12.20}$$

It is now time that we substituted some numbers into the formulae that we have introduced in this chapter. We return, therefore, to the demand-for-money data set in Table 9.1. For this data set we already have, from [9.25]–[9.27], the basic building blocks

$$\sum x_i^2 = 666.86, \qquad \sum x_i y_i = 116.60, \qquad \sum y_i^2 = 26.403. \tag{12.21}$$

We also have, from [9.29] and [9.28], the OLS estimators

$$a = 0.021\,2 \qquad b = 0.174\,85 \tag{12.22}$$

Once a and b have been obtained, the next step in any regression analysis is always to obtain the residual sum of squares from [12.17], using b and two of the basic building blocks:

$$\sum e_i^2 = 26.403 - 0.174\,85 \times 116.60 = 6.0155. \tag{12.23}$$

We can now use [12.16] to obtain

$$s^2 = \frac{6.0155}{28} = 0.2148.$$

Finally, we can use [12.19] to obtain s_a^2 and s_b^2:

$$s_a^2 = \frac{0.2148 \times 1274.66}{30 \times 666.86} = 0.013\ 6, \qquad [12.24]$$

$$s_b^2 = \frac{0.2148}{666.86} = 0.000\ 322\ 1. \qquad [12.25]$$

Note that in [12.24] we have obtained $\sum X_i^2 = 1274.66$ from Table 9.2. The *estimated standard errors* of a and b are then obtained as

$$s_a = \sqrt{0.013\ 65} = 0.1170, \qquad [12.26]$$

$$s_b = \sqrt{0.000\ 322\ 1} = 0.017\ 95. \qquad [12.27]$$

It is worth pausing again, at this point, to consider what the estimated standard errors in [12.26] and [12.27] are actually measuring. Recall that different samples give different values for the OLS estimators a and b. That is, a and b have sampling distributions which have variances and hence standard deviations. The values s_a and s_b in [12.26] and [12.27] are *our estimates* of these standard deviations obtained from the single sample that we have taken. It is the values s_a and s_b that allow us to make inferences about the true α and β.

Confidence intervals for α and β

Using results [12.19], it is now possible to obtain confidence intervals for α and β, the intercept and slope of the population regression equation. Recall that, when using the t distribution, confidence intervals take the general form [3.17]. In this case, we therefore have:

> 95% confidence interval for α is $a \pm t_{0.025} s_a$, $\qquad [12.28]$

and

> 95% confidence interval for β is $b \pm t_{0.025} s_b$, $\qquad [12.29]$

where the $t_{0.025}$ values depend on the degrees of freedom $n - 2$. If we require 99% intervals then the $t_{0.025}$ value is simply replaced by the relevant $t_{0.005}$ value.

Referring back again to the demand-for-money data set of Table 9.1, we can now compute a 95% confidence interval for the slope parameter, β, that measures the increase in the demand for money per unit increase in GDP. We already have, working to three significant figures, $b = 0.175$ and $s_b = 0.0180$. The sample size $n = 30$, so we have 28 d.f. Hence $t_{0.025} = 2.048$. Substituting into [12.29] gives the required interval (to three decimal places) as

$$0.175 \pm 2.048 \times 0.0180 \rightarrow 0.175 \pm 0.037.$$

We can obtain a similar 95% confidence interval for α. In this case we have $a = 0.021\ 2$ and $s_a = 0.117$ so, using [12.28], we obtain the interval

$$0.021\ 2 \pm 2.048 \times 0.117 \rightarrow 0.021 \pm 0.240.$$

Hypothesis testing

The results [12.19] can also be used to test hypotheses about α and β. The most common hypothesis tested in regression analysis is the null hypothesis H_0: $\beta = 0$. To understand this, consider again the population regression equation

$$E(Y) = \alpha + \beta X.$$

If $\beta \neq 0$, then this implies that X must influence Y. If, however, $\beta = 0$ then Y is clearly un-influenced by X and is simply equal to a constant plus a disturbance. Thus if H_0: $\beta = 0$ is rejected against H_A: $\beta \neq 0$, *this implies that X influences Y*. A test statistic for testing H_0 is easily obtained from the second of the basic results in [12.20]. If H_0: $\beta = 0$ is true, then it follows that

$$TS = \frac{b}{s_b} \text{ has a Student's } t \text{ distribution with } n - 2 \text{ d.f.} \qquad [12.30]$$

The test statistic [12.30] is often referred to as a *t-ratio*, because it is the *ratio of the OLS estimator to its estimated standard error*.

In the present situation, if β is non-zero then we expect β to be positive, since an increase in GDP should result in a *rise* in the demand for money. We therefore test

$$H_0: \beta = 0 \quad \text{against} \quad H_A: \beta > 0.$$

Clearly, we will reject H_0 if b, our estimator of β, is sufficiently greater than zero. That is, we use a one-tail test as illustrated in Fig. 12.3. Using a 0.05 level of significance, the critical t value, with 28 d.f., is $t_{0.05} = 1.701$. Thus our decision criterion in this case is:

reject H_0 if $TS > 1.701$, reserving judgement otherwise.

Given $b = 0.175$ and $s_b = 0.0180$, we have

$$TS = \frac{b}{s_b} = \frac{0.175}{0.0180} = 9.72.$$

This t-ratio is considerably greater than 1.701. Thus, we can strongly reject H_0 at the 0.05 level of significance and conclude that a country's GDP influences its demand for money.

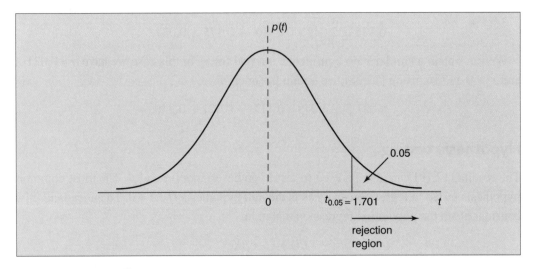

Figure 12.3 Testing $\beta = 0$

Clearly, it is also possible to test hypotheses about the intercept parameter α. Recall that if $\alpha = 0$, then the population regression equation becomes $E(Y) = \beta X$, so that $E(Y)$ is directly proportional to X. We saw in Chapter 9 that monetary theory suggests that the demand for money might be directly proportional to GDP, so it is of obvious interest to test the hypotheses

$$H_0: \alpha = 0 \quad \text{against} \quad H_A: \alpha \neq 0$$

for the data set in Table 9.1.

Note that, because either $\alpha > 0$ or $\alpha < 0$ implies a nonproportional relationship between $E(Y)$ and X, we have adopted $\alpha \neq 0$ as our alternative hypothesis. Thus we will need to perform a two-tail test.

An appropriate test statistic can be obtained from the first basic result in [12.20]. Given $H_0: \alpha = 0$, it follows that

$$TS = \frac{a}{s_a} \text{ has a Student's } t \text{ distribution with } n-2 \text{ d.f.} \qquad [12.31]$$

Since we are utilizing a two-tail test, we will reject H_0 if the test statistic in [12.31] is either sufficiently larger or sufficiently smaller than zero. At the 0.05 level of significant, the critical t value, with $n-2$ d.f., is $t_{0.025} = 2.048$. Our decision criterion is therefore:

reject H_0 if $|TS| > 2.048$, reserving judgement otherwise.

Given $a = 0.0212$ and $s_a = 0.117$, we obtain

$$TS = \frac{0.0212}{0.117} = 0.181.$$

Thus it is clear we cannot reject H_0 at the 0.05 level of significance. Thus the data in Table 9.1 suggest that the demand for money may indeed be directly proportional to GDP.

Presentation of regression results

It is customary to write out an OLS sample regression equation, such as $\hat{M} = a + bG$, with the t-ratios presented in parentheses underneath the OLS estimates. That is, for the demand-for-money data set, we would write

$$\hat{M} = 0.021 + 0.175G.$$
$$(0.181) \quad (9.72)$$

Alternatively, the estimated standard errors of a and b may appear in parentheses.

The null hypothesis in regression analysis is not always H_0: $\alpha = 0$ or H_0: $\beta = 0$, so that the appropriate test statistic is not always the t-ratio. The following worked example should make this clear.

Worked Example

It may be assumed that a simple linear relationship,

$$C = a + bY + \varepsilon,$$

holds between consumption C and income Y. ε is a disturbance, obeying all classical assumptions. If a sample of 37 observations yields

$$\Sigma(C - \bar{C}) = 52\,400, \qquad \Sigma(Y - \bar{Y}) = 56\,100, \qquad \Sigma(C - \bar{C})(Y - \bar{Y}) = 48\,700,$$

test the hypothesis that the marginal propensity to consume (MPC) exceeds 0.7.

Solution

We redefine consumption as Y and income as X so that, in terms of deviations of variables from their means, the sample information becomes

$$\Sigma y^2 = 52\,400, \qquad \Sigma x^2 = 56\,100, \qquad \Sigma xy = 48\,700.$$

In this example, the population MPC is β, so that the hypotheses to be tested are:

$$H_0: \beta = 0.7, \qquad H_A: \beta > 0.7.$$

We can now obtain a test statistic. Under H_0, substitution of $\beta = 0.7$ into the second result in [12.20] yields

$$TS = \frac{b - 0.7}{s_b} \text{ has a Student's } t \text{ distribution with } n - 2 \text{ d.f.}$$

Notice that in this situation the test statistic is not equal to the t-ratio b/s_b.

With $n - 2 = 35$ d.f., the critical t value is $t_{0.05} = 1.69$. Using a one-tail test, because we are asked to test $\beta > 0.7$, the required decision criterion is therefore:

reject H_0 if $TS > 1.69$, but reserve judgement otherwise.

Finally, we need to compute the test statistic. Firstly,

$$b = \frac{\Sigma xy}{\Sigma x^2} = \frac{48\ 700}{56\ 100} = 0.868.$$

The residual sum of squares is

$$\Sigma e^2 = \Sigma y^2 - b \Sigma xy = 52\ 400 - 0.868 \times 48\ 700 = 10\ 128.$$

The estimated disturbance variance is

$$s^2 = \frac{\Sigma e^2}{n - 2} = \frac{10\ 128}{35} = 289.4,$$

and the estimated variance of b is

$$s_b^2 = \frac{s^2}{\Sigma x^2} = \frac{289.4}{56\ 100} = 0.005\ 159 \rightarrow s_b = 0.0718.$$

The value of the test statistic is therefore

$$TS = \frac{b - 0.7}{s_b} = \frac{0.868 - 0.7}{0.0718} = 2.34.$$

Thus, applying the above decision criterion, we reject H_0 at the 0.05 level of significance. So we have sufficient evidence to say that the MPC exceeds 0.7.

The computations involved in two-variable regression are lengthy and quite complicated; those of Chapters 9 and 12 are brought together in Box 12.2. As usual, it is best to tackle the inferential aspects of two-variable regression using a hand calculator first, before resorting to any computer software. This will assist in a full understanding of the topic. You should now tackle the following three examples in this manner.

Box 12.2 Computational procedure for two-variable regression

Step 1. Compute the quantities $\sum X_i$, $\sum Y_i$, $\sum X_i^2$, $\sum Y_i^2$ and $\sum X_i Y_i$.

Step 2. Compute basic building blocks:

$$\sum x_i^2 = \sum X_i^2 - (1/n)(\sum X_i)^2,$$
$$\sum y_i^2 = \sum Y_i^2 - (1/n)(\sum Y_i)^2,$$
$$\sum x_i y_i = \sum X_i Y_i - (1/n)(\sum X_i)(\sum Y_i).$$

Step 3. Compute OLS estimates:

$$b = \frac{\sum x_i y_i}{\sum x_i^2}, \qquad a = \frac{\sum Y_i}{n} - b \frac{\sum X_i}{n}.$$

Step 4. Compute residual sum of squares and s^2:

$$\sum e_i^2 = \sum y_i^2 - b \sum x_i y_i, \qquad s^2 = \frac{\sum e_i^2}{n-2}.$$

Step 5. Compute estimated standard errors of $\hat{\alpha}$ and β:

$$s_a^2 = \frac{s^2 \sum X_i^2}{n \sum x_i^2}, \qquad s_b^2 = \frac{s^2}{\sum x_i^2}.$$

Example 12.1

The following data, first used in Example 9.4, refer to a sample of 15 developed economies, where Y is per-capita income (in thousands of dollars) and X is the percentage of labour force engaged in agriculture. Lower-case letters denote deviations of variables from their means.

$$\sum x^2 = 95.73, \qquad \sum y^2 = 28.93, \qquad \sum xy = -47.13.$$

Assuming a relationship of the kind $E(Y) = \alpha + \beta X$:
(a) test the hypothesis that X influences Y;
(b) if $\sum X^2 = 859$, find a 99% confidence interval for α and interpret your result.

Example 12.2

A sample of 180 quarterly observations (first referred to in Example 9.6), on percentage unemployment, U, and quit rate, Q (per 1000 employees) yields the following information:

$$\sum q_i^2 = 3237.7, \qquad \sum u_i^2 = 1745.2, \qquad \sum u_i q_i = -2084.3.$$

It is claimed that a rise of one percentage point in the unemployment rate results in a fall in the quit rate of one quit per 1000 employees. Test this claim at the 0.05 level of significance.

Example 12.3

The following data refer to the transactions demand for cash balances M (in billions of dollars) and national income Y (also in billions of dollars) over 11 consecutive years.

M	Y	M	Y
21.3	80.6	30.1	120.8
24.2	95.1	33.2	134.4
26.4	103.4	34.7	139.2
27.1	110.3	37.2	150.3
28.5	114.3	39.0	156.2
29.2	117.3		

$\sum m^2 = 298.9, \qquad \sum y^2 = 5386.7, \qquad \sum my = 1265.9$

(Lower-case letters denote deviations from means.)

Assume a relationship of the type $M = \alpha + \beta Y + \varepsilon$.

(a) Calculate the OLS estimates of α and β.

(b) Using a 0.01 level of significance, test the hypothesis $\alpha = 0$ and interpret your result.

(c) Find a 95% confidence interval for β.

Computer Exercise 12.1

In this exercise, you will check the additional results obtained in this chapter for the demand-for-money data set of Table 9.1. Call up your regression programme and access the file DATASET1 containing the demand-for-money data. Repeat the procedure you followed in Computer Exercise 9.1, obtaining the regression of M on G. Obtain a printout of the regression. The result should be identical to Fig. 9.11, but we are now able to interpret more of the output. The relevant statistics are again highlighted in Fig. 12.4.

Firstly, the column denoted 'Standard Error' gives the estimated standard errors of a and b, that is, s_a and s_b. Apart from some rounding error in the hand calculations made earlier in this chapter, the values in the printout are identical with those obtained as [12.26] and [12.27]. Secondly, the column headed 'T-Ratio[Prob] gives the t-ratios and p-values for a and b. The t-ratio is as defined in this chapter, that is, it is the ratio of the relevant OLS estimate to its estimated standard error. p-values were explained in Section 5.4. For example, the value 0.856 opposite INTER simply gives the probability of error when rejecting

```
                    Ordinary Least Squares Estimation
********************************************************************************
 Dependent variable is M
 30 observations used for estimation from 1 to 30
********************************************************************************
 Regressor            Coefficient        Standard Error         T-Ratio[Prob]
 INTER                   .021258                .11576          .18364[.856]
 G                       .174585                .017950        9.7408[.000]
********************************************************************************
 R-Squared                     .77214   R-Bar-Squared                   .76400
 S.E of Regression             .46353   F-stat.   F( 1,  28)   94.8827[.000]
 Mean of Dependent Variable    .79061   S.D. of Dependent Variable      .95416
 Residual Sum of Squares       6.0160   Equation Log-likelihood       -18.4665
 Akaike Info. Criterion      -20.4665   Schwarz Bayesian Criterion    -21.8677
 DW-statistic                  1.2825
********************************************************************************



                           Diagnostic Tests
********************************************************************************
 *    Test Statistics    *     LM Version        *      F Version           *
********************************************************************************
 *                       *                       *                          *
 * A:Serial Correlation *CHSQ(  1)=  4.1520[.042]* F(  1,  27)=  4.3370[.047]*
 *                       *                       *                          *
 * B:Functional Form     *CHSQ(  1)=  2.1167[.146]* F(  1,  27)=  2.0497[.164]*
 *                       *                       *                          *
 * C:Normality           *CHSQ(  2)= 27.6684[.000]*       Not applicable     *
 *                       *                       *                          *
 * D:Heteroscedasticity *CHSQ(  1)=  2.5583[.110]* F(  1,  28)=  2.6103[.117]*
********************************************************************************
    A:Lagrange multiplier test of residual serial correlation
    B:Ramsey's RESET test using the square of the fitted values
    C:Based on a test of skewness and kurtosis of residuals
    D:Based on the regression of squared residuals on squared fitted values
```

Figure 12.4 A typical OLS regression printout

H_0: $\alpha = 0$. In general, the higher the t-ratio, the smaller the p-value. Remember, though, that the t-ratios and p-values are only relevant when testing H_0: $\alpha = 0$ or H_0: $\beta = 0$.

The other ringed values in the printout are easy to interpret. The 'S.E. of Regression' is simply s, the square root of s^2, the estimated variance of the disturbance. Check this with the s^2 given above [12.24]. Note that [12.23] gives the same residual sum of squares $\sum e_i^2$ as on the printout, apart from rounding error. The mean and variance of the dependent variable are simply $\overline{M}$ and $V(M)$, two useful summary statistics.

Although your software may give a slightly different printout, you still should be able to pick out the statistics found above.

Computer Exercise 12.2

Rework examples 12.1, 12.2 and 12.3, using your regression programme instead of a hand calculator. The number of observations is implausibly small in two of the examples, but this will give you useful practice in using the programme. Input the data in the manner described in Computer Exercise 9.2 and obtain a printout of each regression equation, checking the important statistics in each case.

12.4 **Nonlinear regression again**

It is also possible to apply the above inferential techniques in nonlinear regression, provided the population regression equation is 'linear in the parameters' as defined in Chapter 10.7. For example, in that chapter we used the demand-for-carrots data set in Table 10.1 to estimate the double-log regression [10.14],

$$\widehat{\ln(Y)} = 6.73 - 0.744 \ln(X).$$

Recall that, in a double-log regression, the negative of the OLS estimator, $-b$, gives us an estimated value of the price elasticity of demand. Thus we estimated this elasticity by $-b = 0.744$. Since $-b < 1$, this implies that the demand for carrots is inelastic. But b is only an estimate of the true β and a more convincing procedure would be to test whether $-\beta < 1$, that is, whether $\beta > -1$.[8] Let us therefore formulate the hypotheses

$$H_0: \beta = -1, \qquad H_A: \beta > -1.$$

Under H_0 [12.20] yields

$$TS = \frac{b+1}{s_b} \text{ has a Student's } t \text{ distribution with } n - 2 \text{ d.f.}$$

Notice that the test statistic is based on $b - (-1)$, that is, we compare b with -1 or, equivalently, we compare the elasticity $-b$ with $+1$. If the difference between $-b$ and $+1$ is sufficiently large we reject the null hypothesis of a unitary elasticity.

Using a one-tail test, with $n - 2 = 28$ d.f., $t_{0.05} = 1.701$ so that our decision criterion is:

reject H_0 if $TS > 1.701$, reserving judgement otherwise.

Working in terms of the transformed variables $X^* = \ln(X)$ and $Y^* = \ln(Y)$, we have, below [10.12],

$$\sum x_i^{*2} = 2.875, \qquad \sum y_i^{*2} = 2.239, \qquad \sum x_i^* y_i^* = -2.140.$$

We now have all the information we need to work out s_b and the test statistic. Thus,

$$\sum e_i^{*2} = \sum y_i^{*2} - b \sum x_i^* y_i^* = 2.239 - (-0.744)(-2.140) = 0.647.$$

Hence,

$$s^2 = \frac{\sum e_i^{*2}}{n-2} = \frac{0.647}{28} = 0.0231,$$

so that

$$s_b^2 = \frac{s^2}{\sum x_i^{*2}} = \frac{0.0231}{2.875} = 0.008\ 035 \longrightarrow s_b = 0.0896$$

The test statistic therefore takes the value

$$TS = \frac{b+1}{s_b} = \frac{-0.744+1}{0.0896} = 2.857.$$

Referring back to the decision criterion, we see that we can reject H_0: $\beta = -1$ at the 0.05 level of significance. $-\beta$ appears to be less than unity, that is, the demand for carrots is inelastic with respect to price.

Example 12.4

Take the data set in Example 10.5 and check that a log-linear regression yields

$$\widehat{\ln(P)} = 5.363 - 0.511\ \ln(S).$$

Hence test the hypothesis that the price elasticity of supply is more negative than -2.

Example 12.5

Data on the output, Q, and the average costs per unit of output, C, of a firm in six consecutive years yields

C	600	218	294	153	173	247
Q	9	31	18	52	39	25
$A = 1/Q$	0.111	0.032	0.056	0.019	0.026	0.040

If lower-case letters denote the deviations of variables from their respective means, then

$$\sum q^2 = 1170, \qquad \sum cq = -10\ 537, \qquad \sum c^2 = 135\ 100.$$

(a) Plot the data on a scatter diagram, with C on the vertical axis and Q on the horizontal, and fit the OLS linear regression of C on Q to the scatter.

(b) If $\sum a^2 = 0.005\ 68$ and $\sum ac = 27.67$, fit an appropriate curve to the scatter you plotted in (a) and comment. Compute the coefficients of determination for your two regressions and comment.

(c) Estimate the firm's *fixed* costs. Find a 99% confidence interval for fixed costs.

Making predictions

In Chapter 9 we explained how sample regression equations could be used to make predictions. For example, we used the sample regression [9.30] to predict the demand for money for a hypothetical country, Westeuro. On page 271, we substituted Westeuro GDP per head into [9.30] and obtained the value $\hat{Y}_0 = 1.51$ for Westeuro's predicted demand for money per head. However, we pointed out that we could say nothing about the reliability or precision of the prediction. We are now in a position to rectify this omission and place a confidence interval around the prediction.

Suppose, as usual, we have a population regression equation of the type [9.5] that has been estimated by an OLS sample regression equation [9.10]. A new observation X_0 has become available (this might be GDP for a new country, Westeuro). To make a prediction for the corresponding value of Y, we simply substitute the known X_0 into [9.10] and obtain

$$\hat{Y}_0 = a + bX_0, \tag{12.32}$$

where $\hat{Y}_0$ is the predicted value for Y_0.

The predicted value $\hat{Y}_0$ will not normally coincide with the actual unknown value Y_0 which is given by

$$Y_0 = \alpha + \beta X_0 + \varepsilon_0. \tag{12.33}$$

The difference between Y_0 and $\hat{Y}_0$ is normally termed the *predicted* or *forecast error*, f.[9] That is, using [12.32] and [12.33],

$$\begin{aligned} f &= \hat{Y}_0 - Y_0 \\ &= (a - \alpha) - (b - \beta)X_0 - \varepsilon_0. \end{aligned} \tag{12.34}$$

Thus the forecast error depends on:

(a) $a - \alpha$ and $b - \beta$, the sampling errors resulting from having to estimate α and β;

(b) the magnitude of X_0;

(c) the magnitude of ε_0, the disturbance associated with X_0.

Of these factors only (b) is known. Factor (a) is the result of not knowing, but having to estimate, α and β. Such error can be reduced by increasing the sample size, but factor (c) is beyond our control, because it is the result of the innate randomness in the relationship between Y and X.

Since the forecast error f must vary from sample to sample, it has a sampling distribution. Under classical assumptions it can be shown that f is normally distributed with a mean of zero and a variance

$$\sigma_f^2 = \sigma^2 \left[1 + \frac{1}{n} + \frac{(X_0 - \overline{X})^2}{\sum x_i^2} \right] \tag{12.35}$$

where $\bar{X}$ and $\sum x_i^2$ refer to the n original sample observations. Thus, σ_f^2 is the *variance of the forecast error*.

The above can be summarized as

$$f \text{ has a } N(0, \sigma_f^2) \text{ distribution.}$$

Hence

$$\frac{f}{\sigma_f} = \frac{\hat{Y}_0 - Y_0}{\sigma_f} \text{ has a } N(0, 1) \text{ distribution.} \qquad [12.36]$$

The problem with [12.36] is that σ_f^2 depends on the disturbance variance σ^2, which is unknown. However, as usual, we can replace σ^2 by its unbiased estimator $s^2 = \sum e_i^2/(n-2)$. This enables us to estimate σ_f^2 by

$$s_f^2 = s^2 \left[1 + \frac{1}{n} + \frac{(X_0 - \bar{X})^2}{\sum x_i^2} \right] \qquad [12.37]$$

Using [12.36], we can now switch to the t distribution in the usual manner and write

$$\frac{\hat{Y}_0 - Y_0}{s_f} \text{ has a Student's } t \text{ distribution with } n - 2 \text{ d.f.} \qquad [12.38]$$

It follows that a 95% confidence interval for the forecast error f must be

$$0 \pm t_{0.025} s_f$$

Of greater interest is a 95% confidence interval for the unknown Y_0, which takes the form

$$\hat{Y}_0 \pm t_{0.025} s_f \qquad [12.39]$$

Notice that the point prediction $\hat{Y}_0$ is at the centre of the interval. Thus, when taking a sample, we can say that the interval [12.39] has a 0.95 probability of containing the true Y_0. For a 99% confidence interval $t_{0.005}$ replaces $t_{0.025}$.

The width of the prediction interval [12.39] depends on s_f^2, the estimated variance of the forecast error, given by [12.37]. This in turn depends on s^2 and on the terms in parentheses in [12.37]. Notice, in particular, that the further X_0 is from $\bar{X}$, the sample mean of the X values, the wider the prediction interval; that is, the less precise is our forecast. This is to be expected as, not surprisingly, it is easier to forecast when the value of X_0 is closer to values that we have already experienced. Out-of-samples forecasts are naturally less precise.

This is illustrated in Fig. 12.5 in which the sample regression line is shown. For any X_0, this line gives the point forecast $\hat{Y}_0$. For given X_0, the two curves mark the upper and lower limits of the confidence interval for Y_0. The further we are from $\bar{X}$, the wider is the interval.

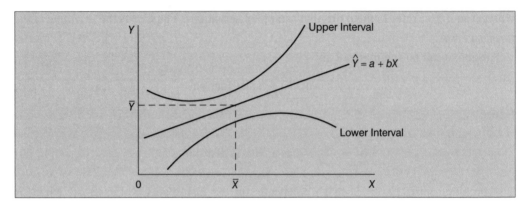

Figure 12.5

Referring back to the demand-for-money data set in Table 9.1, we have already obtained a point prediction for the demand for money in Westeuro. When GDP $X_0 = 8.5$, we predicted the demand for money to be $\hat{Y}_0 = 1.51$. Using [12.39], we are now able to provide a prediction interval for Y_0. Firstly, we use [12.37] to find s_f^2. We have $n = 30$, $s^2 = 0.2418$, using [12.23], and $\sum x_i^2 = 666.86$, from [12.21]. Since $\overline{X} = 4.40$, we can compute

$$(X_0 - \overline{X})^2 = (8.5 - 4.40)^2 = 16.8.$$

Substituting in [12.37] gives

$$s_f^2 = 0.24\left[1 + \frac{1}{30} + \frac{16.8}{667}\right] = 0.24 \times 1.058 = 0.25.$$

With $n - 2 = 28$ d.f., $t_{0.025} = 2.048$, the required prediction interval is then given by substituting in [12.39]. The interval is thus

$$1.51 \pm 2.048\sqrt{0.25} = 1.51 \pm 1.02.$$

Example 12.6

Use the data and results for Example 12.3 to predict the demand for cash balances M in year 12, when national income $Y = 158.5$. Find a 95% confidence interval for your prediction.

Discuss ways in which you might predict the demand for cash balances in year 13, if national income were expected to be $Y = 163.1$ in that year.

Example 12.7

Use the data and results from Example 12.5 to predict average costs per unit of output, C, when output, Q, takes the values
(a) 2   (b) 29   (c) 205.

Obtain 99% confidence intervals for each of these predictions and comment on the width of these intervals.

Computer Exercise 12.3

In the above section we used the demand-for-money data set of Table 9.1 to form a prediction interval for the demand for money per head of a country, Westeuro, with GDP $X_0 = 8.5$. In this exercise, you will use your computer programme to replicate this interval and also to obtain prediction intervals for two further countries, Centeuro, with GDP $X_0 = 6.0$, and Easteuro, with GDP $X_0 = 3.3$.

Access the file DATASET1 and view the data set. Interest is still restricted to just two variables M and G, but this time we will make use of all 33 observations rather than the first 30 used previously. Note that we have placed the X_0 values for Westeuro, Centeuro and Easteuro in the G column at observations 31, 32, 33. Nothing appears in the M column for these observations.

Re-estimate the regression equation obtained in Computer Exercise 9.1, again using the first 30 observations. Check that it is the same equation that you obtained in Exercise 9.1. On this occasion, however, key in a request for forecasts using the observations 31, 32, 33. Your programme will have a facility for making such forecasts, although the details will vary, depending on which programme you are using.

You should obtain something like the result presented in Fig. 12.6, which was produced by Microfit 4 software. It shows the required forecasts, with corresponding forecast standard errors. In Fig. 12.6, the first value in the column headed 'Prediction', refers to observation 31, and gives the value 1.51 (to 3 significant figures), the predicted demand for money for Westeuro. The first value in the 'S.D. of Error' column gives the square root of s_f^2 as defined in [12.37]. Given $t_{0.025} = 2.048$, as above, we can now substitute into [12.39] again, to replicate the 95% prediction interval for Westeuro as

$$1.5075 \pm 2.048 \times 0.4769 = 1.51 \pm 1.02.$$

```
                    Single Equation Static Forecasts
****************************************************************************
 Based on OLS regression of M on:
 INTER         G
 30 observations used for estimation from     1 to 30
****************************************************************************
 Observation       Actual        Prediction        Error      S.D. of Error
     31            *NONE*           1.5075          *NONE*         .47690
     32            *NONE*           1.0704          *NONE*         .47206
     33            *NONE*            .47586         *NONE*         .47230
****************************************************************************
```

Figure 12.6 A typical predictions printout

Finally, use the other values in the 'Prediction' and 'S.D. of Error' columns to obtain the prediction intervals for Centeuro and Easteuro as, respectively,

$$1.07 \pm 0.967 \quad \text{and} \quad 0.48 \pm 0.967.$$

Summary

- The **two-variable classical regression model** was developed for use in the physical sciences. Many of its **assumptions** are implausible when the model is applied to **economic data**.

- The classical model contains a series of assumptions concerning (a) the **explanatory X variable** and (b) the **disturbance ε**. The **properties** of the **OLS estimators** depend crucially on which of the assumptions are valid.

- In the classical model standard **inferential procedures** exist for **testing hypotheses** about and forming **confidence intervals** for the regression parameters α and β.

- It is best to handle **computations** regarding two-variable regression with a **hand calculator** until you are thoroughly familiar with the procedures. Only then should you start using computer software.

Notes

1. Under more general conditions, of course, sampling distributions arise because of both varying X and varying Y.

2. Only if all the extra X values are exactly equal to the mean $\bar{X}$ of the original sample, will S remain unchanged.

3. From [12.2], Y_i is the sum of a constant and a normally distributed variable. But adding a constant to a normally distributed variable merely shifts the distribution along the horizontal axis, leaving its shape unchanged. Thus Y_i must also be normally distributed.

4. But see, for example, Thomas (1997, pp. 141–2).

5. See, for example, Thomas (1997, p. 164).

6. See, for example, Thomas (1997, p. 165).

7. This is directly analogous to the switch from the $N(0, 1)$ to the t distribution when σ is replaced by s in the test statistic $(\bar{X} - q)/(s/\sqrt{n})$ while testing $H_0: \mu = q$.

8. Remember that multiplying an equality throughout by −1 always changes the direction of the inequality.

9. We have used the terms 'forecast' and 'prediction' interchangeably in this section. However, in some situations the two are defined differently. See Thomas (1997, p. 167).

13

An introduction to multiple regression

Objectives

When you have completed your study of this chapter, you should be able:

1. to appreciate that the OLS approach can also be applied to estimating the parameters of a multiple regression equation;

2. to understand the way that the classical model can be extended to the case of more than two regressors;

3. to understand how two-variable inferential procedures can be extended to the multiple regression model;

4. to use simple regression software to estimate a multiple regression equation and conduct inference on its parameters;

5. to realize that when variables are added to or deleted from a regression equation, the values of OLS estimated coefficients will almost certainly change;

6. to understand the problems that can arise when two or more variables in a regression equation are multicollinear;

7. to appreciate that when multicollinearity results in an undesirable rise in standard errors, the only genuine solution to the problem is to obtain additional data;

8. to apply regression F-tests for the overall importance of variables in a regression equation and for the importance of variables that are added to or deleted from such an equation.

Introduction

In the previous chapter we considered the application of OLS regression to relationships involving just one explanatory variable. Unfortunately, it is frequently the case in economics that relationships involve two, three, or even more explanatory variables. For example, the demand for a good depends not only on its price but also on the income of consumers, on the price of substitute goods and so on. Similarly, we used the data in Table 9.1 to estimate a relationship between the demand for money and GDP. But might not the demand for money also be influenced by additional factors such as interest rates and the expected inflation rate?

In this chapter we consider, firstly, how the method of OLS can be generalized to situations in which there are two or more explanatory variables. Then we list the assumptions of the classical multiple regression model and consider problems of inference in the context of this model. Next we take a detailed look at the problem of multicollinearity: a problem that can occur in multiple regression but had no counterpart in two-variable regression. Finally, we consider some regression F-tests.

13.1 Ordinary least squares with more than one explanatory variable

We begin by assuming that a linear relationship exists between a dependent variable Y and $k-1$ explanatory variables, $X_2, X_3, X_4, ..., X_k$:

$$Y = \beta_1 + \beta_2 X_2 + \beta_3 X_3 + \cdots + \beta_k X_k + \varepsilon, \tag{13.1}$$

where ε is a disturbance of similar nature to that of the previous chapter and the β_j's ($j = 1, 2, 3, ..., k$) are constants.[1]

Assuming $E(\varepsilon) = 0$, by taking expectations over [13.1] we have, for given values of the X variables,

$$E(Y) = \beta_1 + \beta_2 X_2 + \beta_3 X_3 + \cdots + \beta_k X_k. \tag{13.2}$$

This is referred to as the *population regression equation*. It is analogous to the population regression equation [9.5] although, in this general case, we cannot depict it on a two-dimensional diagram.

The β_j's in [13.2] are population parameters and it is important to understand exactly what they represent. For example, β_2 measures the effect on $E(Y)$ of a unit change in X_2, *when all the other X variables remain unchanged*. That is, it measures the change in $E(Y)$ per unit change in X_2. Similarly, β_4 measures the change in $E(Y)$ per unit change in X_4, when all variables but X_4 remain unchanged.

Like the population regression equation of Chapter 9, [13.2] remains unknown to any investigator and has to be estimated from sample data. Suppose we have available a sample of size n observations, each observation consisting of a value for Y and values for each of the X variables.

We let Y_i be the value of Y pertaining to the ith observation and X_{ji} the value of X_j ($j = 2, 3, 4, ..., k$) pertaining to the ith observation. For example, X_{43} is simply the value taken by X_4 in the third observation. Similarly, X_{39} is the value taken by X_3 in the ninth observation. ε_i is the unknown disturbance value associated with the ith observation.

If we consider a particular observation, for example the ninth, we therefore have the set of values

$$Y_9, X_{29}, X_{39}, X_{49}, ..., X_{k9}, \tag{13.3}$$

with a disturbance ε_9. Thus, if [13.1] holds for each sample observation, including the ninth, we can substitute the [13.3] values for Y, the X_j and ε into [13.1] and obtain

$$Y_9 = \beta_1 + \beta_2 X_{29} + \beta_3 X_{39} + \cdots + \beta_k X_{k9} + \varepsilon_9.$$

It should be clear that we can perform the same operation for all sample observations. That is, we can write

$$Y_i = \beta_1 + \beta_2 X_{2i} + \beta_3 X_{3i} + \cdots + \beta_k X_{ki} + \varepsilon_i \qquad (i = 1, 2, 3, ..., n). \tag{13.4}$$

The above development is no more than a straightforward generalization of the two-variable analysis of Chapter 9. Similarly, we estimate the population equation [13.2] by a *sample regression equation*

$$\hat{Y} = b_1 + b_2 X_2 + b_3 X_3 + \cdots + b_k X_k, \tag{13.5}$$

where the b_j ($j = 1, 2, 3, ..., k$), are estimators of the unknown β_j's. For the moment, we say nothing about the way in which the β_j's have been estimated. As in two-variable regression, there are a number of possible estimation methods.

As in Chapter 9, $\hat{Y}$ in [13.5] is known as the predicted value of Y because, on substituting the sample values of the X variables into the right-hand side of [13.5], we obtain a set of predicted values of Y, that is $\hat{Y}_i$'s, one for each observation in the sample. For example, for the ninth observation, we can substitute the X_j values from [13.3] into the sample equation [13.5] to obtain

$$\hat{Y}_9 = b_0 + b_1 X_{29} + b_3 X_{39} + \cdots + b_k X_{k9},$$

where $\hat{Y}_9$ is the predicted value of Y for the ninth observation.

In general, we will have

$$\hat{Y}_i = b_1 + b_2 X_{2i} + b_3 X_{3i} + \cdots + b_k X_{ki}, \qquad i = 1, 2, 3, ..., n. \tag{13.6}$$

That is, we will have a predicted $\hat{Y}$ for each observation.

Normally, the predicted $\hat{Y}_i$'s will differ from the actual Y_i's and, as in two-variable regression, the difference is again referred to as a residual. There will therefore be a residual associated with each observation. That is, we have

$$e_i = Y_i - \hat{Y}_i,$$ [13.7]

or, using [13.6] and [13.7],

$$Y_i = b_1 + b_2 X_{2i} + b_3 X_{3i} + \cdots + b_k X_{ki} + e_i, \qquad i = 1, 2, 3, \ldots, n.$$ [13.8]

Since the b_j's and the actual sample values for Y and those for the X variables are known, it is possible to calculate all the residuals using [13.8]. Thus, as in two-variable regression, the residuals are known quantities, although in this general case we cannot depict them on a two-dimensional diagram. Different methods of estimation result in different sample regression equations which will, of course, yield different sets of residuals. As we shall see in a moment, the best-known method of estimation is again OLS.

Worked Example

A population regression equation has the form

$$E(Y) = \beta_1 + \beta_2 X_2 + \beta_3 X_3 + \beta_4 X_4 + \varepsilon$$

and is estimated (using some unspecified method) by the sample regression equation

$$\hat{Y} = 15 - 6X_2 + 3X_3 + 4X_4.$$ [13.9]

What are the estimates of $\beta_1, \beta_2, \beta_3$ and β_4? The first three observations in a sample of size $n > 4$ are

i	1	2	3
Y	2	0	16
X_2	5	7	3
X_3	12	15	19
X_4	−6	−4	−4

Find the residual associated with each sample observation.

Solution

The estimates are $b_1 = 15$, $b_2 = -6$, $b_3 = 3$ and $b_4 = 4$.

Using [13.9], we have

$$\hat{Y}_1 = 15 - 6(5) + 3(12) + 4(-6) = -3, \quad \text{so that} \quad e_1 = 2 - (-3) = 5;$$
$$\hat{Y}_2 = 15 - 6(7) + 3(15) + 4(-4) = 2, \quad \text{so that} \quad e_2 = 0 - 2 = -2;$$
$$\hat{Y}_3 = 15 - 6(3) + 3(19) + 4(-4) = 38, \quad \text{so that} \quad e_3 = 16 - 38 = -22.$$

Ordinary least-squares estimation

Just as in two-variable regression, in OLS estimation we minimize the sum of the squared residuals, $S = \sum e_i^2$, but in the general case the residuals are obtained from [13.8]. That is,

$$e_i = Y_i - b_1 - b_2 X_{2i} - b_3 X_{3i} - \cdots - b_k X_{ki}, \qquad i = 1, 2, 3, \ldots, n. \qquad [13.10]$$

We therefore select the b_j's so as to minimize

$$S = \sum e_i^2 = \sum (Y_i - b_1 - b_2 X_{2i} - b_3 X_{3i} - \cdots - b_k X_{ki})^2. \qquad [13.11]$$

Notice that [9.14] in Chapter 9 is a special case of [13.11]. In the general case, however, we have to differentiate S with respect to each of the b_j's in turn. The idea behind the procedure is no different from that in Chapter 9; it is just that the algebra is more cumbersome. Instead of solving the two normal equations [9.19] and [9.20], in multiple regression we have to solve k normal equations for k variables, the b_j's. If we were to use normal algebra, the expressions for the OLS estimators, the b_j's, would be extremely complex indeed. Even with just two explanatory variables, and hence three estimators b_1, b_2 and b_3, the formulae are considerably more complicated than for the case of just a single explanatory variable. In fact, with $k = 3$, it can be shown that[2]

$$b_1 = \bar{Y} - b_2 \bar{X}_2 - b_3 \bar{X}_3 \qquad [13.12]$$

$$b_2 = \frac{\sum yx_2 \sum x_3^2 - \sum yx_3 \sum x_2 x_3}{\sum x_2^2 \sum x_3^2 - (\sum x_2 x_3)^2}, \qquad [13.13]$$

$$b_3 = \frac{\sum yx_3 \sum x_2^2 - \sum yx_2 \sum x_3 x_2}{\sum x_2^2 \sum x_3^2 - (\sum x_2 x_3)^2}, \qquad [13.14]$$

where, as usual, lower-case letters denote the deviations of values from their sample means. That is, $y_i = Y_i - \bar{Y}$, $x_{2i} = X_{2i} - \bar{X}_2$, and so on.

As the number of explanatory variables rises to three, four, five and more, the formulae for the OLS estimators become ever more complicated. More compact expressions can be obtained using matrix algebra, but these are no easier to compute. Because of this, multiple regression equations are rarely computed by hand calculator and we shall use suitable computer programmes for our exercises. However, it is instructive to begin by tackling by hand the following example.

Example 13.1

Consider the following equation, to be estimated:

$$E(Y_i) = \beta_1 + \beta_2 X_{2i} + \beta_3 X_{3i}.$$

A random sample of size $n = 50$ observations on Y, X_2 and X_3 is taken and yields

$$\Sigma x_2^2 = 163, \quad \Sigma x_2 x_3 = 124, \quad \Sigma x_2 y = 610, \quad \bar{X}_2 = 15,$$
$$\Sigma x_3^2 = 98, \quad \Sigma x_3 y = 523, \quad \bar{X}_3 = 32,$$
$$\Sigma y^2 = 3724, \quad \bar{Y} = 105.$$

Use [13.12]–[13.14] to obtain the OLS sample regression equation.

Computer Exercise 13.1

Recall the data set in Table 9.1, for the demand for money and GDP of 30 countries. The file DATASET1 contains observations, not only on the demand for money per head M and GDP per head G, but also on a rate of interest I and the inflation rate $\dot{P}$ for these countries. Access this file, and use your regression programme to obtain the regression of M on G and I. This is a simple extension of the regression equation of Fig. 9.11.

You should obtain the regression result shown in Fig. 13.1. The values in the column headed 'Coefficient' give the OLS estimators (b_j's for $j = 1, 2, 3$). The regression can therefore be written as

$$\hat{M} = 0.0570 + 0.173G - 0.000\,676I. \tag{13.15}$$

We could have used expressions [13.12]–[13.14] to obtain the coefficients in [13.15] but, obviously, they can be obtained much more quickly using the programme! But, as we keep reminding you, it is always a good idea to know exactly what a piece of software is actually doing for you.

As we shall see, the values in the columns headed 'Standard Error' and 'T-Ratio[Prob]' in Fig. 13.1 have a similar interpretation to that for simple regression. Later we shall use these values to make inferences about the true regression parameters. For the moment just note that the coefficients on the variables G and I have the expected signs, the negative coefficient on I implying that, as the interest rate rises, the demand for money falls.

Next, add the inflation variable $\dot{P}$ to the result in Fig. 13.1. You should obtain the regression result in Fig. 13.2, which we can present as

$$\hat{M} = 0.0894 + 0.170G - 0.000\,169I - 0.002\,20\dot{P}. \tag{13.16}$$

Note that $\dot{P}$ appears as PI in Fig. 13.2.

```
                    Ordinary Least Squares Estimation
*******************************************************************************
Dependent variable is M
30 observations used for estimation from    1 to 30
*******************************************************************************
Regressor           Coefficient         Standard Error          T-Ratio[Prob]
INTER                  .056958                  .12564              .45335[.654]
G                      .17262                   .018320            9.4223[.000]
I                    -.6758E-3                  .8844E-3           -.76413[.451]
*******************************************************************************
R-Squared                      .77696  R-Bar-Squared                    .76044
S.E of Regression              .46701  F-stat.    F(  2,   27)    47.0283[000]
Mean of Dependent Variable     .79061  S.D. of Dependent Variable       .95416
Residual Sum of Squares        6.0160  Equation Log-likelihood        -18.1456
Akaike Info. Criterion       -21.1456  Schwarz Bayesian Criterion     -23.2474
DW-statistic                   1.3969
*******************************************************************************


                            Diagnostic Tests
*******************************************************************************
*   Test Statistics   *     LM Version        *        F Version             *
*******************************************************************************
*                     *                        *                             *
* A:Serial Correlation* CHSQ(  1)=  3.0760[.079]*F(  1,  26)=  2.9704[.097] *
*                     *                        *                             *
* B:Functional Form   * CHSQ(  1)=  2.2830[.131]*F(  1,  26)=  2.1416[.155] *
*                     *                        *                             *
* C:Normality         * CHSQ(  2)= 28.5452[.000]*      Not applicable        *
*                     *                        *                             *
* D:Heteroscedasticity* CHSQ(  1)=  2.6956[.101]*F(  1,  28)=  2.7642[.108] *
*******************************************************************************
    A:Lagrange multiplier test of residual serial correlation
    B:Ramsey's RESET test using the square of the fitted values
    C:Based on a test of skewness and kurtosis of residuals
    D:Based on the regression of squared residuals on squared fitted values
```

Figure 13.1 A typical OLS multiple regression printout

Do not be surprised at the *absolute* size of the coefficients in Figs. 13.1 and 13.2. For example, the coefficient on I may seem very small – only 0.000 169 in Fig. 13.2. But the absolute size of coefficients is dependent on the units of measurement used. For example, the interest rate I has been measured as a percentage. Had we measured I as a proportion, (e.g., 0.16 instead of 16%), then the I values would have been 100 times smaller and the coefficient on I 100 times larger. Check this by re-estimating [13.16] with I defined as a proportion. Similar comments apply to the $\dot{P}$ variable.

Notice that the regression results include values for R^2 of 0.777 and 0.780. In multiple regression R^2 is known as the *coefficient of multiple determination*. It can be defined in terms of the residual, explained and total sums of squares in exactly the same way as in two-variable regression. That is,

$$R^2 = \frac{\text{SSE}}{\text{SST}} = 1 - \frac{\text{SSR}}{\text{SST}}.$$

[13.17]

```
                   Ordinary Least Squares Estimation
*****************************************************************************
Dependent variable is M
30 observations used for estimation from    1 to 30
*****************************************************************************
Regressor            Coefficient         Standard Error        T-Ratio[Prob]
INTER                   .089354                 .13884          .64356[.525]
G                       .17037                  .018943        8.9939[.000]
I                     -.1693E-3                 .0012483       -.13565[.893]
PI                    -.0021970                 .0037733       -.58224[.565]
*****************************************************************************
R-Squared                     .77983   R-Bar-Squared                 .75443
S.E of Regression             .47283   F-stat.   F( 3, 26)    30.6976[.000]
Mean of Dependent Variable    .79061   S.D. of Dependent Variable    .95416
Residual Sum of Squares      5.8129    Equation Log-likelihood     -17.9513
Akaike Info. Criterion     -21.9513    Schwarz Bayesian Criterion  -24.7537
DW-statistic                 1.4576
*****************************************************************************


                          Diagnostic Tests
*****************************************************************************
*    Test Statistics    *      LM Version       *        F Version        *
*****************************************************************************
*                       *                       *                         *
* A:Serial Correlation *CHSQ(  1)=  2.6704[.102]*F( 1, 25)=  2.4428[.131]*
*                       *                       *                         *
* B:Functional Form    *CHSQ(  1)=  2.2685[.132]*F( 1, 25)=  2.0451[.165]*
*                       *                       *                         *
* C:Normality          *CHSQ(  2)= 28.6380[.000]*      Not applicable     *
*                       *                       *                         *
* D:Heteroscedasticity *CHSQ(  1)=  2.7491[.097]*F( 1, 28)=  2.8246[.104]*
*****************************************************************************
   A:Lagrange multiplier test of residual serial correlation
   B:Ramsey's RESET test using the square of the fitted values
   C:Based on a test of skewness and kurtosis of residuals
   D:Based on the regression of squared residuals on squared fitted values
```

Figure 13.2 A further typical regression printout

Thus Fig. 13.1 indicates that 77.7% of the variation in M can be attributed to the variations in G and I.[3]

Notice that R^2 has only risen to 0.780 in Fig. 13.2. Thus the inclusion of the inflation rate does not do much for the explanatory power of the equation. The reason for this will become clear later.

For future reference, create the natural logarithms of all variables, $\ln M$, $\ln G$, $\ln I$ and $\ln \dot{P}$, and estimate the log-linear equivalent of [13.16]. You should obtain the result given in Fig. 13.3, which can be written as

$$\widehat{\ln M} = -1.19 + 1.04 \ln G - 0.292 \ln I + 0.0358 \ln \dot{P}. \qquad [13.18]$$

Note that $\ln \dot{P}$ appears as LNPI in Fig. 13.3.

```
                       Ordinary Least Squares Estimation
****************************************************************************
Dependent variable is LNM
30 observations used for estimation from    1 to 30
****************************************************************************
Regressor              Coefficient        Standard Error        T-Ratio[Prob]
INTER                     -1.1949                .20773        -.5.7522[.000]
LNG                        1.0381               .058468         17.7554[.000]
LNI                       -.29231               .082036        -3.5632[.001]
LNPI                      .035784               .038414          .93152[.360]
****************************************************************************
R-Squared                  .93089    R-Bar-Squared                    .92292
S.E of Regression          .41380    F-stat.    F(  3,  26)   116.7387[.000]
Mean of Dependent Variable -1.1317    S.D. of Dependent Variable       1.4904
Residual Sum of Squares    4.4520    Equation Log-likelihood        -13.9505
Akaike Info. Criterion   -17.9505    Schwarz Bayesian Criterion     -20.7529
DW-statistic               2.0852
****************************************************************************


                              Diagnostic Tests
****************************************************************************
*   Test Statistics    *     LM Version        *        F Version         *
****************************************************************************
*                      *                       *                          *
*A:Serial Correlation *CHSQ(   1)=  .12928[.719]*F(   1,  25)=  .10820[.745]*
*                      *                       *                          *
*B:Functional Form    *CHSQ(   1)= 2.0398[.153]*F(   1,  25)= 1.8239[.189]*
*                      *                       *                          *
*C:Normality          *CHSQ(   2)=  .59391[.743]*       Not applicable     *
*                      *                       *                          *
*D:Heteroscedasticity *CHSQ(   1)= .048110[.826]*F(   1,  28)= .044975[.834]*
****************************************************************************
   A:Lagrange multiplier test of residual serial correlation
   B:Ramsey's RESET test using the square of the fitted values
   C:Based on a test of skewness and kurtosis of residuals
   D:Based on the regression of squared residuals on squared fitted values
```

Figure 13.3 A logarithmic regression printout

For the log-linear regression in Fig. 13.3, the slope coefficients are independent of units of measurement. Thus −0.292 is the interest-rate elasticity whether we measure I as a percentage or as a proportion. Changing units only affects the value of the intercept. Check this by re-estimating.

Finally, notice that the G variable in [13.18] has a positive coefficient and the I variable a negative one, as expected. Is the sign on the inflation-rate coefficient as expected?

13.2 The classical multiple regression model

Just as in the two-variable regression model, the OLS estimators in multiple regression are subject to sampling variability, and the properties of these estimators and their distributions depend very much on the conditions under which they are obtained. We outlined the assumptions of the two-variable classical model in the previous chapter, and the *classical multiple regression model* is a mainly straightforward extension of the two-variable case. There are just two differences. Firstly, assumptions IA, IB and IC now refer to two or more explanatory variables and, secondly, an extra assumption ID is included.

Classical assumptions concerning the explanatory variables in multiple regression

In the classical multiple regression model, *each* explanatory variable X_j ($j = 2, 3, ..., k$) is assumed:

(IA) to be non-stochastic;

(IB) to have values that are fixed in repeated samples;

(IC) to be such that, as the sample size $n \to \infty$, its variance $V(X_j) \to V_j^*$, where V_j^* is some fixed constant.

In addition it is assumed that:

(ID) there exist no exact linear relationships between the sample values of any two or more of the explanatory variables.

Assumptions IA and IB imply the existence of some 'investigator' who fixes the values of *each* X_j variable and maintains the values of each such variable fixed, over many samples. But, from [13.4], the Y_i, values do vary from sample to sample since they are dependent on the disturbances, ε_i, which are stochastic and hence will vary. Consequently, the OLS estimators will also vary in repeated samples since they depend on the Y_i values. For example, in the case of two X variables, it can be seen from [13.12]–[13.14] that b_1, b_2 and b_3 depend not only on the fixed X_{ji} values but also on the Y_i values.

Assumption IC effectively rules out the possibility of trending explanatory X variables. It plays the same role as the corresponding assumption IC in the two-variable case and is intended to rule out the likelihood of spurious correlations in time-series data.

Assumption ID has no equivalent in the two-variable model and is included in order to rule out the possibility of what is termed 'perfect multicollinearity'. We shall deal with multicollinearity in Section 13.3. For now, we simply note that the assumption states that it must *not* be the case that, for example, $X_{4i} = 4 - 6X_{2i}$, for all i, in our sample. Similarly, more complicated linear relationships between more than two explanatory variables, such as $2X_{2i} = -3 + 3X_{4i} - 5X_{3i}$, are also ruled out. As we shall see later, if assumption ID were invalid, then all estimation methods, including OLS, would become infeasible.

The assumptions concerning the disturbances in the classical multiple regression model are exactly the same as those for the two-variable classical model. These assumptions were listed on page 359 in Chapter 12, and you should study them carefully again. They imply that the disturbances are assumed to be normally and independently distributed with zero means and to be non-autocorrelated and homoscedastic.

Properties of the OLS estimators in multiple regression

We stress, as we did in Chapter 12, that, although OLS is the best-known method of estimating regression parameters, it is not necessarily the best. In multiple regression, as in two-variable regression, OLS will only yield estimators, with the desired properties that we listed in Chapter 11, if a whole sequence of assumptions prove to be valid. Given the classical assumptions, in multiple regression the relationship between properties and assumptions is, in fact, almost exactly the same as that given in Box 12.1 for simple regression. The only minor difference is that we require assumption ID for each of the properties. As we noted above, if assumption ID were invalid, then OLS estimation becomes infeasible. You should spend some time studying Box 12.1 again.

As in two-variable regression, the variances of the OLS estimators are dependent on the common variance, σ^2, of the disturbances. For example, with just two explanatory variables, X_2 and X_3, it can be shown that, provided assumptions IIB and IIC are valid – that is, provided the disturbances are both homoscedastic and non-autocorrelated – then the sampling variances of the OLS estimators b_2 and b_3 are given by, respectively,[4]

$$\sigma_{b_2}^2 = \frac{\sigma^2}{\sum x_2^2(1 - r^2)} \qquad [13.19]$$

and

$$\sigma_{b_3}^2 = \frac{\sigma^2}{\sum x_3^2(1 - r^2)} \qquad [13.20]$$

where r is the sample correlation between X_2 and X_3. The square roots of these sampling variances are normally referred to as *standard errors*, as in two-variable regression. The expressions for the $\sigma_{b_j}^2$ are more complicated for the case of more than two explanatory variables and we shall not reproduce them here.

As in two-variable regression, the variance of the disturbances is, of course, unknown but, again as in the two-variable case, it is possible to obtain an unbiased estimator of it. In the general case, the estimator is given by

$$s^2 = \frac{\sum e_i^2}{n - k}, \qquad [13.21]$$

where k is the number of β_j parameters in the regression. Thus, in two-variable regression [13.21] reduces to [12.16] as expected.

For the case given by [13.19] and [13.20] above, we can estimate σ^2 by [13.21] with k set equal to 3. To obtain the residual sum of squares in this case, under classical assumptions we can use

$$\sum e_i^2 = \sum y_i - b_2 \sum x_{2i} y_i - b_3 \sum x_{3i} y_i. \tag{13.22}$$

Notice that [13.22] is a straightforward generalization of the two-variable regression formula [12.17].

We can now replace σ^2 in [13.19] and [13.20] by s^2, as given by [13.21] with $k = 3$, and obtain estimated variances for the OLS estimators, b_2 and b_3, as

$$s_{b_2}^2 = \frac{s^2}{\sum x_2^2(1 - r^2)} \tag{13.23}$$

and

$$s_{b_3}^2 = \frac{s^2}{\sum x_3^2(1 - r^2)} \tag{13.24}$$

The square roots of [13.23] and [13.24] are referred to as *estimated standard errors*.

Example 13.2

Assuming the classical assumptions hold, use the data of Example 13.1 to find, for the equation estimated there:

(a) s^2 using [13.22] and then [13.21];

(b) $s_{b_2}^2$ and $s_{b_3}^2$ using [13.23] and [13.24];

(c) R^2 using [13.17].

Interpret each answer.

Inference in multiple regression

Inference in the multiple regression model is performed analogously to that in simple regression. Under classical assumptions the OLS estimators, the b_j ($j = 1, 2, 3, ..., k$) are normally distributed. That is,

$$\text{each } b_j \text{ has an } N(\beta_j, \sigma_{b_j}^2) \text{ distribution,} \tag{13.25}$$

where $\sigma_{b_j}^2$ is the relevant expression for the variance of the b_j. Thus

$$\frac{b_j - \beta_j}{\sigma_{b_j}} \text{ has a } N(0, 1) \text{ distribution.} \qquad [13.26]$$

But, again as in two-variable regression, when we switch from σ_{b_j} to s_{b_j} we have to use the Student's t distribution rather than the $N(0, 1)$ distribution. That is, for each $j = 1, 2, 3, ..., k$, [13.26] becomes

$$\frac{b_j - \beta_j}{s_{b_j}} \text{ has a Student's } t \text{ distribution with } n - k \text{ d.f.} \qquad [13.27]$$

Notice that in [13.27] the degrees of freedom associated with the Student's t distribution are $n - k$ in the general case, where k is the number of parameters (including the intercept) in the regression equation. This, of course, becomes $n - 2$ for simple regression, as in the previous chapter.

We can now use [13.27] as a basis for finding confidence intervals for and testing hypotheses about any of the individual β_j's.

Firstly, we can test $H_0: \beta_j = 0$ by noting that, under H_0,

$$TS = \frac{b_j}{s_{b_j}} \text{ has a Student's distribution with } n - k \text{ d.f.} \qquad [13.28]$$

Thus, apart from the reduction in degrees of freedom, the test of whether an explanatory variable influences $E(Y)$ is exactly the same as that in simple regression.

Confidence intervals also take a form identical to that in two-variable regression, except that again we use $n - k$ degrees of freedom. In general, a 95% confidence interval is given by the usual formula,

$$b_j \pm t_{0.025} s_{b_j}.$$

Example 13.3

For the data of Examples 13.1 and 13.2,
(a) Using a 0.01 level of significance, test
    (i)   whether X_2 influences Y (ii) the hypothesis $\beta_3 < 20$.
(b) Find a 98% confidence level for β_3.

In multiple regression, we do not normally use hand calculators as we did in Examples 13.1 and 13.2. Rather, we perform any required inference directly on the relevant computer-estimated equations. The following worked example illustrates the procedure.

Worked Example

Consider the population regression equations

$$M = \beta_1 + \beta_2 G + \beta_3 I + \beta_4 \dot{P} + \varepsilon, \tag{1}$$

$$\ln M = \beta'_1 + \beta'_2 \ln G + \beta'_3 \ln I + \beta'_4 \ln \dot{P} + \varepsilon', \tag{2}$$

where the variables are defined as in Computer Exercise 13.1.

(a) For equation [1], use the result in Fig. 13.2 to test the hypotheses $\beta_2 = 0$ and $\beta_3 = 0$. Find a 95% confidence interval for β_4.

(b) For equation [2], use the result in Fig. 13.3 to test the hypotheses $\beta'_2 = 1$ and $\beta'_3 = 0$.

Comment on your tests of $\beta_3 = 0$ and of $\beta'_3 = 0$.

Solution

(a) To test $H_0: \beta_2 = 0$, we require the test statistic b_2/s_{b_2}. From Fig. 13.2, we have $b_2 = 0.170\ 37$ and $s_{b_2} = 0.018\ 94$, so $TS = 8.99$. Since, with $n - k = 26$ d.f., $t_{0.05} = 1.706$, we can clearly reject H_0 and conclude that GDP per head, G, influences the demand for money, M. Note that the value of TS is simply the t-ratio for G given in Fig. 13.2.

To test $H_0: \beta_3 = 0$, we use $TS = b_3/s_{b_3}$. From Fig. 13.2, TS is given by the t-ratio for the interest-rate variable I. Its absolute value is only 0.14, so in this case we certainly cannot reject H_0. We have found no evidence, from this result, that I influences the demand for money. In fact the p-value for I indicates there would be a 0.893 probability of error if we claimed I affected M.

A 95% confidence interval for β_4, the coefficient on the inflation-rate variable $\dot{P}$, is given by

$$b_4 \pm t_{0.025} s_{b_4}$$

or

$$-0.002\ 197 \pm 2.056 \times 0.003\ 773 = -0.021\ 97 \pm 0.007\ 757.$$

(b) In equation [2], the variables are in logarithms, so the parameter β'_2 is the GDP or 'income' elasticity of the demand for money. For testing $H_0: \beta'_2 = 1$, the test statistic can be found using [13.27]. Thus $TS = (b'_2 - 1)/s_{b'_2}$, which, in this case, is not the t-ratio in Fig. 13.3. Using a two-tail test, we have $t_{0.025} = 2.056$, whereas $TS = 0.65$, using the results in Fig. 13.3. So we cannot reject H_0 and conclude that the income elasticity may well be unity as implied by some theories.

To test $\beta_3' = 0$, we simply use $TS = b_3'/s_{b_3'}$, which is the t-ratio on $\ln I$ in Fig. 13.3. This has an absolute value of 3.56, which clearly exceeds $t_{0.05} = 1.706$. This result, in contrast to the result obtained using Fig. 13.2, suggests that the interest rate I does influence the demand for money. The interest elasticity is in fact 0.29.

The fact that we appear to reach different conclusions regarding the I variable in (a) and (b) above is a consequence of the different specifications adopted in equations [1] and [2]. The significance of the coefficient on $\ln I$ in [2] rather suggests that a log-linear function could be superior to a simple linear function for this demand-for-money data set. However, this suggestion is not conclusive since it is possible that yet further variables should be included in the equation.

Example 13.4

Consider the OLS regression result

$$C = 245 \quad + \quad 0.673Y \quad + \quad 0.226L \quad - \quad 0.564P, \qquad n = 25, \qquad R^2 = 0.875,$$
$$ (86) \qquad (0.085) \qquad (0.154) \qquad (0.231)$$

where C is real consumer expenditure, Y is real disposable income, L is the real liquid asset stock of consumers and P is a general price index. Figures in parentheses are estimated standard errors.

Carrying out appropriate t-tests, interpret the regression equation.

Multiple versus simple regression coefficients

Let us consider again the demand-for-money data set of Computer Exercise 13.1. Consider the population regression equation

$$\mathrm{E}(M) = \beta_1 + \beta_2 G + \beta_3 I, \qquad\qquad [13.29]$$

where the variables are defined as before. For the moment, we ignore the variable $\dot{P}$.

Recall that β_2 measures the change in $\mathrm{E}(M)$ per unit change in G, under the *ceteris paribus* assumption that I remains unchanged. Similarly, β_3 measures the change in $\mathrm{E}(M)$ per unit change in I under the assumption of constant G; β_3 is likely to be negative.

Suppose an investigator wishes to assess the magnitude and sign of the unknown parameters β_2 and β_3. In the physical sciences, it might be possible for the investigator to carry out a controlled experiment in which a variable such as I was held constant, the variable G allowed to vary, and the corresponding values of M recorded. Since I is held constant, we can rewrite [13.29] as

$$\mathrm{E}(M) = \beta_1' + \beta_2 G, \qquad\qquad [13.30]$$

where $\beta_1' = \beta_1 + \beta_3 I'$ and I' is the constant value of I.

Equation [13.30] is formally equivalent to [9.5], so that we are back in the world of simple two-variable regression. An estimate of the parameter β_2 can be obtained by simple regression from the scatter diagram of M on G. Similarly, a further controlled experiment, with G this time held constant, would provide an estimate of the parameter β_3 from the observation of the scatter of M on I.

Unfortunately, in economics, such controlled experiments are almost never possible. In practice, it is highly unlikely that we would find sample data in which either G or I happened to be constant. G and I will almost certainly both vary. In such situations, variations in, for example, the I variable make it very unlikely that we could obtain 'good' estimates of the parameter β_2 from a scatter of M on G. Similarly, 'good' estimates of β_3 cannot usually be obtained from observing a simple scatter of M on I.

Clearly, what is required is some statistical procedure that 'mimics' the *ceteris paribus* assumptions that have to be made in two-variable regression. And this is exactly what multiple regression does.[5]

We present here two log-linear regressions, estimated using the data set on the file DATASET1:

$$\widehat{\ln M} = -1.91 + 1.045 \ln G, \qquad [13.31]$$

$$\widehat{\ln M} = -1.25 + 1.027 \ln G - 0.249 \ln I. \qquad [13.32]$$

Replicate [13.31] and [13.32] using your regression programme. Notice immediately that the OLS estimates of the intercept and the coefficient on $\ln G$, β_2, differ between the two equations. In fact, the value of b_2 in [13.32] represents an attempt to assess the influence on $E(\ln M)$ of a change in $\ln G$ under the *ceteris paribus* assumption that $\ln I$ is constant. This is done by including the $\ln I$ variable in the estimating equation to allow for the variation in that variable in the given sample. The value of b_2 in equation [13.31] is different because, in this equation, no allowance is made for any variation in the $\ln I$ variable.

The extent to which regression coefficients change, when additional variables are included in an estimating equation, depends on the extent to which the variables already included are correlated with the variables that are introduced. In the present case, the correlation between $\ln G$ and $\ln I$ is as low as 0.08, and this is the reason why there is so little change in the coefficient on $\ln G$ when the extra variable is introduced.

A simple algebraic model should make the above clear. Suppose Z is determined by two variables, X and Y:

$$Z = \beta_1 + \beta_2 X + \beta_3 Y. \qquad [13.33]$$

Suppose also that X and Y happen to be linked by simple linear equation

$$Y = \alpha_1 + \alpha_2 X. \qquad [13.34]$$

In this model, there are two ways in which X can influence Z. Firstly, there is a direct effect, determined by the coefficient β_2 in [13.33]. Secondly, there is an indirect effect acting via Y in [13.34]. Firstly, X affects Y, which in turn affects Z. To measure the total effect, both direct and indirect, we need to substitute for Y in [13.33], giving

$$Z = \beta_1 + \beta_2 X + \beta_3(\alpha_1 + \alpha_2 X)$$

or

$$Z = \beta_1' + \beta_2' X, \qquad \text{[13.35]}$$

where $\beta_1' = \beta_1 + \alpha_1\beta_3$ and $\beta_2' = \beta_2 + \alpha_2\beta_3$. The coefficient β_2' in [13.35] measures the total effect, both direct and indirect, on Z of a unit change in X.

It should now be clear that, if we use multiple regression to estimate [13.33], then the coefficient we obtain on the X variable measures the direct effect on Z alone. That is, it measures the effect obtained when Y is held constant, so that there is no indirect effect. However, the simple regression of Z on X yields an estimate of β_2' in [13.35], that is, it measures the total effect.

We can now see that the coefficients β_2 and β_2' will be the same only when $\alpha_2 = 0$, that is, when X is unconnected with Y. But if X does influence Y then the coefficient β_2 will differ from β_2'.

It should now be possible to see intuitively why the introduction of the I variable into [13.31] had so little effect on the G coefficient. There is hardly any link between G and I, as the tiny correlation coefficient indicates.

The algebraic model is a deterministic one, that is, it contains no stochastic disturbances. When both [13.33] and particularly [13.34] contain disturbances, the situation is a little more complicated, but the general idea remains the same. We now have to work with estimators of the β and α parameters in [13.33] and [13.34]. There are now two unlikely extreme cases, with an infinite series of intermediate cases. One extreme is when the correlation between X and Y is either +1 or −1. This implies the absence of a disturbance in [13.34] and an exact relationship between X and Y. As we shall see in the next section, such a correlation between X and Y results in a breakdown in the OLS estimation procedure when applied to [13.33].

The other extreme is that of zero correlation between X and Y, which can only occur if $\alpha_2 = 0$. But, as we saw, this implies that the addition of Y has no influence on the coefficient of X in a multiple regression equivalent of [13.33]. In between the two extreme cases are the intermediate possibilities where the correlation between X and Y can lie anywhere between −1 and +1. In general, the greater the correlation (positive or negative) between X and Y, the greater will be the change in the OLS estimator b_2 when a second variable Y is added to an equation containing X only.

It is particularly the case with economic time-series data that explanatory variables exhibit similar trends and hence are highly correlated over time. Consequently, with such data, the addition or subtraction of variables from a regression equation usually has a serious effect on the OLS coefficients of variables retained in the equation.

Example 13.5

Thirty observations on the demand for oranges Q, the relative price of oranges P and an index of consumer disposable income Y gave the following OLS regressions equations:

$$\widehat{\ln(Q)} = 1.33 - 0.853 \ln(P), \qquad R^2 = 0.56;$$
$$\qquad\quad (6.22) \ (5.31)$$

$$\widehat{\ln(Q)} = 0.63 - 0.251 \ln(P) + 0.874 \ln(Y), \qquad R^2 = 0.77.$$
$$\qquad\quad (2.46) \ (1.54) \qquad\quad (7.31)$$

(Figures in parentheses are t-ratios.)

Comment on the size and statistical significance of the price elasticity of the demand for oranges.

13.3 Multicollinearity

Recall that assumption ID of the classical multiple regression model states that no exact linear relationship is permitted to exist between any two or more of the explanatory variables. If this assumption is invalid, then the OLS estimation procedure itself will break down.

To see why this is the case, suppose we wish to estimate a population regression equation with just two explanatory variables,

$$E(Y) = \beta_1 + \beta_2 X_2 + \beta_3 X_3. \qquad [13.36]$$

Suppose, further, that estimation of [13.36] is attempted using sample data in which the linear relationship $X_{2i} = 5 + 2X_{3i}$ holds exactly *for every sample observation*. Thus, assumption ID has clearly been violated.

Now let us assume, for the moment, that an OLS *sample* regression equation were to exist that minimizes the sum of the squares of the residuals, $SSR = \sum e_i^2$, and has the form

$$\hat{Y} = 6 + 12X_2 + 8X_3. \qquad [13.37]$$

Given what we have just assumed, it may appear that the numbers 6, 12 and 8 in [13.37] must represent the OLS estimates of the parameters β_1, β_2 and β_3 in [13.36]. But there is a problem. Obviously, we can write [13.37] as

$$\hat{Y} = 6 + 2X_2 + 10X_2 + 8X_3. \tag{13.38}$$

Since, for all sample observations, we have $X_2 = 5 + 2X_3$, we can therefore rewrite [13.38] as

$$\hat{Y} = 6 + 2X_2 + 10(5 + 2X_3) + 8X_3$$
$$= 56 + 2X_2 + 28X_3. \tag{13.39}$$

Since $X_{2i} = 5 + 2X_{3i}$ holds for all sample observations, the predicted values of Y, the $\hat{Y}_i$, obtained from [13.39] by substituting in the sample values for X_2 and X_3 must be identical to the $\hat{Y}_i$ obtained from the use of [13.37]. Since the actual Y_i in the sample must remain unchanged, it follows that the residuals $e_i = Y_i - \hat{Y}_i$ must also remain unchanged, as must the residual sum of squares SSR $= \Sigma\, e_i^2$. Thus both the sample regression equations [13.37] and [13.39] have the same residual sum of squares. But the OLS estimation method is designed to select estimators b_1, b_2 and b_3 that minimize the residual sum of squares. Unfortunately, in this case, there is no such unique set of OLS estimators because, clearly, if [13.37] minimizes the SSR then so must [13.39].

Moreover, we need not stop here. Given that $X_{2i} = 5 + 2X_{3i}$ holds for all sample observations, it is easy to construct any number of sample regressions all giving the same 'minimum' $\Sigma\, e_i^2$. Again using [13.37], another such equation would be

$$\hat{Y} = 6 + 8X_2 + 4X_2 + 8X_3$$
$$= 6 + 8X_2 + 4(5 + 2X_3) + 8X_3$$
$$= 26 + 8X_2 + 16X_3. \tag{13.40}$$

In fact, there must be an infinite number of sets of values for the estimated b_j's all giving the same 'minimum' residual sum of squares. Consequently, there are no unique OLS estimators, so this method of estimation breaks down.[6]

Example 13.6

Consider the following the sample data set:

i	1	2	3	4	5
X_2	7	3	6	11	5
X_3	3	7	4	-1	5
Y	61	42	54	79	49

(a) An exact linear relationship exists between the sample values of X_2 and X_3. What is this linear relationship?

(b) Consider the sample regression equation

$$\hat{Y} = -5 + 8X_2 + 3X_3.$$

Find the residuals that result from this equation and hence calculate the residual sum of squares, SSR.

(c) Use the linear relationship found in (a) to obtain three other sample regression equations with the same SSR as that of the equation in (b). Check that the SSRs are really equal.

When an exact linear relationship between explanatory variables exists, the situation is referred to as one of *complete* or *perfect multicollinearity*. We are in a situation of complete uncertainty regarding the values of the parameters β_1, β_2 and β_3 in [13.36]. We can have no idea whether to estimate them by, for example, the 6, 12 and 8 appearing in [13.37], the 56, 2 and 28 in [13.39] or the 26, 8 and 16 of [13.40], and so on.

Such complete multicollinearity almost never occurs in practice. But what does happen quite frequently, particularly in time-series work, is a situation where there is not an exact but an approximate linear relationship between two or more of the explanatory variables in a multiple regression equation. This situation can cause serious estimation problems, and the closer the approximation to a linear relationship that occurs, the more serious these problems tend to become.

Suppose that when estimating [13.36] we find that the relationship $X_{2i} = 5 + 2X_{3i}$ holds merely approximately but not exactly for all sample observations. In this situation there will be a unique set of estimates b_1, b_2 and b_3 that minimize $\sum e_i^2$. That is, the OLS method does not break down completely and there will be a unique sample regression equation. But the problem now is that there are many sets of such estimates b_1, b_2 and b_3 (i.e., many sample regression equations), all with residual sums of squares not equal to, but 'very close' to the minimum $\sum e_i^2$ yielded by the OLS regression equation. In such a situation, we will lack confidence and be uncertain about the precision of the OLS estimates obtained because there are so many other sets of values for b_1, b_2 and b_3 which are 'almost as good'. In fact, the closer is the approximation to a linear relationship between the X variables, the higher is the *degree* of the multicollinearity present and, other things being equal, the greater is the extent of our uncertainty about the true population values β_1, β_2 and β_3 in [13.36]. Thus, while complete multicollinearity results in complete uncertainty about population values, a high degree of multicollinearity leads to a high degree of uncertainty about population values. This problem will be illustrated in the following computer exercise.

Computer Exercise 13.2

In the file DATASET2, which can be accessed from the learning centre, you will find observations on four variables: defined as S = sales of tee shirts, E = total spending on clothes, P = relative price of tee shirts, and A = index of advertising expenditure. There are 40 monthly observations in all, the first 19 of which are shown in Table 13.1. They refer to a distinctive tee-shirt sold by a well-known chain of department stores. S and E are measured in thousands of pounds sterling at constant prices. P is the ratio of the price of the tee-shirt to the price of a rival tee-shirt sold by a different chain. A is an index of the advertising expenditure directed at the tee-shirt.

Table 13.1 Data for tee shirt spending				
Month	S	E	P	A
1997M1	23.4	32.1	1.21	76.3
1997M2	24.1	32.3	1.19	76.9
1997M3	24.5	32.5	1.13	77.5
1997M4	25.1	32.6	1.1	77.8
1997M5	26	32.9	1.08	78.5
1997M6	26.3	33.1	1.09	79.5
1997M7	25.6	33.2	1.13	79.7
1997M8	26.5	33.5	1.09	80.4
1997M9	27.2	34.1	1.02	82.3
1997M10	27.2	34.6	1.16	83.8
1997M11	27.3	34.6	1.14	83.9
1997M12	27.7	34.8	1.14	84.6
1998M1	27.6	35.1	1.14	85.3
1998M2	27.7	35.2	1.13	85.8
1998M3	28.4	35.9	1.13	87.5
1998M4	29.1	36.3	0.96	88.9
1998M5	29.4	36.4	0.97	89.3
1998M6	29.3	36.8	0.99	90.5
1998M7	30.1	37.1	1.01	91.2

Our purpose in this exercise is to develop a regression model which both indicates the most important factors determining the demand for tee-shirts and also enables us to forecast that demand in future months.

Before we undertake our exercise, we will illustrate the effect of attempting to estimate a sample regression equation in the presence of perfect multicollinearity among the explanatory variables. Form the artificial variable

$$F = 4 - 3E,$$

[13.41]

```
                    Ordinary Least Squares Estimation
*****************************************************************************
Dependent variable is S
40 observations used for estimation from 1997M1 to 2000M4
*****************************************************************************
Regressor          Coefficient      Standard Error       T-Ratio[Prob]
INTER                 4.0774             2.4695           1.6511[.107]
E                      .69426            .068179          10.1829[.000]
*****************************************************************************
R-Squared                    .73181   R-Bar-Squared                  .72475
S.E of Regression            1.4351   F-stat.   F( 1,  38)   103.6908[000]
Mean of Dependent Variable  29.1175   S.D. of Dependent Variable     2.7354
Residual Sum of Squares     78.2625   Equation Log-likelihood      -70.1813
Akaike Info. Criterion     -72.1813   Schwarz Bayesian Criterion   -73.8702
DW-statistic                 .29390
*****************************************************************************



                    Ordinary Least Squares Estimation
*****************************************************************************
Dependent variable is S
40 observations used for estimation from 1997M1 to 2000M4
*****************************************************************************
Regressor          Coefficient      Standard Error       T-Ratio[Prob]
INTER                 4.9196             2.2816           2.1563[.037]
A                      .27498            .025807          10.6552[.000]
*****************************************************************************
R-Squared                    .74923   R-Bar-Squared                  .74263
S.E of Regression            1.3877   F-stat.   F( 1,  38)   113.5336[000]
Mean of Dependent Variable  29.1175   S.D. of Dependent Variable     2.7354
Residual Sum of Squares     73.1790   Equation Log-likelihood      -68.8381
Akaike Info. Criterion     -70.8381   Schwarz Bayesian Criterion   -72.5270
DW-statistic                 .25339
*****************************************************************************



                    Ordinary Least Squares Estimation
*****************************************************************************
Dependent variable is S
40 observations used for estimation from 1997M1 to 2000M4
*****************************************************************************
Regressor          Coefficient      Standard Error       T-Ratio[Prob]
INTER                56.2539             3.7043           15.1860[.000]
P                   -25.7889             3.5102           -7.3468[.000]
*****************************************************************************
R-Squared                    .58685   R-Bar-Squared                  .57598
S.E of Regression            1.7812   F-stat.   F( 1,  38)    53.9761[000]
Mean of Dependent Variable  29.1175   S.D. of Dependent Variable     2.7354
Residual Sum of Squares    120.5647   Equation Log-likelihood      -78.8237
Akaike Info. Criterion     -80.8237   Schwarz Bayesian Criterion   -82.5126
DW-statistic                 .71829
*****************************************************************************
```

Figure 13.4 Three two-variable regressions

where E is defined above. Move to the data window and verify that the relationship between the F values and the E values holds for every observation. Now attempt to obtain the OLS regression of sales S on the two explanatory variables E and F.

Your programme will simply give you an error message. This is the result of the exact linear relationship [13.41] between E and F. We stressed earlier that the OLS estimation process breaks down when perfect multicollinearity is present among the explanatory variables.

Deleting the artificial variable F, we can now give our attention to the four genuine variables and set about trying to explain the behaviour of sales, S. In Fig. 13.4 you will find three simple two-variable regressions of the dependent variable S on each of the three explanatory variables, E, A and P in turn. You should replicate these results using your programme.

The R^2s for these regressions may seem encouraging, but in fact they tell us little more than we should expect. The advertising and total expenditure coefficients have positive signs, with large t-ratios, while the relative price coefficient has a negative sign, again with a large t-ratio. These are the signs that economics predicts, since they imply that S varies directly with E and A but inversely with P. So at least we are getting the signs that we expect! It is sometimes the case in econometrics that we get statistical results that are not as expected.

Unfortunately, the results in Fig. 13.4 merely confirm what can be deduced by studying the data set in the current file, part of which is shown in Table 13.1. In fact, each regression in Fig. 13.4 simply confirms the general trends in any two of the variables. A study of data plots for the variable S and E indicates that generally S rises when E rises but falls when E falls. Further plots indicate that S also rises when A rises and falls when A falls. Conversely, S falls when P rises but rises when P falls. The problem we need to resolve is this. When S rises, does it rise because of the rise in E? Or does S rise because A rises? Or does S rise because P has fallen? Or does S rise because two or three of the variables E, A and P all move in the required direction? Since all four variables move in the directions that economic theory suggests, then, intuitively, you should be able to see that we are going to have difficulty solving the problem we posed a moment ago. The question is whether multiple regression analysis will be of any assistance.

The obvious approach to take now is to compute the multiple regression of S on at least two of the three variables E, A and P and see what happens. Since the simple regressions, using E and using A, have the highest R^2, it might seem sensible to include both E and A in a multiple regression equation. The result of doing this is shown in Fig. 13.5, and again you should replicate this equation.

It should be clear from Fig. 13.5 that the t-ratios on both the E and A variables are relatively small, particularly that on E. In fact, with $n - k = 37$ d.f., the critical value of t is $t_{0.05} = 1.69$. Thus at the 0.05 level of significance we can find no evidence that either total expenditure or the advertising index influences S! Yet in Fig. 13.4, in the simple regressions, E and A had t-ratios as high as 10.18 and 10.66, respectively.

```
                    Ordinary Least Squares Estimation
*******************************************************************************
Dependent variable is S
40 observations used for estimation from 1997M1 to 2000M4
*******************************************************************************
Regressor          Coefficient      Standard Error        T-Ratio[Prob]
INTER                   4.6240              2.4380          1.8966[.066]
E                       .13086              .34797           .37607[.709]
A                       .22470              .13621          1.6497[.107]
*******************************************************************************
R-Squared                   .75019   R-Bar-Squared                    .73668
S.E of Regression           1.4037   F-stat.   F( 2,  37)       55.5549[000]
Mean of departent Variable 26.1175   S.D. of Dependent Variable       2.7354
Residual Sum of Squares    72.9004   Equation Log-likelihood       -68.7618
Akaike Info. Criterion    -71.7618   Schwarz Bayesian Criterion    -74.2951
DW-statistic                .24993
*******************************************************************************


                           Diagnostic Tests
*******************************************************************************
*    Test Statistics    *     LM Version        *      F Version           *
*******************************************************************************
*                       *                       *                          *
* A:Serial Correlation  * CHSQ( 12)= 29.0850[.004]* F( 12,  25)= 5.5514[.000]*
*                       *                       *                          *
* B:Functional Form     * CHSQ(  1)=  8.4179[.004]* F(  1,  36)= 9.5954[.004]*
*                       *                       *                          *
* C:Normality           * CHSQ(  2)=  1.7877[.409]*    Not applicable       *
*                       *                       *                          *
* D:Heteroscedasticity  * CHSQ(  1)=   .92742[.336]* F(  1,  38)= .90196[.348]*
*******************************************************************************
 A:Lagrange multiplier test of residual serial correlation
 B:Ramsey's RESET test using the square of the fitted values
 C:Based on a test of skewness and kurtosis of residuals
 D:Based on the regression of squared residuals on squared fitted values
```

Figure 13.5 Two collinear regressions

These apparently strange results are simply the result of the fact that the E and A variables are very highly correlated. In fact the correlation between E and A is 0.98. We saw, earlier in this section, that a high degree of multicollinearity between explanatory variables leads to great uncertainty about the true values of regression parameters. This uncertainty manifests itself in *large standard errors* and, more importantly, large estimated standard errors (and hence low *t*-ratios), for the OLS estimators.[7] Such large standard errors imply that confidence intervals for estimated coefficients will be wide. For example, using the result in Fig. 13.5, we can compute a 95% confidence interval for β_2, the total expenditure slope parameter as

$$b_2 \pm t_{0.025} s_{b_2} \quad \text{or} \quad 0.131 \pm 0.706. \qquad [13.42]$$

The confidence range [13.42] is very wide, from −0.575 to +0.837. Our estimate of the true β_2 is therefore highly uncertain and imprecise. A confidence interval for β_3 is similarly wide.

The most serious consequence of a high degree of multicollinearity is likely to be large standard errors and hence small t-ratios, as in Fig. 13.5. This makes it difficult to disentangle the influences of the collinear explanatory variables. Notice that R^2 in Fig. 13.5 is as high as 0.75, so that E and A *together* can explain 75% of the variation in sales. Yet, individually, we cannot reject either $\beta_2 = 0$ or $\beta_3 = 0$. At least one of the two variables seems to influence S but we cannot tell from this sample whether it is E or A or some combination of both variables.

If you add the relative price variable to your estimating equation you should obtain the result shown in Fig. 13.6. Notice the t-ratio on the P variable is much larger than the values for E and A. In fact the t-ratio is sufficiently large for you to reject H_0: $\beta_4 = 0$ and conclude that relative price influences sales of tee-shirts. In addition, notice that the price variable has the correct negative sign. Unfortunately, the t-ratios on the E and A variables remain small.

```
                   Ordinary Least Squares Estimation
*******************************************************************************
Dependent variable is S
40 observations used for estimation from 1997M1 to 2000M4
*******************************************************************************
Regressor            Coefficient      Standard Error          T-Ratio[Prob]
INTER                    20.9548              6.6413         3.1552[.003]
E                        .25662               .32692          .78496[.438]
A                        .10717               .13432          .6497[.430]
P                       -10.0011              3.8232        -2.6159[.013]
*******************************************************************************
R-Squared                     .79009  R-Bar-Squared                  .77259
S.E of Regression             1.3044  F-stat.   F( 3,  36)    45.1665[000]
Mean of Dependent Variable  29.1175   S.D. of Dependent Variable     2.7354
Residual Sum of Squares     61.2564   Equation Log-likelihood      -65.2813
Akaike Info. Criterion     -69.2813   Schwarz Bayesian Criterion   -72.6591
DW-statistic                  .25735
*******************************************************************************


                              Diagnostic Tests
*******************************************************************************
*    Test Statistics    *     LM Version          *      F Version          *
*******************************************************************************
*                       *                         *                         *
* A:Serial Correlation* CHSQ( 12)= 30.2596[.003]* F( 12, 24)=  6.2133[.000]*
*                       *                         *                         *
* B:Functional Form     * CHSQ(  1)= 12.0239[.001]* F(  1, 35)= 15.0427[.000]*
*                       *                         *                         *
* C:Normality           *  CHSQ(  2)=  2.1496[.341]*    Not applicable       *
*                       *                         *                         *
* D:Heteroscedasticity* CHSQ(  1)=  .13666[.712]* F(  1, 38)=  .13027[.720]*
*******************************************************************************
A:Lagrange multiplier test of residual serial correlation
B:Ramsey's RESET test using the square of the fitted values
C:Based on a test of skewness and kurtosis of residuals
D:Based on the regression of squared residuals on squared fitted values
```

Figure 13.6 Adding the *P* variable to the equation

The fact that the *P* variable 'shows up' as an influence on *S* is partly because the correlations between *P* and *E* and between *P* and *A* are much smaller than the correlation of 0.98 found between *E* and *A*. The correlation between *P* and *A* is 0.73, and that between *P* and *E* is just 0.70. Thus the collinearity of *P* with the other variables is insufficient for it to mask the separate influence of *P* on *S*.

Our inability to disentangle the separate influences of *E* and *A* on the dependent variable *S* is a consequence of the nature of our data set. As we noted earlier, and as is apparent from Table 13.1, the variables *E* and *A* move together, with each variable rising or falling as the other rises or falls. Since *S* also moves in this manner we cannot tell which of *E* or *A* (or both) influences *S*. To break this deadlock we need data in which the *E* and *A* variables move in different directions. With such data, we can then observe what happens to *S*.

```
                    Ordinary Least Squares Estimation
*********************************************************************************
 Dependent variable is S
 40 observations used for estimation from 1997M1 to 2000M4
*********************************************************************************
 Regressor          Coefficient       Standard Error        T-Ratio[Prob]
 INTER                  19.8249               6.4701         3.0641[.004]
 E                       .27831               .093242        2.9848[.005]
 A                       .098756              .043824        2.2535[.030]
 P                     -8.9246               3.66929        -2.4167[.021]
*********************************************************************************
 R-Squared                      .80071   R-Bar-Squared                 .78410
 S.E of Regression             1.2710    F-stat.    F( 3,  36)  48.2135[.000]
 Mean of Dependent Variable  29.1175     S.D. of Dependent Variable    2.7354
 Residual Sum of Squares     58.1566     Equation Log-likelihood     -64.2427
 Akaike Info. Criterion      -68.2427    Schwarz Bayesian Criterion  -71.6205
 DW-statistic                  .30419
*********************************************************************************


                            Diagnostic Tests
*********************************************************************************
 *    Test Statistics    *      LM Version       *       F Version          *
*********************************************************************************
 *                       *                       *                          *
 * A:Serial Correlation* CHSQ( 12)= 31.0718[.002]* F( 12, 24)=   6.9603[.000]*
 *                       *                       *                          *
 * B:Functional Form   * CHSQ(  1)=  8.2468[.004]* F(  1, 35)=   9.0900[.005]*
 *                       *                       *                          *
 * C:Normality         * CHSQ(  2)=  2.0847[.353]*    Not applicable        *
 *                       *                       *                          *
 * D:Heteroscedasticity* CHSQ(  1)=   .28143[.569]* F(  1, 38)=    .26925[.607]*
*********************************************************************************
 A:Lagrange multiplier test of residual serial correlation
 B:Ramsey's RESET test using the square of the fitted values
 C:Based on a test of skewness and kurtosis of residuals
 D:Based on the regression of squared residuals on squared fitted values
```

Figure 13.7 Effect of artificially changing the data

As an experiment, using the file DATASET2 again, change the E and A values in the first observation so that $E = 21.3$ and $A = 86.3$. That is, we have artificially reduced the value of E but increased the value of A. This considerably reduces the correlation between E and A, because now we have included an observation with a high A but a low E. Now, re-run the regression of S on all three explanatory variables E, A and P. You should obtain the result shown in Fig. 13.6. All three variables now have t-ratios in excess of 2, so that the multicollinearity deadlock has been removed.

Of course, in practice, it is not legitimate arbitrarily to change your data![8] But the above experiment demonstrated that multicollinearity is a property of the *sample data*. It is not the fact that there is any *population* relationship between E and A. It just happens that A and E move together in our sample. In another sample there might be no serious correlation between E and A.

The consequences of multicollinearity

We have seen that multicollinearity is essentially a sample problem and that, when approximate linear relationships exist between the sample values of explanatory variables, we are likely to encounter estimation problems. If these relationships are close to being exact, it is very likely that some of the estimated standard errors on our explanatory variables will be large. There are a number of consequences of this, as was illustrated in the above computer exercise.

Firstly, large standard errors imply that confidence intervals for the true regression parameters, the β_j's will be wide, so that our estimates of these β_j's will lack precision.

Secondly, as we saw in the computer exercise, when multicollinearity is present it can become very difficult to disentangle the separate effects of different explanatory variables. The large standard errors imply small t-ratios and, consequently, we often find ourselves unable to reject hypotheses of the type H_0: $\beta_j = 0$ when, actually, such a hypothesis is false. That is, our tests lack power, in the sense described in Chapter 4, and we may well find ourselves concluding that an explanatory variable has no influence on the dependent variable when in fact the reverse is true.

Thirdly, because the OLS estimators now have large standard errors – that is, large sampling variances – even slight additions or variations in the data set can lead to large changes in the values of OLS estimated coefficients, that is, in the b_j's. We saw in the above exercise that changes in just one observation can have marked effects. In fact this is another aspect of the uncertainty introduced into our procedure when multicollinearity is present. This sampling variability means that specific estimates of any of the β_j's in a given sample, may have large errors. Since we take just one sample, we can be very 'unlucky' in the sample we take and hence in the estimates we obtain.

Fourthly, when multicollinearity is present and regression coefficients are non-significantly different from zero, it is very tempting to drop the variable with 'the least significant coefficient' from an equation. For example, consider the regression equation of Fig. 13.5, in which both E and A have high standard errors and t-ratios of 0.38 and 1.65, respectively. The temptation is to drop the E variable from the equation. But the apparent lack of influence of E may be solely the result of the high correlation we found between E and A. Dropping the E variable is, in fact, a serious case of 'missing-variable error' and has a major effect on the A coefficient, as shown in Fig. 13.4.

When considering the possible consequences of multicollinearity, it must be remembered that multicollinearity itself does not imply any violation in the classical assumptions of Section 13.2. Hence, the OLS estimators retain all their desired properties of unbiasedness and consistency, etc. Also, their estimated standard errors remain unbiased. That is, OLS remains the best estimation method available. Unfortunately, when multicollinearity is present the 'best available' may not be particularly good. It is not that we cannot trust our procedures; it is just that our procedures may not tell us anything useful. Confidence intervals tend to be wide and our significance tests lack power.

Example 13.7

Twenty-five annual observations on a firm's output Q, its capital input K, its labour input L and its raw material input M yielded the following OLS regressions:

$$\hat{Q} = 0.37 + 0.48L + 0.57K, \qquad R^2 = 0.83;$$
$$\phantom{\hat{Q} = 0.37} (0.42)\ (0.38)\ (0.51)$$

$$\hat{Q} = 0.11 + 0.44L + 0.53K + 0.15M, \qquad R^2 = 0.91.$$
$$\phantom{\hat{Q} = 0.11} (0.37)\ (0.35)\ \ (0.49)\ \ (0.06)$$

Figures in parentheses are estimated standard errors and all variables are in natural logarithms.

Comment on the above results. Do you think that the firm's productive process exhibits constant returns to scale?

Handling and detecting multicollinearity

Students generally find it difficult to come to terms with multicollinearity. They are usually happier with topics such as autocorrelation and heteroscedasticity, which we deal with in Chapter 15. The problem is that there is no formal statistical test for multicollinearity. Statistical tests normally involve population parameters such as the β_j's in regression analysis, but we have seen that multicollinearity involves merely the sample and not the population.

Another problem is that a given degree of multicollinearity *does not always have the same effect on the estimation process*. For example, consider a sample regression equation with just two variables such as

$$\hat{Y} = b_1 + b_2 X_2 + b_3 X_3.$$

If you look back to equations [13.23] and [13.24], you will see that the sizes of the estimated variances and standard errors of the b_j's in such an equation is dependent on *factors other than the simple correlation between the two explanatory variables*. In fact, the size of standard errors also depends (a) directly on the overall goodness of fit of the equation (as measured by s^2, the variance of the residuals), and (b) inversely on the extent of the variation in the sample values of the explanatory variables (as measured by $\sum x_2^2 = \sum (X_2 - \bar{X}_2)^2$ and $\sum x_3^2 = \sum (X_3 - \bar{X}_3)^2$).

The result of this is that it is possible to obtain small standard errors even when the degree of multicollinearity (as measured by the sample correlation between X_2 and X_3) is high, provided the overall fit of the equation is very good and/or there is a sufficiently large variation in the values of the X variables. Conversely, small standard errors may be a result not of multicollinearity but of a poor overall fit for the estimated equation. This would simply imply that neither X_2 nor X_3 has much, if any, influence on Y.

The upshot of all this is that, when we have an equation with well-determined coefficients and small standard errors, we need not be too concerned about multicollinearity, although it may be severe. Recall that under classical assumptions the OLS estimators remain BLUE, and consistent and estimated standard errors remain unbiased.

It is when standard errors turn out to be large that we may suspect that multicollinearity, if present, is masking the importance of some of the explanatory variables. For example, large standard errors combined with a good overall fit for the equation (measured by s^2 or R^2) are a certain indicator of multicollinearity. The result in Fig. 13.5 provides an excellent example of this. Neither of the coefficients on E and A is significantly different from zero, yet E and A together can explain 75% of the variation in S.

It is, however, important to resist the temptation of attributing all large standard errors to multicollinearity. A variable may have a coefficient with a large standard error simply because it is unimportant! But the most confusing situation occurs when large standard errors occur for some or all of the explanatory variables in an equation with a good overall fit. If multicollinearity is present it is then tempting to blame any non-significance in coefficient values on the multicollinearity. However, *there can be no guarantee that in the absence of multicollinearity these coefficients would have proved significant*. Large standard errors may be the result of multicollinearity but they can also occur simply because variables are unimportant.

Assessing the extent of multicollinearity is straightforward when an estimating equation contains just two explanatory variables. Its extent can be measured simply by computing the simple sample correlation between the X variables.[9] But it must be remembered that, in an equation with three or more explanatory variables, approximate linear relationships between any two or more of the X variables can cause similar multicollinearity problems. Furthermore, relationships such as $X_{4i} = -2 + 3X_{2i} - 5X_{3i}$, that hold for all sample observations, are much harder to detect. The existence of such relationships can also result in the problems (large standard errors and so on) that we met with the simplest kind of multi-collinearity. It is in these situations that disentangling the separate effects of different explanatory variables can become almost impossible. In such circumstances we are in the situation of attempting, quoting Johnston (1984), to make bricks without straw. The problem can only be resolved *by getting some more data*, preferably data in which the relevant X variables are no longer so highly correlated.

Example 13.8

Consider the following aggregate savings functions ($n = 48$ and figures in parentheses are t-ratios):

$$\hat{S} = -24.2 \quad + \quad 0.122Y \qquad\qquad\qquad R^2 = 0.868$$
$$\phantom{\hat{S} = } (6.32) \qquad (7.48)$$

$$\hat{S} = -38.4 \quad + \quad 0.103Y \quad + \quad 0.012W \quad + \quad 6.43R \quad R^2 = 0.964$$
$$\phantom{\hat{S} = } (5.64) \qquad (5.97) \qquad\quad (0.833) \qquad\quad (4.81)$$

where S is real aggregate savings, Y is real aggregate disposable income, W is a measure of real personal wealth, and R is a short-term interest rate.

(a) Derive a 99% confidence interval for the marginal propensity to consume income.

(b) Test the hypothesis that a rise in wealth results in an increase in consumption.

(c) Given that the sample correlation between Y and W is 0.91, do you think that such collinearity is disguising the effect of wealth on consumption?

Example 13.9

Consider the following two OLS regression results, obtained from two different countries:

$$\hat{Y} = 0.356 \quad + \quad 0.765X_2 \quad + \quad 1.342X_3, \qquad R^2 = 0.854;$$
$$\phantom{\hat{Y} = } (3.12) \qquad (0.431) \qquad\quad (0.654)$$

$$\hat{Y} = 0.644 \quad + \quad 1.112X_2 \quad + \quad 0.943X_3, \qquad R^2 = 0.187.$$
$$\phantom{\hat{Y} = } (2.76) \qquad (0.644) \qquad\quad (0.482)$$

Figures in parentheses are *t*-ratios. For each regression result consider the extent to which X_2 and X_3 really influence Y.

13.4 **Some regression *F*-tests**

Consider again the population regression equation [13.2]. It is often the case in econometrics that we wish to test some *restriction* on the parameters of such a regression equation. To test such restrictions involves first estimating a so-called *unrestricted equation* and then comparing this with a *restricted equation* in which the required restrictions have been imposed. For example, we might wish to test whether two of the β_j parameters in [13.2] were equal or not. More generally, when variables are in logarithmic form, we often might wish to test hypotheses regarding the sum of the β_j parameters. For example, if [13.2] were a logarithmic production function, then we might well wish to test the hypothesis of constant returns, since this would imply that the sum of the β_j parameters was unity. Similarly, demand theory predicts that the sum of the income and price elasticities in a demand equation should always be zero. This prediction could be tested by expressing the demand equation in logarithmic form, since this prediction would then imply that the sum of the β_j parameters should be zero.

Later in this book we shall present a general method of testing restrictions on regression parameters, but in this section we shall just look at two special cases of the test. These cases involve the simple situations where all or at least some of the β_j parameters are zero.

Testing the overall significance of a regression equation

Recall again the regression result in Fig. 13.5, in which we could reject neither $H_0: \beta_2 = 0$ nor $H_0: \beta_3 = 0$. That is, the explanatory variables E and A both have coefficients that are non-significantly different from zero, although the coefficient of determination R^2 is as high as 0.75. Thus, although we could detect no individual influences for either E or A, the variables together could explain 75% of the variation in sales, S. Such a situation obviously invites some method of testing to see whether the combined influence of the explanatory variables is statistically significant.

For the equation estimated in Fig. 13.5, suppose we formulate the hypotheses

$$H_0: \beta_2 = \beta_3 = 0,$$
$$H_A: \text{at least one of } \beta_2, \beta_3 \text{ is non-zero.}$$

The null hypothesis implies that neither of the variables E and A influences S, while the alternative hypothesis implies that either E or A or both influence S. Note, carefully however, that H_A does not state that both β_j parameters are non-zero.[10]

Recall from [13.17] that the total sum of squares in an OLS multiple regression equation can be split into an explained sum of squares and a residual sum of squares:

$$SST = SSE + SSR.$$

Since the total sum of squares (SST) is constant for a given regression, it follows that the larger the explained sum of squares (SSE), the smaller must be the residual sum of squares (SSR) and vice versa. If H_0 above were true, and neither E and A influences S, then we would expect the SSE (that proportion of SST that *can* be explained by E and A), to be small relative to the SSR (that proportion of SST that *cannot* be explained). Hence, under H_0, we expect the ratio SSE/SSR to be small. The idea behind the regression F-test is that we reject H_0 if the ratio SSE/SSR is 'sufficiently large', because if H_0 is false then H_A must true and at least one of the two variables E and A must influence S.

Finally, we need to interpret what is meant by 'sufficiently large', that is, we require a formal test statistic. Not surprisingly, the test statistic is based on the ratio SSE/SSR. In fact, under H_0, it can be shown that the test statistic

$$TS = \frac{SSE/(k-1)}{SSR/(n-k)} \text{ has an } F \text{ distribution with } (k-1, n-k) \text{ d.f.} \qquad [13.43]$$

We reject H_0 if the test statistic is larger that the relevant critical F value. In [13.43], n is the sample size and k the number of β_j parameters (including the intercept).

For the regression in Fig. 13.5, $n = 40$ and $k = 3$, so we have an F distribution with $(2, 37)$ degrees of freedom. At the 0.05 level of significance the critical F-value is $F_{0.05} = 3.26$. The value of the test statistic is in fact highlighted in Fig. 13.5 as $F(2, 37) = 55.55$. We can therefore confidently reject H_0 and say that at least one of the variables E and A influences S. An alternative way of phrasing this result is to say that the 'combined influence of E and A is statistically significant'.

It is possible to express the test statistic [13.43] in terms of the coefficient of multiple determination R^2. Dividing both numerator and denominator in TS by the total sum of squares, SST, gives

$$TS = \frac{\dfrac{SSE}{SST(k-1)}}{\dfrac{SSR}{SST(n-k)}} = \frac{\dfrac{SSE}{SST(k-1)}}{\dfrac{SST-SSE}{SST(n-k)}} = \frac{R^2/(k-1)}{(1-R^2)/(n-k)}. \qquad [13.44]$$

It is clear that, the larger is R^2, the larger is the value of the test statistic. It can now be seen that this F-test is in fact a test to see whether R^2 is sufficiently larger than zero for us to reject the null hypothesis that neither of the explanatory variables affects S. Since $R^2 = 0.7502$ in Fig. 13.5, substituting into [13.44] again gives a value of 55.55 for the test statistic.

Obviously, the test statistic [13.43] can be extended to cases of more than two explanatory variables.

Example 13.10

Consider the following OLS regression result for $n = 76$:

$$\hat{Z} = 0.67 \quad + \quad 1.13X \quad - \quad 0.77Y \quad + \quad 1.56W, \qquad R^2 = 0.375.$$
$$\quad (2.72) \qquad (0.98) \qquad (2.89) \qquad (2.36)$$

Figures in parentheses are estimated standard errors.

(a) Perform *t*-tests to find out whether any of the variables has any individual influence on Z.

(b) Test whether the combined influence of X, Y and W on Z is statistically significant.

Comment on your results.

Variable addition and deletion tests

Frequently, we find ourselves either adding or removing variables from a regression equation. When this involves a single variable, the standard *t*-test will tell us when we should add or delete the variable. Problems arise, however, when two or more multicollinear variables are to be added or deleted.

Consider the third regression in Fig. 13.4, which has only one explanatory variable, P. Compare this with the result in Fig. 13.6, which also includes the two additional variables E and A. Neither E nor A has a statistically significant coefficient, yet adding the two new variables results in a rise in R^2 from 0.587 (in Fig. 13.4) to 0.790 (in Fig. 13.6). The rise in R^2 strongly suggests that at least one of the variables E and A has some contribution to make to the explanation of variations in S, over and above that of variations in P. The correlation of 0.98 between E and A may well be again masking the true influences of these variables.

We write the underlying population regression equation as

$$E(S) = \beta_1 + \beta_2 P + \beta_3 E + \beta_4 A, \tag{13.45}$$

and adopt as null and alternative hypotheses

$$H_0: \beta_3 = \beta_4 = 0,$$
$$H_A: \text{at least one of } \beta_3, \beta_4 \text{ is non-zero.}$$

Under H_0, [13.45] becomes

$$E(S) = \beta_1 + \beta_2 P. \tag{13.46}$$

In this situation [13.45] is sometimes termed the *unrestricted* equation and [13.46] the *restricted* equation. Rejecting H_0 implies that at least one of the variables E and A influences S.

Figures 13.6 and 13.4 contain estimated versions of [13.45] and [13.46], respectively. It makes sense to reject H_0 if the 'extra explanation', provided by adding the variables E and A to the original equation, is sufficiently great. If we let SSE_U and SSE_R be the explained sum of squares obtained from the estimated versions of the unrestricted equation [13.45] and the restricted [13.46], then we can measure the 'extra explanation' by taking the increase in the explained sum of squares, that is, $SSE_U - SSE_R$.

Since the total sum of squares SST is the same for both equations we have, for the two equations [13.45] and [13.46],

$$SST = SSE_U + SSR_U \quad \text{and} \quad SST = SSE_R + SSR_R. \tag{13.47}$$

We can therefore write

$$SSE_U - SSE_R = (SST - SSR_U) - (SST - SSR_R) = SSR_R - SSR_U$$

Thus the increase in the explained sum of squares, that results from adding the two new variables, is the same as the reduction in the residual sum of squares. The idea behind the following test is that we reject H_0 above if the proportionate reduction in the residual sum of squares, that is, $(SSR_R - SSR_U)/SSR_R$, is sufficiently large.

As usual it remains to decide what is meant by 'sufficiently large'. It turns out that, under H_0, the test statistic

$$TS = \frac{(SSR_R - SSR_U)/h}{SSR_U/(n-k)} \text{ has an } F \text{ distribution with } (h, n-k) \text{ d.f.} \tag{13.48}$$

In [13.48], h is the number of variables added (or deleted), n is the sample size and k is the number of β_j parameters in the equation with the larger number of explanatory variables. We reject H_0 (and say that the new variables do provide some 'extra explanation') if the test statistic [13.48] exceeds the relevant critical value of F.

Returning to the equations in Figs. 13.4 and 13.6, we obtain the two residual sums of squares as $SSR_R = 120.56$ and $SSR_U = 61.26$. With $n = 40$, $k = 4$ and $h = 2$, the test statistic therefore takes the value

$$TS = \frac{(120.56 - 61.26)/2}{61.26/36} = 17.4.$$

With $(2, 36)$ degrees of freedom the 0.05 critical value for F is $F_{0.05}(2, 36) = ?$. Hence we can strongly reject H_0 at this level of significance and conclude that at least one of the two new variables E and A influences S. We find that the combined extra influence of E and A is 'statistically significant'.

It is possible to express the test statistic [13.48] in terms of the difference between the coefficients of determination for the two equations. For the two equations,

$$R_U^2 = \frac{\text{SST} - \text{SSR}_U}{\text{SST}}$$

and

$$R_R^2 = \frac{\text{SST} - \text{SSR}_R}{\text{SST}}.$$

Dividing both numerator and denominator in [13.48] by the common SST yields, with a little manipulation,

$$TS = \frac{(R_U^2 - R_R^2)/h}{(1 - R_U^2)/(n - k)} \qquad [13.49]$$

Substituting in the values $R_U^2 = 0.790$ and $R_R^2 = 0.587$ again gives a value of 17.4.

Example 13.11

Consider the following OLS regression results:

$$\hat{Y} = 3.15 \quad - \quad 5.12X_2, \qquad\qquad \Sigma\, e^2 = 652.1;$$
$$\phantom{\hat{Y} = }(3.71) \qquad (6.18)$$

$$\hat{Y} = 2.13 \quad - \quad 4.76X_2 \quad - \quad 2.56X_3 \quad + \quad 2.19X_4, \qquad \Sigma\, e^2 = 634.7.$$
$$\phantom{\hat{Y} = }(2.84) \qquad (1.86) \qquad\quad (0.76) \qquad\quad (0.49)$$

Figures in parentheses are t-ratios and the sample size is $n = 59$.

   Carrying out appropriate t- and F-tests, what do you conclude about the influences of X_2, X_3 and X_4 on Y?

Example 13.12

Consider the following OLS regression equations estimated from 112 cross-sectional observations on the demand for food, D, real income, Y, and the relative price of food, P:

$$\hat{D} = 52.1 \quad - \quad 35.4P \quad + \quad 0.643Y \qquad R^2 = 0.347;$$
$$\phantom{\hat{D} = }(12.3) \qquad (7.43) \qquad\;\; (1.92)$$

$$\hat{D} = 58.3 \quad - \quad 28.4P \qquad\qquad\qquad\quad R^2 = 0.325.$$
$$\phantom{\hat{D} = }(11.6) \qquad (5.67)$$

(t-ratios are in parentheses.)

(a) When Y is dropped from the equation, the coefficient on P becomes less negative. Why should this be so?

(b) Perform two tests of the hypothesis that $\beta_3 = 0$. Can you deduce how the two tests are related? Will the two tests always give the same result?

Summary

- The **OLS estimation procedure** can be extended to equations **with two or more explanatory X variables**. But, in such cases, hand computation is more lengthy and we therefore usually resort to **regression software**.

- In the **classical multiple regression model**, the two-variable assumptions are extended to the case of two or more **non-stochastic** explanatory variables. Also, **no linear relationships are permitted** between **sample values** of the X variables.

- Adding variables to a simple two-variable regression **almost always results in changes in the values of the estimated coefficients attached to explanatory variables**.

- Under classical assumptions, in multiple regression **inference** proceeds, as in simple regression, via the **t distribution**. The notion of a **coefficient of determination** can be extended to the multiple regression case.

- When **perfect multicollinearity** between explanatory variables exists, all estimation methods, including OLS, **break down**. When an **approximate** but not exact **linear relationship** exists between the X variables, OLS estimators are **likely** to have **large standard errors**.

- A high degree of multicollinearity does **not necessarily** lead to large standard errors. Also, large standard errors are **not necessarily** the result of multicollinearity. However, a **high R^2**, combined with **large estimated standard errors**, is a **certain indicator** of multicollinearity.

- Multicollinearity is a problem relating to the **particular sample** you have taken. It therefore **cannot be tested for** in the statistical sense. If multicollinearity is adversely affecting your results, the only solution is **to get more data**.

- **Regression F-tests** are useful for testing the **combined influence** of the X variables in a regression. They are also useful for assessing the effect of **adding or deleting** two or more **collinear X variables** in a regression.

Notes

1. It is standard notation to denote the first explanatory variable by X_2 rather X_1. In fact, it is often convenient to interpret the intercept β_1 as the coefficient on a variable X_1 that always takes the value unity.

2. See, for example, Thomas (1997, pp. 201–2).

3. On the regression printouts, the R-bar-squared value – or adjusted R^2 as it is often called – is one of a series of 'goodness of fit' measures that allow for variations in the number of explanatory variables in an equation. R^2 itself cannot, by definition, fall when extra variables are added to a regression equation and will almost certainly increase, often markedly. R-bar-squared, in contrast, can be used to compare equations with different numbers of X variables. The Akaike information criterion and the Schwarz criterion, also shown on the printouts, are similar measures.

4. Like the OLS estimators, they are more easily expressed in matrix form. See, for example, Thomas (1997, pp. 188–9).

5. See Stewart (1984, pp. 88–95) for a good explanation of this.

6. Effectively, trying to obtain the OLS estimators in these circumstances involves dividing certain quantities by zero.

7. It is the *true* standard errors σ_{β_2} and σ_{β_3} that are larger. But since the *estimated* standard errors s_{β_2} and s_{β_3} which we compute, are unbiased estimators of σ_{β_2} and σ_{β_3}, they too will be larger.

8. However, some of the strange methods used to 'correct' for multicollinearity do something almost as invalid.

9. Sample correlations were defined in Section 6.3.

10. The equation containing the two explanatory variables, E and A, is an unrestricted equation. But, once the restrictions $\beta_2 = 0$ and $\beta_3 = 0$ are imposed the equation becomes simply $S = \beta_1 + \varepsilon$, which, in the jargon, is termed a restricted equation. You will become more familiar with such terminology in future chapters.

14

Models with qualitative effects

Objectives

When you have completed your study of this chapter, you should be able:

1. to construct simple intercept and slope dummy variables to allow for sudden changes in the parameters of a regression equation;

2. to make use of seasonal dummies to allow for seasonal variations when estimating a regression equation from quarterly unadjusted time-series data;

3. to test a regression equation for parameter stability and predictive failure, using the Chow tests;

4. to appreciate the problems that arise when a dependent variable is dichotomous;

5. to understand the procedure for using latent variables in the probit and logit models;

6. to use simple econometric software to estimate a logit model and draw conclusions from it.

Introduction

It is frequently the case in econometrics that variables cannot be adequately measured in precise quantitative terms. It is therefore necessary to introduce *qualitative* factors into the analysis. For example, consider

$$Q_t = \alpha + \beta Y_t + \varepsilon_t \qquad\qquad [14.1]$$

to be estimated from time-series data, where Q is the per-capita demand for beef, in constant pounds sterling, and Y is per-capita disposable income, also in constant pounds sterling. Suppose we suspect that the underlying structure of beef demand may change for several periods because of a serious Creutzfeldt–Jakob disease (CJD) scare. How can we deal with such a qualitative factor?

One simple approach is to define a *dichotomous variable* (i.e., an either–or variable), such that, in period t

$$D_t = 1 \qquad \text{when consumers fear getting CJD,}$$
$$D_t = 0 \qquad \text{when consumers do not fear getting CJD.}$$

In the first section of this chapter we consider how we can integrate such dichotomous *explanatory* variables into the classical regression model.[1]

An alternative way of analysing the effect of fear of CJD on the demand for beef would be to use available *cross-sectional data* on consumers and define another dichotomous variable where, for consumer i,

$$B_i = 1 \qquad \text{when a consumer does not purchase beef,}$$
$$B_i = 0 \qquad \text{when a consumer does purchase beef.}$$

Clearly B_i, would have to be, in some sense, the *dependent variable* in a cross-sectional regression equation. The explanatory variables would be such factors as the number of cows infected with BSE (the bovine form of the disease). Models with dichotomous dependent variables will be considered in Section 14.3.

14.1 Dummy variables

Let us return to the simple demand-for-beef equation [14.1]. For simplicity, we shall abstract from any price effects. We assume that we have monthly data for five consecutive years ($n = 60$), and that for the 12 months of the second year of the sample and the first six months of the third year there is a CJD scarce. Thus

$$D_t = 1 \qquad \text{for } t = 13, \dots , 30,$$
$$D_t = 0 \qquad \text{for all other } t.$$

Suppose we believed that the CJD scare had no influence on the parameter β in [14.1] (that is, it had no influence on the marginal propensity to buy beef), but simply affected the intercept term α. We can allow for such behaviour by specifying the equation

$$Q_t = \alpha + \delta D_t + \beta T_t + \varepsilon_t. \qquad [14.2]$$

When $D_t = 0$, and there is no CJD scare, [14.2] simply reduces to the original [14.1]:

$$Q_t = \alpha + \beta Y_t + \varepsilon_t. \qquad [14.1]$$

In other months, however, when there is a CJD scare, $D_t = 1$ and [14.2] become

$$Q_t = (\alpha + \delta) + \beta Y_t + \varepsilon_t, \qquad [14.3]$$

where we expect $\delta < 0$.

To estimate [14.2] requires the construction of a dichotomous *dummy variable*, D_t taking the value unity when the CJD scare is operating and the value zero when it is not. For the 60 months, values of the variable would thus be: 0, 0, 0, 0, 0, 0, 0, 0, 0, 0, 0, 0, 1, 1, 1, 1, 1, 1, 1, 1, 1, 1, 1, 1, 1, 1, 1, 1, 1, 1, 1, 0, 0, 0, 0, 0, 0, 0, 0, 0, 0, 0, 0, 0, 0, 0, 0, 0, 0, 0, 0, 0, 0, 0, 0, 0, 0, 0, 0, 0. Such values can be entered into a regression programme, included in a multiple regression equation and *treated just like any other normal variable*.

For example, suppose we obtained an estimated version of [14.2] given by

$$\hat{Q}_t = 25 - 12 D_t + 0.02\, Y_t \qquad [14.4]$$

This would imply, setting $D_t = 1$ in [14.4],

$$\hat{Q} = 13 + 0.02\, Y_t \qquad \text{during the CJD scare.} \qquad [14.5]$$

But, setting $D_t = 0$, we obtain

$$\hat{Q}_t = 25 + 0.02\, Y_t \qquad \text{in other months.} \qquad [14.6]$$

The situation is illustrated in Fig. 14.1. It can be seen that, given the present model, the operation of the CJD scare results in a parallel downward shift in the demand-for-beef equation. It implies that the scare led to a fall of £12 per capita in beef purchases in every month that it was operative. This fall of £12 was constant and independent of the level of income Y. To test whether this fall was statistically significantly different from zero in the statistical sense, we would need to examine the t-ratio and p-value on the coefficient D_t in [14.4]. The dichotomous variable D_t is, for obvious reasons, often referred to as an *intercept or additive dummy*.

Notice that we actually need to estimate *just one equation*, [14.4], to assess the effect of the CJD scare. Once [14.4] has been estimated, we obtain [14.5] and [14.6] by substituting the values $D_t = 0$ and $D_t = 1$ into [14.4].

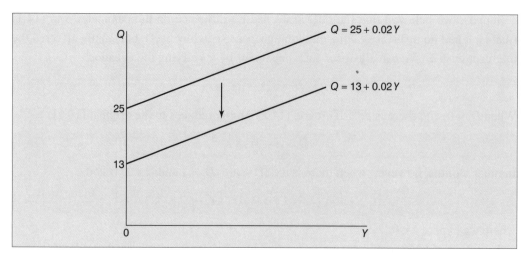

Figure 14.1 Downward shift in the demand-for-beef equation

It is possible that the influence of a CJD scare may be more subtle. For example, it could be argued that it is the marginal propensity to consume beef, β, that is affected by the scare, rather than the intercept, α. We can handle this possibility by specifying

$$Q_t = \alpha + \beta Y_t + \delta Y_t D_t + \varepsilon_t. \qquad [14.7]$$

Given [14.7], when $D_t = 0$ and there is no scare, we again obtain [14.1]:

$$Q_t = \alpha + \beta Y_t + \varepsilon_t. \qquad [14.1]$$

However, this time when $D_t = 1$ in [14.7], and there is a CJD scare, we obtain

$$Q_t = \alpha + (\beta + \delta)Y_t + \varepsilon_t. \qquad [14.8]$$

Assuming δ is again negative and that $\beta + \delta > 0$, the model implies no change in the intercept but a marginal propensity to consume beef falling from β, when there is no scare, to $\beta + \delta$, when there is a scare.

To estimate [14.7] it is necessary to construct the variable $Y_t D_t$, where D_t is the dichotomous variable defined earlier. We must therefore construct $Y_t D_t$ as follows:

$$\text{when } D_t = 1 \quad Y_t D_t = Y_t$$
$$\text{when } D_t = 0 \quad Y_t D_t = 0.$$

Thus, $Y_t D_t$ takes a value equal to income Y_t when there is a CJD scare but a value equal to zero when there is no scare. Such a variable may be included in a regression equation in the normal way. For example, suppose we estimated

$$\hat{Q}_t = 25 + 0.02\, Y_t - 0.01\, Y_t D_t. \qquad [14.9]$$

It follows that, when $D_t = 0$ and there is no scare, the model results in

$$\hat{Q}_t = 25 + 0.02\ Y_t.$$

However when $D_t = 1$, and there is a CJD scare, we obtain from [14.9],

$$\hat{Q}_t = 25 + 0.01\ Y_t. \qquad [14.10]$$

Thus the marginal propensity to consume beef falls from 0.02 to 0.01 when there is a CJD scare. The variable $Y_t D_t$ is often referred to as a *slope or multiplicative dummy*.

As illustrated in Fig. 14.2, it is now the β coefficient rather than the α coefficient that varies according to whether there is a CJD scare or not. Notice, again, that only one equation, namely [14.7], has to be estimated.

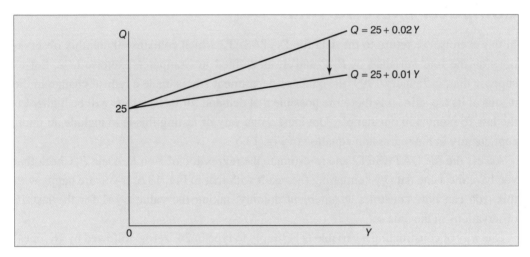

Figure 14.2 A change in the slope of the demand-for-beef equation

The dummy variable technique can easily be generalized for the situation where we have more than one explanatory variable. For example, suppose the demand-for-beef equation was

$$Q_t = \beta_1 + \beta_2 Y_t + \beta_3 P_t + \beta_4 G_t + \varepsilon_t, \qquad [14.11]$$

where P is an index of beef prices and G is a general price index. With an intercept dummy, [14.11] becomes

$$Q_t = \beta_1 + \delta D_t + \beta_2 Y_t + \beta_3 P_t + \beta_4 G_t + \varepsilon_t, \qquad [14.12]$$

where D_t is defined as above.

Similarly, if we wished to assess the effect of a CJD scare on all of the 'slope' parameters we could specify

$$Q_t = \beta_1 + \beta_2 Y_t + \delta_2 D_t Y_t + \beta_3 P_t + \delta_3 D_t P_t + \beta_4 G_t + \delta_4 D_t G_t + \varepsilon_t. \qquad [14.13]$$

If $D_t = 0$, then [14.13] reduces to [14.11], whereas if $D_t = 1$ then we have

$$Q_t = \beta_1 + (\beta_2 + \delta_2) Y_t + (\beta_3 + \delta_3) P_t + (\beta_4 + \delta_4) G + \varepsilon_t.$$

The use of both intercept and multiplicative dummies is widespread in econometrics. They are a most useful extension to normal regression analysis since they often enable us to allow for factors which cannot be measured quantitatively.

Computer Exercise 14.1

In this exercise we return to the data file DATASET2 which contains 40 monthly observations on the four variables S, E, P and A, as defined in Computer Exercise 13.2. Let us suppose that, in January 1999, the chain of department stores made a radical change in the design of its tee-shirt. It is therefore possible that demand for its tee-shirts will be higher for the last 16 months in our sample. Obviously, one way of testing this is to include an intercept dummy in the regression equation of Fig. 13.6.

Access the file DATASET2 and re-estimate the regression of S on E, A and P. Check that you have the same data by comparing the result with that in Fig. 13.6. If you are happy with this, you can now construct an intercept dummy, taking the value $D = 1$ for the last 16 observations in the data set.

One way of constructing a variable D is simply to type in 24 'zeros' followed by 16 'ones' in the appropriate column in the data window but, almost certainly, your regression programme will have a facility for short-cutting this process. Either way, compute the regression of S on D, E, A and P. You should obtain the result shown in Fig. 14.3.

The result in Fig. 14.3 is a little different from that in Fig. 13.6. Firstly, the intercept dummy has a coefficient of 2.22 with a t-ratio as high as 9.53, compared with a critical value of $t_{0.05} = 1.69$. This suggests that the design change has resulted in an increase in tee-shirt sales of £2200 per month during the last 16 months of sample. This increase is independent of the values of E, A and P.

Secondly, while the coefficients on the E and A variables are little changed, that on the relative price variable is now about −6, rather than the −10 in Fig. 13.6. Thus demand appears less sensitive to relative prices than was first thought.

Finally, recall from Computer Exercise 13.2 that collinearity between E and A resulted in relatively high estimated standard errors and low t-ratios for these variables in Fig. 13.6.

```
                      Ordinary Least Squares Estimation
*****************************************************************************
Dependent variable is S
40 observations used for estimation from 1997M1 to 2000M4
*****************************************************************************
Regressor            Coefficient        Standard Error        T-Ratio[Prob]
INTER                    15.8436                3.5937         4.4087[.000]
D                         2.2217                .23322         9.5262[.000]
E                         .23507                .17494         1.3438[.188]
A                         .11879               .071878         1.6526[.107]
P                        -6.2213                2.0837        -2.9857[.005]
*****************************************************************************
R-Squared                   .94157   R-Bar-Squared                   .93490
S.E of Regression           .69795   F-stat.    F(  4,   35)  141.0128[.000]
Mean of Dependent Variable 29.1175   S.D. of Dependent Variable      2.7354
Residual Sum of Squares   17.0497    Equation Log-likelihood       -39.7026
Akaike Info. Criterion   -44.7026    Schwarz Bayesian Criterion    -48.9248
DW-statistic                .85998
*****************************************************************************
```

Figure 14.3 Adding an intercept dummy D

Now notice that, in Fig. 14.3, the t-ratios on E and A are both larger and are now 1.34 and 1.65, respectively. The A coefficient, at least, is now close to being significantly different from zero at the 5% level. The standard errors on both variables have risen, yet the correlation between E and A is, obviously, unchanged. How can this be? To understand this, recall from Chapter 13.3 that the consequences of multicollinearity depend not only on the correlation between explanatory variables, but also on the extent of variation in the values of explanatory variables and on the *overall goodness of fit of a regression equation*. In fact in Fig. 13.6, we have $R^2 = 0.790$, whereas in Fig. 14.3 R^2 is as high as 0.942. It is this improvement in overall fit that has reduced, if not quite eliminated, the consequences of the multicollinearity.

Next, let us see how slope dummies fare when they are introduced into the equation. A slope dummy for spending, E, can be created by keying in $DE = D*E$ in the relevant space. Next create $DP = D*P$ and $DA = D*A$. Check this by examining the data in the relevant window. Including both intercept dummy and the three slope dummies will yield the result shown in Fig. 14.4.

Only one of the slope dummies, DP, has a significant coefficient (t-ratio 2.494). Unfortunately it is large and *positive*, implying that, when $D = 1$, for the last 16 months in the sample, a rise in relative price *increases* demand. This seems improbable and, moreover, in Fig. 14.4 the intercept dummy loses significance. We therefore prefer the result shown in Fig. 14.3.

Setting $D = 1$ in Fig. 14.3 gives the following equation for the last 16 months:

$$\hat{S} = 18.1 + 0.235E + 0.119A - 6.22P.$$

```
                      Ordinary Least Squares Estimation
**********************************************************************************
Dependent variable is S
40 observations used for estimation from 1997M1 to 2000M4
**********************************************************************************
Regressor          Coefficient        Standard Error         T-Ratio[Prob]
INTER                  16.6585               4.0729           4.0901[.000]
D                     -13.6380               8.2045          -2.6623[.106]
E                       .18724                .21855           .85673[.398]
DE                      .13735                .32245           .42595[.673]
A                       .14274               .088672          1.6097[.117]
DA                     -.034467               .13302          -.25912[.797]
P                      -7.3345               2.1937          -3.3435[.002]
DP                     13.4792               5.4053           2.4937[.018]
**********************************************************************************
R-Squared                      .95506   R-Bar-Squared                   .94523
S.E of Regression              .64015   F-stat.    F(  7,  32)    97.1574[.000]
Mean of Dependent Variable  29.1175   S.D. of Dependent Variable      2.7354
Residual Sum of Squares     13.1135   Equation Log-likelihood       -34.4529
Akaike Info. Criterion     -42.4529   Schwarz Bayesian Criterion    -49.2084
DW-statistic                 1.1646
**********************************************************************************
```

Figure 14.4 Adding slope dummies DE, DA and DP

But for the earlier 24 months ($D = 0$) we obtain

$$\hat{S} = 15.8 + 0.235E + 0.119A - 6.22P.$$

Seeing separate equations for the two periods, it may occur to you that we could estimate totally separate equations, for the first 24 months and then for the last 16 months. Do this. That is, regress S on E, A and P (without any dummies!) for each of the periods. Your programme is certain to have a facility for varying your sample period. Results are given in Figs 14.5a and 14.5b.

Can you recognize the connection between the equations in Figs 14.5a and 14.5b and the equation in Fig. 14.4?

Example 14.1

The following production function is estimated for 40 annual observations:

$$\widehat{\ln Q_t} = 0.64 + 0.02\, D_t + 0.34 \ln L_t + 0.03\, D_t \ln L_t + 0.63 K_t,$$

where Q is output and L, K, are labour and capital inputs, respectively. D is a dummy variable reflecting a sudden improvement in labour quality resulting from an intense training programme:

$$D = 1 \quad \text{for years after } t = 19,$$
$$D = 0 \quad \text{for } t = 19 \text{ and before.}$$

Obtain the production functions that hold for the two periods.

```
(a)                         Ordinary Least Squares Estimation
******************************************************************************
Dependent variable is S
24 observations used for estimation from 1997M1 to 1998M12
******************************************************************************
Regressor          Coefficient        Standard Error        T-Ratio[Prob]
INTER                  16.6585                4.3135          3.8620[.001]
E                       .18724                .23146           .80895[.428]
A                       .14274               .093909          1.5200[.144]
P                      -7.3345                2.3232         -3.1570[.005]
******************************************************************************
R-Squared                       .93763   R-Bar-Squared                  .92828
S.E of Regression               .67796   F-stat.    F( 3, 20)  100.2254[.000]
Mean of departent Variable   27.8667     S.D. of Dependent Variable     2.5315
Residual Sum Of Squares         9.1927   Equation Log-likelihood      -22.5387
Akaike info. Criterion       -26.5387    Schwarz Bayesian Criterion   -28.8948
DW-statistic                    .69518
******************************************************************************

(b)                         Ordinary Least Squares Estimation
******************************************************************************
Dependent variable is S
16 observations used for estimation from 1999M1 to 2000M4
******************************************************************************
Regressor          Coefficient        Standard Error        T-Ratio[Prob]
INTER                   3.0205                6.3596          .47496 [.643]
E                       .32458                .21170          1.5332 [.151]
A                       .10827               .088533         1.2229 [.245]
P                       6.1447                4.4112         1.3930 [.189]
******************************************************************************
R-Squared                       .92243   R-Bar-Squared                  .90304
S.E of Regression               .57161   F-stat.    F( 3, 12)   47.5694[.000]
Mean of departent Variable   30.9937     S.D. of Dependent Variable     1.8357
Residual Sum Of Squares         3.9209   Equation Log-likelihood      -11.4528
Akaike info. Criterion       -15.4528    Schwarz Bayesian Criterion   -16.9980
DW-statistic                    2.1465
******************************************************************************
```

Figure 14.5 Separated sample periods

Example 14.2

In the demand-for-beef example at the beginning of this section, it is unlikely that the CJD scare will suddenly just disappear at $t = 31$, as implied by the dummy variable D. How might you redefine the dummy variable to allow for this?

Example 14.3

The following equation is to be estimated from 60 daily observations:

$$Y_t = \beta_0 + \gamma_1 D_{1t} + \gamma_2 D_{2t} + \beta_1 X_t + \varepsilon_t,$$

where

$$D_{1t} = 1 \text{ for } t = 1, 2, 3, \dots, 30, \qquad D_{1t} = 0 \text{ otherwise,}$$

$$D_{2t} = 1 \text{ for } t = 21, 22, \dots, 60, \qquad D_{2t} = 0 \text{ otherwise.}$$

What equation is implied for: (a) $t = 1, \dots, 20$? (b) $t = 21, \dots, 30$? (c) $t = 31, \dots, 60$?

Seasonal dummies

Often more than one dummy variable has to be included in a regression equation. The most frequent reason for this is to allow for seasonal variations when using unadjusted quarterly data. Econometricians normally prefer dealing with raw unadjusted rather than seasonally adjusted data. The reason for this is that it is not always clear what processes have been applied to the data to obtain a seasonally adjusted series. However, with raw data, it is necessary, of course, to allow for any seasonal pattern in the data series, and one of the simplest ways of doing this is to use seasonal dummy variables.

For example, suppose we suspected that the intercept in a demand-for-food equation varied from quarter to quarter (e.g., food demand might be greater in the winter quarter). If Q is the per-capita demand for food, Y is per-capita real disposable income and P is an index of the relative price of food, we might specify

$$Q_t = \alpha + \beta Y_t + \gamma P_t + \delta_1 D_{1t} + \delta_2 D_{2t} + \delta_3 D_{3t} + \varepsilon_t. \qquad [14.14]$$

where

$$D_{1t} = 1 \text{ for spring quarter,} \qquad D_{1t} = 0 \text{ otherwise,}$$
$$D_{2t} = 1 \text{ for summer quarter,} \qquad D_{2t} = 0 \text{ otherwise,}$$
$$D_{3t} = 1 \text{ for autumn quarter,} \qquad D_{3t} = 0 \text{ otherwise.}$$

This implies, for the winter quarter, $D_{1t} = D_{2t} = D_{3t} = 0$, so that [14.14] becomes

$$Q_t = \alpha + \beta Y_t + \gamma P_t + \varepsilon_t \quad \text{(winter quarter).}$$

For the spring quarter, $D_{1t} = 1$ but $D_{2t} = D_{3t} = 0$, so that [14.14] implies

$$Q_t = (\alpha + \delta_1) + \beta Y_t + \gamma P_t + \varepsilon_t \text{ (spring quarter).}$$

Similarly, for the other quarters, we obtain

$$Q_t = (\alpha + \delta_2) + \beta Y_t + \gamma P_t + \varepsilon_t \quad \text{(summer quarter),}$$
$$Q_t = (\alpha + \delta_3) + \beta Y_t + \gamma P_t + \varepsilon_t \quad \text{(autumn quarter).}$$

The statistical importance of the seasonal effects can now be assessed by studying the t-ratios and p-values of the estimates of δ_1, δ_2 and δ_3 in [14.14]. Notice that, *again, we need to estimate just one equation*: this time [14.14]. Equations for each quarter can be obtained by substituting the relevant D values into [14.14].

Notice, also, that *only three seasonal dummies*, D_1, D_2 and D_3 are necessary to capture the full seasonal effects. We do not need to include a fourth seasonal dummy D_4 to allow for the winter quarter. Firstly, we already have separate equations for all four quarters. More importantly, consider what would happen if we included in [14.14] a fourth dummy of the kind

$$D_{4t} = 1 \text{ for winter quarter}, \qquad D_{4t} = 0 \text{ otherwise.}$$

For each observation in our data we would find that the linear relationship

$$D_{1t} + D_{2t} + D_{3t} + D_{4t} = 1$$

held between the four dummy variables. But this is a violation of assumption ID of the classical regression model. As we saw in Chapter 13.3, such perfect multicollinearity between explanatory variables results in a complete breakdown in all estimation procedures. This is sometimes called the 'dummy variable trap'. Fortunately, we do not need a fourth quarterly dummy.[2]

Seasonal variation might, of course, affect parameters other than the intercept. For example, if it were suspected that the marginal propensity to consume food, β, in [14.14] varied seasonally then we could specify

$$Q_t = \alpha + \beta Y_t + \delta_1 Y_t D_{1t} + \delta_2 Y_t D_{2t} + \delta_3 Y_t D_{3t} + \gamma P_t + \varepsilon_t \qquad [14.15]$$

which implies marginal propensities of β, $\beta + \delta_1$, $\beta + \delta_2$ and $\beta + \delta_3$ during the winter, spring, summer and autumn quarters, respectively.

Example 14.4

The following sample regression equation is obtained from quarterly data:

$$\hat{Q} = -0.74 + 3.46Y + 0.69D_1Y + 0.18D_2Y - 0.37D_3Y,$$

where variables are defined as above. Write down the equations obtained, together with the marginal propensities, for each of the four quarters.

Computer Exercise 14.2

Access the data file DATASET3 from the learning centre. This contains UK quarterly data on four variables:

  E = consumer expenditure on drink and tobacco in constant 1995 prices
  E-dash = consumer expenditure on drink on and tobacco in current prices,
  T = total consumer expenditure in constant 1995 prices,

T-dash = total consumer expenditure in current prices.

The data are not 'seasonally adjusted' and are taken from the *Economic Trends Annual Supplement* for 2000 and cover the 60 quarters 1955Q1 to 1969Q4. All series are measured in millions of pounds.

In time-series work it is usually preferable to work with quarterly data (if available) rather than annual data, because of the larger sample implied. For example, for a given span of years from 1961 to 1980, there will be 80 quarterly observations but only 20 annual observations. But we should be a little cautious when increasing the sample size in this way. For example, if a quarterly series has been derived by simply interpolating an annual series then, effectively, we are simply counting each annual observation four times! In practice, most quarterly data are rather more genuine than that and such series usually contain more information than the corresponding annual series. But it is as well to realize that the information content of a quarterly series is, almost certainly, less than four times that of the annual series. Because of this fact, we shall use a 0.01 rather than 0.05 level of significance for inferential work with quarterly data.

The above four data series can be used to obtain the 'implied deflators' of real expenditure on drink and tobacco, *E*, and of real total expenditure, *T*. Create the required variables as

$$P = E\text{-}dash/E, \qquad G = T\text{-}dash/T.$$

P will serve as a price index for drink and tobacco and *G* as a general price index.[3] Go to your data window and check that these series look sensible. Now create a relative price index for drink and tobacco using *REL = P/G*.

The three basic series, which we will be using in this exercise, are *E*, *T* and the relative price index *REL*. Study the time paths of these variables by looking both at the data series and also at plots of the variables against time, using your programme. The time paths are shown in Fig. 14.6.

The time series for drink and tobacco spending, *E*, and total spending, *T*, exhibit clear seasonal patterns. There is a sharp increase, particularly in the *E* series, in the fourth (festive!) quarter, followed by an equally sharp decline in the next. The trend in both these series is consistently upwards. The relative price variable, *REL*, however, behaves rather differently. There is no obviously seasonal pattern and neither is there any clear trend, upward or downward.

We have stressed several times already that it is not difficult to obtain very high values of R^2 when using time series which show strong trends. The apparent strength of such relationships may be at least partly spurious. To illustrate this point, you can create a time trend variable. Such a variable could be obtained by simply keying the values 1, 2, 3, 4, 5, … into any convenient column in the data window. However, your programme will have a facility for doing this for you. Call the variable *TREND*.

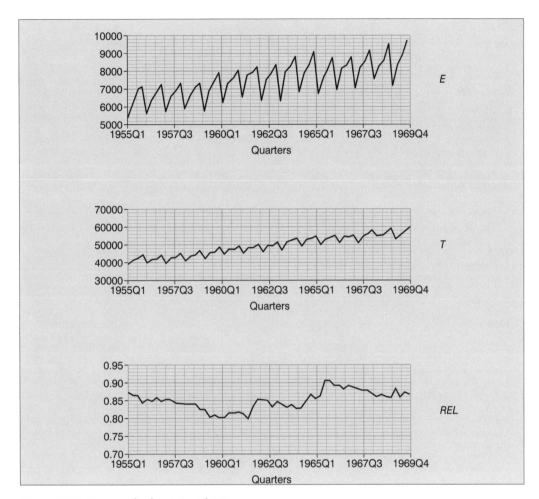

Figure 14.6 Time paths for *E*, *T* and *REL*

Now, use your programme to regress *E* on the trend term, remembering to include an intercept. You should get the result shown in Fig. 14.7a. Clearly over 50% of the variation in *E* can simply be explained by the trend.

But we have not yet allowed for the seasonal pattern. Now create seasonal intercept dummies. Again, your programme should have an easy way of doing this. If you now look in the data window, you will see that four intercept dummies of the kind described below [14.14] have been created. Name these variables *S1*, *S2*, *S3* and *S4*, but avoid the dummy variable trap by including *S1*, *S2* and *S3* only in your estimating equation. You should obtain the result shown in Fig. 14.7b. We are now able to explain as much as 96.7% of the variation in *E* by the time trend and the seasonal dummies. Note, for future reference, that the residual sum of squares for this equation is 2.2×10^6.

```
(a)                    Ordinary Least Squares Estimation
**********************************************************************
Dependent variable is E
60 observations used for estimation from 1955Q1 to 1969Q4
**********************************************************************
Regressor            Coefficient      Standard Error      T-Ratio[Prob]
INTER                     6253.5            182.7331      34.2218[.000]
TREND                    45.2543              5.2100       8.6861[.000]
**********************************************************************
R-Squared                 .56537    R-Bar-Squared                .55788
S.E of Regression       698.8937    F-stat.    F(  1,  58)   75.4482[000]
Mean of Dependent Variable 7633.7   S.D. of Dependent Variable   1051.1
Residual Sum of Squares  2.83E+07   Equation Log-likelihood   -477.0892
Akaike Info. Criterion  -479.0892   Schwarz Bayesian Criterion -481.1835
DW-statistic              2.3767
**********************************************************************


(b)                    Ordinary Least Squares Estimation
**********************************************************************
Dependent variable is E
60 observations used for estimation from 1955Q1 to 1969Q4
**********************************************************************
Regressor            Coefficient      Standard Error      T-Ratio[Prob]
INTER                     7100.9             70.0893     101.3122[.000]
TREND                    42.8531              1.4880      28.7990[.000]
S1                       -1801.3             72.8720     -24.7188[.000]
S2                     -826.3604             72.7960     -11.3517[.000]
S3                     -469.1469             72.7503      -6.4487[.000]
**********************************************************************
R-Squared                 .96652    R-Bar-Squared                .96409
S.E of Regression       199.1933    F-stat.    F(  4,  55)  396.9505[000]
Mean of Dependent Variable 7633.7   S.D. of Dependent Variable   1051.1
Residual Sum of Squares  2182289    Equation Log-likelihood   -400.1825
Akaike Info. Criterion  -405.1825   Schwarz Bayesian Criterion -410.4184
DW-statistic              1.3653
**********************************************************************
```

Figure 14.7 Regression equations containing only trend term and seasonal dummies

When two variables are subject to similar seasonal patterns, they are likely to be highly correlated even if there is no 'economic' relationship between them at all. For example, the number of hours of sunshine in the UK has a strong seasonal pattern and is likely to be inversely related to alcoholic drink and tobacco spending. Thus, just as two time series with similar trends can be spuriously related, so can two time series with similar seasonal patterns. In such situations, it is therefore very easy to obtain high R^2s, such as that in Fig. 14.7b, when any time series are subject to strong trends and seasonal patterns.

What we can do is to use the result in Fig. 14.7b as a standard to assess the true nature of any relationship between E and, for example, total real expenditure T and relative price REL. Firstly, use your programme to regress E on T and REL alone. You should get the result shown in Fig. 14.8a. Here, both the explanatory variables have coefficients that are significantly different from zero with the correct signs. The high R^2 and large t-ratio on T is a consequence of the common trends in E and T. As expected, E rises when total expenditure T rises and falls when relative price REL rises. But only 84% of the variation in E can be explained by variations in T and REL. This compares poorly with the result shown in Fig. 14.7b.

```
(a)                    Ordinary Least Squares Estimation
************************************************************************
Dependent variable is E
60 observations used for estimation from 1955Q1 to 1969Q4
************************************************************************
Regressor          Coefficient       Standard Error       T-Ratio[Prob]
INTER                 4338.7               1832.1          2.3682[.021]
T                     .17284               .010634         16.2530[.000]
REL                  -6218.4               2363.6          -2.6308[.011]
************************************************************************
R-Squared                 .83700    R-Bar-Squared                .83128
S.E of Regression      431.7452      F-stat.   F( 2,  57)  146.3436[.000]
Mean of Dependent Variable  7633.7  S.D. of Dependent Variable   1051.1
Residual Sum of Squares  1.06E+07    Equation Log-likelihood   -477.6676
Akaike Info. Criterion  -450.6676    Schwarz Bayesian Criterion -453.8092
DW-statistic            2.0412
************************************************************************


(b)                    Ordinary Least Squares Estimation
************************************************************************
Dependent variable is E
60 observations used for estimation from 1955Q1 to 1969Q4
************************************************************************
Regressor          Coefficient       Standard Error       T-Ratio[Prob]
INTER                 3738.6               608.8532        6.1403[.000]
T                     .14260               .0038166        37.3631[.000]
REL                  -3195.3               800.8886        -3.9900[.000]
S1                   -1136.3               56.5742         -20.0852[.000]
S2                   -527.7011             53.2479         -9.9103[.000]
S3                   -211.0894             53.1857         -3.9689[.000]
************************************************************************
R-Squared                 .98306    R-Bar-Squared                .98150
S.E of Regression      142.9770      F-stat.   F( 5,  54)  626.9235[000]
Mean of Dependent Variable  7633.7  S.D. of Dependent Variable   1051.1
Residual Sum of Squares  1103891     Equation Log-likelihood   -379.7365
Akaike Info. Criterion  -385.7365    Schwarz Bayesian Criterion -392.0196
DW-statistic            1.9323
************************************************************************
```

Figure 14.8 Regression equations including T and REL

So far, however, we have not allowed for any deterministic seasonal pattern. Adding the seasonal dummies $S1$, $S2$ and $S3$ to the regression will give the result shown in Fig. 14.8b. The dummies have strongly significant negative coefficients which we will interpret shortly. What is of interest is that the residual sum of squares is now only 1.1×10^6, compared with SSR $= 2.2 \times 10^6$ in the purely deterministic Fig. 14.7a. Moreover, despite the presence of the dummies, the 'genuine' explanatory variables, total expenditure, T, and relative price remain significant, with t-ratios of 37.4 and −4.0, respectively.

If you now add the time trend to the equation in Fig. 14.8b, you should find that its coefficient is not significantly different from zero, with a very low t-ratio. It therefore seems that the relationship between E, T and REL, that we have uncovered, is probably genuine and not purely the result of the common trends in the E and T variables. Let us now consider the seasonal aspects of the relationship.

Firstly, if we set $S1 = S2 = S3 = 0$ in the equation of Fig. 14.8b, we obtain an expenditure equation for drink and tobacco, in the fourth quarter, of the form, (figures given to 3 sig. figs),

$$\hat{E} = 3740 + 0.143T - 3200\,REL \qquad \text{(fourth quarter)}$$

To obtain the corresponding equation for the first quarter, we set $S1 = 1$ and $S2 = S3 = 0$. This yields

$$\hat{E} = 2600 + 0.143T - 3200\,REL \qquad \text{(first quarter)}$$

Similarly, for the second and third quarters we obtain

$$\hat{E} = 3210 + 0.143T - 3200\,REL \qquad \text{(second quarter)}$$

and

$$\hat{E} = 3530 + 0.143T - 3200\,REL \qquad \text{(third quarter)}$$

It now can be seen that the linear relationship between E, T and REL shifts up in the fourth quarter, falls back sharply in the following first quarter, before rising again gradually in the second and third quarters.[4] The t-ratios on the dummy variables in Fig. 14.8b indicate that these shifts are statistically significant. They are the effects we would expect, given that the fourth quarter is the Christmas spending period.

Notice that the coefficients on the T and REL variables are very different, with that on T small and that on REL much larger. But this is simply the result of the absolute magnitudes of the values of the two variables.[5] To obtain a proper feel for the effects of changes in the explanatory variables, we can compute total expenditure and relative price elasticities at the point of sample means. The mean values of the variables are in fact

$$\bar{E} = 7634,\ \bar{T} = 49\,660,\ \text{and}\ \overline{REL} = 0.8504.$$

From Fig. 14.8b, we have $\mathrm{d}E/\mathrm{d}T = 0.143$ and $\mathrm{d}E/\mathrm{d}REL = -3200$. Hence, we can now compute the total expenditure elasticity as

$$\eta^{E} = \frac{\mathrm{d}E}{\mathrm{d}T}\frac{\bar{T}}{\bar{E}} = 0.143\,\frac{49\,700}{7630} = 0.931,$$

and the relative price elasticity as

$$\eta^{R} = \frac{-\mathrm{d}E}{\mathrm{d}REL}\left(\frac{\overline{REL}}{\bar{E}}\right) = 3200\,\frac{0.850}{7630} = 0.356.$$

Expenditure on drink and tobacco is therefore rather inelastic with respect to relative prices. The total expenditure elasticity is slightly less than unity, implying that this category of expenditure is, if anything, a necessity rather than a luxury.

You should now experiment with slope dummies. For example, create the variables $TS1 = T*S1$, etc. Try to interpret the results you obtain.

*14.2 **The Chow tests**

In the last section, we saw that it is possible to include intercept and slope dummies in a regression equation. In fact, in Computer Exercise 14.1, we estimated an equation that included both an intercept dummy and slope dummies corresponding to each explanatory variable. In effect, we were estimating *separate equations* for the two periods when $D = 0$ and when $D = 1$. In such a situation, it is natural to want to test whether there is any significant overall difference between the set of true parameter values for the one period and those for the other. The *Chow test for parameter stability* does just that.[6]

For example, suppose we are faced with a regression equation of the kind

$$E(Y) = \beta_1 + \beta_2 X_2 + \beta_3 X_3 + \beta_4 X_4,$$

and suspect a clear switch in parameter values at some point in the sample period. The sample can therefore be divided into two subsamples, one prior to the switch, of size n_1, and one after the switch, of size n_2. The Chow test for parameter stability proceeds as follows.

Firstly, we formulate the null hypothesis of parameter stability,

$$H_0: \beta_j = \text{constant for all } j; \tag{14.16}$$

that is, each β_j remains unchanged over both subperiods.

OLS regressions are now estimated for both subperiods and also for the full or 'pooled' sample, consisting of all $n_1 + n_2$ observations. Suppose the residual sums of squares for the three regressions are $\sum e_1^2$, $\sum e_2^2$ and $\sum e_p^2$, respectively. Now consider the quantity

$$\frac{\sum e_p^2 - (\sum e_1^2 + \sum e_2^2)}{\sum e_1^2 + \sum e_2^2}. \tag{14.17}$$

The numerator in [14.17] measures the change in the sum of the squared residuals (SSR) that occurs when a single regression equation is estimated for the pooled data, rather than allowing the 'greater freedom' of fitting separate regressions for each of the subsamples. Expression [14.17] itself simply measures the *proportionate* change in the SSR, rather than the absolute change, that results from pooling. Under H_0, we would not expect this reduction in freedom to make much difference to the residuals, so that [14.17] is likely to be 'small'. If, however, H_0 is false and the parameters change, then we expect [14.17] to be larger. The situation is illustrated in Figs 14.9a and 14.9b, where we have ignored all variables other than E and T.

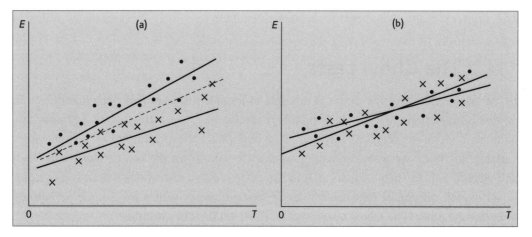

Figure 14.9 The pooling of observations

In each figure, points belonging to the first subsample are shown as dots, whereas points belonging to the second subsample are shown as crosses. Figure 14.9a illustrates the scatter that might be obtained when H_0 is false and the parameters change. The two solid lines show the regression lines for the two subsamples, while the dotted line represents the single regression fitted to all the points, both dots and crosses. Recall that residuals measure the vertical distance between points in a scatter and the relevant sample regression line. For the present situation, it is clear that pooling the data leads to a large increase in the absolute size of the residuals and, hence, in the total residual sum of squares. Thus, in this case, [14.17] is large.

Figure 14.9b illustrates the case where H_0 is true, and the parameters are stable. Now, replacing the two separate regressions by a single line (not shown), fitted to all points, would lead to only a small rise in the residual sum of squares so that, consequently, [14.17] would be small.

The problem, of course, is that we need to know how 'large' [14.17] has to be, before we can safely reject H_0 and maintain that the parameters are unstable. Fortunately, it can be shown that, under H_0,

$$TS = \frac{[\sum e_p^2 - (\sum e_1^2 + \sum e_3^2)]/k}{[\sum e_1^2 + \sum e_2^2]/(n_1 + n_2 - 2k)} \text{ has an } F \text{ distribution with } (k, n_1 + n_2 - 2k) \text{ d.f.} \qquad [14.18]$$

In [14.18], n_1 and n_2 are the sizes of the two subsamples and k is the number of parameters to be estimated.[7]

Notice that [14.18] is a constant multiple of [14.17], the proportionate increase in the sum of the squared residuals. But the advantage of [14.18] is that we can assess the extent to which the SSR has risen by comparing it with critical values taken from standard F tables. We can, in fact, perform this test on the data in the file DATASET2, used in Computer Exercise 14.1.

In Computer Exercise 14.1 we used dummy variables to explore the effect of a change in the parameters of a regression equation. In Figs 14.5a and 14.5b, data from the file DATASET2 were used to split the sample period and compute regressions for the two subsamples, those before and after the change in tee-shirt design. A regression equation for the whole 40 observations was presented in Fig. 13.6.

We now have enough information to compute the above Chow test statistic, the null hypothesis being that of no change in parameter values when the new tee-shirt design is introduced.

From Fig. 13.6, the residual sum of squares for the pooled data is $\sum e_p^2 = 61.3$, whereas, from Figs 14.5a and 14.5b, the residual sums of squares are $\sum e_1^2 = 9.2$ and $\sum e_2^2 = 3.9$ for the first and second subperiods respectively. Notice that there is a large increase in the SSR when the data are pooled, strongly suggesting a clear change in parameter values.

In fact (with $n_1 = 24$, $n_2 = 16$ and $k = 4$), the Chow statistic [14.18] can easily be calculated as 29.4, well above its 0.01 critical F value. Thus this result supports our finding in Computer Exercise 14.1 that the new tee-shirt design has a significant effect.

There are occasions when a sensible division of the data is not feasible because one of the two subperiods is simply too small. This happens whenever, for example, the original n_1 observations are augmented by further n_2 observations, where $n_2 < k$ so that the regression for the second subsample, and hence $\sum e_2^2$, cannot be computed.[8] An alternative procedure is therefore required.

There is a second Chow test in which the null hypothesis is again [14.16]. This time, however, consider the quantity

$$\frac{\sum e_p^2 - \sum e_1^2}{\sum e_1^2}, \qquad [14.19]$$

which measures the proportionate increase in the sum of squared residuals that results from fitting an OLS regression to the whole $n_1 + n_2$ observations rather than just the first n_1. That is, it is the result of adding the extra n_2 observations to the regression. There will be, inevitably, some increase in the SSR but it should be clear that, if the increase is 'sufficiently large', we are likely to reject H_0.

This situation is illustrated in Fig. 14.10, for the case where H_0 is false and the parameters change. The dots again represent the first n_1 observations, that is, the original sample. The solid line represents the regression line for this sample. The crosses indicate the (few) extra observations. Since H_0 is false, and parameter(s) have changed, the crosses lie some way away from the solid line. Consequently, if a dotted line is fitted to all $n_1 + n_2$ observations, there is a 'large' increase in the sum of squared residuals. However, if H_0 were true, then the crosses would lie close to the original solid line and the residuals would be largely unchanged.

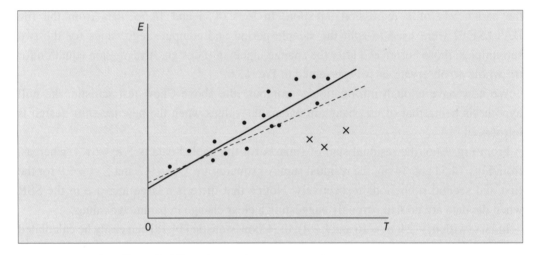

Figure 14.10 The effect of adding observations to a sample

As usual, we have to judge what is meant by 'sufficiently large'. Clearly, there must be some increase in the SSR because of the extra observations, but it can be shown that, if H_0 is true, then

$$TS = \frac{(\Sigma\, e_p^2 - \Sigma\, e_1^2)/n_2}{\Sigma\, e_1^2/(n_1 - k)} \text{ has an } F \text{ distribution with } (n_2, n_1 - k) \text{ d.f.,} \qquad [14.20]$$

where n_1, n_2 and k are defined as for the first Chow test.[9] Notice that the test statistic [14.20] is a simple multiple of [14.19], so we can reject H_0 if TS exceeds the appropriate critical F value.

A problem with the second Chow test is that it is really a test of *predictive failure* rather than parameter stability.[10] That is, it is based on predictions of the dependent variable for the extra n_2 observations, obtained from an equation estimated from the first n_1 observations. The null hypothesis of stable parameters implies that the prediction errors have a zero mean.[11] But zero-mean predictions do not necessarily imply stable parameters. Thus, while rejection of H_0 implies unstable parameters, it is not the case that a failure to reject H_0 implies that the parameters are stable. The failure to reject may simply imply zero-mean predictions.

Note that, although we introduced the second Chow test for the case $n_2 < k$, it is now frequently used for the case where $n_2 > k$ as well. In fact the two Chow tests are often applied together. We shall therefore now carry out the second Chow test using the data file DATASET2, with the same two subperiods.

For our test, the values of n_1, n_2 and k are unchanged. Also, we again have $\sum e_p^2 = 61.3$ and $\sum e_1^2 = 9.2$, but on this occasion we do not require $\sum e_2^2$. The value of the test statistic comes out to 7.1, which also exceeds the relevant critical F value. Thus again we can conclude that the change in tee-shirt design influenced sales.

Notice that the Chow tests have nothing to say about *which* parameter may have changed. If we want information about any particular parameter, we need to resort to dummy variable analysis.

The Chow tests can also be applied to *cross-sectional* data, as the following worked example illustrates.

Worked Example

To test the hypothesis that there is no difference between cross-sectional consumption functions for manual and white-collar workers, the following OLS equations were estimated:

manual workers (sample size = 35)

$$\hat{C} = 120 + 0.90Y, \qquad R^2 = 0.32, \qquad \sum(C - \overline{C})^2 = 3261$$

white-collar workers (sample size = 30)

$$\hat{C} = 160 + 0.82Y, \qquad R^2 = 0.35, \qquad \sum(C - \overline{C})^2 = 4532$$

pooled sample

$$\hat{C} = 250 + 0.70Y, \qquad R^2 = 0.91, \qquad \sum e^2 = 5620$$

What conclusion do you draw, using a 5% level of significance?

Solution

We apply the first Chow test. Our hypotheses are

$$H_0: \beta_j \text{ parameters are the same for both types of worker,}$$
$$H_A: \text{at least one of the } \beta_j \text{ parameters is different.}$$

Under H_0, the test statistic [14.18] has an F distribution with $[k, n_1 + n_2 - 2k]$ d.f. We have $n_1 = 35$, $n_2 = 30$ and $k = 2$, so the test statistic has (2, 61) d.f. Hence, using a 0.05

level of significance, $F_{0.05} = 3.15$. Our decision criterion is therefore

$$\text{reject } H_0 \text{ if } TS > 3.15.$$

Using [13.17], we have SSR $= (1 - R^2)\text{SST}$ or $\sum e^2 = (1 - R^2)\sum(C - \bar{C})^2$. Thus, for manual workers,

$$\sum e_1^2 = 0.68 \times 3261 = 2217.48;$$

for white-collar workers,

$$\sum e_2^2 = 0.65 \times 4532 = 2945.8;$$

and for the pooled sample,

$$\sum e_p^2 = 5620.$$

Substituting into [14.18], we have

$$TS = \frac{[5620 - (2217.48 + 2945.8)]/2}{[2217.48 + 2945.8]/61} = 2.70.$$

Thus we cannot reject H_0 at the 0.05 level of significance but must reserve judgement. We do not have sufficient evidence to say that the parameters differ between the two types of worker.

Example 14.5

Application of OLS to 34 quarterly observations on a firm's aggregate production function yielded

$$\widehat{\ln(Q)} = 0.83 + 0.64 \ln(L) + 0.42 \ln(K), \qquad \sum e^2 = 1.662.$$

Ten fresh observations become available. Application of OLS to the new observations only yields

$$\widehat{\ln(Q)} = 0.43 + 0.71 \ln(L) + 0.36 \ln(K), \qquad \sum e^2 = 0.412.$$

When a single equation is estimated for the 44 pooled observations, the sum of squared residuals for this regression was 2.543. Perform two tests of the stability of parameters in this production function. If the two tests yield different results, explain how this can be.

Example 14.6

In a sample of 25 observations,

$$\Sigma\, C_t = 4560, \qquad \Sigma\, Y_t = 5080,$$
$$\Sigma\, (C_t - \overline{C})^2 = 58\,880, \qquad \Sigma\, (Y_t - \overline{Y})^2 = 64\,650,$$
$$\Sigma(C_t - \overline{C})(Y_t - \overline{Y}) = 54\,180.$$

Use OLS to estimate the consumption function $E(C_t) = \alpha + \beta Y_t$. Hence, estimate the income elasticity of consumption at the point of sample means.

When two additional observations become available, re-estimation of the consumption function, using all observations, results in $R^2 = 0.664$. If all observations yield $\Sigma(C_t - \overline{C})^2 = 63\,990$, test the hypothesis that the two additional observations are generated by the same consumption function that generated the original 25.

**14.3 Dichotomous dependent variables

At the beginning of this chapter, we considered a situation where a consumer might or might not purchase beef during a CJD scare. We defined a dichotomous variable B_i such that

$$B_i = 1 \quad \text{if consumer } i \text{ does not purchase beef,}$$
$$B_i = 0 \quad \text{if consumer } i \text{ does purchase beef.}$$

Whether a consumer purchases beef or not will depend on numerous factors. Some will relate to the CJD scare (e.g., the number of BSE cow deaths in the vicinity), others will be unrelated to the scare (e.g., the consumer's eating habits and income/wealth). For the moment, to simplify matters, let us assume that B_i is a linear function of a single variable X, the number of cow deaths in the statistical region where a consumer lives. That is,

$$B_i = \alpha + \beta X_i + \varepsilon_i, \qquad \text{for all } i = 1, 2, 3, \dots, n, \tag{14.21}$$

where ε is a disturbance and there are n consumers in all. Assuming $E(\varepsilon_i) = 0$, for all i, we therefore have

$$E(B_i) = \alpha + \beta X_i, \qquad \text{for all } i. \tag{14.22}$$

Since B_i can take only one of two values, 0 or 1, its expected value $E(B_i)$ has an unusual interpretation. Recalling the binomial population of Chapter 5.3, suppose $\pi_i = \Pr(B_i = 1)$ so that $\Pr(B_i = 0) = 1 - \pi_i$. Following an identical approach to that in Chapter 5.3, we have

$$E(B_i) = 1.\Pr(B_i = 1) + 0.\Pr(B_i = 0)$$
$$= 1.\pi_i + 0(1 - \pi_i).$$

Hence

$$E(B_i) = \pi_i \quad \text{for all } i. \tag{14.23}$$

Thus, $E(B_i)$ is simply the probability that consumer i refrains from purchasing beef and we can rewrite [14.22] as

$$\pi_i = \alpha + \beta X_i \quad \text{for all } i. \tag{14.24}$$

Equation [14.24] is usually termed the *linear probability model* and can be estimated by regressing B_i on X_i, as suggested by [14.22]. The values of B_i are simply a sequence of 1s and 0s and the variable B is entered in the regression equation just like any other dependent variable. Given estimates of α and β, in [14.24], the model therefore provides estimates of the probability of any given consumer being a beef purchaser.

Worked Example

Consider the estimated linear probability model,

$$\hat{\pi}_i = 0.44 + 0.001\, X_i,$$

where π_i and X_i are defined as above.

Consumer number 7 knows that there have been 69 BSE deaths in his region. There are only 8 BSE deaths in consumer 22's region. For consumers 7 and 22, estimate the probability that (s)he will refrain from purchasing beef.

Solution

For consumer 7, we have $X_7 = 69$. Hence

$$\hat{\pi}_7 = 0.44 + 0.001(69) = 0.509.$$

For consumer 22, we have $X_{22} = 8$. Hence

$$\hat{\pi}_{22} = 0.44 + 0.001(8) = 0.448.$$

Thus there are probabilities of 0.509 and 0.448, respectively, that these consumers will not purchase beef.

Unfortunately, use of the linear probability model raises several problems. Firstly, the disturbance ε in [14.21] cannot be normally distributed. Using [14.21], it must be the case that

$$\begin{aligned} \text{when } B_i = 1, \quad &\text{then} \quad \varepsilon_i = 1 - \alpha - \beta X_i, \\ \text{when } B_i = 0, \quad &\text{then} \quad \varepsilon_i = -\alpha - \beta X_i. \end{aligned}$$

That is, since, for any given consumer, B can take only two values, it must be the case that ε can take only two values. Thus ε cannot be normally distributed as is assumed in the classical model.

More worryingly, the disturbance ε turns out to be heteroscedastic. That is, it does not obey classical assumption IIB, of the previous chapter, that $V(\varepsilon_i)$ should be constant. Since $E(\varepsilon_i) = 0$ for all i, it follows that

$$V(\varepsilon_i) = E(\varepsilon_i^2) = \sum \varepsilon_i^2 P_i,$$

where summation is over the two values of ε given above and the P_i probabilities are π_i and $1 - \pi_i$, respectively. Thus

$$V(\varepsilon_i) = (1 - \alpha - \beta X_i)^2 \pi_i + (-\alpha - \beta X_i)^2 (1 - \pi_i).$$

But [14.24] states that $\pi_i = \alpha + \beta X_i$. Thus

$$\begin{aligned}
V(\varepsilon_i) &= (1 - \pi_i)^2 \pi_i + \pi_i^2 (1 - \pi_i) \\
&= \pi_i (1 - \pi_i).
\end{aligned} \qquad [14.25]$$

This is, in fact, the same result for a binomial population that we obtained in Chapter 5.3.

It is clear from [14.25] that, since the variance of the disturbance depends on π_i, it must vary across consumers. Thus ε must be heteroscedastic. As we shall see in the next chapter, such disturbances have serious consequences for OLS regression analysis. Most seriously, the main inferential procedures become invalid.

But there is an even more fundamental problem with the linear probability model. Suppose we estimated [14.22]/[14.24], by OLS or any other method, obtaining

$$\hat{B}_i = a + b X_i \qquad \text{for all } i, \qquad [14.26]$$

where a and b are the estimates of α and β respectively.[12] Estimates $\hat{B}_i$ of the probability that consumer i will purchase beef should clearly lie between zero and unity. But we compute [14.26] by fitting a line to data on B_i and X_i. Therefore, since the actual B_i take values of either 0 or 1, a scatter diagram of B_i against X_i must look something like Fig. 14.11.

The line [14.26] fitted to the scatter will clearly have a negative intercept, $a < 0$. Thus, for any low X value we will obtain a predicted $\hat{B}_i < 0$. But, of course, probabilities cannot be negative. Moreover, for sufficiently high values of X, we will obtain estimated probabilities that exceed unity.

The recognized method of tackling these problems is to define a continuous *latent variable*, U^*, given by

$$U_i^* = \alpha + \beta X_i + \varepsilon_i \qquad \text{for all } i. \qquad [14.27]$$

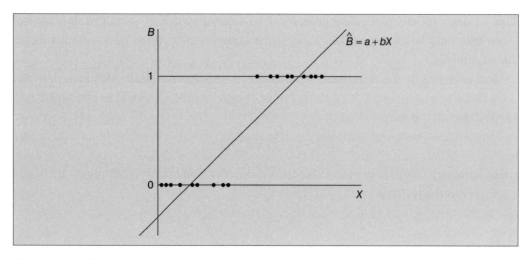

Figure 14.11 Fitting the linear probability model

U^* can be positive or negative and could represent the utility/disutility or 'fear' caused by the level of BSE cases in the neighbourhood. The precise nature of U^* need not be absolutely clear, since it is unobservable. Equation [14.27] replaces [14.21] in the linear probability model, and instead of [14.22] we have

$$E(U_i^*) = \alpha + \beta X_i, \qquad \text{for all } i. \qquad [14.28]$$

The unobservable U_i^* needs to be linked to the observable dichotomous variable B_i. Suppose

$$B_i = 1 \quad \text{if } U_i^* \geqslant 0,$$
$$B_i = 0 \quad \text{if } U_i^* < 0.$$

$U_i^* = 0$ now becomes a threshold value for 'fear'. Whenever $U_i^* \geqslant 0$, a consumer has $B_i = 1$ and does not purchase beef. However, whenever $U_i^* < 0$, a consumer has $B_i = 0$ and does purchase beef.

Unlike in the linear probability model, $\pi_i = \Pr(B_i = 1)$ is no longer given by [14.24]. Instead

$$\begin{aligned}
\pi_i = \Pr(B_i = 1) &= \Pr(U_i^* > 0) \\
&= \Pr(\alpha + \beta X_i + \varepsilon_i > 0) \qquad \text{(using [14.27])} \\
&= \Pr(\varepsilon_i > -[\alpha + \beta X_i]). \qquad\qquad\qquad\quad [14.29]
\end{aligned}$$

Assuming that the distribution of the ε_i is symmetric about zero, it follows that

$$\Pr(\varepsilon_i > -[\alpha + \beta X_i]) = \Pr(\varepsilon_i < \alpha + \beta X_i)$$

so that, using [14.29],

$$\pi_i = \Pr(B_i = 1) = \Pr(\varepsilon_i < \alpha + \beta X_i). \qquad [14.30]$$

The value π_i, (i.e., $E(B_i)$, since the population is binomial) will therefore depend on the shape of the *cumulative* probability distribution for ε_i.[13] As assumed above, the distribution for the ε_i is no longer restricted to being binary, as in the linear probability model, But, to obtain estimates of α and β and hence of the π_i, we have to make some alternative assumption about the shape of the distribution for the disturbances and hence their cumulative distribution.

One possible assumption is that the ε_i have a standard normal distribution and this gives rise to what is referred to as the *probit model*. Another possibility is to represent [14.30] by a cumulative *logistic curve*. This leads to the so-called *logit model*, which we will describe in more detail in the following subsection. Both give rise to a cumulative distribution for the ε_i of the shape indicated in Fig. 14.12.[14]

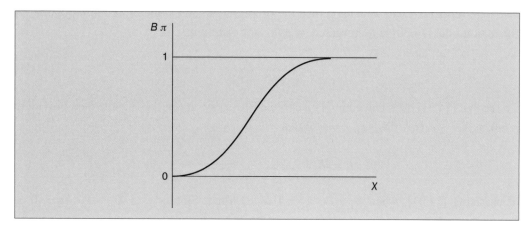

Figure 14.12 A cumulative distribution for E

Notice that both models constrain π_i to lie between zero and unity, as is required. Moreover, as $X_i \to \infty$, $\pi_i \to 1$, and as $X_i \to 0$, $\pi_i \to 0$. Consequently, a curve such as that in Fig. 14.12 is better able to fit the scatter shown in Fig. 14.11 than is the linear probability model. The linear model implies, from [14.24], that

$$\frac{d\pi_i}{dX_i} = \beta = \text{constant},$$

that is, a unit rise in X_i always results in the same rise in the probability, π_i, that consumer i refrains from purchasing beef. But, in practice, we would expect π_i, the probability of not purchasing beef, to increase rapidly at low levels of X_i when the first incidence of cattle disease is felt. At much higher levels of X_i, the value π_i, will rise much more slowly as the maximum value of unity is approached. The relationship between X_i and π_i clearly cannot be linear and is better represented by a curve such as that illustrated in Fig. 14.12.

The estimation of probit and logit models is complicated. Recall that we require estimates of the parameters α and β in equations [14.28] and [14.30], which determine the shape of the curve in Fig. 14.12. We can then use the curve to estimate the value of the probability B_i for any given X_i.

The problem is that actual values of B_i must equal either 0 or 1. That is, a consumer either purchases beef or (s)he does not. A maximum likelihood method has therefore to be used. It can be applied to both probit and logit models, but the method itself is beyond our scope. However, many computer packages have a facility for estimating both models. But, before moving on to a computer exercise, we need to consider the logit model in more detail.

** The logit model

The logit model is easier to handle than the probit model and is therefore more popular. In the logit model [14.30] is represented by a *logistic function*:

$$\pi_i = \frac{1}{1 + \exp[-(\alpha + \beta X_i + \varepsilon_i)]} \qquad \text{for all } i. \qquad [14.31]$$

To see that [14.31] does indeed imply a curve of the shape in Fig. 14.12, note that, providing $\beta > 0$, as $X_i \to \infty$, $(\alpha + \beta X_i + \varepsilon_i) \to \infty$, so that

$$\exp[-(\alpha + \beta X_i + \varepsilon_i)] = \frac{1}{\exp(\alpha + \beta X_i + \varepsilon_i)} \to 0.$$

Thus, using [14.31], when $X_i \to \infty$, $\pi_i \to 1$ as required. Similarly as $X_i \to -\infty$, $\pi_i \to 0$ as required.

Next, it is possible to show that[15]

$$1 - \pi_i = \frac{\exp[-(\alpha + \beta X_i + \varepsilon_i)]}{1 + \exp[-(\alpha + \beta X_i + \varepsilon_i)]}.$$

Hence

$$\frac{\pi_i}{1 - \pi_i} = \frac{1}{\exp[-(\alpha + \beta X_i + \varepsilon_i)]} = \exp[\alpha + \beta X_i + \varepsilon_i].$$

It follows that

$$\ln\left(\frac{\pi_i}{1 - \pi_i}\right) = \alpha + \beta X_i + \varepsilon_i. \qquad [14.32]$$

The quantity $\pi_i/1-\pi_i$ is the ratio of the probability that $B_i = 1$ to the probability that $B_i = 0$. It is therefore referred to as the *odds ratio*. For example, if the probability of consumer i not purchasing beef is $\pi_i = 0.8$, then the odds ratio is $0.8/0.2$ or 4. Thus the odds are 4 to 1 that consumer i does not purchase beef. The natural logarithm of the odds ratio, given by [14.32], is termed the *logit*.

Note that, in the logit model [14.32], π_i is not linearly related to X_i as in the linear probability model [14.24]. This is clear from Fig. 14.12. In fact, it is not difficult to show that

$$\frac{d\pi_i}{dX_i} = \beta\pi_i(1 - \pi_i).$$
[14.33]

Clearly it is possible to generalize [14.32] to the case of more than one explanatory variable. In general

$$\ln\left(\frac{\pi_i}{1 - \pi_i}\right) = \beta_1 + \beta_2 X_{2i} + \beta_3 X_{3i} + \cdots + \beta_k X_{ki} + \varepsilon_i.$$
[14.34]

In this general case, the response of π_i to a unit change in any of the explanatory variables is given by

$$\frac{\partial\pi_i}{\partial X_j} = \beta_j\pi_i(1 - \pi_i) \qquad \text{for all } i \text{ and } j.$$
[14.35]

Equation [14.35] can be used to compute *marginal effects*, $\partial\pi_i/\partial X_j$, for each of the explanatory variables. Notice, from [14.35], that as each π_i rises from 0 to 1, the marginal effects all first rise and then decline to zero.

Goodness-of-fit statistics

In all regression analysis it is necessary to check how well a model fits the sample data. Study of Fig. 14.12 should convince you that the normal coefficient of determination R^2 is as unsuitable a measure of fit for logit and probit models as it is for the linear probability model. There are a number of alternative measures of goodness of fit for logit and probit models, but we will consider just two.

The McFadden *pseudo-R^2* compares a given logit/probit equation with one in which the following restrictions are imposed on [14.34]. The null hypothesis is

$$H_0\colon \beta_2 = \beta_3 = \beta_4 = \cdots = \beta_k = 0,$$

that is, we compare the preferred logit model with one in which the logit is uninfluenced by any of the explanatory X variables. Given H_0, in standard OLS regression the F statistic [13.28] would be used to test the overall fit of an equation. But when maximum likelihood methods are used to estimate logit/probit models the maximized likelihoods for the two equations have to be computed. These can be used to find a value for the psuedo-R^2 which, like the usual coefficient of determination, must lie between zero and unity. Unfortunately, the psuedo-R^2 does not have the useful interpretation in terms of SSR/SST that the normal R^2 has for OLS regression.

Another popular measure is the so-called *count-R^2*. We define a predicted $\hat{B}_i^*$ such that

$$\hat{B}_i^* = 1 \quad \text{if } \hat{B}_i > 0.5,$$
but
$$\hat{B}_i^* = 0 \quad \text{if } \hat{B}_i < 0.5.$$

The count-R^2 is defined as the number of correct predictions (zero or one) divided by the total number of observations. That is, the count-R^2 statistic is simply the proportion of correct prediction. The main problem with the count-R^2 statistic is that it often does not have sufficient discriminatory power to enable us to choose between different models.

Computer Exercise 14.3

In this exercise we estimate a dichotomous dependent variable model relating to whether a householder is an owner-occupier or not. In the data file entitled DATASET4 in the learning centre, you will find a cross-sectional sample containing data on 50 households involving, firstly, the dependent variable

$$B = 1 \quad \text{if the householder is an owner-occupier,}$$
$$B = 0 \quad \text{if the householder rents the house.}$$

The explanatory variables to be considered are:

$$INC = \text{total annual income of the household;}$$
$$AGE = \text{age of the householder;}$$
$$SEX = 1 \quad \text{if the householder is male,}$$
$$SEX = 0 \quad \text{if the householder is female;}$$
$$COHAB = 1 \quad \text{if the householder has a long-term partner,}$$
$$COHAB = 0 \quad \text{if not.}$$

Access the DATASET4 file and study the data series. Notice the dichotomous nature of not only the dependent variable B but also of *SEX* and *COHAB*.

We begin by estimating a linear probability model, that is, a generalization of [14.24] with four explanatory variables. We can do this by simply applying OLS and regressing B on *INC*, *AGE*, *SEX* and *COHAB*. You should obtain the result shown in Fig. 14.13. Notice that all four of the regressors have coefficients with the expected positive sign and three of them have t-ratios in excess of 2. However, the SEX variable has a very low t-ratio and does not appear to influence the dependent variable.

```
                    Ordinary Least Squares Estimation
*******************************************************************************
Dependent variable is B
50 observations used for estimation from    1 to 50
*******************************************************************************
Regressor             Coefficient        Standard Error       T-Ratio[Prob]
INTER                   -.43174               .15117          -2.8560[.006]
INC                     .1266E-4              .3366E-5          3.7618[.000]
AGE                     .012746               .0052165         2.4433[.019]
SEX                     .012599               .098977           .12729[.899]
COHAB                   .22664                .10975           2.0650[.045]
*******************************************************************************
R-Squared                     .66184    R-Bar-Squared                 .63178
S.E of Regression             .30551    F-stat.   F( 4,  45)  22.0178[.000]
Mean of Dependent Variable    .54000    S.D. of Dependent Variable    .50346
Residual Sum of Squares      4.2000     Equation Log-likelihood      -9.0235
Akaike Info. Criterion    -14.0235      Schwarz Bayesian Criterion  -18.8035
DW-statistic               1.6656
*******************************************************************************


                         Diagnostic Tests
*******************************************************************************
*    Test Statistics    *      LM Version       *         F Version         *
*******************************************************************************
*                       *                       *                           *
* A:Serial Correlation* CHSQ( 1)=  1.0246[.311]*F( 1,  44)=   .92050[.343]*
*                       *                       *                           *
* B:Functional Form     * CHSQ( 1)=  7.7595[.005]*F( 1,  44)=  8.0828[.007]*
*                       *                       *                           *
* C:Normality           * CHSQ( 2)=  1.0215[.600]*     Not applicable       *
*                       *                       *                           *
* D:Heteroscedasticity* CHSQ( 1)=   .10729[.743]*F( 1,  48)=   .10322[.749]*
*******************************************************************************
A:Lagrange multiplier test of residual serial correlation
B:Ramsey's RESET test using the square of the fitted values
C:Based on a test of skewness and kurtosis of residuals
D:Based on the regression of squared residuals on squared fitted values
```

Figure 14.13 OLS estimation of error probability model

The equation in Fig. 14.13 can be used to predict probabilities for households with any values for *INC*, *AGE*, *SEX* and *COHAB*. For example, a household of income £25 000 per annum, whose head is aged 36 and who is male with a long-term partner is predicted to have a probability of being an owner-occupier of

$$\hat{B} = -0.432 + 0.000\ 012\ 7(25\ 000) + 0.0127(36) + 0.0126(1) + 0.227(1) = 0.582.$$

We outlined the problems with the linear probability model earlier. We can illustrate one of them by considering a household with *INC* = 65 000, *AGE* = 56, *SEX* = 1 and *COHAB* = 1. By substituting these values into the linear equation in Fig. 14.13 you will obtain $\hat{B} = 1.34$. The estimated probability of such a household being an owner-occupier is thus 1.34, which is clearly inadmissible.

Next move to the logit/probit section of your program. Enter in the variables B, *INTER*, *AGE*, *SEX*, *COHAB* and *INC* as before and select the option for a logit model. This should provide the maximum likelihood estimated logit equation shown in Fig. 14.14.

```
                  Logit Maximum Likelihood Estimation
            The estimation method converged after 10 iterations
**********************************************************************************
Dependent variable is B
50 observations used for estimation from    1 to 50
**********************************************************************************
Regressor             Coefficient        Standard Error        T-Ratio[Prob]
INTER                   -.27.6440               .13.3631      -2.0687[.044]
INC                      .5739E-3               .2818E-3        2.0363[.048]
AGE                      .024383                .14177          1.7199[.092]
SEX                     1.6261                  2.1969           .74021[.463]
COHAB                   3.1958                  3.7504          2.1619[.251]
**********************************************************************************
Factor for the calculation of marginal effects = .094252
Maximized value of the log-likelihood function = -4.3142
Akaike Information Criterion = -9.3142
Schwarz Bayesian Criterion = -14.0943
Hannan-Quinn Criterion = -11.1345
Mean of B =    .54000
Mean of fitted B =     .54000
Goodness of fit =      .96000
Pesaran-Timmermann test statistic = .24155[.809]
Pseudo-R-Squared =     .87494
**********************************************************************************
```

Figure 14.14 Estimation of a logit model

The equation in fig 14.14 was computed using Microfit 4 software and the dependent variable is given as B, but it is an equation of the form [14.34] that has been estimated. That is, we have (t-ratios in parentheses)

$$\ln\left(\frac{\widehat{\pi}}{1-\pi}\right) = -27.6 + 0.000\,574\,INC + 0.244\,AGE + 1.63\,SEX + 3.20\,COHAB. \quad [14.36]$$
$$\quad\quad\quad\quad (2.07)\quad (2.04)\quad\quad\quad (1.72)\quad\quad (0.74)\quad\quad (1.16)$$

Notice again that the SEX variable has a low *t*-ratio.

You will find below the main regression result a series of diagnostic and goodness-of-fit statistics. We shall consider just three of these. Firstly, an estimated value of $\pi(1 - \pi)$, termed the 'Factor for the calculation of marginal effects' is quoted. We will return to this later. The 'Goodness of fit' value of 0.96, quoted in Fig. 14.14, is in fact the count-R^2, defined earlier, and indicates that, for 48 out of 50 households, a correct prediction concerning owner-occupation has been made. 'Pseudo-R-Squared' is in fact McFadden's pseudo-R^2, and takes a value of 0.875.

A moment ago, we used the linear probability model to predict the probability of owner-occupation for a household that had $INC = 65\,000$, $AGE = 56$, $SEX = 1$ and $COHAB = 1$. The model gave a predicted probability in excess of unity. We can now use the logit model to predict this probability. Using [14.36] gives

$$\text{Ln } \widehat{(\pi/1-\pi)} = -27.6 + 0.000\,574(65\,000) + 0.244(56) + 1.63(1) + 3.20(1) = 28.2$$

Thus $\widehat{\pi/1-\pi} = e^{28.2} = 1.77 \times 10^{10}$, so $\hat{\pi}$ (or $\hat{B}$) is therefore just a tiny fraction less than unity. The household is therefore almost certain to be an owner-occupier. This contrasts with the infeasible probability yielded by the linear probability model.

You should find that many of the fitted probabilities are very close to either unity or zero. This is a consequence of our having fitted a logistic curve to a scatter such as that of Fig. 14.12. The 'fitted values' are those used to compute the count-R^2 statistic.

There are several variables in [14.36] with t-ratios below 2 and, as in Fig. 14.13, the variable SEX does not seem to be important. Omitting this variable will yield the result in Fig. 14.15. The b_j coefficients are in fact little changed from Fig. 14.14 but the count-R^2 value has actually risen to 0.98 (49 correct predictions out of 50). The pseudo-R^2 has, as expected, fallen slightly.

```
                  Logit Maximum Likelihood Estimation
             The estimation method converged after 10 iterations
*****************************************************************************
Dependent variable is B
50 observations used for estimation from    1 to 50
*****************************************************************************
Regressor          Coefficient          Standard Error         T-Ratio[Prob]
INTER               -.24.0057               10.8007           -2.2226[.031]
AGE                  .20767                 0.12507            1.6604[.104]
COHAB               3.2203                  2.3654             1.3614[.180]
INC                  .5320E-3               .2463E-3           2.1608[.036]
*****************************************************************************
Factor for the calculation of marginal effects = .098962
Maximized value of the log-likelihood function = - 4.6288
Akaike Information Criterion = -8.6288
Schwarz Bayesian Criterion = -12.4528
Hannan-Quinn Criterion = -10.0850
Mean of B =   .54000
Mean of fitted B =   .52000
Goodness of fit =   .98000
Pesaran-Timmermann test statistic = .26391[.792]
Pseudo-R-Squared =   .86582
*****************************************************************************
```

Figure 14.15 Omitting the *SEX* variable

We can use the result in Fig. 14.15 to calculate marginal effects, that is, to estimate how sensitive the probability of owner-occupation, π, is to *INC*, *AGE* and *COHAB*.

To do this we need an estimated value for $\pi(1 - \pi)$ that we can substitute into the right-hand side of [14.35]. The obvious way to find such a value is to take the predicted value of π, obtained when the explanatory variables *INC*, *AGE* and *COHAB* take their sample mean values. These are in fact $\overline{INC} = 32\,630$, $\overline{AGE} = 34.3$, $\overline{COHAB} = 0.5$. Substitution of these values into the result in Fig. 14.15, gives $\ln(\widehat{\pi/1 - \pi}) = 2.08$ and hence $\hat{\pi} = 0.889$. It follows that $\hat{\pi}(1 - \hat{\pi}) = 0.099$, and this is what we can substitute into [14.35]. This is the value 0.099 (to two sig. figs) that appears immediately below the logit regression in Fig. 14.15 as the 'Factor for the calculation of marginal effects'. We can now calculate these marginal effects.

For income, the marginal effect is $0.000\,532 \times 0.099$ or $0.000\,052\,7$. Thus a rise in income of £1000 leads to the probability of owner-occupation π rising by about 0.053. For age, the marginal effect is $0.208 \times 0.099 = 0.021$. Thus an increase of 10 years in age results in π rising by about 0.21. Finally, a switch in the *COHAB* variable from 0 to 1 leads to a rise in π of 3.22×0.099 or 0.32. Thus if a householder acquires a long-term partner then there is a sharp rise in the probability of owner-occupation.

As noted above, the probit model is more difficult to handle than the logit model. While [14.30] holds for both models, there is no simple equivalent version of [14.33] for the probit model.[16] However, it is possible, again, to obtain maximum likelihood estimates of coefficients in a probit equation using most good regression software. If you can obtain such a probit equation, then you will find that the fitted values obtained are very similar to those of the logit model.

Summary

- **Dummy variables** can be introduced into regression equations to allow for **qualitative factors**. Both **intercept dummies** and **slope dummies** can be used to allow for variations in the magnitude of regression parameters.

- Econometricians prefer to use **non-adjusted** quarterly data rather than **seasonally adjusted** data. **Seasonal dummies** are then used to allow for quarterly **seasonal variations**.

- The **Chow tests** can be used to test for any overall **variation in regression parameters** over different time periods or cross-sectional samples.

- **Dependent variables** can also be **dichotomous**. Such a regression model is referred to as the **linear probability model**, but there are several problems with this model.

- Firstly, the **disturbances** cannot be **normally distributed**. They must also be **heteroscedastic**. Moreover, the model can yield **predicted probabilities** outside the range of **zero to unity**.

- These problems are normally tackled by introducing an unobservable **latent variable**. This leads to the **logit model** and/or the **probit model**.

- In the probit model, the disturbances are assumed to be **normally distributed**. In the logit model the cumulative **logistic curve** is used instead.

- R^2 is a **poor measure of goodness of fit**, when the dependent variable is dichotomous. Better measures are the **pseudo-R^2** and the **count-R^2**.

Notes

1. Such dichotomous explanatory variables can, of course, also be used in cross-sectional data.

2. However, if the intercept α in [14.15] is suppressed, then all four quarterly dummies need to be included. The estimated seasonal effects will then be identical to those of [14.15].

3. Recall that the real wage rate is obtained by deflating the nominal wage rate by a general price index. In a similar way, real total expenditure E is obtained by deflating nominal total expenditure E-dash by a price index G. That is $E = E\text{-}dash/G$. Similarly, $T = T\text{-}dash/P$.

4. Study of the four quarterly equations reveals that, for given values of T and REL, expenditure E falls by £1140 million in the first quarter but then rises by 610, 320 and 210 in the succeeding quarters.

5. For example, if we multiplied REL by 100, so that in 1995 the relative price index would equal 100, the coefficient on the REL variable would become only $-3200/100 = -3.2$.

6. See Chow (1960).

7. If you have problems remembering the degrees of freedom for this test, they can easily be deduced. Since $\sum e_1^2$ and $\sum e_2^2$ have $n_1 - k$ and $n_2 - k$ d.f., respectively, $\sum e_1^2 + \sum e_2^2$ must have $n_1 + n_2 - 2k$ d.f. Thus the degrees of freedom in the denominator must be $n_1 + n_2 - 2k$. However, the pooled sample has $n_1 + n_2$ observations so that $\sum e_p^2$ has $n_1 + n_2 - k$ d.f. It follows that $\sum e_p^2 - (\sum e_1^2 + \sum e_2^2)$ has $n_1 + n_2 - k - (n_1 + n_2 - 2k) = k$ d.f. Thus the degrees of freedom in the numerator must be k.

8. In Chapter 9, we saw that in two-variable regression we required $n > 2$ if OLS estimation is to be feasible. Similarly, in multiple regression we require $n > k$.

9. The degrees of freedom for this test are also easy to remember. Recall from note 7 that $\sum e_p^2$ has $n_1 + n_2 - k$ d.f., whereas $\sum e_1^2$ has $n_1 - k$ d.f. Thus the numerator $\sum e_p^2 - \sum e_1^2$ must have $n_1 + n_2 - k - (n_1 - k) = n_2$ d.f. The denominator of course has $n_1 - k$ d.f.

10. See again Chow (1960).

11. That is, $E(Y_0) = \hat{Y}_0$, where Y_0 is the actual value and $\hat{Y}_0$ is the predicted value (see the subsection on 'Making predictions' in Section 12.4).

12. Since [14.22] and [14.24] are equivalent, an equally valid notation would be to replace $\hat{B}_i$ in [14.26] with $\hat{\pi}_i$. $\hat{B}_i$ and $\hat{\pi}_i$ are therefore interchangeable.

13. Cumulative distributions were discussed in the prerequisites chapter.

14. The logistic distribution has, in fact, slightly 'fatter' tails than the standard normal distribution.

15. If we let $k = \alpha + \beta X_i + \varepsilon_i$, then

$$\pi_i = \frac{1}{1 + \exp(-k)}.$$

Thus

$$1 - \pi_i = 1 - \frac{1}{1 + \exp(-k)} = \frac{1 + \exp(-k) - 1}{1 + \exp(-k)} = \frac{\exp(-k)}{1 + \exp(-k)}.$$

16. That is, not without employing the integral sign.

15

Some problems with the classical model

Objectives

When you have completed your study of this chapter, you should be able:

1. to appreciate that, when explanatory X variables are stochastic, OLS will yield biased and inconsistent estimators if the disturbance of a regression equation is correlated with any of its respective X variables;

2. to realize that such correlations can arise because of errors of measurement in the values of X variables and/or because of the simultaneous nature of many economic relationships;

3. to use simple econometric software to obtain general instrumental variable estimators when it is suspected that disturbances and explanatory variables are correlated;

4. to understand the problem of heteroscedasticity, test for its presence and apply simple corrective procedures when the problem is believed to be present;

5. to understand the problem of autocorrelation, and test for the presence of auto-correlation in the residuals from a sample regression equation;

6. to realize that statistically significant autocorrelation statistics may signify not auto-correlation in the disturbances but a misspecified regression equation.

Introduction

In this chapter we examine the consequences of breakdowns in the assumptions of the classical regression model. In addition, we consider what can be done if any of these assumptions become invalid.

The assumptions in the classical model that students normally find most implausible are those relating to the explanatory X variables. Clearly, it is difficult to accept the idea of some independent investigator holding fixed the values of all X variables, over many samples. In fact, in almost all situations, the explanatory variables are *stochastic*, rather than non-stochastic as assumed in Chapters 12–14. That is, they are outside the control of any hypothetical investigator. In this chapter therefore we consider, first, the consequences of relaxing the assumption of non-stochastic explanatory variables and, second, what alternative estimation procedures are available.

Later, we shall see that the classical assumptions regarding the disturbances are also invalid in many circumstances. In particular, disturbances may be heteroscedastic or they may be autocorrelated. We outline methods of detecting these problems and suggest some alternative procedures. Finally, we consider a problem the effects of which can be confused with those of autocorrelated disturbance: that of a misspecified regression equation.

15.1 **Stochastic explanatory variables**

If the explanatory X variables in a regression equation are stochastic, then it turns out that what matters is the relationship (if any) between these variables and the disturbance in the equation.

Firstly, we take the case of a single stochastic X variable, so that we can work with a simple two-dimensional diagram. The population regression equation is then

$$E(Y) = \alpha + \beta X \qquad [15.1]$$

and, given a disturbance ε, we have

$$Y = \alpha + \beta X + \varepsilon. \qquad [15.2]$$

Equation [15.1] is shown as the broken line in Fig. 15.1.

Now let us assume that $\text{Cov}(X, \varepsilon) > 0$, so that there is a positive correlation between X and ε. As we shall see later in this section, there are good reasons why such a correlation might occur. Recall that the disturbance ε represents the distance of any point in a scatter from the population regression line in Fig. 15.1. If the correlation between ε and X is positive, this implies that 'high' values of X tend to coincide with 'high' values of ε. Since $E(\varepsilon) = 0$, high

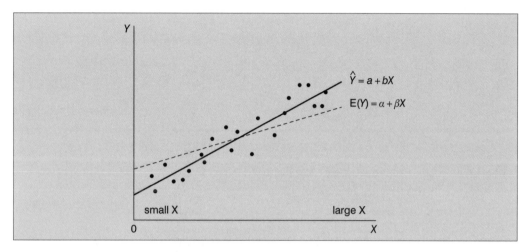

Figure 15.1 A positive correlation between X and E

values of ε imply positive values of ε, that is, points in the scatter above the population regression line. Hence, when X values are high or large, we tend to get points above the line, as illustrated in Fig. 15.1.

Similarly, given $\text{Cov}(X, \varepsilon) > 0$, whenever X is 'low', then the disturbance ε tends to take a 'low' value. This means that ε is likely to be less than its mean of zero and hence negative, the relevant point lying below the regression line. Thus low or small X values usually result in points below the line. Such points are also illustrated in Fig. 15.1.

Recall that the population regression line remains unknown; all a research worker ever observes are the points in the scatter. But we use the *points* to estimate a line that we cannot see. Obviously, if we use OLS to fit a line to a scatter such as that in Fig. 15.1, we will almost certainly obtain a *sample* regression line, $\hat{Y} = a + bX$ (illustrated as a solid line), with a slope that is too large and an intercept that is too small. In other words the OLS estimator is *biased upwards*, that is, $\text{E}(b) > \beta$. Similarly the OLS estimator a is *biased downwards*, that is $\text{E}(a) < \alpha$.

Notice that an increase in sample size will not solve this problem. More sample observations will simply lead to more points above the regression line, when X takes a large value, and more points below the line, when X is small. The bias in the OLS estimators will persist however large we make the sample size. Thus a and b are not only biased but also *inconsistent* estimators of the true parameters α and β.

Similar problems occur when $\text{Cov}(X, \varepsilon) < 0$, so that the correlation between X and ε is negative. This situation is illustrated in Fig. 15.2. Now it can be seen that OLS estimation leads to a downward bias in b and an upward bias in a. That is, $\text{E}(b) < \beta$ and $\text{E}(a) > \alpha$.

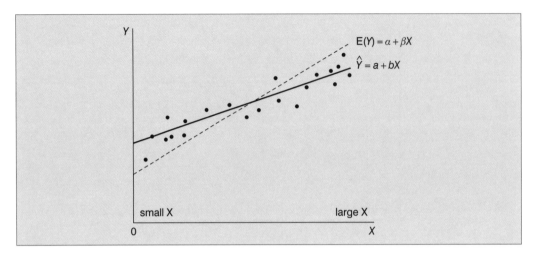

Figure 15.2 A negative correlation between X and E

Figures 15.1 and 15.2 demonstrate that a non-zero correlation between X and ε is certain to lead to bias and inconsistency in the OLS estimators. When the explanatory variable is stochastic, it is intuitively obvious that a lack of correlation between X and ε is going to improve the properties of the OLS estimators. However, it turns out that, only if X and ε are not merely uncorrelated but also *independent* of each other, will OLS yield both unbiased and consistent estimators.[1] Figures 15.1 and 15.2 refer to a situation where X and ε are correlated and therefore cannot be independent. In fact, in such a situation, OLS estimators turn out to be both biased and inconsistent.[2]

Stochastic explanatory variables cause similar problems in multiple regression. If the OLS estimators are to retain the properties of unbiasedness and consistency then it is necessary that *each* stochastic explanatory variable be *independent* of the disturbance. Clearly, this is a very big 'if' and there are many circumstances in which OLS may not be an appropriate estimating procedure.

In the next two subsections, we consider situations in which correlations between explanatory variables and disturbances are very likely.

Errors of measurement

It is rare for economists to be faced with perfectly accurate data and, moreover, theoretical economic concepts often do not quite match empirical quantities. So-called *errors of measurement* are one reason why correlations, of the kind described in Figs 15.1 and 15.2, occur.

Consider the population relationship

$$Y_i = \alpha + \beta X_i + \varepsilon_i \qquad \text{(for all } i\text{)}. \qquad [15.3]$$

Suppose that [15.3] holds for the 'true' values of X and Y and that ε is *classical disturbance*, that is, it obeys all the assumptions of the classical models. However, suppose further that, instead of observing the true values of X and Y, we observe, for all i, X^* and Y^*, where

$$X_i^* = X_I + v_i \quad \text{and} \quad Y_i^* = Y_i + w_i.$$ [15.4]

The v_i and w_i are the errors made in the measurement of X and Y.

Suppose we have to estimate α and β in [15.3], using X^* and Y^* rather than the true X and Y. Using [15.4] and substituting into [15.3], the regression equation becomes

$$Y_i^* = \alpha + \beta X_i^* + (\varepsilon_i + w_i - \beta v_i).$$ [15.5]

Without data on X and Y we are forced to estimate [15.5], using X^* and Y^*, whether we know it or not. Equation [15.5] has the 'composite' disturbance

$$\varepsilon_i^* = \varepsilon_i + w_i - \beta v_i.$$ [15.6]

But we know that the explanatory variable in [15.5] is

$$X_i^* = X_i + v_i.$$

Thus both explanatory variable X^* and disturbance ε^* in [15.5] are dependent on v_i. For example, if $\beta > 0$ then, when v_i rises, we can expect ε_i^* to fall and X_i^* to rise. That is, we expect ε_i^* and X_i^* to be negatively correlated. In fact, if the errors v and w follow classical assumptions, then it is not difficult to show that X^* and ε^* are correlated with $\text{Cov}(X^*, \varepsilon^*) = -\beta \sigma_v^2$, where σ_v^2 is the variance of the v error.[3] We know that such a non-zero correlation leads to biases in the OLS estimators of α and β.

The correlation between X^* and ε^* obviously depends on the sign of β, the slope parameter in the original equation [15.3]. If $\beta > 0$, then the correlation is negative and the situation is as illustrated in Fig. 15.2, whereas if $\beta < 0$ then the correlation is positive, as illustrated in Fig. 15.1.

Notice that it is the error in the measurement of X that leads to bias. If there are no errors in measuring X, that is, if $v_i = 0 = $ constant, so that $\sigma_v^2 = 0$, $\text{Cov}(X^*, \varepsilon^*)$ must be zero and there is no bias. Hence, errors in the measurement of Y alone do not lead to bias. Clearly, however, measurement errors in X are a problem that cannot be dealt with by using OLS.

**Identification and simultaneous equation bias

It is rare for an economic relationship to exist in isolation from other relationships. More usually, an equation is but a single relationship in a system containing at least one other such relationship. In this subsection we consider the extent to which a set of simultaneous equations, in which a particular equation is embedded, affects the manner in which we attempt to estimate that equation.

As an example, suppose we wish to estimate the 'demand equation' for a typical non-durable good, which we might write as

$$Q = a_0 + a_1 P + a_2 Y + u, \qquad [15.7]$$

where Q is the quantity demanded of the good, P is its relative price and Y is an index of the real income of purchasers. u is a classical disturbance, as defined in Chapter 12 and 13.

Suppose, further, we were fortunate to have weekly data available on Q and P for a period of many weeks, in which real income Y happened to be constant. Thus [15.7] becomes, for this period,

$$Q = a_0^* + a_1 P + u \qquad (a_0^* = a_0 + a_2 Y = \text{const.}). \qquad [15.8]$$

It might be tempting, now, to apply simple OLS to [15.8] and claim that we had estimated, under the *ceteris paribus* assumption of constant real income, a 'demand curve' of the kind found in elementary economics textbooks.

However, we might then wonder, given that we estimated a demand curve in the above way, how we would estimate a supply curve. After all, a supply curve is also a relationship drawn up between quantity Q and price P, under the *ceteris paribus* assumption that all other relevant variables are held constant. Suppose the supply equation is, in fact

$$Q = \beta_0 + \beta_1 P + \beta_2 C + v, \qquad [15.9]$$

where C is an index of supply costs and v is another classical disturbance. To simplify matters, we assume the market for the good always clears, so that we can use the same symbol Q for both demand and supply.

If C happened (fortunately) to be constant, during the period we collect data, [15.9] would become, for this period,

$$Q = \beta_0^* + \beta_1 P + v \qquad (\beta_0^* = \beta_0 + \beta_2 C). \qquad [15.10]$$

Notice that the statistical forms of equations [15.8] and [15.10] are identical. They both express Q as a linear function of P plus a disturbance.

The original equations [15.7] and [15.9] form a *simultaneous system* of two equations. Often economic systems involve many more such equations, but we will keep life simple! Equations [15.7] and [15.9] represent the so-called *structural form* of the system or model and are termed *structural equations*. Our two-equation model, comprised of [15.7] and [15.9], is designed to determine the values of Q and P *for given values of Y and C*. Q and P are referred to as *endogenous* variables. That is, they are variables that are determined by or within the model. Y and C, however, are *exogenous* variables, which implies that they are determined outside the model or system. The division of variables into endogenous and exogenous variables is very common in econometrics and it is important to grasp its significance.[4]

Suppose, for the sake of argument, that, during the time we observe Q and P, the two variables Y and C actually do remain constant, so that the structural equations [15.7] and [15.9] reduce to [15.8] and [15.10]. Moving even further from reality, suppose just for the moment that, during the weeks in which we collect data, the disturbances u and v are always identically equal to zero. In such circumstances, all we could ever observe would be a single pair of values for P and Q, those of the intersection point of the unobserved but stationary curves $Q = \alpha_0^* + \alpha_1 P$ and $Q = \beta_0^* + \beta_1 P$. This is illustrated in Fig. 15.3. No 'scatter' of points could be obtained because, for example, a sample of size n weeks would consist of n identical values of P and n identical values of Q. That is, the same point would be observed each

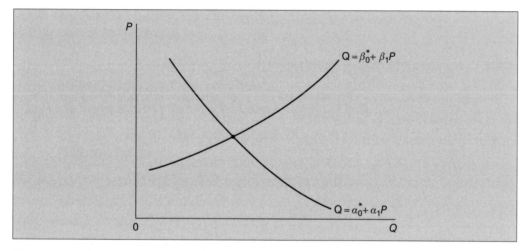

Figure 15.3 The intersection of stationary demand and supply curves

week.[5]

We must now start to relax the powerful assumptions that we made above. Firstly, even if the disturbances were non-zero, and varied from week to week, all we would observe in any particular week (for given u and given v) is the point of intersection of two curves. Any scatter of points over a sample of weeks would merely be a sequence of such intersection points, generated by shifting demand and supply curves.[6] This situation is illustrated in Fig. 15.4, where D_i and S_i denote the demand and supply curves for week i.

Clearly, if we attempted to fit a regression line to such a scatter, by OLS or any other method, we can hardly expect the regression coefficients obtained to be sensible estimators of either α_0^* and α_1 in the demand equation [15.8], or β_0^* and β_1 in the supply equation [15.10]. We will have estimated a 'mongrel' equation, which is some unspecified combination of both demand and supply curves.

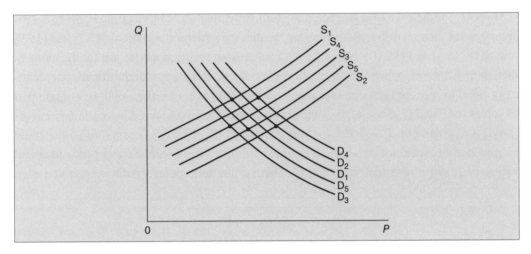

Figure 15.4 Shifting demand and supply curves

To make this clear, let us suppose that λ and μ are any two constants. Then multiplying [15.8] by λ, multiplying [15.10] throughout by μ, and then adding, yields, after dividing by $\lambda + \mu$,

$$Q = \left(\frac{\lambda a_0^* + \mu \beta_0^*}{\lambda + \mu} \right) + \left(\frac{\lambda a_1 + \mu \beta_1}{\lambda + \mu} \right) P + \frac{\lambda u + \mu v}{\lambda + \mu}, \qquad [15.11]$$

where the terms in parentheses are constants.

If [15.8] and [15.10] are valid equations then, under present assumptions, [15.11] must be equally valid. But [15.11] *has exactly the same statistical form as [15.8] and [15.10]*, simply expressing Q as a linear function of P plus a disturbance, which is a function of the original u and v. Equation [15.11] is, in fact, a weighted average of [15.8] and [15.10], and is the equation that we referred to above as a mongrel equation. Since λ and μ can be any constants, under present conditions the model generates an infinite number of such mongrel equations, all of the same statistical form as [15.8] or [15.10]. Clearly, if we regressed Q on P, using OLS *or any other method of estimation*, we would have no idea whether we were estimating the demand curve, the supply curve, or any of the infinite number of equations of the form of [15.11].

The problem we have just encountered is a simple version of what is known as the *identification problem*. We are unable to identify which equation we are estimating.

It is fairly easy to see that identification of either curve can only be achieved provided it remains stationary over time while, week by week, the other curve shifts about in the (P, Q) plane. For example, if the supply curve shifts but the demand curve remains stationary, then we would obtain a situation like that illustrated in Fig. 15.5. The intersections obtained now trace out the demand curve. The demand equation is now said to be *identified*.

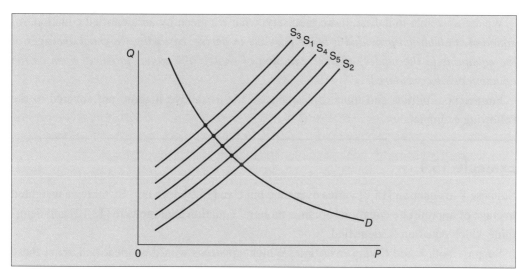

Figure 15.5 Shifting supply curve but stationary demand curve

There are two reasons why the supply curve might shift around. Firstly, the disturbance v might vary strongly over time. For example, v might vary because of fluctuations in the weather. Secondly, if the cost variable C were to vary over time instead of remaining unchanged, then this would again cause shifts in the supply curve.[7] In each case, it would be the demand curve that would be traced out and hence identified.

Of course, we could face the reverse situation. If it were the demand curve that shifts, either because of large variations in v, or because of changes in Y over time, then it would be the supply curve that would be observed and identified.

Let us look at these possibilities algebraically. Suppose, firstly, that it is the cost variable C that varies, while the income variable Y remains unchanged. Our model now consists of equations [15.8] and [15.9]. Taking a weighted average of these equations, in the same manner as above, yields

$$Q = \left(\frac{\lambda\alpha_0^* + \mu\beta_0}{\lambda + \mu}\right) + \left(\frac{\lambda\alpha_1 + \mu\beta_1}{\lambda + \mu}\right)P + \left(\frac{\mu\beta_2}{\lambda + \mu}\right)C + \frac{\lambda u + \mu v}{\lambda + \mu}. \qquad [15.12]$$

It should be clear that there is no way in which the demand equation [15.8] can be confused with the mongrel equation [15.12] because, like the supply equation [15.9], the mongrel equation contains the variable C, whereas the demand equation does not. In this situation the demand equation [15.8] is said to be identified. This is the algebraic equivalent of Fig. 15.5. In contrast, the supply equation [15.9] *can* be confused with the mongrel equation, because it contains both P and C. It is therefore said to be *unidentified*. Notice that it is the appearance of C in the *supply* equation that serves to identify the *demand* equation.

We are now able to define, more precisely, what we mean by an identified equation. *An equation is identified provided it is* not *possible to derive, by taking weighted averages of the equations in the model, another equation of exactly the same statistical form as the equation being considered.*

Further possibilities and their consequences, for the above market, are covered in the following example.

Example 15.1

Suppose Y in equation [15.7] varies over time but C in [15.9] does not. By taking a weighted average of appropriate equations obtain a mongrel equation analogous to [15.12] and determine which equation is identified.

Suppose both Y and C vary over time. Which equations would be identified under these conditions?

Worked Example

Consider the following two-equation model in which Y_1 and Y_2 are endogenous variables, X_1 and X_2 are exogenous, and u and v are disturbances:

$$Y_1 = a_0 + a_1 Y_2 + a_2 X_1 + a_3 X_2 + u, \tag{1}$$

$$Y_2 = b_0 + b_1 Y_1 + b_3 X_2 + v. \tag{2}$$

Determine which equations (if any) are identified.

Solution

Rearranging the second equation yields

$$Y_1 = \frac{-b_0}{b_1} + \frac{1}{b_1} Y_2 - \frac{b_3}{b_1} X_2 - \frac{v}{b_1}. \tag{3}$$

Any weighted average of [1] and [3] must have the form

$$Y_1 = \gamma_0 + \gamma_1 Y_2 + \gamma_2 X_1 + \gamma_3 X_2 + w, \tag{4}$$

where the γs are functions of the as and the bs, and w is a composite disturbance.

Since [4] has the same statistical form as [1], it follows that [1] is not identified. However, [2] does not include the variable X_1 and hence cannot be confused with either [1] or [4] which do contain X_1. Thus equation [2] is identified.

Example 15.2

In the previous worked example, how would your answer be affected: (a) if $a_3 = 0$ in equation [1]; (b) if $a_2 = 0$ in equation [1]; (c) $b_3 = 0$ in equation [2]?

It should be clear from the above discussion that, if an equation is unidentified, there is *no way in which unbiased or even consistent estimators of its parameters can be obtained.* However, if an equation is identified, then in principle it is possible to obtain consistent estimators of its parameters. Unfortunately, however, *it is not normally possible to obtain consistent estimators by the application of OLS.* Other methods of estimation have to be adopted.

The reason why OLS is not usually applicable, even for identified equations, can be understood by referring back to the demand/supply model of equations [15.7] and [15.9].

$$Q = a_0 + a_1 P + a_2 Y + u \tag{15.7}$$

$$Q = \beta_0 + \beta_1 P + \beta_2 C + v \tag{15.9}$$

From Example 15.1, we know that both demand and supply equations are identified. However, as we shall show in a moment, the endogenous P variable, appearing as an explanatory variable in both [15.7] and [15.9], turns out to be correlated with both the disturbances u and v. Consequently, we find ourselves in a situation akin to those illustrated in Figs 15.1 and 15.2. That is, *the OLS estimators in both equations are biased and inconsistent.*

To see why this is the case, we need to find the *reduced form* of the two-equation system. The reduced form of a model can always be found by expressing the endogenous variables as functions of the exogenous variables alone.[8] In this case we must express the endogenous Q and P (the values of which are determined by the model) in terms of the exogenous Y and C (the values of which are determined outside the model). This is most easily done by equating the right-hand sides of [15.7] and [15.9].

$$a_0 + a_1 P + a_2 Y + u \ = \ \beta_0 + \beta_1 P + \beta_2 C + v.$$

Hence

$$(a_1 - \beta_1)P \ = \ \beta_0 - a_0 + \beta_2 C - a_2 Y + v - u,$$

so that

$$P = \frac{\beta_0 - a_0}{a_1 - \beta_1} + \left(\frac{\beta_2}{a_1 - \beta_1}\right)C - \left(\frac{a_2}{a_1 - \beta_1}\right)Y + \frac{v - u}{a_1 - \beta_1}, \tag{15.13}$$

which is the reduced-form equation for P because it expresses the endogenous P in terms of the exogenous C and Y alone.

To obtain the corresponding equation for Q, we need to use [15.13] to substitute for P in either [15.7] or [15.9]. Substituting into [15.7] yields

$$Q = a_0 + a_1 \left[\frac{\beta_0 - \alpha_0}{\alpha_1 - \beta_1} + \left(\frac{\beta_2}{\alpha_1 - \beta_1} \right) C - \left(\frac{a_2}{\alpha_1 - \beta_1} \right) Y + \frac{v - u}{\alpha_1 - \beta_1} \right] + a_2 Y + u.$$

Finally, simplifying gives

$$Q = \frac{a_1 \beta_0 - a_0 \beta_1}{\alpha_1 - \beta_1} + \left(\frac{a_1 \beta_2}{\alpha_1 - \beta_1} \right) C - \left(\frac{a_2 \beta_1}{\alpha_1 - \beta_1} \right) Y + \frac{a_1 v - \beta_1 u}{\alpha_1 - \beta_1},$$ [15.14]

which is the reduced-form equation for Q, since it expresses Q in terms of the exogenous C and Y alone.

Equations [15.13] and [15.14] constitute the reduced form of the model, as opposed to the structural equations [15.7] and [15.9].

It can now be easily seen, from the reduced-form equations, that Q, and more importantly P, because it appears on the right-hand side of both [15.7] and [15.9], depend on both disturbances u and v. Thus, in [15.7], there is a correlation between P and the disturbance u. Similarly, in [15.9], there is a correlation between P and the disturbance v. In each case the correlations cause bias and inconsistency in the OLS estimators.

The composite disturbance, that from [15.13] influences P, is

$$\left(\frac{1}{\alpha_1 - \beta_1} \right) v - \left(\frac{1}{\alpha_1 - \beta_1} \right) u.$$ [15.15]

Since we have clear *a priori* expectations about the parameters in the structural equations, it is now possible to deduce the directions of the OLS bias. Economic theory leads us to expect that demand will fall and supply will rise as price rises. That is, $\alpha_1 < 0$ and $\beta_1 > 0$. Thus [15.15] implies that, in equation [15.7], P must be positively correlated with u because $-1/(\alpha_1 - \beta_1) > 0$. It follows that the OLS estimator of α_1 in [15.7] (the demand equation) will be biased upwards in a manner similar to that illustrated in Fig. 15.1.

However, when we consider [15.9], the supply equation, it is clear from [15.15] that P is negatively correlated with the disturbance v, because $1/(\alpha_1 - \beta_1) < 0$. Thus the OLS estimator of β_1 in [15.9] will be biased downwards.

The type of bias we have been considering is normally termed *simultaneous equation bias*. It arose because of the simultaneous existence of the relationships [15.7] and [15.9]. Such bias arises frequently with economic data. The structural equations of simultaneous equation systems typically include endogenous variables on their right-hand sides and, as in the above situation, these variables will typically be correlated with the corresponding disturbances.

It should be stressed that the simultaneous equation problem is a separate problem from that of identification, although the two problems are obviously connected. But, *even if an equation is identified, OLS will still not provide unbiased or consistent estimators*. This is because of the problem of simultaneous equation bias.

Example 15.3

Use [15.13] to substitute for P in [15.9], instead of [15.7], to obtain the reduced-form equation for Q. Verify that it is identical to [15.14].

Worked Example

Consider the simple Keynesian model of income determination:

$$C = \alpha + \beta Y + u, \qquad \alpha > 0, \ 0 < \beta < 1, \qquad\qquad [15.16]$$

$$Y = C + A, \qquad\qquad [15.17]$$

where C is consumption, Y is income and A is autonomous expenditure. u is a classical disturbance.

Will an OLS estimator of the marginal propensity to consumer β be biased? If so, what will be the direction of the bias?

Solution

We have a two-equation model which determines the values of the two endogenous variables C and Y. A is an exogenous variable.

It should be clear that the consumption function [15.16] is identified. Any weighted average of [15.16] and [15.17] must contain the variable A. The consumption function, which does not contain A, can be distinguished from any mongrel equation and hence must be identified.

Since [15.16] is identified it is possible in principle to obtain consistent estimators of α and β. But will OLS do the trick? To find out, we derive the reduced form as usual. That is, we express the endogenous C and Y in terms of the exogenous A alone. This is easily done by substituting for Y in [15.16].

$$C = \alpha + \beta(C + A) + u \quad \rightarrow \quad C(1 - \beta) = \alpha + \beta A + u.$$

Thus the reduced-form equation for C is

$$C = \frac{\alpha}{1 - \beta} + \left(\frac{\beta}{1 - \beta}\right)A + \frac{u}{1 - \beta}. \qquad\qquad [15.18]$$

We can now use [15.16] to find the reduced form equation for Y:

$$Y = \frac{\alpha}{1 - \beta} + \left(\frac{\beta}{1 - \beta}\right)A + \frac{u}{1 - \beta} + A,$$

so that

$$C = \frac{\alpha}{1-\beta} + \left(\frac{1}{1-\beta}\right)A + \frac{u}{1-\beta}. \qquad [15.19]$$

Equations [15.18] and [15.19] constitute the reduced form of the model.

We can now see from [15.19] that Y is correlated with u, the disturbance in the consumption function [15.16]. Since the endogenous Y appears on the right-hand side of [15.16], this means the OLS estimators of α and the marginal propensity β will be biased.

The direction of the bias can also be ascertained from [15.19]. Since $0 < \beta < 1$, it follows that $1/(1-\beta) > 0$. Hence, Y must be positively correlated with u. It follows that the OLS estimator β is biased upwards, the situation being similar to that illustrated in Fig. 15.1.

Example 15.4

Consider the model

$$Y = a_0 + a_1 X + a_2 A + a_3 B + u, \qquad a_1 > 0, \qquad [1]$$

$$X = b_0 + b_1 Y + b_2 A + v, \qquad b_1 < 0. \qquad [2]$$

X and Y are endogenous variables, while A and B are exogenous. u and v are disturbances and the as and bs are unknown parameters.

(a) Which if any of the two equations are identified? If a_3 were equal to zero, how would this affect your answer?

(b) Obtain the reduced form of the model. For any equation that is identified, discuss the direction (s) of any OLS biases.

Example 15.5

Consider the following two-equation model:

$$Y_1 = a_0 + a_1 Y_2 + a_2 X_1 + a_3 X_2 + v, \qquad [1]$$

$$Y_2 = b_0 + b_1 X_1 + b_2 X_2 + w. \qquad [2]$$

The Ys are endogenous and the Xs exogenous. v and w are classical disturbances.

Obtain the reduced form for this model. Which (if any) of the equations could be estimated by OLS?

15.2 **An alternative to ordinary least squares**

The simplest method of countering problems regarding contemporaneous correlations between explanatory variables and disturbances is that of *instrumental variable estimation*. This method is best understood if we revert to two-variable regression for a moment.

Consider the population relationship

$$Y_i = \alpha + \beta X_i + \varepsilon_i. \tag{15.20}$$

If we sum [15.20] over all sample observations we obtain

$$\sum Y_i = n\alpha + \beta \sum X_i + \sum \varepsilon_i. \tag{15.21}$$

Similarly, if we multiply [15.20] throughout by X_i and then sum, we obtain

$$\sum X_i Y_i = \alpha \sum X_i + \beta \sum X_i^2 + \sum X_i \varepsilon_i. \tag{15.22}$$

Provided the sample size n is large, $\sum \varepsilon_i$ will be close to zero, so that [15.21] becomes virtually identical to [9.19], the first normal equation for two-variable regression. If X and ε are uncorrelated, so that $\text{Cov}(X, \varepsilon) = 0$, then for large samples $\sum X_i \varepsilon_i$ will be close to zero, so that [15.22] becomes virtually identical to [9.20], the second normal equation for two-variable regression.[9]

We know that solving the normal equations results in the OLS estimators. Thus we can see that, *provided* $\sum \varepsilon_i = \sum X_i \varepsilon_i = 0$, solving [15.21] and [15.22] will give the OLS estimators that we know are unbiased and consistent estimators of α and β.

But what if X and ε are correlated so that $\sum X_i \varepsilon_i$ is very different from zero even in large samples? Obviously, solving [15.21] and [15.22] will give a different result and will no longer yield consistent estimators. However, provided we can find some variable Z whose values are uncorrelated with ε, we can proceed as follows.

We multiply [15.20] throughout by Z_i to obtain not [15.22] but

$$\sum Z_i Y_i = \alpha \sum Z_i + \beta \sum Z_i X_i + \sum Z_i \varepsilon_i. \tag{15.23}$$

Since, *in large samples*, $\sum Z_i \varepsilon_i$ will be close to zero if Z and ε are uncorrelated, [15.23] becomes[10]

$$\sum Z_i Y_i = \alpha \sum Z_i + \beta \sum Z_i X_i. \tag{15.24}$$

Since $\sum \varepsilon_i$ is again close to zero in large samples, [15.21] again becomes identical to [9.19]:

$$\sum Y_i = n\alpha + \beta \sum X_i. \tag{15.25}$$

Equations [15.24] and [15.25] can now be solved to provide estimators of α and β. These estimators are easily shown to be[11]

$$b^* = \frac{\sum z_i y_i}{\sum z_i x_i} \quad \text{and} \quad a^* = \overline{Y} - b^*\overline{X}. \tag{15.26}$$

The estimators in [15.26] are known as *instrumental variable* (IV) *estimators* and the variable Z is referred to as an *instrument*. Unlike the OLS estimators, IV estimators remain consistent even in the presence of correlation between X and ε.[12]

Unfortunately, although IV estimators are consistent, they may not be particularly efficient, asymptotically. Only if the instrument Z happens to be highly correlated with the explanatory variable X will the sampling variances of a^* and b^* be small. Since, in addition, Z needs to be uncorrelated with ε if IV estimators are to be consistent, this means that suitable instruments may be difficult to find.

*General instrumental variables estimators

Nowadays, attempts to overcome the above problem generally involve the use of *generalized instrumental variables estimators* (GIVEs). Suppose we have m possible instruments, $Z_1, Z_2, Z_3, \ldots, Z_m$, all uncorrelated with ε. The first stage of the GIVE procedure involves computing the OLS regression of X on all the Zs,

$$\hat{X} = \hat{\gamma}_1 Z_1 + \hat{\gamma}_2 Z_2 + \hat{\gamma}_3 Z_3 + \cdots + \hat{\gamma}_m Z_m, \tag{15.26}$$

where the $\hat{\gamma}$s are OLS estimated coefficients. X is referred to as an *instrumental variable* as opposed to an *instrument*.

The second stage of the GIVE procedure involves using OLS to regress Y on the instrumental variable $\hat{X}$ to obtain

$$\hat{Y} = a^* + b^*\hat{X}; \tag{15.27}$$

a^* and b^* in [15.27] are the GIVEs of α and β.

The fact that all the instruments Z_i are uncorrelated with ε implies that $\hat{X}$ is uncorrelated with ε and this ensures that the GIVEs are consistent. Moreover, the use of [15.26] means that the correlation between $\hat{X}$ and the original Zs has been maximized. As a result, GIVEs turn out to be more efficient that simple IV estimators.

IV estimators and GIVEs can also be used in multiple regression. In simple IV estimation it is necessary to find instruments (i.e., Zs) for every explanatory variable. Each such instrument needs to be uncorrelated with the disturbance but correlated (highly, if possible) with the corresponding explanatory variable. Any explanatory variable that is already uncorrelated with the disturbance may serve as its own instrument.

In generalized estimation each explanatory variable has to be regressed on the m instruments to form a corresponding instrumental variable. The dependent variable Y is then regressed on all the instrumental variables.[13]

Computer Exercise 15.1

In this exercise we introduce a new data set. The file DATASET5 which, as usual, can be accessed from the learning centre, contains annual time series for five variables on the Irish economy from 1958 to 1997:

> DW = annual percentage change in wage rates,
> DP = annual percentage change in consumer prices,
> U = aggregate unemployment rate,
> S = annual total of days lost due to industrial disputes,
> DWP = and world inflation rate.

We investigate the equation

$$DW = a_1 + a_2DP + a_3U + a_4S + u;$$ [15.28]

[15.28] is known as a 'Phillips curve'. S is included as an index of 'union militancy'. Theory would suggest that $a_2 = 1$, since workers perceive that it is changes in *real* wages $DW - DP$ that influence their actions. We expect $a_3 < 0$ and $a_4 > 0$. The DWP variable we will use later, as an instrument in the estimation of [15.28].

Access the file DATASET5 and study the data for a moment, looking at plots of the variables against time. Create an intercept in the usual manner and estimate [15.28] using OLS. You should obtain the result shown in Fig. 15.6a.

The t-ratios and p-values in Fig. 15.6a indicate that the coefficients on the variables DP and U are both significantly different from zero (with $n - k = 36$ d.f., $t_{0.05} = 1.69$). These coefficients also have the expected sign; wage inflation rises with price inflation but falls as unemployment rises. The variable S, however, has a lower t-ratio and its coefficient, although possessing the correct sign, is not significantly different from zero. Dropping S from the equation should yield the second result shown in Fig. 15.6b.

As noted above, a strict interpretation of the Phillips curve suggests that the coefficient on DP should be unity. In fact a_2 is only about 0.83. But we can test the hypothesis of a unitary DP coefficient. With H_0: $a_2 = 1$ and H_A: $a_2 \neq 1$, we can use the results in Fig. 14.6b to compute the test statistic

$$TS = \frac{a_2 - 1}{s_{a_2}}.$$ [15.29]

Since, under H_0, TS has a Student's t distribution with $n - k = 37$ d.f., we can reject H_0 at the 0.05 level of significance if $|TS| > t_{0.025} = 2.03$. Given $a_2 = 0.830$ and $s_{a_2} = 0.0948$, we obtain $|TS| = 1.79$, so that we cannot reject H_0. Thus our result is consistent with the theoretical prediction that $a_2 = 1$.

```
(a)                    Ordinary Least Squares Estimation
*************************************************************************
Dependent variable is DW
40 observations used for estimation from 1958 to 1997
*************************************************************************
Regressor         Coefficient      Standard Error      T-Ratio[Prob]
INTER                 6.0793              1.7602        3.4537[.001]
DP                    .78629              .099229       7.9240[.000]
U                    -.23701              .11370       -2.0846[.044]
S                     .0029434            .0021798      1.3503[.185]
*************************************************************************
R-Squared                    .74387   R-Bar-Squared                .72252
S.E of Regression            3.6005   F-stat.    F(  3,  36)  34.8509[.000]
Mean of Dependent Variable  10.3308   S.D. of Dependent Variable   6.8353
Residual Sum of Squares    466.6995   Equation Log-likelihood   -105.8937
Akaike Info. Criterion    -109.8937   Schwarz Bayesian Criterion -113.2714
DW-statistic                 2.1342
*************************************************************************


(b)                    Ordinary Least Squares Estimation
*************************************************************************
Dependent variable is DW
40 observations used for estimation from 1958 to 1997
*************************************************************************
Regressor         Coefficient      Standard Error      T-Ratio[Prob]
INTER                 7.3089              1.5230        4.7990[.000]
DP                    .83029              .094766       8.7614[.000]
U                    -.28542              .10909       -2.6164[.013]
*************************************************************************
R-Squared                    .73090   R-Bar-Squared                .71635
S.E of Regression            3.6404   F-stat.    F(  3,  36)  50.2468[.000]
Mean of Dependent Variable  10.3308   S.D. of Dependent Variable   6.8353
Residual Sum of Squares    490.3356   Equation Log-likelihood   -106.8818
Akaike Info. Criterion    -109.8818   Schwarz Bayesian Criterion -112.4151
DW-statistic                 2.0058
*************************************************************************
```

Figure 15.6 Estimation of the Irish wage equation

We have estimated [15.28] by OLS. But is this estimation method appropriate? There are in fact several reasons why the explanatory variable DP in our wage equation could be correlated with the disturbance u in [15.28]. Firstly, the wage equation could be part of what is sometimes referred to as a 'wage–price spiral'. That is, not only may DP influence DW, but also DW may influence DP. Rises in aggregate wages may put pressure on the aggregate price level. Suppose changes in prices are determined by the equation

$$DP = \beta_1 + \beta_2 DW + \beta_3 C_1 + \beta_4 C_2 + v, \qquad [15.30]$$

where C_1 and C_2 represent changes in various non-wage costs. Now [15.28] and [15.30] represent a two-equation simultaneous system, which can be used to determine the values of the two endogenous variables, DW and DP, for given values of the exogenous variables U, S, C_1 and C_2.

The above system is very similar to that of Example 15.4 and you should have no difficulty in showing that the endogenous DP in the wage equation [15.28] is, almost certainly, positively correlated with the disturbance u. The OLS estimator of α_2 in [15.28] is therefore biased upwards. This suggests that our conclusion that $\alpha_2 = 1$, as theory suggests, may be suspect. We shall therefore re-estimate [15.28] using a GIVE method.

In the file DATASET5 you will find a fifth variable, DWP, which is a measure of world inflation. We shall use DWP as an instrument for DP. DWP can be regarded as exogenous to the Irish economy so, hopefully, should be uncorrelated with u in [15.28]. It is also likely to be correlated with the Irish inflation rate DP and, hence, could make a good instrument. The other variables, U and S, are exogenous to our two equation system and will serve as their own instruments in [15.28].

Key in the wage equation again (including the S variable). This time, use a GIVE procedure (some regression programmes may refer to GIVEs as two-stage least-squares (2SLS) estimators). You will need to select at least four instruments (including the intercept).[14] Select the intercept, DWP, U and S. This should give the GIVE regression equation shown in Fig. 15.7a.

In Fig. 15.7a, the coefficient on the industrial disputes variable S is again not significantly different from zero. Drop this variable from the equation and re-estimate using just three instruments (intercept, DWP and U). You should obtain the regression shown in Fig. 15.7b.

Notice that the coefficients on the price-change variable DP are slightly lower in the GIVE equations than they are in the OLS equations. This is what we might expect if the OLS estimators are in fact biased upwards. But the differences are small and we must remember that GIVEs are only consistent so that the bias correction may not be felt in samples as small as our $n = 40$.

There is another problem with the GIVE result. Unfortunately the correlation between our instrument, world price change DWP, and the Irish price change, DP, is only 0.21. But we know that the efficiency of a GIVE depends on the sizes of the correlations between variables and instruments. Hence the GIVE of α_2 is not likely to be particularly efficient. That this is the case can be seen by looking at the estimated standard errors of the OLS estimator a_2 and the GIVE a_2^*. Comparing the results in Figs 15.6a and 15.7a, a_2 has a standard error of 0.099, whereas that of a_2^* is much larger at 0.177. Confidence intervals for the true α_2 will therefore be much larger using the GIVE method than they would be using OLS. There are similar differences when the S variable is dropped.

Although the GIVE a_2^* is slightly smaller than the OLS estimator a_2, its larger standard error means that we are still unable to reject H_0: $\alpha_2 = 1$. The test statistic [15.29] this time gives a value of just 1.11. As an exercise, you should obtain data on the UK inflation rate for your sample period and use this as an alternative instrument for DP. The correlation between DP and the UK inflation rate should be much higher.

```
(a)                     Instrumental Variable Estimation
*********************************************************************************
Dependent variable is DW
List of instruments:
INTER          DWP          U                   S
40 observations used for estimation from 1958 to 1997
*********************************************************************************
Regressor          Coefficient          Standard Error          T-Ratio[Prob]
INTER                  6.1864               1.9531               3.1676[.003]
DP                     .76773               .17685               4.3411[.000]
U                     -.23940               .11530              -2.0762[.045]
S                     .0030773             .0024229              1.2701[.212]
*********************************************************************************
R-Squared                      .74362    R-Bar-Squared                   .72225
S.E of Regression              .43134    GR-Bar-Squared                  .38396
Mean of Dependent Variable     3.6023    F-stat.   F(  3,  36)    34.8054[.000]
Residual Sum of Squares       10.3308    S.D. of Dependent Variable      6.8353
Akaike Info. Criterion       467.1532    Value of IV Minimand            .0000
DW-statistic                   2.1280
*********************************************************************************


(b)                     Instrumental Variable Estimation
*********************************************************************************
Dependent variable is DW
List of instruments:
INTER          DWP          U
40 observations used for estimation from 1958 to 1997
*********************************************************************************
Regressor          Coefficient          Standard Error          T-Ratio[Prob]
INTER                  7.3805               1.9825               3.7228[.001]
DP                     .82301               .16001               5.1435[.000]
U                     -.28743               .11481              -2.5035[.017]
*********************************************************************************
R-Squared                      .73085    R-Bar-Squared                   .71631
S.E of Regression              .36505    GR-Bar-Squared                  .33073
Mean of Dependent Variable     3.6407    F-stat.   F(  2,  37)    50.2359[.000]
Residual Sum of Squares       10.3308    S.D. of Dependent Variable      6.8353
Akaike Info. Criterion       490.4136    Value of IV Minimand            .0000
DW-statistic                   2.0011
*********************************************************************************
```

Figure 15.7 GIVE estimation of the wage equation

We can use the GIVE result in Fig. 15.7b to obtain an estimate of the so-called non-accelerating inflation rate of unemployment (NAIRU).[15] Assuming an aggregate rate of productivity growth of 4%, we have, approximately,

$$DW = DP + 4. \tag{15.31}$$

Substituting for DW in the second result of Fig. 15.7 then gives

$$DP + 4 = 7.38 + 0.823DP - 0.287U. \tag{15.32}$$

Thus

$$0.177DP = 3.38 - 0.287U. \qquad [15.33]$$

Finally, substituting $DP = 0$ into [15.33] gives a value for the NAIRU of $U = 11.8$. That is, only at a rate of unemployment of around 12% can the price level be kept unchanged. Do you think this is a sensible value for the NAIRU?

Computer Exercise 15.2

In this exercise we return to the file DATASET1, which we used to estimate a cross-sectional demand-for-money function for 40 countries. Recall that we estimated a function of the form

$$M = \alpha_0 + \alpha_1 G + \alpha_2 I + u, \qquad \alpha_1 > 0, \ \alpha_2 < 0, \qquad [15.34]$$

where G represented GDP per head, I was an interest-rate variable and u is a disturbance.

In Computer Exercise 13.1, we conveniently omitted any discussion of supply-of-money. functions. But in any economy there also exists a supply function to pair with any demand-for-money function. To simplify matters, let us assume that we can write the supply of money as

$$M = \beta_0 + \beta_1 M^* + \beta_2 I + v, \qquad \beta_1 > 0, \ \beta_2 > 0, \qquad [15.35]$$

where M^* is the stock of 'high-powered' money. A data series for M^* is provided in the data file. v in [15.35] is another disturbance. You are now asked to perform two tasks:

(a) Assuming that money markets always clear and that GDP G and high-powered money M^* can be treated as exogenous, obtain reduced-form equations for M and I. Hence, assess the bias in the OLS estimator of α_2 in [15.34].

(b) Using M^* as one of the instruments, obtain a GIVE version of the demand-for-money equation. Compare this with your OLS regression.

15.3 **Heteroscedasticity**

Assumptions IIA, IIB, IIC and IID in the classical model all concern the disturbance in the regression equation. With the possible exception of IIA, each of these assumptions tends to break down with economic data. In this section and the next, we examine these problems, assuming this time that all assumptions concerning the explanatory variable remain valid.

Recall that assumption IIB states that

$$V(\varepsilon_i) = E(\varepsilon_i^2) = \sigma^2 = \text{constant}, \qquad \text{for all } i; \qquad [15.36]$$

that is, the disturbances are *homoscedastic*. If this assumption proves to be invalid and $V(\varepsilon_i)$ is not constant, but depends on i, then the disturbances are said to be heteroscedastic and assumption IIB has to be replaced by

$$V(\varepsilon_i) = e(\varepsilon_i^2) = \sigma_i^2, \qquad \text{for all } i; \qquad\qquad [15.37]$$

that is, for example, the variance of the disturbance ε_6 has a value σ_6^2, which is different from σ_{15}^2, the variance of ε_{15}.

There are three main consequences of heteroscedacticity, which can be deduced from Box 12.1 in Chapter 12.

Firstly, provided assumption IIA remains valid, the OLS estimators retain the properties of unbiasedness and consistency. These properties do not depend on the validity of assumption IIB.

Secondly, because of the breakdown of assumption IIB, the OLS estimators are no longer BLUE or efficient. Since this lack of efficiency exists regardless of sample size, it follows that the estimators, although still consistent, are no longer asymptotically efficient.

Thirdly, and less obviously, the normal formulae for the estimated standard errors of the OLS estimators are no longer unbiased estimators of the true standard errors. When disturbances are homoscedastic, the true variances of the OLS estimators depend on the true constant disturbance variance σ^2. But under heteroscedasticity there is no constant σ^2 so that, obviously, the expressions for the true variances and standard errors must be different.[16] For example, in two-variable regression, the usual formulae [12.19] for estimating standard errors depend on replacing the non-existent σ^2 by the s^2 of [12.16], and so cannot be correct.

Students often confuse the second and third of the above difficulties. The fact that the OLS estimators are no longer efficient, or even BLUE, implies that their *true* standard errors are larger than they need be. However, the fact that the *estimated* standard errors are biased estimators of the true standard errors is a completely separate problem.

BOX 15.1 Consequences of heteroscedastic/autocorrelated disturbances

1. OLS estimators remain unbiased and consistent.

2. OLS estimators are no longer BLUE nor asymptotically efficient.

3. The normal formulae for estimating the standard errors of OLS estimators become biased.

(3) is the most serious consequence, since it implies that the usual classical inferential procedures become *invalid*.

Biased estimated standard errors are the most serious consequence of heteroscedasticity. We need unbiased standard errors if we are to form correct confidence intervals or to test hypotheses about the true regression parameters in a valid manner. Thus, if we apply OLS in the presence of heteroscedasticity, all our normal inferential procedures become invalid. The consequences of a breakdown in assumption IIB are summarized in Box 15.1. As we shall see in the next section, the consequences of autocorrelation are exactly the same.

In two-variable regression, it is often the case that the disturbance variance σ_i^2 in [15.37] increases with X_i, particularly if there is a large variation in the X_i, the values of the explanatory variable. Suppose, for example, that

$$E(Y_i) = 7 + 0.8X_i. \qquad [15.38]$$

Suppose $X_3 = 10$, so that [15.38] implies $E(Y_3) = 15$. Similarly, if $X_{30} = 100$, $E(Y_{30}) = 87$. This situation is illustrated in Fig. 15.8. Actual values of Y_i obviously differ from $E(Y_i)$, because of the relevant disturbance values. But suppose that, over many samples, actual Y_3 varies between 15 ± 5, so that there exists a range of 10 about an $E(Y_3)$ of 15. Will the range of Y_{30} values also be just 10, centred about $E(Y_{30}) = 87$? That is, will Y_{30} vary between 87 ± 5? This would imply disturbance variances that are, at least approximately, constant.

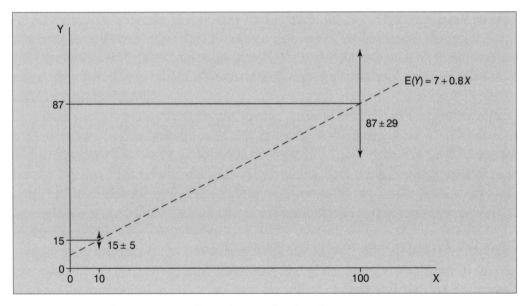

Figure 15.8 Disturbance variance dependent on the size of X

In fact, the range of Y_i values is more likely to be roughly proportionate to the size of $E(Y)$ rather than constant. For example, Y_{30} might vary between 87 ± 29, as suggested in

Fig. 15.8. Such behaviour clearly implies disturbance variances which are non-constant. That is, the disturbances display heteroscedasticity.

The consequences of heteroscedasticity are so serious, particularly for estimated standard errors, that clearly we need to test for it statistically. The problem is that heteroscedasticity is a property of the disturbances in a regression equation and the disturbances are unknown. In practice, therefore, we have to hope that the (known) residuals from a sample regression equation will prove adequate estimators of the (unknown) disturbances.

Many tests use residuals, e_i's instead of ε_i's and check for any variations in $V(e_i)$ rather than the unknown $V(\varepsilon_i)$. For example, suppose we are faced with a multiple regression equation of the standard form [13.2] but we fear that $V(\varepsilon_i)$ varies positively with the magnitude of X_3. For example, it might be the case that $V(\varepsilon_i) = E(\varepsilon_i^2) = hX_{3i}$, where h is some unknown constant. Alternatively we might have $V(\varepsilon_i) = hX_{3i}^2$. The $E(\varepsilon_i^2)$ are unknown, but we can estimate them by the squared residuals, e_i^2, from the OLS estimation of [13.2]. We can then plot values of e_i^2, against values of X_{3i} or X_{3i}^2 and look for any patterns indicative of heteroscedasticity. For example, suppose we obtained a scatter similar to that of Fig. 15.9. The pattern in Fig. 15.9 strongly suggests heteroscedasticity, with $V(\varepsilon_i)$ increasing with the size of X_{3i}.

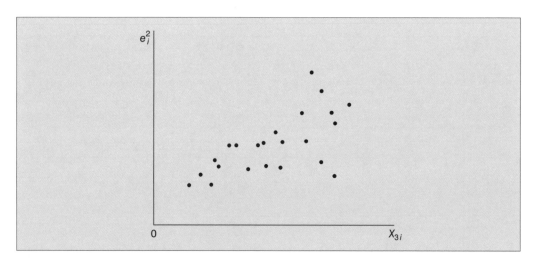

Figure 15.9 Squared residuals suggesting heteroscedasticity

Lagrange multiplier tests

The best-known quantitative tests for heteroscedasticity belong to the class of so-called *Lagrange multiplier* (LM) tests.[17] The reasons for this terminology need not concern us, but for example, suppose

$$V(\varepsilon_i) = e(\varepsilon_i^2) = \alpha + \beta[E(Y_i)]^2, \qquad [15.39]$$

where $E(Y_i)$ can depend on any number of explanatory variables. If $\beta = 0$ then the disturbances are homoscedastic. Since we have no data on $E(Y_i)$ or $E(\varepsilon_i^2)$, we replace them by Y_i and e_i^2, that is, the predicted values and squared residuals from the OLS estimation of [13.2]. Thus we actually estimate

$$e_i^2 = a + bY_i^2 + u_i. \qquad [15.40]$$

If $\beta \neq 0$ in [15.39], then the disturbances are heteroscedastic and, when [15.40] is estimated, its coefficient of determination R^2 should be non-zero. We can assess the extent of heteroscedasticity by considering the size of R^2. In fact, it can be shown that, under $H_0: \beta = 0$ and with a sample size n, the test statistic nR^2 has a χ^2 distribution with just one degree of freedom. Thus we reject H_0, the hypothesis of homoscedasticity, if the test statistic exceeds the relevant χ^2 critical value.

The above LM test is often referred to as a test for *dependent-variable heteroscedasticity*. It is given as part of the standard output of many regression packages.

Another frequently used test is the *Breusch–Pagan* (BP) test, which is also, in fact, an LM test. The BP test assumes that

$$V(\varepsilon_i) = f(\alpha_1 + \alpha_2 W_2 + \alpha_3 W_3 + \alpha_4 W_4 + \cdots + \alpha_m W_m), \qquad [15.41]$$

where the αs are constants. Thus $V(\varepsilon_i)$ is a function of a linear relationship in the Ws, which are themselves variables that we believe might influence $V(\varepsilon_i)$. The Ws may include some of the explanatory X variables in the relevant regression but can also include variables that do not appear in the regression. [15.41] states that $V(\varepsilon_i)$ is some unspecified function of the linear relationship in parentheses. The null hypothesis is $H_0: \alpha_2 = \alpha_3 = \alpha_4 = \cdots = \alpha_m = 0$. Thus, from [15.41], H_0 implies $V(\varepsilon_i) = f(\alpha_1) = $ constant, so that ε is homoscedastic.

The advantage of the Breusch–Pagan test is its generality; it is not necessary to know the precise form of the function f in [15.41]. We will not quote the form of the BP statistic here,[18] but, like the previous statistic, it is given by virtually all econometric software packages. Under H_0, the BP statistic has a χ^2 distribution with $m - 1$ degrees of freedom, where m is the number of αs in [15.41]. Thus, its value can be assessed by consulting χ^2 tables.

Worked Example

The following OLS result is obtained from 28 observations:

$$\hat{Y} = 2.342 + 0.731X.$$

(a) When [15.40] is estimated, $R^2 = 0.38$. Test for dependent-variable heteroscedasticity.

(b) When it is assumed that $V(\varepsilon) = \alpha_1 + \alpha_2 X + \alpha_3 X^2$, the BP statistic takes a value of 15.86. However, if it is assumed that $V(\varepsilon) = \alpha_1 + \alpha_2 X_1 + \alpha_3 Z^2$, where Z is an exogenous variable, the BP statistic takes a value of 14.13. Test for heteroscedasticity.

Solution

(a) The test statistic in this case takes the value $nR^2 = 10.64$. With just 1 d.f., we have a critical value of $\chi^2_{0.05} = 3.841$. Thus we reject the null hypothesis of homoscedasticity at the 0.05 level of significance.

(b) In both cases $V(\varepsilon)$ depends on X but in the first function the second W variable is X^2, whereas in the second function it is Z. However, in each case, the BP test has $m - 1 = 2$ d.f., so the critical value is $\chi^2_{0.05} = 5.991$. Thus we reject the null hypotheses of homoscedasticity against both $V(\varepsilon)$ functions.

Tackling heteroscedasticity

*The White procedure

Clearly, if the null hypothesis of homoscedasticity is rejected, so that OLS estimated standard errors are biased, then some corrective procedure is needed.

Recall that the OLS estimators remain unbiased and consistent under homoscedasticity. Although they are no longer efficient, the main problem with OLS is the biased nature of the estimated standard errors. White (1980) suggests that, since σ^2 in [15.36] is no longer constant under heteroscedasticity, we should estimate all the σ_i^2's in [15.37] by the e_i^2's, obtained from an OLS regression. In large samples, White's procedure leads to what are called *heteroscedasticity-consistent estimators* (HCEs), and these can then be used to make inferences about the true regression parameters in the usual manner. The White procedure is one of the options in many regression programmes.

The problem with HCEs is that, even though they are consistent, because of the heteroscedasticity they are still inefficient even in large samples. If efficiency is an important aim then an alternative procedure needs to be followed.

Generalized least-squares estimation

Generalized least-squares (GLS) estimators are normally obtained by *applying an appropriate transformation to the original data series and* then *applying OLS*. As an example, suppose that

$$Y_i = \beta_1 + \beta_2 X_{2i} + \varepsilon_i, \quad \text{with} \quad V(\varepsilon_i) = kX_{2i}^2, \qquad [15.42]$$

where k is an unknown constant; that is, ε_i is heteroscedastic with a variance proportional to the square of X_{2i}.

The key to the GLS process is that, if we divide all the ε_i values by the corresponding value of X_{2i}, we obtain a transformed disturbance $\varepsilon_i^* = \varepsilon_i/X_{2i}$ that is homoscedastic. That is,

$$V(\varepsilon_i^*) = V\left(\frac{\varepsilon_i}{X_{2i}}\right) = \frac{1}{X_{2i}^2} V(\varepsilon_i) = k = \text{constant.} \qquad [15.43]$$

But if we divide the disturbance in [15.42] by X_{2i} then clearly we must divide the whole of [15.42] by X_{2i}. We then obtain

$$\frac{Y_i}{X_{2i}} = \frac{\beta_1}{X_{2i}} + \beta_2 + \frac{\varepsilon_i}{X_{2i}} \qquad [15.44]$$

or

$$Y_i^* = \beta_2 + \beta_1 X_{2i}^* + \varepsilon_i^*, \qquad \text{where } Y_i^* = \frac{Y_i}{X_{2i}} \text{ and } X_{2i}^* = \frac{1}{X_{2i}}. \qquad [15.45]$$

Because ε_i^* is homoscedastic, it is now possible to estimate [15.45] by OLS, using the transformed variables Y_i^* and X_{2i}^*. That is, we construct the transformed variables and then simply regress Y_i^* on X_{2i}^*. Provided all the other classical assumptions are valid, the estimators of β_1 and β_2 obtained in this way will be efficient as well as unbiased and, moreover, the estimated standard errors obtained from the use of [15.45] will be unbiased.[19]

Example 15.6

The following equation has to be estimated:

$$Y_i = \beta_1 + \beta_2 X_{2i} + \beta_3 X_{3i} + \beta_4 X_{4i} + \varepsilon_i.$$

The disturbance ε_i is heteroscedastic with variance proportional to the square of X_{3i}. How would you proceed if efficient estimators are required?

Example 15.7

Consider the following two-variable model:

$$Y_i = \beta_1 + \beta_2 X_i + \varepsilon_i \qquad \text{where } V(X_i) = \sigma X_i.$$

What transformations must be made to X_i and Y_i if OLS is to be applied? Would the estimated standard errors be unbiased?

Computer Exercise 15.3

This exercise involves dealing with suspected heteroscedasticity. The data file DATASET6, which can be accessed from the learning centre, contains new cross-sectional data for 50 single-earner households on five variables:

> S = household saving per annum
> Y = household income per annum
> A = age of single earner,
> E = number of years in full-time education beyond the age of 16
> N = and size of household, N.

Suppose we require as precise an estimate as is possible of the marginal propensity to save (MPS) out of household income. Clearly we need to allow for the factors A, E and N when considering the relationship between S and Y, so we begin by estimating the equation

$$S = \beta_1 + \beta_2 Y + \beta_3 A + \beta_4 E + \beta_5 N + \varepsilon,$$ [15.46]

```
                    Ordinary Least Squares Estimation
*******************************************************************************
Dependent variable is S
50 observations used for estimation from    1 to 50
*******************************************************************************
Regressor          Coefficient        Standard Error        T-Ratio[Prob]
INTER                  3034.9              558.7238           5.4319[.000]
Y                      .13346              .020236            6.5954[.000]
A                     27.2509              9.2864             2.9345[.005]
E                    -37.4917             94.0745            -.39853[.692]
N                    -1951.4             144.7847           -13.4779[.000]
*******************************************************************************
R-Squared                     .82236   R-Bar-Squared                  .80657
S.E of Regression             1110.5   F-stat.    F(  4,  45)   52.0792[.000]
Mean of Dependent Variable    1249.4   S.D. of Dependent Variable     2525.0
Residual Sum of Squares     5.55E+07   Equation Log-likelihood     -418.9414
Akaike Info. Criterion     -426.9414   Schwarz Bayesian Criterion  -428.7215
DW-statistic                  2.5837
*******************************************************************************


                           Diagnostic Tests
*******************************************************************************
*    Test Statistics    *       LM Version       *       F Version         *
*******************************************************************************
*                       *                        *                         *
* A:Serial Correlation* CHSQ(  1)=   5.4141[.020]* F(  1,  44)=  5.3430[.026]*
*                       *                        *                         *
* B:Functional Form     * CHSQ(  1)=    .81729[.366]* F(  1,  44)=   .73117[.397]*
*                       *                        *                         *
* C:Normality           * CHSQ(  2)=   1.2057[.547]*      Not applicable     *
*                       *                        *                         *
* D:Heteroscedasticity* CHSQ(  1)=  12.7333[.000]* F(  1,  48)= 16.4007[.000]*
*******************************************************************************
A:Lagrange multiplier test of residual serial correlation
B:Ramsey's RESET test using the square of the fitted values
C:Based on a test of skewness and kurtosis of residuals
D:Based on the regression of squared residuals on squared fitted values
```

Figure 15.10a OLS estimation of a household saving function

where ε is a disturbance. We expect the MPS, β_2, to lie between zero and unity and also expect β_3 and β_4 to be positive since households which have high incomes and/or are well educated are likely to be able to save more. However, we expect β_5 to be negative since, for given Y, A and E, the larger the size of the household, the more likely S is to be small or negative. (Note that negative values of S imply dis-saving.)

Using the data in the file, first estimate [15.46] using OLS. You should obtain the result shown in Fig. 15.10a. In this equation the intercept and the variables Y, A and N have the expected signs, with t-values well above the critical level $t_{0.05} = 1.68$, but the 'education' variable E has an unexpected negative sign on its coefficient and a small t-ratio. The reason for this is unclear, but it may be because better-educated individuals usually earn more income. That is, the effect on saving of education is masked by that of income. Notice that

```
                    Ordinary Least Squares Estimation
*******************************************************************************
Dependent variable is S
50 observations used for estimation from    1 to 50
*******************************************************************************
Regressor              Coefficient          Standard Error        T-Ratio[Prob]
INTER                     2972.6                531.4816          5.5931[.000]
Y                         .12787                .014443           8.8532[.000]
A                        27.7934                9.1017            3.0536[.004]
N                       -1944.8                142.5087         -13.6467[.000]
*******************************************************************************
R-Squared                     .82173    R-Bar-Squared                  .81010
S.E of Regression             1100.3    F-stat.    F( 3,  46)    70.6784[.000]
Mean of Dependent Variable    1249.4    S.D. of Dependent Variable     2525.0
Residual Sum of Squares    5.57E+07     Equation Log-likelihood     -419.0295
Akaike Info. Criterion    -423.0295     Schwarz Bayesian Criterion  -426.8535
DW-statistic                  2.5979
*******************************************************************************


                           Diagnostic Tests
*******************************************************************************
*    Test Statistics    *     LM Version      *        F Version             *
*******************************************************************************
*                       *                     *                              *
* A:Serial Correlation* CHSQ(   1)=   2.5940[.118]* F(  1,  45)=  5.6688[.022]*
*                       *                     *                              *
* B:Functional Form     * CHSQ(   1)=   .85917[.354]* F(  1,  45)=  .78677[.380]*
*                       *                     *                              *
* C:Normality           * CHSQ(   2)=   1.2165[.544]*       Not applicable   *
*                       *                     *                              *
* D:Heteroscedasticity* CHSQ(   1)=  13.3081[.000]* F(  1,  48)= 17.4096[.000]*
*******************************************************************************
A:Lagrange multiplier test of residual serial correlation
B:Ramsey's RESET test using the square of the fitted values
C:Based on a test of skewness and kurtosis of residuals
D:Based on the regression of squared residuals on squared fitted values
```

Figure 15.10b Omission of the education variable

household size N seems to be a particularly important influence on saving. Its coefficient is large in absolute value, with a t-ratio of 13.5, and implies that each extra individual in a household leads to a reduction of £1951 in household saving. This compares with a mean value for saving of £1249.

Dropping the insignificant E variable from the equation leads to the result in Fig. 15.10b.

At this moment, the numbers of most interest in Fig. 15.10 are the diagnostic statistics below the main results. We will consider the tests A and B later in this chapter, but it is tests C and D that are of most interest for this data set. C is the Jarque–Bera statistic which tests assumption IID in the classical model, that of normality of the disturbances.[20] Under the null hypothesis of normality, the statistic has a χ^2 distribution with 2 d.f. The critical value $\chi^2_{0.05}$ is 5.99, so that the values of 1.21 and 1.22 obtained for the statistic imply that the normality assumption is clearly satisfied.

The statistic D refers to the LM statistic for dependent-variable heteroscedasticity, outlined earlier in this section. Under a null hypothesis of homoscedasticity, the statistic has a χ^2 distribution with 1 d.f. Its critical value is therefore $\chi^2_{0.05} = 3.84$. Unfortunately, the values for the statistic, obtained in Figs 15.10, are 12.7 and 13.3, so that it appears that the disturbances are heteroscedastic.

Recall that the most serious consequence of heteroscedasticity is that the estimated standard errors in the OLS procedures are biased. In the Figs 15.10, we cannot therefore rely on the standard error on the estimated MPS b_2. This problem is often handled by obtaining White heteroscedasticity-adjusted standard errors, as explained earlier in this section. Your programme should have an option for obtaining White-type HCEs and you should now use it, again omitting the E variable. You will obtain the result shown in Fig. 15.11.

Comparing the results in Fig. 15.10b and Fig. 15.11, it is clear that the adjusted standard errors in Fig. 15.11 are rather different from the OLS standard errors in Fig. 15.10b. For income Y, the adjusted standard error is much larger than that in Fig. 15.10b, whereas for the

```
                    Ordinary Least Squares Estimation
              Based on White's Heteroscedasticity adjusted S.E.'s
***************************************************************************
Dependent variable is S
50 observations used for estimation from    1 to 50
***************************************************************************
Regressor            Coefficient          Standard Error          T-Ratio[Prob]
INTER                     2972.6               433.2468            6.8613[.000]
Y                        .12787               .025344             5.0454[.000]
A                       27.7934                5.8528             4.7487[.000]
N                       -1944.8               149.1011          -13.0433[.000]
***************************************************************************
```

Figure 15.11 Heteroscedasticity-consistent estimation of the saving function

age variable A the adjusted standard error is much smaller than that in Fig. 15.10b. Notice, however, that the b_j estimators are unchanged from Fig. 15.10b. This is because we are still using OLS, although we are using a different method of estimating standard errors.

The White-adjusted result indicates that the precision with which we can estimate the MPS out of income may be less than we hoped. A 95% confidence interval for β_2 obtained from Fig. 15.11 is as wide as 0.128 ± 0.051. However, we know that another consequence of heteroscedasticity is a lack of efficiency in the OLS estimators, and this is reflected in the width of the confidence interval. Maybe we can find a GLS transformation, similar to that adopted in Example 15.6, that will reduce the standard error on any estimate of the MPS.

Display the result in Fig. 15.10b again and save the residuals from this regression. Name the residuals e. Now create e^2, and then obtain a scatter of e^2 against the income values, similar to that in Fig. 15.9. Print out this scatter and obtain similar scatters of e^2 against A and then N. You should get the scatters shown in Fig. 15.12.

Examination of the scatters suggests a positive relation between e^2 and Y but no apparent links between e^2 and A or between e^2 and N. Thus $V(\varepsilon)$ may increase with Y or, more likely, Y^2. There is a very wide range in the Y values (from less than £3000 to over £50 000), and this may be the cause of the heteroscedasticity.

We can now attempt the GLS procedure outlined earlier in this section. The obvious transformation is that of Example 15.6. This is to divide [15.46] throughout by Y, obtaining

$$\frac{S}{Y} = \beta_2 + \beta_1 \frac{1}{Y} + \beta_3 \frac{A}{Y} + \beta_4 \frac{N}{Y} + \varepsilon^*, \qquad [15.47]$$

where $\varepsilon^* = \varepsilon/Y$ is, hopefully, homoscedastic.

Create the variables S/Y, $1/Y$, A/Y and N/Y and use OLS to estimate [15.47] and obtain the GLS estimators of the β_j together with their estimated standard errors. You should obtain the result shown in Fig. 15.13.

Looking at the diagnostic statistics first, it is clear that all the χ^2 statistics are improved. In particular, the heteroscedasticity statistic is now only 0.567. Consequently, we can rely on not only the OLS estimators but also their estimated standard errors. However, do not be impressed by the increase in R^2 between Figs. 15.10b and 15.13. In the former regression we were explaining variations in Y, whereas this time, the dependent variable is S/Y.[21]

Notice that *it is the intercept in Fig. 15.13 that gives us an estimate of the MPC β_2.* This should be clear from a comparison of equations [15.46] and [15.47]. Similarly, it is the coefficient on $1/Y$ in Fig. 15.13 that gives us an estimate of β_1, the intercept in the original [15.46]. Using [15.47] in fact gives our GLS estimated saving function as

$$\hat{S} = 331 + 0.112Y + 26.7A - 1983N. \qquad [15.48]$$

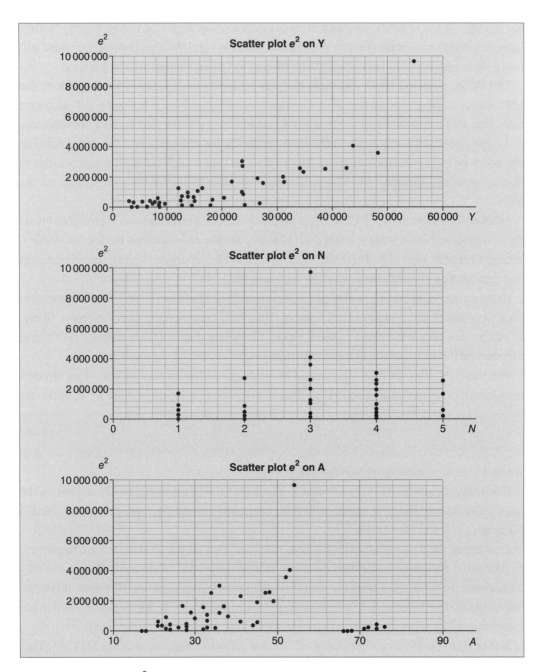

Figure 15.12 Plots of e^2 against Y, N and A

```
                 Ordinary Least Squares Estimation
*******************************************************************************
Dependent variable is SY
50 observations used for estimation from    1 to 50
*******************************************************************************
Regressor              Coefficient        Standard Error          T-Ratio[Prob]
INTER                      .11182                .014101           7.9297[.000]
R                          3305.1               226.2769          14.6066[.000]
AY                        26.6951                2.9492            9.0518[.000]
NY                       -1983.2                85.0843          -23.3090[.000]
*******************************************************************************
R-Squared                  .95684    R-Bar-Squared                      .95403
S.E of Regression          .056155   F-stat.   F( 3,  46)   339.9720[.000]
Mean of Dependent Variable .12816    S.D. of Dependent Variable         .26191
Residual Sum of Squares    .14506    Equation Log-likelihood          75.1195
Akaike Info. Criterion    71.1195    Schwarz Bayesian Criterion       67.2955
DW-statistic               2.3598
*******************************************************************************


                          Diagnostic Tests
*******************************************************************************
*    Test Statistics    *      LM Version       *        F Version          *
*******************************************************************************
*                       *                       *                           *
* A:Serial Correlation* CHSQ(   1)=  2.1682[.141] * F(   1,  45)= 2.0398[.160]*
*                       *                       *                           *
* B:Functional Form     * CHSQ(   1)=  5.5885[.018] * F(   1,  45)= 5.6625[.022]*
*                       *                       *                           *
* C:Normality           * CHSQ(   2)=  3.5841[.167] *       Not applicable     *
*                       *                       *                           *
* D:Heteroscedasticity* CHSQ(   1)=   .5667[.452] * F(   1,  48)= .55034[.462]*
*******************************************************************************
A:Lagrange multiplier test of residual serial correlation
B:Ramsey's RESET test using the square of the fitted values
C:Based on a test of skewness and kurtosis of residuals
D:Based on the regression of squared residuals on squared fitted values
```

Key to variables: $SY = S/Y$, $R = 1/Y$, $AY = A/Y$, $NY = N/Y$

Figure 15.13 GLS estimation of the saving function

The standard error on b_2, obtained from Fig. 15.13, is 0.0141, so this time we obtain a 95% confidence interval for the MPS of 0.112 ± 0.028 compared with the 0.128 ± 0.051 obtained earlier. As hoped, the GLS procedure has yielded a narrower confidence interval and hence a more precise estimate of β_2.

15.4 **Autocorrelation**

Recall from Chapters 12 and 13 that assumption IIC of the classical regression model states that $\text{Cov}(\varepsilon_i, \varepsilon_j) = 0$ for all $i \ne j$. That is, any two different disturbances must be uncorrelated. Unfortunately, it is often the case, particularly with time-series data, that $\text{Cov}(\varepsilon_i, \varepsilon_j)$ is non-zero for many, if not all, $i \ne j$. For example, ε_7 might be correlated with ε_{24}. The disturbances are then said to be *autocorrelated*.

As we saw in Chapter 12.1, a frequent problem with time series is that random shocks or disturbances tend to 'spill over' from one time period to the next. Such *autocorrelation* often occurs because of the 'momentum' in many economic time series which creates self-sustaining upswings and downswings. Thus the disturbance in period t, ε_t, is likely to be influenced by the disturbance in the previous period, ε_{t-1}. Consequently, $\text{Cov}(\varepsilon_t, \varepsilon_{t-1}) \ne 0$ and assumption IIC is violated. When autocorrelation occurs in this way with time series it is often referred to as *serial correlation*.

The consequences of autocorrelated disturbances for the OLS estimators are similar to those of heteroscedasticity. Study of Box 12.1 indicates that the OLS estimators remain unbiased and consistent. But the violation of assumption IIC means that the estimators are no longer BLUE or asymptotically efficient. In addition, and more seriously, in the presence of autocorrelation *the normal formulae for estimated standard errors become biased so that this invalidates normal OLS inferential procedures*. Thus, as in the heteroscedastic case, we can no longer rely on our usual confidence interval formulae or our normal hypothesis testing procedures. The consequences of autocorrelation were summarized in Box 15.1.

Modelling and testing for autocorrelated disturbances

Probably the best-known method of attempting to model autocorrelation is the *first-order autoregressive process*. In this model the normal classical assumptions about the disturbance are replaced by the process

$$\varepsilon_t = \rho\varepsilon_{t-1} + u_t, \tag{15.49}$$

where ρ is a parameter lying between 1 and −1 and u is a further disturbance that does in fact obey all the classical assumptions.[22] Thus the disturbance value in one period is linked to the disturbance value in the previous period.

It should be noted that, when $\rho = 0$ in [15.49], $\varepsilon_t = u_t$ so that ε itself is a non-autocorrelated classical disturbance. As we will see in a moment, this special case of $\rho = 0$, implying the absence of autocorrelation, is used as the null hypothesis when testing for this kind of process. The possible alternative hypotheses are then $\rho > 0$, $\rho < 0$ or $\rho \ne 0$.

The case $\rho > 0$ is often referred to as *positive autocorrelation* because it implies a tendency for positive values of ε_{t-1} to be followed by further positive values of ε_t. Similarly, negative values of ε_{t-1} tend to be followed by further negative values of ε_t. Consequently, we tend to obtain positive or negative 'runs' of disturbance values over time. As a result, this model can be good at capturing the tendency, described earlier, for disturbances to spill over from one period to the next.

If $\rho < 0$ then *negative autocorrelation* is said to be present and positive values of ε_{t-1}, tend to be followed by negative values of ε_t and vice versa. This is possibly less likely with economic time series, although occasionally a positive disturbance can occur as 'compensation' for a previous negative disturbance.

Testing for autocorrelation

Although, initially, we abandoned all the classical assumptions regarding the disturbance, it can be shown that if $\rho \neq 0$, then ε_t in the first-order scheme [15.49] *will satisfy all classical assumptions apart from that of non-autocorrelation.*[23] This enables us to concentrate on the problem of autocorrelation alone.

The well-known Durbin–Watson statistic is frequently used to test H_0: $\rho = 0$ in a first-order autoregressive process. It is defined as

$$dw = \frac{\sum_{t=2}^{\infty}(e_t - e_{t-1})^2}{\sum_{t=1}^{\infty} e_t^2},\qquad [15.50]$$

where the e_t are the residuals from an OLS regression.

It is possible to show intuitively that, under H_0: $\rho = 0$, dw will lie somewhere between 0 and 4, but with a value probably close to 2. If we treat the residuals e_t as estimates of the unknown ε_t in [15.49], then if ρ were to take its maximum value of $+1$, we would obtain $e_t = e_{t-1} + u_t$. Hence, since $E(u_t) = 0$, we have, 'on average', $e_t - e_{t-1} = 0$ so that [15.50] yields $dw \approx 0$. If, on the other hand, $\rho = -1$ in [15.49] then we obtain 'on average' $e_t = -e_{t-1}$ so that $e_t - e_{t-1} = 2e_t$. Substituting in [15.50] then gives $dw \approx 4$.

Values of the Durbin–Watson statistic are therefore expected to lie between 0 and 4. Values close to zero suggest $\rho > 0$, with a maximum of $\rho = 1$, and hence positive autocorrelation. Values close to 4 suggest $\rho < 0$, with a minimum of $\rho = -1$, and hence negative autocorrelation.

If no autocorrelation is present then $\rho = 0$, which is a value mid-way between the extremes of $+1$ and -1. Hence, under H_0: $\rho = 0$, when ε is non-autocorrelated, it should be clear intuitively that we can expect a value for dw of around 2, or mid-way between its extremes of 0 and 4.

It must be remembered, however, that dw, like all test statistics, has a sampling distribution. Even under H_0, it is still possible, simply by chance, to obtain a value of dw which is quite far away from the expected value of 2. The null hypothesis H_0: $\rho = 0$ is therefore normally rejected if the Durbin–Watson statistic takes a value which is *sufficiently different from 2*. Values below 2 indicate possible positive autocorrelation, whereas values above 2 suggest negative autocorrelation.

Tables of critical values for the *dw* statistic are often found in econometrics textbooks although, unfortunately, there are many problems in using such tables. Firstly, there is an inconclusive range of values for the statistic such that, sometimes, it is impossible to tell whether we should reject H_0 or not. Secondly, it is also the case that *the dw statistic is biased towards 2 in the presence of a lagged dependent variable.*[24] Consequently, in such situations, the *dw* statistic clearly cannot be used to test for autocorrelation. More fundamentally, it tests only for first-order processes such as [15.49]. But autocorrelation can arise for many reasons, not just because of a first-order process. It may well be more appropriate to model the spill-over effect between disturbances either by, for example, the process

$$\varepsilon_t = \rho_1 \varepsilon_{t-1} + \rho_2 \varepsilon_{t-2} + u_t, \qquad [15.51]$$

or perhaps

$$\varepsilon_t = u_t + \theta u_{t-1}, \qquad [15.52]$$

or even

$$\varepsilon_t = u_t + \theta_1 u_{t-1} + \theta_2 u_{t-2}, \qquad [15.52]$$

here u_t is again a classical disturbance.

Equations [15.49] and [15.51] are both autoregressive processes, [15.51] being a *second-order process*. However, [15.52] and [15.53] are examples of so-called *moving-average processes*, of orders 1 and 2, respectively. The Durbin–Watson statistic, being a test for a first-order autoregressive process, is not appropriate in such situations. Consequently, nowadays econometricians regard the *dw* statistic as no more than a rough indication of the presence of autocorrelation in the *residuals* of an estimated equation. For example, a value of *dw* outside the range 1.7 and 2.3 might cause concern.

Fortunately, there is available a general test for autocorrelation of up to pth order for both autoregressive and moving-average processes. This is the *Breusch–Godfrey* (BG) test, also known as the *Lagrange multiplier test for autocorrelation*. Under the null hypothesis of no autocorrelation, the Breusch–Godfrey statistic has a χ^2 distribution with p degrees of freedom, where p is the highest order of autocorrelation being tested for. The construction and theory behind the BG test are difficult and we do not include them here, but we shall make use of this statistic in later computer exercises.[25]

Tackling autocorrelation

We saw earlier that autocorrelation has serious consequences for the OLS estimating procedure, particularly for its inferential aspects. The type and order of autocorrelation determine the form of any alternative estimation approach adopted. For example, suppose we wish to estimate

$$Y_t = \beta_1 + \beta_2 X_{2t} + \beta_3 X_{3t} + \varepsilon_t, \tag{15.54}$$

where ε_t follows the first-order autoregressive process [15.49]. Suppose, for the moment, that the parameter ρ in [15.49] is known. From [15.49], we know that $u_t = \varepsilon_t - \rho \varepsilon_{t-1}$ is a classical disturbance. We now apply a transformation to [15.54]. Multiplying [15.54] by ρ and 'lagging' the equation by one period yields

$$\rho Y_{t-1} = \rho \beta_1 + \rho \beta_2 X_{2t-1} + \rho \beta_3 X_{3t-1} + \rho \varepsilon_{t-1}. \tag{15.55}$$

Next, subtracting [15.55] from [15.54] gives

$$Y_t - \rho Y_{t-1} = \beta_1(1-\rho) + \beta_2(X_{2t} - \rho X_{2t-1}) + \beta_3(X_{3t} - \rho X_{3t-1}) + \varepsilon_t - \rho \varepsilon_{t-1}. \tag{15.56}$$

We can rewrite [15.56] as

$$Y_t^* = \beta_1^* + \beta_2 X_{2t}^* + \beta_3 X_{3t}^* + u_t, \tag{15.57}$$

where $Y_t^* = Y_t - \rho Y_{t-1}$, etc., $\beta_1^* = \beta_1(1-\rho)$ and $u_t = \varepsilon_t - \rho \varepsilon_{t-1}$.

The β_j's may now be estimated by applying OLS to [15.57] because u is a classical disturbance. Higher autoregressive processes can be tackled in similar ways. The process just outlined is another example of generalised least sqaures (GLS) estimation, and the estimators of the β_j's, obtained from [15.57], are referred to as GLS estimators.

The problem with such techniques is that, to construct the transformed variables Y^*, X_2^* and X_3^* we have to assume that the value of the parameter ρ is known. In practice, of course, ρ is not known and has to be estimated.

Example 15.8

The following equation is to be estimated:

$$Y_t = \alpha_0 + \alpha_1 X_{1t} + \alpha_2 X_{2t} + \varepsilon_t,$$

where the disturbance follows the second-order scheme

$$\varepsilon_t = \rho_1 \varepsilon_{t-1} + \rho_2 \varepsilon_{t-2} + u_t.$$

Assuming that u_t obeys the classical assumptions, how would you proceed?

Example 15.9

Consider the regression equation

$$Y_t = \beta_1 + \beta_2 X_t + \varepsilon_t.$$

The equation has to be estimated from quarterly time-series data for which

$$\varepsilon_t = \rho \varepsilon_{t-4} + v_t,$$

where v is a classical disturbance. Why might the disturbance ε follow such an auto-regressive process? How would you estimate β_1 and β_2 and test hypotheses about them?

We shall not detail the various methods of estimating ρ parameters that are available, for two reasons. Firstly, to apply them, we need to know for certain that ε_t in [15.54] does indeed follow a first-order regressive process. In practice, we will not normally know whether this is so. Secondly, significant values for test statistics such as the *dw* statistic or the *B– G* statistic *may indicate something rather different from an autocorrelated disturbance*. It is to this problem that we will turn in the final section of this chapter.

Computer Exercise 15.4

In Computer Exercise 13.2 we used the data in the file DATASET2 to estimate an equation for sales of tee-shirts, S. Our OLS result was reproduced as Fig. 13.6. In that exercise we were mainly concerned about the collinearity between earnings, E, and advertising expenditure, A. But there are other serious problems with this result. From Fig. 13.6, we can see that the Durbin–Watson statistic is as low as 0.257! Also, looking at the diagnostic tests below the main result, we see an LM statistic for serial correlation. This is, in fact, the Breusch– Godfrey statistic described earlier in this section.

As indicated, the value given is that for the BG statistic for up to 12th-order auto-correlation. This is because we were employing monthly data in our regression. With 12 d.f., the critical value of χ^2 is $\chi^2_{0.05} = 21.03$. Hence since the BG statistic is 30.26, we have to reject the null hypothesis of no autocorrelation up to the 12th order. Thus both the DW and the BG statistics indicate autocorrelation problems.

Your programme should enable you to investigate the nature of the autocorrelation present more closely. Re-estimate the equation in Fig. 13.5 and access the LM tests for autocorrelation. You will now be asked to choose the order of the LM test you want to make. Ask for BG test statistics for up to fourth-order autocorrelation. You should obtain an output similar to that shown in Fig. 15.14a, at the foot of which the value of the statistic is shown. Under the null hypothesis of no autocorrelation it has a χ^2 distribution with 4 d.f. Given $\chi^2_{0.05} = 9.49$ and a BG statistic of 29.45, it can be seen that autocorrelation is again indicated.

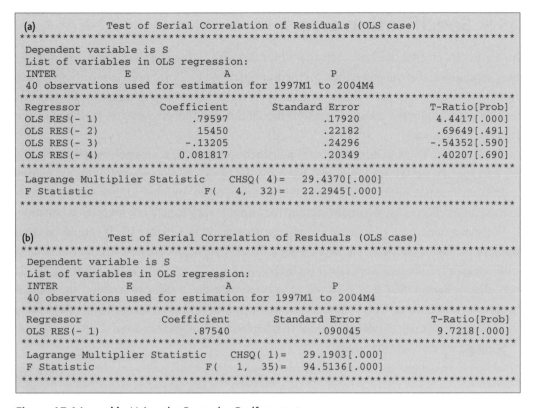

Figure 15.14a and b Using the Breusch–Godfrey test

The estimated equation indicated in the main section of Fig. 15.14a represents an attempt to estimate the fourth-order autoregressive process

$$\varepsilon_t = \rho_1 \varepsilon_{t-1} + \rho_2 \varepsilon_{t-2} + \rho_3 \varepsilon_{t-3} + \rho_4 \varepsilon_{t-4} + u_t, \qquad [15.58]$$

which is simply a generalization of [15.49] and is sometimes called the *auxiliary equation*.

When testing for autocorrelation up to the fourth order, the null hypothesis is $\rho_1 = \rho_2 = \rho_3 = \rho_4 = 0$. Since the ε_t are unknown, the residuals e_t from the original OLS sales equation are used instead in the estimation of [15.58]. The *t*-ratio on OLS RES(−1), that is on e_{t-1}, is as high as 4.44, and this is clearly a major reason for the significant BG statistic.

The test for first-order autocorrelation alone is shown in Fig. 15.14b. The LM statistic is now 29.2 (c.f. $\chi^2_{0.05} = 3.84$, with 1 d.f.), so, not surprisingly, we again find evidence of auto-correlation. The auxiliary equation estimated this time is simply [15.49], which gives an estimate for ρ of 0.875 in the first-order process.

It is tempting to use the value $\rho = 0.875$ to construct the transformed variables needed to estimate a version of [15.57]. But before we rush into GLS estimation we need to consider the problem covered in the next section.

15.5 **Specification errors**

So far in this chapter, we have considered breakdowns in the classical assumptions under the presumption that the population regression equation [13.2] has been *correctly specified*. But [13.2] is as much a part of the classical model as the sets of assumptions I or II, so in this section we consider the consequences for the OLS estimators of a *misspecified* population regression equation.

There are two kinds of error we can make when specifying a regression equation. Firstly, we can specify the wrong functional form for the equation. For example, the population regression equation might be log-linear but we might try to estimate a linear sample regression equation. Secondly, we might include the 'wrong' variables in our regression equation.

We spent some time considering nonlinear regression in Chapter 10. It should be clear that, for example, the OLS estimators from a linear regression equation will normally have little meaning if the true population relationship is nonlinear. Only if the range of data is sufficiently narrow that it is possible to approximate the nonlinear function by a linear 'segment' would linear OLS estimation be of much use. However, the problem of choosing the 'wrong' explanatory variables needs to be considered in greater detail.

Suppose we estimate the equation

$$Y = \beta_1 + \beta_2 X_2 + u \qquad [15.59]$$

when, in fact, the true population equation is

$$Y = \beta_1 + \beta_2 X_2 + \beta_3 X_3 + \varepsilon, \qquad \beta_3 \neq 0. \qquad [15.60]$$

In [15.59] we have omitted a 'relevant' variable X_3 which influences Y.

Recall that the disturbance in a regression equation is included to allow for purely random factors and also to capture *the influence of any other variables, apart from those already included in the equation*. When we estimate [15.59], we are therefore forcing the disturbance u to include the influence of X_3. In fact, it is obvious that $u = \beta_3 X_3 + \varepsilon$. Now if X_2 and X_3 happen to be correlated, it follows that u, which depends on X_3, must also be correlated with X_2. That is, in [15.59], the explanatory variable X_2 is correlated with the disturbance u. But we know, from Chapter 15.1, that such a correlation leads to biased and inconsistent OLS estimators. That is, the omission of X_3 from [15.59] results in biased estimators of β_1 and β_2. This bias is referred to as *omitted-variable bias*.[26]

Omitted variable(s) usually result in such bias. In fact, we mentioned this finding, when introducing multiple regression in Chapter 13.2. We saw then that only when the omitted variable is totally uncorrelated with any of the variables already included in the regression equation can this bias be zero.

Now, suppose that [15.60] is again the 'correct' equation, but this time we estimate

$$Y = \beta_1 + \beta_2 X_2 + \beta_3 X_3 + \beta_4 X_4 + v. \tag{15.61}$$

In this situation we have included an 'irrelevant' variable X_4 in our estimating equation; that is, a variable that has no influence on Y.

'Irrelevant' variables are easier to tackle. If X_4 does not affect Y, then obviously $\beta_4 = 0$. But there is nothing in the classical model to say that β_4 has to be non-zero. We can still apply OLS to [15.61] and obtain unbiased estimators of the β_j's. The fact that $E(b_4) = \beta_4 = 0$ does not matter. OLS simply gives us an unbiased estimate of this zero.

However, the presence of an irrelevant variable X_4 in [15.61] does have one important consequence. The OLS estimators are unlikely to be efficient. The unnecessary X_4 may well be correlated with X_2 and/or X_3 in [15.61], and this introduces an extra and unnecessary degree of multicollinearity between the explanatory variables in the equation. As we saw in Chapter 13.3, this leads to an unnecessary increase in standard errors and, consequently, the OLS estimators of β_1, β_2 and β_3 lack the precision they would have in the absence of X_4. Only if the 'irrelevant' X_4 happens to be totally uncorrelated with either X_2 or X_3 will the OLS estimators remain efficient when X_4 is included.

It can be seen that the consequences of misspecifying either the functional form or the explanatory variables of a regression equation are likely to be serious. It is therefore important that we should be able to detect such specification errors and the simplest way of doing this is to examine the residuals from fitted regression equations.

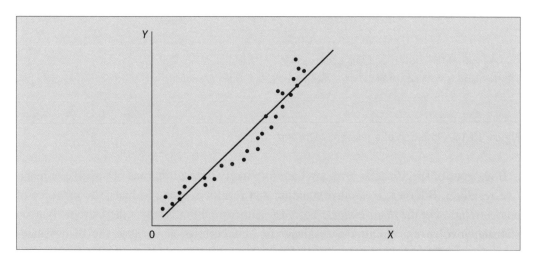

Figure 15.15 Fitting a linear regression to a non-linear scatter

For example, in two-variable regression the population regression equation might be log-linear and result in a scatter of points similar to those in Fig. 15.15. Without studying the scatter visually, we might attempt to fit a linear sample regression to the data, as illustrated in Fig. 15.15. The residuals from the fitted equation are, as usual, given by the vertical distances of points from the line. But study of Fig. 15.15 indicates that, as X increases, we obtain first a 'run' of positive residuals, then a run of negative residuals, and finally another run of positive residuals. Runs of positive and negative residuals are often an indication of functional form misspecification. Such indications are even more important in multiple regression where, of course, we cannot represent the data in a simple scatter diagram.

Runs of positive and/or negative residuals are equally important when checking for omitted-variable errors. For example, suppose we estimate equation [15.59] when in fact the true population equation is [15.60]. If the omitted X_3 exhibits a strong positive trend over time, the residuals from the fitted version of [15.59] are almost certain to reflect this. The likely pattern is shown in Fig. 15.16, with on this occasion time on the horizontal axis. The pattern shows a run of negative residuals followed by a run of positive residuals.

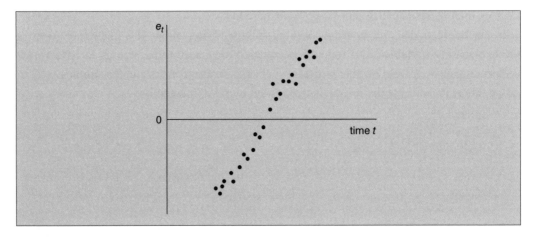

Figure 15.16 Omission of a relevent regressor

Both types of specification error are therefore likely to result in runs of positive or negative *residuals*. But there is another situation that results in such residuals; the presence of autocorrelation in the *disturbances*. Tests for autocorrelation, such as the Durbin–Watson statistic, involve examining the residuals for autocorrelation because the disturbances are unknown. But, if we find the residuals autocorrelated, is this because of genuine autocorrelation in the disturbances or because of some misspecification in the regression equation itself?

Nowadays econometricians distinguish between *tests of specification* and *tests of misspecification* or *diagnostic tests*. In a test of specification, clear null and alternative hypotheses are needed. For example, when testing for a first-order autoregressive process using the *dw* statistic, we test H_0: $\rho = 0$ against the clear alternative that ρ is non-zero. This is therefore a test of specification.

In contrast, in a diagnostic or misspecification test, there is no clear alternative hypothesis. H_0: $\rho = 0$ implies a classical disturbance, but rejection of H_0 could imply a first-order process or an omitted variable or an incorrect functional form. In using the *dw* statistic in this way, we are conducting a test of misspecification.

Nowadays, almost all the well-known tests for autocorrelation and heteroscedasticity are used as diagnostic tests. For example, if the Durbin–Watson and Breusch–Godfrey statistics indicated autocorrelation in the residuals of a regression, most investigators would start searching for a better-specified model, rather than applying some complicated procedure for eliminating autocorrelation.

One general set of tests for misspecification are the so-called RESET tests (Regression Error Specification Tests), developed from the work by Ramsey (1969). One of the RESET test statistics is employed in the following computer exercise, but, rather than relying on test statistics, it is often a good idea to study the data series for yourself. Econometricians are sometimes accused of failing to actually look at their data. In fact, *visual inspection of data series can often give you important clues about possible problems before you resort to sophisticated analysis*.

Computer Exercise 15.5

In this exercise we return to the file DATASET2. In Computer Exercise 15.4 we discovered serious problems with some of the diagnostic statistics for the sales equation. Both the *dw* statistic and the LM statistic for autocorrelation were well beyond their critical values. However, we have seen, in this section, that these statistics may often signal not genuine autocorrelation but some kind of specification error.

Looking back to Fig. 13.6, you will find that the second diagnostic test below the main regression result gives a χ^2 statistic for 'functional form'. This is, in fact, one of the Ramsey RESET statistics referred to earlier in this section. In this case any possible nonlinearity in the regression is allowed for by the addition of the squared values of Y from the original OLS regression. The resultant statistic has a χ^2 distribution with just one degree of freedom and its value is also clearly beyond the critical value of $\chi^2_{0.05} = 3.841$, suggesting that our linear formulation of the sales equation may be incorrect.

Using the data in DATASET2, you should at least try log-linear and other nonlinear specifications for the sales function, checking the autocorrelation and RESET statistics on each occasion. You will find that varying the specification in this way does not help.

The other type of misspecification we should always be on the lookout for, particularly with time-series data, is omitted-variable error. We saw earlier that omitting a relevant variable not only can result in OLS bias but also often shows up in the autocorrelation statistics.

With time series it is often the case that the omitted variables turn out to be values of the explanatory variables for previous periods. For example, often it is necessary to include not only the current value of a given variable X but also its value in some past period(s). That is, the regressors should include both X_t and at least X_{t-1}. The reason why such lagged variables are required is that often it takes time for a dependent variable (such as sales in the present example) to adjust completely to changes in some or all of the explanatory variables. A failure to allow for lagged responses of this kind is normally referred to as a *dynamic misspecification*, and we shall have much more to say about this in the final chapters of this book.

Since the sales data are monthly data, we can suspect strongly that lagged responses by the sales variable, S, to the variables expenditure E, advertising A and relative price P are likely. Create the lagged variable S_{t-1}, (sales in month $t-1$) by typing in $S1 = S(-1)$. Similarly, create $E1$, $A1$ and $P1$ as the values for E, A and P for month $t-1$. Now look in your data window again. You will find values for S_{t-1}, E_{t-1}, A_{t-1} and P_{t-1}, for months $t = 2, \dots, 40$, but no values for S_0, E_0, A_0 or P_0 because these are unknown.

Next regress S_t on E_t, A_t, P_t and the lagged values of all variables. You should obtain the result shown in Fig. 15.17. For the moment, you can regard the variable S_{t-1} as simply reflecting 'habit', since its inclusion implies that sales in month t are influenced by sales in the previous month $t-1$. In the next chapter we will consider the role of such 'lagged dependent variables' in more detail.

Notice that the result shown in Fig. 15.17 uses only 39 rather than 40 observations. This is because, as we noted above, we have no values of the lagged variables for the first month.

It is immediately apparent that the problems with the diagnostic tests in the sales equation have been partly solved. The RESET statistic is now very good and the LM statistics have improved. While the LM statistic for up to 12th-order autocorrelation is still slightly larger than its critical value $\chi^2_{0.05} = 21.03$, you should find that the first- and fourth-order statistics are now below their critical values. It seems, then, that the problems with the original equation in Fig. 13.6 may be, at least partly, the result of the omission of relevant variables rather than genuine autocorrelation in the disturbances. Notice, however that the normality statistic (with 2 d.f.) has deteriorated and now exceeds its critical value of $\chi^2_{0.05} = 5.99$. It is not easy to get all the diagnostic statistics moving in the required direction!

```
                    Ordinary Least Squares Estimation
*********************************************************************************
Dependent variable is S
39 observations used for estimation from 1997M2 to 2000M4
*********************************************************************************
Regressor          Coefficient        Standard Error         T-Ratio[Prob]
INTER                  .77830                3.6918           .21082[.834]
E                      .36925                 .15160         2.4357[.021]
E1                    -.26067                 .17220        -1.5137[.140]
A                      .023455               .069646          .33677[.739]
A1                    -.014514               .078791         -.18421[.855]
P                    -3.2917                 1.9754         -1.6663[.106]
P1                    2.9627                 1.9857          1.4920[.146]
S1                     .82670                 .071963       11.4879[.000]
*********************************************************************************
R-Squared                       .96565   R-Bar-Squared                    .95790
S.E of Regression               .53495   F-stat.    F(  7,  31)   124.5103[.000]
Mean of departent Variable    29.2641    S.D. of Dependent Variable       2.6071
Residual Sum Of Squares        8.8713    Equation Log-likelihood        -26.4642
Akaike info. Criterion       -34.4642    Schwarz Bayesian Criterion     -41.1184
DW-statistic                   2.1312
*********************************************************************************


                            Diagnostic Tests
*********************************************************************************
*     Test Statistics     *     LM Version         *      F Version           *
*********************************************************************************
*                         *                        *                          *
* A:Serial Correlation*  CHSQ( 12)=  22.2799[.035] * F( 12, 19)=  2.1098[.071]*
*                         *                        *                          *
* B:Functional Form      * CHSQ(  1)=  .081051[.776] * F(  1, 30)= .062477[.804]*
*                         *                        *                          *
* C:Normality            * CHSQ(  2)=  8.5971[.014] *      Not applicable     *
*                         *                        *                          *
* D:Heteroscedasticity*  CHSQ(  1)=  086260[.769] * F(  1, 37)= .082018[.776]*
*********************************************************************************
A:Lagrange multiplier test of residual serial correlation
B:Ramsey's RESET test using the square of the fitted values
C:Based on a test of skewness and kurtosis of residuals
D:Based on the regression of squared residuals on squared fitted values
```

Figure 15.17 Inclusion of one-period lags in the sales function

Although the Durbin–Watson statistic in Fig. 15.17 is quite close to 2, do not be too impressed by this. Recall, from section 15.4, that the *dw* statistic is biased towards the value 2, in the presence of a lagged *dependent* variable. Thus, the presence of lagged sales S_{t-1} in our equation makes the *dw* statistic invalid as a test of autocorrelation and also as a test for misspecification.

Notice that both the advertising variables A and $A1$ have very low *t*-values. Obviously it makes sense to see whether these variables should be dropped from the equation. But remember that low *t*-values can be the result of multicollinearity and A and $A1$ are almost certainly highly correlated. We can check this by using the F statistic [13.48] for adding (or dropping) explanatory variables in a regression equation. Your programme will have a facility for doing this, but it will again be instructive to do this via hand calculator.

It can be seen that the equation in Fig. 15.17 has a residual sum of squares $SSR_U = 8.871$. If the variables A and $A1$ are dropped from the sales equation, you should obtain the result shown in Fig. 15.18. This equation has a residual sum of squares of $SSR_R = 8.904$, a slight increase on that in Fig. 15.17. To test the additional explanatory power of the two advertising variables, we use [13.48] to compute, with $h = 2$ and $n - k = 39 - 8 = 31$ d.f.,

$$TS = \frac{(8.904 - 8.871)/2}{8.871/31} = 0.058.$$

```
                   Ordinary Least Squares Estimation
****************************************************************************
Dependent variable is S
39 observations used for estimation from 1997M2 to 2000M4
****************************************************************************
Regressor            Coefficient        Standard Error         T-Ratio[Prob]
INTER                  1.0264               3.5126               .29221[.722]
E                       .41706              .049387             8.4448[.000]
E1                     -.28895              .068909            -4.1933[.000]
P                     -3.4352              1.8723              -1.8347[.076]
P1                     2.9592              1.9166               1.5440[.132]
S1                      .82634              .068817            12.0077[.000]
****************************************************************************
R-Squared                     .96553   R-Bar-Squared                    .96030
S.E of Regression             .51944   F-stat.    F( 5, 33)    184.8583[.000]
Mean of Dependent Variable  29.2641   S.D. of Dependent Variable       2.6071
Residual Sum of Squares      8.9038   Equation Log-likelihood        -26.5355
Akaike Info. Criterion     -32.5355   Schwarz Bayesian Criterion     -37.5262
DW-statistic                 2.0935
****************************************************************************


                           Diagnostic Tests
****************************************************************************
*    Test Statistics     *     LM Version         *       F Version         *
****************************************************************************
*                        *                        *                         *
* A:Serial Correlation* CHSQ( 12)= 17.9834[.116] * F( 12, 21)= 1.4974[.202]*
*                        *                        *                         *
* B:Functional Form      * CHSQ(  1)= .048335[.826] * F(  1, 32)= .039709[.843]*
*                        *                        *                         *
* C:Normality            * CHSQ(  2)= 9.8572[.007] *      Not applicable      *
*                        *                        *                         *
* D:Heteroscedasticity* CHSQ(  1)= 089894[.764] * F(  1, 37)= .085481[.772]*
****************************************************************************
A:Lagrange multiplier test of residual serial correlation
B:Ramsey's RESET test using the square of the fitted values
C:Based on a test of skewness and kurtosis of residuals
D:Based on the regression of squared residuals on squared fitted values
```

Figure 15.18 Omission of the advertising variables A and $A1$

With (2, 31) d.f., the critical value $F_{0.05} = 3.31$. Thus we can see that the advertising variables make no contribution to explaining variations in sales. The poor t-ratios on A and $A1$ cannot be regarded as solely due to the correlation between these variables.

The diagnostic statistics for the equation in Fig. 15.18 are similar to those in Fig. 15.17, with an improvement in the LM statistic for up to 12th-order autocorrelation (now less than its critical value) and a further slight deterioration in the normality statistic. On balance, it certainly looks as if the problems with the autocorrelation statistics in Fig. 13.6 were the result not of serial correlation in the disturbances, but of the omission of lagged variables from the regression equation. That is, the estimation of the equation in Fig. 13.6 involved a dynamic misspecification. We shall return to the equation in Fig. 15.18 in the next chapters.

Example 15.10

Consider again the result in Fig. 15.18. Both the price variables P and $P1$ have t-values that are less than 2. But, like A and $A1$, P and $P1$ are likely to be highly correlated. Re-estimate the equation without the price variables and test the joint hypothesis that neither of the price variables influences sales.

Summary

- The **explanatory X variables** in a regression equation are **rarely non-stochastic** as assumed in the classical model.

- When any stochastic X variables in a regression equation are **correlated** with the disturbance in that equation, **OLS** provides **biased** and **inconsistent** estimators of regression parameters.

- Such correlation can occur because of **errors of measurement** in the values of variables and because of the **simultaneity** of many economic relationships. **Instrumental variable** methods of estimation are often used to combat such problems.

- Disturbances are frequently **homoscedastic** when data are **cross-sectional** and **auto-correlated** when data refer to **time series**.

- Heteroscedasticity or autocorrelation results in OLS estimators becoming **inefficient** although they **remain unbiased** and **consistent**. A more serious problem is that estimated standard errors become **biased estimators** of the **true standard errors**.

- Tests for heteroscedasticity and autocorrelation use **residuals** as **estimates** of the unknown **disturbances**. Well-known general tests for these problems are the **Lagrange multiplier tests**.

- When heteroscedasticity or autocorrelation is present then they can be allowed for by using **data transformations**. This leads to **general least-squares** estimators with unbiased estimated standard errors.

- Autocorrelated **residuals** can also be the result of a **misspecified** regression equation. Misspecification can occur both because of the selection of an **incorrect functional form** and because of the selection of the **wrong regressors**.

- The **omission** of a **relevant** explanatory variable will, almost always, lead to **biased estimators** of regression parameters. The **inclusion** of an **irrelevant** variable will not cause bias but will, usually, result in **less efficient** estimators.

Notes

1. See, for example, Thomas (1997, pp. 207–8). If X and ε are uncorrelated but *not independent* of each other, then it is possible to show that the OLS estimators are consistent but *biased* in small samples. For reasons which need not concern us here, this situation is sometimes referred to as the *contemporaneously uncorrelated case*; see, for example, (Thomas 1997, p. 209).

    If X and ε are independent, then clearly they must be uncorrelated and, as noted in the main text, the OLS estimators are both unbiased and consistent. For obvious reasons this is known as the *independence case*.

2. This is referred to as the *contemporaneously correlated case* when the OLS estimators are not only biased but inconsistent.

3. See, for example, Thomas (1997, p. 212).

4. A thorough consideration of this distinction is provided in Thomas (1999, Chapter 4).

5. When the intercept on the Q-axis, of either curve, changes then that curve must shift. In this case the intercepts are the constants α_0^* and β_0^* which remain unchanged because Y and C remain unchanged.

6. If u and v vary over time, the intercepts (which are now given by $\alpha_0^* + u$ and $\beta_0^* + v$) must also vary. Thus the curves will shift about over time.

7. The intercept of the supply curve is $\beta_0^* = \beta_0 + \beta_2 C$. So when C varies the intercept varies and the curve must shift.

8. In the reduced form there will always be a reduced-form equation for *each* endogenous variable. Each reduced-form equation must contain *only* exogenous variables on its

right-hand side. Thus, in this system, there will be just two reduced-form equations – one for Q and one for P. Only the exogenous variables Y and C will appear on the right-hand side.

9. In large samples, $\sum X_i \varepsilon_i / n$ can be shown to be the *sample* covariance between X and ε. Again, in large samples the sample covariance is virtually identical to the population covariance $\text{Cov}(X_i, \varepsilon_i)$. Note that

$$\sum X_i \varepsilon_i = \sum (X_i - \bar{X}) \varepsilon_i \quad \text{(since } \sum \bar{X} \varepsilon_i = \bar{X} \sum \varepsilon_i = 0 \text{ in large samples)}$$
$$= \sum (X_i - \bar{X})(\varepsilon_i - \bar{\varepsilon}) \quad \text{(since } \bar{\varepsilon} \sum (X_i - \bar{X}) = \bar{\varepsilon} \sum x_i = 0),$$

which, when divided by n, gives the sample covariance. It follows that if $\text{Cov}(X_i, \varepsilon_i) = 0$, then $\sum X_i \varepsilon_i = 0$.

10. If ε and Z are uncorrelated then $\text{Cov}(Z_i, \varepsilon_i) = 0$. By arguments identical to those in note 9, in large samples $\sum Z_i \varepsilon_i / n$ is equivalent to the sample covariance between Z and ε.

11. Since [15.24] and [15.25] are only valid in large samples, it follows that the estimators [15.26] are only valid in large samples.

12. It is necessary that m, the number of instruments, be at least as great as the number of explanatory variables (including the intercept). The intercept may serve as one of the instruments.

13. See note 12.

14. U and S serve as their own instruments.

15. See Dornbusch and Fisher (1987) for a discussion of the NAIRU.

16. See, for example, Thomas (1997, p. 283).

17. See, for example, Thomas (1997, p. 288).

18. See, for example, Greene (2000, p. 541).

19. Notice that, when estimating [15.45], it is the intercept b_2 that gives an estimate of the coefficient on X_2 in the original equation [15.42]. Similarly, it is the coefficient on the X_2^* variable in [15.45] that gives an estimate of the intercept in the original [15.42].

20. It does this by testing for skewness and kurtosis of OLS residuals.

21. In fact the high R^2 for the GLS regression is partly spurious. Both dependent and explanatory variables have income Y in their denominators. Thus we can expect correlations between S/Y, $1/Y$, A/Y and N/Y because of their common denominator.

22. That is, u_t is normally distributed with $E(u_t) = 0$ for all t, $E(u_t^2) = $ constant for all t, and $E(u_t u_s) = 0$ for all $t \neq s$. Notice that when discussing serial correlation i subscripts are normally replaced by t subscripts.

23. See, for example, Thomas (1997, pp. 298–9).

24. For example, when estimating $E(Y_t) = \alpha + \beta X_t + \gamma Y_{t-1}$, the presence of the lagged dependent variable Y_{t-1} among the regressors invalidates the Durbin–Watson statistic. See, for example, Thomas (1997, p. 312).

25. See, for example, Thomas (1997, pp. 305–6).

26. The direction of the bias will depend on (a) the direction of the correlation between X_2 and X_3 and (b) the sign of β_3 in [15.60].

16

Introducing dynamic econometrics

Objectives

On completion of your study of this chapter you should be able:

1. to realize that, with time-series data, dependent variables usually respond to explanatory variables with a distributed lag, so that impact and long-run multipliers differ;

2. to recognize a Koyck or geometric lag and appreciate the problems of estimating a regression equation that involves such a lag;

3. to understand and distinguish between the partial adjustment model and adaptive expectations model, and appreciate the limitations of the latter;

4 to appreciate that, when time series are non-stationary, the standard large-sample theory relating to regression models breaks down.

Introduction

In Computer Exercise 15.5 we introduced the idea that, in the current period, a dependent variable may not react fully or immediately to changes in one or more of the explanatory variables. Thus lagged values of some of the explanatory variables need to appear in the estimating equation. For example, consumption may depend not only on current income but also, for reasons of habit or simple inertia, on past levels of income. Similarly, a firm may need time to adjust its capital stock in response to a rise in the demand for its product.

In this chapter, we begin by introducing some basic ideas concerning dynamic econometrics and explain the meaning of a Koyck distributed lag. Then we describe two well-known simple dynamic models, the partial adjustment model and the adaptive expectations model. Finally, we define what we mean by a stationary time series and examine the consequences of non-stationarity for the estimation of dynamic equations.

16.1 **Basic ideas**

Consider the following equation:

$$Y_t = \alpha + \beta_0 X_t + \beta_1 X_{t-1} + \beta_2 X_{t-2} + \beta_3 X_{t-3} + \varepsilon_t. \qquad [16.1]$$

Here Y_t depends not only on the current value of X_t but also on the lagged values X_{t-1}, X_{t-2} and X_{t-3}. The lag pattern in [16.1] is referred to as a *distributed lag*. In this case the so-called *maximum lag* is just three periods but often, with quarterly data, the maximum lag length m can be quite large and possibly infinite.

Equations such as [16.1] imply that the long-run response of Y to a once-and-for-all change in X is different from the short-run immediate response. For example, suppose that X is held constant at the level $X = Z$. This implies that $X_t = X_{t-1} = X_{t-2} = X_{t-3} = Z$. Assuming $E(\varepsilon_t) = 0$, then, given [16.1], we have

$$\begin{aligned}
E(Y_t) &= \alpha + \beta_0 Z + \beta_1 Z + \beta_2 Z + \beta_3 Z \\
&= \alpha + (\beta_0 + \beta_1 + \beta_2 + \beta_3)Z \\
&= \alpha + (\Sigma \beta_j)Z,
\end{aligned} \qquad [16.2]$$

where the summation is from $j = 0$ to 3. Equation [16.2] gives us the *long-run* or *equilibrium* value of Y when X is held constant at the value Z.

Now suppose that, at period t, the value of X rises from $X_t = Z$ to $X_t = Z + 1$ and remains at this level. Using [16.2], we have

$$\begin{aligned}
E(Y_t) &= \alpha + \beta_0(Z + 1) + (\beta_1 + \beta_2 + \beta_3)Z \\
&= \alpha + \beta_0 + (\beta_0 + \beta_1 + \beta_2 + \beta_3)Z \\
&= \alpha + \beta_0 + (\Sigma \beta_j)Z.
\end{aligned} \qquad [16.3]$$

Comparing [16.3] with [16.2], it can be seen that the rise in X by one unit has led to an immediate rise in $E(Y)$ of β_0 units. Hence β_0, the coefficient on X_t in [16.1], measures the immediate or *short-run* or *impact* effect on $E(Y)$ of a unit change in X. β_0 is sometimes called the *short-run* or *impact multiplier*.

The impact effect is not, however, the final effect. By period $t + 1$, X has been at its new level for two periods, so that, again using [16.1],

$$\begin{aligned}
\mathrm{E}(Y_{t+1}) &= \alpha + (\beta_0 + \beta_1)(Z + 1) + (\beta_2 + \beta_3)Z \\
&= \alpha + (\beta_0 + \beta_1) + (\Sigma\,\beta_j)Z
\end{aligned} \qquad [16.4]$$

Similarly,

$$\mathrm{E}(Y_{t+2}) = \alpha + (\beta_0 + \beta_1 + \beta_2) + (\Sigma\,\beta_j)Z \qquad [16.5]$$

and, finally,

$$\begin{aligned}
\mathrm{E}(Y_{t+3}) &= \alpha + (\beta_0 + \beta_1 + \beta_2 + \beta_3) + (\Sigma\,\beta_j)Z \\
&= \alpha + \Sigma\,\beta_j + (\Sigma\,\beta_j)Z \\
&= \alpha + (\Sigma\,\beta_j)(Z + 1).
\end{aligned} \qquad [16.6]$$

Thus, when X has been at its new level, $X = Z + 1$, for three periods, $\mathrm{E}(Y)$ attains the level given by [16.6]. Moreover, unless X were to change again, $\mathrm{E}(Y)$ remains at this final equilibrium level, since it is easy to see that, using [16.1] repeatedly,

$$\mathrm{E}(Y_{t+3}) = \mathrm{E}(Y_{t+4}) = \mathrm{E}(Y_{t+5}) = \mathrm{E}(Y_{t+6}) = \ldots$$

Comparing [16.6] with [16.2], we can deduce two facts. Firstly, we can see that the long-run or equilibrium effect on a unit change in X is a change in $\mathrm{E}(Y)$ of $\Sigma\,\beta_j$, that is, the sum of the β_j in [16.1]. The quantity $\Sigma\,\beta_j$ is often termed the *long-run* or *equilibrium multiplier*.

It should also be fairly clear, looking at [16.2] and [16.6], that the long-run equilibrium relationship between X and Y is

$$\mathrm{E}(Y_t) = \alpha + (\Sigma\,\beta_j)X_t. \qquad [16.7]$$

That is, if we substitute any value for X (whether it be Z or $Z + 1$ or any other value) into [16.7], we will obtain the long-run equilibrium value of $\mathrm{E}(Y_t)$.

Students are frequently confused over the meaning of 'long run' in this context. Here, when we talk about the long run, we are considering equilibrium values. The long run does not necessarily involve a large number of periods or years. A new equilibrium may be reached very quickly or, alternatively, very slowly. In the above example, the maximum lag length is $m = 3$ so that a new equilibrium is reached after only three periods.

Equations [16.2]–[16.6] trace the path of $\mathrm{E}(Y)$ as it moves from its initial to its new equilibrium. Such a path is illustrated in Fig. 16.1. Such analysis of *movements* between equilibria is termed a *dynamic analysis* in econometrics, while models that involve such analysis are termed *dynamic models*.

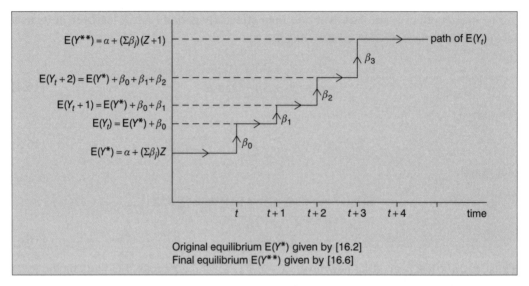

Figure 16.1 Time path of $E(Y_6)$

This type of analysis can be undertaken for any maximum lag length m. The generalization of [16.1] is

$$Y_t = \alpha + \beta_0 X_t + \beta_1 X_{t-1} + \beta_2 X_{t-2} + \beta_3 X_{t-3} + \cdots + \beta_m X_{t-m} + \varepsilon_t. \qquad [16.8]$$

This implies an impact effect of β_0 and a long-run effect again given by $\Sigma \beta_j$, where the summation is over all the β_j in the equation. Similarly, the equilibrium relationship between X and $E(Y)$ is again given by [16.7], regardless of the value of m.

Example 16.1

Determine the impact and long-run multipliers of a unit change in X when:

(a) $Y_t = 0.31 + 0.94X_t + 0.48X_{t-1} + 0.46X_{t-2} + 0.73Y_{t-3} + 0.68X_{t-4} + 0.45X_{t-5}$;

(b) $Y_t = 1.64 + 2.08X_t - 2.01X_{t-1} + 1.53X_{t-2} - 1.58X_{t-3}$.

16.2 Geometric lag distributions

A serious problem in estimating distributed lag models such as [16.8] is the large number of lagged values of X that have to be included in the equation. If m is large, we encounter what are referred to as 'degrees-of-freedom problems'. If m is large relative to n, the sample size, the degrees of freedom in the regression, $n - m - 1$, will be small. As a result, the normal OLS hypothesis tests will lack power since t-tables reveal that $t_{0.05}$, for example, can be relatively large. For instance, with just 2 d.f., $t_{0.05} = 2.92$, compared with 1.64 for very large samples. Under these circumstances, the probability of rejecting a null hypothesis when it is false can be relatively small.

Even with large n, there will be problems because the various lagged values of X are likely to be highly multicollinear, so that standard errors are large. This makes it difficult to estimate the β_j in [16.8] with any precision.

Because of these difficulties, it is unusual for models such as [16.8] to be estimated directly. Rather, some *a priori restriction* is often *imposed* on the pattern of the β_j coefficients, so as to reduce the number of parameters that have to be estimated and to cut down the number of regressors.

The best-known and simplest restriction that can be placed on the β_j is that they should decline geometrically. That is,

$$Y_t = \alpha + \beta_0 X_t + \beta_0 \theta X_{t-1} + \beta_0 \theta^2 X_{t-2} + \beta_0 \theta^3 X_{t-3} + \cdots + \varepsilon_t \qquad [16.9]$$

where $-1 \leqslant \theta \leqslant 1$.

In [16.9], the β_j of [16.8] follow the sequence $\beta_0 = \beta_0 \theta^j$ ($j = 0, 1, 2, 3, \ldots$). That is,

$$\beta_0, \quad \beta_0 \theta, \quad \beta_0 \theta^2, \quad \beta_0 \theta^3, \quad \beta_0 \theta^4, \ldots. \qquad [16.10]$$

Thus the coefficients follow a geometric progression, with first term β_0 and a common ratio θ having an absolute value between zero and unity. In this case the maximum lag is infinite, but successive lagged values of X have a continually declining influence on Y. Such a lag distribution is usually referred to as *geometric* or *Koyck lag*.[1]

In [16.9], while we have reduced the number of parameters in the model to three (α, β_0 and θ), we still have the same number of lagged values of X on the right-hand side. However, the model can be further simplified by applying what is known as a *Koyck transformation*.

Firstly, we lag equation [16.9] by one period. That is, Y_t becomes Y_{t-1}, X_t becomes X_{t-1}, X_{t-1} becomes X_{t-2} and so on. Secondly, if we multiply the resulting equation by θ, we obtain

$$\theta Y_{t-1} = \theta \alpha + \beta_0 \theta X_{t-1} + \beta_0 \theta^2 X_{t-2} + \beta_0 \theta^3 X_{t-3} + \cdots + \theta \varepsilon_{t-1}. \qquad [16.11]$$

Finally, subtracting [16.11] from the original [16.9] gives

$$Y_t - \theta Y_{t-1} = \alpha(1 - \theta) + \beta_0 X_t + \varepsilon_t - \theta \varepsilon_{t-1}$$

or

$$Y_t = \alpha(1 - \theta) + \beta_0 X_t + \theta Y_{t-1} + u_t, \qquad [16.12]$$

where

$$u_t = \varepsilon_t - \theta \varepsilon_{t-1} \qquad [16.13]$$

is a first-order moving-average disturbance of the kind described in Section 15.4.

The advantage of the formulation [16.12] is not only that it involves just three parameters, but also that, with only three regressors (including the intercept), it is easy to estimate. For example, suppose we obtain the regression

$$\hat{Y} = 48 + 0.3X_t + 0.6Y_{t-1}. \qquad [16.14]$$

Comparing [16.14] with [16.12], we see that we can estimate β_0 in [16.12] by $b_0 = 0.3$, θ by $\hat{\theta} = 0.6$ and, since we can equate $a(1 - \hat{\theta})$ with 48, a by $a = 48/0.4 = 120$. In fact, substituting these values into [16.9] yields

$$Y_t = 120 + 0.3X_t + 0.18X_{t-1} + 0.108X_{t-1} + 0.0648X_{t-3} + \cdots + \varepsilon_t. \qquad [16.15]$$

[16.15] is the distributed-lag formulation of the model. Notice how the coefficients of the X variables decline geometrically with common ratio 0.6.

The impact multiplier for X is easily seen to be 0.3 and we can find the long-run multiplier by summing the series [16.10]. The sum to infinity of the series is $\beta_0/(1 - \theta)$, which we can estimate by $b_0/(1 - \hat{\theta}) = 0.75$.

Unfortunately, there are severe problems with the estimation of [16.12]. We have already noted that the disturbance u_t in that equation is of a moving-average type, and so will, almost certainly, be autocorrelated.[2] But there is an even more serious problem. Even if X is non-stochastic, the other regressor in [16.12], Y_{t-1}, clearly is not. Y_{t-1} depends on the disturbance u_{t-1} and so must be stochastic.

If u_t had been non-autocorrelated, the presence of Y_{t-1}, a stochastic variable in [16.12], would not have mattered too much. From Chapter 15.1, we know that OLS estimators, although biased in small samples, remain consistent in such conditions. Moreover, in the absence of any lagged dependent variables, an autocorrelated disturbance alone means that OLS estimators remain unbiased and consistent, although they are no longer efficient. It is *the combination of both autocorrelation and a lagged dependent variable that causes major problems*. Now the OLS estimators become *both biased and inconsistent*.

To understand this intuitively, note from [16.12] and [16.13] that Y_{t-1} depends on u_{t-1} and hence on ε_{t-1}. But, since u_t is a moving-average disturbance, it must also depend on ε_{t-1}. Hence Y_{t-1} and u_t must be related. Since Y_{t-1} is one of the regressors in [16.12], we have a correlation between a disturbance and a right-hand-side variable. But we know, from Chapter 15.1, that such correlation means that OLS estimators will be both biased and inconsistent.

In fact serial correlation in the disturbances always causes such problems when lagged dependent variables appear on the right-hand side of an estimating equation. This makes the proper testing of the disturbance for autocorrelation a crucial matter. Recall that the Durbin–Watson statistic is biased towards 2 in the presence of a lagged dependent variable. In such a situation the *dw* statistic is therefore inappropriate and other tests such as the LM statistics for serial correlation, discussed in Chapter 15.4, must be used.

If consistent estimators of the parameters in [16.12] are required, then a possible approach is to make use of the instrumental-variable techniques of Chapter 15.2. The obvious method is to use X_t as its own instrument and X_{t-1} as the instrument for the lagged dependent variable Y_{t-1}. X_{t-1} is uncorrelated with ε_t, by assumption, but is likely to be highly correlated with Y_{t-1}, so it makes a suitable instrument. Unfortunately, however, X_t and X_{t-1} are likely to be highly correlated themselves so that, although instrumental variable estimators will be consistent, they are not likely to be particularly efficient. The alternative is to estimate α, β_0 and θ in [16.12] by maximum likelihood techniques, described in Chapter 11.4, but this process is complicated and we do not pursue it here.[3]

Example 16.2

Estimation of a Koyck model by ML methods yields

$$\hat{Y} = 25 + 0.72X_t + 0.45Y_{t-1}.$$

Using the notation of this section, obtain estimates of α, β_0 and θ. Write down the distributed-lag formulation of the model.

Worked Example

A model is estimated by an instrumental variable technique:

$$\hat{Y}_t = 1.4 + 2.1X_t + 1.7Y_{t-1}.$$

How would you interpret this model?

Solution

Comparing the estimated equation with [16.12] yields $\hat{\theta} = 1.7$, $b_0 = 2.1$ and hence $a = 1.4/(-0.7) = -2$. This is therefore not a Koyck model, since $\hat{\theta} > 1$. The distributed-lag formulation can be obtained using [16.9], and is

$$\hat{Y}_t = -2 + 2.1X_t + 3.57X_{t-1} + 6.07X_{t-2} + 10.3X_{t-3} \dots.$$

The b_j coefficients in this equation form a divergent geometric series. The impact multiplier appears to be 2.1, with a long-run multiplier, obtained by summing the b_j coefficents, that is apparently infinite! In fact, this an example of a dynamic model which exhibits the phenomenon of non-stationarity. We discuss such models in Chapter 16.4.

Example 16.3

Interpret the regression results

(a) $\hat{Y}_t = -4 \;-\; 0.4X_t \;+\; 0.8Y_{t-1}$,

(b) $\hat{Y}_t = \; 0.85 \;+\; 0.6X_t \;-\; 0.7Y_{t-1}$.

---

*16.3 The partial adjustment and adaptive expectations models

In this section we discuss two well-known economic models that result in a geometric or Koyck lag, similar to that in the previous section.

The partial adjustment model

Suppose the desired value of Y at time t, Y_t^*, depends on some expanatory variable X so that

$$Y_t^* = \alpha + \beta X_t + \varepsilon_t, \qquad\qquad [16.16]$$

where ε_t is a classical disturbance. For example, a household's optimal level of consumption might depend on its income, or a firm's desired level of capital stock might depend on its level of sales.

However, it may take time for the actual value of Y to become fully adjusted to its desired or optimal Y^*. Thus Y and Y^* may differ, at least in the short term. That is, a complete adjustment of Y in response to a change in X does not occur instantaneously. For example, habit or inertia may delay a household's adjustment to changes in its income. Similarly, a firm cannot adjust its capital stock instantaneously; investment in and the instalment of new equipment takes time.

Suppose that the relationship between actual Y and desired Y^* is as follows:

$$Y_t - Y_{t-1} = \lambda(Y_t^* - Y_{t-1}), \qquad 0 \leqslant \lambda \leqslant 1, \qquad [16.17]$$

or

$$Y_t = \lambda Y_t^* + (1 - \lambda)Y_{t-1}. \qquad\qquad [16.18]$$

Thus, if desired Y in period t exceeds actual Y in the previous period (i.e., if $Y_t^* - Y_{t-1} > 0$), then actual Y in period t is adjusted upwards above its level in the previous period, (i.e., $Y_t - Y_{t-1} > 0$). But this adjustment is not by the full extent of the difference between Y_t^* and Y_{t-1} (otherwise we would have $Y_t - Y_{t-1} = Y_t^* - Y_{t-1}$ and hence $Y_t = Y_t^*$). That is, the *adjustment* is only *partial* and not complete, the extent of the upward movement in Y depending on the size of the *adjustment parameter* λ, which lies between 0 and 1, inclusive.[4] At one extreme, $\lambda = 1$ and adjustment is immediate and complete, implying, from [16.18], that

$$Y_t = Y_t^*, \qquad\qquad [16.19]$$

that is, actual and desired Y are always the same. At the other extreme, $\lambda = 0$ and there is no adjustment at all, implying from [16.18], that

$$Y_t = Y_{t-1}, \qquad\qquad [16.20]$$

that is, actual Y remains unchanged, regardless of any change in X or Y^*. In practice, of course, we expect λ to lie somewhere between zero and unity. In general, the larger is λ, the larger is the extent of the adjustment in the current period and the more rapidly Y adjusts to X over time.

Substituting for Y_t^* in [16.18], using [16.16], gives

$$Y_t = \alpha\lambda + \beta\lambda X_t + (1-\lambda)Y_{t-1} + \lambda\varepsilon_t. \qquad\qquad [16.21]$$

This equation constitutes the *partial adjustment model*. A major advantage of [16.21] is that it involves only variables that can be observed, that is, X and Y. In contrast, [16.16] involves desired Y, that is Y^*, which is not a variable that we will normally have data for. The point of the partial adjustment equation [16.18], provided it is valid, is that it takes us from the unestimatible [16.16] to the estimatible [16.21].

Notice that [16.21] is very similar to the Koyck equation [16.12] in the previous section, with $\theta = 1 - \lambda$ and $\beta_0 = \beta\lambda$. There is, however, one important difference between the two models. In [16.12] the disturbance u_t is autocorrelated (it is of moving-average kind). But in [16.21] the disturbance is simply λ times the disturbance in [16.16]. Since there is no reason why ε_t in [16.16] should be autocorrelated, it follows that the disturbance $\lambda\varepsilon_t$ in [16.21] can also be regarded as non-autocorrelated. It follows that [16.21] can be estimated by OLS, although because of the lagged dependent variable the estimators will be consistent but not unbiased.

Suppose we were to obtain again the regression result [16.14]. We could now interpret it in terms of the partial adjustment model. Comparing [16.14] with [16.21], we have

$$a\hat\lambda = 48, \qquad b\hat\lambda = 0.3, \qquad 1 - \hat\lambda = 0.6.$$

Thus we would estimate λ by $\hat\lambda = 0.4$, β by $b = 0.3/0.4 = 0.75$ and a by $\alpha = 48/0.4 = 120$. That is, the underlying relationship [16.16] is estimated by

$$Y_t^* = 120 + 0.75X_t$$

and the adjustment parameter in [16.17] by $\hat\lambda = 0.4$. This value of 0.4 implies that 40% of any difference between desired Y^* and actual Y in the previous period is made up in the current period.

The partial adjustment model was much used in early applied econometrics, although nowadays it is usually regarded as too simple, particularly when data are quarterly. We will consider an important generalization of this model in the next chapter.

Finally, since the partial adjustment model can be expressed in the form [16.21], which is identical in form to [16.12] apart from the disturbance, it must imply a geometric lag of the type [16.9].[5]

Example 16.4

The following partial adjustment model is estimated by OLS:

$$\hat{Y}_t = 18 + 1.2X_t + 0.7Y_{t-1}.$$

Obtain estimates of the underlying parameters and interpret them.

Example 16.5

Optimal Y_t^* is determined by

$$Y_t^* = \alpha + \beta_1 X_{1t} + \beta_2 X_{2t} + \varepsilon_t,$$

while actual Y adjusts to Y^* via the partial adjustment process [16.17]. The following equation was estimated by OLS:

$$\hat{Y}_t = 5 + 0.8X_{1t} + 0.4X_{2t} + 0.8Y_{t-1}.$$

Obtain estimates of α, β_1, β_2 and the adjustment parameter λ.

Estimate the short- and long-run multipliers for X_1 and X_2.

**The adaptive expectations model

Students often confuse the partial adjustment model with the model we will describe in this subsection. This is surprising because, although both models lead eventually to a geometric lag, they are fundamentally different.

Suppose that Y depends not on the actual value of X, but on its expected, normal or 'permanent' value, X^*:

$$Y_t = \alpha + \beta X_t^* + \varepsilon_t. \tag{16.22}$$

The most common interpretation of X^* is that it represents 'permanent' income in the Friedman sense. Y might then represent consumption or the demand for money. However, X^* might also be, for example, a firm's expected output.

A comparison of [16.22] with [16.16] indicates that it is X^* in [16.22] that is the 'unobservable' variable rather than Y^* as in [16.16]. It is this that makes the models so different. We now have to propose some hypothesis regarding the formation of the expected variable X^*. One of the best-known such hypotheses is the *adaptive expectations model* where

$$X_t^* - X_{t-1}^* = \mu(X_t - X_{t-1}^*), \qquad 0 \leqslant \mu \leqslant 1, \qquad\qquad [16.23]$$

or

$$X_t^* = \mu X_t + (1 - \mu)X_{t-1}^*. \qquad\qquad [16.24]$$

Thus [16.23] is a relationship which links X^* to X, whereas the partial adjustment equation [16.17] links Y^* to Y. Equation [16.23] is an example of a so-called *learning process*, because in each period actual X is compared with the expected or normal X^* from the period before.[6] If actual X exceeds previous expected X^* (i.e., $X_t - X_{t-1}^* > 0$ in [16.23]), then our idea of what is normal or expected X is adjusted upwards (i.e., $X_t^* - X_{t-1}^* > 0$ in [16.23]). On the other hand, if actual X_t is less than X_{t-1}^*, then normal or expected X^* is adjusted downwards. In general, the extent of the adjustment in X^* is determined by the size of the *adjustment parameter μ* which lies between zero and unity, inclusive.

At one extreme, $\mu = 1$ and X^* is always completely adjusted to current actual X; that is, using [16.24],

$$X_t^* = X_t. \qquad\qquad [16.25]$$

Thus, in these circumstances expected X^* is always the same as actual X. For example, consumers then always regard their actual current income to be normal, expected or permanent.

At the other extreme, $\mu = 0$ and there is no adjustment at all, so that X^* is totally uninfluenced by changes in actual X; that is, using [16.24],

$$X_t^* = X_{t-1}^*. \qquad\qquad [16.26]$$

In other words, X^* never changes, whatever the value of actual X. That is, the consumer maintains his fixed optimistic (or pessimistic) idea about what his normal income is, regardless of whatever his actual current income turns out to be.

To estimate the parameters in the model we must first use [16.24] to substitute for X^* in [16.22]. This yields

$$Y_t = \alpha + \beta[\mu X_t + (1 - \mu)X_{t-1}^*] + \varepsilon_t$$

or

$$Y_t = \alpha + \beta\mu X_t + \beta(1 - \mu)X_{t-1}^* + \varepsilon_t. \qquad\qquad [16.27]$$

Next, we multiply [16.22] by $1 - \mu$ and lag the whole equation by one period.[7] This gives

$$(1 - \mu)Y_{t-1} = \alpha(1 - \mu) + \beta(1 - \mu)X_{t-1}^* + (1 - \mu)\varepsilon_{t-1}. \qquad [16.28]$$

Finally, if we subtract [16.28] from [16.27], we obtain an equation that involves just the actual values of X and Y:

$$Y_t - (1 - \mu)Y_{t-1} = \alpha\mu + \beta\mu X_t + \varepsilon_t - (1 - \mu)\varepsilon_{t-1}$$

or

$$Y_t = \alpha\mu + \beta\mu X_t + (1 - \mu)Y_{t-1} + v_t, \qquad [16.29]$$

where $v_t = \varepsilon_t - (1 - \mu)\varepsilon_{t-1}$ is a moving-average disturbance.

Notice that [16.29] no longer includes the unobservable variable X^* and can therefore, in principle, be estimated. For example, if we again obtained the regression result [16.14] then, comparing [16.29] with [16.14], we could estimate μ by $\hat{\mu} = 0.4$, α by $a = 48/0.4 = 120$ and β by $b = 0.3/0.4 = 0.75$.

Given these values we could now estimate the underlying relationship [16.22] as

$$Y_t = 120 + 0.75X_t^* \qquad [16.30]$$

and the adjustment parameter μ in [16.23] as $\hat{\mu} = 0.4$. Such a value for μ would imply that 40% of any difference between actual X and previous expected X^* is reflected in a revised expected X^*.

Unfortunately, there are major problems in the estimation and interpretation of [16.29]. Firstly, the disturbance v_t is autocorrelated, being of first-order moving-average type. The presence of the lagged dependent variable Y_{t-1} means that OLS estimators will be biased and inconsistent. The estimation of the adaptive expectations model is, therefore, more difficult than that of the partial adjustment model of the previous subsection. In fact, the problems with the adaptive expectations equation [16.29] are identical to those of the Koyck equation [16.12], described in Section 16.2. The form of [16.29] also implies a geometric or Koyck lag and, as noted there, estimation usually requires maximum likelihood methods.

But there are more fundamental problems with the partial adjustment and adaptive expectations models. Suppose again we have obtained the estimated equation [16.14]. We saw above that we could interpret this equation in terms of an adaptive expectations model with adjustment coefficient $\hat{\mu} = 0.4$. But we could equally well interpret it in terms of the partial adjustment equation [16.21] with an adjustment coefficient $\hat{\lambda} = 0.4$. In fact, that is exactly what we did in the previous subsection. Without prior knowledge of what model is appropriate, we cannot know whether the importance of the lagged dependent variable Y_{t-1}, (and hence of the implied geometric lag) is the result of a partial adjustment mechanism or of a non-instantaneous adjustment of expected X^* to actual X. The confusion arises, of course, because each of the models makes use of an unobservable variable: desired Y^* in the partial adjustment model [16.16], and expected X^* in the adaptive expectations model [16.22].[8] In applied econometrics, it is often the case that the lag structure in an equation can be satisfactorily uncovered. Unfortunately, interpreting the lags in terms of underlying behavioural relationships is frequently a different matter.

During the 1950s and 1960s, the adaptive expectations model proved very popular with applied econometricians, particularly those working on the demand for money or the consumption function. Gradually, however, the mechanical and backward-looking nature of the model became apparent. It was pointed out, for example, that adaptive expectations imply irrational behaviour by economic agents, when a variable grows at a constant rate over time. Unfortunately, the 1970s proved to be a period when a number of key economic indices – particularly general price indices – grew at an exponential rate.

It is easy to show that, if expectations are formed in an adaptive way, and if a variable X grows at a constant positive rate, then the predicted value of X always turns out to be less than the actual value that eventually occurs.[9] In such circumstances, we should expect economic agents to adjust their expectations-forming process and allow for the errors that they are making. Unfortunately, the adaptive expectations model, being a both backward-looking and rigid hypothesis, permits no such corrections for past and current forecast errors.

A more general criticism of the adaptive expectations model is based on the Lucas (1976) critique of econometric policy evaluation. As noted above, adaptive expectations models imply a fixed relationship between expectations and the lagged past values of certain variables. A change in economic policy regime, however, provided it is recognized by economic agents, should affect expectations, despite the fixed nature of past values of these variables. Consequently, the parameters of any forecasting equation must change whenever the policy regime changes. But this is inconsistent with an adaptive expectations equation with its fixed parameters. Economic agents are being irrational if they continue to make adaptive expectations, even when there is change of policy regime.

In the late 1970s and 1980s economists developed the *rational expectations model* as an alternative to the adaptive expectations model. A procedure for estimating such models was first developed by McCallum (1976), but it is beyond the scope of this book.

Example 16.6

Maximum likelihood methods are used to estimate the following adaptive expectations model:

$$\hat{Y}_t = 0.26 + 0.42X_t + 0.82Y_{t-1}.$$

Obtain estimates of and interpret all underlying parameters.

Example 16.7

An instrumental variable method is used to obtain the following equation:

$$\hat{Y}_t = 1.36 + 2.23X_t + 0.36Y_{t-1}.$$

Estimate and interpret all underlying parameters: (a) if the equation is the result of a partial adjustment process; (b) if it results from an adaptative expectations process.

Computer Exercise 16.1

In this exercise we shall make a preliminary investigation of the US consumption function using annual data from 1959 to 1997. In the file DATASET7 you will find data on just three variables:

> RY = real personal disposable income per capita, measured in constant 1996 dollars:
> RC = real non-durable consumption expenditure per capita, measured in constant 1996 dollars:
> NC = nominal non-durable consumption expenditure per capita, measured in *current* US dollars.

The simplest and oldest formulation of the consumption function is the Keynesian-type specification, presented here in natural logarithm form:

$$\ln RC_t = \alpha + \beta \ln RY_t + \varepsilon_t. \qquad [16.31]$$

Notice that [16.31] is specified in real terms. Suppose, however, we add a general price variable P to our equation:

$$\ln RC_t = \alpha + \beta \ln RY_t + \delta \ln P_t + \varepsilon_t \qquad [16.32]$$

It is important to realize that, on strict theoretical terms, *the coefficient δ on the price variable in [16.32] should be zero*. Do not fall into the trap of expecting δ to be negative because of some vague feeling that a rise in prices should lead to a decline in consumption expenditure!

It is worth considering exactly why we should expect $\delta = 0$ in [16.32]. Recall that a regression coefficient such as δ measures the effect of a unit change in $\ln P$ when all other explanatory variables are held constant. In [16.32], the only other regressor is real income $\ln RY$. However, a general price rise, with real income held constant, must imply an equiproportional rise in nominal income. But economic theory predicts that equiproportionate changes in prices and nominal income should leave demand (i.e., $\ln RC$) unchanged. This, of course, implies $\delta = 0$ in [16.32].

Access the file DATASET7, from the learning centre. The data series for RC and NC can be used to derive a price index for non-durable consumption. RC is equal to NC divided by a price index P, which is termed the *implied deflator* of consumption expenditure. Thus, since $RC = NC/P$, we have $P = NC/RC$.

Create the index P, using the data transformation section of your programme. Now view the data series P. As expected, its value rises steadily from about 0.22 in 1960 to 1.02 in 1997. Its value is exactly 1 in 1996. This reflects the fact that RC is measured in 1996 prices.[10]

Create an intercept in the usual manner, and estimate [16.31] and [16.32] by OLS in natural logarithmic terms. Use data for 1961–97. The observations for 1959 and 1960 will be utilized later in the chapter and in the next chapter. You should obtain the results shown in Figs 16.2a and 16.2b.

```
                   Ordinary Least Squares Estimation
*******************************************************************************
Dependent variable is LNRC
37 observations used for estimation from 1961 to 1997
*******************************************************************************
Regressor            Coefficient        Standard Error         T-Ratio[Prob]
INTERCEPT               -.26267                .10649        -2.4666[.019]
LNRY                    1.0150                 .011040        91.9409[.000]
*******************************************************************************
R-Squared                   .99588   R-Bar-Squared                   .99576
S.E of Regression           .016543  F-stat.   F(  1,  35)     8453.1[.000]
Mean of Dependent Variable  9.5249   S.D. of Dependent Variable      .25401
Residual Sum of Squares     .0095780 Equation Log-likelihood       100.2946
Akaike Info. Criterion      98.2946  Schwarz Bayesian Criterion     96.6836
DW-statistic                .41476
*******************************************************************************


                           Diagnostic Tests
*******************************************************************************
*    Test Statistics     *      LM Version       *       F Version          *
*******************************************************************************
*                        *                       *                          *
* A:Serial Correlation*  CHSQ(   1)= 21.9376[.000] * F(  1, 34)= 49.5193[.000] *
*                        *                       *                          *
* B:Functional Form    *  CHSQ(   1)= 20.4359[.000] * F(  1, 34)= 41.9472[.000] *
*                        *                       *                          *
* C:Normality          *  CHSQ(   2)=  .36728[.832] *      Not applicable     *
*                        *                       *                          *
* D:Heteroscedasticity*  CHSQ(   1)=  3.2603[.071] * F(  1, 35)=  3.3821[.074] *
*******************************************************************************
 A:Lagrange multiplier test of residual serial correlation
 B:Ramsey's RESET test using the square of the fitted values
 C:Based on a test of skewness and kurtosis of residuals
 D:Based on the regression of squared residuals on squared fitted values
```

Figure 16.2a US consumption function

In fig 16.2a you may be initially impressed by an R^2 as high as 0.996 and a t-ratio on ln RY as large as 91.9! But alarm bells should ring when you notice a Durbin–Watson statistic of only 0.41 and that two of the diagnostic χ^2 statistics are well beyond critical values. What has happened?

```
                    Ordinary Least Squares Estimation
*********************************************************************************
Dependent variable is LNRC
37 observations used for estimation from 1961 to 1997
*********************************************************************************
  Regressor           Coefficient        Standard Error          T-Ratio[Prob]
  INTERCEPT               .36076               .47434              .76055[.452]
  LNRY                    .95260               .047571           20.0249[.000]
  LNP                     .029398              .021810            1.3479[.187]
*********************************************************************************
R-Squared                     .99609   R-Bar-Squared                     .99586
S.E of Regression             .016353  F-stat.   F( 2,  34)      4326.1[.000]
Mean of Dependent Variable    9.5249   S.D. of Dependent Variable        .25401
Residual Sum of Squares       .0090921 Equation Log-likelihood         101.2577
Akaike Info. Criterion        98.2577  Schwarz Bayesian Criterion       95.8413
DW-statistic                  .43361
*********************************************************************************


                              Diagnostic Tests
*********************************************************************************
*    Test Statistics     *       LM Version          *        F Version       *
*********************************************************************************
*                        *                           *                        *
* A:Serial Correlation*  CHSQ(  1)=  22.4398[.000]  * F(  1, 33)= 50.8586[.000]*
*                        *                           *                        *
* B:Functional Form     *  CHSQ(  1)=  24.9434[.000]  * F(  1, 33)= 68.2725[.000]*
*                        *                           *                        *
* C:Normality           *  CHSQ(  2)=   .038952[.981]  *      Not applicable    *
*                        *                           *                        *
* D:Heteroscedasticity* CHSQ(  1)=   4.7120[.030]  * F(  1, 35)=  5.1078[.030]*
*********************************************************************************
  A:Lagrange multiplier test of residual serial correlation
  B:Ramsey's RESET test using the square of the fitted values
  C:Based on a test of skewness and kurtosis of residuals
  D:Based on the regression of squared residuals on squared fitted values
```

Figure 16.2b Addition of the price variable

In fact, it is very easy to obtain very high R^2 values using time-series data on consumption and income. Over the period since World War II, both these variables have exhibited strong upward trends. A quick look at your data should convince you of that. But we have stressed several times, earlier in this text, that common trends in time-series variables can lead to spurious correlations between such variables. While virtually everyone would accept that there must be *some* relationship between *RC* and *RY*, their common trends are severely exaggerating any correlation that is present.

The results in Fig. 16.2b reflect similar problems. The price variable also exhibits a strong trend, as we have seen, but it is interesting to note that the coefficient on the price variable is positive and, although not significant, its *t*-ratio is as high as 1.35. Similar, and more markedly significant, results for US data were firstly noted by Branson and Klevorick (1969) and were regarded as evidence of 'money illusion' in the consumption function.

Such results implied that equiproportionate rises in prices and hence in money income lead to increases in consumption. This was interpreted as meaning that consumers *mistake a rise in money income for a rise in real income* and consequently increase spending.

Earlier in this section we saw that lagged dependent variables are sometimes included in regression equations to allow for geometric distributed lags. Consumption function work in the 1950s and 1960s provided an example of this. Econometricians of that time employed both the partial adjustment model [16.17] and the adaptive expectations model [16.23] to justify the inclusion of the lagged dependent variable $\ln RC_{t-1}$ in [16.31] and [16.32].

It is possible to create lagged variables in all time-series econometric programmes. For example, it is usually possible to create the variable $\ln RC_{t-1}$ simply by typing $LnRC1 = LnRC(-1)$. Again using the sample period 1961–97, re-estimate [16.31] and [16.32], with the lagged dependent variable $\ln RC_{t-1}$ included. You should obtain the results shown in Figs 16.3a and 16.3b.

```
                    Ordinary Least Squares Estimation
*******************************************************************************
Dependent variable is LNRC
37 observations used for estimation from 1961 to 1997
*******************************************************************************
Regressor            Coefficient        Standard Error        T-Ratio[Prob]
INTERCEPT             -.068374              .099673           -.68598[.497]
LNRY                   .54220               .11423            4.7466[.000]
LNRC1                  .45942               .11064            4.1525[.000]
*******************************************************************************
R-Squared                    .99726    R-Bar-Squared                  .99710
S.E of Regression            .013672    F-stat.    F(  2,   34)   6196.7[.000]
Mean of Dependent Variable  9.5249     S.D. of Dependent Variable     .25401
Residual Sum of Squares     .0063551   Equation Log-likelihood      107.8836
Akaike Info. Criterion      104.8836   Schwarz Bayesian Criterion   102.4672
DW-statistic                 .87264
*******************************************************************************


                            Diagnostic Tests
*******************************************************************************
*     Test Statistics    *      LM Version       *        F Version         *
*******************************************************************************
*                        *                       *                          *
* A:Serial Correlation *  CHSQ(   1)=  12.9844[.001] * F(  1, 33)= 16.0054[.000] *
*                        *                       *                          *
* B:Functional Form      *  CHSQ(   1)=  15.1214[.000] * F(  1, 33)= 22.8078[.000] *
*                        *                       *                          *
* C:Normality            *  CHSQ(   2)=   2.9057[.234] *     Not applicable       *
*                        *                       *                          *
* D:Heteroscedasticity *  CHSQ(   1)=    .64691[.421] * F(  1, 35)=   .62283[.435] *
*******************************************************************************
A:Lagrange multiplier test of residual serial correlation
B:Ramsey's RESET test using the square of the fitted values
C:Based on a test of skewness and kurtosis of residuals
D:Based on the regression of squared residuals on squared fitted values
```

Figure 16.3a Addition of the lagged dependent variable

```
                    Ordinary Least Squares Estimation
*******************************************************************************
Dependent variable is LNRC
37 observations used for estimation from 1961 to 1997
*******************************************************************************
Regressor            Coefficient       Standard Error        T-Ratio[Prob]
INTERCEPT               .012001               .41274        .029076[.977]
LNRY                    .54225                .11588         4.6796[.000]
LNP                     .0039538              .019685         .20085[.842]
LNRC1                   .45121                .11944         3.7776[.001]
*******************************************************************************
R-Squared               .99727     R-Bar-Squared                  .99702
S.E of Regression       .013869    F-stat.    F(  3,   33)   4014.5[.000]
Mean of Dependent Variable  9.5249 S.D. of Dependent Variable     .25401
Residual Sum of Squares .0063473   Equation Log-likelihood      107.9062
Akaike Info. Criterion  103.9062   Schwarz Bayesian Criterion   100.6843
DW-statistic            .86895
*******************************************************************************


                           Diagnostic Tests
*******************************************************************************
*      Test Statistics    *       LM Version       *       F Version         *
*******************************************************************************
*                         *                        *                         *
* A:Serial Correlation *  CHSQ(   1)=  13.5826[.000] * F(   1, 32)= 18.5607[.000] *
*                         *                        *                         *
* B:Functional Form    *  CHSQ(   1)=  21.4238[.000] * F(   1, 32)= 44.0132[.000] *
*                         *                        *                         *
* C:Normality          *  CHSQ(   2)=   2.8683[.238] *      Not applicable     *
*                         *                        *                         *
* D:Heteroscedasticity *  CHSQ(   1)=    .74283[.389] * F(   1, 35)=   .71708[.403] *
*******************************************************************************
A:Lagrange multiplier test of residual serial correlation
B:Ramsey's RESET test using the square of the fitted values
C:Based on a test of skewness and kurtosis of residuals
D:Based on the regression of squared residuals on squared fitted values
```

Figure 16.3b Addition of price variable to model with geometric lag

The coefficient on the lagged dependent variable has *t*-ratios of 4.15 and 3.78. This makes it clear that we cannot expect to explain variations in US consumption by looking at the *current* values of variables alone. Lags, and hence dynamic factors, must be important. Unfortunately, the problem of the common upward trends in all the variables means that, at this stage, there is little more that we can say. However, we shall return to this data set in our final chapter.

Example 16.8

Assume that the equation estimated in Fig. 16.3b is the result of an underlying consumption function of the kind

$$RC_t = \alpha + \beta RY_t^p + \delta P_t + \varepsilon_t,$$

where RY^p is permanent real income. Suppose that permanent income is determined by an adaptive expectations process

$$RY^p_t - RY^p_{t-1} = \mu(RY_t - RY^p_{t-1}), \qquad 0 < \mu < 1.$$

All variables are in natural logarthms.

Ignoring any econometric problems of estimation, and adding the variable P_{t-1} to the result in Fig. 16.3b, attempt the estimation of α, β, δ and μ. What values are implied for the short- and long-run income elasticities of consumption?

**16.4 The problem of non-stationarity

In this text, we have several times stressed the problems that can arise when applying regression analysis to trending time series. A trending or non-stationary regressor implies that assumption IC of the classical model has been violated, so that the normal large-sample theory underpinning the classical regression model can no longer be relied upon. It is, therefore, time to look more directly at the question of non-stationarity.

Suppose we have a set of random variables, $X_1, X_2, X_3, X_4, X_5, \ldots$, where the subscripts denote successive time periods. For example, X_1 might be the value of a variable in period 1, X_2 its value in period 2 and so on, but each X has its own probability distribution and, together, they make up what is termed a *stochastic process*. If, for each period, the relevant X takes a particular value, then we have a *time series* of observations, again each observation referring to a different variable. We refer to the above process/time series as X_t $(t = 1, 2, \ldots)$.

Generally, each X_t will have its own mean $E(X_t)$ and variance $V(X_t)$. In addition, non-zero covariances can exist for different X_t. It is not necessarily the case that these means, variances and covariances will remain unchanged over time. For example, if $E(X_t)$ increases

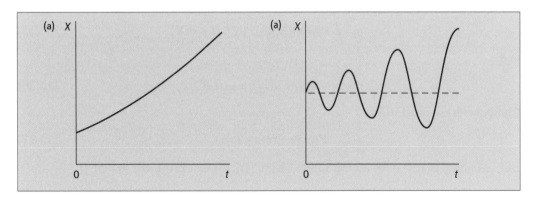

Figure 16.4 Two non-stationary time series

over time then the time path for X_t might look like that in Fig. 16.4a. Alternatively, even if $E(X_t)$ remains unchanged but $V(X_t)$ increases over time, then the time series for X_t might look like that in Fig. l6.4b.

A time series X_t is said to be *stationary* if:

(a) $E(X_t)$ is constant for all t,

(b) $V(X_t)$ is constant for all t, and

(c) $Cov(X_t, X_{t+k})$ is constant for all t and all $k \neq 0$;

A time series is therefore stationary if its mean, variance and covariances remain constant over time. It is *non-stationary* if it fails to satisfy any part of the above definition.[11] For example, either of the two series in Fig. 16.4 is almost certain to be non-stationary.

Whether or not a time series is stationary *will depend on the values of the parameters that characterize the underlying stochastic process*. For example, suppose that

$$X_t = k + \theta X_{t-1} + \varepsilon_t, \qquad \theta > 0, \tag{16.33}$$

where k and θ are parameters and ε_t is a classical disturbance. Successive substitution in [16.33] yields

$$X_1 = k + \theta X_0 + \varepsilon_1$$

$$X_2 = k + \theta X_1 + \varepsilon_2 = k + \theta k + \theta^2 X_0 + (\varepsilon_2 + \theta \varepsilon_1)$$

$$X_3 = k + \theta X_2 + \varepsilon_3 = k + \theta k + \theta^2 k + \theta^3 X_0 + (\varepsilon_3 + \theta \varepsilon_2 + \theta^2 \varepsilon_1)$$

$$\vdots \qquad \vdots \qquad \vdots \qquad \vdots$$

$$X_t = k + \theta X_{t-1} + \varepsilon_t = \quad m_t \quad + \quad v_t \tag{16.34}$$

where

$$m_t = k + \theta k + \theta^2 k + \cdots + \theta^{t-1} k + \theta^t X_0 \tag{16.35}$$

and

$$v_t = \varepsilon_t + \theta \varepsilon_{t-1} + \theta^2 \varepsilon_{t-2} + \cdots + \theta^{t-1} \varepsilon_1. \tag{16.36}$$

Consequently, using [16.34]

$$E(X_t) = E(m_t) + E(v_t). \tag{16.37}$$

But, assuming $E(\varepsilon_t) = 0$ for all t, it follows from [16.36] that $E(v_t) = 0$, so that

$$E(X_t) = E(m_t),$$

where m_t is given by [16.35].

Now suppose that in [16.33], $0 < \theta < 1$. As $t \to \infty$, $\theta^t \to 0$, so that it can be seen from [16.35] that m_t tends to the sum of a convergent geometric series, with first term k and common ratio θ. That is, $m_t \to k/(1 - \theta)$, which is a constant. It follows that $E(m_t)$ and hence $E(X_t)$ must also tend to this same constant $k/(1 - \theta)$.

It should now be clear, at least when t is large, that if $0 < \theta < 1$, X_t obeys the first of the conditions for stationarity given at the beginning of this section. In fact, it is not too difficult to show that X_t obeys the second and third conditions also.[12]

However, if $\theta \geq 1$, then the conditions for stationarity cannot be met. For example, if $\theta = 1$, then using [16.35]

$$m_t = k(1 + 1 + 1 + \cdots + 1) + X_0 = kt + X_0$$

so that, using [16.37], we now have $E(X_t) = X_0 + kt$. This implies that $E(X_t)$ increases with time, showing no sign of approaching a constant value as $t \to \infty$. Thus the time series X_t is non-stationary. If $\theta > 1$, then, from [16.35], m_t becomes a divergent series and X_t is again non-stationary.

As we have noted in previous chapters, there is nothing unusual in economic variables displaying such non-stationary behaviour, since they frequently display regular trends both upwards and downwards. However non-stationarity may well have serious consequences for estimation. For example, in the geometric lag model [16.12], if Y_t increases at a constant rate over time, then so must Y_{t-1}. It follows that one of the regressors, namely Y_{t-1}, in [16.12] displays such an upward trend. But this implies that assumption IC in the classical model is invalid. Consequently, *we cannot make use of conventional large-sample theory when estimating [16.12]*.

In estimation the value of parameters, such as θ above, is clearly of the greatest importance. For example, it is desirable to be able to test H_0: $\theta = 1$ against H_A: $\theta < 1$. The obvious way of doing this is to construct the usual t statistic $(\hat{\theta} - 1)/s_{\hat{\theta}}$, where $\hat{\theta}$ is the OLS estimator of θ in [16.33] and $s_{\hat{\theta}}$ is its estimated standard error. Such a test is usually referred to as a unit root test. Unfortunately, since normal large-sample theory breaks down when $\theta = 1$, this test is inapplicable even in large samples because the sampling distribution for the test statistic is no longer the t distribution.

Much work was done in the 1980s discovering the shape of the distribution for the above test statistic, in both small and large samples. It is nowadays referred to as the *Dickey–Fuller distribution* and it has become one of the standard tools of the modern applied econometrician.[13] Unfortunately, we do not have time to go into this matter in any further detail.

Equation [16.12] is of very simple form, although it can arise from either partial adjustment or adaptive expectations processes. But similar problems arise when any dynamic equation, with lagged dependent variables on its right-hand side, has to be estimated. If the implied time path for the dependent variable is non-stationary, then conventional large-sample theory is not applicable. Consequently, close attention must be played to the dynamic properties of such models, to determine whether time paths violate classical assumptions.

Example 16.9

Consider the following equations, in which ε_t is a classical disturbance,:

(a) $Y_\tau = 10 + 0.6Y_{t-1} + \varepsilon_t$;

(b) $Y_\tau = 0.5 + 1.3Y_{t-1} + \varepsilon_t$;

(c) $Y_\tau = 40 - 0.8Y_{t-1} + \varepsilon_t$;

(d) $Y_\tau = 0.4 + 0.8Y_{t-1} + 0.4Y_{t-2} + \varepsilon_t$;

(e) $Y_\tau = -14 + 7.3X_t + 0.7Y_{t-1} + \varepsilon_t$;

(f) $Y_\tau = 0.8X_t - 0.7Y_{t-1} + \varepsilon_t$.

If the time paths for X are exogenous, which of the time series for Y are stationary?

In this chapter and the next, there are many econometric equations containing variables lagged by one or more periods. Although it is often very difficult to comprehend or deduce the behavioural relationships underlying such equations, provided the variables are stationary in the sense described above, it is always possible to compute the values of relevant impact and long-run multipliers, as the following worked example illustrates.

Worked Example

The following equation is estimated, using stationary time series on the variables Y, X and Z:

$$\hat{Y}_t = 0.74 + 0.35X_t + 0.24X_{t-1} + 1.56Z_t - 0.74Z_{t-1} + 0.12Z_{t-2} - 0.45Y_{t-1} + 0.26Y_{t-2}.$$

Obtain estimates of the impact and long-run multipliers for both X and Z.

Solution

As usual, impact multipliers can be obtained by looking at the coefficients on the unlagged explanatory variables, in this case X_t and Z_t. Thus the impact multipliers for X and Z can be estimated as 0.35 and 1.56, respectively.

To obtain long-run multipliers, we need to derive the equilibrium relationship between Y, X and Z. In equilibrium, it must be the case that

$$Y_t = Y_{t-1} = Y_{t-2} = \dots ,$$
$$X_t = X_{t-1} = X_{t-2} = \dots ,$$
$$Z_t = Z_{t-1} = Z_{t-2} = \dots .$$

Thus, substituting in the estimated equation, we have

$$Y_t(1 + 0.45 - 0.26) = 0.74 + X_t(0.35 + 0.24) + Z_t(1.56 - 0.74 + 0.12).$$

Hence

$$1.19Y_t = 0.74 + 0.59X_t + 0.94Z_t$$

so that the equilibrium relationship must be

$$Y_t = 0.62 + 0.50X_t + 0.79Z_t.$$

The long-run multipliers for X and Z can, therefore, be estimated as 0.50 and 0.79, respectively. Notice that the long-run effect of a unit change in Z is less than the impact effect.

Example 16.10

The following equation is estimated:

$$\hat{Z}_t = 0.61 + 0.74X_t + 0.48X_{t-1} + 0.26X_{t-2} + 0.38Y_t - 0.36Y_{t-1} + 0.13Z_{t-1} + 0.09Z_{t-2}.$$

If all variables are in logarithmic form, estimate the short-run and long-run elasticities of Z with respect to X and Y.

Summary

- **Dynamic models** involve equations containing the **lagged values** of dependent and/or explanatory variables. They enable us to analyse the behaviour of a model when it is out of equilibrium and to compute both **impact** and **long-run multipliers**.

- When many lags of an explanatory variable appear in an equation, the variable is said to appear as a **distributed lag**. The simplest form of distributed lag is the **Koyck** or **geometric lag**. It can be estimated most simply by the inclusion of the **lagged dependent variable**.

- Both the **partial adjustment model** and the **adaptive expectations model** imply geometric distributed lags.

- **OLS estimators** of the parameters of the Koyck and the adaptive expectations models are both **biased** and **inconsistent**. **OLS estimators** of the parameters of a partial adjustment model are **biased** in small samples but **consistent**.

- When time series are **non-stationary**, the standard **large-sample** theory regarding regression analysis **breaks down**. For example, we cannot always rely on estimators being consistent, let alone unbiased.

- Many **economic time series** possess **strong trends**, both upwards and downwards. Consequently these time series are highly likely to be **non-stationary**.

Notes

1. See Koyck (1954).

2. Only if ε_t in [16.9] happens to be subject to a first-order autoregressive process with parameter $\rho = \theta$, so that $\varepsilon_t = \theta \varepsilon_{t-1} + u_t$, will u_t in [16.12] be non-autocorrelated. The condition $\rho = \theta$ is, of course, rather unlikely.

3. The procedure was first outlined by Klein (1958).

4. If $Y_t^* - Y_{t-1} < 0$ then, of course, Y_t is adjusted downwards, that is, $Y_t - Y_{t-1} < 0$.

5. In fact, successive substitution for $Y_{t-1}, Y_{t-2}, \ldots$ in [16.21] gives

$$Y_t = \alpha + \beta \lambda X_t + \beta \lambda (1 - \lambda) X_{t-1} + \beta \lambda (1 - \lambda)^2 X_{t-2} + \cdots + u_t,$$

where

$$u_t = \lambda \varepsilon_t + \lambda (1 - \lambda) \varepsilon_{t-1} + \lambda (1 - \lambda)^2 \varepsilon_{t-2} + \cdots .$$

6. Equation [16.23] is sometimes presented slightly differently as

$$X_{t+1}^* - X_t^* = \mu (X_t - X_t^*).$$

7. We are, in fact, again applying the so-called Koyck transformation; that is, we lag [16.22] by one period and then multiply by a suitable constant – in this case $1 - \mu$.

8. In fact, if the models are combined to incorporate both partial adjustment and adaptive expectations, then this problem is resolved; see, for example, Gujarati (1988, p. 521).

9. See, for example, Thomas (1991, p. 127).

10. Alternatively, we could multiply all P values by 100 to give a 1996 value of 100. You may be more familiar with indices expressed in this manner.

11. The third condition for stationarity, that of constant covariances, implies that the correlation between any two values of X depends only on the distance apart in time of the two values but does not vary with time itself. For example,

$$\text{Cov}(X_3, X_{18}) = \text{Cov}(X_8, X_{23}) = \text{Cov}(X_{14}, X_{29}) \text{ etc.,}$$

but $\text{Cov}(X_3, X_{18})$ is not the same as $\text{Cov}(X_3, X_{23})$.

12. For example, using [16.36], we have

$$V(v_t) = V(\varepsilon_t) + \theta^2 V(\varepsilon_{t-1}) + \theta^4 V(\varepsilon_{t+1}) + \cdots.$$

We know that $\sigma^2 = V(\varepsilon_t) = $ constant for all t. It follows that, when $0 < \theta < 1$, $V(v_t)$ tends to $\sigma^2/(1 - \theta^4)$ as $t \to \infty$. The proof that all covariances are constant is more complicated.

13. See, for example, Dickey and Fuller (1979).

17

A possible best-practice methodology

Objectives

When you have completed your study of this chapter you should be able:

1. to appreciate the distinction between the 'simple to general' and the 'general to specific' approaches to econometric investigation and recognize the advantages of the latter;

2. to understand the usefulness of nesting various regressions within a general model;

3. to use the F distribution to test restrictions on the parameters of a regression equation and, hence, undertake a simplification search;

4. to appreciate the advantage of using error correction models, particularly when time series are non-stationary;

5. to realize that only when variables are cointegrated can a long-run relationship between such variables exist.

Introduction

In this final chapter we examine an econometric methodology that can make a strong claim to be that of best practice, at least in the UK – the so-called 'general to specific' approach. Closely linked to this methodology is a type of dynamic equation that is usually termed an 'error correction model'. As we shall see, error correction models are extremely valuable tools for dealing with non-stationary time series.

*17.1 **The general to specific approach**

In the thirty years after World War II, most econometricians tended to adopt an approach to finding the 'best' model that has been termed *simple to general*. They might begin by estimating the simplest equation that was consistent with the relevant economic theory. If such a model proved 'unsatisfactory', as it often did, then various 'improvements' could be made, this process continuing until a 'satisfactory' model was obtained.[1] Often, the final model might be far more complicated than the initial model. For example, suppose an econometrician wished to model the demand for beef, D. He might have started by estimating

$$E(D_t) = \beta_1 + \beta_2 RY_t + \beta_3 RP_t, \qquad [17.1]$$

where RY_t is the real disposable income of consumers and RP_t is the relative price of beef, suitably defined.

If OLS estimation of [17.1] proved 'satisfactory' then the search for the best model might well have ended there. More likely, however, such an equation might be deemed unsatisfactory in some way. For example, the coefficient on RP might be non-significantly different from zero and even have an incorrect sign. Alternatively, the Durbin–Watson statistic might be well below 2, or R^2 might be thought too low.

Various attempts might now be made to 'improve' the equation in some way. For example, faced with a low dw statistic, one of the procedures, described in Chapter 15, for tackling an assumed first-order process in the disturbances might be adopted. Alternatively, another explanatory variable might be included in the equation to improve the R^2. Another favourite possibility might be to add the lagged dependent variable D_{t-1} to the right-hand side. Eventually a 'satisfactory' model would be uncovered, often considerably more complicated and 'general' than the initial equation [17.1].

The difficulty with the process outlined above was that, in many cases, investigators would fail to abandon the ideas embodied in their initial equations. They were simply searching for equations or evidence in support of hypotheses that they already believed in.

As Gilbert (1986) pointed out, they wished merely to 'illustrate' the theories that they were determined to support, come what may. Consequently, it was quite possible for two different investigators to come up with different conclusions, even when using the same data!

In the past 25 years an alternative approach to finding the most appropriate model has been developed, initially and particularly at the London School of Economics. The approach is especially associated with Professor D.F. Hendry, the British econometrician.

Unlike the simple to general approach, the Hendry approach involves *starting* with the estimation of a very general and possibly quite complicated model. This general model will contain within it a number of competing but simpler models, which are special cases of the general model. The simple models should, hopefully, represent all alternative economic hypotheses that require consideration. Such an approach has been termed *general to specific*, in contrast to the simple to general methodology described above. To take a straightforward case, returning to our demand for beef example, a suitable general model might be (with all variables perhaps in natural logarithms)

$$D_t = \alpha_0 + \alpha_1 RY_t + \alpha_2 RP_t + \alpha_3 Z_t + \beta_1 RY_{t-1} + \beta_2 RP_{t-1} + \beta_3 Z_{t-1} + \chi D_{t-1} + \varepsilon_t, \quad [17.2]$$

where RY_t and RP_t are as defined above and Z_t is some other exogenous variable (e.g., an index of non-beef meat prices or the proportion of vegetarians in the population) that the investigator believes may also influence the demand for beef. Notice that [17.2] includes, on its right-hand side, the lagged values of all variables, including the lagged value of the dependent variable D.

A number of special cases of [17.2] can be obtained by *imposing restrictions* on its parameters. For example, if we set $\beta_1 = \beta_2 = \beta_3 = 0$ in [17.2] we obtain

$$D_t = \alpha_0 + \alpha_1 RY_t + \alpha_2 RP_t + \alpha_3 Z_t + \chi D_{t-1} + \varepsilon_t, \quad [17.3]$$

which could be interpreted as a simple geometric lag model in which optimal demand depends on RY, RP and Z.

Another special case is obtained if the restrictions $\alpha_2 = \beta_2 = \chi = 0$ are imposed. Equation [17.2] then becomes

$$D_t = \alpha_0 + \alpha_1 RY_t + \alpha_3 Z_t + \beta_1 RY_{t-1} + \beta_3 Z_{t-1} + \varepsilon_t. \quad [17.4]$$

Here, demand depends only on real income and on the exogenous Z, with short one-period lags.

Yet another possibility is to impose $\alpha_2 = \alpha_3 = \beta_1 = \beta_2 = \beta_3 = 0$, so that [17.2] becomes

$$D_t = \alpha_0 + \alpha_1 RY_t + \chi D_{t-1} + \varepsilon_t. \quad [17.5]$$

In this case, demand depends only on real income, but again with a geometric lag.

When it is possible to obtain an estimating equation by imposing restrictions on some general model, then the equation is said to be *nested* within the general model. For example, [17.3], [17.4] and [17.5] are all nested within the general equation [17.2].

It is often the case that a nested equation will itself have even simpler models nested within it. For example, if the restriction $\alpha_1 + \beta_1 = 1$ is imposed on [17.4] then, provided the equation is estimated in natural logarithms, this implies that the long-run real income elasticity of demand must be unity. Substituting $\beta_1 = 1 - \alpha_1$ into [17.4] gives

$$D_t = \alpha_0 + \alpha_1 RY_t + \alpha_3 Z_t + (1 - \alpha_1)RY_{t-1} + \beta_3 Z_{t-1} + \varepsilon_t$$

or

$$D_t = \alpha_0 + \alpha_1(RY_t - RY_{t-1}) + RY_{t-1} + \alpha_3 Z_t + \beta_3 Z_{t-1} + \varepsilon_t$$

We cannot estimate this equation as it stands, because if we did that we would almost certainly not obtain the required coefficient of unity on the RY_{t-1} variable. So RY_{t-1} must be taken to the left-hand side to give

$$D_t - RY_{t-1} = \alpha_0 + \alpha_1(RY_t - RY_{t-1}) + \alpha_3 Z_t + \beta_3 Z_{t-1} + \varepsilon_t. \qquad [17.6]$$

If we now construct the variables $A_t = D_t - RY_{t-1}$ and $B_t = RY_t - RY_{t-1}$ from the data set, we can estimate [17.6] by regressing A_t on B_t, Z_t and Z_{t-1}. This yields estimates of α_0, α_2, α_3 and β_3. An estimate of β_1 can then be obtained, using the restriction $\beta_1 = 1 - \alpha_1$.

Example 17.1

Consider the estimating equation

$$Y_t = \alpha_0 + \alpha_1 X_t + \alpha_2 X_{t-1} + \alpha_3 X_{t-2} + \beta_1 Y_{t-1} + \beta_2 Y_{t-2} + \varepsilon_t.$$

In each case, find the equation that is obtained if the following restrictions are imposed. Comment on each equation.

(a) $\alpha_2 = \alpha_3 = \beta_2 = 0$, $0 \leqslant \beta_1 \leqslant 1$ [ε_t is $N(0, \sigma^2)$]

(b) $\beta_1 = \beta_2 = \alpha_3 = 0$

(c) $\alpha_1 + \alpha_2 = 0$, $\alpha_3 = 0$

(d) $\beta_2 = 0$, $0 \leqslant \beta_1 \leqslant 1$ [ε_t is $N(0, \sigma^2)$]

(e) $\alpha_1 + \alpha_2 = 1$, $\alpha_3 = 0$, $\beta_1 = \beta_2 = 0$

(f) $\alpha_2 = \alpha_3 = \beta_2 = 0$, $0 \leqslant \beta_1 \leqslant 1$ [$\varepsilon_t = u_t - \lambda u_{t-1}$]

(g) $\alpha_1 + \alpha_2 = 0$, $\beta_1 = 1$, $\beta_2 = \alpha_3 = 0$ [ε_t is $N(0, \sigma^2)$]

Are any of the equations (a)–(g) nested within any other equation in this set?

Example 17.2

Consider the general model

$$W_t = \kappa + \alpha_0 X_t + \alpha_1 X_{t-1} + \beta_0 Y_t + \beta_1 Y_{t-1} + \delta W_{t-1} + \varepsilon_t,$$

where all variables are in logarithmic form. Which equations should be estimated when the following restrictions are imposed?

(a) $\kappa = 0$, $\delta = 1$, $\alpha_0 + \alpha_1 = 0$, $\beta_0 + \beta_1 = 0$;

(b) $\delta = 0$, $\alpha_0 + \alpha_1 = \beta_0 + \beta_1 = 1$;

(c) $\alpha_0 + \alpha_1 + \delta = 1$.

Suppose the (three) restrictions

$$\alpha_0 + \alpha_1 = \beta_0 + \beta_1 = 1 - \delta$$

are imposed on the general model. Which equation should now be estimated? Is this final equation nested within any of the equations obtained in (a), (b) or (c)?

The structure linking the various equations [17.2]–[17.6] is shown in Fig. 17.1. Of course, for a large general model with many regressors, a 'tree diagram' linking all the various special case can be quite complicated. For this reason the econometrician will undertake what is called a *simplification search* or a *testing-down procedure*.

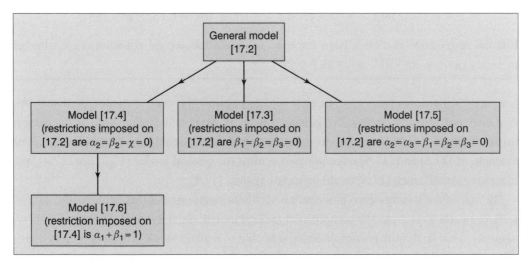

Figure 17.1 Structure linking equations [17.2]–[17.6]

Each special case is normally tested against the general model using an F-test. The imposition of a restriction on a regression equation virtually always results in an increase in the residual sum of squares (SSR). A restriction is held to be rejected if the resulting proportionate increase in the SSR is 'sufficiently large'. Under the null hypothesis of valid restriction(s), it can be shown that

$$TS = \frac{(SSR_R - SSR_U)/h}{SSR_U/(n-k)} \text{ has an } F \text{ distribution with } (h, n-k) \text{ d.f.} \qquad [17.7]$$

SSR_U and SSR_R refer to the residual sums of squares of the original (unrestricted) and restricted regression equations, respectively. h is the number of restrictions being tested, n is the sample size and k the number of parameters in the unrestricted equation. As usual, the null hypothesis is rejected if TS exceeds the relevant critical F value.

The test statistic [13.48] (for variable addition or deletion) is, in fact, a special case of the test statistic [17.7]. The only difference is that in [13.48] the restrictions are all of the form $\beta_j = 0$.

Example 17.3

The following equation is estimated from a sample of size $n = 48$:

$$\hat{Y}_t = -0.84 + 0.56X_t - 0.48X_{t-1} + 0.81Z_t - 0.83Z_{t-1} + 0.94Y_{t-1} \qquad (R^2 = 0.97, \Sigma\, e^2 = 246).$$

When restrictions are imposed on the regression coefficients, a second equation is estimated:

$$\widehat{Y_t - Y_{t-1}} = 0.38(X_t - X_{t-1}) + 0.79(Z_t - Z_{t-1}) \qquad (R^2 = 0.18, \Sigma\, e^2 = 268).$$

List the restrictions that have been imposed to obtain the second equation. Test whether these restrictions are valid, using an F-test.

In the testing-down procedure, models rejected against the general model are discarded. A model not rejected against the general model is examined further and, if necessary, further restrictions are imposed to see whether further simplification is possible. For example, if [17.3] and [17.5] were rejected against the general model [17.2] but [17.4] was 'data-acceptable', then [17.6] could be tested against [17.4].

The aim of the testing-down procedure is to find a simple model that explains the data as well, or nearly as well, as the complicated general model. Such a model is said to be *parsimonious*. That is, despite its simple form, it is able to explain much. The approach is therefore rooted in the well-known scientific principle that, for a given information set, simple explanations are to be preferred to complicated explanations.[2]

A major advantage of the general to specific methodology is that specification errors are hopefully limited to those that occur because of the presence of irrelevant variables rather than the omission of relevant ones. As we saw in Chapter 5.5, omitted-variable error is the more serious problem because it leads to bias and inconsistency. Provided the initial general model incorporates all competing hypotheses and likely variables, with a sufficient number of lags, omitted-variable bias should not be a problem. Moreover, any lack of efficiency due to the initial inclusion of irrelevant variables should be gradually reduced as the testing-down procedure proceeds and unimportant variables are dropped from the equation.

The simplification search can be more difficult than it might first seem. Use of the F statistic for testing a nested model against the general model needs to be buttressed by the full battery of diagnostic tests. For example, accepting a simpler model on the basis of a satisfactory F-test is of little use if the omitting of regressors leads to severe autocorrelation of the residuals.

Furthermore, a simplification search will frequently lead us to a situation where we have to choose between two non-nested models. For example, [17.4] and [17.5] are said to be non-nested because neither model can be obtained by placing restrictions on the parameters of the other. But if both [17.4] and [17.5] are data acceptable, compared with the general model [17.2], then we face something of an impasse. Since [17.4] and [17.5] are non-nested models, we cannot choose between them in the normal way because the usual F-test is inapplicable. Although a number of approaches for dealing with non-nested models have been suggested by econometricians, unfortunately these tests are far more complicated and we do not discuss them here.[3]

Worked Example

Consider the general model

$$Y_t = \kappa + \alpha_0 X_t + \alpha_1 X_{t-1} + \beta_1 Y_{t-1} + \beta_2 Y_{t-2} + \varepsilon_t.$$

Which of the following equations are nested in the general model and which are not? ($\Delta Y_t = Y_t - Y_{t-1}$, $\Delta Y_{t-1} = Y_{t-1} - Y_{t-2}$, etc.)

(a) $\Delta Y_t = \kappa + \alpha_0 \Delta X_t + \varepsilon_t$
(b) $Y_t = \alpha_1 X_{t-1} + \alpha_2 X_{t-2} + \beta_2 Y_{t-1} + \varepsilon_t$
(c) $\Delta Y_t = \kappa + \alpha_0 \Delta X_t + \gamma Y_{t-1} + \varepsilon_t$
(d) $Y_t - X_{t-1} = \alpha_0 \Delta X_t + \beta_1 Y_{t-1} + \varepsilon_t$
(e) $\Delta Y_t = \kappa_1 \Delta X_t + \kappa_2 \Delta X_{t-1} + \eta_1 \Delta Y_{t-1} + \varepsilon_t$

For the nested equations state, in each case, the restrictions that have been placed on the general model.

Solution

(a) This equation can be written as

$$Y_t - Y_{t-1} = \kappa + a_0(X_t - X_{t-1}) + \varepsilon_t$$

or as

$$Y_t = \kappa + a_0 X_t - a_0 X_{t-1} + Y_{t-1} + \varepsilon_t.$$

Thus (a) can be obtained from the general model by imposing the restrictions $a_0 + a_1 = 0$, $\beta_1 = 1$ and $\beta_2 = 0$. It is therefore nested in the general model.

(b) This equation is not nested in the general model because it contains X_{t-2}, which has not been included in the general model.

(c) This equation can be written as

$$Y_t - Y_{t-1} = \kappa + a_0(X_t - X_{t-1}) + \gamma Y_{t-1} + \varepsilon_t$$

or as

$$Y_t = \kappa + a_0 X_t - a_0 X_{t-1} + (1 + \gamma) Y_{t-1} + \varepsilon_t.$$

The restrictions that have to be imposed are $a_0 + a_1 = 0$ and $\beta_2 = 0$. This yields (c), with β_1 simply rewritten as $1 - \gamma$. Therefore (c) is nested in the general model. (Note that $\beta_1 = 1 - \gamma$ is *not* a restriction since γ is a *new* parameter that did not appear in the general model.)

(d) The equation can be rewritten as

$$Y_t = a_0 X_t + (1 - a_0) X_{t-1} + \beta_1 Y_{t-1} + \varepsilon_t.$$

It is therefore nested in the general model with $\kappa = 0$, $\beta_2 = 0$ and $a_0 + a_1 = 1$.

(e) The equation can be rewritten as

$$Y_t - Y_{t-1} = \kappa_1(X_t - X_{t-1}) + \kappa_2(X_{t-1} - X_{t-2}) + \eta_1(Y_{t-1} - Y_{t-2}) + \varepsilon_t$$

or as

$$Y_t = \kappa_1 X_t + (\kappa_2 - \kappa_1) X_{t-1} - \kappa_2 X_{t-2} + (1 + \eta_1) Y_{t-1} - \eta_2 Y_{t-2} + \varepsilon_t.$$

While we can set $\kappa = 0$ and define new parameters $\kappa_1 = a_0$, $\kappa_2 = a_0 + a_1$, $\eta_1 = \beta_1 - 1$ and $\eta_2 = -\beta_2$, it remains the case that equation (e) contains the variable X_{t-2}, which does not appear in the general model. Thus, this equation is not nested within the general model.

Example 17.4

Consider the following general model:

$$Y_t = \kappa + \alpha_0 X_t + \alpha_1 X_{t-1} + \beta_0 Z_t + \beta_1 Z_{t-1} + \gamma Y_{t-1} + \varepsilon_t.$$

What restrictions have to be imposed on the general model to obtain the following equations?

(a) $\Delta Y_t = \alpha_0 \Delta X_t + \beta_0 \Delta Z_t + \varepsilon_t;$

(b) $Y_t = \kappa + \alpha_0 X_t + \beta_0 Z_t + \gamma Y_{t-1} + \varepsilon_t;$

(c) $Y_t - Z_t = \kappa + \alpha_0 (X_t - Z_t) + \gamma Y_{t-1} + \varepsilon_t;$

(d) $Y_t - X_{t-1} = \kappa + \alpha_0 \Delta X_t + \gamma Y_{t-1} + \varepsilon_t;$

(e) $Y_t - X_{t-1} - Z_{t-1} = \kappa + \alpha_0 \Delta X_t + \beta_0 \Delta Z_t + \gamma Y_{t-1} + \varepsilon_t.$

Which of the equations (a)–(d) are nested in equation (e) and which are not? ($\Delta Y_b = Y_t - Y_{t-1}$, etc.)

Computer Exercise 17.1

In this section we will make use of the US consumption and income data, in the file DATASET7, to illustrate the general-to-specific approach just described. The variables are defined as in Computer Exercise 16.1.

Since the data series are annual we can, with some safety, limit maximum lag lengths to just two periods and formulate, in logarithmic form, the following general model:

$$\ln RC_t = \alpha + \beta_0 \ln RY_t + \beta_1 \ln RY_{t-1} + \beta_2 \ln RY_{t-2}$$
$$+ \delta_0 \ln P_t + \delta_1 \ln P_{t-1} + \delta_2 \ln P_{t-2}$$
$$+ \gamma_1 \ln RC_{t-1} + \gamma_2 \ln RC_{t-2} + \varepsilon_t. \qquad [17.8]$$

Construct the required lagged variables. (For example, $\ln RY_{t-2}$ may be created by typing in $lnRY2 = lnRY(-2)$ and so on.) Now estimate the general model [17.8] for the sample period 1961–97. You should obtain the result shown in Fig. 17.2.

Notice, first, that all the diagnostic tests beneath the main result are passed, so there appears to be no problem with the functional specification and no sign of omitted-variable error. The R^2 value of 0.999 is of little import, merely reflecting the strong common trend in the variables. Note also that the equation is estimated for the sample period 1961–97, because the observations for 1959 and 1960 are needed to construct the lagged variables. For the sake of comparisons, the same sample period was employed in Computer Exercise 16.1.

```
                     Ordinary Least Squares Estimation
************************************************************************
Dependent variable is LNRC
37 observations used for estimation from 1961 to 1997
************************************************************************
Regressor          Coefficient       Standard Error        T-Ratio[Prob]
INTERCEPT             -.49436              .32634          -1.5149[.141]
LNRY                   .74258              .11751           6.3191[.000]
LNRY1                 -.30026              .18900          -1.5887[.123]
LNRY2                  .036737             .19683            .18665[.853]
LNP                   -.34114              .15371          -2.2194[.035]
LNP1                   .28199              .30749            .91707[-367]
LNP2                   .041782             .17676            .23638[.815]
LNRC1                  .62836              .20304           3.0948[.004]
LNRC2                 -.060474             .18600           -.32512[.748]
************************************************************************
R-Squared                     .99906   R-Bar-Squared                .99880
S.E of Regression            .0088093   F-stat.   F(  8,  28)   3738.0[.000]
Mean of Dependent Variable    9.5249   S.D. of Dependent Variable   .25401
Residual Sum of Squares      .0021729   Equation Log-likelihood    127.7376
Akaike Info. Criterion       118.7376   Schwarz Bayesian Criterion 111.4885
DW-statistic                  1.8773
************************************************************************


                          Diagnostic Tests
************************************************************************
*    Test Statistics    *      LM Version      *     F Version        *
************************************************************************
*                       *                      *                      *
* A:Serial Correlation* CHSQ(  1)=   2.4834[.115] * F(  1, 27)=  1.9426[.175] *
*                       *                      *                      *
* B:Functional Form     * CHSQ(  1)=   1.5880[.208] * F(  1, 27)=  1.2107[.281] *
*                       *                      *                      *
* C:Normality           * CHSQ(  2)=   1.9247[.382] *        Not applicable     *
*                       *                      *                      *
* D:Heteroscedasticity* CHSQ(  1)=  .0062139[.937] * F(  1, 35)=.0058790[.939] *
************************************************************************
A:Lagrange multiplier test of residual serial correlation
B:Ramsey's RESET test using the square of the fitted values
C:Based on a test of skewness and kurtosis of residuals
D:Based on the regression of squared residuals on squared fitted values
```

Figure 17.2 The estimated general model

What is more interesting is the fact that the second-order lagged variables, $\ln RY_{t-2}$, $\ln P_{t-2}$ and $\ln RC_{t-2}$, all have t-ratios less than 0.5. An obvious first step in a simplification search is therefore to drop these variables from the equation. Estimating such an equation for the same sample period 1961–97 yields the result shown in Fig. 17.3.

Apart from the intercept, all the variables in this equation have coefficients with significant t-ratios (with 31 d.f., $t_{0.05} = 1.70$). The equation in Fig. 17.3 is clearly nested in the equation in Fig. 17.2, so we can use the F statistic [17.7] to test the three restrictions $\beta_2 = \delta_2 = \gamma_2 = 0$ that have been imposed. From Figs 17.2 and 17.3, we have the residual sums

```
                    Ordinary Least Squares Estimation
**************************************************************************
Dependent variable is LNRC
37 observations used for estimation from 1961 to 1997
**************************************************************************
Regressor            Coefficient      Standard Error       T-Ratio[Prob]
INTERCEPT               -.54613              .28832        -1.8942[.068]
LNRY                     .76294             .097702         7.8089[.000]
LNRY1                   -.31167              .15685        -1.9871[.056]
LNP                     -.37436             .091815        -4.0773[.000]
LNP1                     .35437             .084444         4.1965[-000]
LNRC1                    .60122              .10846         5.5433[.000]
**************************************************************************
R-Squared                       .99905  R-Bar-Squared                .99890
S.E of Regression             .0084165  F-stat.  F( 5,  31)    6552.0[.000]
Mean of Dependent Variable      9.5249  S.D. of Dependent Variable    .25401
Residual Sum of Squares       .0021960  Equation Log-likelihood     127.5422
Akaike Info. Criterion        121.5422  Schwarz Bayesian Criterion  116.7094
DW-statistic                    1.8697
**************************************************************************


                            Diagnostic Tests
**************************************************************************
*     Test Statistics     *      LM Version        *       F Version        *
**************************************************************************
*                         *                        *                        *
* A:Serial Correlation*    CHSQ(   1)=  .14646[.702] * F(   1, 30)=  .11922[.732]*
*                         *                        *                        *
* B:Functional Form   *    CHSQ(   1)=  .82560[.364] * F(   1, 30)=  .68469[.415]*
*                         *                        *                        *
* C:Normality         *    CHSQ(   2)=  2.1695[.338] *      Not applicable    *
*                         *                        *                        *
* D:Heteroscedasticity*    CHSQ(   1)= .0035090[.953] * F(   1, 35)=.0033197[.954]*
**************************************************************************
A:Lagrange multiplier test of residual serial correlation
B:Ramsey's RESET test using the square of the fitted values
C:Based on a test of skewness and kurtosis of residuals
D:Based on the regression of squared residuals on squared fitted values
```

Figure 17.3 Omitting all second-order lagged variables

of squares $SSR_U = 0.002\ 173$ and $SSR_R = 0.002\ 196$. With $h = 3$, $n = 37$ and $k = 9$, the test statistic takes the value

$$\frac{(SSR_R - SSR_U)/h}{SSR_U/(n-k)} = \frac{(0.002\ 196 - 0.002\ 173)/3}{0.002\ 173/28} = 0.099.$$

With $(3, 28)$ d.f., the 5% critical value for F is $F_{0.05} = 2.95$, so that the restrictions are not rejected. Moreover, imposing the restrictions causes no obvious deterioration in the diagnostic statistics, so it is clear that omitting second-order lags from the equation is data acceptable.

For the moment, it is not obvious what direction we should take next in our simplification search. Moreover, the interpretation of the model in Fig. 17.3 is not clear. For example, what are the implications of the negative coefficients on the variables $\ln RY_{t-1}$ and $\ln P_t$? Some answers to these questions will be provided later in the chapter.

What we can investigate at this point is the relationship between our general model and the models presented in Figs 16.2b and 16.3b. These equations are clearly nested in the general model [17.8] and hence the restrictions imposed can be subjected to an F-test. Since these models were also estimated over the sample period 1961–1997, they are directly comparable with the general model of Fig. 17.2.

You should find that the simple geometric lag model of Fig. 16.2b has a residual sum of squares $SSR_R = 0.009\,092$. Six variables have been omitted from the general model in this case so that, using [17.7] with $h = 6$, $n = 37$ and $k = 9$, you should obtain a value of the F statistic of 14.87. With (6, 28) d.f., the critical F value is $F_{0.05} = 2.45$, so this model is clearly rejected by the data.

Next, test the model in Fig. 16.3b against the general model. You should find that the F statistic takes a value of 10.76. Thus, this geometric lag model also has to be strongly rejected. These results confirm that the poor diagnostic statistics obtained in Computer Exercise 16.1 are at least partly the result of the omission of relevant lagged variables. That is, the equation suffered from a dynamic misspecification.

*17.2 Error correction models

We have stressed, in this and earlier chapters, that high R^2s and large t-ratios, obtained particularly from time-series data, do not necessarily imply any causal link between dependent and explanatory variables. When time-series variables exhibit strong trends and so are, almost certainly, non-stationary, high correlations may be at least partly spurious. Unfortunately, for many years, applied econometricians paid little attention to this problem. This was despite the fact that such trending stochastic time series rendered invalid many of the large-sample properties of classical regression analysis.

An early token attempt to deal with such data was to *first-difference* all variables. For example, suppose that

$$Y_t = \beta_0 + \beta_1 X_t + \varepsilon_t, \tag{17.9}$$

but that both variables in [17.9] exhibit strong trends, either upwards or downwards. Lagging [17.9] one period gives

$$Y_{t-1} = \beta_0 + \beta_1 X_{t-1} + \varepsilon_{t-1}. \tag{17.10}$$

A first-differenced equation is then obtained by subtracting [17.10] from [17.9] to obtain

$$Y_t - Y_{t-1} = \beta_1(X_t - X_{t-1}) + \varepsilon_t - \varepsilon_{t-1}. \qquad [17.11]$$

Equation [17.11] involves the *changes* or first differences in the two variables, $\Delta Y_t = Y_t - Y_{t-1}$ and $\Delta X_t = X_t - X_{t-1}$, not their *levels*, Y_t and X_t. Even if the levels of variables exhibit trends, it is often the case that changes in such variables do not. For example, a general price level almost always trends upwards, but the change in the price level, (i.e., the inflation rate), usually shows no upward trend in the long run.

The variables in [17.11] are, hence, likely to be stationary, so it was hoped that such equations could be estimated without invalidating classical assumptions. Unfortunately there were other problems with first-differenced equations.

Firstly, it is obvious that the disturbance in [17.11], $\varepsilon_t - \varepsilon_{t-1}$, is of first-order moving-average form and will be autocorrelated. Secondly, in estimating the first-differenced equation [17.11], we focus purely on the short-run relationship between the ΔY and ΔX variables and ignore important information about the levels of the variables.

It is worth explaining in detail what is implied by this second point. To begin with, it is clear that [17.11] can provide no estimate of β_0, the intercept in the original [17.9]. Thus, even if the long-run level of X is known, we cannot determine the long-run level of Y. More importantly, the relationship between the first differences, ΔY_t and ΔX_t, is unlikely to be independent of the levels of the variables. But [17.11] wrongly suggests such an independence. The simple numerical example of Table 17.1 should make this clear.

Table 17.1 A numerical example

$ED_{t-1} = Y_{t-1} - 5 - 0.8X_{t-1}$	ΔX_t	ΔY_t
0	5	3
4	5	1.4
8	5	−0.2
−8	5	6.2
−4	5	4.6

Suppose the long-run or equilibrium relationship between X and Y happens to be

$$Y_t = 5 + 0.8X_t. \qquad [17.12]$$

That is, if X remains at some constant value Z for sufficiently long, then Y will eventually approach the value $5 + 0.8Z$. Now, let us define ED_t as

$$ED_t = Y_t - 5 - 0.8X_t. \qquad [17.13]$$

If Y and X are in long-run equilibrium, then [17.12] must hold so that $ED_t = 0$. But few economic systems are ever in long-run equilibrium. In practice, normally, either Y_t is above its equilibrium value (in which case $Y_t > 5 + 0.8X_t$) or Y_t lies below its equilibrium value (in which case $Y_t < 5 + 0.8X_t$). In general, ED_t measures the *extent of disequilibrium* in the system. When Y_t exceeds its equilibrium value, $ED_t > 0$, and whenever Y_t is below its equilibrium value, $ED_t < 0$. ED_t is often referred to as a *disequilibrium error*.

The columns in Table 17.1 refer to possible values for the disequilibrium error in period $t-1$ (the previous period), an exogenous value for the current-period change in X, ΔX_t, and the typical resultant current-period change in Y, that is, ΔY_t. For the moment, do not be too concerned with where these values come from.

In the first row of Table 17.1, X and Y are in equilibrium in period $t-1$, so that $ED_{t-1} = 0$. The change in X is determined exogenously as $\Delta X_t = 5$ and suppose the resultant change in Y is $\Delta Y_t = 3$.[4] Now suppose, as in row 2, that $ED_{t-1} = 4 > 0$. That is, Y_{t-1} is *above* its equilibrium value given by [17.12]. For the same change $\Delta X_t = 5$, we can expect ΔY_t now to be *less* than its value of 3 in row 1. This is because the value of Y has to be 'reined back' towards its equilibrium value. Thus ΔY_t takes a value of perhaps 1.4.

In row 3, ED_{t-1} is even larger, that is, Y_{t-1} is even further above its equilibrium, so that for the same change in X, the value of ΔY_t is reined back even further, perhaps even becoming negative.

In row 4 of the table, $ED_{t-1} = -8 < 0$. This implies that Y_{t-1} is *below* its equilibrium given by [17.12]. Thus, for the same constant $\Delta X_t = 5$, we can expect the change in Y_t to be greater than the value of 3 found in row 1. This is because Y_t now needs to do some 'catching up' on its equilibrium value. It therefore takes a value greater than 3, perhaps 6.2.

In row 5, ED_{t-1} is still negative but Y_{t-1} is not as far below its equilibrium value, so that the catching up needed is less pronounced. ΔY_t therefore takes a value of perhaps only 4.6.

The main point of this numerical example is that the change in Y depends not only on the change in X, but also *on the extent of disequilibrium in the previous period*. That is, it depends on the relationship between *the levels of the variables in the previous period*. Thus, if we ignore information on the levels of variables we are, almost certainly, misspecifying any estimating equation. This is the main problem with the first-differenced equation [17.11]; no use is made of information on the levels of variables, Y_t and X_t.

The figures in Table 17.1 were, in fact, derived from the following underlying model:

$$\Delta Y_t = 0.6\,\Delta X_t - 0.4(Y_{t-1} - 5 - 0.8X_{t-1}). \qquad [17.14]$$

[17.14] expresses ΔY_t as a simple linear function of ΔX_t and the lagged disequilibrium error $ED_{t-1} = Y_{t-1} - 5 - 0.8X_{t-1}$, that is, the extent of disequilibrium in the previous period. For obvious reasons, [17.14] is referred to as an *error correction model*. Disequilibrium errors in one period are at least partially corrected in the next.

In practice, error correction models have always been closely linked with the general to specific approach described in the previous section. As we shall see, shortly, their use has several important advantages.

In the two-variable case, the general form of the equilibrium or long-run relationship is

$$Y_t = \alpha + \beta X_t, \qquad\qquad [17.15]$$

while, with disturbance added, the general form of [17.14] is

$$\Delta Y_t = b\,\Delta X_t - \mu(Y_{t-1} - \alpha - \beta X_{t-1}) + \varepsilon_t \qquad\qquad [17.16]$$

or

$$\Delta Y_t = b\,\Delta X_t - \mu ED_{t-1} + \varepsilon_t, \qquad\qquad [17.17]$$

where $ED_{t-1} = Y_{t-1} - \alpha - \beta X_{t-1}$ and μ is an adjustment parameter lying between zero and unity.

When handling trending time-series variables, the possibility of high but spurious correlations in the data makes it difficult to determine whether or not there is any genuine long-term relationship between the variables. However, luckily, there is a very important econometric theorem that states that, *if a long-run relationship between* X *and* Y *does exist, then it is always possible to represent the short-run relationship between* X *and* Y *by an error correction model.*[5]

The ability to use an error correction model to represent the relationship between X and Y depends crucially on the size and statistical significance of the parameter μ in [17.16]. If μ proves to be non-significantly different from zero, then the disequilibrium error term falls out of the equation and we no longer have an error correction type of model.

More importantly, the above theorem also works in reverse. If an error correction model can be found that satisfies the data, that is, if we obtain a non-zero μ, then a long-run relationship between X and Y *must exist*. That is, a high R^2 cannot be entirely spurious. It is possible to see this intuitively. A non-zero parameter, as in the above numerical example, implies that any non-zero disequilibrium errors must work to pull Y back towards some long-run equilibrium value. Thus, such a long-run or equilibrium relationship must exist. When such a long-run relationship exists between two variables then these variables are said to be *cointegrated*.

Another useful property of error correction models is that they make the distinction between short- and long-run effects quite clear. The parameters α and β in the error correction term of [17.16] also appear in [17.15]. They are therefore long-run parameters and, once estimated, provide us with an estimated version of the long-run relationship [17.15]. b and μ, however, are short-run parameters. b is simply the short-run or impact effect of a unit change in X. The adjustment parameter μ influences the speed over time with which Y

approaches its equilibrium value. The larger is μ, the stronger is the effect on Y of a given disequilibrium error.

Error correction models such as [17.16] cannot be estimated as they stand. That is, without knowledge of α and β, we cannot simply regress ΔY_t on ΔX_t and the disequilibrium error ED_{t-1}. However, the model can be estimated if we first 'multiply out' [17.16]. This yields

$$\Delta Y_t = \mu\alpha + b\,\Delta X_t - \mu Y_{t-1} + \mu\beta X_{t-1} + \varepsilon_t, \qquad [17.18]$$

that is,

$$\Delta Y_t = a + b\,\Delta X_t + cY_{t-1} + dX_{t-1} + \varepsilon_t, \qquad [17.19]$$

where $a = \mu\alpha$, $c = -\mu$ and $d = \mu\beta$.

If ΔY_t is regressed on ΔX_t, Y_{t-1} and X_{t-1}, then estimates of a, b, c and d are obtained. Since $\mu = -c$, it follows that $\alpha = -a/c$ and $\beta = -d/c$. Thus, given the estimates of a, c and d, we can obtain estimates of μ, α and β. Note that, here, we have abandoned our rule of using English letters only for sample statistics. In this area, it has become usual to use English letters for short-run parameters such as b above, and we have also used them for the products of short- and long-run parameters (e.g., a for $\mu\alpha$). We shall write estimators of, for example, μ as $\hat{\mu}$ and so on.

Econometricians have made frequent use of error correction models in the past twenty years. They are an important tool in time-series analysis, particularly when variables are trending.

Worked Example

The long-run relationship between Y, X and Z is given by

$$Y = KX^\beta Z^\gamma$$

or

$$y = \alpha + \beta x + \gamma z,$$

where $\alpha = \ln(K)$, and y, x and z are the natural logarithms of Y, X and Z. β and γ are long-run elasticities. However, because the variables are never in equilibrium, a short-run relationship has to be estimated instead. This is in the form of the following error correction model:

$$\widehat{\Delta y_t} = 0.32 + 0.63\,\Delta x_t - 0.45\,\Delta z_t + 0.37 x_{t-1} - 0.42 z_{t-1} - 0.63 y_{t-1}.$$

Obtain estimates of the short- and long-run elasticities of Y with respect to X and Z. Interpret the coefficient on Y_{t-1}.

Solution

The estimated equation can be rewritten as

$$\Delta y_t = 0.63\,\Delta x_t - 0.45\,\Delta z_t - 0.63\,(y_{t-1} - 0.51 - 0.59x_{t-1} + 0.67z_{t-1}).$$

Since the variables are in logarithmic form, the coefficients on Δx_t and Δz_t, 0.63 and -0.45, are the short-run elasticities for X and Z, respectively.

The expression in parentheses is the disequilibrium error, so the long-run relationship must be

$$y = 0.51 + 0.59x_t - 0.67z_t.$$

Thus, in terms of the original variables,

$$Y = 1.7X^{0.59}Z^{-0.67}.$$

The long-run elasticities with respect to X and Z are 0.59 and -0.67, respectively. The coefficient of -0.63 on Y_{t-1} in the original estimated equation implies an adjustment parameter of $\mu = 0.63$. Thus we can say that 63% of the disequilibrium in a given period is eliminated in the next period.

Example 17.5

An estimated version of [17.16] is

$$\widehat{\Delta Y}_t = 2.6 + 0.7\,\Delta X_t - 0.83Y_{t-1} - 1.2X_{t-1}.$$

Estimate all long-run and short-run parameters.

Example 17.6

The following error correction model is estimated from annual data:

$$\widehat{\Delta \ln(C_t)} = 0.53\,\Delta \ln(Y_t) - 0.67[\ln(C_{t-1}) - \ln(Y_{t-1})],$$

where C is consumption and Y income. Interpret this result.

Computer Exercise 17.2

In this exercise we return to the file DATASET7 and the US income and consumption data. We begin by estimating a slightly generalized version of the error correction model [17.16] in which the postulated long-run consumption function is with variables defined as in

Computer Exercise 16.1,

$$\ln RC_t = \alpha + \beta \ln RY_t + \delta \ln P_t. \tag{17.20}$$

The disequilibrium error is thus

$$\ln RC_{t-1} - \alpha - \beta \ln Y_{t-1} - \delta \ln P_{t-1}$$

and the error correction model has the logarithmic form

$$\Delta \ln RC_t = b_1 \Delta \ln RY_t + b_2 \Delta \ln P_t$$
$$- \mu(\ln RC_{t-1} - \alpha - \beta \ln RY_{t-1} - \delta \ln P_{t-1}) + \varepsilon_t, \tag{17.21}$$

where the first-differenced variables can be created as $\Delta \ln RC_t = \ln RC_t - \ln RC_{t-1}$ and so on.

Without knowledge of the long-run parameters, we cannot estimate [17.21] but must again 'multiply out' to obtain

$$\Delta \ln RC_t = \alpha\mu + b_1 \Delta \ln RY_t + b_2 \Delta \ln P_t$$
$$- \mu \ln RC_{t-1} + \beta\mu \ln RY_{t-1} + \delta\mu \ln P_{t-1} + \varepsilon_t; \tag{17.22}$$

that is,

$$\Delta \ln RC_{t-1} = b_0 + b_1 \Delta \ln RY_t + b_2 \Delta \ln P_t$$
$$+ c_0 \ln RC_{t-1} + c_1 \ln RY_{t-1} + c_2 \ln P_{t-1} + \varepsilon_t \tag{17.23}$$

where $b_0 = \alpha\mu$, $c_0 = -\mu$, $c_1 = \beta\mu$ and $c_2 = \delta\mu$.

OLS estimation of [17.23], over 1961–97, should yield the result shown in Fig. 17.4. The first thing to notice in Fig. 17.4 is that the residual sum of squares for this equation is 0.002 196, which is exactly the same as that for the equation in Fig. 17.3, which we estimated in Computer Exercise 17.1. Compare carefully Figs 17.4 and 17.3. Many of the other quantities, for example the autocorrelation statistics, are also identical. In fact, this is not surprising since the two equations are exactly the same! If we substitute $\Delta \ln RC_t = \ln RC_t - \ln RC_{t-1}$, etc., in [17.23], rearranging soon gives

$$\ln RC_t = b_0 + b_1 \ln RY_t + b_2 \ln P_t + (c_0 + 1) \ln RC_{t-1}$$
$$+ (c_1 - b_1) \ln RY_{t-1} + (c_2 - b_2) \ln P_{t-1} + \varepsilon_t. \tag{17.24}$$

It should be clear that [17.24] contains the same dependent and explanatory variables as the result in Fig. 17.3. So the two equations are indeed the same. Moreover, since the result in Fig. 17.3 is nested in the general model [17.8], so is the error correction model of Fig. 17.4. In fact, the general to specific approach often results in a search for the most appropriate error correction model.

```
                    Ordinary Least Squares Estimation
*************************************************************************
Dependent variable is LNRC
37 observations used for estimation from 1961 to 1997
*************************************************************************
Regressor           Coefficient        Standard Error        T-Ratio[Prob]
INTERCEPT             -.54613               .28832            -1.8942[.068]
DLNRY                  .76294               .097702            7.8089[.000]
DLNP                  -.37436               .091815           -4.0773[.000]
LNRC1                 -.39878               .10846            -3.6767[.001]
LNRY1                  .45127               .11489             3.9279[.000]
LNP1                  -.019989              .013655           -1.4639[.153]
*************************************************************************
R-Squared                     .80508   R-Bar-Squared                 .77365
S.E of Regression             .0084165 F-stat.   F( 5,  31)   25.6085[.000]
Mean of Dependent Variable    .023893  S.D. of Dependent Variable    .017690
Residual Sum of Squares       .0021960 Equation Log-likelihood       127.5422
Akaike Info. Criterion        121.5422 Schwarz Bayesian Criterion    116.7094
DW-statistic                  1.8697
*************************************************************************


                         Diagnostic Tests
*************************************************************************
*   Test Statistics    *     LM Version        *      F Version       *
*************************************************************************
*                      *                       *                      *
* A:Serial Correlation * CHSQ(   1)= .14646[.702] * F(  1, 30)= .11922[.732] *
*                      *                       *                      *
* B:Functional Form    * CHSQ(   1)= 4.1691[.041] * F(  1, 30)= 3.8096[.060] *
*                      *                       *                      *
* C:Normality          * CHSQ(   2)= 2.1695[.338] *      Not applicable      *
*                      *                       *                      *
* D:Heteroscedasticity * CHSQ(   1)= 1.4855[.223] * F(  1, 35)= 1.4640[.234] *
*************************************************************************
A:Lagrange multiplier test of residual serial correlation
B:Ramsey's RESET test using the square of the fitted values
C:Based on a test of skewness and kurtosis of residuals
D:Based on the regression of squared residuals on squared fitted values
```

Figure 17.4 An estimated error correction model

Notice that $R^2 = 0.805$ in Fig. 17.4 is much lower than the value of 0.999 obtained in Fig. 17.3. However, the two values are not comparable, because the first equation has $\ln RC$ as dependent variable, whereas the second has $\Delta \ln RC$. But at least the use of first-differenced variables will have, hopefully, removed the problem of common trends in the levels variables.

In Fig. 17.4, the levels variable $\ln P_{t-1}$ ($LNP1$) has a t-ratio of just 1.46, rather below its 5% critical value. Consequently, take your simplification search another step further by dropping this variable from the model. This should yield the result shown in Fig. 17.5.

In this model, all the variables have more than adequate t-ratios and the serial correlation statistics are good. There is no suggestion that any relevant variables have been omitted.

```
                    Ordinary Least Squares Estimation
*********************************************************************************
 Dependent variable is LNRC
 37 observations used for estimation from 1961 to 1997
*********************************************************************************
 Regressor           Coefficient         Standard Error        T-Ratio[Prob]
 INTERCEPT              -.13397                .063187          -2.1202[.042]
 DLNRY                   .79185                .097380           8.1315[.000]
 DLNP                   -.29472                .075272          -3.9154[.000]
 LNRC1                  -.38821                .11014           -3.5248[.001]
 LNRY1                   .39919                .11118            3.5906[.001]
*********************************************************************************
 R-Squared                    .79161   R-Bar-Squared                    .76556
 S.E of Regression          .0085655   F-stat.    F( 4,  32)   30.3896[.000]
 Mean of Dependent Variable .023893   S.D. of Dependent Variable       .017690
 Residual Sum of Squares    .0023478   Equation Log-likelihood         126.3056
 Akaike Info. Criterion     121.3056   Schwarz Bayesian Criterion      117.2783
 DW-statistic                1.8537
*********************************************************************************


                           Diagnostic Tests
*********************************************************************************
 *    Test Statistics  *       LM Version          *        F Version          *
*********************************************************************************
 *                     *                     *                     *
 * A:Serial Correlation* CHSQ(  1)=  .13973[.709] * F(  1, 31)=  .11751[.734] *
 *                     *                     *                     *
 * B:Functional Form   * CHSQ(  1)= 4.6897[.030] * F(  1, 31)= 4.4995[.042] *
 *                     *                     *                     *
 * C:Normality         * CHSQ(  2)= 1.8989[.387] *     Not applicable        *
 *                     *                     *                     *
 * D:Heteroscedasticity* CHSQ(  1)= 3.7873[.052] * F(  1, 35)= 3.9911[.054] *
*********************************************************************************
 A:Lagrange multiplier test of residual serial correlation
 B:Ramsey's RESET test using the square of the fitted values
 C:Based on a test of skewness and kurtosis of residuals
 D:Based on the regression of squared residuals on squared fitted values
```

Figure 17.5 Omission of long-run price variable

There is, however, one further restriction that could be placed on our equation. The ratio of the coefficients on $\ln RY_{t-1}$ and $\ln RC_{t-1}$ is $c_1/c_0 = -0.399/0.388 = -1.03$. This is very close to -1, suggesting that the long-run income elasticity of consumption, β, may be unity. (To see this, note that $c_0 = -\mu$ and $c_1 = \beta\mu$, so that $c_1/c_0 = -\beta$.)

To impose the restriction $\beta = 1$ on the model involves imposing the restriction $c_1/c_0 = -1$, or $c_1 = -c_0$ on the coefficients of the equation. We can do this by using the fact that

$$-\mu(\ln RC_{t-1} - \alpha - \beta \ln RY_{t-1}) = c_0 \ln RC_{t-1} + b_0 + c_1 \ln RY_{t-1}$$
$$= b_0 + c_0(\ln RC_{t-1} - \ln RY_{t-1}),$$

since $c_1 = -c_0$. Thus we need to replace the two separate variables $\ln RC_{t-1}$ and $\ln RY_{t-1}$ by the single constructed variable

$$(CY)_t = \ln RC_{t-1} - \ln RY_{t-1}.$$

Create the (CY) variable and re-estimate the equation with $(CY)_t$ replacing the $\ln RC_{t-1}$ and $\ln RY_{t-1}$ variables. You should obtain the result shown in Fig. 17.6.

```
                    Ordinary Least Squares Estimation
*******************************************************************************
Dependent variable is DLNRC
37 observations used for estimation from 1961 to 1997
*******************************************************************************
Regressor          Coefficient      Standard Error       T-Ratio[Prob]
INTER               -.023986             .012158         -1.9729[.057]
DLNRY                .72552              .092763           7.8212[.000]
DLNP                -.28427              .077434         -3.6711[.001]
CY1                 -.36082              .11252          -3.2066[.003]
*******************************************************************************
R-Squared                    .77117   R-Bar-Squared                   .75037
S.E of Regression          .0088387   F-stat.    F(  3,  33)   37.0703[.000]
Mean of Dependent Variable  .023893   S.D. of Dependent Variable     .017690
Residual Sum of Squares    .0025781   Equation Log-likelihood      124.5745
Akaike Info. Criterion     120.5745   Schwarz Bayesian Criterion   117.3526
DW-statistic                 1.6697
*******************************************************************************


                           Diagnostic Tests
*******************************************************************************
*     Test Statistics    *      LM Version       *       F Version          *
*******************************************************************************
*                        *                       *                          *
* A:Serial Correlation*  CHSQ(  1)=   .68793[.407] * F(  1, 32)=  .60624[-442] *
*                        *                       *                          *
* B:Functional Form     *  CHSQ(  1)=  4.3984[.036] * F(  1, 32)=  4.3172[.046] *
*                        *                       *                          *
* C:Normality           *  CHSQ(  2)=  2.3084[.315] *     Not applicable      *
*                        *                       *                          *
* D:Heteroscedasticity* CHSQ(  1)=   .11649[.733] * F(  1, 35)=  .11055[.742] *
*******************************************************************************
A:Lagrange multiplier test of residual serial correlation
B:Ramsey's RESET test using the square of the fitted values
C:Based on a test of skewness and kurtosis of residuals
D:Based on the regression of squared residuals on squared fitted values
```

Figure 17.6 Imposing a unitary long-run income elasticity

Imposing this restriction results in a slight rise in the residual sum of squares from 0.002 348 in Fig. 17.5 to 0.002 578 in Fig. 17.6. Perform the F-test to check whether this restriction is acceptable. You should find that it is.

This is our final preferred equation. It is parsimonious, in that it contains only four regressors (including the intercept), compared with nine in the general model [17.8]. The diagnostic statistics, particularly the ones for autocorrelation, are satisfactory, suggesting again that no relevant variables have been omitted. There is a slight problem in that the functional form statistic is significant at the 5% level, but we will leave the reader to investigate alternative forms for the model.[6]

Before attempting to interpret our final preferred equation, it is always important to compare it with the general model that we started with. The estimated version of our general model [17.8] is given in Fig. 17.2 and has a residual sum of squares of 0.002 173, compared with 0.002 578 for our final model. List the five restrictions that have been imposed and perform a joint F-test of their validity.

To 3 significant figures, the final model is

$$\Delta \ln RC_t = -0.0240 + 0.726 \, \Delta \ln RY_t - 0.284 \, \Delta \ln P_t$$
$$- 0.361 \ln RC_{t-1} + 0.361 \ln RY_{t-1}. \qquad [17.25]$$

Using the expressions below [17.23], equation [17.25] therefore yields estimators

$$\hat{b}_0 = -0.0240 = \hat{\alpha}\hat{\mu}, \qquad \hat{b}_1 = 0.726, \qquad \hat{b}_2 = -0.284,$$
$$\hat{c}_0 = -0.361 = -\hat{\mu}, \qquad \hat{c}_1 = 0.361 = \hat{\beta}\hat{\mu} \qquad \hat{c}_2 = 0.$$

Thus the adjustment parameter is estimated as $\hat{\mu} = 0.361$, implying that 36% of any disequilibrium between income and consumption in the previous year is made up in the current period. Estimated long-run parameters are

$$\hat{\alpha} = \frac{-0.0240}{0.361} = -0.0665, \qquad \hat{\beta} = 1.$$

The long-run relationship between income and consumption is therefore estimated to be

$$\ln RC_t = -0.0665 + \ln RY_t \quad \text{or} \quad RC_t = 0.936 \, RY_t. \qquad [17.26]$$

Note that $\ln(0.936) = -0.0665$ in [17.26].

Our model thus implies a long-run income elasticity of unity and a long-run average propensity to consume of 0.936.

The estimated short-run income elasticity is $\hat{b}_1 = 0.726$, smaller than the long-run elasticity, as expected. Thus a 1% change in income results in approximately only a 0.7% increase in consumption in the short run but a 1% increase in the long run.

In the long run there appear to be no significant price effects on consumption. As we saw in Computer Exercise 16.1, this is what economic theory suggests. But what are we to make of the significant and *negative* short-run price elasticity of $\hat{b}_2 = -0.284$?

As we saw in Computer Exercise 16.1, a positive coefficient on the price variable, whether this be in the short or long run, can be interpreted as implying 'money illusion' in the consumption function. But we have a negative sign, at least in the short run. Similar results have, in fact, been obtained for UK consumption functions both in the short and long run. And, if you refer back to Fig. 17.4, you will note that the long-run price coefficient is also negative, albeit not significantly so.

Think about what such negative price coefficients might imply. Remember that the coefficient measures the effect on consumption when the price level rises with real income remaining unchanged.

Summary

- The **general to specific** approach to time-series econometrics involves the specification of a **general model** within which are **nested** a series of special cases. These special cases should ideally cover all theories and short-run adjustment processes concerning the relevant variables.

- A **simplification search** or a **testing-down** procedure is adopted to determine the final preferred special case. This should be a **parsimonious** model which is able to 'explain' the data almost as well as the general model.

- The general model is a short-run equation which frequently takes the form of an **error correction model**. Such models are generally preferred to **first-differenced equations** because they take account of any previous departures from equilibrium.

- When a long-run relationship between two variables exists, the two variables are said to be **cointegrated**. If the short-run relationship between two variables can be modelled as an error correction model, then the two variables must be cointegrated.

- **Cointegration analysis** is an important tool in helping econometricians determine whether high correlations between **trending** variables are **spurious** or not.

Notes

1. The limited capacity of early computers almost certainly made a simple to general approach seem attractive.

2. This principle is often referred to as 'Occam's razor', after the fourteenth-century philosopher, William of Occam.

3. But see, for example, Mizon and Richard (1986).

4. Do not fall into the trap of looking at [17.12] and expecting ΔY_t to be $0.8 \Delta X_t = 4$. Equation [17.12] is the equilibrium relationship and there is no guarantee that Y_t will remain in equilibrium.

5. This is the well-known *Granger representation theorem.* See, for example, Engel and Granger (1987).

6. Other possibilities would be to estimate linear and semi-log versions of the model.

Solutions to Examples

Prerequisites

P.1 Mean = 11.94, median = 10, mode = 7. After change, mean = 18.19, median = 11.5, mode = 7.

P.2 Arithmetic mean = 47.6, Geometric mean = 34.75. AM > GM.

P.3 Geometric mean = 10.20. AM > GM.

P.4 **(a)** 21.52. **(b)** Since $\sum X_i = 206$, weighted mean = 26.3. **(c)** Since $\sum(1/X_i) = 0.632$, weighted mean = 15.8. **(c)** is the smallest because the greater is X_i, the smaller is the weight allocated to it.

P.5 42.18.

P.6 Mean = 53.25, st dev = 16.7. **(a)** The mean will increase by 5, with the standard deviation unchanged. **(b)** Both the mean and the standard deviation will increase by one-fifth.

P.7 Mean deviation = 5.31, standard deviation = 6.49. MD < SD.

P.8 Mean deviation = 14.25. MD < SD.

P.9 Frequencies are 2, 1, 0, 1, 1, 3, 0, 3, 3, 1, 2. Cumulative frequencies are 2, 3, 3, 4, 5, 8, 8, 11, 14, 15, 17.

P.10

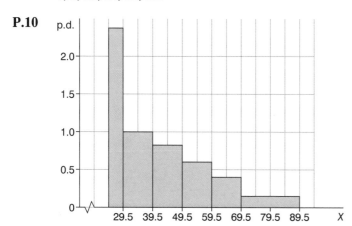

P.11 **(a)** 0.04; **(b)** 0.27; **(c)** 0.25; **(d)** $1 - 0.27 = 0.73$.

P.12 **(a)** 1/13; **(b)** 1/26; **(c)** 1/2; **(d)** 1/26; **(e)** 2/13. The addition rule is used in (b), (d) and (e).

P.13 **(a)** 0.36; **(b)** 0.45.

P.14 **(a)** 0.010 08; **(b)** 0.040 32; **(c)** 0.959 68.

Chapter 1

1.1 Sample space is

HHHH	THHH	THHT	HTTT	TTTT
	HTHH	THTH	THTT	
	HHTH	TTHH	TTHT	
	HHHT	HTTH	TTTH	
		HTHT		
		HHTT		

$\Pr(Y = 3) = 0.25$

1.2 Sample space is

1, 1	2, 1	3, 1	4, 1	5, 1	6, 1
1, 2	2, 2	3, 2	4, 2	5, 2	6, 2
1, 3	2, 3	3, 3	4 ,3	5, 3	6, 3
1, 4	2, 4	3, 4	4, 4	5, 4	6, 4
1, 5	2, 5	3, 5	4, 5	5, 5	6, 5
1, 6	2, 6	3, 6	4, 6	5, 6	6, 6

(a) 1/36 **(b)** 5/12 **(c)** 1/2 **(d)** 11/36

1.3

Y	0	1	2	3	4
$p(Y)$	0.0625	0.25	0.375	0.25	0.0625

1.4

Y	0	1	2	3	4
$C(Y)$	0.0625	0.3125	0.6875	0.9375	1.0000

1.5 Sample space is identical to that for Example 1.1 with $H = S$ (sale) and $T = N$ (no sale). $\Pr(X \leqslant 2) = 0.8208$.

1.6 Sample space is SSS, FSS, SFS, SSF, SFF, FSF, SFF, FFF (S = satisfactory, F = non-satisfactory)

With replacement:

X	0	1	2	3
$p(X)$	1/64	9/64	27/64	27/64

Without replacement:

X	1	2	3
$p(X)$	3/28	15/28	10/28

(In the second case FFF cannot occur, so that $\Pr(X = 0) = 0$.)

1.7 $E(Y) = 2$, $E(Y^2) = 5$, $E(Y^3) = 14$, $E(Y + 2) = 4$. $[E(Y)]^2 = 4 \neq E(Y^2)$, $[E(Y)]^3 = 8 \neq E(Y^3)$, $E(Y) + 2 = 4 = E(Y + 2)$.

1.8 $E(X) = 7.5$, $V(X) = 14.375$. Since $\sigma = 3.79$, we can say that the X-values are roughly 3.8 away from their mean, on average. $E(1/X) = 0.183$, but $1/E(X) = 0.133$.

1.9 $E(T) = 165$, $V(T) = 5625$. $\sigma = 75$. Thus T values are roughly £75 from their mean of £165, on average.

1.10 (a) $E(X) = 2.25$, $E(X^2) = 5.625$, $V(X) = 0.5625$, $E(X^4) = 41.0625$
  (b) $E(X) = 2.25$, $E(X^2) = 5.464$, $V(X) = 0.4018$, $E(X^4) = 37.6071$
   $E(X^4) > [E(X^2)]^2$ in each case.

1.11 £37.50.

1.12

X	0	1	2	3	4
$p(X)$	0.1296	0.3456	0.3456	0.1536	0.0256

$E(X) = 1.6$, $V(X) = 0.96$

1.13 $\Pr(X = 11) = 0.5$, $\Pr(X = 9, 10) = 0.25$, $\Pr(X = 12, 13, 14, 15) = 0.25$

1.14 (a) 0.3; (b) 0.4; (c) 0.3. Axis values become 0.001 and 0.002, instead of 0.01 and 0.02.

1.15 (a) $E(Z) = 44$, $V(Z) = 45$. If st. dev. of X doubles then st. dev. of Z will double.
  (b) $E(Y) = -14$, $V(Y) = 50$.

1.16 Expected value and standard deviation are £13 000 and £2750.

1.17 He should bid £15 000. However, the probability distribution for profit P is

Y	2200	−£5800	4200
$p(P)$	0.6	0.1	0.3

Hence, if he cannot afford a loss of 5800, under any circumstances, he would not make this bid, because there is a probability of 0.1 of such a loss.

1.18 Since expected profit is +£4000, the novel should be published.

1.19 With $\pi = 0.5$ and n = 3,

$$p(X) = \frac{3!}{(3-X)!X!} 0.5^X 0.5^{n-X}.$$

Substituting $X = 0, 1, 2, 3$ gives the distribution in Table 1.2. The binomial distribution may be used because there are only two outcomes (head or tail) to the experiment and Pr(H) is constant.

1.20

X	0	1	2	3	4	5	6
$C(X)$	0.004	0.041	0.179	0.455	0.766	0.953	1.000

$C(3) = 0.455$.

1.21 (a) 0.168 07;   (b) 0.3087;   (c) $1 - 002\ 43 = 0.997\ 57$.
$\Pr(X = 1) = 0.028\ 35$. Thus, getting $X = 1$ is highly unlikely if $\pi = 0.7$, so that π is almost certainly less than believed.

1.22

X	0	1	2	3
$p(X)$	0.027	0.189	0.441	0.343

Probability that alarm is triggered $= 1 - 0.027 = 0.973$.

1.23

X	0	1	2
$p(X)$	0.2	0.6	0.2

$E(X) = 1$
The binomial distribution cannot be used because if the eggs are not replaced then Pr(bad egg) is no longer constant.

1.24 $R = 9$

1.25 1.53×10^{-22} (very small probability).

1.26 (a) 0.0153;   (b) 0.905.

1.27 (a) 3.67×10^{-5};   (b) 0.999 751

1.28 0.065 536

Chapter 2

2.1 (a) 0.4772;   (b) 0.4406;   (c) 0.9178;   (d) 0.0228;   (e) 0.9406.

2.2 (a) 0.0071;   (b) 0.0021;   (c) 0.7745;   (d) 0.9386;   (e) 0.0968;
(f) 0.3827;   (g) 0.9893.

2.3 (a) 0.0548;   (b) 0.9452;   (c) 0. (Since Z is a continuous variable, the probability
of getting a value exactly equal to 1.6 must be infinitesimally small).

2.4 (a) 0.74;   (b) –0.74;   (c) –1.23;   (d) 1.96;   (e) 2.575.

2.5 $Y = X - 3$ is $N(9, 25)$ and hence $W = Y/5$ is $N(1.8, 1)$.

2.6 (a) 0.1587;   (b) 0.6915.

2.7 0.0802

2.8 Pr(burn out) = 0.5111. s = 706.8 hours.

2.9 Pr(without) = 0.0228. Starting stock = 308.

2.10 (a) 0.0274;   (b) 0.9726.   (c) Assuming incomes are given to the nearest pound,
$\Pr(X = 95) = \Pr(94.5 < X < 95.5) \approx 0.005$.

2.11 Airplane A should be selected because it has the greater probability of flying over
26 hours.

2.12 95% within the range £1232 to £2864. Two-thirds within the range £1640 to £2456.

2.13 (a) (i) 0.0062;   (ii) 0.0668.   (b) Since $\Pr(X < 4.9) = 0$, it is highly unlikely that
the mean and variance are as stated.

2.14 0.3935

2.15 $\Pr(65.5 < X < 84.5) = 0.7239$. $\Pr(X < 70.5) = 0.0853$. $\Pr(X < 59.5) = 0.0015$. This
probability is so small that the supermarket should revise its estimate.

2.16 0.0162.

2.17 $\Pr(203.5 < X < 206.5) = 0.080$. $\Pr(200.5 < X < 201.5) = 0.03$.

2.18 0.112.

Chapter 3

3.1 $E(\bar{X}) = £31.24$, $V(\bar{X}) = 3.411$.   **(a)** 1.706   **(b)** 0.853

3.2 $\mu = 20$ and $\sigma^2 = 80$

3.3 **(a)** 0.9266;   **(b)** 0;   **(c)** 0 if X is a continuous variable.

3.4 **(a)** 0.0228   **(b)** 0.0228

3.5 0.0143

3.6 The probability is 0.0023. Thus $X < 500$ is very unlikely. Since $Pr(X < 400) = 0$, it is virtually impossible that $X < 400$. Thus the true μ must be less than 600

3.7 Bus A.

3.8 $\bar{X} = 800$; $s^2 = 462\ 771.4$.

3.9 **(a)** 28.87   **(b)** 29.15

3.10 **(a)** 36 ± 1.10 **(b)** $n = 385$

3.11 $n = 531$

3.12 $n = 217$, at a cost of £108.50. Doubling precision requires $n = 865$, at cost £432.50. That is, doubling precision results in a quadrupling of cost.

3.13 Probability is 0.0764. Since $Pr(X > 28) = Pr(p > 0.35) = 0.0010$, it is very unlikely that only 21% of cows are sick.

3.14 $p = 0.2$. Interval is 0.2 ± 0.23.

3.15 Interval is 0.35 ± 0.03. Sample size of 8739 is required.

3.16 **(a)** $n = 81$;   **(b)** taking π as 0.5, $n = 97$. Doubling precision requires $n = 323$ and $n = 385$, respectively.

Chapter 4

4.1 $H_0: \mu = 3200$, $H_A: \mu < 3200$. $TS = -1.45$. Do not reject H_0. Complaints do not appear to be justified.

4.2 $H_0: \mu = 23$, $H_A: \mu \neq 23$. $TS = 2.71$. Reject H_0. Rate of clearing appears to have changed.

4.3 $H_0: \mu = 850, H_A: \mu > 850$. $TS = 3.87$. Reject H_0. Claim appears to justified.

4.4   Level of significance $= 0.01$. OC curve lies above the OC curve for $\alpha = 0.05$.

4.5 $H_0: \mu = 80, H_A: \mu > 80$. $TS = 1.54$. Accept H_0 but we do not know the probability of a type II error. If $\mu = 82$, then $\Pr(\text{type II})$ equals $\Pr(TS < 1.64 \mid \mu = 82) = \Pr(Z < 0.10) = 0.504$.

4.6 $\Pr(\text{type I error}) = \Pr(\text{type II error}) = 0.0367$. The criterion is sensible because any change will lead to a fall in the probability of one error but a rise in the probability of the other. The rise in probability of the former will exceed the fall in probability of the latter.

4.7 $H_0: \mu = 50, H_A: \mu \neq 50$. $TS = -2.05$. You can reject H_0 at the 0.05 but not at the 0.01 level of significance. If you allow yourself a 0.05 chance of error, you can safely reject H_0. However, if you allow yourself only a 0.01 chance of error, then you cannot reject H_0 because, if you did, the chance of error would be greater than the 0.01 you allowed. That is, you are 95% certain you are right to reject H_0 but you are not 99% certain.

4.8   The following mistakes have been made.
   (i)   The hypotheses should involve μ not $\bar{X}$.
   (ii) H_0 should contain an equality sign.
   (iii)   The TS depends on $\bar{X} - 80\ 000$ not $\bar{X} - \mu$.
   (iv)   One-tail test is required so decision criterion should be 'reject H_0 if $TS < -2.33$'.
   (v)   Decision should be 'do not reject H_0'.
   (vi)   The 0.01 probability of error only applies when H_0 is rejected, but in this case H_0 cannot be rejected.

4.9 $H_0: \mu = 2, H_A: \mu > 2$. $TS = 1.81$. Reject H_0 (i.e., the claim appears to be false) at the 0.05 but not at the 0.01 level of significance. See answer to Example 4.7.

4.10 $H_0: \mu = 6, H_A: \mu \neq 6$. $TS = 3.6$. Reject H_0 at 0.05 and 0.01 levels of significance. Evidence appears to contradict claim.

4.11 $H_0: \mu = 24, H_A: \mu < 24$. $TS = -7.07$. Reject H_0 at 0.05 and 0.01 levels of significance. Reduction appears to be the result of global warming.

4.12 $H_0: \mu = 25\ 000, H_A: \mu < 25\ 000$. $TS = -2.55$. Reject H_0 at 0.05 and 0.01 levels of significance. Claim appears to be excessive.

4.13 $H_0: \mu = 500, H_A: \mu > 500$. $TS = 1.64$. Do not reject H_0. Insufficient evidence to back claim. We allowed ourselves only a 0.05 chance of error when rejecting H_0. Thus we cannot reject H_0 since, if we did so, the chance of error would exceed 0.05.

4.14 H_0: $\mu = 0.75$, H_A: $\mu < 0.75$. $TS = -1.5$. Do not reject H_0 at the 0.05 or 0.01 levels of significance. Insufficient evidence to say that complaint is justified. Since H_0 is not rejected, neither type I nor type II errors are being committed. The 0.05 and 0.01 probabilities, which refer to type I errors, therefore do not apply.

4.15 The powers are given by 0.8051, 0.3483 and 0.0823, respectively. With a 0.01 level of significance, Pr(type I error) is reduced but the probabilities of a type II error must rise. Thus the powers of the test must all fall. 2.33 replaces 1.64 in the expression for the power.

4.16 The powers for the test are 0.0158 and 0.3015, respectively.

Chapter 5

5.1 H_0: $\mu = 82$, H_A: $\mu \neq 82$. $t_{0.05} = 2.201$. $TS = 1.92$. Do not reject H_0 at 0.05 level of sig. Insufficient evidence that weights are different this year.

5.2 H_0: $\mu = 40$, H_A: $\mu < 40$ (claim invalid). $t_{0.05} = 1.895$. Sample yields $\bar{X} = 39$ with $s = 0.95$. $TS = -2.98$. Reject H_0 at 0.05 level of sig. Claim appears to be invalid.

Assumption is that population is normally distributed with variance unknown. Hence, t distribution may be used.

5.3 H_0: $\mu = 2050$, H_A: $\mu > 2050$. Use z-test rather than t-test because σ^2 is known. $TS = 1.71$. Reject H_0. New practice appears to work.

5.4 Interval is $\bar{X} \pm t_{0.01}s/\sqrt{n}$. $t_{0.01} = 2.998$. Hence the required interval is 39 ± 1. A large sample is clearly needed for such precision, so use $z_{0.01} = 2.33$. $n = 490$ is required.

5.5 H_0: $\mu = 10$, H_A: $\mu > 10$ (line is faulty). $TS = 1.54$. Do not reject H_0. Insufficient evidence to say line is faulty.

H_0: $\sigma^2 = 0.0001$, $\sigma^2 > 0.0001$ (line is faulty). Reject H_0 if $TS > \chi^2_{0.05} = 120$. $TS = 167.3$. Reject H_0. The line appears to be faulty in terms of the variance.

5.6 H_0: $\sigma^2 = 150$, H_A: $\sigma^2 > 150$ (specification incorrect). Reject H_0 if $TS > \chi^2_{0.05} = 19.675$. $TS = 15.03$. Do not reject H_0. Insufficient evidence to say specification is incorrect.

5.7 H_0: $\pi = 0.3$, H_A: $\pi < 0.3$. $p = 0.26$, $TS = -2.47$. Reject H_0 at 0.05 but not 0.01 level of significance. If allowed 5% chance of error, we can safely reject H_0. But if allowed only 1% chance of error, we cannot reject H_0 since, if we did, chance of error would exceed 1%.

5.8 H_0: $\pi = 1/6$ (no ESP), H_A: $\pi > 1/6$ (ESP). $p = 112/600$, $TS = 1.31$. Cannot reject H_0 at 0.05 level of sig. Insufficient evidence to say there is ESP.

Given $p = 72/600 < 1/6$, this suggests that the two individuals are subconsciously resisting any ESP. Adopting H_A: $\pi < 1/6$, $p = 0.12$ gives $TS = -3.07$. In this case, we reject H_0, suggesting resistance.

5.9 H_0: $\pi = 0.4$, H_A: < 0.4 (claim is excessive). Criterion: reject H_0 at 0.05 level of sig. if $TS < -1.64$. $TS = 0.46$. Cannot reject H_0. Clearly, claim is not excessive!

5.10 p-value is 0.0106, thus p-value lies between 0.01 and 0.05. You could reject H_0 with probability of error of 0.011. You are 98.9% certain that H_0, is false.

5.11 p-value is 0.046. Thus, you could have rejected H_0 with a 0.0496 probability of error. That is, you are 95.4% certain that you were correct in rejecting H_0.

5.12 (a) Interval is 0.437 ± 0.056.
(b) H_0: $\pi = 0.5$, H_A: $\pi < 0.5$ (claim is invalid). $TS = -2.18$. Reject H_0 at 0.05 but not 0.01 level of significance.

5.13 (a) 0.0228   (b) (i) 0.8438   (ii) 0.1469
If sample size is increased then we have
(a) 0.00   (b) (i) 1.00   (ii) 0.00

5.14 H_0: $\mu = 6$, H_A: $\mu > 6$. $t_{0.05} = 1.833$. Sample yields $\bar{X} = 6.5$, with $s^2 = 5.2$. $TS = 0.65$. Do not reject H_0. Insufficient evidence to justify concern.

5.15 H_0: $\mu = 190$, H_A: $\mu \neq 190$. $t_{0.005} = 2.861$. $TS = -1.83$. Insufficient evidence to suggest problem with temperature level.

H_0: $\sigma^2 = 3$, $\sigma^2 > 3$. $\chi^2_{0.01} = 36.19$. $TS = 38$. Reject H_0. Temperature variation appears too large.

5.16 H_0: $\mu = 0.425$, H_A: $\mu < 0.425$ (company is incorrect). At 0.05 level of sig., reject H_0 if $(\bar{X} - 0.425)/(s/\sqrt{n}) < -1.64$. That is, if $\bar{X} < 0.422$.

5.17 H_0: $\mu = 0.25$, H_A: $\mu < 0.25$. $p = 0.21$. $TS = 1.307$. Do not reject H_0 at 0.05 level of sig. Insufficient evidence to say that commercial was effective. By interpolation, p-value is 0.096.

Chapter 6

6.1   Distributions are shown below:

X Y	0	1	2	3	$g(Y)$
0	0	0	1/16	1/16	1/8
1	0	2/16	3/16	1/16	3/8
2	1/16	3/16	2/16	0	3/8
3	1/16	1/16	0	0	1/8
$f(X)$	1/8	3/8	3/8	1/8	

$V(X) = 0.75$, $V(Y) = 0.75$.

6.2   Sum rows and columns to find marginal distributions. $E(X) = 410$, $E(Y) = 195$. Distribution for Z is

Z	300	400	500	600	700	800	900
$p(Z)$	0.01	0.09	0.23	0.31	0.24	0.11	0.01

$E(Z) = 605$. Thus $E(Z) = E(X) + E(Y)$.

6.3 $E(X) = 32.2$, $V(X) = 151.16$. $E(Y) = 28.6$, $V(Y) = 98.04$.

6.4 $E(X) = E(Y) = 1.5$. $E(X + 2Y) = 4.6$. Thus $E(X + 2Y) = E(X) + 2E(Y)$. $E(XY) = 1.75$.
Thus $E(XY) \neq E(X)E(Y)$.
$E(X^2Y^2) = 4.75$. $E(X^2) = E(Y^2) = 3$. Thus $E(X^2Y^2) \neq E(X^2)E(Y^2)$.

6.5 $E(XY) = 922$. $E(XY) \neq E(X)E(Y)$.
$E(2X - Y) = 35.8$. Thus $E(2X - Y) = 2E(X) - E(Y)$. $E(X/Y) = 1.2625$.
But $E(X)/E(Y) = 1.1259$.

6.6   Expected profits are 31.8 and 8.69.

6.7 $E(Z) = 665.2$.

6.9 $Cov(X, Y) = -0.5$. There is an inverse relationship between X and Y as expected, given the definitions of X and Y.

6.10 $Cov(X, Y) = -150$. There is an inverse relationship between the outputs of the two firms.

6.11 $Cov(X, Y) = 1.08$. There is a direct relationship between home and overseas output.

6.12 $V(2X - Y) = 4V(X) + V(Y) - 4Cov(X, Y) = 4(0.75) + 0.75 - 4(-0.5) = 5.75.$

6.13 $E[X - E(X)][Y - E(Y)] = -3E[X - E(X)]^2 \quad E[X - E(X)]^2 E[Y - E(Y)]^2 =$
$9E[X - E(X)]^2 E[X - E(X)]^2.$ Thus correlation $= -3/\sqrt{9} = -1.$

6.14 $\rho = -0.67.$ This is a moderately high negative correlation, as expected given the nature of X and Y.

6.15 The joint distribution is

X \ Y	0	1	2	3
0	0	0	0	1/8
1	0	0	3/8	0
2	0	3/8	0	0
3	1/8	0	0	0

All the non-zero probabilities lie on a main 'diagonal line'.

$Cov(X, Y) = -0.75.$ The correlation is -1 because there is an exact negative linear relationship between X and Y. The relationship is in fact $Y = 3 - X.$

6.16 **(a)** $\rho = -0.022.$ The negative relationship found in Example 6.10 is a very weak one.

(b) $\rho = 0.0089.$ The positive relationship found in Example 6.11 is a very weak one.

6.17 $E(X) = 2, E(Y) = 1.5, E(XY) = 3.$ Thus $Cov(X, Y) = 0,$ so that X and Y are uncorrelated. But they are not independent since the product of marginal probabilities does not always give the joint probability.

6.18 Since X and Y are independent, the product of the relevant marginal products always gives the required joint probability. Thus the joint distribution must be

X \ Y	10	20	40	80
30	0.02	0.08	0.06	0.04
40	0.05	0.20	0.15	0.10
50	0.03	0.12	0.09	0.06

$E(X) = 37, E(Y) = 41, E(XY) = 1517.$ Thus $E(XY) = E(X)E(Y)$ so that, as expected, X and Y are uncorrelated.

6.19 $E(X) = 1.5, E(Y) = 2, E(XY) = 3.$ Thus $Cov(X, Y) = 0.$ Hence, X and Y are uncorrelated. But they are not independent since products of marginal probabilities do not give joint probabilities.

6.20 $E(X) = 5$, $V(X) = 4$, $E(Y) = 4$, $V(Y) = 9$.

$E(Z) = E(2X - 3Y) = 2E(X) - 3E(Y) = -2$.

$V(Z) = V(2X - 3Y) = 4V(X) + 9E(Y) = 97$ (X, Y are independent).

Since Z is a linear function of two normally distributed variables, X and Y, it must itself be normally distributed. Thus Z is $N(-2, 97)$. Hence, $\Pr(Z > 2.5) = 0.324$.

6.21 $H_0: \mu_1 = \mu_2$, $H_A: \mu_1 \neq \mu_2$. Large samples. $TS = 3.74$. Reject H_0 at 0.05 and 0.01 levels of significance.

6.22 $H_0: \mu_A = \mu_B$, $H_A: \mu_A < \mu_B$. $\bar{X}_A = 600$, $s_A^2 = 2250$, $\bar{X}_B = 654$, $s_B^2 = 2052$, $s^2 = 2131.2$. $TS = -2.00$, $t_{0.05} = 1.812$. Reject H_0. Mean wages appear lower at location A.

6.23 $H_0: \sigma_1^2 = \sigma_2^2$, $H_A: \sigma_1^2 \neq \sigma_2^2$. d.f. $= (7, 10)$, $F_{0.025} = 3.95$. $TS = s_1^2/s_2^2 = 1.36$. Do not reject H_0 at 0.05 level of sig. Insufficient evidence to say variances differ.

6.24 $H_0: \pi_1 = \pi_2$, $H_A: \pi_1 > \pi_2$. $p_1 = 0.713$, $p_2 = 0.636$, $p = 0.673$. $TS = 3.08$ Reject H_0 at 0.05 and 0.01 levels of sig. It appears that more are opposed in rural areas.

6.25 $H_0: \mu_A = \mu_B$, $H_A: \mu_A > \mu_B$. $\bar{X}_A = 300$, $s_A^2 = 150$, $\bar{X}_B = 290$, $s_B^2 = 100$. $s^2 = 125$. $TS = 1.79$, $t_{0.01} = 1.761$, $t_{0.01} = 2.624$. Reject H_0 at 0.05 but not 0.01 level of sig. We assume populations are normally distributed with a common variance.

6.26 $H_0: \pi_1 = \pi_2$, $H_A: \pi_1 \neq \pi_2$. $p_1 = 0.38$, $p_2 = 0.685$, $p = 0.55$. $TS = -5.01$. Reject H_0 at 0.05 and 0.01 levels of sig. Parties appear to differ.

6.27 (a) $H_0: \mu_A = \mu_B$, $H_A: \mu_A > \mu_B$. Large samples. $TS = 3.90$. Reject H_0 at 0.05 and 0.01 levels of sig.

(b) Interval is $(1400 - 1350) \pm 1.96\sqrt{164.11} = = 50 \pm 25.1$.

6.28 $H_0: \mu = 200$, $\mu < 200$ (unfair practice). Large sample. $TS = -2.17$. Do not reject H_0 at 0.01 level of sig. If allow a 0.01 probability of error, we cannot say there is unfair practice.

6.29 (a) $H_0: \sigma_1^2 = \sigma_2^2$, $H_A: \sigma_1^2 \neq \sigma_2^2$. $TS = s_2^2/s_1^2 = 1.65$, $F_{0.05}(8,11) = 2.948$. Do not reject H_0. No apparent difference in variances.

(b) $H_0: \mu_2 - \mu_1 = 4$, $H_A: \mu_2 - \mu_1 \neq 4$. TS based on $\bar{X}_2 - \bar{X}_1 - 4$. $s^2 = 250$, $TS = 0.86$. $t_{0.025} = 2.093$. Do not reject H_0 at 0.05 level of sig.

(c) Interval is $(494 - 484) \pm t_{0.05}\sqrt{6.97} = 10 \pm 12.1$.

6.30 $H_0: \sigma_1^2 = \sigma_2^2$, $H_A: \sigma_1^2 \neq \sigma_2^2$. $s_1^2 = 47.5$, $s_2^2 = 42.8$. d.f. $= (4, 5)$, $F_{0.025} = 7.39$. $TS = s_1^2/s_2^2 = 1.11$. Do not reject H_0. Variances do not appear to differ.

$H_0: \mu_1 = \mu_2$, $H_A: \mu_1 < \mu_2$. $\bar{X}_1 = 34$, $\bar{X}_2 = 37$. $s^2 = 44.9$ (estimate of common variance). d.f. $= 9$. $t_{0.05} = 1.83$. $TS = -0.74$. Do not reject H_0 Do not buy new machine. Assume populations are normally distributed.

Chapter 7

7.1 H_0: Attitudes are independent of party. d.f. = 4, $\chi^2_{0.1} = 13.28$. $TS = 25.6$. Reject H_0. Not independent.

7.2 H_0: Stores used are independent of income. d.f. = 6, $\chi^2_{0.01} = 16.8$. Top left-hand value of $(o_i - e_i)^2/e_i = 52.7$. Hence $TS > 16.8$. Reject H_0. Not independent.

7.3 H_0: $\pi_A = \pi_B = \pi_C = \pi_D$, (where π_A = proportion of firm A workers who are part-time, etc.). H_A: At least one π is different. d.f. = 3, $\chi^2_{0.05} = 7.815$. $TS = 1.63$. Do not reject H_0. Insufficient evidence to suggest part-time working varies across firms.

7.4 **(a)** H_0: $\pi_{WT} = \pi_{MT} = \pi_{UT}$, $\pi_{WB} = \pi_{MB} = \pi_{UB}$, d.f. = 4, $\chi^2_{0.01} = 13.28$. Using tabloid column, $TS > 33.6 > 13.28$. Reject H_0. Habits appear to differ across classes.
   (b) H_0: $\pi_{MB} = \pi_{WB}$, H_A: $\pi_{MB} > \pi_{WB}$. $p_{MB} = 0.365$, $p_{WB} = 0.160$, pooled $p_B = 0.2625$. $TS = 4.66 > 2.33$. Reject H_0 at 0.01 level of sig. Middle-class proportion appears to exceed working-class proportion.

7.5 **(a)** H_0: X is binomial with $\pi = 0.5$. $n = 6$, d.f. = 5, $\chi^2_{0.05} = 11.07$. $TS = 1.32$. Do not reject H_0. Distribution appears to be binomial.
   (b) H_0: X is binomial with unknown π. If p is estimate of π, then $np = \Sigma\, xp(x) = 2.91$. Hence $p = 0.485$. d.f. = 4, $\chi^2_{0.05} = 9.49$. $TS = 0.30$. Again, do not reject H_0.

7.6 H_0: X is Poisson with unknown λ. Estimated $\lambda = 2.154$ per week, which can be used to calculate Poisson probabilities for $X = 0$ to 6. Multiplying by 52 gives estimated frequencies. d.f. = 6, $\chi^2_{0.05} = 12.59$. $TS = 2.49$. Do not reject H_0. Frequencies appear to be Poisson.

7.7 H_0: $\mu = 25$, H_A: $\mu < 25$. $E(X) = 7.5$, $V(X) = 3.75$. 10 minuses, hence $p = 0.33$. $TS = -1.29$. Since $T > -1.64$, do not reject H_0. Insufficient evidence to say visitors spend less than £25. For t-test, $\bar{X} = 20.47$, $s^2 = 86.41$. d.f. = 14, $t_{0.05} = 1.761$. $TS = -1.88$. In this case, reject H_0, since $|TS| > 1.771$. If population had a normal distribution, t-test would be more powerful since it uses more information. Hence H_0 is rejected.

7.8 H_0: $\mu_1 = \mu_2$, H_A: $\mu_1 \neq \mu_2$. Median = 92.5. $n_1 = 13$, $n_2 = 9$, $k = 11$ and $X = 9$. Hence $n_1 - X = 4$, $k - X = 2$, $n_2 - k + X = 7$. $\chi_{0.05} = 3.841$, $TS = 4.7$. Reject H_0. Varieties appear to differ. For t-test, $\bar{X}_1 = 90.31$, $s_1^2 = 34.06$, $\bar{X}_2 = 96.67$, $s_2^2 = 25.87$, $s^2 = 30.79$. d.f. = 20, $t_{0.025} = 2.086$. $TS = 2.65$. Again, reject H_0.

7.9 H_0: $\mu_1 = \mu_2$, H_A: $\mu_1 \neq \mu_2$. Median = 51. Ignoring median observation, $n_1 = 9$, $n_2 = 9$, $k = 9$, $X = 4$. Hence, $n_1 - X = 5$, $k - X = 5$, $n_2 - k + X = 4$. $\chi^2_{0.05} = 3.841$. $TS = 0.22$. Do not reject H_0. No apparent difference between groups.

7.10 H_0: $\mu_1 = \mu_2$, H_A: $\mu_1 \neq \mu_2$. A-level ranks are 1, 2, 7, 9, 10, 14, 15, 17, 18, 19. Non-A-level ranks are 3, 4, 5, 6, 8, 11, 12, 13, 16. Thus, $n_1 = 10$, $n_2 = 9$, $R_2 = 78$. $U = 62$, $E(U) = 45$, $V(U) = 150$. $TS = 1.39$. Do not reject H_0 since $|TS| < 1.96$. Same result as Example 7.9.

7.11 H_0: $\mu_1 = \mu_2$, H_A: $\mu_1 \neq \mu_2$. [*Note*: there are three wages of 380, occupying ranks 3, 4 and 5. Thus each such wage is given a rank of 4.] Firm A ranks are 1, 4, 8, 9.5, 11.5, 11.5, 13, 14.5, 16. Firm B ranks are 2, 4, 4, 6, 7, 9.5, 14.5. Thus $n_1 = 9$, $n_2 = 7$, $R_2 = 48$. $U = 52$, $E(U) = 31.5$, $V(U) = 89.25$. $TS = 2.17$. Reject H_0 since $|TS| > 1.96$. Average wages appear to differ.

For t-test $\bar{X}_A = 433.33$, $\bar{X}_B = 404.29$, $s_A^2 = 2350$, $s_B^2 = 1262$, so that $s^2 = 1883.7$. d.f. = 14, $t_{0.025} = 2.145$. $TS = 1.33$. In this case, we cannot reject H_0.

7.12 H_0: Random outcomes. No. of g outcomes is $n_1 = 66$, No. of d outcomes is $n_2 = 15$. $U = 19$, $E(U) = 25.44$, $V(U) = 7.164$. $TS = -2.40$. Since $|TS| > 1.96$, reject H_0 of randomness.

7.13 H_0: Random outcomes. Median = 6. Reading column by column yields the sequence a–––bba–aaabbbaababababababab–bb. Thus $n_a = 12$, $n_b = 13$. $U = 18$, $E(U) = 13.48$, $V(U) = 5.97$. Hence $TS = 1.85$. Since $TS < 1.96$, do not reject H_0 of randomness.

Chapter 9

9.2 Canada: $\hat{Y} = 2.435$, $e = -0.426$. Indonesia: $\hat{Y} = 0.1121$, $e = -0.0563$. Spain: $\hat{Y} = 0.7656$, $e = +0.241$.

9.3 For Easteuro, $\hat{Y} = 0.411$.

9.4 **(b)** $\sum x^2 = 95.733$, $\sum xy = -47.13$, $\sum y^2 = 28.93$.
(c) $b = -0.4923$, $a = 14.58$, so that $\hat{Y} = 14.6 - 0.492X$.
(e) $\bar{X} = 7.133$, $\bar{Y} = 11.067$, so elasticity $= b\bar{X}/\bar{Y} = -0.317$.

9.5 Let the Y variable be consumption and the X variable be income.
(a) In this notation, $\sum y^2 = 8890$, $\sum x^2 = 33\,000$, $\sum xy = 16\,800$
(b) The marginal propensity to consume can be estimated by $b = 0.509$.
(c) $a = 24.45$ so the OLS line is $\hat{Y} = 24.45 + 0.509X$. Thus, when $X = 350$, $Y = £202.60$.

9.6   Let $Y = Q$ and $X = U$. Thus $\sum y^2 = 3237.7$, $\sum x^2 = 1745.2$, $\sum xy = -2084.3$.

   (a) The OLS line is $\hat{Y} = 22.7 - 1.19X$, that is $\hat{Q} = 22.7 - 1.19U$.

   (b) When unemployment rises by one percentage point, the quit rate falls by 1.19 per 1000 employees.

9.7 $R^2 = 0.802$, $R = -0.896$.

9.8 $R^2 = 0.763$.

Chapter 10

10.1   **(a)**

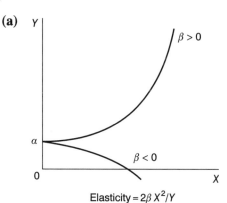

Elasticity $= 2\beta\, X^2/Y$

   (b)

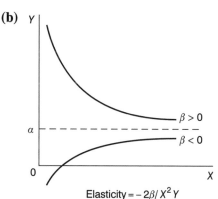

Elasticity $= -2\beta/\, X^2\, Y$

   (c)

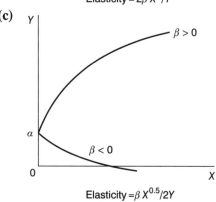

Elasticity $= \beta\, X^{0.5}/2Y$

   (d)

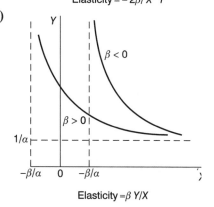

Elasticity $= \beta\, Y/X$

10.2   Figure 10.6a: $Y = Ae^{\beta X}$, with $\beta > 0$, $A > 0$. Figure 10.6b: $Y = \alpha + \beta(1/X)$, with $\beta > 0$, $\alpha > 0$. Figure 10.6c: $Y = AX^\beta$, with $0 < \beta < 1$, $A > 0$. Figure 10.6d: $Y = \alpha + \beta \ln X$ with $\beta < 0$, $\alpha < 0$.

10.3   Let $Y = \ln M$ and $X = \ln G$. $\sum x^2 = 52.67$, $\sum xy = 55.026$. Thus $b = 1.0447$. $\bar{Y} = -1.1317$, $\bar{X} = 0.74721$. Thus $a = -1.912$. The double-log OLS equation is $\widehat{\ln M} = -1.91 + 1.045 \ln G$. The income elasticity is therefore 1.045, close to the value found in Chapter 9.

10.4   **(a)** Let $Y = W$ and $X = U$. Thus $\sum y^2 = 15.81$, $\sum x^2 = 1.137$, $\sum xy = -3.934$, $\bar{Y} = 4.714$, $\bar{X} = 1.543$. OLS line is $\hat{W} = 10.05 - 3.46U$, with $R^2 = 0.86$.

(b) Let $Y = W$ and $X = 1/U$. Thus $\sum y^2 = 15.81$, $\sum x^2 = 0.1771$, $\sum xy = 1.628$, $\bar{Y} = 4.714$, $\bar{X} = (1/n)\sum(1/U) = 0.689$. OLS line is $\hat{W} = -1.62 + 9.19(1/U)$ with $R^2 = 0.95$. The R^2s are comparable so the curve fits the data rather than a straight line.

(c) In 1964, $\hat{W} = 4.1$ (cf. $W = 4.4$), whereas, in 1967, $\hat{W} = 2.2$ (cf. $W = 5.1$). Thus the curve seems to have shifted up.

10.5   **(a) (i)**   Let $Y = P$ and $X = S$. Thus $\sum x^2 = 647\ 100$, $\sum y^2 = 148.8$, $\sum xy = -8858$, $\bar{Y} = 12.15$, $\bar{X} = 441.67$. The OLS line is $\hat{P} = 18.2 - 0.01369S$.

(ii)   Let $Y = A = \ln P$ and $X = B = \ln S$. Thus $\sum x^2 = 4.061$, $\sum y^2 = 1.063$, $\sum xy = -2.076$, $\bar{Y} = 2.41$, $\bar{X} = 5.78$. The OLS line is $\widehat{\ln P} = 5.36 - 0.511 \ln S$ or $\hat{P} = 213S^{-0.511}$.

(b) $R^2 = 0.815$ for the linear function. $R^2 = 0.998$ for the double-log function. This may be suggestive, but the R^2s are not comparable.

(c) The curve fits the scatter better than a straight line.

(d) For the linear function, elasticity $= \beta(\bar{X}/\bar{Y}) = -0.498$. For the double-log function, elasticity $= -0.511$. The estimates of the *sales* elasticity are 2.01 and 1.96

10.6 $\bar{M} = 0.32248$. The regressions are $\hat{M}^* = 0.066 + 0.542G$ with SSR $= 57.85$, and $\widehat{\ln M}^* = -0.78 + 1.045 \ln G$ with SSR $= 6.93$. $Z = 8.35$, $TS = 31.83$. $\chi^2_{0.01} = 6.635$. Nonlinear fit is best.

10.7 $\bar{P} = 11.1406$. Regressions are $\hat{P}^* = 1.63 - 0.012\ 295$ with SSR $= 0.222$, and $\widehat{\ln P}^* = 2.95 - 0.511 \ln S$ with SSR $= 0.001\ 96$. $Z = 113$, $TS = 14.19$. $\chi^2_{0.01} = 6.635$. Nonlinear fit is best.

Chapter 11

11.1   Considering many samples, X_1 and X_8 will be normally distributed with $E(X_1) = E(X_8) = \mu$ and $V(X_1) = V(X_8) = \sigma^2$. m^* is a linear function of X_1 and X_8 and hence must itself be normally distributed.

$E(m^*) = 0.5E(X_1) + 0.5E(X_8) = \mu$, so that m^* is unbiased, $V(m^*) = 0.25\ V(X_1) + 0.25\ V(X_8) = \sigma^2/2$. But, with $n = 8$, $V(\bar{X}) = \sigma^2/8$ so that $V(m^*) > V(\bar{X})$.

11.2   Over many samples X_1, X_2 and X_3 are normally distributed with each $E(X_i) = \mu$ and each $V(X_i) = \sigma^2$. X^* is a linear function of the X_i and so is normally distributed. $E(X^*) = 0.6E(X_1) + 0.3E(X_2) + 0.1E(X_3) = \mu$. Thus X^* is unbiased. $V(X^*) = 0.36V(X_1) + 0.09V(X_2) + 0.01V(X_3) = 0.46\sigma^2$. But, with $n = 3$, $V(\bar{X}) = \sigma^2/3$, so that $V(X^*) > V(\bar{X})$. Thus X^* is less efficient than $\bar{X}$.

With $\sigma^2 = 200/23$, X^* is $N(\mu, 4)$. Thus $Z = (X^* - \mu)/2$ is $N(0, 1)$. The required probability is $\Pr(X^* > \mu + 2) + \Pr(X^* < \mu - 2) = 2\,\Pr(Z > 1) = 0.3174$.

11.3 $\hat{m}$, $\tilde{m}$, m^* are all linear functions of $\bar{X}$ which is itself a linear estimator. Thus, $\hat{m}$, $\tilde{m}$ and m^* are also linear estimators. X^* is a linear function of the sample observations and must, hence, be a linear estimator.

11.4 $\text{MSE}(\hat{m}) = \sigma^2/n + 100$. $\text{MSE}(\tilde{m}) = \sigma^2/n + 25/n^2$.
$\text{MSE}(m^*) = (n-1)^2/(n-2)^2(\sigma^2/n) + \mu^2/(n-2)^2$.
For the given values, $\tilde{m}$ has the smallest MSE.

11.5 $E(\tilde{X}) = \mu$, $V(\tilde{X}) = \sigma^2/(n + m)$. $V(\bar{X}_n) = \sigma^2/n$. $\tilde{X}$ is the more efficient. As n and $m \to \infty$, both $V(\tilde{X})$ and $V(\bar{X}_n) \to 0$. Thus both $\tilde{X}$ and $\bar{X}_n$ are consistent. Since, for any large n and $n + m$, $V(\tilde{X}) < V(\bar{X}_n)$, $\tilde{X}$ is asymptotically more efficient.

11.6   **(a)** Since the population is normally distributed, the asymptotic distributions for $\bar{X}_1$, $\bar{X}_2$, $\bar{X}_3$ and $\bar{X}$ will be normal. Since $\tilde{X}$ is a linear function of $\bar{X}_1$, $\bar{X}_2$ and $\bar{X}_3$, its asymptotic distribution will also be normal.
(b) Since $E(\tilde{X}) = \mu$ and $V(\tilde{X}) \to 0$ as n_1, n_2 and $n_3 \to \infty$, $\tilde{X}$ is consistent.
(c) $\bar{X}$ is also consistent and is asymptotically more efficient than $\tilde{X}$.

11.7   **(a)** $\tilde{X}$ and X^* are unbiased but $\hat{X}$ is biased and hence cannot be efficient. X^* is more efficient than $\tilde{X}$.
(b) $\tilde{X}$ and X^* are consistent. If $n_1 > n_2 > n_3$, then X^* is asymptotically more efficient than $\tilde{X}$.

11.8 Values of $L = \pi(1 - \pi)^2$ for values of π between 0 and 1 yield the likelihood function shown below.

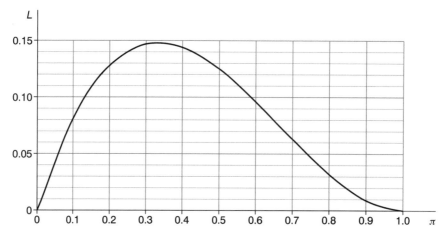

Checking L values for π between 0.3 and 0.35 suggests an ML estimate of about 0.33–0.34. This not a surprising result, since one-third of the components in the sample are defective.

11.9 Only when $\alpha = 4$ is the likelihood non-zero. Thus the MLE of α is 4.

11.10 Since $X = 2$, the likelihood function is $L = \lambda^2(1 - \lambda)$. Values of L for $\lambda = 0, 0.1, 0.2, 0.3, 0.4 \ldots$ yield the sketch shown below.

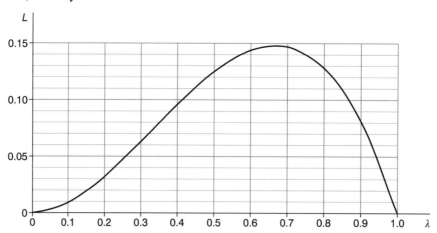

L takes its maximum value for λ between 0.6 and 0.7. Checking L for λ values in this range suggests an MLE for λ of 0.66 to 0.67. (Note also that since $E(X) = \lambda/(1 - \lambda)$, setting $E(X) = 2$ gives $2 = \lambda/(1 - \lambda)$ or $\lambda = 2/3$.)

Chapter 12

12.1 (a) H_0: $\beta = 0$, H_A: $\beta < 0$ (on a priori grounds). $b = -0.4923$, $\Sigma e^2 = 5.73$, $s_b = 0.068$. $TS = -7.25$, $t_{0.01} = 2.65$. Reject H_0 at 0.01 level of sig. X appears to influence Y.

(b) $a = 14.58$, $s_a = 0.5136$, $t_{0.005} = 3.012$. Interval: 14.58 ± 1.55.

12.2 H_0: $\beta = -1$ (claim is valid), $\beta \neq -1$. $b = -1.19$, $\Sigma e^2 = 757.4$, $s_b = 0.049\,38$. $TS = (b + 1)/s_b = -3.85$. $t_{0.025} = 1.96$. Reject H_0 at 0.05 level of sig. Claim appears to be invalid.

12.3 (a) Let M be the Y variable and Y be the X variable. $b = 0.235$. $\bar{Y} = 30.08$, $\bar{X} = 120.17$. $a = 1.84$.

(b) H_0: $\alpha = 0$, H_A: $\alpha \neq 0$. $\Sigma X^2 = 164\,243$, $s_a = 0.729$. $TS = 2.52$. $t_{0.005} = 3.25$. Do not reject H_0 at 0.01 level of sig. A zero intercept implies that M is proportionate to Y.

(c) $s_b = 0.0054$, $t_{0.025} = 2.262$. Interval is 0.235 ± 0.012.

12.4 If $P = AS^\beta$, then $S = (1/A)^{1/\beta} P^{1/\beta}$. That is, elasticity is $1/\beta$. H_0: $\beta = -0.5$ H_A: $\beta < -0.5$. $b = -0.511$, $s_b = 0.100$, $TS = (b + 0.5)/s_b = -1.1$. $t_{0.05} = 2.132$. Do not reject H_0 at 0.05 level of sig. Elasticity not more negative than -2.

12.5 (a) $\hat{C} = 542 - 9.01Q$, $R^2 = 0.70$.

(b) $\hat{C} = 51.1 + 4854(1/Q)$, $R^2 = 0.99$. Nonlinear fit best.

(c) Since $C = \alpha + \beta(1/Q)$, Total cost $= CQ = \alpha Q + \beta$. Thus, fixed costs $= \beta$. Interval is 4854 ± 1091.

12.6 $\hat{M} = 39.09$. $s_f = 0.463$. Interval is 39.1 ± 1.0.

12.7 (a) $\hat{C} = 2478$, $s_f = 109$, 2478 ± 502.

(b) $\hat{C} = 218.5$, $s_f = 19.5$, 218.5 ± 89.8.

(c) $\hat{C} = 74.8$, $s_f = 21.8$, 74.8 ± 100.4.

The further $1/Q$ is from its mean, 0.0473, the wider interval.

Chapter 13

13.1 $\hat{Y} = -282 - 8.48X_2 + 16.1X_3$.

13.2 (a) $s^2 = 10.47$.   (b) $s_{b_2}^2 = 1.74$, $s_{b_3}^2 = 2.89$.   (c) $R^2 = 0.87$.

13.3 (a) (i) $H_0: \beta_2 = 0$, $H_A: \beta_2 \neq 0$. $TS = b_2/s_{b_2} = -6.42$. d.f. $= 47$, $t_{0.005} = 2.68$. Reject H_0. X_2 appears to influence Y.

(ii) $H_0: \beta_3 = 20$, $H_A: \beta_3 < 20$. $TS = (b_3 - 20)/s_{b_3} = -2.31$. $t_{0.01} = 2.41$. Do not reject H_0. β_3 not less than 20.

(b) 16.1 ± 4.1.

13.4   d.f. $= 21$, $t_{0.05} = 1.72$. Intercept, Y and P have sig. t-ratios of 2.85, 7.92 and 2.44, but L has non-sig. t-ratio of 1.47. 87.5% of variations in C can be explained by variations in Y, A and P. Y and maybe L influence C with correct signs. Coeff. on P is sig. different from zero with negative sign. This result is inconsistent with theory.

13.5   First equation: d.f. $= 28$, $t_{0.05} = 1.701$. Elasticity $= 0.853$ with large t-ratio of 5.31. Second equation: d.f. $= 27$, $t_{0.05} = 1.703$. Elasticity falls to 0.251 with non-sig. t-ratio $= 1.54$. Inclusion of Y (large t-ratio $= 7.31$) results in sharp rise in R^2.

Conclusion: It is an error to omit Y. Thus the elasticity is much smaller than first thought and its value is not significantly different from zero.

13.6   (a) $X_2 + X_3 = 10$.   (b) Residuals are 1, 2, −1, −1 and −1, with $\Sigma\, e^2 = 8$.

13.7   First equation: d.f. $= 22$, $t_{0.05} = 1.717$. t-ratios are 0.88, 1.26, 1.12. Neither L nor K appears to influence Q, yet 83% of variation in Q can be explained. L and K are multicollinear.

Second equation: d.f. $= 21$, $t_{0.05} = 1.721$. t-ratios on L and K little changed. t-ratio on M is 2.5. M appears to influence Q.

Conclusion: Multicollinearity is masking the influence of L and K. In double-log equations, coefficients are elasticities. Sum of L and K elasticities is 0.97, which is less than 1. But low t-ratios mean we cannot reject constant returns.

13.8   Second equation is preferred because of high t-ratio on R.

(a) d.f. $= 44$, $t_{0.005} = 2.69$. $s_{b_2} = b_2/t\text{-ratio} = 0.017\ 25$. Interval is 0.103 ± 0.046.

(b) $H_0: \beta_3 = 0$, $H_A: \beta_3 > 0$. $TS = 0.833$. Wealth has no influence.

(c) No. W coefficient has low t-ratio but t-ratio on Y is much larger.

13.9   First equation: t-ratios low but R^2 is large. Collinearity is masking influence of X_2, and/or X_3.

Second equation: t-ratios low but now R^2 is also small. Suggests that X_2 and X_3 have little influence on Y.

13.10   d.f. $= 72$, $t_{0.025} = 1.99$. t-ratios on X, Y and W are 1.15, 0.27, 0.66. Unable to reject $H_0: \beta = 0$ for any variable. $H_0: \beta_2 = \beta_3 = \beta_4 = 0$, H_A: at least one β is non-zero. Using [13.44], $TS = 14.4$, $F_{0.05} = 2.73$. Reject H_0. Multicollinearity is masking influence of individual variables.

13.11   First equation: X_2 appears to influence Y.

Second equation: X_2 loses significance and X_3, X_4 have low t-ratios, yet SSR has fallen.

H_0: $\beta_3 = \beta_4 = 0$, H_A: at least one β is non-zero. $h = 2$, $n = 59$, $k = 4$. $\text{SSR}_\text{R} = 652.1$, $\text{SSR}_\text{U} = 634.7$. $TS = 0.75$, $F_{0.05} = 3.17$. Combined influence of X_3 and X_4 not significant. Fall in t-ratio for X_2 suggests correlation with X_3 and/or X_4.

13.12   (a) Because Y is positively correlated with P.

(b) t-test: $TS = 1.92$, $t_{0.025} = 1.982$. F-test: using [13.49] with $h = 1$, $TS = 3.67$, $F_{0.05} = 3.93$. Reject H_0: $\beta_3 = 0$ in each case. Using the test statistics, $t^2 = F$ (i.e., $1.92^2 = 3.67$). Also $t_{0.025}^2 = F_{0.05}$. Thus the tests will always give the same result.

Chapter 14

14.1   After $t = 19$: $\widehat{\ln Q} = 0.66 + 0.37 \ln L + 0.63 \ln K$.   Before $t = 19$: $\widehat{\ln Q} = 0.64 + 0.34 \ln L + 0.63 \ln K$.

14.2   For example, a value $D = 0.5$ might be used for $t = 31, 32, 33$.

14.3 $t = 1, \ldots, 20$: $Y = \beta_0 + \gamma_1 + \beta_1 X + \varepsilon$.
$t = 21, \ldots, 40$: $Y = \beta_0 + \gamma_1 + \gamma_2 + \beta_1 X + \varepsilon$.
$t = 40, \ldots, 60$: $Y = \beta_0 + \gamma_2 + \beta_1 X + \varepsilon$.

14.4   Spring: $Q = -0.74 + 4.15Y$. Summer: $Q = -0.74 + 3.64Y$.
Autumn: $Q = -0.74 + 3.09Y$. Winter: $Q = -0.74 + 3.46Y$.

14.5   Chow test I: $TS = 3.17$, $F_{0.05} = 2.86$. Reject H_0.
Chow test II: $TS = 1.64$, $F_{0.05} = 2.15$. Do not reject H_0.
First Chow test uses more information and hence has greater power than second test.

14.6 $\hat{C} = 12.1 + 0.838Y$. Elasticity 0.93.
$\Sigma e_1^2 = 13\ 474$. $\Sigma e_\text{p}^2 = \Sigma c^2(1 - R^2) = 21\ 501$. Using second Chow test, $TS = 6.85$.
$F_{0.05} = 3.42$. Reject H_0. Change in parameters suggested.

Chapter 15

15.1   Mongrel equation is

$$Q = \left(\frac{\lambda a_0 + \mu \beta_0^*}{\lambda + \mu}\right) + \left(\frac{\lambda a_1 + \mu \beta_1}{\lambda + \mu}\right)P + \left(\frac{\lambda a_2}{\lambda + \mu}\right)Y + \frac{\lambda u + \mu v}{\lambda + \mu}.$$

The supply equation is identified because it cannot be confused with the mongrel equation.

If Y and C vary then both equations are identified.

15.2   **(a)** Both equations are identified;   **(b)** neither identified;
(c) [1] is not identified but [2] is identified as before.

15.4   **(a)** Equation (ii) can be rewritten as

$$Y = -\frac{b_0}{b_1} + \frac{1}{b_1}X - \frac{b_2}{b_1}A - \frac{v}{b_1}.$$

Thus [2] is identified but not [1]. If $a_3 = 0$, then neither equation is identified.

(b) Substituting for X in [1] leads to the reduced-form equation

$$Y = \left(\frac{a_0 + a_1 b_0}{1 - a_1 b_1}\right) + \left(\frac{a_2 + a_1 b_2}{1 - a_1 b_1}\right)A + \left(\frac{a_3}{1 - a_1 b_1}\right)B + \frac{u + a_1 v}{1 - a_1 b_1}.$$

Substituting for Y in [2] then gives the reduced-form equation

$$X = \left(\frac{b_0 + b_1 a_0}{1 - a_1 b_1}\right) + \left(\frac{b_2 + b_1 a_2}{1 - a_1 b_1}\right)A + \left(\frac{b_1 a_3}{1 - a_1 b_1}\right)B + \frac{v + b_1 u}{1 - a_1 b_1}.$$

Since [1] is not identified it cannot be consistently estimated. In [2], Y is related to v via the first reduced-form equation which has composite disturbance $(u + a_1 v)/(1 - a_1 b_1)$. Since $a_1 > 0$ and $b_1 < 0$, Y is positively correlated with v. Thus OLS will yield biased estimators, with $E(\hat{b}_1) > b_1$, $E(\hat{b}_0) < b_0$ and $E(\hat{b}_2) < b_2$.

15.5   Equation [2] contains only exogenous variables on its RHS and is therefore the reduced-form equation for Y_2. Substituting for Y_2 in [2] gives the reduced-form equation for Y_1:

$$Y_1 = (a_0 + a_1 b_0) + (a_2 + a_1 b_1)X_1 + (a_3 + a_1 b_2)X_2 + v + a_1 w.$$

Both equations could be estimated by OLS, [2] because all regressors are exogenous and [1] because the endogenous Y_2 in this equation is not related to the disturbance v.

15.6   Since $V(\varepsilon) = kX_3^2$, $V(\varepsilon/X_3) = (1/X_3^2)V(\varepsilon) = k$. We therefore transform the equation by dividing throughout by X_3 to obtain

$$Y^* = \beta_3 + \beta_1 X_3^* + \beta_2 X_2^* + \beta_4 X_4^* + \varepsilon^*,$$

where $Y^* = Y/X_3$, $X_3^* = 1/X_3$, $X_2^* = X_2/X_3$, $X_4^* = X_4/X_3$ and $\varepsilon^* = \varepsilon/X_3$. Since ε^* is homoscedastic, efficient estimators of the βs can be obtained by regressing Y^* on X_3^*, X_2^* and X_4^*. Note, however, that it is the intercept and the coefficient on X_3^* in the regression that yields estimates of β_3 and β_1, respectively.

15.7   Since $V(\varepsilon) = \sigma X$, $V(\varepsilon/\sqrt{X}) = (1/X)V(\varepsilon) = \sigma$. We therefore transform the equation by dividing by $\sqrt{X}$ to obtain

$$Y^* = \beta_1 X_1^* + \beta_2 X_2^* + \varepsilon^*,$$

where $Y^* = Y/\sqrt{X}$, $X_1^* = 1/\sqrt{X}$, $X_2^* = \sqrt{X}$ and $\varepsilon^* = \varepsilon/\sqrt{X}$. OLS may now be applied, regressing Y^* on X_1^* and X_2^* with intercept supressed. The estimated standard errors will then be unbiased.

15.8   Since u_t is a classical disturbance, OLS may be applied to

$$Y_t^* = \alpha + \alpha_1 X_{1t}^* + \alpha_2 X_{2t}^* + u_t,$$

where $\alpha = \alpha_0(1 - \rho_1 - \rho_2)$, $Y_t^* = Y_t - \rho_1 Y_{t-1} - \rho_2 Y_{t-2}$, $X_{1t}^* = X_{1t} - \rho_1 X_{1t-1} - \rho_2 X_{1t-2}$, $X_{2t}^* = X_{2t} - \rho_1 X_{2t-1} - \rho_2 X_{2t-2}$, and $u_t = \varepsilon_t - \rho_1 \varepsilon_{t-1} - \rho_2 \varepsilon_{t-2}$. Note, however, that ρ_1 and ρ_2 are unknown and would have to be estimated before using OLS.

15.9   Given an estimate of ρ, OLS can be applied to

$$Y_t^* = \beta + \beta_2 X_t^* + v_t$$

where $Y_t^* = Y_t - \rho Y_{t-4}$, $\beta = \beta_1(1 - \rho)$, $X_t^* = X_t - \rho X_{t-4}$ and $v_t = \varepsilon_t - \rho \varepsilon_{t-4}$. With quarterly data, the values of disturbances are more likely to be related to disturbance values four quarters previous.

15.10   The hypothesis that neither price variable influences sales is rejected. At least one of these variables influences sales but their significance is masked by their collinearity. Omitting the variables would therefore be a dynamic misspecification.

Chapter 16

16.1   Impact and long-run multipliers are, respectively **(a)** 0.94 and 3.74; **(b)** 2.08 and 0.02.

16.2 $\theta = 0.45$, $b_0 = 0.72$, $a = 45.5$, implying a geometric lag of form

$$Y_t = 45.5 + 0.72X_t + 0.324X_{t-1} + 0.146X_{t-2} + 0.066X_{t-3} \dots .$$

16.3 (a) $\theta = 0.8$, $b_0 = -0.4$, $a = -2$, implying
$$Y_t = -2 - 0.4X_t - 0.32X_{t-1} - 0.256X_{t-2} - 0.205X_{t-3} \dots .$$
(b) $\theta = -0.7$, $b_0 = 0.6$, $a = 0.5$, implying
$$Y_t = 0.5 + 0.6X_t - 0.42X_{t-1} + 0.294X_{t-2} - 0.206X_{t-3} \dots .$$

16.4 $\hat{\lambda} = 0.3$, $b = 4$, $a = 60$, implying $Y_t^* = 60 + 4X_t$. 30% of the difference between Y and Y^* is eliminated in each period.

16.5 The model gives $Y_t = \lambda a + \lambda \beta_1 X_{1t} + \lambda \beta_2 X_{2t} + (1 - \lambda)Y_{t-1} + \lambda \varepsilon_t$. Thus $\hat{\lambda} = 0.2$, $a = 25$, $b_1 = 4$, $b_2 = 2$. For X_1, short- and long-run multipliers are 0.8 and 4, while, for X_2, they are 0.4 and 2.

16.6 $\hat{\mu} = 0.18$, $b = 2.33$, $a = 1.44$. Thus $Y_t = 1.44 + 2.33X_t^*$. 18% of the difference between X and X^* is eliminated in each period.

16.7 (a) $\hat{\lambda} = 0.64$, $b = 3.48$, $a = 2.13$. Thus $Y_t^* = 2.13 + 3.48X_t$. 64% of the difference between Y and Y^* is eliminated in the period.
(b) $Y_t = 2.13 + 3.48X_t^*$. 64% of the difference between X and X^* is eliminated in the period.

16.8 The estimating equation is
$$RC_t = \alpha\mu + \beta\mu RY_t + \delta P_t - \delta(1 - \mu)P_{t-1} + (1 - \mu)RC_{t-1} + u_t.$$
OLS yields
$$RC_t = -0.744 + 0.630RY_t - 0.496P_t + 0.466P_{t-1} + 0.441RC_{t-1}.$$
The coefficient on RC_{t-1} gives $\hat{\mu} = 0.559$, which implies $b = 1.13$ and $a = -1.33$. Also, clearly, $d = -0.496$. But there is a problem. The ratio of the coefficients on P_t and P_{t-1} provides us with a second estimate of μ! This is $1 - \hat{\mu} = 0.94$, so that we obtain $\hat{\mu} = 0.06$, a value very different from that found earlier. It is therefore necessary to re-estimate our equation subject to the restriction that the two estimates of μ are identical. Such estimation is tackled in the next chapter. For the moment, we simply obtain the short-run income elasticity as $b\hat{\mu} = 0.630$ and the long-run elasticity as $b = 0.630/0.550 = 1.13$.

16.9 (a) Stationary;   (b) non-stationary;   (c) stationary;
(d) successive substitution indicates that the process is non-stationary;
(e) stationary about long-run path $Y_t = -14 + 7.3X_t$;
(f) stationary about long-run path $Y_t = 0.8X_t$.

16.10 Short run elasticities with respect to X and Y are 0.74 and 0.38 respectively. Long-run elasticities are 1.90 and 0.026.

Chapter 17

17.1 (a) $Y_t = \alpha_0 + \alpha_1 X_t + \beta_1 Y_{t-1} + \varepsilon_t$ (partial adjustment model).

(b) $Y_t = \alpha_0 + \alpha_1 X_t + \alpha_2 X_{t-1} + \varepsilon_t$ (Y depends on X, with short lag).

(c) $Y_t = \alpha_0 + \alpha_1 \Delta X_t + \beta_1 Y_{t-1} + \beta_2 Y_{t-2} + \varepsilon_t$ where $\Delta X_t = X_t - X_{t-1}$ (Y depends on ΔX, not X).

(d) $Y_t = \alpha_0 + \alpha_1 X_t + \alpha_2 X_{t-1} + \alpha_3 X_{t-2} + \beta_1 Y_{t-1} + \varepsilon_t$ (partial adjustment model with Y^* depending on X_t, X_{t-1} and X_{t-2}).

(e) $Y_t - X_{t-1} = \alpha_0 + \alpha_1 \Delta X_t + \varepsilon_t$ (long-run X-elasticity is unity).

(f) $Y_t = \alpha_0 + \alpha_1 X_t + \beta_1 Y_{t-1} + \varepsilon_t$ (adaptive expectations model).

(g) $\Delta Y_t = \alpha_0 + \alpha_1 \Delta X_t + \varepsilon_t$ (equation is in differences not levels).

Models (a), (b), (e) and (g) are nested in (d). Model (g) is also nested in (c).

17.2 (a) $\Delta W_t = \alpha_0 \Delta X_t + \beta_0 \Delta Y_t + \varepsilon_t$ where $\Delta W_t = W_t - W_{t-1}$ etc.

(b) $W_t - X_{t-1} - Y_{t-1} = \kappa + \alpha_0 \Delta X_t + \beta_0 \Delta Y_t + \varepsilon_t$

(c) $W_t - W_{t-1} = \kappa + \alpha_0 (X_t - W_{t-1}) + \beta_0 Y_t + \alpha_1 (X_{t-1} - W_{t-1}) + \beta_1 Y_{t-1} + \varepsilon_t$

The final equation to be estimated is

$$W_t - X_{t-1} - Y_{t-1} = \kappa + \alpha_0 \Delta X_t + \beta_0 \Delta Y_t + \delta(W_{t-1} - X_{t-1} - Y_{t-1}) + \varepsilon_t.$$

Final equation is nested in (c).

17.3 Restrictions on $Y_t = \beta_0 + \beta_1 X_t + \beta_2 X_{t-1} + \gamma_1 Z_t + \gamma_2 Z_{t-1} + \delta Y_{t-1}$ are $\beta_1 + \beta_2 = 0$, $\gamma_1 + \gamma_2 = 0$ and $\delta = 1$.

Under H_0 (all restrictions valid), we have $h = 3$, $n = 48$, $k = 6$, with $\mathrm{SSR}_U = 246$ and $\mathrm{SSR}_R = 268$. Hence, $TS = 1.25$. Since $F_{0.05} = 2.83$, the restrictions cannot be rejected. They appear to be valid.

17.4 (a) $\kappa = 0$, $\alpha_0 + \alpha_1 = 0$, $\beta_0 + \beta_1 = 0$, $\gamma = 1$.

(b) $\alpha_1 = \beta_1 = 0$.

(c) $\alpha_0 + \beta_0 = 1$, $\alpha_1 = \beta_1 = 0$.

(d) $\beta_0 = \beta_1 = 0$, $\alpha_0 + \alpha_1 = 1$.

(e) $\alpha_0 + \alpha_1 = 1$, $\beta_0 + \beta_1 = 1$.

None of (a), (b), (c) or (d) are nested in (e).

17.5 Short-run parameters are $b = 0.7$ and $\mu = 0.83$. Long-run parameters are $\alpha = 3.13$ and $\beta = -1.45$.

17.6 Short-run income elasticity is 0.53. In the short run, 67% of any previous period disequilibrium between C and Y is made up in the current period. The long-run relationship between income consumption is $C_t = Y_t$. Thus both the long-run income elasticity and the long-run average propensity to consume equal unity.

Appendix:
Statistical Tables

Table A.1 Areas under the standard normal curve

z'	0.00	0.01	0.02	0.03	0.04	0.05	0.06	0.07	0.08	0.09
0.0	0.0000	0.0040	0.0080	0.0120	0.0160	0.0199	0.0239	0.0279	0.0319	0.0359
0.1	0.0398	0.0438	0.0478	0.0517	0.0557	0.0596	0.0636	0.0675	0.0714	0.0753
0.2	0.0793	0.0832	0.0871	0.0910	0.0948	0.0987	0.1026	0.1064	0.1103	0.1141
0.3	0.1179	0.1217	0.1255	0.1293	0.1331	0.1368	0.1406	0.1443	0.1480	0.1517
0.4	0.1554	0.1591	0.1628	0.1664	0.1700	0.1736	0.1772	0.1808	0.1844	0.1879
0.5	0.1915	0.1950	0.1985	0.2019	0.2054	0.2088	0.2123	0.2157	0.2190	0.2224
0.6	0.2257	0.2291	0.2324	0.2357	0.2389	0.2422	0.2454	0.2486	0.2517	0.2549
0.7	0.2580	0.2611	0.2642	0.2673	0.2704	0.2734	0.2764	0.2794	0.2823	0.2852
0.8	0.2881	0.2910	0.2939	0.2967	0.2995	0.3023	0.3051	0.3078	0.3106	0.3133
0.9	0.3159	0.3186	0.3212	0.3238	0.3264	0.3289	0.3315	0.3340	0.3365	0.3389
1.0	0.3413	0.3438	0.3461	0.3485	0.3508	0.3531	0.3554	0.3577	0.3599	0.3621
1.1	0.3643	0.3665	0.3686	0.3708	0.3729	0.3749	0.3770	0.3790	0.3810	0.3830
1.2	0.3849	0.3869	0.3888	0.3907	0.3925	0.3944	0.3962	0.3980	0.3997	0.4015
1.3	0.4032	0.4049	0.4066	0.4082	0.4099	0.4115	0.4131	0.4147	0.4162	0.4177
1.4	0.4192	0.4207	0.4222	0.4236	0.4251	0.4265	0.4279	0.4292	0.4306	0.4319
1.5	0.4332	0.4345	0.4357	0.4370	0.4382	0.4394	0.4406	0.4418	0.4429	0.4441
1.6	0.4452	0.4463	0.4474	0.4484	0.4495	0.4505	0.4515	0.4525	0.4535	0.4545
1.7	0.4554	0.4564	0.4573	0.4582	0.4591	0.4599	0.4608	0.4616	0.4625	0.4633
1.8	0.4641	0.4649	0.4656	0.4664	0.4671	0.4678	0.4686	0.4693	0.4699	0.4706
1.9	0.4713	0.4719	0.4726	0.4732	0.4738	0.4744	0.4750	0.4756	0.4761	0.4767
2.0	0.4772	0.4778	0.4783	0.4788	0.4793	0.4798	0.4803	0.4808	0.4812	0.4817
2.1	0.4821	0.4826	0.4830	0.4834	0.4838	0.4842	0.4846	0.4850	0.4854	0.4857
2.2	0.4861	0.4864	0.4868	0.4871	0.4875	0.4878	0.4881	0.4884	0.4887	0.4890
2.3	0.4893	0.4896	0.4898	0.4901	0.4904	0.4906	0.4909	0.4911	0.4913	0.4916
2.4	0.4918	0.4920	0.4922	0.4925	0.4927	0.4929	0.4931	0.4932	0.4934	0.4936
2.5	0.4938	0.4940	0.4941	0.4943	0.4945	0.4946	0.4948	0.4949	0.4951	0.4952
2.6	0.4953	0.4955	0.4956	0.4957	0.4959	0.4960	0.4961	0.4962	0.4963	0.4964
2.7	0.4965	0.4966	0.4967	0.4968	0.4969	0.4970	0.4971	0.4972	0.4973	0.4974
2.8	0.4974	0.4975	0.4976	0.4977	0.4977	0.4978	0.4979	0.4979	0.4980	0.4981
2.9	0.4981	0.4982	0.4982	0.4983	0.4984	0.4984	0.4985	0.4985	0.4986	0.4986
3.0	0.4987	0.4987	0.4987	0.4988	0.4988	0.4989	0.4989	0.4989	0.4990	0.4990

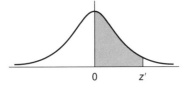

The above table shows the area beneath the standard normal curve between zero (the mean of the $N(0, 1)$ distribution) and z', a point on the horizontal axis. It therefore gives areas such as that shaded in the figure. For example, if $z' = 1.47$ then the shaded area is 0.4292. Thus if z is $N(0, 1)$ then $\Pr(0 < z < z') = 0.4292$.

Since (a) the standard normal curve is symmetrical about the vertical axis and (b) the total area under it is unity, the area beneath the curve between any two points on the z-axis can be found using the table.

Table A.2 Percentage points of the Student's *t* distribution

Area α under right-hand tail

v	0.4	0.25	0.1	0.05	0.025	0.01	0.005	0.0025	0.001	0.0005
1	0.325	1.000	3.078	6.314	12.706	31.821	63.657	127.320	318.310	636.620
2	0.289	0.816	1.886	2.920	4.303	6.965	9.925	14.089	22.327	31.598
3	0.277	0.765	1.638	2.353	3.182	4.541	5.841	7.453	10.214	12.924
4	0.271	0.741	1.533	2.132	2.776	3.747	4.604	5.598	7.173	8.610
5	0.267	0.727	1.476	2.015	2.571	3.365	4.032	4.773	5.893	6.869
6	0.265	0.718	1.440	1.943	2.447	3.143	3.707	4.317	5.208	5.959
7	0.263	0.711	1.415	1.895	2.365	2.998	3.499	4.029	4.785	5.408
8	0.262	0.706	1.397	1.860	2.306	2.896	3.355	3.833	4.501	5.041
9	0.261	0.703	1.383	1.833	2.262	2.821	3.250	3.690	4.297	4.781
10	0.260	0.700	1.372	1.812	2.228	2.764	3.169	3.581	4.144	4.587
11	0.260	0.697	1.363	1.796	2.201	2.718	3.106	3.497	4.025	4.437
12	0.259	0.695	1.356	1.782	2.179	2.681	3.055	3.428	3.930	4.318
13	0.259	0.694	1.350	1.771	2.160	2.650	3.012	3.372	3.852	4.221
14	0.258	0.692	1.345	1.761	2.145	2.624	2.977	3.326	3.787	4.140
15	0.258	0.691	1.341	1.753	2.131	2.602	2.947	3.286	3.733	4.073
16	0.258	0.690	1.337	1.746	2.120	2.583	2.921	3.252	3.686	4.015
17	0.257	0.689	1.333	1.740	2.110	2.567	2.898	3.222	3.646	3.965
18	0.257	0.688	1.330	1.734	2.101	2.552	2.878	3.197	3.610	3.922
19	0.257	0.688	1.328	1.729	2.093	2.539	2.861	3.174	3.579	3.883
20	0.257	0.687	1.325	1.725	2.086	2.528	2.845	3.153	3.552	3.850
21	0.257	0.686	1.323	1.721	2.080	2.518	2.831	3.135	3.527	3.819
22	0.256	0.686	1.321	1.717	2.074	2.508	2.819	3.119	3.505	3.792
23	0.256	0.685	1.319	1.714	2.069	2.500	2.807	3.104	3.485	3.767
24	0.256	0.685	1.318	1.711	2.064	2.492	2.797	3.091	3.467	3.745
25	0.256	0.684	1.316	1.708	2.060	2.485	2.787	3.078	3.450	3.725
26	0.256	0.684	1.315	1.706	2.056	2.479	2.779	3.067	3.435	3.707
27	0.256	0.684	1.314	1.703	2.052	2.473	2.771	3.057	3.421	3.690
28	0.256	0.683	1.313	1.701	2.048	2.467	2.763	3.047	3.408	3.674
29	0.256	0.683	1.311	1.699	2.045	2.462	2.756	3.038	3.396	3.659
30	0.256	0.683	1.310	1.697	2.042	2.457	2.750	3.030	3.385	3.646
40	0.255	0.681	1.303	1.684	2.021	2.423	2.704	2.971	3.307	3.551
60	0.254	0.679	1.296	1.671	2.000	2.390	2.660	2.915	3.232	3.460
120	0.254	0.677	1.289	1.658	1.980	2.358	2.617	2.860	3.160	3.373
∞	0.253	0.674	1.282	1.645	1.960	2.326	2.576	2.807	3.090	3.291

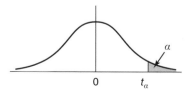

The table gives critical values for t, written t_α, cutting off an area α under the right-hand tail as indicated by the shaded area in the figure. v = number of degrees of freedom. For example, if $v = 24$ and $\alpha = 0.05$ then $t_{0.05} = 1.711$; if $v = 12$ and $\alpha = 0.025$ then $t_{0.025} = 2.179$.

Table A.3 Percentage points of the χ^2 distribution

v	\multicolumn{4}{c}{Area α under right-hand tail}				
	0.995	**0.99**	**0.975**	**0.95**	**0.05**	**0.025**	**0.01**	**0.005**
---	---	---	---	---	---	---	---	---
1	0.0000393	0.000157	0.000982	0.00393	3.841	5.024	6.635	7.879
2	0.0100	0.0201	0.0506	0.103	5.991	7.378	9.210	10.597
3	0.0717	0.115	0.216	0.352	7.815	9.348	11.345	12.838
4	0.207	0.297	0.484	0.711	9.488	11.143	13.277	14.860
5	0.412	0.554	0.831	1.145	11.070	12.832	15.086	16.750
6	0.676	0.872	1.237	1.635	12.592	14.449	16.812	18.548
7	0.989	1.239	1.690	2.167	14.067	16.013	18.475	20.278
8	1.344	1.646	2.180	2.733	15.507	17.535	20.090	21.955
9	1.735	2.088	2.700	3.325	16.919	19.023	21.666	23.589
10	2.156	2.558	3.247	3.940	18.307	20.483	23.209	25.188
11	2.603	3.053	3.816	4.575	19.675	21.920	24.725	26.757
12	3.074	3.571	4.404	5.226	21.026	23.337	26.217	28.300
13	3.565	4.107	5.009	5.892	22.362	24.736	27.688	29.819
14	4.075	4.660	5.629	6.571	23.685	26.119	29.141	31.319
15	4.601	5.229	6.262	7.261	24.996	27.488	30.578	32.801
16	5.142	5.812	6.908	7.962	26.296	28.845	32.000	34.267
17	5.697	6.408	7.564	8.672	27.587	30.191	33.409	35.718
18	6.265	7.015	8.231	9.390	28.869	31.526	34.805	37.156
19	6.844	7.633	8.907	10.117	30.144	32.852	36.191	38.582
20	7.434	8.260	9.591	10.851	31.410	34.170	37.566	39.997
21	8.034	8.897	10.283	11.591	32.671	35.479	38.932	41.401
22	8.643	9.542	10.982	12.338	33.924	36.781	40.289	42.796
23	9.260	10.196	11.689	13.091	35.172	38.076	41.638	44.181
24	9.886	10.856	12.401	13.848	36.415	39.364	42.980	45.558
25	10.520	11.524	13.120	14.611	37.652	40.646	44.314	46.928
26	11.160	12.198	13.844	15.379	38.885	41.923	45.642	48.290
27	11.808	12.879	14.573	16.151	40.113	43.194	46.963	49.645
28	12.461	13.565	15.308	16.928	41.337	44.461	48.278	50.993
29	13.121	14.256	16.047	17.708	42.557	45.722	49.588	52.336
30	13.787	14.953	16.791	18.493	43.773	46.979	50.892	53.672

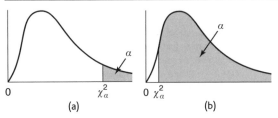

(a)   (b)

The table gives critical values for χ^2, written χ_α^2, cutting off the area α to the right of χ_α^2, under the distribution as indicated by the shaded areas in the figures. Note that α can be a small area, as in (a) or a large area as in (b). v = number of degrees of freedom. For example, if $v = 24$ and $\alpha = 0.05$ then $\chi_{0.05}^2 = 36.415$; if $v = 12$ and $\alpha = 0.95$ then $\chi_{0.95}^2 = 5.226$.

Table A.4 Critical values of the *F* distribution

(a) Upper 5% points

v_1 = degrees of freedom for the numerator

v_2	1	2	3	4	5	6	7	8	9
1	161.45	199.50	215.71	224.58	230.16	230.99	236.77	238.88	240.54
2	18.513	19.000	19.164	19.247	19.296	19.330	19.353	19.371	19.385
3	10.128	9.5521	9.2766	9.1172	9.0135	8.9406	8.8867	8.8452	8.8123
4	7.7086	6.9443	6.5914	6.3882	6.2561	6.1631	6.0942	6.0410	5.9988
5	6.6079	5.7861	5.4095	5.1922	5.0503	4.9503	4.8759	4.8183	4.7725
6	5.9874	5.1433	4.7571	4.5337	4.3874	4.2839	4.2067	4.1468	4.0990
7	5.5914	4.7374	4.3468	4.1203	3.9715	3.8660	3.7870	3.7257	3.6767
8	5.3177	4.4590	4.0662	3.8379	3.6875	3.5806	3.5005	3.4381	3.3881
9	5.1174	4.2565	3.8625	3.6331	3.4817	3.3738	3.2927	3.2296	3.1789
10	4.9646	4.1028	3.7083	3.4780	3.3258	3.2172	3.1355	3.0717	3.0204
11	4.8443	3.9823	3.5874	3.3567	3.2039	3.0946	3.0123	2.9480	2.8962
12	4.7472	3.8853	3.4903	3.2592	3.1059	2.9961	2.9134	2.8486	2.7964
13	4.6672	3.8056	3.4105	3.1791	3.0254	2.9153	2.8321	2.7669	2.7144
14	4.6001	3.7389	3.3439	3.1122	2.9582	2.8477	2.7642	2.6987	2.6458
15	4.5431	3.6823	3.2874	3.0556	2.9013	2.7905	2.7066	2.6408	2.5876
16	4.4940	3.6337	3.2389	3.0069	2.8524	2.7413	2.6572	2.5911	2.5377
17	4.4513	3.5915	3.1968	2.9647	2.8100	2.6987	2.6143	2.5480	2.4943
18	4.4139	3.5546	3.1599	2.9277	2.7729	2.6613	2.5767	2.5102	2.4563
19	4.3807	3.5219	3.1274	2.8951	2.7401	2.6283	2.5435	2.4768	2.4227
20	4.3512	3.4928	2.0984	2.8661	2.7109	2.5990	2.5140	2.4471	2.3928
21	4.3248	3.4668	3.0725	2.8401	2.6848	2.5727	2.4876	2.4205	2.3660
22	4.3009	3.4434	3.0491	2.8167	2.6613	2.5491	2.4638	2.3965	2.3419
23	4.2793	3.4221	3.0280	2.7955	2.6400	2.5277	2.4422	2.3748	2.3201
24	4.2597	3.4028	3.0088	2.7763	2.6307	2.5082	2.4226	2.3551	2.3002
25	4.2417	3.3852	2.9912	2.7587	2.6030	2.4904	2.4047	2.3371	2.2821
26	4.2252	3.3690	2.9752	2.7426	2.5868	2.4741	2.3883	2.3205	2.2655
27	4.2100	3.3541	2.9604	2.7278	2.5719	2.4591	2.3732	2.3053	2.2501
28	4.1960	3.3404	2.9467	2.7141	2.5581	2.4453	2.3593	2.2913	2.2360
29	4.1830	3.3277	2.9340	2.7014	2.5454	2.4324	2.3463	2.2783	2.2229
30	4.1709	3.3158	2.9223	2.6896	2.5336	2.4205	2.3343	2.2662	2.2107
40	4.0847	3.2317	2.8387	2.6060	2.4495	2.3359	2.2490	2.1802	2.1240
60	4.0012	3.1504	2.7581	2.5252	2.3683	2.2541	2.1665	2.0970	2.0401
120	3.9201	3.0718	2.6802	2.4472	2.2899	2.1750	2.0868	2.0164	1.9588
∞	3.8415	2.9957	2.6049	2.3719	2.2141	2.0986	2.0096	1.9384	1.8799

v_2 = d.f. for the denominator

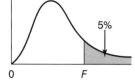

The entries in the table give the critical values of *F* cutting off 5% in the right-hand tail of the distribution. v_1 gives the degrees of freedom in the numerator, v_2 those in the denominator.

Table A.4 (*continued*)

(a) Upper 5% points (*continued*)

v_1 = d.f. for the numerator

v_2	10	12	15	20	24	30	40	60	120	∞
1	241.88	243.91	245.95	248.01	249.05	250.10	251.14	252.20	253.25	254.31
2	19.396	19.413	19.429	19.446	19.454	19.462	19.471	19.479	19.487	19.496
3	8.7855	8.7446	8.7029	8.6602	8.6385	8.6166	8.5944	8.5720	8.5494	8.5264
4	5.9644	5.9117	5.8578	5.8025	5.7744	5.7459	5.7170	5.6877	5.6581	5.6281
5	4.7351	4.6777	4.6188	4.5581	4.5272	4.4957	4.4638	4.4314	4.3985	4.3650
6	4.0600	3.9999	3.9381	3.8742	3.8415	3.8082	3.7743	3.7398	3.7047	3.6689
7	3.6365	3.5747	3.5107	3.4445	3.4105	3.3758	3.3404	3.3043	3.2674	3.2298
8	3.3472	3.2839	3.2184	3.1503	3.1152	3.0794	3.0428	3.0053	2.9669	2.9276
9	3.1373	3.0729	3.0061	2.9365	2.9005	2.8637	2.8259	2.7872	2.7475	2.7067
10	2.9782	2.9130	2.8450	2.7740	2.7372	2.6996	2.6609	2.6211	2.5801	2.5379
11	2.8536	2.7876	2.7186	2.6464	2.6090	2.5705	2.5309	2.4901	2.4480	2.4045
12	2.7534	2.6866	2.6169	2.5436	2.5055	2.4663	2.4259	2.3842	2.3410	2.2962
13	2.6710	2.6037	2.5331	2.4589	2.4202	2.3803	2.3392	2.2966	2.2524	2.2064
14	2.6022	2.5342	2.4630	2.3879	2.3487	2.3082	2.2664	2.2229	2.1778	2.1307
15	2.5437	2.4753	2.4034	2.3275	2.2878	2.2468	2.2043	2.1601	2.1141	2.0658
16	2.4935	2.4247	2.3522	2.2756	2.2354	2.1938	2.1507	2.1058	2.0589	2.0096
17	2.4499	2.3807	2.3077	2.2304	2.1898	2.1477	2.1040	2.0584	2.0107	1.9604
18	2.4117	2.3421	2.2686	2.1906	2.1497	2.1071	2.0629	2.0166	1.9681	1.9168
19	2.3779	2.3080	2.2341	2.1555	2.1141	2.0712	2.0264	1.9795	1.9302	1.8780
20	2.3479	2.2776	2.2033	2.1242	2.0825	2.0391	1.9938	1.9464	1.8963	1.8432
21	2.3210	2.2504	2.1757	2.0960	2.0540	2.0102	1.9645	1.9165	1.8657	1.8117
22	2.2967	2.2258	2.1508	2.0707	2.0283	1.9842	1.9380	1.8894	1.8380	1.7831
23	2.2747	2.2036	2.1282	2.0476	2.0050	1.9605	1.9139	1.8648	1.8128	1.7570
24	2.2547	2.1834	2.1077	2.0267	1.9838	1.9390	1.8920	1.8424	1.7896	1.7330
25	2.2365	2.1649	2.0889	2.0075	1.9643	1.9192	1.8718	1.8217	1.7684	1.7110
26	2.2197	2.1479	2.0716	1.9898	1.9464	1.9010	1.8533	1.8027	1.7488	1.6906
27	2.2043	2.1323	2.0558	1.9736	1.9299	1.8842	1.8361	1.7851	1.7306	1.6717
28	2.1900	2.1179	2.0411	1.9586	1.9147	1.8687	1.8203	1.7689	1.7138	1.6541
29	2.1768	2.1045	2.0275	1.9446	1.9005	1.8543	1.8055	1.7537	1.6981	1.6376
30	2.1646	2.0921	2.0148	1.9317	1.8874	1.8409	1.7918	1.7396	1.6835	1.6223
40	2.0772	2.0035	1.9245	1.8389	1.7929	1.7444	1.6928	1.6373	1.5766	1.5089
60	1.9926	1.9174	1.8364	1.7480	1.7001	1.6491	1.5943	1.5343	1.4673	1.3893
120	1.9105	1.8337	1.7505	1.6587	1.6084	1.5543	1.4952	1.4290	1.3519	1.2539
∞	1.8307	1.7522	1.6664	1.5705	1.5173	1.4591	1.3940	1.3180	1.2214	1.0000

v_2 = d.f. for the denominator

Table A.4 (*continued*)

(b) Upper 2.5% points

v_1 = d.f. for the denominator

v_2	1	2	3	4	5	6	7	8	9
1	647.79	799.50	864.16	899.58	921.85	937.11	948.22	956.66	963.28
2	38.506	39.000	39.165	39.248	39.298	39.331	39.355	39.373	39.387
3	17.443	16.044	15.439	15.101	14.885	14.735	14.624	14.540	14.473
4	12.218	10.649	9.9792	9.6045	9.3645	9.1973	9.0741	8.9796	8.9047
5	10.007	8.4336	7.7636	7.3879	7.1464	6.9777	6.8531	6.7572	6.6811
6	8.8131	7.2599	6.5988	6.2272	5.9876	5.8198	5.6955	5.5996	5.5234
7	8.0727	6.5415	5.8898	5.5226	5.2852	5.1186	4.9949	4.8993	4.8232
8	7.5709	6.0595	5.4160	5.0526	4.8173	4.6517	4.5286	4.4333	4.3572
9	7.2093	5.7147	5.0781	4.7181	4.4844	4.3197	4.1970	4.1020	4.0260
10	6.9367	5.4564	4.8256	4.4683	4.2361	4.0721	3.9498	3.8549	3.7790
11	6.7241	5.2559	4.6300	4.2751	4.0440	3.8807	3.7586	3.6638	3.5879
12	6.5538	5.0959	4.4742	4.1212	3.8911	3.7283	3.6065	3.5118	3.4358
13	6.4143	4.9653	4.3472	3.9959	3.7667	3.6043	3.4827	3.3880	3.3120
14	6.2979	4.8567	4.2417	3.8919	3.6634	3.5014	3.3799	3.2853	3.2093
15	6.1995	4.7650	4.1528	3.8043	3.5764	3.4147	3.2934	3.1987	3.1227
16	6.1151	4.6867	4.0768	3.7294	3.5021	3.3406	3.2194	3.1248	3.0488
17	6.0420	4.6189	4.0112	3.6648	3.4379	3.2767	3.1556	3.0610	2.9849
18	5.9781	4.5597	3.9539	3.6083	3.3820	3.2209	3.0999	3.0053	2.9219
19	5.9216	4.5075	3.9034	3.5587	3.3327	3.1718	3.0509	2.9563	2.8801
20	5.8715	4.4613	3.8587	3.5147	3.2891	3.1283	3.0074	2.9128	2.8365
21	5.8266	4.4199	3.8188	3.4754	3.2501	3.0895	2.9686	2.8740	2.7977
22	5.7863	4.3828	3.7829	3.4401	3.2151	3.0546	2.9338	2.8392	2.7628
23	5.7498	4.3492	3.7505	3.4083	3.1835	3.0232	2.9023	2.8077	2.7313
24	5.7166	4.3187	3.7211	3.3794	3.1548	2.9946	2.8738	2.7791	2.7027
25	5.6864	4.2909	3.6943	3.3530	3.1287	2.9685	2.8478	2.7531	2.6766
26	5.6586	4.2655	3.6697	3.3289	3.1048	2.9447	2.8240	2.7293	2.6528
27	5.6331	4.2421	3.6472	3.3067	3.0828	2.9228	2.8021	2.7074	2.6309
28	5.6096	4.2205	3.6264	3.2863	3.0626	2.9027	2.7820	2.6872	2.6106
29	5.5878	4.2006	3.6072	3.2674	3.0438	2.8840	2.7633	2.6686	2.5919
30	5.5675	4.1821	3.5894	3.2499	3.0265	2.8667	2.7460	2.6513	2.5746
40	5.4239	4.0510	3.4633	3.1261	2.9037	2.7444	2.6238	2.5289	2.4519
60	5.2856	3.9253	3.3425	3.0077	2.7863	2.6274	2.5068	2.4117	2.3344
120	5.1523	3.8046	3.2269	2.8943	2.6740	2.5154	2.3948	2.2994	2.2217
∞	5.0239	3.6889	3.1161	2.7858	2.5665	2.4082	2.2875	2.1918	2.1136

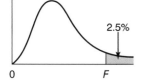

2.5%

The entries in the table give the critical values of F cutting off 2.5% in the right-hand tail of the distribution. v_1 gives the degrees of freedom in the numerator, v_2 in the denominator.

Table A.4 (*continued*)

(b) Upper 2.5% points (*continued*)

ν_1 = d.f. for the denominator

ν_2	10	12	15	20	24	30	40	60	120	∞
1	968.63	976.71	984.87	993.10	997.25	1001.4	1005.6	1009.8	1014.0	1018.3
2	39.398	39.415	39.431	39.448	39.456	39.465	39.473	39.481	39.400	39.498
3	14.419	14.337	14.253	14.167	14.124	14.081	14.037	13.992	13.947	13.902
4	8.8439	8.7512	8.6565	8.5599	8.5109	8.4613	8.4111	8.3604	8.3092	8.2573
5	6.6192	6.5245	6.4277	6.3286	6.2780	6.2269	6.1750	6.1225	6.0693	6.0153
6	5.4613	5.3662	5.2687	5.1684	5.1172	5.0652	5.0125	4.9589	4.9044	4.8491
7	4.7611	4.6658	4.5678	4.4667	4.4150	4.3624	4.3089	4.2544	4.1989	4.1423
8	4.2951	4.1997	4.1012	3.9995	3.9472	3.8940	3.8398	3.7844	3.7279	3.6702
9	3.9639	3.8682	3.7694	3.6669	3.6142	3.5604	3.5055	3.4493	3.3918	3.3329
10	3.7168	3.6209	3.5217	3.4185	3.3654	3.3110	3.2554	3.1984	3.1399	3.0798
11	3.5257	3.4296	3.3299	3.2261	3.1725	3.1176	3.0613	3.0035	2.9441	2.8828
12	3.3736	3.2773	3.1772	3.0728	3.0187	2.9633	2.9063	2.8478	2.7874	2.7249
13	3.2497	3.1532	3.0527	2.9477	2.8932	2.8372	2.7797	2.7204	2.6590	2.5955
14	3.1469	3.0502	2.9493	2.8437	2.7888	2.7324	2.6742	2.6142	2.5519	2.4872
15	3.0602	2.9633	2.8621	2.7559	2.7006	2.6437	2.5850	2.5242	2.4611	2.3953
16	2.9862	2.8890	2.7875	2.6808	2.6252	2.5678	2.5085	2.4471	2.3831	2.3163
17	2.9222	2.8249	2.7230	2.6158	2.5598	2.5020	2.4422	2.3801	2.3153	2.2474
18	2.8664	2.7689	2.6667	2.5590	2.5027	2.4445	2.3842	2.3214	2.2558	2.1869
19	2.8172	2.7196	2.6171	2.5089	2.4523	2.3937	2.3329	2.2696	2.2032	2.1333
20	2.7737	2.6758	2.5731	2.4645	2.4076	2.3486	2.2873	2.2234	2.1562	2.0853
21	2.7348	2.6368	2.5338	2.4247	2.3675	2.3082	2.2465	2.1819	2.1141	2.0422
22	2.6998	2.6017	2.4984	2.3890	2.3315	2.2718	2.2097	2.1446	2.0760	2.0032
23	2.6682	2.5699	2.4665	2.3567	2.2989	2.2389	2.1763	2.1107	2.0415	1.9677
24	2.6396	2.5411	2.4374	2.3273	2.2693	2.2090	2.1460	2.0799	2.0099	1.9353
25	2.6135	2.5149	2.4110	2.3005	2.2422	2.1816	2.1183	2.0516	1.9811	1.9055
26	2.5896	2.4908	2.3867	2.2759	2.2174	2.1565	2.0928	2.0257	1.9545	1.8781
27	2.5676	2.4688	2.3644	2.2533	2.1946	2.1334	2.0693	2.0018	1.9299	1.8527
28	2.5473	2.4484	2.3438	2.2324	2.1735	2.1121	2.0477	1.9797	1.9072	1.8291
29	2.5286	2.4295	2.3248	2.2131	2.1540	2.0923	2.0276	1.9591	1.8861	1.8072
30	2.5112	2.4120	2.3072	2.1952	2.1359	2.0739	2.0089	1.9400	1.8664	1.7867
40	2.3882	2.2882	2.1819	2.0677	2.0069	1.9429	1.8752	1.8028	1.7242	1.6371
60	2.2702	2.1692	2.0613	1.9445	1.8817	1.8152	1.7440	1.6668	1.5810	1.4821
120	2.1570	2.0548	1.9450	1.8249	1.7597	1.6899	1.6141	1.5299	1.4327	1.3104
∞	2.0483	1.9447	1.8326	1.7085	1.6402	1.5660	1.4835	1.3883	1.2684	1.0000

ν_2 = d.f. for the denominator

Table A.4 (*continued*)

(c) Upper 1% points

ν_1 = d.f. for the denominator

ν_2	1	2	3	4	5	6	7	8	9
1	4052.2	4999.5	5403.4	5624.6	5763.6	5859.0	5928.4	5981.1	6022.5
2	98.503	99.000	99.166	99.249	99.299	99.333	99.356	99.374	99.388
3	34.116	30.817	29.457	28.710	28.237	27.911	27.672	27.489	27.345
4	21.198	18.000	16.694	15.977	15.522	15.207	14.976	14.799	14.659
5	16.258	13.274	12.060	11.392	10.967	10.672	10.456	10.289	10.158
6	13.745	10.925	9.7795	9.1483	8.7459	8.4661	8.2600	8.1017	7.9761
7	12.246	9.5466	8.4513	7.8466	7.4604	7.1914	6.9928	6.8400	6.7188
8	11.259	8.6491	7.5910	7.0061	6.6318	6.3707	6.1776	6.0289	5.9106
9	10.561	8.0215	6.9919	6.4221	6.0569	5.8018	5.6129	5.4671	5.3511
10	10.044	7.5594	6.5523	5.9943	5.6363	5.3858	5.2001	5.0567	4.9424
11	9.6460	7.2057	6.2167	5.6683	5.3160	5.0692	4.8861	4.7445	4.6315
12	9.3302	6.9266	5.9525	5.4120	5.0643	4.8206	4.6395	4.4994	4.3875
13	9.0738	6.7010	5.7394	5.2053	4.8616	4.6204	4.4410	4.3021	4.1911
14	8.8618	6.5149	5.5639	5.0354	4.6950	4.4558	4.2779	4.1399	4.0297
15	8.6831	6.3589	5.4170	4.8932	4.5556	4.3183	4.1415	4.0045	3.8948
16	8.5310	6.2262	5.2922	4.7726	4.4374	4.2016	4.0259	3.8896	3.7804
17	8.3997	6.1121	5.1850	4.6690	4.3359	4.1015	3.9267	3.7910	3.6822
18	8.2854	6.0129	5.0919	4.5790	4.2479	4.0146	3.8406	3.7054	3.5971
19	8.1849	5.9259	5.0103	4.5003	4.1708	3.9386	3.7653	3.6305	3.5225
20	8.0960	5.8489	4.9382	4.4307	4.1027	3.8714	3.6987	3.5644	3.4567
21	8.0166	5.7804	4.8740	4.3688	4.0421	3.8117	3.6396	3.5056	3.3981
22	7.9454	5.7190	4.8166	4.3134	3.9880	3.7583	3.5867	3.4530	3.3458
23	7.8811	5.6637	4.7649	4.2636	3.9392	3.7102	3.5390	3.4057	3.2986
24	7.8229	5.6136	4.7181	4.2184	3.8951	3.6667	3.4959	3.3629	3.2560
25	7.7698	5.5680	4.6755	4.1774	3.8550	3.6272	3.4568	3.3439	3.2172
26	7.7213	5.5263	4.6366	4.1400	3.8183	3.5911	3.4210	3.2884	3.1818
27	7.6767	5.4881	4.6009	4.1056	3.7848	3.5580	3.3882	3.2558	3.1494
28	7.6356	5.4529	4.5681	4.0740	3.7539	3.5276	3.3581	3.2259	3.1195
29	7.5977	5.4204	4.5378	4.0449	3.7254	3.4995	3.3303	3.1982	3.0920
30	7.5625	5.3903	4.5097	4.0179	3.6990	3.4735	3.3045	3.1726	3.0665
40	7.3141	5.1785	4.3126	3.8283	3.5138	3.2910	3.1238	2.9930	2.8876
60	7.0771	4.9774	4.1259	3.6490	3.3389	3.1187	2.9530	2.8233	2.7185
120	6.8509	4.7865	3.9491	3.4795	3.1735	2.9559	2.7918	2.6629	2.5586
∞	6.6349	4.6052	3.7816	3.3192	3.0173	2.8020	2.6393	2.5113	2.4073

ν_2 = d.f. for the denominator

The entries in the table give the critical values of F cutting off 1% in the right-hand tail of the distribution. ν_1 gives the degrees of freedom in the numerator, ν_2 in the denominator.

Table A.4 (*continued*)

(c) Upper 1% points (*continued*)

v_1 = d.f. for the denominator

v_2	10	12	15	20	24	30	40	60	120	∞
1	6055.8	6106.3	6157.3	6208.7	6234.6	6260.6	6286.8	6313.0	6339.4	6365.9
2	99.399	99.416	99.433	99.449	99.458	99.466	99.474	99.482	99.491	99.499
3	27.229	27.052	26.872	26.690	26.598	26.505	26.411	26.316	26.221	26.125
4	14.546	14.374	14.198	14.020	13.929	13.838	13.745	13.652	13.558	13.463
5	10.051	9.8883	9.7222	9.5526	9.4665	9.3793	9.2912	9.2020	9.1118	9.0204
6	7.8741	7.7183	7.5590	7.3958	7.3127	7.2285	7.1432	7.0567	6.9690	6.8800
7	6.6201	6.4691	6.3143	6.1554	6.0743	5.9920	5.9084	5.8236	5.7373	5.6495
8	5.8143	5.6667	5.5151	5.3591	5.2793	5.1981	5.1156	5.0316	4.9461	4.8588
9	5.2565	5.1114	4.9621	4.8080	4.7290	4.6486	4.5666	4.4831	4.3978	4.3105
10	4.8491	4.7059	4.5581	4.4054	4.3269	4.2469	4.1653	4.0819	3.9965	3.9090
11	4.5393	4.3974	4.2509	4.0990	4.0209	3.9411	3.8596	3.7761	3.6904	3.6024
12	4.2961	4.1553	4.0096	3.8584	3.7805	3.7008	3.6192	3.5355	3.4494	3.3608
13	4.1003	3.9603	3.8154	3.6646	3.5868	3.5070	3.4253	3.3413	3.2548	3.1654
14	3.9394	3.8001	3.6557	3.5052	3.4274	3.3476	3.2656	3.1813	3.0942	3.0040
15	3.8049	3.6662	3.5222	3.3719	3.2940	3.2141	3.1319	3.0471	2.9595	2.8684
16	3.6909	3.5527	3.4089	3.2587	3.1808	3.1007	3.0182	2.9330	2.8447	2.7528
17	3.5931	3.4552	3.3117	3.1615	3.0835	3.0032	2.9205	2.8348	2.7459	2.6530
18	3.5082	3.3706	3.2273	3.0771	2.9990	2.9185	2.8354	2.7493	2.6597	2.5660
19	3.4338	3.2965	3.1533	3.0031	2.9249	2.8442	2.7608	2.6742	2.5839	2.4893
20	3.3682	3.2311	3.0880	2.9377	2.8594	2.7785	2.6947	2.6077	2.5168	2.4212
21	3.3098	3.1730	3.0300	2.8796	2.8010	2.7200	2.6359	2.5484	2.4568	2.3603
22	3.2576	3.1209	2.9779	2.8274	2.7488	2.6675	2.5831	2.4951	2.4029	2.3055
23	3.2106	3.0740	2.9311	2.7805	2.7017	2.6202	2.5355	2.4471	2.3542	2.2558
24	3.1681	3.0316	2.8887	2.7380	2.6591	2.5773	2.4923	2.4035	2.3100	2.2107
25	3.1294	2.9931	2.8502	2.6993	2.6203	2.5383	2.4530	2.3637	2.2696	2.1694
26	3.0941	2.9578	2.8150	2.6640	2.5848	2.5026	2.4170	2.3273	2.2325	2.1315
27	3.0618	2.9256	2.7827	2.6316	2.5522	2.4699	2.3840	2.2938	2.1985	2.0965
28	3.0320	2.8959	2.7530	2.6017	2.5223	2.4397	2.3535	2.2629	2.1670	2.0642
29	3.0045	2.8685	2.7256	2.5742	2.4946	2.4118	2.3253	2.2344	2.1379	2.0342
30	2.9791	2.8431	2.7002	2.5487	2.4689	2.3860	2.2992	2.2079	2.1108	2.0062
40	2.8005	2.6648	2.5216	2.3689	2.2880	2.2034	2.1142	2.0194	1.9172	1.8047
60	2.6318	2.4961	2.3523	2.1978	2.1154	2.0285	1.9360	1.8363	1.7263	1.6006
120	2.4721	2.3363	2.1915	2.0346	1.9500	1.8600	1.7628	1.6557	1.5330	1.3805
∞	2.3209	2.1847	2.0385	1.8783	1.7908	1.6964	1.5923	1.4730	1.3246	1.0000

v_2 = d.f. for the denominator

Table A.4 (*continued*)

(d) Upper 0.5% points

v_1 = d.f. for the numerator

v_2	1	2	3	4	5	6	7	8	9
1	16211	20000	21615	22500	23056	23437	23715	23925	24091
2	198.50	199.00	199.17	199.25	199.30	199.33	199.36	199.37	199.39
3	55.552	49.799	47.467	46.195	45.392	44.838	44.434	44.126	43.882
4	31.333	26.284	24.259	23.155	22.456	21.975	21.622	21.352	21.139
5	22.785	18.314	16.530	15.556	14.940	14.513	14.200	13.961	13.772
6	18.635	14.544	12.917	12.028	11.464	11.073	10.786	10.566	10.391
7	16.236	12.404	10.882	10.050	9.5221	9.1553	8.8854	8.6781	8.5138
8	14.688	11.042	9.5965	8.8051	9.3018	7.9520	7.6941	7.4959	7.3386
9	13.614	10.107	8.7171	7.9559	7.4712	7.1339	6.8849	6.6933	6.5411
10	12.826	9.4270	8.0807	7.3428	6.8724	6.5446	6.3025	6.1159	5.9676
11	12.226	8.9122	7.6004	6.8809	6.4217	6.1016	5.8648	5.6821	5.5368
12	11.754	8.5096	7.2258	6.5211	6.0711	5.7570	5.5245	5.3451	5.2021
13	11.374	8.1865	6.9258	6.2335	5.7910	5.4819	5.2529	5.0761	4.9351
14	11.060	7.9216	6.6804	5.9984	5.5623	5.2574	5.0313	4.8566	4.7173
15	10.798	7.7008	6.4760	5.8029	5.3721	5.0708	4.8473	4.6744	3.5364
16	10.575	7.5138	6.3034	5.6378	5.2117	4.9134	4.6920	4.5207	4.3838
17	10.384	7.3536	6.1556	5.4967	5.0746	4.7789	4.5594	4.3894	4.2535
18	10.218	7.2148	6.0278	5.3746	3.9560	4.6627	4.4448	3.2759	4.1410
19	10.073	7.0935	5.9161	5.2681	4.8526	4.5614	4.3448	4.1770	4.0428
20	9.9439	6.9865	5.8177	5.1743	4.7616	4.4721	4.2569	4.0900	3.9564
21	9.8295	6.8914	5.7304	5.0911	4.6809	4.3931	4.1789	4.0128	3.8799
22	9.7271	6.8064	5.6524	5.0168	4.6088	4.3225	4.1094	3.9440	3.8116
23	9.6348	6.7300	5.5823	4.9500	3.5441	4.2591	4.0469	3.8822	3.7502
24	9.5513	6.6609	5.5190	4.8898	4.4857	4.2019	3.9905	3.8264	3.6949
25	9.4753	6.5982	5.4615	4.8351	4.4327	4.1500	3.9394	3.7758	3.6447
26	9.4059	6.5409	5.4091	4.7852	4.3844	4.1027	3.8928	3.7297	3.5989
27	9.3423	6.4885	5.3611	4.7396	4.3402	4.0594	3.8501	3.6875	3.5571
28	9.2838	6.4403	5.3170	4.6977	4.2996	4.0197	3.8110	3.6487	3.5186
29	9.2297	6.3958	5.2764	4.6591	4.2622	3.9831	3.7749	3.6131	3.4832
30	9.1797	6.3547	5.2388	4.6234	4.2276	3.9492	3.7416	3.5801	3.4504
40	8.8279	6.0664	4.9758	4.3738	3.9860	3.7129	3.5088	3.3498	3.2220
60	8.4946	5.7950	4.7290	4.1399	3.7599	3.4918	3.2911	3.1344	3.0083
120	8.1788	5.5393	4.4972	3.9207	3.5482	3.2849	3.0874	2.9330	2.8083
∞	7.8794	5.2983	4.2794	3.7151	3.3499	3.0913	2.8968	2.7444	2.6210

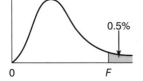

The entries in the table give the critical values of F cutting off 0.5% in the right-hand tail of the distribution. v_1 gives the degrees of freedom in the numerator, v_2 in the denominator.

Table A.4 (*continued*)

(d) Upper 0.5% points (*continued*)

v_1 = d.f. For the numerator

v_2	10	12	15	20	24	30	40	60	120	∞
1	24224	24426	24630	24836	24940	25044	25148	25253	25359	25464
2	199.40	199.42	199.43	199.45	199.46	199.47	199.47	199.48	199.49	199.50
3	43.686	43.387	43.085	42.778	42.622	42.466	42.308	42.149	41.989	41.828
4	20.967	20.705	20.438	20.167	20.030	19.892	19.752	19.611	19.468	19.325
5	13.618	13.384	13.146	12.903	12.780	12.656	12.530	12.402	12.274	12.144
6	10.250	10.034	9.8140	9.5888	9.4742	9.3582	9.2408	9.1219	9.0015	8.8793
7	8.3803	8.1764	7.9678	7.7540	7.6450	7.5345	7.4224	7.3088	7.1933	7.0760
8	7.2106	7.0149	6.8143	6.6082	6.5029	6.3961	6.2875	6.1772	6.0649	5.9506
9	6.4172	6.2274	6.0325	5.8318	5.7292	5.6248	5.5186	5.4104	5.3001	5.1875
10	5.8467	5.6613	5.4707	5.2740	5.1732	5.0706	4.9659	4.8592	4.7501	4.6385
11	5.4183	5.2363	5.0489	4.8552	4.7557	4.6543	4.5508	4.4450	4.3367	4.2255
12	5.0855	4.9062	4.7213	4.5299	4.4314	4.3309	4.2282	4.1229	4.0149	3.9039
13	4.8199	4.6429	4.4600	4.2703	4.1726	4.0727	3.9704	3.8655	3.7577	3.6465
14	4.6034	4.4281	4.2468	4.0585	3.9614	3.8619	3.7600	3.6552	3.5473	3.4359
15	4.4235	4.2497	4.0698	3.8826	3.7859	3.6867	3.5850	3.4803	3.3722	3.2602
16	4.2719	4.0994	3.9205	3.7342	3.6378	3.5389	3.4372	3.3324	3.2240	3.1115
17	4.1424	3.9709	3.7929	3.6073	3.5112	3.4124	3.3108	3.2058	3.0971	2.9839
18	4.0305	3.8599	3.6827	3.4977	3.4017	3.3030	3.2014	3.0962	2.9871	2.8732
19	3.9329	3.7631	3.5866	3.4020	3.3062	3.2075	3.1058	3.0004	2.8908	2.7762
20	3.8470	3.6779	3.5020	3.3178	3.2220	3.1234	3.0215	2.9159	2.8058	2.6904
21	3.7709	3.6024	3.4270	3.2431	3.1474	3.0488	2.9467	2.7408	2.7302	2.6140
22	3.7030	3.5350	3.3600	3.1764	3.0807	2.9821	2.8799	2.7736	2.6625	2.5455
23	3.6420	3.4745	3.2999	3.1165	3.0208	2.9221	2.8197	2.7132	2.6015	2.4837
24	3.5870	3.4199	3.2456	3.0624	2.9667	2.8679	2.7654	2.6585	2.5463	2.4276
25	3.5370	3.3704	3.1963	3.0133	2.9176	2.8187	2.7160	2.6088	2.4961	2.3765
26	3.4916	3.3252	3.1515	2.9685	2.8728	2.7738	2.6709	2.5633	2.4501	2.3297
27	3.4499	3.2839	3.1104	2.9275	2.8318	2.7327	2.6296	2.5217	2.4079	2.2867
28	3.4117	3.2460	3.0727	2.8899	2.7941	2.6949	2.5916	2.4834	2.3690	2.2470
29	3.3765	3.2110	3.0379	2.8551	2.7594	2.6600	2.5565	2.4479	2.3331	2.2102
30	3.3440	3.1787	3.0057	2.8230	2.7272	2.6278	2.5241	2.4151	2.2998	2.1760
40	3.1167	2.9531	2.7811	2.5984	2.5020	2.4015	2.2958	2.1838	2.0636	1.9318
60	2.9042	2.7419	2.5705	2.3872	2.2898	2.1874	2.0789	1.9622	1.8341	1.6885
120	2.7052	2.5439	2.3727	2.1881	2.0890	1.9840	1.8709	1.7469	1.6055	1.4311
∞	2.5188	2.3583	2.1868	1.9998	1.8983	1.7891	1.6691	1.5325	1.3637	1.0000

v_2 = d.f. for the denominator

References

Bowers, D. (1991) *Statistics for Economics and Business*. Macmillan, London.

Box, G.E.P. and Cox, D.R. (1964) An analysis of transformations. *Journal of the Royal Statistical Society*, **B26**, 211–52.

Branson, W.H. and Klevorick, A.K. (1969) Money illusion and the aggregate consumption function. *American Economic Review*, **59**, 832–49.

Chow, G. (1960) Tests of equality between sets of coefficients in two linear regressions. *Econometrics*, **28**, 591–605.

Dickey, D.A. and Fuller, W.A. (1979) Distribution of the estimators for autoregressive time series with a unit root. *Journal of the American Statistical Association*, **74**, 427–31.

Dornbusch, R. and Fischer, S. (1987) *Macroeconomics*, 4th edition. McGraw-Hill, New York.

Engel, R.F. and Granger, C. (1987) Co-integration and error correction: interpretation, estimation and testing. *Econometrics*, **66**, 251–76.

Gilbert, C.L. (1986) Professor Hendry's econometric methodology. *Oxford Bulletin of Economics and Statistics*, **48**, 283–307.

Greene, W.H. (2000) *Econometric Analysis*, 4th edition. Prentice Hall, New York.

Gujarati, D.N. (1988) *Basic Econometrics*, 2nd edition. McGraw-Hill, New York.

Hoel, P.G. (1962) *Introduction to Mathematical Statistics*, 3rd edition. Wiley, New York.

Johnston, J. (1984) *Econometric Methods*, 3rd edition. McGraw-Hill, New York.

Klein, L.R. (1958) The estimation of distributed lags. *Econometrica*, **26**, 559–65.

Koyck, L.M. (1954) *Distributed Lags and Investment Analysis*. North Holland, Amsterdam.

Lucas, R.E. (1976) Economic policy evaluation: a critique. In *The Phillips Curve and Labour Markets* (K. Brunner and D. Meltzer, eds). North Holland, Amsterdam.

McCallum, R.T. (1976) Rational expectations and the estimation of econometrics models: an alternative procedure. *International Economic Review*, **17**, 484–90.

Ramsey, J.B. (1969) Tests for specification error in classical least squares regression analysis. *Journal of the Royal Statistical Society*, **B31**, 250–71.

Samuelson, P.A., Koopmans, T.C. and Stone, J.R.N. (1954) Report of the evaluative committee for Econometrica. *Econometrica*, **22**, 141–6.

Stewart, J. (1984) *Understanding Econometrics*, 2nd edition. Hutchinson, London.

Thomas, R.L. (1993) *Introductory Econometrics: Theory and Applications*, 2nd edition. Longman, London.

Thomas, R.L. (1997) *Modern Econometrics: An Introduction.* Addison-Wesley, Harlow.

Thomas, R.L. (1999) *Using Mathematics in Economics.* Addison-Wesley, Harlow.

White, H. (1980) A heteroskedastic-consistent covariance matrix estimator and a direct test of heteroskedasticity. *Econometrics*, **48**, 817–38.

Zarembka, P. (1968) Functional form in the demand for money. *Journal of the American Statistical Association*, **63**, 502–11.

Index